ETHICS OF THE ALGORITHM

Ethics of the Algorithm

DIGITAL HUMANITIES AND HOLOCAUST MEMORY

TODD PRESNER

WITH CONTRIBUTIONS BY

Anna Bonazzi, Rachel Deblinger, Lizhou Fan, Michelle Lee, Kyle Rosen, and Campbell Yamane

PRINCETON UNIVERSITY PRESS

PRINCETON AND OXFORD

Published by Princeton University Press
41 William Street, Princeton, New Jersey 08540
99 Banbury Road, Oxford OX2 6JX

press.princeton.edu

All Rights Reserved

Library of Congress Cataloging-in-Publication Data

Names: Presner, Todd Samuel, author.
Title: Ethics of the algorithm : digital humanities and Holocaust memory /
    Todd Presner ; with contributions by Anna Bonazzi, Rachel Deblinger,
    Lizhou Fan, Michelle Lee, Kyle Rosen, and Campbell Yamane.
Other titles: Digital humanities and Holocaust memory
Description: Princeton : Princeton University Press, [2024] | Includes
    bibliographical references and index.
Identifiers: LCCN 2024012546 (print) | LCCN 2024012547 (ebook) |
    ISBN 9780691258966 (hardback) | ISBN 9780691258980 (ebook)
Subjects: LCSH: Holocaust, Jewish (1939–1945)—Study and teaching. | History—
    Data processing. | Digital humanities—Moral and ethical aspects. | Computer
    algorithms—Moral and ethical aspects. | BISAC: HISTORY / Modern /
    20th Century / Holocaust | COMPUTERS / Programming / Algorithms
Classification: LCC D804.33 .P739 2024 (print) | LCC D804.33 (ebook) |
    DDC 940.53/18071—dc23/eng/20240422
LC record available at https://lccn.loc.gov/2024012546
LC ebook record available at https://lccn.loc.gov/2024012547

British Library Cataloging-in-Publication Data is available
Editorial: Fred Appel and James Collier
Production Editorial: Nathan Carr
Text Design: Carmina Alvarez
Jacket / Cover Design: Karl Spurzem
Production: Erin Suydam
Publicity: William Pagdatoon
Copyeditor: Lachlan Brooks

This book has been composed in Arno

Printed in the United States of America

10 9 8 7 6 5 4 3 2 1

CONTENTS

At the nexus of Holocaust studies and computational methods, the research described in this book is the product of more than ten years of collaborative work with many people and institutional partners who have given generously of their time, ideas, and expertise. At UCLA, I convene a Digital Humanities Holocaust Research Lab: https://holocaustresearchlab.com/. It is an experimental, vertically integrated humanities lab consisting of researchers who bring together cross-disciplinary perspectives ranging from history, literary studies, philosophy, and linguistics to statistics, computer science, information studies, and design. Lab members are undergraduate students in our digital humanities program, doctoral students in various humanities fields, librarians and information studies specialists, and data scientists. Over the years, we have been fortunate to work with several institutions, including the USC Shoah Foundation, the Yale Fortunoff Video Archive, the US Holocaust Memorial Museum, and the Voices of the Holocaust project at the Illinois Institute of Technology. They have generously shared data, testimonies, and feedback with our team.

The research performed in my lab is emblematic of "big humanities" precisely because the work connects multiple disciplines, methodologies, and media forms to investigate both big problems and big data. The "big problem" is this: Without objectifying survivors or reducing the study of the Holocaust to quantitative abstractions, how can computational methods be used in ethical ways to further our understanding of the memory and history of the Holocaust? The "big data" are hundreds of thousands of hours of recorded Holocaust testimony—audio and video—composed of more than a billion words in dozens of languages, and the millions of pieces of associated descriptive metadata. Preserved in a range of digital archives across the world, these hundreds of thousands of hours of recorded testimony would take lifetimes to watch and comprehend. In approaching testimonial archives as big data, this book argues for the necessity and urgency of developing forms of witnessing guided by an "ethics of the algorithm."

This link between ethics and algorithms to study the Holocaust was first articulated in my coauthored book on emerging genres and methods in the digital humanities. We asked:

> What would it mean to subject the 52,000 Holocaust video testimonies in the USC Shoah Foundation Institute archives to machine reading and algorithmic analyses? Averaging two hours apiece, it would take a person 24 years to watch them all, assuming he or she watched 12 hours every day of the year. There is simply no way we can process and make sense of the volume of cultural data—including traditional printed materials—without the help of a computer to process, index, select, and cluster data on a comprehensible scale. But what are the implications of turning Holocaust testimonies into units of data, statistical analyses, and compact visualizations? Does this sort of quantitative analysis not inevitably, or perhaps by definition, subject the victims to further objectification, another dehumanizing process? Might there be an "ethics of the algorithm" that could mediate between the ethical demands of listening to individual Holocaust testimonies and the macrocosmic view enabled by a statistical representation of the total event? It is here that we need digital humanists to bring together the tools of technological analysis and the values, critical skills, and historical knowledge that animate the humanities disciplines.[1]

Over the past decade, members of my lab have asked these and many other questions as we proposed methods to study the Holocaust at varying scales commensurate with the testimonies, documents, and data that we have. As we show in this book, algorithmic processes can inform experimental methods that help humanities scholars to create new knowledge, new data, new narratives, and new interpretative possibilities. But to do so, we need to develop an "ethics of the algorithm" in which computational methods are employed responsibly and thoughtfully in ways that humanize rather than objectify.

Far from something that a single scholar can undertake alone, the research documented in this book is the product of many long-term collaborations, experiments, and practices in developing and applying mixed methodologies to study digital archives and testimonies. The work of our lab has taken place over years and explores a new paradigm for training humanities undergraduate and graduate students to help advance a larger research project, rather than to develop siloed specializations. To this end, my students and team members have coauthored parts of this book and have contributed centrally to the development of the methodologies, algorithms, visualizations, and datasets, as well as the analyses.

Throughout the book's narrative, there are intentional shifts between "I" and "we" subjects to signal these contributions and the multiplicity of voices engaged with the ideas.

While my digital humanities lab works mostly with data, spreadsheets, transcripts, videos, and computational processes, participants in the lab have also had the chance to meet and speak with Holocaust survivors. The spontaneity and physicality of the in-person experience inflects the analytical work of the lab and foregrounds the need to tarry with ethical questions in concrete ways. In fact, for the entire time my lab has existed, I have served as the faculty advisor of a program called "Bearing Witness" in which students meet and interview Holocaust survivors.[2] Over the years, dozens of survivors have participated and told their stories to us. Survivors sit together over lunch with groups of students who listen and reflect. We hear their voices; we breath the same air; we learn about their experiences; and we hug one another. The survivors are not data, even if our access to the testimonies, stories, histories, and archives will be mediated almost entirely by digital technologies in the very near future.

The research undertaken in our digital humanities lab is thus guided by a "values infrastructure" that is prior to the technological cyberinfrastructure used to carry out our computational work. This values infrastructure, informed by critical interventions such as the FemTechNet Manifesto and inspired by projects at UCLA such as "Big Data for Justice" and "Million Dollar Hoods," is grounded in an ethic of care, critical computation, and a reparative justice framework that seeks to honor the voices of the survivors by helping us to listen, read, and interpret testimonial narratives in new ways.[3] It is a transgenerational undertaking rooted in empathy, responsibility, and engagement with stories of pain and loss. At every moment in our work, intellect, emotion, mind, and body are intimately linked.[4] While the risk of datafication is real, we seek to model approaches to computation that resist objectification and, instead, bring about new possibilities for intersubjective relationality, thoughtfulness, and attentiveness. Rather than seeing algorithmic processes to produce definitive "results" or yield final answers, we consider our methods and data in the mode of the subjunctive—that is to say, as possible approaches, still in development, for asking new questions, posing new interpretations, and producing new data and narratives.

Although much of the analysis that follows engages with "big data," the methods are not deployed to prioritize structures over people, but rather to humanize individuals, identify differences, and perceive collectively shared experiences and events. As we will see, multiscalar zoom is an important part of the approach since it allows us to move from the analysis of an entire archive or corpus to a shared experience perceived through a multiplicity of testimonies, down to the language of semantic networks derived from individual testimonies and, finally, to singular utterances of agency and discrete phonetic expressions.[5] The units of analysis span metadata related to tens of thousands of testimonies and thousands of testimony transcripts down to the words in individual expressions: for example, "I removed the yellow patch" is a single expression of agency in the context of Nazi discriminatory violence; or the spectrographic analysis of four fraught words—"I see you tonight," said by survivor Erika Jacoby—registers phonetically the layered traumas in this utterance about family separation on the ramp at Auschwitz. Our datascapes always return us to the expressivity of singular individuals: Abraham Kimmelmann, Anna Kovitzka, Renee Firestone, Erika Jacoby, Edith Serras, Mala Zimetbaum, Abraham Bomba, Fritzie Fritzshall, Robert Ness, Efraim Hoffman, and many others.

Nearly all the testimonies and the associated metadata analyzed in this book were provided to us by the organizations that created them and/or currently steward them. While members of our team were fortunate to be able to speak with two Auschwitz survivors whose testimonies are discussed in this book (Erika Jacoby and Renee Firestone), we did not conduct or record formal interviews.[6] The USC Shoah Foundation generously provided thousands of testimony transcripts, mostly created by ProQuest, dozens of audio and video files, as well as select transcripts and user data related to the Dimensions in Testimony (DiT) project. They also provided us with metadata, including their thesaurus and video indexing tags, related to about fifty thousand testimonies in the Visual History Archive. The Yale Fortunoff Archive provided UCLA with full access to their testimonial corpus (approximately 4,400 testimonies), and they also provided us with several hundred testimony transcripts and the accompanying metadata. Additional testimony transcripts came from the US Holocaust Memorial Museum and the Illinois Institute of Technology, where the Voices of the Holocaust project is housed. The latter includes approximately 120 testimony transcripts as well as the original sound recordings done by David Boder in 1946. All of the Holocaust testimonies analyzed in this book come from these digital archives and are available for listening and analysis in accordance with each institution's terms of use and informed consent agreements. Without implying their agreement with the analyses documented here, we are extremely appreciative of their support of this research.

We did not create or help shape any of these testimonies or archives. Instead, we are the distant witnesses who have inherited them. And what an inheritance we have before us: hundreds of thousands of hours of survivor testimony in a multiplicity of digital platforms, languages, and archives. We sit at the cusp of a historical moment in which the last surviving witnesses are passing away and the recording of eyewitness testimonies of the Holocaust will be complete. We also inhabit a very different world than that of the survivors. Ours is constituted by new technologies—the web, search algorithms, big data, machine learning, and generative AI—that have fundamentally transformed how we comport ourselves toward one another *and* toward the dead. The repercussions are massive and felt everywhere because they affect our understanding of history, ethics, epistemology, aesthetics, politics, and society. At stake is nothing short of our relationship to the past. What can—and should—we responsibly do with the inheritance of these massive archives of testimony? How can we develop ethical forms of listening and analysis that bring together humanistic and computational methods? What does it mean to engage in distant witnessing and what are the ethical questions that might inform such a subject position? Without being prescriptive or definitive, this book starts to map answers to such questions.

ACKNOWLEDGMENTS

First and foremost, I would like to thank the dozens of students who have participated in—and helped shape—the research in this book. Nearly a decade ago, I began offering capstone courses and internships in my Holocaust research lab for undergraduate and graduate students in our digital humanities program. The students have consistently been thoughtful interlocutors, dexterously navigating humanistic and computational questions that have deepened our understanding of digital archives and testimony. In particular, I wish to thank Somashree Biswas, Anna Bonazzi, Erin Caracristi, Christina Cha, Lizhou (Leo) Fan, Michelle Lee, Seul Lee, Camille Lent, Hana Lim, Lindsey Mardona, Keertana Namuduri, Ulysses Pascal, Kyle Rosen, Andrew Rosenstein, Audrey Tey Teng, Andrew Thompson, Connor Thompson, Laurel Woods, Campbell Yamane, Jiaxin Yang, and Haiqi Zhou.

Over the years, a number of former UCLA students have also worked at the lab as researchers and contributed invaluable insights. In addition to Lizhou Fan, Michelle Lee, and Campbell Yamane, they include Violet Guo, Omar Hassan, Mahati Kumar, Jack Schaefer, Chereen Tam, Aileen Tang, Monit Tyagi, Richard Wang, and Wanxin Xie. They have worked alongside many extraordinary staff-scholars at UCLA, including Zoe Borovsky, Anthony Caldwell, Yoh Kawano, David Shepard, and Lisa Snyder—all of whom have supported various phases of this project. I also thank Keyi Cheng, Stefan Inzer, Adrian Leung, and Xiaoxian Shen, the students who participated in the 2022 summer Research Experience for Undergraduates at UCLA.

A few of these students worked as members of my lab for years and contributed to the development of the methods, analyses, visualizations, and project write-ups, which have, in different ways, become part of this book. In particular, I thank Anna Bonazzi (PhD, UCLA, Germanic Languages, 2025), who began her graduate career with me delving into David Boder's corpus of testimonies and is completing a dissertation on digital migrant archives of testimony. Her research has applied and further developed some of the digital humanities methodologies described in this book. She brought her formidable linguistics and computational background to the project (as seen in our jointly written analysis of the "gray zone" in Abraham Kimmelmann's testimony) and is also to thank for developing the project's website. I thank Lizhou (Leo) Fan, a digital humanities and statistics major (BS, UCLA, 2021; PhD, University of Michigan, 2024), who served as a research associate in the lab for two years (2020–2022). Leo played a formative role in developing methods of natural language processing for testimony analysis. His thoughtfulness, collaboration, and creativity inspired many of our digital humanities approaches to testimonial analysis (as seen in our jointly conceived chapter on using semantic triplets to analyze expressions of agency). I thank Michelle Lee, who graduated from UCLA in digital humanities and statistics (BS, 2022) and worked in our lab for two years, during which time she developed the methodologies for classifying and clustering interview questions. Her visualizations are featured on the lab's website, and we coauthored the digital project, "What Were Survivors Asked?" And I thank Campbell Yamane, a digital humanities and cognitive science major (BS, UCLA, 2018), who worked as a research intern for the lab in its formative years and helped lay the foundation for our approaches to voice and audio analysis. Campbell presented his research, "Using Computational Techniques to Analyze Holocaust Testimonies" (2018), as a poster at UCLA's Undergraduate Research Week and helped catalyze our investigations of vocal patterns and memory. Several of Campbell's visualizations are featured in chapter 5.

Since this project began over ten years ago, I have had the chance to work closely with Rachel Deblinger (PhD, UCLA, History, 2014), Director of the Modern Endangered Archives Program at the UCLA Library. Rachel has been integral to our explorations of the many intersections between digital humanities, Holocaust studies, history, and ethics. We have had countless conversations on these topics with students and colleagues as well as presented papers together and jointly authored the concluding chapter to this book. I thank Rachel for her genuine openness and engagement with this project. And last but not least, I want to express my deep appreciation to Kyle Rosen (PhD, UCLA, Germanic Languages, 2023). I worked closely with Kyle during his entire graduate career at UCLA as he formulated a comparative project on the ethics of testimony focusing on the poetic voices of Paul Celan and M. NourbeSe Philip. Kyle not only participated in numerous digital instantiations of our lab over the years, but he consistently offered thoughtful guidance and constructive critiques that helped sharpen our work. He read the entire manuscript in its penultimate form, and we engaged in many highly generative dialogues over the book. Although his name appears only in footnotes, his voice is woven through many of the pages here.

Over more than a decade, the support of the staff at the USC Shoah Foundation has been instrumental to this project, most recently through my participation in the Scholar Lab on Antisemitism (2021–2022). I express my thanks to the following individuals: Douglas Ballman, Crispin Brooks, Mills Chang, Sam Gustman, the late Kia Hays, Anita Pace, Badema Pitic, Michael Russell, Stephen Smith, Kori Street, Martha Stroud, and Claudia Wiedeman. I especially want to thank Badema, Claudia, and Martha for their intellectual friendship and guidance over the years, as they have seen the project grow in various ways and have always been so generous with their support. The findings described in this book do not necessarily reflect the views of the USC Shoah Foundation Institute. I also want to thank Wolf Gruner, founding director of USC's Dornsife Center for Advanced Genocide Research, for his interest in the project and collaborative approach to Holocaust studies.

At the US Holocaust Memorial Museum (USHMM), I would like to thank Kierra Crago-Schneider, Robert Ehrenreich, Emil Kerenji, Wendy Lower, Jürgen Matthäus, and Leah Wolfson. They have provided tremendous inspiration to me over the years. I also want to express my gratitude to the USHMM team that invited me to deliver the 2018 Meyerhoff Lecture in Holocaust Studies.

At Yale's Fortunoff Archive, I thank Director Stephen Naron, who has been a wonderfully engaged interlocutor and colleague over the years. His vision for the archive and willingness to collaborate on numerous digital humanities projects have transformed the way we interact with Holocaust testimony. At the Illinois Institute of Technology, I thank Adam Strohm, Director of Distinctive Collections and Digital Strategy at the Paul V. Galvin Library. Finally, I thank the staff at UCLA's Charles E. Young Research Library Special Collections and the staff at the Drs. Nicholas and Dorothy Cummings Center for the History of Psychology at the University of Akron, Ohio.

In the field of Holocaust studies, I wish to thank Paris Papamichos Chronakis, Deb Donig (who graciously invited me to present some of these ideas on her podcast, "Technically Human"), Claudio Fogu, Saul Friedländer, Laura Jockusch, Wulf Kansteiner, Noah Shenker, Gábor Tóth, and Elisabeth Weber. Some of the initial ideas in this book were presented at a conference dedicated to Saul Friedländer and Hayden White, later published in *Probing the Ethics of Holocaust Culture* (Cambridge, MA: Harvard University Press, 2016), coedited with Fogu and Kansteiner. I also want to acknowledge the generosity of the "Geographies of the Holocaust" team—in particular, Tim Cole, Alberto Giordano, Paul Jaskot, and Anne Knowles. With their students and colleagues, they have pioneered the development of digital mapping and modeling in Holocaust studies. It is no exaggeration to say that their collective work has propelled the "spatial turn" in Holocaust studies. I wish to thank Anne and Paul in particular for their friendship, thoughtfulness, and generosity. They both read numerous versions of this book and always offered their honest, reflective, and constructive critiques. Their work in digital humanities has been inspirational to me, and they embody the kind of scholar I strive to be.

At UCLA, I would like to thank my colleagues in Jewish Studies, in particular, Aomar Boum, Lia Brozgal, Vivian Holenbeck, Mark Kligman, Miriam Koral, Aliza Luft, David Myers, Michael Rothberg, and Sarah Stein. I want to acknowledge David for his unwavering support of this book over the years and also to thank him for his intellectual openness and disposition of care toward this project. The Michael and Irene Ross Endowment for Yiddish and Jewish Studies provided the majority of funding to support the students and research in this book. I gratefully acknowledge that indispensable support here. Within UCLA's Digital Humanities and Urban Humanities programs, I would like to thank Dana Cuff, Chris Johanson, Anastasia Loukaitou-Sideris, Peter Lunenfeld, Miriam Posner, Ashley Sanders, Lisa Snyder, Francis Steen, and Maite Zubiaurre. In and beyond my department, I thank Ali Behdad, Munia Bhaumik, Cisca Brier, David Kim, John McCumber, Kalani Michell, Dominic Thomas, Juliet Williams, and Yasemin Yildiz. I wish to acknowledge the support of UCLA's Office for Research and Creative Activities, specifically that of Vice Chancellor Roger Wakimoto and Executive Director Mary Okino. And finally, publication is made possible by the Michael and Irene Ross Endowment for Yiddish and Jewish Studies at UCLA.

Outside of UCLA, I wish to honor my teacher and friend, the late Hayden White, who, over nearly two decades, engaged in numerous conversations with me about Holocaust studies, ethics and narrative, and even algorithmic forms of representation. He was instrumental in introducing me to the field of "conceptual history" and was always a model of intellectual generosity. I have also had the good fortune to present parts of this book to colleagues in various fields. In particular, I wish to thank colleagues at Duke University, specifically Esther Gabara, N. Katherine Hayles, Paul Jaskot, Mark Olson, Kristine Stiles, and Victoria Szabo; colleagues at Harvard University, specifically Eric Rentschler and Judith Ryan; colleagues at UC Santa Barbara, specifically Sven Spieker and Elisabeth Weber; as well as Nathaniel Deutsch (UC Santa Cruz), Amir Eshel (Stanford University); and members of the Hebrew University's Lab for the Computational Analysis of Holocaust Testimonies: Renana Keydar, Amit Pinchevski, and Eitan Wagner.

I want to express my gratitude to the anonymous readers of this manuscript and my editors at Princeton, Fred Appel, Nathan Carr, and James Collier, for their guidance and support of this project. The readers provided exceptionally thoughtful feedback on the project and helped me sharpen many of the arguments in this book.

Finally, I wish to thank my family: my parents, Harvey and Susan; my brother Brad, my sister-in-law, Kiesha, and their son, Dylan; and most of all, my husband, Jaime, and our son, Mateo, who have truly lived alongside this project for the last decade. Not only have they patiently engaged in countless dinner conversations about ethics, algorithms, and Holocaust testimony, but they have also offered generous guidance and support as I sought ways to move this project forward. I thank them for their companionship, thoughtfulness, and care. This project is dedicated to them both with love.

* * *

The initial ideas for this book, now part of chapter 4, were previously published as: Todd Presner, "The Ethics of the Algorithm: Close and Distant Listening to the Shoah Foundation Visual History Archive," in *Probing the Ethics of Holocaust Culture*, ed. Claudio Fogu, Wulf Kansteiner, and Todd Presner, 175–202 (Cambridge, MA: Harvard University Press, 2016). We thank Harvard University Press for permission to reproduce that material here. Parts of chapters 3 and 4 were also previously published as: "Digitale Geisteswissenschaften und Holocaustzeugnisse: Anmerkungen zu einer globalen Genealogie," trans. Lena Hein, in *Globalgeschichten der deutschen Literatur*, ed. Urs Büttner and David Kim, 93-117 (Stuttgart: J. B. Metzler, 2022). We thank Springer Nature for permission to reprint that material. An earlier version of part of the digital project on Abraham Kimmelmann was published as: Anna Bonazzi, "N-Gram-Based Content Indexing: Semiautomated Analysis of Holocaust Testimonies," in *Jewish Studies in the Digital Age*, ed. Gerben Zaagsma, Daniel Stökl Ben Ezra, Miriam Rürup, Michelle Margolis, and Amalia S. Levi, 89–104 (Berlin: De Gruyter Oldenbourg, 2022). That material has been republished with permission from De Gruyter. Finally, part of chapter 6 was published as: Lizhou Fan and Todd Presner, "Algorithmic Close Reading: Using Semantic Triplets to Index and Analyze Agency in Holocaust Testimonies," *Digital Humanities Quarterly* 16, no. 3 (2022). It is reproduced in accordance with the journal's open access license.

ETHICS OF THE ALGORITHM

Technologies of Testimony and Distant Witnessing

Shortly after the death of Auschwitz survivor and president of the Illinois Holocaust Museum and Education Center, Fritzie Fritzshall, on June 19, 2021, I decided to spend some time talking with Fritzshall through the USC Shoah Foundation's Dimension in Testimony project (Figure 0.1). I logged into the IWitness platform from my home computer and decided to ask her a number of questions. Periodically shifting in the chair in which she sat, her head shook slightly back and forth; she evidenced a welcoming smile and changed the position of her hands and fingers ever so slightly, as if she was waiting for me to begin. I started with a simple "Hello, how are you?," to which she responded, "I am fine." I then asked her why she did this project. She responded by saying that although "it opens a wound" each time she tells her story, she feels an "obligation to teach" and "leave my story behind so the next generation can learn from me [about] what I have gone through."

When I ask her how she arrived in Auschwitz, she recounts a detailed and horrific story of being deported in a locked train with starving and sick people struggling to breathe, mothers holding dead and dying infants, and the overwhelming stench of human waste spilling over in the boxcar. The story ends with her arrival in Auschwitz, where she describes the last time she saw her mother. On the selection platform, she says that she told her mother to stand in a different line from her, anticipating that it would save them both from certain punishment. Later, she found out that her mother was sent immediately to her death, and she wonders: "Did I send my mother to the gas chambers? I don't know. Would she have lived? I don't know. I don't know." Hesitantly, I mustered the courage to ask: "Do you really think you sent your mother to her death?" The answer played does not seem quite right since it is about her mother's courage and care of her children in the ghetto and the boxcar. So, I rephrase my question: "Why did you tell your

FIGURE 0.1: Fritzie Fritzshall, Dimensions in Testimony,
IWitness platform, USC Shoah Foundation.

mother to stand in the other line?" She responds by describing the brutal punishments she saw on the platform of women being hit with rifle butts and
slapped around. Clasping and opening her hands, she continues by saying:
"The fear was there and you just wanted to do what they asked you to do so you
wouldn't be punished. So, I remember standing with my mother in this line, I
remember motioning to her and telling her to go into the next line, I don't remember anything else. I don't remember any conversation, I don't remember
a goodbye, I don't remember . . . I don't remember."

While speaking about the same traumatic event, her two answers provide
different accounts of her memory and are delivered in markedly different
voices. In fact, the words alone in the final quotation do not indicate anything
about the creakiness of her voice, her tone of almost pleading with me to understand her, the hesitant pursing of her lips, or her labored breathing. The
quoted transcript omits the fact that the single ellipsis represents a pause of
almost ten seconds in duration. It also obscures the fundamental phonetic differences of the last two expressions of "I don't remember," the second of which
is uttered as she chokes up and can barely express the words, perhaps in disbelief at her own lack of memory.

I decided to shift my questions to ask her if she had recorded a testimony with the USC Shoah Foundation or if she had recorded any testimony previously. To both questions, she gives the same answer: "The project we're doing here I think is amazing. I think technology is great and I love it. I think it's a great project." It turns out that this answer is played often for questions related to recording technologies and even to questions about whether she considers herself to be a "hologram" or "AI." When I try to test the system's illusion of immediacy and presence by asking "What do you think of the world today?" and "What do you think the world will look like in 100 years from now?," I get the same answer: "I don't know when you're talking to me but I hope that it is better now," evidencing the fact that our interaction is still fundamentally bound to the time-kernel of its moment of recording. When I go further by asking "do you have any questions for me?," she responds by reminding me: "I'm actually a recording so I can't answer that question."

But when I rephrase the question to be "Do you think this is the future of Holocaust testimony?," I receive a somewhat surprising answer: "I don't think I remember things accurately. I don't think anybody that's lived as long as I have, three hundred years at this point. . . . No, I don't. I have certain pictures that are in my mind and certain facts that I am really sure of but certain things, did it really happen, is it a memory, did I really see it, do I remember it . . . no, I'm not sure that I remember every single thing that happened during that particular time." She smiles as she says three hundred years, perhaps signaling to us that she knows we are both participating in the same illusion, but surely also hoping that she will live on, far into the distant future, through the technology to transmit her testimony. The desired infallibility of digital technology is in tension with the fallibility, finiteness, and contingency of human memory. And even though the answer does not quite fit the question asked, her words reveal the imbrication of the promises of technology with what might be considered the "necropolitics" of the digital archive.[1] While Achille Mbembe uses the latter term to refer to the sovereign's power over life and death, the necropolitics of the digital archive points to the ways in which the testimonial archive is not only a record of whose lives are preserved and in what modality (and whose lives are not or could never be) but also, more generally, who and what is in the database, who and what is searchable, and who and what can be heard beyond the facticity of death.

Of course, I was never "talking to" or "interviewing" Fritzshall. Instead, I was providing data to an automatic speech recognition tool that interpreted my words into text before the platform, running a set of natural language processing and machine-learning algorithms, matched the best, prerecorded answer to what it decided was the intended meaning of my question. And yet the illusion of immediacy is compelling. She shifts in her chair, blinks her eyes, and moves her hands, seemingly waiting for me to pose more questions, as if to say: *Here I am, ready to listen and engage with you.* But what does it mean for the algorithm to "hear," "listen," and "interpret" my speech? Has the ethical obligation of the listener to be open to the testimony of the other shifted to an obligation of the algorithm to be open to my questions? We need to ask: Is there an ethics behind the decision-making of this algorithm? Or more generally, what are the ethics of any algorithmic engagement with a digital archive?

Dimensions in Testimony is a project of "distant witnessing" that raises fundamental questions of what it means for an ethics of testimony to intersect with an ethics of the algorithm. Starting in 2014, the USC Shoah Foundation, in partnership with the USC Institute for Creative Technologies, began to record survivors for this interactive form of volumetrically captured testimony. Initially (although somewhat erroneously) described as "holograms," the testimonies were recorded in a special studio to capture the survivor in 360 degrees in order to allow for three-dimensional projection and interaction.[2] Available both through a web interface and in physical installations across the world in museums, several dozen Jewish Holocaust survivors have been recorded to date, as well as one survivor of the Nanjing Massacre, two liberators, and one war crimes prosecutor.[3] Often asked over a thousand questions, the answers given by the interviewees are marked up and become part of a machine-learning system to allow the general public to pose questions interactively in real time. Unlike audiovisual testimonies that play linearly in a fixed fashion, each interaction with an interviewee in Dimensions in Testimony is a new experience, contingent upon the questions posed by the user, the system's parsing of the user's speech, and the calculations of the machine-learning algorithm that determine what clip is the most appropriate answer to play.

While the technologies upon which the project are built were only developed recently, it is not fortuitous that it launched at a time in which a profound generational shift is occurring: the last surviving witnesses of the Holocaust are passing away. It is no surprise that numerous museums and educational centers have developed interactive apps, virtual reality projects, and augmented reality experiences to foster forms of digital Holocaust memory.[4] At the same time, the final recordings of eyewitness testimonies—including the USC Shoah Foundation's "Last Chance Testimony Collection" initiative, its Dimensions in Testimony project, and the "Forever Project" backed by the UK National Holocaust Museum—are being undertaken with great urgency. Most of the survivors of camps who are still able to tell their stories are in their mid to late 90s. Some lack the physical and mental stamina to sit for hours and recount the horrors of their childhood and early adult years. Holocaust testimony is shifting from experiential narratives of embodied memories to archived histories mediated by digital interfaces, databases, and algorithms. From the moment I logged onto the IWitness platform, my interaction with Fritzie Fritzshall was entirely mediated by technology, from clicking on the microphone icon to ask my question—and the automatic speech recognition tool that subsequently parsed the question into tokens for natural language processing—to the machine-learning algorithm that decided on the best match from the database of video clips and the video playback in my browser-based interface. The algorithmic layers between the user interface and the recorded archival content play an absolutely critical role in constituting the testimony and conditioning what an ethical engagement with the witness and the archive can be. These algorithmic layers are a central part of what we probe in this book.

Before we do so, we need to look back at the history of the genre of Holocaust testimony to gain a broader perspective on the significance of the changing media and technologies for both constituting and interacting with testimonial archives. As a genre of attestation to the destruction of the Jewish communities of Europe, Holocaust testimony—in the form of diaries, letters, photographs, narrative documentation, and collection building—began almost immediately after Nazi Germany invaded Poland in September of 1939.[5] Following the establishment of Jewish ghettos in the early 1940s, secret archives were founded in Bialystok, Kovno, Lodz, Vilna, and Warsaw, where victims documented the catastrophe unfolding around them.[6] Started by Emanuel Ringelblum in November of 1940, the Oyneg Shabes archive in the Warsaw ghetto was the most extensive and collected a trove of documents, including letters, diaries, clippings from the Jewish press, cultural and literary artifacts, posters, and ephemera of everyday life.[7] As the ghetto was evacuated and came under siege, the archive was buried in milk canisters under the city in the summer of 1942 and spring of 1943. Not unlike the precariousness and hopefulness of a message in a bottle, the archive—with its diversity of voices—was intended to be sent, as it were, to the future. After the war, it was partially salvaged when it was rediscovered and excavated in 1946. The technology of the milk cannister enabled an intentional form of witnessing in which testimonial inscriptions were preserved, stored, and transmitted beyond human mortality.

Collection efforts by historical commissions and documentation centers began before the war was over in Polish cities liberated by the red army and expanded throughout Europe in the immediate aftermath of the war, especially in Germany, Austria, Italy, and France. According to Laura Jockusch, "The survivor documentarians . . . pioneered the development of victim-focused Holocaust historiography . . . [using sources that] reflect the life stories, experiences, and self-perceptions of their creators, [such] as diaries, letters, autobiographies, and memoirs, along with testimony drawn from survivors' memories."[8] In addition to documenting information about displaced people (family background, addresses, languages, nationality), the historical commissions developed questionnaires to collect information about family separations, displacements, the fate of families, time in camps, liberation, and surviving family members.[9]

As a complement (or perhaps antidote) to the silent news reel footage of liberated camps, the first audio interviews with Holocaust survivors were recorded in 1946 by a man named David Boder.[10] Trained as a psychologist and linguist, he developed his own interview methodology to document and understand the traumatic impact of the Pan-European catastrophe. Using a wire recorder, Boder interviewed about 120 displaced people, mostly Jewish survivors of concentration camps, in displaced persons camps in Germany, Italy, France, and Switzerland.[11] Survivors were interviewed in nine languages, with the goal of translating and disseminating the testimonies across the Anglophone world.[12] As dialogically mediated, first-person narratives wrought with emotion, Boder considered the interviews to be a new form of "literature." This is because they represented forms of narrative characterized by a range of linguistic choices, emplotment decisions, storytelling devices, and translation effects. According to Boder, the "verbatim recorded narratives" not only demanded the development of an "art of listening" but also necessitated the development of mixed methodologies—qualitative and quantitative, humanistic and proto-computational—to analyze the traumatic language and emotional content.[13]

In the years that followed, formalized institutions of Holocaust memory were founded in the United States, Europe, and Israel. Holocaust survivor testimony became the centerpiece of their collecting initiatives.[14] Many of the early testimonies in Yad Vashem's collection were written down or recorded before it was formally established in 1953. Today, Yad Vashem has an archive of more than 131,000 testimonies across various media formats (of which about 36,000 are recorded voices and/or video). The Holocaust Survivors Film Project and the

Video Archive for Holocaust Testimonies at Yale (which later became integrated into the Fortunoff Archive) began recording audiovisual interviews in 1979, guided initially by the collaboration between television personality Laurel Vlock and child survivor and psychiatrist Dori Laub. Today, the archive has more than 4,400 testimonies and consists of some 10,000 hours of video footage. It is not coincidental, as Annette Wieviorka points out, that the impulse to record audiovisual testimonies in the late 1970s and early 1980s was spurred by televisual realities that returned to the immediacy of first-person accounts by survivors at the 1961 trial of Adolf Eichmann. These broadcasts and recordings set the stage for the public impact of the television miniseries *Holocaust* (1979), Claude Lanzmann's monumental film of witnessing, *Shoah* (1985), and the global reception of Steven Spielberg's *Schindler's List* (1993).[15] Founded in the wake of *Schindler's List*, the Survivors of the Shoah Visual History Foundation (which later became the USC Shoah Foundation Visual History Archive) began interviewing survivors in 1994. Today, with some 55,000 video testimonies, in over forty languages, the more than 120,000 hours of testimony comprise the largest such archive in the world.

To preserve this content and make it globally accessible on the web, archives and libraries have undertaken multiple processes of media migration and digitization, each of which has changed how the testimonies are heard, accessed, and searched.[16] Boder's analog wire recordings were transferred to reel-to-reel tape by the Library of Congress and later recorded on U-matic or VHS tape. In 1999, the Paul V. Galvin Library at the Illinois Institute of Technology (IIT) obtained copies of the recordings as Digital Audio Tape (DAT) files, and those DAT copies were transferred to WAV files in 2007–2008. They were encoded as digital flash files and are now playable as WAV files on the IIT website. The interviews are searchable by way of the extensive Text Encoding Initiative (TEI) mark-up created by the IIT team.[17] When Yale's Fortunoff Archive began recording testimonies in 1979, they were recorded on 3/4-inch U-matic videocassettes, before being transferred to VHS, and now digital streaming formats. The Shoah Foundation began recording testimonies in 1994 on thirty-minute Beta SP videotapes. In the early 2000s, the 235,000 tapes were digitized as Motion JPEG 2000 digital files, the industry standard for preservation. According to Stephen Smith, the former executive director of the USC Shoah Foundation, an "ethic of data integrity" informs the Foundation's commitment to "bit level preservation . . . of every byte of data (for its own sake)."[18] The eight petabytes of data are stored on Oracle StorageTek SL8500 machines, which are checked nightly for any errors.[19] Maintained by USC's Information Technologies data center, painstaking preservation systems are used to protect and regularly backup all of the data to within one bit per five terabytes of data.[20] In certain ways, this commitment to the fidelity of both the digital files and the system's hardware—networked, backed-up, distributed, and mirrored—underscores how the archive aims to be a transgenerational refuge or asylum for the survivors' testimonies. The ethics of archiving are deeply rooted in ensuring a future for the testimonies to be heard.

During these critical decades of recording, archive creation, and media preservation, the testimony of Holocaust survivors was subject to much discussion and debate. Some historians asked if testimonies, many of which were collected decades after the events, were "factual" enough to be admitted as evidence into the historical record, especially if these testimonies contained inaccuracies; on the other hand, psychoanalysts like Laub argued that first-person testimonies were less about evaluating their historical accuracy and more about their role as documents of emotional realities, traumatic experiences, and epistemological frameworks—in other words, subjective ways of knowing, experiencing, and narrating.[21] Although certain Holocaust historians such as Raul Hilberg and Lucy Dawidowicz distanced themselves from the use of first-person testimony,[22] others such as Christopher Browning, Jan Gross, and Omer Bartov have shown how survivor testimony can be critical for historical work, especially when few or no other sources are available.[23] In his acclaimed study of the Starachowice slave-labor camps, Browning used nearly three hundred eyewitness accounts, spanning 1945 through 2008, as nearly all other evidence about the camps was destroyed. While survivor accounts, according to Browning, are often recognized for their "authenticity" (as they are drawn from the wellsprings of memory), they can also be problematic for historians because the memories may, for instance, become mixed with "iconic Holocaust tropes" in popular culture.[24] Nevertheless, Browning argues that it is possible for first-person accounts to be squared with "factual accuracy" to get at a "core memory" of the events, even if they—like all historical sources—do not provide "perfect evidence."[25] Instead, they open up spaces of evaluation and judgment for historical work to take place.

Derived from the Latin word *testimonium*, meaning "evidence, proof, witness, attestation," the root *testis* refers to a witness or to someone who attests, especially as a third party (or *terstis*) in a trial or court of law.[26] Witnesses deliver testimony of something known, observed, or experienced in light of having been present at the event to which they are testifying.[27] When testimony is evaluated by a judge or a historian, the ability to verify the testimony's factual accuracy and reliability remains paramount.[28] However, as we argue in the analyses that follow, testimony need not be evaluated—certainly not exclusively—for strict factuality or the extent to which it accurately represents the reality of the past. Testimony is a widely variant form of narrative performance in which a survivor makes subjective choices about how to voice personal experiences of trauma. At its core, testimony is a narrative form of emplotment with an implicit promise to be truthful. It is presented and preserved as an act of truth-telling for others to hear, see, or read. Thus the dialogical process of telling and listening is just as important as the language describing the reality of experiences.

Connecting the dialogical aspects of interview-guided testimony to transgenerational responsibility, Geoffrey Hartman, one of the founders and original project directors of the Yale Fortunoff Archive, distilled what he considered to be the ethical dimension of video testimony: the "duty to listen and to restore a dialogue."[29] For Hartman, video testimony offers an "optic" for non-survivors to mediate the geographic, temporal, experiential, and psychological distance that they (or, we) have with respect to the events of the Holocaust. This mediation happens initially through the relationship between the interviewer and the survivor and, after that, through the generations of viewers who contribute to the creation of an "affective community" of witnesses to the witnesses.[30] For Hartman, the specific media technology of the audiovisual recording documents an ethical encounter between interviewer and survivor, which becomes, through each act of watching, an ethical encounter between viewer and survivor. In this sense, testimony functions as a performative embodiment of Martin Buber's "Ich-du" (I-you) relationship,[31] in which we—the non-survivors— enter into a "contract" through acts of listening, bearing witness, hearing, and being heard.[32] Survivors, Laub writes, have a need to be heard, to tell their stories to a listener who is actively present for the other, listening to both silence and speech, trauma and survivorship.[33] "The unlistened-to story," as in Primo Levi's recurring nightmare in *Survival in Auschwitz*, is a trauma akin to reexperiencing the event itself.[34]

Because bearing witness is a dialogical appeal that needs a listener, Hartman will explicitly situate it within a framework derived from the philosopher of relational ethics, Emmanuel Levinas. It is the philosophy of Levinas, perhaps more than any other, that has informed much postwar scholarship on the Holocaust related to ethics as obligation and responsibility to the other.[35] In survivor testimony, the physical face of the other—the traumatized, wounded face of the survivor—enters into a relationship of proximity, vulnerability, and closeness with the listener's own face. For Levinas, ethics is defined by an intersubjective relationship with and responsibility for the other. He considers it a first philosophy, prior to the establishment of identity, origin, or any attempt to ground being. For Hartman, Laub, and many others, the ethics of testimony rests upon the presence of a relational listener: "Here I am," ready to listen attentively; I am all ears, standing open and ready to be summoned to this infinite demand, to this injunction to "hear."[36]

But what, specifically, constitutes an "ethics of response for secondary witnesses—interviewers, oral historians, and commentators,"[37] as Dominick LaCapra has asked? And, more pointedly for our contemporary situation, what might an "ethics of response" mean for us—the tertiary witnesses—whose acts of witnessing are mediated by computer interfaces, algorithms, and databases?[38] We consider the survivor to be the primary witness, the interviewer to be the secondary witness, and all of us listening to the testimonies via forms of digital mediation and computation to be tertiary or distant witnesses. I will use the term "distant witnessing" to refer to this subject position. The question is: How can we develop an ethics of witnessing in a world in which our temporal relationship to the voices of the dead is becoming more and more distant, but our ability to call up vast amounts of information from the digital archive is becoming more and more instantaneous?

Although many viewers will continue to engage with video testimony in ways that reflect the ethics of relationality and empathy central to its initial creation, the recording of Holocaust testimony is reaching an end.[39] As we approach the threshold of a generational shift in which living witnesses will have passed away, the character of the ethical relationship between survivor and listener is also changing: going forward, that relationship will be largely mediated by digital technologies, information architectures, and algorithms. Concretely speaking, this means search boxes, web interfaces, databases, query languages, mark-up and encoding protocols, speech recognition, natural language processing, visualizations, and a wide range of algorithmic methods and tools for reading, listening, creation, and analysis. Because the digital archive is structured, accessed, and interpreted by computational technologies and algorithmic methods, the futures of Holocaust memory and history will be shaped increasingly through these technologies and methods. Our relationship to the voices of the dead will be mediated through forms of distant witnessing, some of which already exist and others of which will emerge in the future. Not only do the scale and complexity of the digital records far exceed our human cognitive and empathetic capacities for listening, reading, and interpreting,[40] but new questions about the future of authenticity and digital provenance have also taken center stage in light of the possibilities unleashed by generative AI.

While this book focuses primarily on digital archives of survivor testimony, the mass digitization of artifacts and documents related to all aspects of the history and memory of the Holocaust is well underway. We might mention, in passing, some of the collecting and digitization efforts at other major museums and archives, for instance: the fifty million records in the International Tracing Service archive that reference the fates of 17.5 million people at the Arolsen Archives;[41] the millions of individuals and life stories in Yad Vashem's Central Database of Shoah Victims' Names; the US Holocaust Memorial Museum's encyclopedias and databases of more than 44,000 concentration camps, ghettos, forced labor camps, detention centers, and other sites of persecution between 1933 and 1945.[42] And these figures do not even include the millions of documents, artifacts, photographs, films, and books that are steadily becoming digitized in each of these archives and museums, or new database projects such as those carried out under the aegis of the Claims Conference.[43] Beyond these institutional projects, we might mention the global investigatory work of Yahad-In Unum, an international human rights and educational organization that has documented—through forensic evidence, witness interviews, survivor testimonies, and digital maps—more than three thousand execution sites of Jews in Ukraine, Russia, Belarus, and the Baltic countries between 1941 and 1944.[44] The mass digitization of documentation represents the condition of possibility for newly emergent fields of research at the intersection of digital humanities, memory studies, public history, and the computational and social sciences.

While it may have made sense at one time to argue that the Holocaust was "an event without witnesses" to make a point about the destructiveness of the genocidal will and the inability to assume an outside frame of reference during the event,[45] the Holocaust is clearly an event with hundreds of thousands of witnesses who have contributed and helped to produce a staggering amount of testimonial evidence, documents, and data sources. In addition to recording and stewarding these testimonies, these institutional archives have also produced new data and documentary evidence about the Holocaust, especially through the critically important mark-up and encoding of testimonies, the creation of extensive metadata scaffoldings, and the production of new documentary databases. Today, computational forms of analysis can work in tandem with documentary, historical, and social analyses to produce new frames of reference and perspectives to examine evidence, patterns, relationships, narratives, motives, micro- and macrolevel events, and more.

Even though the records and testimonies of the Holocaust have been (and continue to be) digitized on a massive scale, the use of computational methods and digital humanities tools for analysis is still in its early stages in the field of Holocaust studies. This may be because of a justified concern over replicating the violence caused by certain forms of quantification and the use of technologies that have the potential to dehumanize. Computation and quantification seem to present humanists with a "limit" on responsible modes of interpretation and representation.[46] Although not referencing computation specifically, LaCapra raised the question as to whether "there is something inappropriate about modes of representation which in their very style or manner of address tend to overly objectify, smooth over, or obliterate the nature and impact of the events they treat."[47] This could happen, he warns, through "excessive objectification, purely formal analysis, and narrative harmonization"[48]—all of which are potentialities of computation.

But, as we argue in this book, computational technologies and algorithmic methods do not necessarily lead to objectification, reduction, or simplification. These technologies and methods are not inherently unsuitable, but they do raise fundamental epistemological, aesthetic, and ethical questions, not unlike the questions raised several decades ago about appropriate and inappropriate modes of historical emplotment.[49] Inspired by Saul Friedländer who sought to develop "an integrative and integrated history" of the Holocaust to express the convergence of distinct elements, perspectives, and experiences, we are proposing an *integrated methodology* composed of computational and humanistic approaches to analyzing testimony. Such a methodology allows us to move between macro, meso, and micro scales of analysis, reflecting the size and complexity of the documentation in the archives. At the same time, because digital archives are now the primary access points and storage systems for testimony, integrated methodologies can yield new reading and listening practices as well as critical modes of engagement with the archive.

To do this, we need to proceed from the position that computational methods are not neutral, value-free, or objective. While they may sometimes help us discover or verify facts, these methods do interpretative and discursive work, which allows us to imagine possibilities, test hypotheses, change the scale of analysis, and represent knowledge in new ways. As architectural historian Paul Jaskot has pointed out, digital humanities scholars have developed and applied computational methods to expand our understanding of traditional sources by modeling contexts, bringing together new data, and scaling up interpretations in ways that explore new research questions.[50] Some of the pioneering work, for example, at the nexus of digital mapping, 3D visualization, and data-driven research has been led by the collective associated with the "Geographies of the Holocaust" project. They use the measurements derived from Historical Geographic Information Systems (H-GIS) in ways that foreground probability, uncertainty, and qualitative visualization rather than objectivist forms of mapping.[51] Their research humanizes the victims and expands our understanding of historical dynamics by moving between macro-level systems at the continental scale to cities, ghettos, blocks, and individual experiences articulated in testimonial narratives.[52]

Advances in related fields such as computational linguistics, natural language processing, and machine learning have opened up new methods for mining and analyzing large textual corpora and promise to have a transformative impact on how scholars, archivists, and librarians work with digitized historical records.[53] Under the broad leadership of organizations such as the European Holocaust Research Infrastructure (EHRI) working in collaboration with the Common Language Resources and Technology Infrastructure (CLARIN), robust digital infrastructures are emerging to support transnational Holocaust research and education. Their goals are to provide access to archival materials, facilitate interoperability, preserve collections, and share resources and knowledge. As documented by CLARIN, a number of institutions have already developed technical pipelines, workflows, and datasets for transforming oral history interviews into interoperable research data.[54] Focusing mostly on language technologies, the research includes standardized text mark-up and annotation, text encoding, text summarization, transcription and translation, voice and text alignment, interface development, and semantic and spatial search. For example, in partnership with the Yale Fortunoff Archive, the USC Shoah Foundation, and the USHMM, Gábor Tóth has used computational linguistics and text mining tools to identify recurrent experiences in testimonial fragments across these three corpora. His project, "Let Them Speak," offers a new, searchable interface for identifying shared experiences and showing how "the experience of the *Drowned* can be rendered through the pieces of collective suffering."[55] Employing data mining and natural language processing, Tóth created a custom search interface that allows users to explore 2,681 testimonies attuned to recurrent linguistic features in the transcripts and their underlying linguistic networks.

Using empirical data and systematic analyses, researchers have also used quantitative methods from the social, political, and computational sciences to analyze historical phenomena related to the events of the Holocaust.[56]

Yad Vashem has developed a comprehensive Holocaust deportation database, which includes quantitative information and source materials about every transport organized by the Nazis.[57] The data—arranged by individual transports, dates, number of people deported, number of survivors, nationality, the route taken, agencies involved, and, when available, gender and age breakdown—are now being used to advance social science research in Holocaust studies.[58]

And yet, I do not think we should ignore any lingering uncertainty or skepticism that we may feel when it comes to using digital technologies, quantitative methodologies, algorithms, or computational tools to study the Holocaust. After all, we have to depart from the knowledge that technologies and methods of calculative reasoning shaped the foundation of the social engineering policies of dehumanization that gave rise to the Holocaust. As Zygmunt Bauman famously argued, bureaucratic forms of rationality, coupled with technologies of quantification and abstraction, were deeply linked to the modern management of society that formed one of the conditions of possibility for the Holocaust.[59] When those forces—the product of modern science, modern technology, and modern forms of state power—came together with racialized forms of instrumental reason driven by biostatistics, bureaucratic distantiation, and hierarchical quantification, the result was social engineering, eugenics, and eventually genocide. Bureaucratic operations, Bauman argued, substituted "technical for moral responsibility," allowing people to be dealt with as railway "cargo" and human beings to be "reduced . . . to pure, quality-free measurements."[60]

Not unlike the operations of certain algorithms, bureaucracy, according to Bauman, "is programmed to seek the optimal solution. It is programmed to measure the optimum in such terms as would not distinguish between one human object and another, or between human and inhuman objects. What matters is the efficiency and lowering of costs of their processing."[61] To the extent that science achieved its aim of becoming "value-free," it became, in the process, "morally blind and speechless," replacing the previous authority of religion and ethics with a "cult of rationality."[62] The technological instruments it spawned—grounded in calculation, bureaucracy, and distantiation—were unable to prevent the crimes of the state and, instead, became complicit with them. Today, we are, once again, living in a moment in which science, in concert with industry and big tech, sometimes claims (quite dubiously and erroneously) that algorithms are objective or that rationalist calculations are value-free, even as AI reshapes the idea of the human. The risk of technology becoming morally blind, speechless, and complicit is still very much with us.

We must thus urgently ask: How can we use technology without replicating the violence of objectivist logics? How can computation and algorithms be morally engaged and able to speak in ways that humanize others, serve to bear witness to past crimes, and help inform reparative approaches to historical injustices? As we endeavor to answer these questions, Bauman may have given us an indication of a possible way forward that is not an either-or choice. In his Amalfi Prize Lecture of 1990, he concludes by citing the admonitions of computer scientist Joseph Weizenbaum and calling for "a new ethics, an ethics of distance and distant consequences, an ethics commensurable with the uncannily extended spatial and temporal range of the effects of technological action."[63] Although Bauman does not give any further explanation of what this may entail, he helps us identify the problem in a way that offers a sense of possibilities: "a new ethics" would have to be responsive to distance and address how technologies of distance enable new kinds of actions, mediations, and responsibilities. As we will see, an ethics of distant witnessing goes hand-in-hand with the need to imagine an ethics of the algorithm.

As technologies of calculation, decision-making, and prediction, algorithms are all too often disassociated from human experiences of time, space, and inter-subjective relationality precisely because they can be deployed anywhere, at any time, and in virtually any context. Far from being outside of history and society, algorithms and, more broadly, computational methods and quantitative thinking, need to be understood as deeply embedded, culturally contingent forms of power with a dialectical potential to humanize as well as dehumanize. They give rise to ways of knowing the world and constituting realities that could be—and, we argue, *should be*—yoked to an ethical framework enabled by human judgment and guided by values that are life-affirming. If there is to be a new ethics, human judgment must not be relinquished, overcome, or outsourced to algorithmic forms of decision-making. Instead, algorithms can function as heuristics with which to discover, devise, investigate, invent, compose, reflect, and, ultimately, humanize—provided algorithmic decision-making is guided by ethics as its first priority. Concretely, this means fostering human dignity, plurality, attentiveness, and care.

It would not be an exaggeration to say that we are in the midst of a paradigm shift in which digital technologies, algorithmic processes, and computational tools will soon mediate and structure our access to and knowledge of all historical events, not just the Holocaust, and to the dead more generally. What might it mean to bring together a new epistemology—guided and informed by algorithms—for the creation and analysis of testimony, on the one hand, and an ethics—guided and informed by testimony—for the development and deployment of algorithms, on the other? The risks and dangers of datafication, the logic of objectivism, and instrumental reason loom large and have deep historical roots. Throughout this book, we will confront them dialectically, demonstrating both the humanizing possibilities and the dehumanizing perils of technology. If there is to be an ethics of testimony after the passing of the generation of eyewitnesses, it will be constituted, we argue, by forms of distant witnessing guided by what we are calling an ethics of the algorithm. And so, it is with algorithms that we must begin.

1

What Should Algorithms Have to Do with Ethics?

Algorithms are ubiquitous and yet remain largely unknown and inscrutable in our digital worlds. Algorithms rank search results, personalize and recommend purchases, optimize traffic routes, calculate credit scores, detect fraud, trade stock, and determine what we see and who we interact with on our social networks, among many other things. In their most basic sense, algorithms are instructions, originally created by humans, for computers to run certain processes. Those instructions are represented symbolically through numbers, letters, equations, and logic sequences. While rarely revealed for public scrutiny, algorithms not only generate and evaluate data but they are also trained on data, often with the aim of solving more general problems: for instance, how to understand intention and determine relevance, how to increase attention and drive sales, how to get from point A to point B as efficiently as possible, how to measure risk, or how to diagnose disease. These complex calculations are happening all the time, as real-time inputs and outputs are reconfigured through feedback loops to make decisions, render predictions, screen for security, moderate social media feeds, make recommendations, and generate capital. Modeled on how neurons function in the brain, neural network algorithms engage in "deep learning" to train artificial intelligence (AI) in the ever-expanding domains of natural language processing, computer vision, speech recognition, language generation, and information extraction and retrieval.

Due to their ability to manage and parse complex data at extraordinary speeds, AI algorithms (and the computational power behind them) do many things at a massive scale: instantaneous image classification and speech recognition, predictive modeling in domains ranging from market forecasting to weather forecasting, trend and pattern detection, feature extraction and dimensionality reduction for data visualization, and natural language processing for search and text generation.

IBM's Watson machine-learning platform, for example, is used by the USC Shoah Foundation to automatically recognize speech and match questions asked by people interacting with Dimensions in Testimony to answers given by Holocaust survivors in real time. Google's Bidirectional Encoder Representations from Transformers (BERT) is one of the most widely used neural network algorithms for understanding intention and meaning in search queries. We used a variation of BERT, alongside an unsupervised machine-learning algorithm called "K-means clustering," to group and classify nearly ninety-thousand interview questions asked to Holocaust survivors. Our team also developed a prototype for a rule-based algorithm to extract "semantic triplets" from survivor testimonies in order to identify expressions of agency (statements of who did what and to whom) as well as applied a neural network algorithm to create a training model to disambiguate pronouns. Among the outputs that will be examined and discussed are a series of processual visualizations and "testimonial ensembles" derived from these algorithmic processes.

While some of these tasks could have been done manually, they certainly could not be done at scale, nor would it have been possible to identify, visualize, and analyze patterns and relationships across corpora without computational processing. Rather than seeing algorithmic methods to be antithetical to human interpretation (or even just distinct domains), we are proposing an approach to humanistic computing in which they are deeply intertwined and potentially complementary.[1] Not unlike other epistemologically transformative technologies (we might think of the camera, the clock, or the printing press), computers and the algorithms that run on them offer new ways of engaging, perceiving, framing, knowing, interacting with, and, ultimately, constituting the world. None of these technologies was ever neutral or value-free, but each helps us to see, perceive, and analyze the world around us, including helping us to determine what is worth knowing about and how. We *think with* these technologies, but we do not set them free to decide and judge automatically what is true, important, and useful.

For our purposes here, we use the term "algorithm" as a collective singular to refer to a wide range of computational processes that take the form of instructions, calculations, and decision logics. These include everything from ruled-based instructions, search queries, and sorting and filtering processes to classification and clustering tools, data mining, language extraction and modeling, and machine-learning algorithms trained on massive datasets. Algorithms are not data, but they do ingest data, generate data, transform data, arrange data, get trained on data, and output data, which we analyze, visualize, interpret, and reinterpret. Algorithms and computational processes overlap insofar as the former are embedded within the latter in various programs, tools, and software. Together, they help construct methods, in the sense of forging pathways, to explore problems and offer possible solutions.

Our overarching question can be formulated quite succinctly: *How can we think, listen, compose, and interpret ethically with algorithms and computational methods?* To explore answers to this question, we will bring algorithmic analyses and computational tools to bear on the study of the Holocaust, with a specific focus on thousands of witness testimonies given by Holocaust survivors from 1946 to the present. Spoken in various languages, recorded in (and transferred across) various media, as well as transcribed, translated, indexed, and marked up in different ways, these testimonies form an exceptionally rich body of materials to delve into fundamental questions of Holocaust memory and history. Because of their size, variability, and complexity, they may be accurately described as "big data." Owing to the nature of the content, Holocaust testimonies provide a test case for employing computational methods of analysis attuned to ethics and responsibility as well as a chance to develop an "ethics of the algorithm" through principles that can be applied more broadly and generally.

In what follows, we will first delve into the field of critical algorithm studies in order to understand some of the problems, limits, and assumptions of algorithmic processes and decisionist logics. Our initial focus will be on the kinds of agency sometimes given to algorithms to make decisions and the need to articulate how that agency is distinct from—but can be complementary to—human judgment. We argue that algorithms do not have and should not be endowed with ethical agency—that is, the ability to make ethical decisions about what we should or ought to do. Instead, this book is an argument for how to think and interpret with algorithms to provide guidance and insight *for* human judgment, *for* our acts of distant witnessing. We are not arguing that ethics "inheres" or "belongs" to any particular algorithm or that there is a single algorithm or set of algorithms to which ethics can be inherently attached. Instead, the phrase "ethics of the algorithm" points to the many ways that algorithms raise fundamental ethical questions in their formal functions, have ethical consequence, involve human judgment, and can contribute to our ethical thinking. Far from value-free or neutral, algorithms make decisions through various kinds of calculations, but by themselves, they are not capable of ethical reasoning. Algorithms can be harnessed to do interpretative work because they help us hear, read, and see differently; they can help us develop new kinds of attentiveness; they can change the scale of analysis and pluralize narratives; and they can open up new fields of possibility for generating knowledge and engaging with others. In the final analysis, the ethical question is how we should judge and act *with* and *in light of* algorithms.

* * *

If we glance at the origins of the concept of "algorithm," we see immediately that it had nothing to do with computers, since the term appears to be derived from the surname of Muḥammad ibn Mūsā al-Khwārizmī (c. 780–850 CE), a Persian scholar of mathematics and astronomy. When his writings on Hindu-Arabic numerals were translated into Latin in the twelfth century as *Algoritmi de numero Indorum* (Al-Khwārizmī on the Hindu art of reckoning), the word "algorithm" was introduced in the West. Initially denoting Al-Khwārizmī's methods of arithmetic calculation and symbol manipulation, the term algorithm only became closely allied with the formal logic of "decision-making" and computational processes in the twentieth century. The common usage of the term dates to the 1960s and 70s when algorithms—as mathematical instructions—could be run on computers to generate outputs from a set of inputs.[2] While it is the latter usage that will occupy most of our attention, it is worth bearing in mind that algorithmic processes are grounded in fundamental arithmetic and algebraic operations.

Today, the terms "algorithm" and "algorithmic" have much broader meanings. As Tarleton Gillespie points out, the word "algorithm" evidences a tremendous amount of lability, depending on the domain in which it is used: Software engineers and technical specialists consider an algorithm to be "a logical series of steps for organizing and acting on a body of data to quickly achieve a desired outcome" (such as play the best clip for the question asked). But the term has grown to also connote information technologies and people in an "ill-defined network . . . debating the models, cleaning the training data, designing the algorithms, tuning the parameters, [and] deciding which algorithms to depend on in which context."[3] This "sociotechnical ensemble," as Gillespie calls it, involves people, programs, models, data, information systems, and applications—all of which operate through various kinds of calculations and procedures.[4] As we explore the ethics of "information systems committed (both functionally and ideologically) to the computational generation of knowledge or decisions,"[5] we will lean more heavily on the definition of the algorithm as a "sociotechnical ensemble."

We might start in 1979 when the computer scientist Robert Kowalski famously defined an algorithm as the sum of its "logic" and "control" components. According to Kowalski, the logic component defines *what* is to be done. It determines "the meaning of the algorithm" and the way it behaves. The logic component includes the knowledge to be gathered and used in carrying out the processes, the definitions of the terms (such as variables and data structures), and the data inputs. The control component defines *how* it is to be done. It guides "the problem-solving strategy" and the efficiency by which the algorithm carries out processes.[6] The control component includes the methods for processing the data, executing certain procedures, and storing the data (such as in relational tables in a database or plotting the data on a map). Together, logic ("the what") and control ("the how") determine the meaning and efficiency, respectively, of an algorithm.

Kowalski's ideas formed the basis of an approach called logic programming, in which information and relationships between objects are defined through formal logic and rules. This gave rise to the programming language Prolog (codeveloped by Kowalski), which is widely used for natural language processing and in various domains of artificial intelligence.[7] Emblematic of logic programming, Kowalski's "classic" definition of an algorithm is often cited for its clarity as well as its applicability to other forms of computational representation.[8] Davide Panagia argues, for instance, that in order for an algorithmic model to work, "the parameters of the model need to be defined so as to fix their functional form," which, he says, is precisely what Kowalski's definition proposed. As Panagia writes, "for an algorithm to model reality in such a way as to produce an output means that it must consistently toggle between the outputs it generates and a predefined, optimal actuality," minimizing and reducing the difference in each iteration.[9] Zachary Horton points out that the algorithm and the database follow similar structures: "What is true of algorithms is true of databases: the logic component of a database is its classification structure, while its control component consists of methods of accessing its stored data."[10] But as Horton and other critics contend, the algorithm—like the database—is also a complex cultural form that "embeds cultural meaning and social relationships" by shaping and structuring fields of possibility, strategies for executing procedures, and schemes for organizing information.[11] Indeed, as Taina Bucher argues, "algorithms are much more than simply step-by-step instructions telling the machine what to do"; instead they constitute "a cultural logic" precisely because they "do" certain things that give rise to new agencies, new possibilities, and new forms of power.[12]

Beginning with the narrow definition of algorithms as *merely* instructions, we might enumerate some of their performative attributes and political functions. Algorithms count, sort, filter, rank, extrapolate, cluster, render, distill, correlate, score, measure, order, assign, harvest, and extract, among other things. They also recommend, compose, decide, moderate, predict, value, profile, polarize, and police. It is precisely here—when non-human agents are endowed with the capacity to judge and make decisions of social and ethical consequence—that algorithms take on a potentially dangerous kind of power over life.[13] That power is deployed in numerous, ever more consequential ways from deciding whether we qualify for a home loan to recommending videos on social media platforms and amplifying misinformation[14] to making risk assessments about the future criminality of a defendant to determining if a given neighborhood should be policed more heavily on a given day.[15]

What is missing in Kowalski's succinct definition of the algorithm as the sum of logic ("what") and control ("how") is *why, for whom, in whose name, to what ends, and with what possibilities and limitations?*[16] He defines the algorithm in such a way as to obfuscate any "awareness" of its content, context, or range of possible ends to which it might be applied, not to mention the violence that could result when "the what" and "the how" are never confronted with "why" and "for whom." When an algorithm is radically decontextualized from all social, cultural, political, economic, and historical situatedness, it is endowed with an aura of neutrality, objectivity, and even infallibility, not unlike what Donna Haraway critiqued as "the god trick of seeing everything from nowhere,"[17] or, we might add, doing anything from anywhere. If algorithmic decision-making is contextless, it can just be deployed anywhere, in any community, to whatever ends those in power have prioritized and determined. By contrast, as we will argue here, an ethics of the algorithm cannot be content-agnostic and must, instead, be deeply context-attuned—with the goal of situating knowledge, amplifying voices, and creating spaces for a multiplicity of stories and perspectives to inform the inputs and outputs of any algorithmic process.

All too often, however, as Ian Bogost has argued, the algorithm (and computation more broadly) is perceived as a "transcendental ideal," divorced from the messy, everyday, material reality and labor that make it run.[18] When the algorithm hides (or, more precisely, is hidden) in a "black box," there is little or no accountability, transparency, scrutiny, and participation.[19] And yet, as algorithms are deployed in and applied to nearly every possible cultural, political, social, and economic space, they are endowed, at least by some, with a level of unquestioned trust that, in Bogust's words, "turns computers into gods . . . [and] their outputs into scripture."[20] As we argue here, algorithms are hardly scripture, and computers are anything but gods; instead, they are both deeply situated, contingent cultural forms that produce and process data, which can be used to inform—not replace—human judgment and interpretation.

At the same time, the "what" and the "how" of an algorithm need to be rigorously scrutinized: What data is placed into the system (and what data is not)?

Who created the data and what story does it tell (or make it possible to tell, or not tell at all) by the way in which the data are structured? Whose voices are represented by the data and whose voices are left out? How are an algorithm's weights and thresholds calculated and represented? To whom are they accountable and what constitutes a responsible form of prediction? How is the individual human voice, human experience, human history, human freedom, and human potentiality preserved and safeguarded in the operations of the algorithm? If individuals are brought together, what ethical considerations should inform the construction of an aggregate? How can algorithmic processes help add more perspectives, insights, complexity, and layers into the historical record?

Because of their immense social and cultural impact, algorithms—and, more broadly, the data they generate, arrange, and evaluate—are considerably more than just "instructions" for computers to undertake tasks or find "answers" to problems. They are technologies of power—and, potentially, of empowerment. It is for this reason that algorithms (and the companies that develop them, not to mention the decisions that get made with them) have been subject to intense criticism in recent years. An interdisciplinary body of critical literature has exposed how algorithms are used to disadvantage certain groups, reinforce racism and sexism, replicate inequitable social structures, reify class hierarchies, and amplify extreme viewpoints.[21] Although calls for transparency, accountability, equity, and inclusion have been met with mixed results, global movements for algorithmic and data justice have also begun in earnest.[22]

In her study of the ethics and politics of machine-learning algorithms, Louise Amoore argues that algorithms are generating new "ideas of goodness, transgression, and what society ought to be."[23] She calls for an "ethics of algorithms" articulated as a "cloud ethics," in which the algorithm is "always already an ethicopolitical entity by virtue of being immanently formed through the relational attributes of selves and others."[24] Focusing on the social and technical conditions of their emergence and the consequences of their operations, she underscores the ways in which algorithms make "people and things perceptible"[25] for attention, judgment, and action in situations such as mass surveillance, policing, border control, robotic surgery, and drone warfare, where life and death are ultimately adjudicated. Algorithmic violence occurs when data and algorithms are weaponized to control and restrict the freedom of others, often under the guise of objectivity, neutral outputs, and mathematical certainty. When every person in a neighborhood is reduced, for instance, to a datapoint of fixed dimensionality within a geographically and temporally inscribed bounding box for policing, the supposed "objectivity" of the algorithm (it's just instructions; it's just numeric data) has both curtailed freedom and dehumanized the residents. Divorced from the values of human plurality and freedom, such algorithms make one-directional decisions, never taking into account or weighing the perspectives, experiences, and points of view of those who have been targeted for surveillance. As Amoore argues, citing the NSA's collection and algorithmic analysis of citizens' data, "contemporary algorithms are changing the processes by which people and things are rendered perceptible and brought to attention" for various kinds of action.[26] When algorithms are used to render people into data as a means to some other end (such as profit, social control, or policing) rather than an end in themselves, they can quickly become tools of discrimination and oppression.

There are a number of reasons why this happens: First, humans behave *as if* algorithms are objective, value-free, neutral, and automatic when, in fact, they are always already programmed, structured, and respondent in certain ways (and non-respondent in others). There is nothing "automatic" about how an algorithm functions since it is always grounded in and a function of a series of programmed decisions that encode certain parameters, worldviews, values, and perspectives.[27] And similarly, there is nothing "automatic" about the inputs or outputs of an algorithm: these are a function of human decisions, and both need to be rigorously scrutinized, contextualized, and historicized. In other words, we do not just run algorithms and get answers; instead, we get possibilities that constantly need to be interrogated and interpreted. This leads to the second danger, namely when humans fail to scrutinize and expose how algorithms work, particularly when algorithms reinscribe structural inequities, including gender and racial disparities, and are not held accountable to anyone or anything.[28] And even when algorithms are, indeed, scrutinized for biases, a third danger arises when humans think that the algorithms can be "fixed" by simply inserting a constraint or making a fairness adjustment without interrogating their fundamental epistemologies and relationship to broader structural systems. Such a belief rests on the assumption that algorithms become progressively more objective, factual, and, ultimately, infallible.

Recognizing the potential of algorithms to propagate disparities, some computer scientists, such as Michael Kearns and Aaron Roth, have called for an "ethical algorithm" attuned to equity, fairness, and privacy.[29] Focusing on these social values, Kearns and Roth argue for the need "to encode ethical principles directly into the design of the algorithms that are increasingly woven into our daily lives."[30] For them and others, the principles of fairness, accuracy, transparency, and ethics (FATE)[31] should inform "the emerging science of designing social constraints directly into the algorithm."[32] They argue that biases in training data might be overcome by introducing a "fairness constraint" in machine-learning models and suggest "quantifying and injecting diversity"[33] so that different viewpoints and new clusters of data can break apart "the echo chamber" or "filter bubble" prevalent in social media and news feeds.

While I certainly agree that unethical algorithms and biased data need to be corrected, these views are grounded in a faith that science and/or the companies that develop and benefit from algorithms can (and will) effectively develop and perfect them in ways that are equitable, fair, and transparent for everyone. Not only is this faith enormously misplaced (as the scandals around the failure of Facebook and other social media companies to self-regulate have shown[34]), but it is grounded in a belief that "ethical algorithms" are merely a problem of getting the science right and are something that science and technology companies can (or will eventually) solve. Indeed, when ethics and equity are cast as problems that science can fix by adjusting the parameters of the algorithm, a very limited framework informs the problem and the solutions being proposed. History, design, law, policy, and social and cultural practices, for example, are completely left out of such a rationalist calculus. "Quantifying and injecting diversity" into a system may result in different news stories in a user's feed, but it will not address— and may, in fact, reinforce and embed technologically—the larger, structural inequities put in place by the history of human decision-making. The "science" of ethical algorithms will always fall short because algorithms are not mathematical vessels that can be perfected to behave morally but always already value-laden, interpretative tools embedded in complex and long-standing social relations comprised of humans and machines.

As we argue throughout this book, there are many things that algorithms can do that humans cannot do (or that we cannot do well at scale): processing data to detect underlying correlations and patterns, extracting and structuring massive amounts of data for interpretation, detecting outliers and unique features among a field of data, comparing specific cases to results across an entire corpus, or summarizing data in ways that enable new modes of query and analysis. Precisely because algorithms "read" and "listen" in ways that are fundamentally different from human reading and listening, they detect differences, patterns, precedents, and relationships that human readers and listeners cannot possibly track and remember: word frequencies, co-occurrences, code-switching, paralinguistic cues, topics, and grammatical relationships between words across an entire corpus are just a few examples. An algorithm cannot tell us what something means (such as why a particular word was used or what a change in intonation of someone's voice means in the context of a testimony), but an algorithm can identify such changes and differences for human interpretation, especially ones that may otherwise go undetected by human listeners. And in certain fields, algorithms and AI may reach decisions that are less biased, more informed, and more representative than human decision makers precisely because they rely on more data, consider more outcomes, and can draw on many more precedents for their calculations.[35]

By selecting and drawing attention to certain things, by making decisions, and by doing evaluative work, algorithms help constitute the world, and, therefore, have political, epistemological, and ethical consequence. They have a certain kind of agency to decide and act but do not have a conscience or sense of ethical self-reflexivity. Without reducing "the teeming multiplicity of the world to a precise output,"[36] the question for us is how algorithms can perceive and distill things that help humanize others, deepen understanding, proliferate interpretations, and build toward futures that are open-ended and truly pluralizing. If it is possible to *think with algorithms* in ways that are thoughtful, speculative, and pluralizing, we must not relinquish human judgment to algorithms. We must not claim that they merely unlock factual truths or that they have independent ethical agency. In the next section, we describe why.

Ethical Agency and Judgment

While machines and algorithms have been endowed with agency to make decisions, they do not, we argue, have *ethical agency*—that is, the ability to reflect on whether they should or should not do something according to values and principles that exist in dynamic situations of intersubjectivity, relationality, and historicity. Ethical agency is grounded in the freedom of value-based judgments that not only respond to the question "what should be done?" but also respond to the question "what should *not* be done?" An algorithm does not have the ethical agency and reflexivity to decide—either ahead of time or in the middle of running a process—not to act due to a value judgment grounded in knowledge, responsibility, or a sense of moral obligation. In short, a sense of ethics is not what makes an algorithm decide or act in ways that either harm or help others. While there is no guarantee that ethics will stop a human being from deciding to harm others or act wrongly, human beings do have ethical agency, and we can decide to act, not to act, or to act differently depending on the specific situation, context, knowledge, and history. This is because ethics opens a field of possibilities for human decision-making, choice, and judgment. Although there is no single way to navigate this field, common principles and values—such as protecting human dignity, affirming human life, and fostering human plurality—can guide our judgment.

About a decade after inventing ELIZA (1964–1966), widely considered the world's first natural language processing program to simulate human conversation, Joseph Weizenbaum, a professor of computer science at MIT, published a scathing critique of the power of computers and the risks to the social world unleashed by the ascendancy of instrumental reason. His 1976 book *Computer Power and Human Reason* argued that human judgment was becoming steadily corrupted by the ruthlessness of calculating reason. He urged his readers to consider "the proper place of computers in the social order"[37] and sought to disabuse computers of the power with which they had been endowed by society at large. For Weizenbaum, the computer was the culminating symbol of the modern age of science, which had brought about the rationalization of the world and given rise to a form of thoughtlessness that divorced technology from ethics. In Weizenbaum's words: "When instrumental reason is the sole guide to action, the acts it justifies are robbed of their inherent meanings and thus exist in an ethical vacuum."[38]

Weizenbaum, a German Jewish refugee who escaped Nazi Germany in 1936 with his family, conceived of the book at the height of the Vietnam War and explicitly linked the Holocaust to the logic of instrumental reason: "Germany implemented the 'Final Solution' of its 'Jewish Problem' as a textbook exercise in instrumental reasoning."[39] Indeed, one can hear echoes of the Frankfurt School across the pages of his critique. Citing Max Horkheimer's *Eclipse of Reason*, Weizenbaum criticizes the hegemony of science as the authority of knowledge and urges "the introduction of ethical thought into science . . . [to] combat the imperialism of instrumental reason."[40] The fully enlightened world, guided by the power of instrumental reason, reduces complexity and human choice to rationalized calculations, rule-based processes, and quantitatively driven decisions. The result is the corruption of human choice—the basis of ethics—into "a mechanical act."[41] Referencing the distanciation and dehumanization produced by the conduct of modern warfare, Weizenbaum warns of "decisions [being] made with the aid of, and sometimes entirely by, computers whose programs no one any longer knows explicitly or understands."[42] He further warns of the abdication "of decision-making responsibility" to a technology that is not fully understood and operates precisely by "[removing] responsibility from the shoulders of everyone."[43] Weizenbaum concludes by arguing for the need to preserve the difference between deciding and choosing: instrumental reason decides through logicality and calculation but only humans can choose through ethical judgments.

Although Weizenbaum is widely remembered as the inventor of the first natural language processing program to function (at least ostensibly) like a Turing Test, his strongest critiques of the seductiveness of the computer, the dangers of instrumental reason, and the misguided enthusiasm for and applications of his own work have remained largely unheeded.[44] His critiques—made in the foundational, early years of AI nearly two decades before browsers facilitated access to the Internet via the World Wide Web—sought to sound the alarm bell and have proven to be quite prescient: the computer is a "powerful new metaphor for helping us to understand many aspects of the world, but that it enslaves the mind that has no other metaphors and few other resources to call on."[45] Weizenbaum is not arguing in favor of giving up computers and technology but rather underscoring the dangers inherent in transferring too much power to them without recognizing their fundamental limitations and seductive powers. After rejecting soundly any kind of "imperial rights to science,"[46] he concludes by advocating for the expressiveness of the humanities in helping us to articulate more inclusive, ethical, and humane frameworks for knowledge.[47] Through the humanities, he suggests, multiple epistemological frameworks, diverse perspectives, multilayered histories, and cultural metaphors arise for both understanding the complexity of the world and imagining possible, future worlds. The faculty of human judgment remains at its core and needs to be allied with human dignity.

In realms such as ethics and aesthetics, the faculty of human judgment differs markedly from "algorithmic judgment" because the former derives from freedom and represents a mode of reflection cognizant of history, grounded in intersubjectivity, and part of a common community or *sensus communis*.[48] According to Hannah Arendt, "judgments are not arrived at by either deduction or induction [because] they have nothing in common with logical operations."[49] This is because the faculty of judgment is not a kind of thinking grounded in logic or algorithmic calculations but rather a "public sense" of decision-making grounded in human freedom and plurality. As she explains, "judgment may be one of the fundamental abilities of man [*sic*] as a political being insofar as it enables him to orient himself in the public realm, in the common world."[50] For Arendt, judgment is an activity that happens in "the presence of others" and must consider the "perspectives" of others in building toward potential agreement.[51] Guided by one's sense of being in a community, judgment is a critical part of what she calls "sharing-the-world-with-others" and thus rests on an "expanded way of thinking" (*eine erweiterte Denkungsart*).[52] Such an expanded way of thinking has the potential to imagine new constellations, create new narratives, offer new interpretations, and attune our attention to new possibilities.[53] As she argues in her lectures on Immanuel Kant, the notion of an enlarged or expanded mind happens through the realm of the imagination when we compare "our judgment with the possible rather than the actual judgments of others, and by putting ourselves in the place of any other man [*sic*]."⁵⁴ For this reason, she considers judgment to be a "political" activity carried out "in the sphere of public life and the common world."⁵⁵

However, by itself, algorithmic decision-making is agnostic to others and need not consider the perspectives or presence of anyone. As logic and rule-based calculations, algorithms do not judge as members of a common community or shared world even if they may facilitate an "expanded way of thinking." They would not be part of the public realm as Arendt defines it in *The Human Condition* since "the reality of the public realm relies on the simultaneous presence of innumerable perspectives and aspects in which the common world presents itself and for which no common measurement or denominator can ever be devised."⁵⁶ The public realm is not only characterized by the diversity of many different perspectives, but it is also a chance for "being seen and being heard by others" and the possibility of coming to agreement as participants in "the common world."⁵⁷ This plurality of perspectives and experiences is grounded in the potentialities of human freedom and thus is the condition of possibility for democratic societies. As Linda Zerilli explains Arendt's position, "judging is political . . . because it proceeds by taking into account the perspectives of others and does not rely on an algorithmic decision procedure or the mechanical subsumption of particulars under known rules."⁵⁸ Unlike decisions made by algorithms, human judgment, according to Arendt, is grounded in intersubjectivity, freedom, community, and plurality. For us, however, the questions we will ask are much more intertwined: How can algorithms inform and inflect human judgment through their attunement and perceptions, thus giving rise to an expanded way of thinking? At the same time, how does human judgment inform and inflect how algorithms are attuned and what they perceive?

For Arendt, the faculty of judgment is the ability "to judge particulars . . . [such as] 'this is wrong,' 'this is beautiful,'" and it differs from the faculty of thinking, which deals with representations and things further away, abstract, or invisible.⁵⁹ While thinking, she argues, deals with "representations of things that are absent" and judging deals with "particulars and things close at hand, . . . the two are interrelated in a way similar to the way consciousness and conscience are interconnected."⁶⁰ In other words, consciousness is to thinking as conscience is to judging. Although Arendt does not have more to say about the development of one's conscience, it is clear that ethical judgments—and the freedom to make such judgments—are at the core of what it means to share the world with others. That freedom to act (or not to act) in accordance with such judgments takes place in a field of possible actions in the subjunctive mode, namely a reflection of what we could, should, and ought to do.⁶¹

Of course, there are no guarantees for thinking, judging, and acting according to ethical principles and moral values. One need only recall that Arendt's reflections on judgment were articulated in the aftermath of the trial of Adolf Eichmann, the infamous Nazi officer who coordinated the deportation trains carrying hundreds of thousands of Jews to their deaths. For Arendt, the uniqueness of the evil that Eichmann represented was epitomized by his "sheer thoughtlessness."[62] This thoughtlessness did not mean stupidity but rather the inability to realize and reflect on what he was doing, which she identified as his "lack of imagination" and his "*hostis generis humani*,"[63] which might be translated, in Arendt's terms, as hatred of human plurality.[64] She writes that while his crimes made it "well-nigh impossible for him to know or to feel that he is doing wrong," he unequivocally "supported and carried out a policy of not wanting to share the earth with the Jewish people and the people of a number of other nations . . . [as if he] and [his] superiors had any right to determine who should and who should not inhabit the world."[65] Lacking any reflection on moral behavior or the value of human plurality, Eichmann abdicated all ethical agency and never "[fell] back upon his 'conscience.'"[66] Had he been "thoughtful" in Arendt's sense of reflecting on and recognizing his responsibility for his actions, a sense of ethical agency might have led him to judge right from wrong and to act differently. Instead, as a Nazi ideologue, he administered genocide as a "legal" crime without his conscience or faculty of judgment ever raising a question.[67] In Arendt's assessment, Eichmann never thought about what he was doing. He processed orders and abdicated all ethical agency, reflexivity, and responsibility that might have prompted him to act otherwise. In short, he embodied the extreme danger of purely instrumental, algorithmic reason. He ran processes and never reflected any further.

The concomitant risk involves human beings ceding their judgment to algorithmic processes and letting algorithms make ethical judgments. When humans behave as if algorithms have ethical agency and can make ethical decisions on their own, the faculty of human judgment is, at best, outsourced to the algorithm and, at worst, relinquished to algorithmic decision-making. In his reflections on algorithmic governance and law, Norman Spaulding argues that "what is at stake . . . is the form and function of human judgment": not only because human judgment is already built into AI systems but, more urgently, because human judgment is also displaced by AI.[68] Some of that displacement, he argues, may offer potentially promising possibilities, for instance, in predictive analytics "to liberate us from the biases, errors, and repetition automatism of local knowledge, tradition, and intuition," but "the liberation is to a future heavily determined by rationally calculated abstractions aggregated from observable data of our past choices."[69] Alone and by itself, algorithmic decision-making stands in tension with new world-building because the former produces a future that is derived from the stock of experiences contained in the inputs of the past.[70] As Cathy O'Neil argues: "Big data processes codify the past. They do not invent the future. Doing that requires moral imagination, and that's something only humans can provide. We have to explicitly embed better values into our algorithms, creating Big Data models that follow our ethical lead."[71] *Ethics of the Algorithm* is an attempt to do just that: namely, to use algorithms and develop big data models in ways that complexify, pluralize, add nuance, deepen understanding, and tarry with difference and particularity.

O'Neil's critique is not unlike that made by Hayden White in his most strident critiques of historians who attempt to construct a "specious continuity" between the past, present, and future.[72] In contrast to certain historians who imagined history as a science aimed at objectively uncovering "the past" to create lines of continuity that extend chronologically into the present and point toward the future, White argued for the contingency of narrative emplotment marked by discontinuity and disruption. The "past" was not something that could be known in any totalizing, objective, or definitive sense but rather was a function of choices made in the present for the sake of imagining possible worlds. Far from a scientific process in which facts speak for themselves, historical representation is a "poetic process" of decision-making, construction, and narrative emplotment.[73] Any claim to resuscitate or know the fullness of the past—whether by scientifically-minded historians or algorithms—needs to be subject to intense scrutiny precisely because such methods can lead to a codification of the past into a body of facts all-too-easily instrumentalized for dubious ends. As White writes in his famous essay "The Burden of History": "The historian serves no one well by constructing a specious continuity between the present world and that which preceded it. On the contrary, we require a history that will educate us to discontinuity more than ever before; for discontinuity, disruption, and chaos is our lot."[74]

Far from determinative, historians make judgments that give rise to narratives through the choices they make about their modes of emplotment. When those judgments offer orientation and guidance for present or future action, the past becomes "practical," White argues, in the sense of being useful as well as ethical.[75] The value of studying the past, White contends, is not "an end in itself," but rather rests on providing "perspectives on the present that contribute to the solution of problems peculiar to our own time."[76] The risk, however, is to fall back on objectivist understandings of the past as a totalized "thing" that can be known, uncovered, and constituted in the present from which to predict the future. This strict scientification of the past—whether created by historians or by algorithms—

narrowly defines "the what" and "the how" as properties to be known, managed, and applied rather than as practical, open-ended possibilities oriented toward ethical world-making. How, then, might we engage "the practical past of memory, dream, fantasy, experience, and imagination" in ways that help us answer ethical questions:[77] *What ought I to do, how ought I attune myself to the past, and how might I engage responsibly with the voices of the dead?*

Ethics of the Algorithm argues for the creation of a third space: Humans should not cede their faculties of judgment to algorithms and, instead, could use algorithmic calculations as part of a heuristic to make interpretative and ethical decisions, not unlike the "cognitive assemblages" described by N. Katherine Hayles.[78] When we speak of an "ethics of the algorithm," we mean the possibilities for using algorithms and computational processes to expand our thinking, attune our perception, and inform judgment in ways that advance human dignity, freedom, and plurality. With regard to the study of the memory and history of the Holocaust, we ask: How can algorithms help us explore the complexity and ambiguity of cultural records, appreciate differences, preserve the heteronomous, listen to more voices and perspectives, and, ultimately, provide insights that help to humanize others through various practices of distant witnessing? Can algorithms and computational methods be used against themselves, so to speak, to unmask epistemic assumptions or ideologies built into computational systems? Rather than merely solving problems and providing (seemingly) decisive answers, we aim to show how algorithms can function as devices to ask new questions, thereby enabling humanists to use them as tools for discovery, analysis, and judgment. In so doing, algorithmic methods and computational tools can complement—rather than oppose, undermine, or override—humanistic methods of interpretation.

In the chapters that follow, we use rule-based algorithms, classification algorithms, machine-learning algorithms, and more to think with algorithms, but we do not set them free to do things on their own. By themselves, algorithms are not "thoughtful," "intelligent," or "magical" things endowed with ethical agency or capable of ethical judgment. They are fallible, just like the humans who created them. As such, we scrutinize their formal functions and their outputs; we learn from and we learn with them; we think with them and do not oppose humanistic interpretative methods to algorithmic interpretive methods; we situate their inputs, transformations, and outputs in ways that open up fields of interpretation and possible actions. Algorithms do not provide final answers or closure but rather allow us to ask new kinds of exploratory questions that multiply what we perceive and how we interpret the voices, perspectives, and stories preserved—and not preserved—in cultural records.[79]

As Bucher suggests, algorithms can function as problematizations with "the capacity to produce new orderings or disorderings," which may make it possible for human beings to perceive, listen, know, and act differently.[80] By connecting them to humanistic epistemological and interpretative practices, it becomes possible to move beyond the algorithmic logic of "if . . . then" conditional statements and engage, instead, with a wide range of subjunctive and speculative possibilities: "what if, then possibly . . ." or "what if, then how might . . ." or "what if, how should or how ought I . . ." An ethics of the algorithm is aspirational in that it seeks to deploy algorithms and computational processes to think, imagine, listen, document, interpret, and humanize. To the extent that algorithms help us to "see" and "hear" in new ways, we are able to recognize and appreciate new things, enabling us tell new stories by constantly interpreting and reinterpreting the complexity of the human record at different scales and in creative, life-affirming ways. The question, of course, is: how?

Proposing Methods / Imagining Practices

Our point of departure is a dictum from Simone de Beauvoir: "Ethics does not furnish recipes any more than do science and art. One can merely propose methods."[81] The quotation comes from her seminal book on existentialist ethics, *The Ethics of Ambiguity* (1948), a study of the relationship between human freedom and ethical responsibility. Without absolute truths or higher powers to guide us, de Beauvoir argues that we are responsible for everything we do and must therefore forge an "ethics of ambiguity" in a world of subjective, open possibilities. But how does this freedom and ambiguity give rise to the creation of ethical frameworks for choices and actions? It falls on us, she suggests, to come up with methods—and, we might also add, the failure to come up with methods is also a choice with moral consequences, such as when algorithmic methods devoid of ethical frameworks are presented as value-neutral or objective. A recipe, of course, provides a set of step-by-step instructions, which are known ahead of time and generally produce the same output. Science-by-recipe would merely replicate the results we know already, never allowing for progress, let alone scientific breakthroughs or paradigm shifts. Art-by-recipe would be like painting by numbers; it would be absurd to think that following a set of predefined steps and procedures would create beauty. History-by-recipe would be a historicist approach motivated by the belief that "the past" can be definitively reconstructed through certain scientific methods. Similarly, ethics-by-recipe would mean a moral code or set of instructions that tells us, in all cases, what we ought or ought not to do.

The point is that judgments in ethics, art, science, or history cannot be reduced to definitive, step-by-step instructions or recipes. Instead, we make choices—for instance, about narrative forms of emplotment or methods of attunement—guided by certain principles. While algorithms are often thought to be fixed instructions or recipes to generate answers, we are arguing, instead, that they always encode human choices and generate contingent outputs. Far from being instructions to impose upon archives, data, or historical records, algorithms are propositional methods and need to be considered within an open field of possible tools with which to think. As de Beauvoir argues, if humans are condemned to be free, then we have to *propose* methods by which we judge.

Derived from the Greek root *hodos*, a method is a "road," a possible pathway forward. There are many roads, and, as such, methods have to be developed, forged, tried out, and sometimes abandoned. Methods are experimental, situated, and bound to a time-kernel, rather than linear, objectivist, or universalizing. Methods also need to be evaluated, for not every method is equally good or compelling. And as we propose methods, we need to articulate what principles undergird them. *Ethics of the Algorithm* is anything but a recipe book, an answer guide, or set of instructions. Instead, as an experimental undertaking in proposing methods and imagining practices, it argues for the urgent convergence between the methods proposed in ethics and the methods proposed in computation, both of which should be rooted in principles that care for, honor, and expand human dignity, human life, and human freedom.

To affirm the complexity of life means to develop data generation and computational methods that refuse to use another as a means to some other end or represent individuals as finite sets of datapoints or attributes to be merely calculated.[82] As de Beauvoir argues in *The Ethics of Ambiguity*, "ethics is the triumph of freedom over facticity."[83] Human beings do not live on what she calls "the plane of bare facticity"—the merest factual reality or biological existence—because "no man [*sic*] is a datum . . . passively suffered."[84] On the contrary, every human being is "an absolute value," and each individual's "freedom can be achieved only through the freedom of others."[85] When tyrants or their followers take away the freedom of others through violence "in lynchings, in pogroms, in all the great bloody movements," human beings become enclosed by their "facticity" and treated as "cattle."[86] Essentially, they are reduced to objects, numbers, or what we will call "bare data." By contrast, the fundamental ethical precept, she argues, is "to treat the other . . . as a freedom so that his [*sic*] end may be freedom."[87] If we apply this precept to computational processes, algorithms must not use human beings for some other end that undermines their freedom by enclosing them in a part of their facticity; instead, thinking ethically with algorithms means creating futures for human potentiality, particularity, and heterogeneity.

The chapters of this book unfold in a fugue-like way. We introduce analytical methods and testimonies together, building contrapuntally but also progressively on motifs, voices, and interpretative practices. Chapters alternate between the general and the specific, from zoomed-out views of an archival corpus to individual voices and the radically particular utterance; methods are refined and revisited throughout the book, while voices are encountered across the pages in registers that allow their expressivity to persist. Attuned to the risks of automation, objectivism, and instrumental reason, we are proposing methods in the mode of the subjunctive; that is to say, these are possible methods to help us interpret and reinterpret testimony, all of which build toward an ethics of the algorithm. The results are not final answers and are certainly not intended to provide closure, underlying truths, or singular solutions. They do, however, enable experimental ways of working with digital archives through a wide range of computational methods and algorithmic transformations of data. These have resulted in processual visualizations, modernist modes of storytelling, testimonial ensembles, paratexts, annotated spectrograms, speculative designs, and new structures for and experiences of testimony. While the specific technologies discussed in this book will surely be supplemented and supplanted by others in the future, our methods and practices are intended to form the groundwork for an emerging field of research that foregrounds questions of ethics at the nexus of the humanities and computation.

Without in any way ignoring the unethical potentials of algorithms to simplify, polarize, and control, we seek to explore and model dialectically how algorithms can be used for life-affirming ends: namely, to help us deepen knowledge and understanding, detect patterns and relationships, shift the scales of analysis, identify difference in the archive, and add more perspectives and voices to the cultural record. Algorithms help to proliferate data, stories, and interpretations; they allow us to see and analyze at various scales, from singular individuals to collective, transhistorical experiences. Ultimately, what we are after in the most practical sense are ethical forms of distant witnessing that think and care about the other.

As both the generative force and underbelly of the modern, rationalized world, the use of algorithms is hardly new. In fact, in the 1930s and early 40s, algorithmic processes—using Hollerith punch cards, tabulating machines, and statistics—played a critical role in tracking and registering Jews, compiling deportation lists, and reducing people to bare data through systematic processes of dehumanization. As we will see in the second chapter, under Nazi occupation, the Dutch state's registration authority and its chief inspector for population registration, Jacobus Lentz, assiduously carried out the Nazi orders to register all the Dutch Jews, compile interoperable records of the registration and census data, visualize that data as maps, and process that data to form deportation lists. This is an emblematic— and calamitous—moment in which the failure of human judgment in data gathering, data analysis, data visualization, and data processing became complicit with genocide.

However, this outcome was neither inevitable nor the only possibility for collecting data and thinking with algorithms. We might entertain a thought exercise: Could data gathering, data analysis, data visualization, and data processing have been used for something life-affirming—for instance, as a means to rescue the Jews who were immediately in danger of deportation by planning exit routes to allow them to hide, perhaps, in the countryside or reach the shores of another country, not unlike the ways in which the Danish Jews were ferried to safety in Sweden? What if, instead of aiding the creation of deportation lists, the maps and punch cards were used to identify the most vulnerable people and optimize available transportation routes for moving them out of harm's way? Could some of the same calculations and efficiencies of computation have been used for something life-affirming instead? How could an algorithm of care and refuge have been programmed instead? At the same time, we need to ask about the decisions and calculations made by Lentz himself. As a human being, he could have judged and acted differently; he could have thought about data and algorithmic calculations in fundamentally different ways—for example, to respect and save lives. He could have prioritized human dignity, human freedom, and human plurality, but he did not. He prioritized the voiceless neutrality of administration and the calculus of instrumental reason.

While these kinds of reflections will, of course, always remain counterfactual thought experiments, the bare data produced by Lentz and the Dutch registration authorities has, seven decades later, been transformed into "life-affirming data" through a number of memorial projects. The data have been aggregated, queried, sorted, cross-tabulated, and visualized to give rise to new data, new stories, and new modes of emplotment that span the digital and physical worlds of memorials and memory cultures. In essence, the database and punch cards, which previously formed the deportation lists, have now become a digital refuge for the names, memories, and stories of those who were murdered. As we explore this potentiality, we will situate our analysis vis-à-vis another "big data" project, specifically the Transatlantic Slave Trade Database, in which the critiques of numeracy and the bare data of the archive have also inspired reparative forms of scholarship and knowledge design. How can data collection, databases, and computation more generally be used for life-affirming ends? How can data be gathered, indexed, and processed in ways that open up new possibilities for memorializing human life and adding to our understanding of the cultural record?

The next chapters turn to practices and delve into these questions from the archives of Holocaust studies. The third chapter begins with the immediate postwar period, in which the first audio interviews were recorded with Holocaust survivors in displaced persons camps. These were conducted by an individual named David Boder who used a wire recorder in 1946 to interview about 120 survivors in nine different languages. Where Lentz collected and tallied data that reduced humans to bare life, Boder collected stories and sought to develop practices of listening and analysis informed by humanistic and social scientific methods. Not only do his interviews represent a key origin for the genre of Holocaust testimony, but his analytical methods, we argue, are a key origin for "digital humanities" methodologies. We will endeavor to characterize the uniqueness of the interviews by using a range of computational methods to compare them—in terms of structure and content—to later testimonies, particularly those of the Yale Fortunoff Archive and the USC Shoah Foundation's Visual History Archive.

As a linguist and quantitative psychologist, Boder and his team undertook their own analyses of the testimonies using proto-computational methods to quantify trauma in relationship to narrative and language. His archive-building and analytical work represents a key arc for this book since it raises important humanistic questions at the nexus of quantitative and qualitative analysis, media specificity, early computational linguistics, and trauma theory. While his pioneering archive of spoken testimony is fairly well-known in Holocaust studies, the analytical work carried out by his team—specifically, the mark-up of the testimonies to track and quantify trauma, the analysis of testimonial language in terms of distress and relief structures, and the development of a generalizable traumatological lexicon—is much less known and appreciated. Boder's proto-computational work will function as the point of departure for a series of investigations including the analysis of tens of thousands of interview questions, the development of algorithmic forms of counter-indexing to analyze spaces of ambiguity ("the gray zone") in testimonies, the use of quantitative methods to characterize the changing genre of testimony, and the creation of what we call "testimonial ensembles."

The chapters and digital projects that follow employ various computational methods—including scalable data visualizations, text analysis tools developed for natural language processing, network analysis, phonetic and speech analysis, and machine-learning algorithms—to investigate the genre of spoken Holocaust testimony. This work is documented comparatively and examines the structure of digital archives alongside the creation of specific corpora and individual testimonies. But rather than deploying computational methods in just one direction (namely, to analyze corpora of testimony), we also show how the thousands of testimonies from the aforementioned institutional archives can help shape an ethics for algorithms and computational methods more broadly. The fourth chapter on the USC Shoah Foundation's Visual History Archive takes a "macrohistorical" view using the data related to more than fifty thousand Holocaust and genocide testimonies. It asks the fundamental question of what makes a digital archive, database, information system, and interface ethical? The analysis moves between comparative, whole-corpus visualizations and individual witness accounts in order to examine the changing content and narrative structures of testimonies. It aims to articulate the limits of literalist indexing systems and the need to develop methods of "saying" and "unsaying" the database to continually unleash new potentialities in testimony. At the same time, we raise questions about the "computational tractability" of testimony in the first place and what it means for the Holocaust to be a paradigm for developing digital archives for other genocides: What is at stake when the interviewing and recording techniques, the indexing methodologies and categories, and the information infrastructures are built on a platform that has been "generalized," so to speak, for all Holocaust and genocide testimonies?

The fifth chapter, "The Haunted Voice: On the Ethics of Close and Distant Listening," uses phonetic and speech analysis tools to focus on the voice *as voice*. Attuned to the sonorous dimensions of testimony that are all too often ignored when we privilege semantic content to interpret language and meaning, this chapter turns to the grain of the voice through an analysis of silence and speech, loudness and pitch, and cadence and rhythm. We demonstrate how "close listening" achieved through computational sound analysis can provide insights into testimonial expressivity that cannot be found when the analysis remains solely on the semantic meaning of words in narratives. How might we listen to silence, paralinguistic cues, breathing, and the sonic richness of the whole testimonial environment? At the same time, what are the ethical limits of the datafication of the sonic record of a testimony, especially when we consider the ways these same technologies have been used to create "voice prints" (used from fraud detection to surveillance) and are now being used to train AI to evaluate human performance, qualities, and competencies? In other words, how do we negotiate the borderland between ethical and unethical phonetic measurements with algorithmically informed techniques of listening?

The digital project that follows analyzes nearly ninety thousand questions asked to survivors from 1946 to the present. Here, we critically assess how machine-learning language models can help us classify and understand the changing topics and questions asked to survivors over seven decades, across four testimonial corpora. The outputs are a series of interactive visualizations that allow readers to explore 89,759 questions, organized into 310 specific question topics and twenty-five parent topics. The questions can be explored all at once, by testimonial corpus, or by individual testimony, the last of which allows users to compare the topics covered, by interview, in the order in which they were asked. None of the machine-learning processes are automatic but, instead, rest upon human decisions at each stage in the process. While the outputs can be, by and large, replicated, we consider them to be "subjunctive metadata"—that is, possible and plausible outputs given the constraints we assigned, the interpretative decisions we made, and our understanding of the operations of the algorithms.

The sixth chapter, "Algorithmic Close Reading: Analyzing Vectors of Agency in Holocaust Testimonies," develops and employs a rule-based algorithm to extract, index, and visualize mentions of agency in testimonies. We are interested in analyzing agency—expressions of what people say they did or was done to them—to understand vectors of action ranging from coerced actions to possibilities for resistance and defiance. While names (personal, organizational, geographic), general topics, and historical events tend to be well-identified and tagged in testimonies, individual expressions of agency are harder to find and analyze at scale. Built on the Natural Language Processing tools of the software library spaCy, we developed an algorithm to extract and characterize "semantic triplets"—textual units consisting of subjects, verb relations, and objects—from the testimonial transcripts. Our algorithm categorizes these triplets according to the type of speech used (active, passive, speculative/modal, or coerced speech; subjective evaluations or contextual orientations). For example, "We had to hand in this crystal radio" is a semantic triplet that expresses a coerced action; "I removed the yellow star" is an active expression of victim defiance; "Stones were thrown at us" is a passive expression that references an act of antisemitic behavior without specifying an agent; "We could not go to movie theaters" is a modal expression that names an action no longer permitted or possible for victims.

Altogether, by extracting and indexing expressions of agency, the semantic triplets create a new paratext for a given interview and, thereby, provide a set of additional metadata that can be queried and overlaid on the existing content mark-up. This paratext is not intended to replace the testimonial text but rather to supplement it by providing another set of metadata derived from articulations of agency. We, then, use those expressions of agency to identify unindexed actions, such as "microhistorical" acts of resistance or defiance, to examine the "gray zone" (actions that problematize the crispness of the border between perpetrators and victims), to explore the creation of testimonial ensembles aimed at configuring collective memories (such as how nearly thirty witnesses remember the life and actions of Auschwitz aid provider, Mala Zimetbaum), and to limn the contours of collective experiences (for example, how hundreds of witnesses remember and talk about antisemitism in the 1930s and early 40s). In each case, we underscore the many questions of decision-making in relation to the algorithmic and visualization processes.

The final chapter turns to the affordances—and limitations—of machine-learning algorithms and generative AI for creating new testimonial experiences. Here, we consider how algorithms inform "cultural memory machines," and we reflect on various futures for testimony and distant witnessing. In addition to discussing the USC Shoah Foundation's Dimensions in Testimony (DiT) project, we also analyze two social media projects of Holocaust remembrance: @eva.stories on Instagram and the St. Louis Manifest project on Twitter. For each project, algorithms play a central (although not exclusive) role in generating the testimony, shaping the testimonial experience, and opening up new opportunities for listening and viewing. These projects raise the critical question of what it means for testimony to be composed by people—and technologies—other than the survivor. This is taken to an extreme with AI chatbots and generative AI. We conclude by confronting some of the dangers of testimonial mimicry and call for an ethics of digital provenance for large language models.

Far from reductive, we argue that algorithmic processes and computational methods can contribute to Holocaust memory and history by adding layers of interpretative complexity to how we read, listen to, and understand testimony. More generally, as tools with which to think and reflect, algorithms contribute to the development of experimental methods that generate new data and enable new models for humanistic scholarship. At the same time, there are limitations, shortcomings, biases, and errors that cannot be ignored. This is why human judgment and human interpretation—including, but not limited to, contextualization, historicization, and close reading informed by robust cultural critique—are absolutely necessary at each stage of the analysis. The dangers of instrumental reason, objectivist pretenses, and the calculating logic of mathesis are ever present. And while the individuality of human beings can become lost or overcome in the face of big data, an ethics of the algorithm returns us, over and over again, to the singularity of the human voice, the poetics of specific words, and the individual stories of each survivor. In so doing, this book explores how technologically enabled forms of distant witnessing can be morally engaged. Ultimately, we argue, an "ethics of the algorithm" means reflecting on and thinking with algorithms in ways that humanize data and proliferate stories, foster attentive and relational modes of witnessing, and undertake reparative work that continually documents, interprets, reinscribes, and tarries with the cultural records of past injustices.

2

Computation That (De)humanizes

FROM "BARE DATA" TO HUMAN LIFE

This chapter begins in January of 1941, when Arthur Seyss-Inquart, *Reichskommissar* of the occupied Netherlands who reported directly to Hitler, issued an infamous order requiring all Dutch Jews to register with the state authorities.[1] Over the following months, well over a hundred thousand Jews were forced to provide personal data to the state. Under the leadership of its chief inspector for population registration, the data were used to create a comprehensive Jewish registry. Human beings were reduced to "bare data," a radically delimited set of attributes that could be enumerated, queried, and, finally, mobilized. Computational processes and algorithmic calculations played a critical role in dehumanizing people and facilitating the roundups that ended in mass murder. The first part of this chapter tells the story of the Dutch Jewish registry and the man that oversaw its creation and use. Proceeding dialectically, the second part of this chapter turns to a series of memorials and archiving projects that attempt to humanize bare data using computational processes and digital interfaces. I then consider these projects in a broader, comparative context that brings in the Trans-Atlantic Slave Trade Database and the ethical issues that arise in confronting violent histories of numeracy, bare data, and archival absence. The motivating question is as follows: How can data-oriented methods and computational modalities of representation contribute to the development of ethical relationships by forging thicker bonds of responsibility (to the past), understanding (of what happened), relationality (to others), and attentiveness (to the names, stories, and absences in the archive)?

The Thoughtlessness of Bare Data

Seyss-Inquart's registration order went into effect on January 24, 1941, and demanded that all Jews in the provinces outside of Amsterdam register within four weeks and that Jews living in Amsterdam register within ten weeks. At that time, the local mayors' offices, together with the Head of the National Inspectorate of Population Registries (*Hoofd der Rijksinspectie van de Bevolkingsregisters*), were responsible for maintaining the complete and up-to-date population registry (*bevolkingsregister*). In line with the Nuremberg Race Laws of 1935, which defined Jews according to the number of Jewish grandparents, Order No. 6/41 required anyone with "full or part Jewish blood" to register. This was further stipulated as anyone "descending from [at least] one racially full Jewish grandparent," which was defined as anyone who "belongs or belonged to the Jewish religious community" (Article 2). Any questions about who had Jewish blood were to be resolved by the *Reichskommissar* or the *Generalkommissariat für Verwaltung und Justiz* (General Office for Administration and Justice) since no ambiguity was to be countenanced.

The Dutch state's registration authority—the Census Bureau for Statistics in the Ministry of Interior—was to keep track of each registration and all the data related to each "person of Jewish blood" (Article 7). That office was particularly well-suited for the task, since, starting in 1928, it had led the effort to develop a complete population registration system for the Netherlands. Under the leadership of Jacobus Lentz, an assiduous Dutch civil servant and statistics administrator who held the position of Chief Inspector for Population Registration in the Netherlands, the 1936 National Population Accounting Decree had required every municipality to complete and maintain personal identity cards for each resident.[2] These were to become part of a unified and standardized national population registration system.

At this time, Lentz had already worked for more than two decades in population accounting and was recently decorated by the Dutch government for his administrative achievements. In the late 1930s, he advocated for the introduction of individual identity cards for every citizen, complete with personal data, photograph, and fingerprints, but his proposal was not adopted by the Dutch government over fears of privacy and what some saw to be the implication of criminality across the populace. However, under Nazi occupation, Lentz's proposal of an identity card for the whole populace was greeted with enthusiasm by Berlin's *Kriminaltechnische Institut des Reichskriminalpolizeiamtes* (Criminal-Technical Institute of the Reich's Criminal Police Office), as it was considered to be more advanced than the *Kennkarte* (identity card) introduced in Germany in 1939. Lentz's identity card was virtually forgery-proof.[3] His proposal was, in fact, quickly adopted and implemented across the occupied Netherlands.

Before his collaboration with the Nazis to develop personal identity cards and oversee the registration of the Dutch Jews, Lentz was known and recognized internationally for his professional achievements, partly owing to the positive reviews and reception of his 1936 book, *De Bevolkingsboekhouding* (Population bookkeeping),[4] as well as a series of articles authored by (or coauthored with) his superior, H. W. Methorst, the Director-General of Statistics and Head of the Government Inspection of the Population Registers.[5] The Netherlands was considered a leader in developing population registries (first instituted in 1850, following the 1829 census) that linked personal and familial data to records detailing place of residence and migration history.[6] In his expansive book on population accounting, which was introduced by Methorst, Lentz expounds on his central idea that "the population register can be regarded as a collection of paper people [*papieren menschen*] who represent natural people at a central point in order to provide the government with all the desired information about each person."[7] He speculates that "the collection of data about each person can be perfected to such a degree" that the "paper people" will become the true and complete surrogates of individuals.[8] When coupled with statistical analyses for aggregating and cross-referencing data registries, Lentz argues that population accounting is a critical administrative function because it provides "the government [with] data on the size and composition of the population, data on the movement of the population, and especially data on the individuals from which that population is composed."[9] Among other things, population accounting connects personal and familial information to current and prior places of residence—something that he notes, in passing, "is indispensable for findability"[10]—so that the government has precise knowledge about the current composition of the population at any level of granularity, from the street to the neighborhood to the municipality and the nation.

For the Dutch population register of 1936, Lentz says that the following data was to be collected for each "paper person":

> Family name, first name, date of birth, place of birth, gender, birth certificate number, nationality, religion, profession or job, names of parents and their dates and places of birth, legal or non-legal recognition, name of spouse (or spouses), date and place of birth, date and place of marriage, date and place of divorce, cause of divorce, names of children, their dates and places of birth, death, marriage or absence of children, name changes

or additions, successive residences and addresses of those residences in addition to the dates of registration of changes of residence or address, date and place of death, and death certificate number.[11]

Beyond this, Lentz points out that, in the near future, personal data related to all aspects of social life, economic circumstances, and health should also be collected by the government for the purposes of state finances, public health, immigration, and genetics. Among other things, this would include military and civil service, professional achievements, special licenses or privileges, degree of poverty or affluence, financial obligations (such as alimony), arrest history, abnormalities of the body, physical disabilities, hereditary diseases, mental development (including "insanity"), nomadic tendencies, fertility, and cause of death.[12]

More than just counting people, the population registry was a biopolitical act of population tracking and management because it involved the creation of a whole rubric of knowledge about the biological background, reproductivity, and fitness of the individual bodies that comprise the population.[13] By focusing on lineage (parents, marriage/divorce, children, and their progeny) coupled with birth and death ages, locations, and professions, the registry represented a systematic approach to monitor and manage the economic, biological, and political strength of the Dutch population.[14] As Michel Foucault argued, the era of biopower deployed sex as "a means of access both to the life of the body and the life of the species" since it was "put forward as the index of a society's strength, revealing both its political energy and its biological vigor."[15] And it is for this reason that the state took such an interest in knowing, harnessing, calculating, and regulating sex and, by extension, populations and race. By the mid-nineteenth century, when the analytics of sex were connected to "the prestige of blood,"[16] the state became the guardian and enabler of policies of eugenics that separated racialized bodies that it deemed to be inferior from racialized bodies that it deemed to be superior. Once the former were no longer afforded the protection of the state and stripped of rights, they were deemed unworthy of life. The question undergirding Order No. 6/41 was how to identify, track, and find the Jews so they could be efficiently rounded up and deported.

Much more than a bureaucrat responsible for the logistics of maintaining population registries, Lentz approached his work through a philosophy of social administration that he linked to the state's biopower. For Lentz, population management was *the* imperative of the twentieth-century modern state because of the intensification of interactions between people, especially with regard to health and reproduction, trade and traffic, and mobility and migration, all of which led to the interpenetration of national borders and what he considered to be the need for the state to know and control its population. As he wrote at the start of his 1941 book on the manifold uses of personal identity cards for the state:

> The control of social life, with regard to public affairs and security, is the task of the government and requires its constant care. As the population increases and the development of technology opens up new and limitless avenues for trade and traffic, the more difficult the task and the greater the concern. The confusion of modern life places great demands on continuous improvement and the organization of orderly and safe movement [verkeer] between people. People who do not know each other, who meet in good or bad faith, interact with each other, do business and disappear again, leave behind only an impression: good or evil.[17]

He wrote these words shortly after he finished the oversight of the Dutch Jewish registry for the Nazi occupiers, believing fervently that unforgeable personal identity cards, connected to real people and troves of identificatory data, should be used by the state to achieve "the administrative control of social life."[18]

When Seyss-Inquart issued Order No. 6/41, the conceptual, administrative, and technical infrastructures of state biopower—not to mention the personal dedication and will of Dutch civil servants—were already in place to register the Dutch Jews, and, in fact, the majority of the data already existed in the population registries.[19] What was missing, however, was the racial composition of members of the Jewish community, namely the data enumerating each individual's Jewish grandparents, which is what the Nazis wanted. This is something that Lentz wrote about in his 1944 memoirs reflecting on the creation of the Jewish Registry. He remembers the "undesirability" and "practical impossibility" of using the existing population registers "to build a registration based on racial descent [rassische afkomst]" since the former "only contain the denominational breakdown [kerkelijke verhouding] of the Jews." Indeed, the Dutch population registry did not designate Jews by race or lineage; it only collected information about religious affiliations. He then raises another complication related to determining race: "Even if, with great difficulty, an investigation of race [afstamming] were possible, population accounting would still encounter the difficulty that the starting point for evaluating racial origin [rassische oorsprong] is lacking with regard to all those who are not ecclesiastically identified as Jews in the population registers."[20] In other words, to be completely successful, the Jewish registry would need to locate those racial Jews who did not self-identify religiously as Jewish.

These concerns, however, were largely administrative hurdles, since the necessary data could be newly collected and, then, correlated with the existing registries to identify and track every Dutch Jew, even those who did not identify as Jewish, or may have changed their name or religious affiliation over time.[21] Indeed, Lentz was personally up for the challenge and even expressed enthusiasm for creating the Jewish registry.[22] He described the general process as follows:

> With regard to the registration of Jews . . . I was deeply interested in the role that the population registers could play, which is why I immediately took up the work. I remember that the design was based on a triplicate registration of all Jews in the Netherlands, using the data from the population registers. For each person described as a Jew, the mayors had to create a card in triplicate. One of those cards would remain with the municipality, in order to form, together with all the cards of other Jews, an up-to-date *Judenprotokoll* [Jewish registry]. The other two copies should, if I remember, be sent to the German *Sicherheitsdienst* [Security Service of the SS], which would have two collections compiled. One collection would be kept at the *Sicherheitsdienst* and the other (third) collection would be sent to the Ministry of the Interior.[23]

The registration process itself was conducted locally across the 1,050 municipalities throughout the Netherlands. The Dutch Jews had to submit a form and pay a registration fee, in accordance with Order 6/41, and their personal history would then be double-checked against the existing population registers to be sure that everyone was accounted for and that their data (including place of residence) were up-to-date. "Full-blooded Jews" were designated as "J," while "Bastard Jews I" were designated BI (two Jewish grandparents), and "Bastard Jews II" were designated B2 (one Jewish grandparent).[24]

Functioning as a synecdoche for the state's campaign of racial purification, the registration form was itself an emblem of standardization, bureaucracy, and rationalization (Figure 2.1). It was organized bilaterally into ten fillable fields: first and last name of the registrant, place and date of birth, address (including street and house number), nationality, religion, job or profession, marital status, whether the registrant belonged to the Jewish religious community before and/or after May 9, 1940, whether the registrant was married to a Jew before and/or after May 9, 1940, and, lastly, the number of Jewish grandparents.[25] At the bottom left, a section to be filled in by the local registration office acknowledged whether the appropriate fee was paid or waived, confirmed that the information on the form was cross-checked and compared to both the "personal card" and "residence

Aanmeldingsformulier voor één persoon,

die geheel of gedeeltelijk van joodschen bloede is (Verordening 6/1941)

Invullen met schrijfmachine of met inkt in blokletters

1.	Geslachtsnaam: (een vrouw vult hier alleen haar meisjesnaam in) Voornamen: (alle voluit)	Perlberg Jacob David
2.	Geboorteplaats: (gemeente) Datum van geboorte: (dag, maand en jaar)	Hamburg 23 - 3 - 1909
3.	Woon- of verblijfplaats: Straat en huisnummer:	's-Gravenhage Schalkwijkerstr. 33/2
	Laatste woonplaats in het Groot-Duitsche Rijk (met inbegrip van het Protectoraat Bohemen en Moravië) of van het Gouvernement-Generaal voor het bezette Poolsche gebied: (Invullen voor hen, die na 30 Januari 1933 in Nederland geimmigreerd zijn)	Hamburg
4.	Nationaliteit: en Eventueele vroegere nationaliteiten:	Nederlandsche Deutsche
5.	Kerkelijke gezindte:	Joodsch
6.	Beroep of werkzaamheid: (duidelijk omschrijven)	Kleermaker
7.	Ongehuwd, gehuwd, weduwnaar, weduwe of gescheiden van echt: (naam en voornamen van echtgenoot(e) of gewezen echtgenoot(e) voluit)	gehuwd met: van der Stam, Esther Sarah weduwnaar van: weduwe van: gescheiden van:
8.	De onder 1 vermelde persoon: a. behoorde op 9 Mei 1940 tot de joodsch-kerkelijke gemeente b. is na dien datum daarin opgenomen c. was op 9 Mei 1940 met een jood gehuwd d. is na dien datum met een jood in het huwelijk getreden	 ja/neen ja/neen ja/neen ja/neen
9.	Hoeveel joodsche grootouders in den zin van artikel 2 der verordening (zie keerzijde): (invullen in letters)	Twee
10.	Opmerkingen:	

Niet zelf invullen	Par. ambt.	Ondergeteekende verklaart het vorenstaande naar waarheid te hebben ingevuld.
Ingekomen d.d. Leges { f 1.— { voldaan / niet voldaan Vermindering Reden: tot een bedrag van f Vrijstelling: Vergeleken met en aanduiding geplaatst op: Persoonskaart Verblijfregister Sign. aangebracht Bew. v. aanmelding afgegeven d.d. Verzonden aan { Hoofd R. Insp. { d.d. Ontvangen door { Bevolk. reg. { d.d. ;		Gemeente 's-Gravenhage 6 maart 1941 (handteekening aanmeldingsplichtige) Uitgegeven met toestemming van het hoofd der Rijksinspectie van de bevolkingsregisters beschikking dd. 31 Januari 1941 nr. 5

N.S. 18323

FIGURE 2.1: "Registration form for persons of full or partial Jewish blood (Order 6/1941)," signed by Jacob David Perlberg, a German-Dutch Jew living in The Hague. Bulmash Family Holocaust Collection, 2012.1.557, https://digital.kenyon.edu/bulmash /1386.

register," and that all this information was sent to and received by the Head of the National Inspectorate of Population Registries. The form encoded units of personal data as concisely—and reductively—as possible. The data were to be transmitted centrally where they would be queried and aggregated to abet the state's exercise of power over life.[26] Finally, on the bottom right, the undersigned declared that everything on the form is true and thus is forced to performatively participate in and accede to the state's biopower.

Getting the numbers exactly right and corroborating all the personal data fell to Lentz's office. Before the registration forms were collected and the data tabulated, the Nazis had estimated there were about 300,000 Dutch Jews. But Lentz took issue with this number, arguing that it was, at the most, about 200,000. When the Jewish registration forms were tabulated in the spring and summer of 1941, Lentz recalls having to defend the fact that "the low number of 160,000" was not "the result of sabotage or negligence on our part," but an accurate accounting of the Jewish population in the Netherlands.[27] He further writes: "The number of questions that were put to me by the Germans with respect to the wide variety of data on the distribution of the Jews, religion, the number of Jewish married couples, the breakdown of age, and so forth . . . pushed me more and more in the direction of compiling a systematic series of tables [*samenstellen van een systematische reeks van tabellen*], something that would not be possible by hand." Given the order to produce a full statistical accounting of the number of Jews categorized by race and cross-indexed with the other categories of data in the personal registry, Lentz reports that he "rented a Hollerith [punch card] installation to compile the official statistical overview, which greatly satisfied the Germans and convinced them that my insights had been correct."[28]

The creation of the Jewish registry took many more months than expected (partly owing to requests from Friedrich Wimmer, the *Generalkommissar* of Administration and Justice, about how he wanted the data structured and searchable). Lentz was committed to getting it right and even believed the validity of the registry was "in the interest of the Jews themselves."[29] On May 26, 1941, he was ordered by Wimmer's office to create an alphabetical registry of all Jews, according to racial composition, using a punch card system to create statistical compilations.[30] To do so, he sought out the computational infrastructure of the Hollerith punch card system, a technology that had been in development and use for decades throughout Europe and the United States for the rapid tabulation of census data.[31] Through combinations of holes in individual cards, the punch cards—and the machines that read and collated them—facilitated large-scale data tabulation, information retrieval, and storage. Beyond merely counting, the encoded punch cards stored data (and, hence, functioned as data records) and, just as importantly, they could be used to group, sort, filter, and cross-check data.[32]

The alphabetical encoding and punching of the data took place over a period of months in the spring and summer of 1941. A preliminary summary of the numbers from June 13, 1941, tallied 135,792 Jews of Dutch nationality, twenty-one Jews in colonial Dutch territories, 15,629 German Jews residing in the Netherlands, and 8,066 Jews of other nationalities residing in the Netherlands, for a grand total of 159,508.[33] The following day, on June 14, 1941, the National Inspectorate of Population Registers announced to the *Generalkommissar's* office that it "will 'very soon' start with sorting according to the Hollerith method but first wanted to know 'whether it is desirable to answer certain questions right away.'"[34] With the encoding of the data onto Hollerith cards, Lentz's office was ready to start answering analytical questions about the Jewish population according to demographic segmentation.

But prior to the processing of the registration forms, something else happened at the moment the Jewish registry was created that gives us insight into the workings of the biopolitics of the state and the power of the law: an administrative function—namely, the creation and filling out of a form—reduced the complexity of human beings to what I will call *bare data*. Under Nazi occupation, citizens who happened to be Jewish were reduced to a series of static data fields: name, place and date of birth, address, profession, nationality, marital status, being part of the Jewish community, and number of Jewish grandparents. The answers were explicitly anti-narrative since they were not stories of who the people were or might become but rather data intended to be frozen in time, as a radical reduction of the registrant's state-of-being. Once collected, there was nothing more that needed to be known or documented by the state, and there was no space for the registrant to respond, explicate, change, or speak back. The registration form, like the state or like Lentz, was utterly indifferent to who the registrant was or might become; the only thing that mattered for the Nazis and their collaborators was the absolute facticity of the bare data, the non-consensual biological "facts" that indicated who was Jewish.[35]

The concept of "bare data" is intended to echo Giorgio Agamben's articulation of "bare life," the reduction of human life to mere biological elements by a sovereign power that stakes a biopolitical claim to decide whose life is worth living and whose life is not.[36] Agamben explains that the two Greek words for life, *zoē* and *bios*, refer, respectively, to the biological fact of life and the form or way of living in a social, cultural, and political context. When the modern State places "biological life at the center of its calculations, . . . [it brings] to light the secret tie uniting power and bare life," namely the capacity to reduce *bios* to *zoē* and, thereby, decide who lives and who dies. *Homo sacer* represents a threshold concept for Agamben in that it is human life that may be killed by anyone "with impunity" because the killing is not considered homicide. Agamben argues that "the Jew living under Nazism . . . is a flagrant case of *homo sacer* in the sense of life that may be killed but not sacrificed. His killing . . . constitutes neither capital punishment nor a sacrifice, but simply the actualization of a mere 'capacity to be killed' inherent in the condition of the Jew as such." He continues by pointing out that when the Jews were exterminated "as lice" (as Hitler had announced), they were killed as "bare life."[37] But I want to add that before being killed as bare life, they were reduced to bare data precisely on the basis of their imputed biology (*zoē*), namely their racial composition as determined by the blood of their grandparents. Bare data thus refer to the deliberate reduction of human beings to a set of data points and calculations in order to transform the plurality of human life into a singular means for some other end.

Beyond Lentz's office, the administrative and statistical work was facilitated by local municipalities, which also began to aggregate and visualize the data. In May of 1941, the Amsterdam Bureau of Statistics completed a disturbing map showing "The Distribution of Jews across the Municipality" (Figure 2.2). Drawn at a scale of "one dot" representing ten Jews, the map shows the location and distribution of about eighty thousand Jews throughout the city. The dots are superimposed on a planimetrically accurate base map showing streets, railway lines, shipping channels, canals and bodies of water (in green), and other human-made features of the landscape. While only groups of Jews are represented as dots on the map, the legend also indicates, by neighborhood, the total number of non-Jews (in red) and the total number of Jews (in blue). When correlated with the data collected by the National Inspectorate's office for the Jewish registry, each dot could be resolved into ten people based on family name, gender, age, profession, number of Jewish grandparents, address, and more. In essence, the map functions as a cartographic representation of the *"Blut und Boden"* (blood and soil) ideology of the Nazis: Jewish blood is first to be separated from non-Jewish blood, and then to be extirpated from the soil. The Jews—reduced to clusters of black dots—are to be removed from every neighborhood.

As a work of cartography, this is a radically "thin" map that flattens difference into a seemingly objective, statistical representation. Every dot is the same, and they are clustered together based on the registration data collected by the state. Unlike a "thick map" (or a "thick database") in which multiple narratives, voices, temporalities, uncertainties, and pathways are built into a given model, the

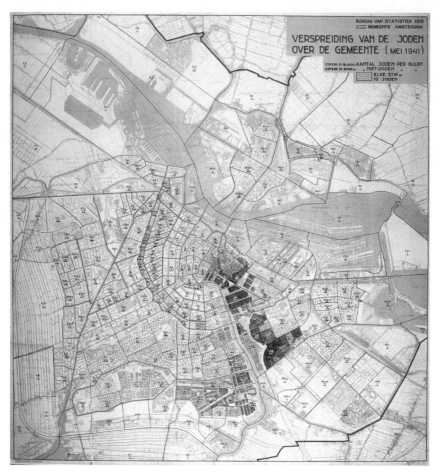

FIGURE 2.2: "Distribution of Jews across the Municipality [of Amsterdam] (May 1941)." Dutch Institute for War, Holocaust, and Genocide Studies (NIOD).

"Distribution of Jews across the Municipality" represents the targeted citizenry as mere data points to be objectively known, plotted, and controlled.[38] The map is inextricable from the power of the state to reduce people to numbers, as the dots have been robbed of their voices and individuality. Working backward from this map, we might wonder: What kind of queries did the municipality make with the data they collected and visualized? Assuming each dot could be resolved into data from the individual registrations, an algorithm might have been created to query neighborhoods or even blocks and streets by age, gender, and profession, perhaps to locate where a reliable workforce of men and women of a certain age could be most expeditiously found. Or, taking the visualization as a geographic information system, kernel density could have been calculated by neighborhood to determine the size of the police force needed to facilitate deportations and the modes of transportation to move people (via tram, train, or truck) to the central train station. Although we do not know what algorithms the Nazis ultimately used, we do know that the data were processed using sorting technologies, calculations, and data visualizations that optimized roundups with chilling efficiency and precision.[39]

On September 5, 1941, *Generalkommissar* Friedrich Wimmer wrote a letter to the *Generalkommissar* of Finance and Economy to report the results of the Jewish registry.[40] He declared that "the execution of Order No. 6/41 by the *Reichskommissar* is as good as finished" and that the National Inspectorate of the Population Registry had succeeded in counting "all the people of Jewish blood and mixed Jewish blood in the Netherlands." The numbers came out to: 140,552 full-blooded Jews, 14,549 half-Jews, and 5,719 quarter Jews. He averred that the central registry of Jews and mixed Jews will henceforth be "an instrument and central information system for all branches of administration, policing, and law enforcement," providing up-to-date information for individual cases and statistical overviews of the population as a whole.[41] In addition to his letter, Wimmer also sent over a massive set of administrative files, which he enumerated as follows: first, a complete directory of all registered Jews according to gender, Jewish blood (full, half, or quarter), nationality, and citizenship; second, a directory of registered Jews by municipality; third, a directory of registered Jews according to the ten largest Jewish communities in the Netherlands; fourth, a binder containing an overview of all the registered Jews according to date of birth (something, he notes, shows the rate of growth and age breakdown of the community, ostensibly proving how "unhealthy" the Jewish population is); and fifth, a statistical overview of the distribution of Jews according to profession.[42] In the final analysis, the files—directories, binders, statistical overviews—were not meant to be "read" for any kind of meaning that would humanize the subjects; rather, they were to be "processed" by card punchers and list creators to enforce the state's ideology of racial purity.[43]

In July of 1942, Lentz submitted his final 104-page report called *Statistiek der bevolking van Joodschen bloede in Nederland: Samengesteld door de Rijksinspectie van de Bevolkingsregisters aan de hand van de formulieren van aanmelding ingevolge verordening No 6 / 1941 van der Rijkscommissaris voor het Bezette Nederlandsche Gebied* (Statistics Regarding the Population of the Jewish Race in the Netherlands: Compiled by the National Inspectorate of the Population Registry based on Registration Forms Submitted Pursuant to Order No. 6/1941 of the *Reichskommissar* of the Occupied Netherlands). In the months leading up to the submission of the final report (after multiple preliminary reports, statistical summaries, and responses to demands about how the data needed to be organized), the number and scope of antisemitic laws aimed at radically isolating the Dutch Jewish community exploded: as of February 1942, Jews were barred from most professional occupations and had to register all their personal property as well as turn in jewelry, art, and precious metals to the Nazis; as of April 29, 1942, all Jews had to publicly wear a Star of David emblazoned on their clothes; as of May 21, 1942, Jews had register their bicycles with the state (and a few weeks later, they were required to turn them in); as of July 1942, Jews were no longer permitted to have telephones; on July 14, 1942, the Nazis arrested seven hundred Jews and threatened to send them to concentration camps should four thousand additional Jews not be selected and deported to labor camps; and on July 15, 1942, the first transport, consisting of over a thousand Jews, was sent from the Westerbork transit camp to Auschwitz-Birkenau. In the following months, provisions were put in place to transport all the Jews from the provinces to Amsterdam so they could be tracked, collected, and deported centrally.[44]

Starting on July 16, 1942, deportation trains departed, on average, twice a week from Westerbork to Auschwitz-Birkenau, for a total of at least sixty-seven trains. While exact numbers varied, many of these transports held close to a thousand Jewish men, women, and children. Upon arrival in Auschwitz-Birkenau, victims were either chosen for slave labor or gassed immediately. Beginning in March of 1943, Dutch Jews were sent to the Sobibor extermination camp on deportation trains carrying over two thousand Jews each. Of the 34,000 Dutch Jews sent to Sobibor, all but nineteen were gassed. Deportation trains continued through September of 1944, with the final deportation trains sent to Buchenwald, Ravensbruck, Bergen-Belsen, and Theresienstadt.[45]

All told, about 104,000 Dutch Jews were killed during the Holocaust, a number that represents more than 75 percent of the Dutch national Jewish population. One reason for this high rate of death was the administrative precision and cooperation of civil servants who collaborated with the Nazis, including the chief commissioner of the Amsterdam police who eagerly complied with the German SS commander of the police and compelled many "ordinary policemen" to carry out the nightly raids.[46] As Bob Moore writes with regard to Dutch civil servants, "it is possible to find examples of Dutch organizations and functionaries exceeding even the expectations of their German overseers."[47] And, as Rob Bakker reminds us, while Lentz gave a distinct "face" to the bureaucratic apparatus, thousands of civil servants, registration officers, inspectors, punch-card operators, police officers, tram operators, and truck and train drivers from 1,050 different municipalities all participated in various aspects of the registration, identification, collection, and deportation of the Dutch Jews.[48]

For his own part, Lentz wrote that he not only knew that the Jewish registry was being used by the *Sicherheitsdienst* to create "transport lists" (*transportlijsten*) of Jews who were to be sent to the Westerbork transit camp and then "deported abroad" (*buitenland afgevoerde Joden*), but he was also aware that the lists had to be frequently updated to correct for inconsistencies, such as misspelled names and erroneous deportation records.[49] He says that he and his team worked directly with the Dutch province of Zeeland, for instance, and that, more than once, he "was able to compile the evacuation specifications" (*de evacuatievoorschriften te mogen samenstellen*). He made "both his technical and administrative officials available [to help and] . . . devoted [himself] entirely to this important work." Assisted by his deputy inspectors, Lentz says that he even chaired numerous "evacuation meetings" across the Netherlands and gave directions to municipalities about how to proceed.[50]

Lentz made these choices freely, without coercion or even prompting. At almost any point, he could have acted otherwise, but he did not. He had ethical agency and failed to use it. He might have asked, "Why is this data being collected, from whom, in the name of whom, and to what ends? What is at stake when people are reduced solely to the number of Jewish grandparents they happen to have?" But there appears to be no ethical reflection on what he did. He carried out the registry, collected and collated the forms, and computed the data. It was solely an administrative and calculative function. It was thoughtless in the same way that Arendt characterized Eichmann's actions: not stupid, but utterly indifferent to and uncaring of others.[51] His data collection, list-making, and computations were an attack on human plurality and freedom.

Shortly after the war ended, Lentz was arrested and brought to trial in 1947 for allowing the Germans access to the population registries, assisting the Germans in finding forced laborers, and colluding with the Germans in the issuance of ration cards. The creation of the Jewish registry and the facilitation of the transport lists were not, however, part of the charges. And as Bakker points out, no Dutch civil servants were ever punished for anti-Jewish collaborations in postwar case law.[52] For his defense, Lentz argued that he felt it was his duty, as a government officer, to carry out his administrative assignments properly and ably.[53] He was found guilty of collusion with the Germans and served three years in jail.

Toward the end of his book *The Destruction of the Dutch Jews*, Jacob Presser remarks in passing: "The extermination of the Jews was in the first place an administrative achievement: genocide as an office-like task" (*De Joden-uitroeiing was in de eerste plaats een administratieve prestatie: genocide als ambtenaarlijke taak*).[54] Indeed, the proliferation of administrative documents included forms, registries, certificates, identification cards, written reports, Hollerith punch-cards, statistical overviews, dot density maps, and transport lists, all of which were created to advance the biopower of the state over the population. But it was also a *computational* achievement because the information collected on the forms had to be organized, counted, tabulated, sorted, cross-checked, visualized, and, ultimately, transmitted and acted upon. The "computers" were not necessarily machines processing algorithmic instructions (although sometimes they were, as in the Hollerith installations) but rather people, like Lentz and his colleagues working at the Office of the National Inspectorate and in local registries. As computers, they processed the forms in accordance with the orders to create transport lists used to carry out evacuations. Biological definitions of Jews based on lineage and blood ("what?") identified, registered, and isolated a group of people from the general population; registration and census punch cards were sorted and queried ("how?") to determine the precise composition of a given Jewish community to plan roundups, deportations, selections, and exterminations ("why and to what ends?"). The processing of bare data is the extreme outcome of Lentz's concept of "paper people," who are no more than the sum of their data for the state's biopolitical policies of social control. Bare data are all that are left when the paper people have been denaturalized and denationalized, when the state uses its power to identify, designate, and exclude through determinations of who belongs and who gets to live. The administrative task of creating bare data never gave rise to ethical questions.

But bare data are neither inevitable nor the only possible outcome of quantification and computation. Proceeding dialectically, we will now consider ways that quantification and computation can be used to affirm lost lives and transform bare data into humanizing, reparative possibilities. Arranged and encountered to facilitate new narratives, embed data in new contexts, and open up possibilities for adding to and reinterpreting the historical record, we will examine how databases, algorithmic calculations, and computational forms of representation can start to *humanize* the multitude of victims of the Holocaust. Far from reducing the victims, once again, to numbers and static data fields, we will examine a group of memorials that, in scaling between the singular individual and the totality of the records in the archive, recontextualize, animate, and reimagine the bare data initially created and collected by the Dutch National Inspectorate.

Humanizing Data: Memory in Pixels and Bricks

Sixty years after the end of World War II, the "Digital Monument to the Jewish Community in the Netherlands" launched as a website.[55] The initial design (2005–2016) was a raster graphic, or bitmap, composed of 831,432 colored pixels organized in a rectangular grid and viewable in a web browser on a computer monitor (Figure 2.3). Altogether, the graphic represented over a hundred thousand Dutch Jews who were killed by the Nazis and was intended to be a public memorial that could be seen from any computer connected to the World Wide Web. Each little box of pixels represented a single person, and they varied in size according to the age of the victim: tall blue bars represented adult men and tall red bars represented adult women; half-length green bars represented boys aged 6–21 and half-length yellow bars represented girls aged 6–21; the shortest bars (light blue and pink) represented children under age six. Groupings of tall and half-length and/or short bars represented families. Clicking on an individual color box brought a viewer to a webpage containing information about the victims, including their names, dates of birth and death (if known), place of birth, and family members, as well as information about whether anyone in the family survived the war. The graphical organization of the monument was based on the alphabetical order of the place of residence of the victims when they were deported.[56]

Consisting of just six colors in a grid formation, the abstract design of the original monument attempted to present the totality of the Dutch Jewish community killed during the Holocaust. Viewers interacted with the website on a computer screen by clicking on a rectangular box to learn about the individuals represented as pixels. The whole de Hond family of Blasiusstraat 88-II in Amsterdam was, for instance, killed in Auschwitz: two young girls, two boys, and their mother, Vogelina, were killed on September 28, 1942, while the father, Nathan, was killed a few months later, on January 31, 1943, possibly because he was separated from the rest of the family and/or selected for forced labor (Figure 2.4). Since 2010, when the online Jewish Monument Community was launched, viewers could respond to the question "do you have extra information about Nathan de Hond and his family?" by uploading photographs, writing stories, and adding names. In so doing, they move from being "viewers" to subjects actively involved in constituting the public memories of the victims.

According to the website, the data come from several different sources: "Jokos files" stored at the Amsterdam municipal archive and built around reparation claims submitted to the Federal Republic of Germany for the looting of household jhm.nl | jhmkindermuseum.nl | hollandscheschouwburg.nl | portugesesynagoge.nl | etshaim.nl | joodsmonument.nl | menassehbenisrael.nl

Community | Toelichting | FAQ | English

Digitaal Monument Joodse Gemeenschap in Nederland

Zoek

Joodse gezinnen in Nederland

Toon de joodse gezinnen uit de plaats

Toon

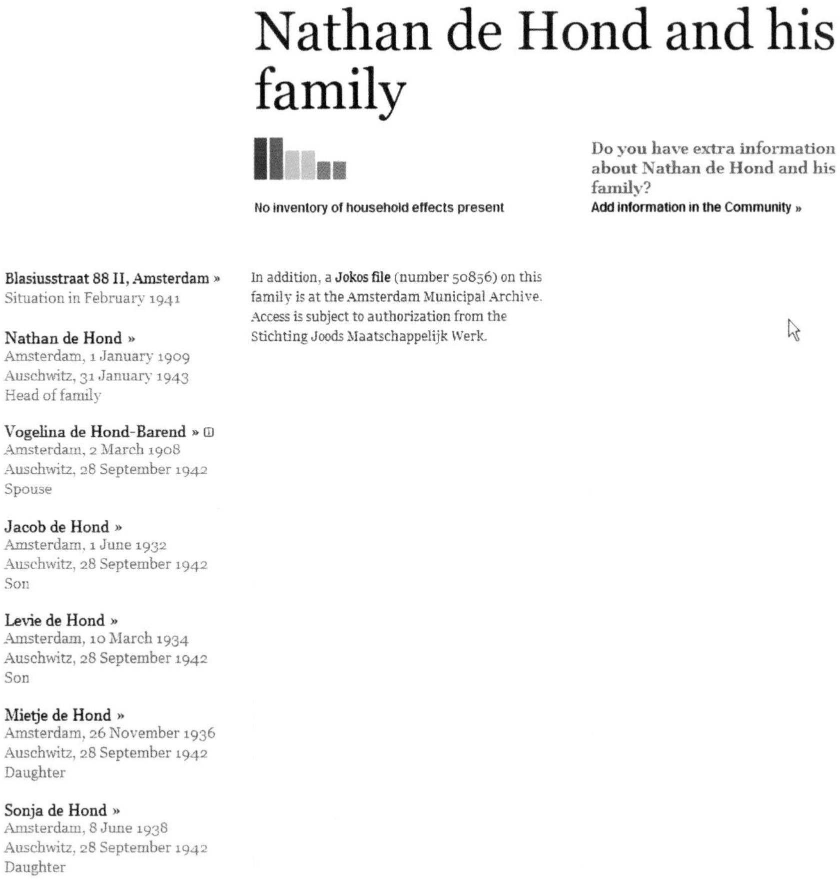

Nathan de Hond and his family

No inventory of household effects present

Do you have extra information about Nathan de Hond and his family?

Add information in the Community »

Blasiusstraat 88 II, Amsterdam »
Situation in February 1941

Nathan de Hond »
Amsterdam, 1 January 1909
Auschwitz, 31 January 1943
Head of family

Vogelina de Hond-Barend » ⓘ
Amsterdam, 2 March 1908
Auschwitz, 28 September 1942
Spouse

Jacob de Hond »
Amsterdam, 1 June 1932
Auschwitz, 28 September 1942
Son

Levie de Hond »
Amsterdam, 10 March 1934
Auschwitz, 28 September 1942
Son

Mietje de Hond »
Amsterdam, 26 November 1936
Auschwitz, 28 September 1942
Daughter

Sonja de Hond »
Amsterdam, 8 June 1938
Auschwitz, 28 September 1942
Daughter

In addition, a **Jokos file** (number 50856) on this family is at the Amsterdam Municipal Archive. Access is subject to authorization from the Stichting Joods Maatschappelijk Werk.

FIGURE 2.4: Database entry for Nathan de Hond and family, 2005–2016. Joods Monument, 2005, www.joodsmonument.nl.

effects during the war; "LiRo cards" at the National Archive in The Hague, named for the agency, a seized bank, that laundered Jewish property and capital assets in the Netherlands (Lippmann, Rosenthal and Company); and the municipal lists of registered Jews compiled by the National Inspectorate's Office.[57] Because it relies on data that were, at least in part, originally collected, enumerated, and structured by the Nazis and their collaborators, there is an ineluctable violence

FIGURE 2.3: Initial design for the Digital Monument to the Jewish Community in the Netherlands (2005–2016). Joods Monument, 2005, www.joodsmonument.nl.

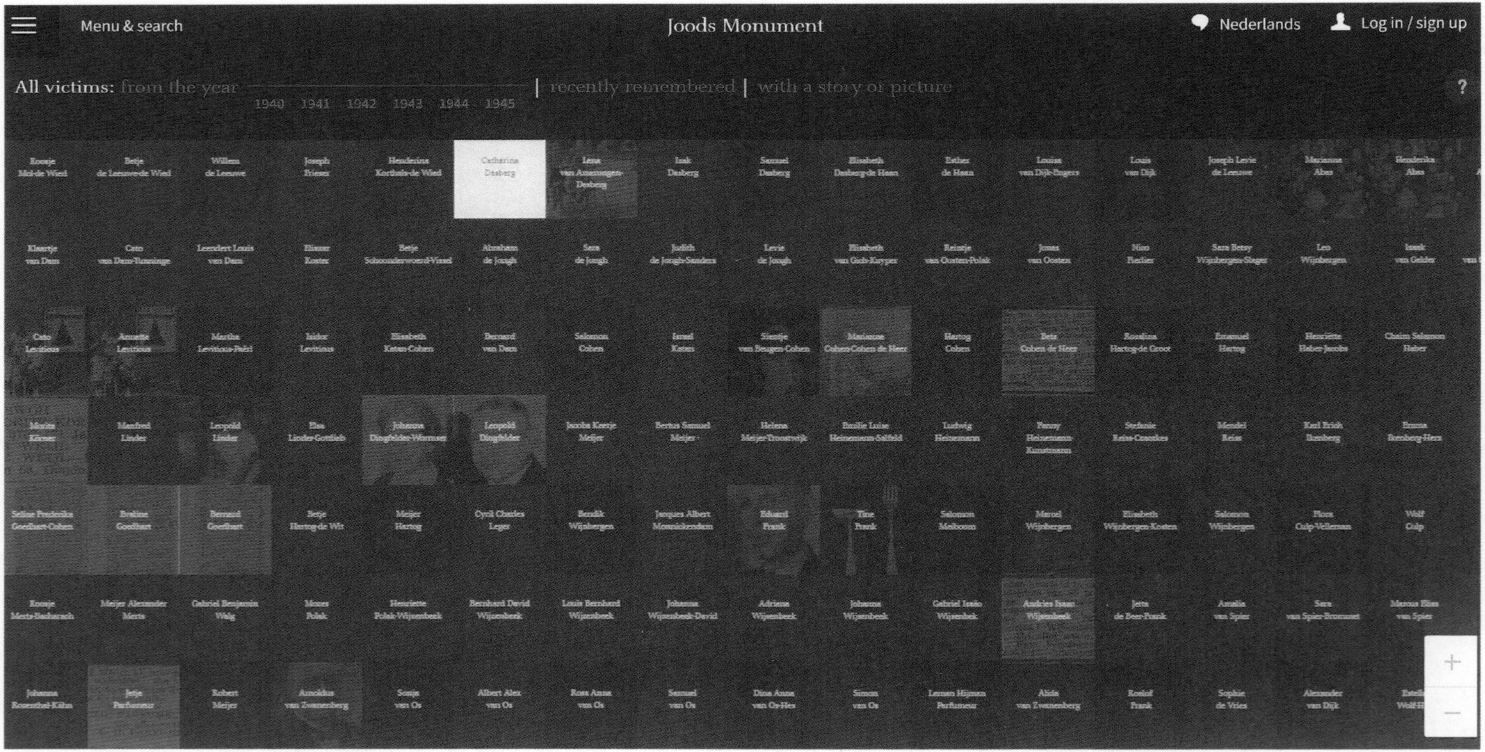

FIGURE 2.5: Digital Monument to the Jewish Community in the Netherlands. Joods Monument, 2016–present, www.joodsmonument.nl.

Stories

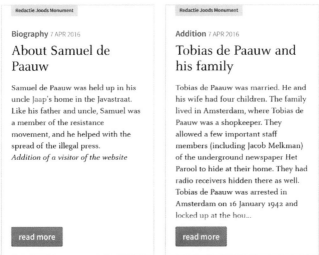

FIGURE 2.6: Jewish Monument showing stories about Samuel de Paauw and family. Joods Monument, 2016–present, www.joodsmonument.nl.

in this archive. But far from ignoring this violence, the monument creates a graphical form for confronting—and also reimagining—bare data. This means putting the data into new contexts, structuring it in new ways, interacting with it through new interfaces, creating narrative possibilities for adding to and extending the data, and, as discussed below, materializing the data in physical memorials throughout the city. As a visualization, the monument scales between the totality of the murdered Dutch Jewish community and the singularity of each known individual, facilitating an open-ended process of exploration and growth that gives rise to new narratives and commemorative pathways.

In April 2016, a new version of the digital monument launched (Figures 2.5–2.6). The updated monument uses much of the same data but has a zoomable interface based on the names and, when available, photographs of the victims, rather than only pixel boxes. The abstract symbolism of the initial bitmap was replaced by an interface organized by a multitude of names and faces, although,

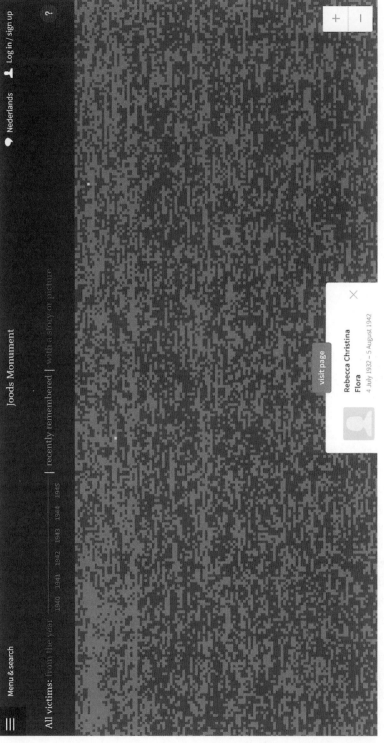

FIGURE 2.7: Jewish Monument showing which people have been recently viewed (orange) and which ones have not (purple). Joods Monument, 2016–present, www.joodsmonument.nl.

upon zooming all the way out, the names and photographs return to a hundred thousand pixelated boxes. In addition to the reimagination of the interface, the records can be queried and sorted in multiple ways, including by year, by which ones have a story and/or picture, and by which ones have been recently viewed (Figure 2.7). For the last, the color of the pixel boxes changes from purple to orange depending on a user's choices, leaving a trace behind for others who later come to the site. Moreover, family members and the broader community can add more data and link to other commemorative sites, something that makes the monument into a living, dynamic memorial. Biographical narratives, family trees, photographs, external weblinks, and additional source materials are available for many of the victims. Searching can be done in many different ways, including by name, date of birth or death, location, occupation, place of death, or by simply clicking on a particular box from the main interface.

Like the first version, the interface, to apply Johanna Drucker's formulation, "*is* information, not merely a means of access to it."[58] This is because the structure, form, and organization of the memorial's interface present information to facilitate acts of interactivity and remembrance. And while the memorial certainly provides a "portal" to data and stories about the murdered Jewish community, it is also a richly generative interface that functions as a mediating structure for knowing, creating, thinking, and even behaving. We may, for instance, be drawn to click on the victims who are marked as not having been recently remembered. Unlike mechanistic interfaces that tend to be goal- and task-oriented for "users," a humanistic interface—like the Dutch Jewish Monument—is "subject-oriented" because it opens up process-oriented, community-driven possibilities for extension and imagination.[59] In this sense, the aesthetic form of the monument fosters values of plurality, participation, and transgenerational obligation.

The data in the Dutch Jewish Monument have also informed the creation of a number of site-specific memorials throughout the Netherlands. This is perhaps most evident in the *Stolpersteine* ("Stumbling Stones") project, a trans-European installation started in 1992 by the artist Gunter Demnig to commemorate the victims of the Nazis (Figure 2.8). Embedded in sidewalks, cobblestones, and pavement, the *Stolpersteine* are location-specific markers, indicating where the victims once lived. The "stones" provide the victims' names, date of birth, and their fate. Thousands of such stones have been laid in the Netherlands and tens of thousands have been installed across Europe.[60] At the same time that each stone commemorates a single life, altogether they help produce a communal network of memory-marking in the everyday, physical landscape. Functioning as a

FIGURE 2.8: Three *Stolpersteine*. The middle one says: "Here lived Samuel de Paauw, born in 1921, deported to Westerbork, murdered on May 31, 1944, in Auschwitz." Stichting Stolpersteine, 2023, https://stichting-stolpersteine.nl.

kind of dialectical image of the 1941 dot density map of Jews, the *Stolpersteine* map of Amsterdam shows some of the hundreds of sites commemorating victims throughout the former Jewish quarter of the city (Figure 2.9). Each of the stones are cross-indexed with the Dutch Jewish Monument and can also be discovered from its online database.

In September 2021, the Dutch Holocaust Memorial of Names (*Holocaust Namenmonument*) opened. Designed by architect Daniel Libeskind, the monument is located along Weesperstraat, a central street within Amsterdam's historical Jewish quarter that was home to the highest concentration of Jewish residents in the early 1940s (Figure 2.10). The monument consists of 102,000 bricks, each of which is inscribed with a victim's first and last names, date of birth, and age at death.[61] The bricks are arranged into two-meter-high walls, and when viewed from above, the memorial spells out the letters of the Hebrew word *lizkor* ("in memory of"). The 102,000 bricks—quite literally a material instantiation of information[62]—are arranged in precise, rectilinear configurations, two meters high in order to fit and be legible within the 1,550-square-meter memorial site. They can be read one by one and also seen as a whole from the webcam that remediates the embodied, physical experience of moving through the site.[63] According to Libeskind, the memorial sought to "[give] a tangible quantification to the many casualties, as well as [leave] 1000 blank bricks that will memorialize the unknown victims."[64]

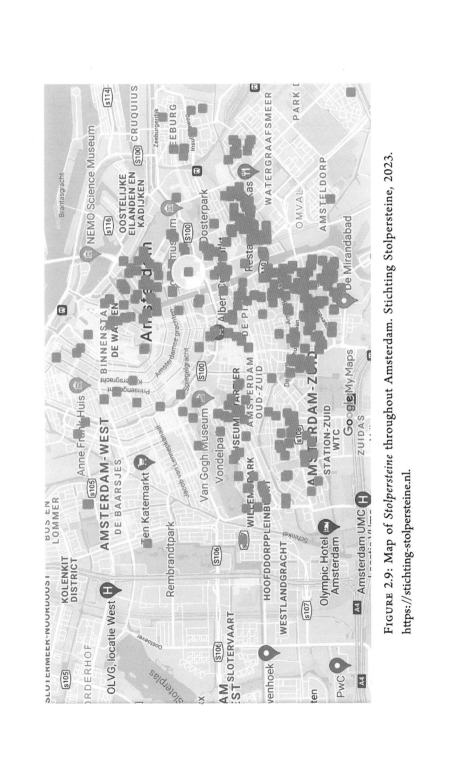

FIGURE 2.9: Map of *Stolpersteine* throughout Amsterdam. Stichting Stolpersteine, 2023. https://stichting-stolpersteine.nl.

FIGURE 2.10: Dutch *Namenmonument*, 2021, designed by Daniel Libeskind. Photograph by Christian Michelides.

If the underlying condition of possibility for the data related to the more than 102,000 victims (names, birth and death dates, street addresses, and so forth) was the Nazi order to register the Jewish population and reduce every Jewish person to bare data, today an ethics of documentation and commemoration attempts to humanize the victims through ever thicker relationships between data and narrative, data and performance, and data and architecture. What was once only bare data has now been restructured, re-presented, and recontextualized in a multiplicity of ways, resulting in new historical and geographical narratives, interfaces, and forms of memorialization. The interconnections between the extensibility of the digital monument and the localized site-specificity of the physical memorials enable reparative possibilities in which bare data have been transformed into forms of testimony, archive building, and collective mourning.

And while there are certainly salient differences between these digital and physical interfaces, they function in complementary ways to create points of contact with representations and materializations of data. With regard to the Dutch Jewish Monument, a visitor anywhere in the world can zoom in and out of the interface in a web browser, click on a name or face by chance, query the database by typing a particular name into the search box, or add new information about a victim.[65] For the physical memorials, visitors "stumble" over the stones or walk along the multisided brick walls (not unlike viewing the engraved, black, granite walls of Maya Lin's Vietnam Veterans Memorial in Washington, DC) to read the names, make paper tracings of the inscriptions, or leave behind objects.[66] In each case, we are talking about performative encounters with memorial surfaces that not only situate the singular victim vis-à-vis the totality of people killed but also place us—as distant witnesses—into a relationship with lost human lives in order to create opportunities for reading, inscribing, remembering, taking responsibility, and acting.

While nearly 60,000 names (in the case of Lin's Vietnam memorial) or 102,000 names (in the case of Libeskind's Dutch memorial) can ostensibly be inscribed in a physical memorial, challenges of scale and feasibility arise when this approach is generalized to represent the totality of Jewish victims of the Holocaust (six million people). In fact, one of the concerns over the original winning proposal submitted by Christine Jackob-Marks for the Berlin Holocaust memorial in 1995 was that there simply was not enough physical space to legibly write the names of some 4.8 million identified victims (let alone account for the additional 1.2 million unknown and unidentified victims).[67] That memorial was never built. The final design for the Memorial to the Murdered Jews of Europe was created by architect Peter Eisenman and realized in 2005. It forgoes any inscriptions, such as victims' names, nationalities, and number of people murdered. Conceived computationally as two superimposed topographies joined together by a grid of columns, the memorial consists of 2,711 concrete pillars of varying height that are slightly tilted along an undulating field. As one's body moves through the narrow spaces between the pillars, the memorial gives rise to an experience of epistemic disorientation, uncertainty, and perhaps a degree of open-ended futurity.

Beneath the southeast portion of Eisenman's memorial is an underground information and Holocaust documentation center, which includes letters, testimonies, and archival evidence related to both victims and perpetrators. Agamben considers the seeming "illegibility" of the field of pillars to foster a productive tension with the information in the underground center, resulting in two kinds of memory: the "unforgettable" (*Unvergessliches*), which "can never be entrusted to an archive" because the names, stories, and testimonies are forever lost, and that which is "rememberable" (*Erinnerbares*) in the documents of the archive and sanctioned forms of collective memory.[68] While this is a profoundly useful distinction (to which we will come back), I tend to agree with Mark Godfrey who has argued that the abstract form of the memorial is far from "illegible" or empty. Instead, as he points out, the memorial produces "a reading of Nazism" that not only counters its ideological obsession with ground (*Blut und Boden*) but also betrays the ways in which Nazism was "a disturbing product of a rational system" that invented an industrial logic of mass death.[69] If the memorial can be said to function indexically "as a kind of sign caused by its referent," its abstract form not only points toward the violence of certain systems of rationality, but it also opens a space for the infinite stories and histories that will never be known, written, or inscribed about the Holocaust.[70]

Totality and Infinity

No physical memorial or digital monument will ever represent the totality of the past or compensate for lost lives. As we think further about digital forms of memorialization and archive building, we need to consider a multiplicity of knowledge design practices for documenting and transforming bare data without replicating the dehumanizing calculus that gave rise to the bare data in the first place. In other words, how can we develop computational methods (interactive interfaces and visualizations, databases, structured data, search and sort queries, and various kinds of algorithmic analyses) to imagine and represent the size, scale, and temporality of events without reproducing the logic of numeracy and dehumanizing systems of rationality?[71] At stake is nothing short of proposing *ethical methods* and *ethical modalities* of representation for understanding, interpreting, conveying, and witnessing in the wake of catastrophic events.

To be sure, there is always infinitely more to the events and people that remains undescribed, unknown, and unaccounted for in any memorial, historical narrative, archive, or database. And this all the more so when we consider that many of the original records created by Nazi collaborators and perpetrators—for example, population registries, registration certificates, card indexes, death certificate reference cards, various "death books" and other tallies of death—were created precisely to debase and dehumanize the subjects (or were the result of that debasement and dehumanization). This is why "totality" can only refer to what remains among the *ruins* of the archive and needs to be linked to "infinity,"[72] a concept that recognizes the surplus or excess of meaning that is always beyond the archive and that which is memorialized. Every single record is a life of infinite complexity and difference that will never be fully and finally known, no matter how much data is inputted, how many histories are written, or how many survivor testimonies are heard.

These questions of method—at once epistemological, aesthetic, political, and ethical—are not new or unique to the Holocaust but speak, more broadly, to the challenges of developing open-ended forms of representation commensurate

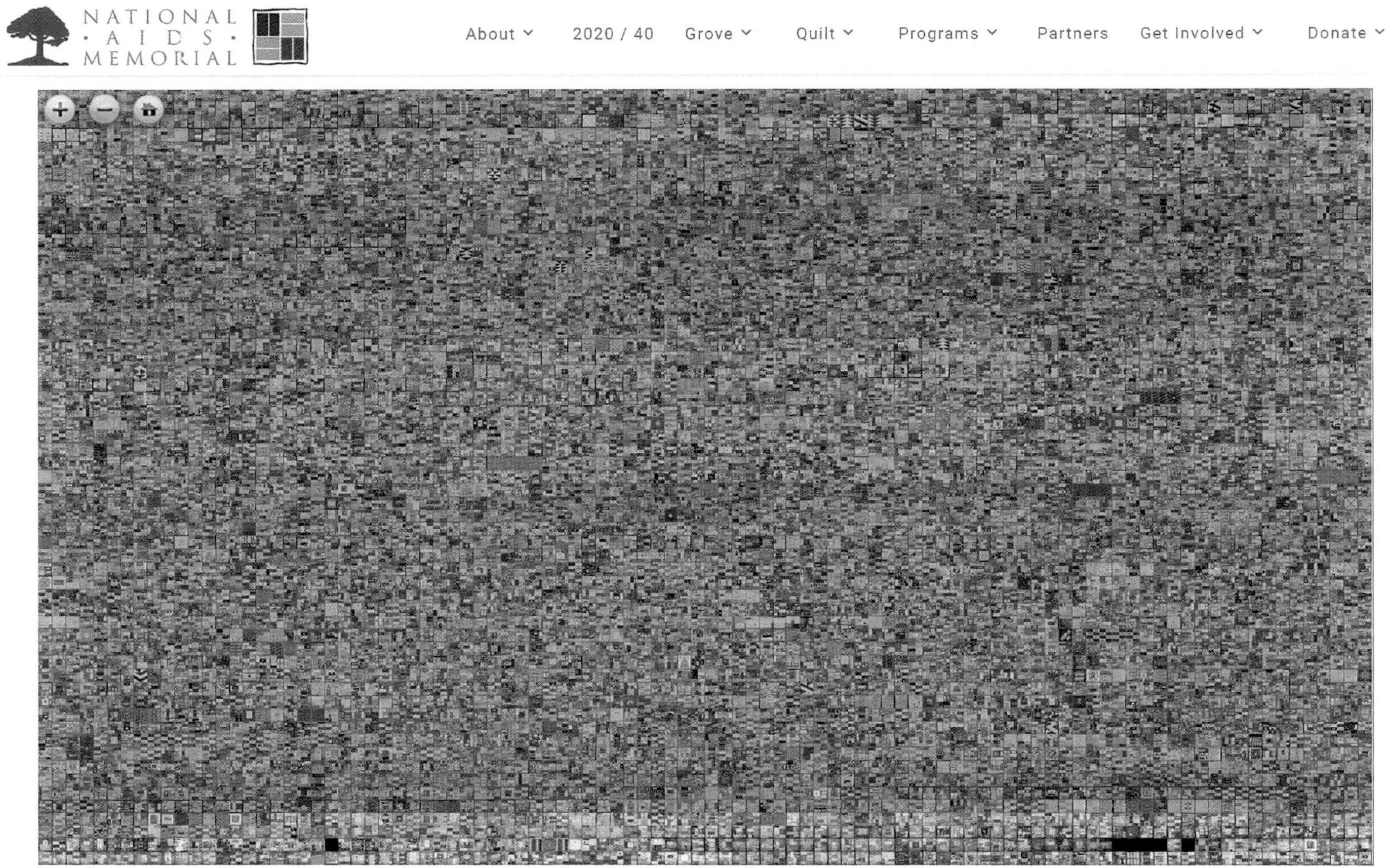

Figure 2.11: National AIDS Memorial, 2023, https://www.aidsmemorial.org/interactive-aids-quilt.

with scale and consequence without becoming reifying. Experimental digital interfaces such as the Dutch Jewish Monument, the National AIDS Memorial (Figure 2.11), or, as we will see, the SlaveVoyages project (Figure 2.12), give us the opportunity to interact with collections in ways that present a synoptic view of the records as well as facilitate granular modes of browsing, querying, disaggregating, reconfiguring, and extending the records.[73] Mitchell Whitelaw uses the term "generous interfaces" to describe the multiplicity of ways that digital archives might "represent the scale and richness" of a collection by inviting exploration through a multiplicity of views and pathways for encountering content.[74] As a digital interface and database built from tens of thousands of physically quilted panels, the National AIDS Memorial functions as a generative, open-ended interface that allows subjects to explore a multiplicity of pathways for discovery and commemoration. In addition to zooming and panning, the names database can be searched; new stories can be added; and new quilt panels can be created to commemorate lost lives. The physical and digital quilts are infinitely extensible, while all being interconnected.

Of course, the representations of and pathways through an archive will never capture the totality of an event, but they can function as traces or pointers to the infinite testimonies and names never recorded. The National AIDS Memorial contains over a hundred thousand names that have been movingly stitched on digitized quilts, but the memorial also points to the more than twenty-five million people who have died of AIDS-related complications globally since the start of the epidemic. For every story in the Dutch Jewish Monument, there is also a story lost, signaled only by the traces of a life contained on the other side of bare data. As the SlaveVoyages project makes clear, having no name inscribed or story recorded was the fate of more than twelve million captives brought to the Americas on transatlantic slave ships.

In his later writings, the philosopher of history Hayden White reflected on some of the challenges of representing "modernist events," which he saw to be new *kinds* of events by virtue of their scale (affecting huge populations and vast areas), immediacy, and impact.[75] The first challenge concerns the enormity, scope, and complexity of the events themselves; the second concerns the lack of homology between the reality of "what happened" and the modes of representation, whether through narrative, visual, architectural, performative, or computational techniques; and the third is the problem of the limited human faculties to observe, comprehend, read, listen to, and adjudicate the vastness of the many aspects and accounts of the events themselves. While realistic modes of historical representation may have been appropriate to narrate events of the nineteenth century, "holocaustal events" (to use his term) such as the Shoah, the firebombing of cities, nuclear annihilation, and genocide seem to "bear little similarity to what earlier historians conventionally took as their objects of study and do not, therefore, lend themselves to understanding by the commonsensical techniques utilized in conventional historical inquiry."[76] By virtue of their catastrophic size, complexity, immediacy, impact, and scale, modernist events resist traditional modes of spectatorship, witnessing, and knowability as much as they betray the limits of historical realism to represent those events realistically and completely.

However, these "modernist" or "holocaustal" events are not simply unrepresentable or unimaginable, according to White. Instead, they demand new forms of representation, which he saw in the strategies of visual and literary modernism, such as those used in more recent historical writings about the Holocaust, particularly Saul Friedländer's *The Years of Extermination*. These strategies include the jolts and "moments of interruption" of victims' voices in letters and diaries that "halt the process of narrativization" to convey a "truth of feeling" and create an effect of disbelief without assuming "the voice of an omniscient narrator" outside of the actions related.[77] Eisenman's Holocaust memorial might be considered another by the ways in which it opens an infinite multiplicity of meanings that situate us—quite literally—inside the form of representation without turning it into a mere object of contemplation or singular narrative.

We need not, however, consider "holocaustal" events in reference only to the atrocities of the twentieth century, since other holocaustal events and genocides—colonialism, indigenous genocides, slavery, and the Middle Passage—took place globally, over centuries, and involved tens or even hundreds of millions of lives. My point here is not to compare or analogize events. Instead, it is to think paratactically, from the standpoint of witnessing in our receding present, about methods and modalities of representation—that is to say, how to conceive of an ethics of the algorithm in light of the brutally violent systems of rationality that produced so many histories of bare life and bare data. Indeed, as Christina Sharpe rightly reminds us: "Slavery's brutal arithmetics are precursive to those of the Holocaust."[78] The question we are after is whether computational methods can ever yield humanizing practices of representation that inform how we think about, imagine, document, analyze, and relate to holocaustal events. Are there approaches to computation and practices from the digital humanities that might help us think of the contour and shape of these events without reifying the victims or subjecting them, once again, to the violence of numeracy?

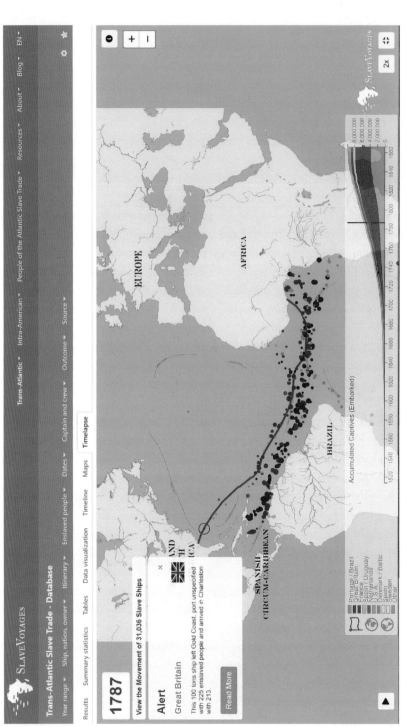

FIGURE 2.12: Screenshot of the "Timelapse" of SlaveVoyages' "Trans-Atlantic Slave Trade Database Page," covering 1515–1866. "Trans-Atlantic Slave Trade—Database," SlaveVoyages, 2019. https://www.slavevoyages.org/voyage/database#timelapse.

Let's consider the animated visualization of 31,036 slave ships, carrying over ten million enslaved people, over a period of 351 years created by the SlaveVoyages project (Figure 2.12).[79] Playable in just six minutes, the visualization depicts chronologically the voyages of 31,036 ships, the vast majority of which left the African continent (Senegambia and the offshore Atlantic, the Gold Coast, the Bight of Benin, the Bight of Biafra and the Gulf of Guinea Islands, West Central and Southeast Africa, and other regions in Africa) to the Caribbean, Brazil, the Spanish mainland Americas, and North America. It compresses a massive amount of time, geographic space, events, and people into a six-minute data visualization on a computer screen. The size of the colored dots represents the number of enslaved people onboard a given ship, and the colors correspond to the ship's nationality. As the visualization plays, the pathways of each ship—from the place of embarkation to the region or port of disembarkation—reveal an intensifying succession of ships and people crisscrossing the Atlantic annually. Clicking on a ship brings up a database entry containing, if known, information about the vessel's name and owner, the nationality of the ship, the ship's tonnage, the ship's crew, the date and duration of the slave voyage, the number of captives onboard at the point of embarkation, the number of captives that disembarked (and, hence, survived the journey), and, when available, information about the gender and age of the enslaved, the outcome of the voyage, and their sale as slaves.[80] The downloadable database of the Trans-Atlantic Slave Trade (from which this visualization is derived) consists of more than thirty-six thousand rows of data organized according to 293 variables that can be searched, configured, and cross-tabulated.

These collections of data have opened up countless research questions and shed new light on the global scale, pace, patterns, and impact of the slave trade. Documentation about the more than thirty-six thousand total voyages allows scholars to investigate economic, social, cultural, political, and demographic changes diachronically as well as pose comparative, synchronic questions. At the same time, as Jessica Marie Johnson reminds us, "the database in and of itself could not function as a window onto the everyday lives of Africans, who remained faceless, anonymous, disembodied" because they were merely enumerated through calculations, measurements, and compilations.[81] David Eltis, one of the project's founding principal investigators, underscores that, in fact, there is almost no record in the archival data of *who* the captives were. Eltis writes: "The data set contains thousands of names of shipowners and ship captains, but it contains almost no names of the millions of slaves carried to the Americas," save "the African names of and personal information about 91,491 captives who were found on board slave vessels detained by naval cruisers attempting to suppress the slave trade in the nineteenth century."[82] The archive is drawn from the extensive but profoundly incomplete, one-sided, and violently haunted records of the perpetrators who catalogued enslaved people as bare data: mostly as numbers and prices, and only sometimes by gender and age. Strikingly, the vast majority of the slave ship records contain the name of the vessel, the name of one or more of the captains, and the name of at least one of the ship's owners.[83]

As the project has grown, additional databases have been created, including a database of the enslaved with more than ninety thousand names and a database of enslavers with more than fifty thousand names (in addition to captains and owners, this database includes buyers, sellers, and crew members). Eltis explains that these databases represent a development of the project from "a ship-based to a people-based record of the movement of people from Africa to and within the Americas."[84] In the "African Origins—Database," not only can we read the names of the enslaved people and query the records by age, gender, language group, ship name, and captive fate, but we can also hear thousands of the names pronounced.[85] As a subject-oriented interface, the site allows users to contribute names and pronunciations as well as submit new data for the Voyages Database. Hearing the names read aloud situates us—as distant witnesses—in a position of listening and responsibility to lives beyond bare data.

As such, we might also consider the project as a digital memorial or refuge to the millions of victims whose names have been lost and whose voices have been forever silenced and un-archived. In their reduction to bare data in the form of cargo and sales, every enslaved person was also robbed of the right to testify and have their stories remembered in their infinite humanity and individuality. No amount of computation, data analysis, or algorithmic processing will bring back their voices and stories. At the same time, as Johnson warns us, the dehumanization and violence that gave rise to this "devastating archive" could be reproduced "in digital architecture" if sustained attention is not given to developing "a methodology attuned to black life and to dismantling the methods used to create the [slave ship] manifests in the first place."[86] Digital archives of slavery, she argues, are grounded in the rationalist enumeration, commodification, and calculation of Black bodies, some of which are "marked" with particular attributes and others of which are completely "unmarked" and thus "defy computation."[87] The challenge is not only to interrogate and listen to the silences of the digital archive but also to find "ways to hold the null values up to the light . . . [by developing] a methodology and praxis that centers the descendants of the enslaved, grapples with the uncomfortable, messy, and unquantifiable, and in doing so, refuses disposability."[88] As Katherine McKittrick writes, referencing practices of numeracy, datafication, and technologies of race that extend right up to the biometrics of our contemporary world: "The numbers set the stage for our stories of survival—what is not there is *living*."[89]

In a similar vein, Vincent Brown points out that because such archives consist of "data [that] are debased, compiled from the records of slavers, the racists, the exploiters, and their bureaucrats," we "can never confuse our sources for the things they describe."[90] As such, he maintains that scholars must "emphasize their qualitative nature . . . [and] exploit the potential of digital tools to craft scholarly designs that appreciate the interdependency of interpretive knowledge and aesthetic expression."[91] Such readings and designs can take many creative forms that confront the silences of the archive and its constitutive record of violence, while also presenting imaginative possibilities for new modes of analysis, storytelling, and witnessing.[92] In this sense, Brown argues, archives are never merely static records but rather "tools" for exploration and interpretation, with "design decisions that communicate our sense of history's possibilities."[93] Indeed, we confront the records of bare data and interpret testimonial archives attuned to history's possibilities.

For scholars such as Christina Sharpe, the many silences and violations of the archive demand the invention of new languages and media forms to undertake "wake work," namely, the urgent work of "[imagining] new ways to live in the wake of slavery, in slavery's afterlives, to survive (and more) the afterlife of property . . . [as] a mode of inhabiting *and* rupturing this episteme with our known lived and un/imaginable lives."[94] Sharpe turns to a wide range of generative possibilities through poetry, literature, performance, and visual arts that stay "in the wake and . . . perform wake work,"[95] cognizant of the impossibility of achieving resolutions or filling the profound gaps in the archive. The "ditto ditto" across the pages of the ships' manifests is but a trace of the extinguished and unnamed lives that fill "the archives of the past" with a dehumanizing "calculus."[96] Not unlike Sharpe, Johnson invokes the creative, life-affirming possibilities of Black digital practice to "[draw] attention to the many ways users, content creators, coders, and programmers have worked ethical, intentional praxis into their work in pursuit of more just and humane productions of knowledge."[97]

While computation may help us limn the contours of the archive as a totality replete with devastating silences, forms of narrative—including history, memoir, literature, and poetry—may help us imagine the infinity of missing voices. As Toni Morrison reflected shortly after completing her novel *Beloved*, "only the act of the imagination can help me" to begin to fill in the absences, gaps, and silences in the archival record.[98] She continues by adding that "the matrix of the work

I do is the wish to extend, fill in, and complement slave autobiographical narratives."[99] The literary imagination is necessary for filling in the truth of the historical record. Similarly, the poet M. NourbeSe Philip takes "the desiccated legal report" regarding the insurance claims made by the owners of the Zong slave ship, whose crew threw some 150 African slaves overboard under the pretense of saving a portion of their "cargo" after the ship became lost at sea, and transforms the report into a space of visual poetics that aims to resurface "the cacophony of voices—wails, cries, moans, and shouts that had earlier been banned from the text."[100] The imaginative act of inscribing, however tentatively, the voices of the drowned into the archive is, at the same time, an ethical act of listening to deafening silences and testifying to violent absences. As the words of her poetry break apart, spread out across the page, and fade into the paper, what emerges are new structures for language, new words and voices, and new forms of encounter with testimony. These are radically different from the sequential rows of numbers on a ledger or the two typeset pages, with justified margins, comprising the six paragraphs of the legal report of the *Gregson v. Gilbert* ruling (1783), which is fundamentally shaped by the dehumanizing language of "property" and "goods."

The work of "critical fabulation," to use Saidiya Hartman's richly generative concept, aims to "imagine doubts, wishes, and possibilities . . . both to tell an impossible story and to amplify the impossibility of its telling."[101] Indeed, no methods will fill in the chasms of absence, the drowned voices, and manifold silences in the archive; but it seems possible that certain kinds of computational and algorithmic work, as exemplified by the SlaveVoyages database and the Dutch Jewish Monument, can help us appreciate the scope, size, and scale of that chasm. In the grammatical form of the subjunctive, Hartman argues, it becomes possible to "imagine what might have happened, what might have been said or might have been done" by the human beings in the midst of this multi-century, transatlantic, holocaustal event.[102] Perhaps, poetry, literature, and art are able to bear witness—chiasmatically with humanizing forms of computation—to extend, reimagine, and speak back to the totality of the archive. In so doing, we might avoid reproducing the constitutive violence of an archive filled with bare data and, instead, imagine more humane, life-affirming futures built, at least in part, from the possibilities unleashed by the confluence of the humanities and the digital.

As we prepare to bring together digital humanities methods and Holocaust testimony, I want to acknowledge that our wake work is fundamentally different from that of scholars of slavery because we have before us hundreds of thousands of first-person, Holocaust survivor testimonies preserved in various archives across the world. These testimonies almost always reference the *Unvergessliches*, the unforgettable dead, the lost, who have no story and may not even have a name. However, the survivors' voices were recorded intentionally to bear witness, in their own words, to the experiences of having lived through bare life and having lived beyond bare data. Attuned to the risks of replicating the violence of numeracy, we aspire to develop computational forms of representation and algorithmic processes of analysis that extend historical knowledge, give rise to new narratives, deepen attention, and foster new possibilities for empathetic witnessing. In other words, we are interested in how algorithms can be deployed in Kant's "practical" sense: to provide guidance and orientation for knowledge, creativity, judgment, and action. It is here that I see numerous points of contact and opportunities for coalitional approaches to digital humanities grounded in just, humane, and caring productions of knowledge.

In the afterword to *The Practical Past*, a set of essays that sought to recuperate the "practical" possibilities of the discipline of history (that is, the ways in which it could provide guidance and contribute to the making of ethical decisions in life), White sought to wrest history away from the seduction of being a science. The nineteenth-century pretenses of objectivity and neutrality had stripped history of its moral impulse as a narrative form that could inform, guide, and teach. He looks, instead, to historical novels, such W. G. Sebald's *Austerlitz* and Toni Morrison's *Beloved*, as examples of narratives that used the possibilities of the poetic imagination to fill in aspects of the historical record that were missing (such as the interior thoughts of the figure of Margaret Garner or how dehumanization felt and might have been expressed). Far from a recitation of facts or an objective cataloging of events long gone, the representation of the practical past in these novels opened up spaces for memory and ethics that confront unresolved, urgent, and timely issues in the present. Histories, according to White, are first and foremost stories and, as such, an author makes choices about how they should, could, or might be emplotted. These choices are critical to the meaning-making of the novels and raise urgent ethical questions that apply, practically, to our here and now.

But one thing White never considered was whether algorithms and computation could *also* help tell stories and whether these (arguably modernist) methods of analysis could open up new vistas of interpretation, composition, and listening. Of course, algorithms are not stories, but it is possible that algorithms can help tell and analyze stories—and do so in a way that may function "as an organon of ethical reflection."[103] This book does not take the records of the past as objective data, nor does it aim to turn history into an algorithmic "science" or elevate computational processes above humanistic interpretative methods. At the same time, we refuse to ignore or bracket off the violent histories of capturing, quantifying, and enumerating bare data about bare lives. Instead, *Ethics of the Algorithm* is aspirational because it strives to use computation to tell and interpret histories in order to advance human dignity and plurality. While algorithms are certainly derived from the computational sciences, they need not—and should not—be driven by mathematical certainties, suffused by pretenses of objectivity, or stripped of humanizing potentialities. Indeed, in the most extreme situations, we have seen what could happen when they are. Over the course of the next five chapters, we will endeavor to explore what is possible when they are not.

3

David Boder and the Origins of Computational Analysis of Survivor Testimonies

David Boder has a unique place in the history of Holocaust testimony because he was the first person to record the voices of displaced survivors in their own words after the end of World War II. In the summer and early fall of 1946, he conducted about 120 oral interviews with Jewish survivors and other displaced persons in nine different languages (mostly in German and Yiddish, but also in Russian, Polish, French, English, Lithuanian, Latvian, and Spanish), using a relatively new technology called a wire recorder (Figure 3.1).[1] As he explained the appeal of the technology in July of 1945, about a year before he secured the funding and clearances to travel to displaced persons camps in Europe:

> The magnetic wire recorder is a highly compact instrument which records sound, speech, and music with high fidelity. The records are made on a wire .004, and a spool equivalent to 33 minutes of conversation is readily carried in one's pocket. The record is permanent and is readily duplicated either on wire or on discs. No processing is required and the instrument plays back the record immediately after it has been taken. The whole apparatus for recording and reproduction weighs about 40 lbs and is definitely "portable."

The recordings, Boder predicts, will be "an immense treasure of indisputable factual material of the details of the recent catastrophy [sic] . . . and [the] unprecedented collection of facts [could also] be used in the ideological struggle against anti-Semitism."[2] Beyond facts and data, Boder also recorded stories and voices.

While Boder used many different terms over the years to describe the recordings, he did not, perhaps surprisingly, call them "testimonies." Instead, he called

FIGURE 3.1: David Boder with wire recorder, 1946. Courtesy of the Boder/Levien Family Trust.

them "personal reports," "documents," "factual material," "personal histories," "verbatim recorded narratives," "tales," and "wire-recorded literature." The genre of Holocaust testimony—in the sense of first-person witness narratives expressed in the words of survivors about their personal experiences during the Holocaust—was just starting to come into existence.[3] And the large-scale interviewing, recording, and archiving projects, such as those of the Yale Fortunoff Archive, the US Holocaust Memorial Museum (USHMM), or the USC Shoah Foundation, were still many decades away.[4] By calling them "tales," Boder alluded to the lurid and tragic dimensions of the stories he heard and even his own occasional skepticism or disbelief as he tried to understand and make sense of the atrocities described by his interviewees.[5] He never, however, questioned their historical truthfulness or social applicability. Indeed, he thought "the unprecedented collection of facts" could help fight antisemitism. Even before he embarked on the project, he said that his intention was to capture the "exact recording of their tale in their own voice" and "in their own language" for historical and psychological purposes.[6] He believed the narratives would be useful not only for historical, behavioral, and social scientific knowledge but also for practical knowledge, ethics, and justice. The question was how to listen to, archive, and analyze these "verbatim recorded narratives."

After returning from Europe and feverishly transcribing and translating some of the interviews into English, he produced a manuscript called the "The D.P. Story" (1948), which included the subtitle: "A Series of Tales of Displaced Persons—Wire Recorded, Translated and Interpreted by David P. Boder."[7] In a letter that same year to the Jewish Publication Society of America, an organization that he had hoped would help publish the work, he referred unabashedly—although incorrectly—to the group of interviews as "the first case in world literature . . . of actually verbatim recorded narratives." He further predicted that the narratives represented the foundation of "a form of literature which is bound to emerge in the future as a result of newly invented recording devices."[8] With regard to the former claim, Boder appears not to have been familiar with the sporadic use of audio recording technologies in the 1930s and early 40s to conduct interviews with former slaves in the United States, perhaps because these recordings were not widely created or available at the time.[9] With regard to the latter claim, Boder was quite prescient about how the genre of testimony would become intimately connected with the recording devices and technological media by which testimonies are captured, stored, and accessed.[10]

In addition to not calling the interviews "testimonies," Boder and his interviewees did not use the term "Holocaust" either, as this term did not come into common usage until the 1950s to describe the Pan-European dimensions of the Nazi genocide of the Jews. He does, however, refer to and attempt to explicate "the concentration camp phenomenon"[11] in the preface to *I Did Not Interview the Dead* and says that the "displaced" and "uprooted" people were "dislocated by a world catastrophe,"[12] perhaps referencing the Hebrew word *Shoah* ("catastrophe") or the Yiddish word *khurbn* ("destruction"), both of which were used by survivors interviewed by Boder to describe the destruction of the Jewish communities of Europe.[13] At the same time, he speaks specifically of the experiences of survivors and "martyrs" in concentration camps and refers to them as slave laborers, forced laborers, and "war sufferers."[14] For example, during an American radio debate in 1948 on whether displaced persons should be allowed to immigrate to the United States, Boder argues for the moral imperative to resettle survivors in light of the individual horrors recounted to him by the "rank and file of martyrs who have seen men and women marched into gas chambers, children burned in open fire pits, and youth killed in electrified fences."[15]

Citing the prominence of newsreel footage and graphic visual imagery captured by Allied powers shortly after the end of the war, Boder wrote in 1945 that he "could not help observing the enormous discrepancy between the abundance of visual materials collected on the subjects of the war and the meagerness of first-hand auditory material available on the same subject."[16] More than a year later, after he returned from the DP camps in Europe and published his first article about the interviews, "The Displaced People of Europe" (1947), he further reinforced his initial observation: "I could not help observing that while literally hundreds of thousands of feet of visual material was collected to preserve the details of the war, practically nothing was preserved for the other perceptual avenue, the avenue of hearing."[17] Recording the voices of survivors in their own words was one way to rectify this imbalance. In his book, *I Did Not Interview the Dead*, which contained eight of the interviews, he recalled the "boundless . . . wonder [expressed by survivors] of hearing their own voices recorded."[18]

In the years that followed, he worked indefatigably to interest a broad, lay public in learning about the experiences of the survivors and displaced people. He appeared on radio programs (where portions of his interviews were sometimes played), took part in public debates over DPs and immigration during the late 1940s and throughout the 1950s, worked with international Jewish relief and resettlement organizations, and sent copies of the translated interviews to libraries across the Anglophone world. In one of his later public presentations, a lecture from 1956 or possibly after, Boder reflected on the impulse behind using the wire recorder to interview survivors, stating that the recorder can capture and preserve the authenticity of stories without abridgement or editing. As he said with regard to the longest—and, according to Boder, still incomplete—interview recorded with Jewish survivor Abraham Kimmelmann: "I never tried to steer him to the end, you see, because I was afraid of abridgement. It was irrelevant to me whether I have the end or the middle or what not. I wanted the interviews! I wanted spoken material!"[19]

While much has been written about Boder's 1946 interviews and their usefulness for understanding the immediate postwar moment, our contribution to the study of Boder and his recordings aims to place his research practice in a different framework. We will focus first on his methodology of collection building and second on his analytical work indexing, encoding, comparing, and interpreting the testimonies using a mixture of quantitative, social-science methods and qualitative, experimental readings. This analytical work, which began almost immediately as the transcriptions and translations were prepared, consumed Boder over the last decade of his life and formed the intellectual groundwork for a computational approach to the study of Holocaust testimonies. As much as he prioritized collection building through the transcription, translation, and annotation of the interviews, he was equally interested in analyzing the testimonies through interdisciplinary social science methods informed by early computational linguistics and the burgeoning fields of the psychological sciences. In other words, he sought to develop an integrated methodology for what would become Holocaust studies.

Trained as a psychologist, Boder worked across languages, the new and the old world, the pre- and post-Holocaust eras, and the social sciences and the humanities through his commitment to quantitative analysis and qualitative interpretation. As he argued in the Addenda to *Topical Autobiographies*, his unpublished magnum opus of seventy transcribed, translated, indexed, and annotated testimonies:

> In addition to the intended scientific purpose and significance of this project, the author, from the start, was well aware of the practical use that may be made of this material outside the realism of the laboratory and clinic; and of the impact that the reading of these interviews may have on the layman. A scientific investigation should not be branded as biased simply because the work, at least from the investigator's standpoint, possesses a concomitant ethical idealism and practical usefulness. That the present material offers thought-provoking reading for the statesman, for the clergyman, and for the soldier should in no way detract from its basic scientific import.[20]

He saw the project to have both scientific significance for the psychological, anthropological, and linguistic study of trauma as well as practical significance for the development of ethics and democracy in the postwar era.

As we will suggest here, David Boder and his team of graduate student researchers at the Illinois Institute of Technology can be considered, avant la lettre, the first digital humanists of Holocaust studies: not because they used digital tools or even had the materials in a digital format (the recordings were all analog on a magnetized metal wire), but because they brought together humanist—historical, documentary, and ethical—concerns with large-scale, experimental, quantitative, and computational analyses. In what follows, we will explore the development of Boder's analytical praxis, focusing on both the humanistic and computational work that he and his students pioneered in the 1950s to mark up and index the narratives, to catalog and quantify trauma, and to develop a set of experimental linguistic analyses of the interviews. In fitting tribute to their efforts, we will analyze their work in the same way, through a mixture of computational, statistical, humanistic, and historical approaches that shed light on the foundations of the genre of "Holocaust testimony." In the chapters that follow, we will return to Boder's interviews and present a number of methodologies for computational analysis, including "counter-indexing" his interview with Abraham Kimmelmann, developing a process of extracting "semantic triplets" from testimonies to study expressions of agency, and using machine learning to classify interviewer questions.

* * *

Born Aron Mendel Michelson (he later changed his name) in 1886 in Libau, Russia (present day Latvia), Boder grew up speaking Yiddish, German, and Russian. He was an Eastern European Jew who had a religious and secular education. He attended the Jewish Teacher's Institute in Vilna, before going to the University of Leipzig (where he studied briefly with Wilhelm Wundt, a leader in experimental psychology), and then the Psycho-Neurological Institute of St. Petersburg. He emigrated to the United States in 1926 and became a US citizen in 1932. He completed his master's degree at the University of Chicago in 1927 in the field of psycholinguistics and his doctorate at Northwestern in 1934 in the field of physiological psychology. In 1927, Boder began teaching at the Lewis Institute in Chicago, and by 1935, he was chair of both the psychology and philosophy departments. In 1940, the Lewis Institute became the Illinois Institute of Technology. There, Boder served as a professor of psychology until 1952, when he moved to UCLA's psychology department. He died in 1961 of a heart attack, at the age of seventy-five.[21]

While the technology for recording sound on wire was invented at the end of the nineteenth century, wire recorders were not practically and commercially available until several decades later. The basic principle involves pulling a thin steel wire (about twice the diameter of a human hair) across a recording head, which magnetizes each point along the wire according to the intensity and polarity of the audio signal. The portable wire recorder brought by Boder to Europe was invented and manufactured at the Illinois Institute of Technology and needed an assortment of converters, transformers, fuses, and wire spools to function properly.[22] Tape recorders became commercially available in 1948 and quickly replaced wire recording because tapes are simply not as bulky or expensive.

Boder conceived of his interviewing project around May of 1945 and spent much of the next fourteen months gathering the financial support and necessary clearances to travel to postwar Europe and conduct research in DP camps. While he originally imagined the project as a broader ethnography (including interviews with victims, perpetrators, bystanders, and "war sufferers" of all kinds), he knew from the start that he would record what he heard using the wire recorder.

About fourteen months after the end of the war, Boder arrived in Europe and began interviewing displaced persons almost every day, for just over two months, starting on July 29, 1946, in Paris. His interviews continued in France, Switzerland, Italy, and finally Germany. They were mostly with Jewish survivors of concentration and slave labor camps, as well as with a smaller group of "friendly Eastern refugees," consisting of Mennonites and other Christians who had fled Soviet territories, primarily Estonia, Latvia, and Lithuania. Of the 118 total interviews for which we have recordings, transcripts, and translations, at least eighty-seven are Jewish survivors, twenty-five are non-Jewish, and six are unknown.[23] Of the seventy interviews transcribed and translated for Boder's anthology *Topical Autobiographies*, sixty are Jewish survivors and ten are non-Jewish. Today, almost all of Boder's interviews are available online, in both their original languages and in English translations, through the Illinois Institute of Technology's Voices of the Holocaust project on the Aviary platform.[24]

Boder conducted the interviews in multiple locations including DP camps, offices of the Organization for Rehabilitation and Training (ORT), the Jewish committee home for refugees, hotels, family homes, orphanages, training schools, the United Nations Rehabilitation and Relief Agency University (UNRRA), and the Wiesbaden synagogue. The ages of the interviewees ranged from ten to seventy-nine, and the interviews ranged from less than twenty minutes to over four hours, with most being about one hour long (the length of two wire spools). Boder actually worried that he was too late because, he argued, memory and emotions were fading over time.[25] To counter such forgetting and provide a rationale for his recordings, he often began his interviews by telling the survivors: "We know very little in America about the things that happened to you in concentration camps. If you want to help us out by contributing information about the fate of the displaced persons, tell your own story. Begin with your name, give your age, and tell where you were when the war started and what has happened to you since."[26]

Boder's interviews played a foundational role in constituting the genre of spoken Holocaust testimony, and many of the methodologies that he developed were later taken up (and variously modified) by other interviewers and organizations dedicated to preserving Holocaust memory. There are a number of reasons for this: First, since Boder's interviews were conducted with displaced persons primarily in DP camps and other transitional locations, they were very close to the events themselves and still within a moment of historical crisis and uncertainty. Second, Boder—like the rest of the world—was just beginning to understand the magnitude of the Holocaust and sought to develop language to make sense of the events, including the historical terms, periodization, agents, places, and overarching narratives. Third, reflecting the Pan-European scale of the catastrophe, Boder's interview project was truly multilingual. As a polyglot himself, he conducted the interviews in nine languages, in four countries, with the intention of disseminating them in the United States and translating them for an Anglophone audience. Boder's interviews represented the beginnings of what would become the global genre of Holocaust testimony. And, finally, as we will see below, he developed the first analytical tools—through the interdisciplinary integration of qualitative and quantitative methods—to interpret the interviews and argue for their general importance as human records.

A Statistical Characterization of Boder's Corpus

To limn the general contours of Boder's corpus of interviews, we will start with a "zoomed-out" view in order to characterize certain statistical features of the interviews.[27] We will look at who is speaking (when and how much, by both word count and time), code-switching between languages, and the number and kinds of questions Boder asked to his interviewees.[28] These empirical measurements are not ends in themselves, but will help us open up broader questions (which we will take up throughout this book) around the changing genre of testimony and the shape of the digital archive. Our data visualizations are primarily produced in Tableau, a web-based visual analytics platform, that we chose in order to allow viewers to manipulate, query, and interact with the data. The visualizations function as empirically grounded interpretations of key aspects of Boder's corpus.[29]

Unlike later Holocaust testimonies where the interviewer tended to retreat into the background to allow the survivor to tell his or her story, Boder tended to conduct his interviews as dialogical investigations, often asking more than one hundred questions in a single interview session and quite frequently interrupting survivors to elicit more information, clarify what had happened to them, or ask them to shift languages.[30] At the same time, there is significant variation among the interviews in terms of number and kind of questions asked, topics covered, the length of the interviews, languages used, and the degree to which the interviewees seem to have felt comfortable narrating the traumas they had just survived. In fact, when considering the whole corpus, we find that the average value of the ratio of words spoken by a given interviewee to words spoken by Boder is 4.06, a fairly low number indicating how much Boder talked during the interviews: about 20 percent of the time.[31] Unlike later interviews—such as those done by the Yale Fortunoff Archive or the USC Shoah Foundation—there is significantly more variation in Boder's interviews, something that can be attrib-

uted to many factors, including Boder's evolving priorities about who to interview, changes in Boder's interview style over the course of his trip, the fact that
he interviewed both Jewish and non-Jewish survivors, and the multilingualism
of the interviews (which often meant additional questions and clarifications were
needed, particularly when Boder and his interviewee did not have equal fluency
in the languages being spoken). Boder was motivated to document the factuality
of the survivors' experiences, and this led him to ask a lot of specific questions.
As interview protocols developed in the years and decades to come (and as historical knowledge of the facts of the Holocaust increased), the role of the interviewer changed from being a "fact finder" to being an engaged listener who
tended to recede more into the background once a space was established to allow
interviewees to express themselves freely and uninterruptedly.

One way to view Boder's corpus of interviews and his role in helping to
shape and steer the dialogue is to "zoom out," so to speak, and visualize the
archive as a whole. Attuned to voice (who was speaking when and for how
long), we sought to visualize the archive by time. But rather than just indicate
the temporal duration of segments, we wanted to be able to compare the interviews synoptically and also know what was being said in each segment. The
following interactive visualization of Boder's corpus (Figure 3.2) is one attempt
to remediate the archive by organizing the voices and content of the interviews
according to the timestamps of the sound recordings. The width of the orange
segments corresponds to Boder's spoken time and hovering over the segment
brings up the English translations (and includes any annotations Boder added
about the question or situation); the blue segments correspond to the interviewee's spoken time and, similarly, hovering over a segment brings up the
English translations. We can see very quickly that certain interviews have many
orange bands (corresponding to many questions asked), while others have
comparatively fewer. We can also see which questions, in the course of an interview, gave rise to longer narrative answers (blue segments) and where they
come in the interview. The presence of Boder's annotations can sometimes
complexify simple data classification since he also includes comments about
emotional state, reflections, and occasionally episodes written from memory,
such as in the final minutes of his interview with Anna Kaletska (Kovitzka).
Figure 3.2 shows Boder's deeply self-reflexive commentary on his entire project
after interviewing Kaletska, which was the last interview he conducted in
Germany.

We ordered the 118 interviews chronologically, starting with Boder's interview
with Polish-Jewish survivor Polia Bisenhaus on July 29, 1946, and ending with

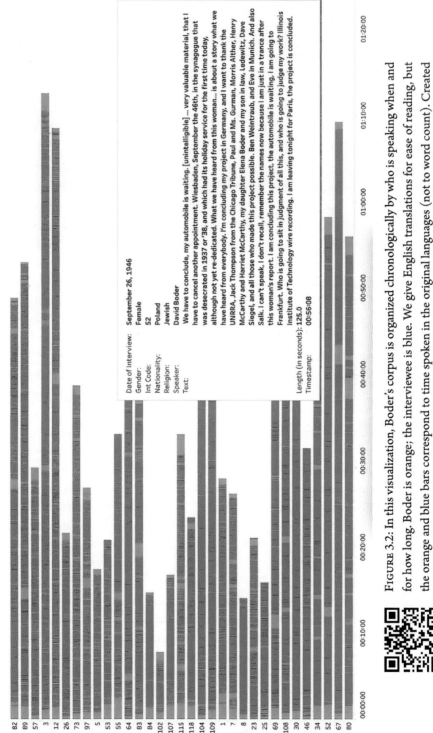

Date of interview: September 26, 1946
Gender: Female
Int Code: 52
Nationality: Poland
Religion: Jewish
Speaker: David Boder
Text: We have to conclude, my automobile is waiting. [unintelligible] ... very valuable material, that I have to cancel another appointment. Wiesbaden, September the 46th, in the synagogue that was desecrated in 1937 or '38, and which had its holiday service for the first time today, although not yet re-dedicated. What we have heard from this woman... is about a story what we have heard from everybody. I'm concluding my project in Germany, and I want to thank the UNRRA, Jack Thompson from the Chicago Tribune, Paul and Ms. Gurman, Morris Alther, Henry McCarthy and Harriet McCarthy, my daughter Elena Boder and my son in law, Ledewitz, Dave Siegel, and all those who made this project possible. Ben Weintraub, and Eve in Munich. And also Salk. I can't speak, I don't recall, remember the names now because I am just in a trance after this woman's report. I am concluding this project, the automobile is waiting, I am going to Frankfurt. Who is going to sit in judgment of all this, and who is going to judge my work? Illinois Institute of Technology wire recording. I am leaving tonight for Paris, the project is concluded.

Length (in seconds): 125.0
Timestamp: 00:56:08

FIGURE 3.2: In this visualization, Boder's corpus is organized chronologically by who is speaking when and for how long. Boder is orange; the interviewee is blue. We give English translations for ease of reading, but the orange and blue bars correspond to time spoken in the original languages (not to word count). Created by Lizhou Fan. Data courtesy of Voices of the Holocaust, Paul V. Galvin Library, Illinois Institute of Technology. Interactive visualization on Tableau: hrl.pub/6d3a9f.

his last interview on October 4 with Dimitri Odinets, a member of the Russian intelligentsia who had settled in Paris and was sent to an internment camp for failing to cooperate when France came under Nazi occupation. The interviews can also be sorted by gender, religion, date, or nationality. For instance, the first few seconds of Boder's interview with Bisenhaus begin with Boder explaining the microphone and recorder: "Now you talk into this," and she responds by saying, "Now what shall I talk," to which Boder responds, "I shall tell you. Now tell me Polia, what is your full name?" Boder proceeds by asking her nearly 125 questions in just over twenty-five minutes. She briefly talks about her experiences working in a forced labor camp before being sent to Bergen-Belsen where she suffered from malnutrition and extreme cold. At the very end of the war, she was sent to Dachau where she was liberated by the Americans. He also asks her a series of questions related to interpreting images from the Thematic Apperception Test (TAT), a psychology test in which interviewees are asked to come up with stories about images shown to them.[32] Boder also tells her that she can record a message to her uncle who lives in Chicago and that he would play it for him when he returns to the United States. He concludes by asking her what message he should relay to her uncle in Chicago, to which she responds, "Whatever you want"—and to let him know that she is doing "well" in Paris with her aunt and uncle.[33]

This visualization is one attempt to represent the structure of the interviews in the archive, but it is far from a totality and makes no claim to being complete or totalizing. There are, of course, many ways to remediate the archive depending on the kind of analysis we seek to undertake. In this case, we are interested in knowing "how much" and "when" Boder spoke relative to the interviewees and what he asked. This is something we can visualize across the entire archive according to the timestamps of the recordings. Chunks of orange at the beginning and end represent Boder's framing of the interview, while chunks of orange in the middle generally represent spool changes, an artifact of the recording technology itself. Interviews that were conducted more like dialogical investigations have many more questions (orange bands) with short answers (blue bands), while interviews with longer-form narrative answers have larger blue segments.

Because the visualization is also connected to a metadata spreadsheet about each interviewee, we can sort the results by gender, religion, nationality, and date of interview, allowing us to pose additional questions such as: Did Boder speak more when interviewing men versus women or with Jewish survivors versus non-Jewish survivors? Did his overall interview style appear to change over time? While overt gender differences seem negligible,[34] his interviews with Jewish survivors are comparatively longer, and over time, he asks fewer questions, which

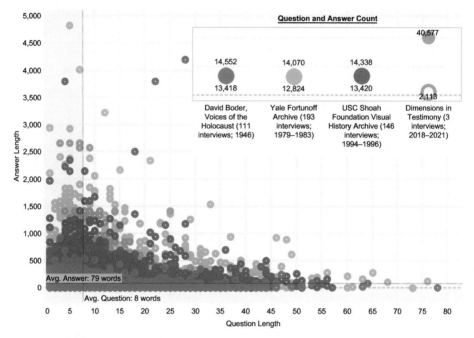

FIGURE 3.3: Comparative distribution of question and answer length across four corpora. Created by Michelle Lee. Interactive visualization on Tableau: hrl.pub/daf8fe.

allows his interviewees to speak for longer blocks of narrative time. Although the sample size is relatively small, it appears that some interviewees were more trusting, willing, and linguistically able to share their experiences with Boder, and, at the same time, he seems to have had more patience, willingness, and linguistic facility to sit with some interviewees than with others. Having a common language with relatively equivalent levels of fluency was an important determinant for how much each interviewee spoke. At the same time, his interviews with non-Jewish displaced persons tend, as a group, to be on the shorter side and cover significantly fewer topics.

Another way to consider the corpus synoptically is to plot all the questions and answers by length (word count) from the 111 interviews Boder recorded with survivors. In the visualization above (Figure 3.3), we include questions and answers from the foundational years of three other corpora as well: the Yale Fortunoff Archive, the USC Shoah Foundation, and the USC Dimensions in Testimony (DiT) project. For the first three (Boder, Fortunoff, and Shoah), we sought

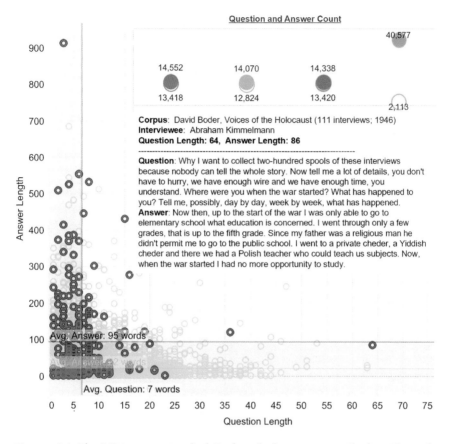

FIGURE 3.4: The 262 instances in which Boder asked questions to Abraham Kimmelmann, visualized by question and answer length. The selection shows one instance of questions and the answer given by Kimmelmann (Boder's translation). The y-axis is scaled to Boder's interviewees. Created by Michelle Lee.

to keep the number of total questions about the same (around 14,000) to compare the distributions. The DiT project is quite different, as we will see in the last chapter, as the system is always accepting new questions and matching them to a fixed number of prerecorded answers. Thus, the distance between the number of questions and the number of answers will continue to grow over time.[35]

In addition to allowing the user to read both the question and the answer by hovering over a circle, users can sort the visualization by interviewee by simply clicking on a name (Figure 3.4). For example, there are 262 instances in which Boder asked questions to Abraham Kimmelmann, and the answers he gave can be examined relative to one another for length as well as where they fit within the overall corpus of questions and answers. In this selection, we see the introductory group of questions asked by Boder to Kimmelmann and his answer.

These kinds of visualizations attempt to remediate the archive through representations that create new "entry points" for exploration, browsing, and comparison. We sought to characterize Boder's corpus by offering a set of synoptic, comparative views that could supplement the mode of viewing enabled by the Voices of the Holocaust interface, which is well-suited for exploring the interviews one-by-one and has numerous possibilities for grouping them by language, gender, date, nationality, duration, and subject categories. The idea was to facilitate a mode of engagement that allows users to toggle between a representation of the whole (all of the testimonies) and the distinctiveness of the particular (the singularity of each individual testimony) within the same representation. Far from totalizing, definitive, or final, a representation of the whole is just that: a representation—and many such representations are possible by taking into account various parameters, metadata, and content. There is always infinitely more to represent and remediate beyond any one synoptic view.

As another comparative lens for considering the interviews in Boder's corpus, we can examine their multilingual dimensions. Many of Boder's interviews were conducted in multiple languages and featured frequent code-switching between languages, especially German, Yiddish, and Polish. In some interviews, Boder interviewed in one language (Russian, German, or English) and the interviewee answered in another language (Polish, Yiddish, or French, respectively). In fact, it was common for the interviews to begin in one language and later shift to another (Figure 3.5). As Anna Bonazzi has analyzed, there are many reasons for the code-switching within the interviews, the most frequent simply being the desire to be understood.[36] Boder had a significant influence over the choice of language spoken during the interview and, at the start of each recording, would frame the interview by date, location, and language to be spoken. About 40 percent of the cases of code-switching occur either because interviewees are trying to help Boder understand them or because Boder asks them to rephrase something.[37]

The level of influence Boder had on the interview language inevitably affected the content of the interviews. When the interviewee struggles with the language or languages of the interview (mostly because they are not speaking in their native tongue), longer narrative answers tend to be infrequent, prompting Boder to ask more questions and record short answers. For instance, Toba Shiver, a Czech Jewish survivor, is interviewed in German while in an Italian DP camp, and her German is far from fluent. Polia Bisenhaus speaks four languages during her interview (German, Yiddish, English, and French). David Lea, a Greek Jew from

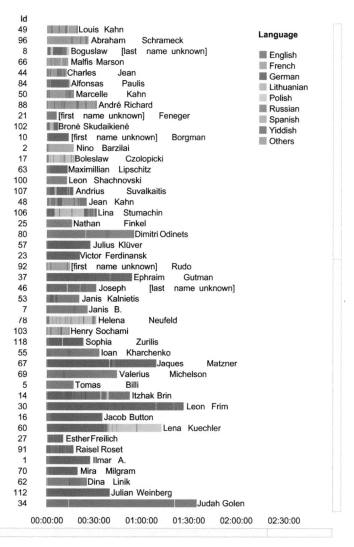

FIGURE 3.5: Language shifts in interviews conducted by David Boder (1946). Created by Anna Bonazzi and Lizhou Fan. Interactive visualization on Tableau: hrl.pub/e58467.

Saloniki, struggles in German and ends up speaking Spanish to Boder in the second half of the interview. Bella Zgnilek, a Jewish-Polish survivor, spoke fluently about her experiences in English, recited parts of camp songs about revenge in German, and recorded a message in Polish about hatred of the Germans for the wrongs they committed against the Jews at the end of her interview.[38] Other times, interviewees switch between languages to describe a particular episode that happened in a different language, or to quote specific words they remember. For example, Otto Feuer, a German Jewish survivor of Buchenwald and an executive of the American Joint Distribution Committee,[39] tells Boder how the Buchenwald commander tried asking the prisoners to help him when over a hundred SS guards were wounded in a targeted American bombing, something he remembers as "a humoristic episode." Feuer says: "While in this moment there were others . . . amongst the dead. There were two . . . about one hundred and fifty SS and of course a lot of wounded . . . This moment, the commander of the camp, he tried . . . *Wir sind alle Kameraden—helft uns Kameraden.* They cried to the prisoners—we are all comrades . . ." and turned to the prisoners—now called comrades—to help carry the wounded SS.[40]

And just as remarkable as the multilingualism of the corpus of interviews is the fact that Boder asked his interviewees over 14,000 individual questions (a number that excludes simple prompting words or repetitions encouraging his interviewees to speak). Figure 3.6 shows an initial breakdown of the questions Boder asked to all 118 people he interviewed. More than half of the interviewees are asked over one hundred questions, and nine interviewees are asked over three hundred questions. As a whole, a little more than a third of Boder's questions were variations of "what," "how," or "where" questions aimed at comprehending the specificity of the survivors' experiences, namely what they went through, what they saw, and how and where it happened. These types of questions predominate significantly over "when," "who," and "why" questions, which are also asked, although much less frequently. About another third of Boder's questions were simple clarifying questions or reactions (such as "yes?," "nu?," "and?," or "well?") aimed at eliciting more information, prompting the interviewee to speak, or correcting a misunderstanding. In this visualization, the total number of questions asked per interview is depicted along the y-axis, and six question types are broken down within each interview (along the x-axis). Interview 8, with a student named Boguslaw involved with the Polish resistance and imprisoned in a concentration camp for his actions, is among the shortest interviews he recorded, and includes only six questions asked by Boder.

In terms of interview topics, Boder usually began by asking his interviewee to explain where they were when the war started and what happened to them. He often asked about their family situation and sometimes their professional life before honing in on their personal experiences during the war. He cautioned his interviewees not to speak about "general politics" and, instead, asked them to focus on what they witnessed and experienced: "What happened to

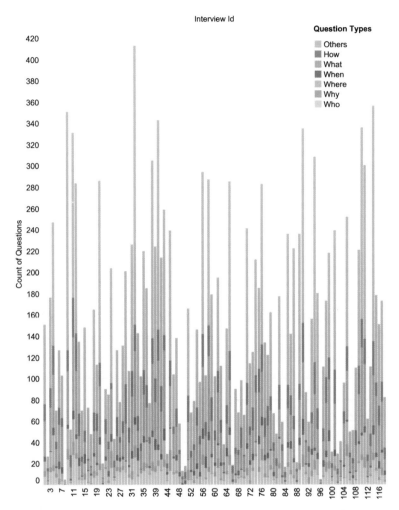

FIGURE 3.6: Visualization of primary question types ("How, What, When, Where, Why, Who, and Other Questions") in David Boder's interviews. Created by Lizhou Fan. Interactive visualization on Tableau: hrl.pub/4c89fa.

you personally?"; "Personally, how were you treated?"; "Were you personally present?"; "How did the Germans behave toward you personally?"; and "Did that really happen to you personally?" are just some of the questions Boder asks. While Boder was certainly interested in obtaining the truth of the eyewitnesses' experiences, he was also interested in comprehending the contours of the Pan-European event that we now call the Holocaust. As such, his questions were sometimes didactic: he confirms, for example, that "Ka-Zet" means concentrations camp; he asks what an "Appell" (roll call) is; he asks why certain people are called "Kapos"; he asks multiple interviewees what a "Muselmann" (living skeleton) is; he asks what "Aussiedlung" (resettlement) means; he asks how far certain concentration camps were from one another; he asks multiple times about toilets on deportation trains; he asks whether a "crematorium" is an "oven" and if "smoke came from the chimneys." Sometimes he probes the traumatic elements of everyday life in the camps, asking, for instance, whether toilet facilities were available for hygiene, what a particular interviewee talked to others about while digging pits, why another was beaten, and why prisoners were screaming.

In the "close-up" that follows, we introduce an algorithmic classification method to analyze the content of all 16,360 questions asked by Boder. In so doing, we seek to obtain insights about his priorities, interview style, and the narrative composition of these early Holocaust testimonies. This method, including its limitations and shortcomings, is explained in more detail in the digital project "What Were Survivors Asked?"

Close-Up:
Analyzing Boder's 16,360
Interview Questions

Created by Michelle Lee and Todd Presner

Utilizing the English language translations completed by Boder for *Topical Autobiographies* (seventy interviews) as well as the English translations completed by the staff at the Illinois Institute of Technology for the remaining forty-one, we extracted all the words spoken by Boder for the 111 interviews conducted with survivors.[41] We removed introductory and concluding remarks about the recordings, ellipses, bracketed comments, and bracketed clarifications from the text.[42] Since we wanted just the questions or statements made by Boder to the interviewee, we extracted all the interrogative sentences as well as any imperative statement or partial statement containing a phrase that prompted the interviewee to speak.[43] We counted a total of 16,360 questions, of which 12,621 were unique questions.

To characterize the different topics among the thousands of questions, we utilized a natural language processing algorithm based on Google's Bidirectional Encoder Representations from Transformers (BERT) called Sentence-BERT (SBERT), which allowed us to compare the semantic similarity of sentences. The output is a multi-dimensional embedding vector for each sentence, which we then grouped together using K-Means clustering (closest neighbors), an iterative machine-learning algorithm. After some experimentation, we decided on one hundred clusters. In the end, we combined seven clusters to reduce the total number of topics to ninety-three, based on what appeared to be redundancy or insufficient justification for separation. In the table below (Table 3.1), we named the ninety-three clusters ("question topic"), coded them according to twenty "parent" topics, and indicated the total count for each question topic and percentage of the parent topic. Parent topics are thematic groups of question topics, and similar colors in the online visualization are meant to show related topic clusters. The labeling of question and parent topics is entirely done by human judgment based on what we determined the questions had in common from the outputs of the algorithms.[44]

In terms of general observations, about half of Boder's questions are focused on fact finding and understanding what the interviewee experienced. These include questions about time markers and temporal durations; locations and places; whether something was true or happened; who did what; how things were done; how many people were present; how long something lasted; whether certain resources were available; what and how events happened; what people had (and lost); what happened to the interviewees and their families; yes/no questions; and questions about what things mean (mostly questions about words and concepts as well as clarifications of something said by the interviewee). These questions appear in various topical categories, such as school, religion, sickness, bodily violations, mistreatment, death, and liberation.

While many of the thematic clusters accord with what we now know about the Holocaust, some are unique to the moment in which Boder was conducting his interviews. For instance, the 128 questions that Boder asks about "Palestine, Judaism, kibbutzim" reflect the uncertainty of the future, as survivors were considering possibilities of emigration and participation in communal societies such as the kibbutzim. Although not appearing as a cluster on its own, questions about Mennonites and Mennonite beliefs (such as pacifism) are fairly common due to the non-Jewish survivors he interviewed. A little more than half of the Jewish survivors are asked very specific questions (156 in total) about bodily violations, hygiene, and toilet facilities: "So what did you do when you needed to go to the toilet?"; "And did men and women use the same latrine?"; "Now tell me what kind of toilet facilities did you have?"; "One could throw out also the feces?"; "From where was your hair cut off?"; "The hair was cut only from your head?"; "Well, when you carried out the dead, could you wash yourselves?" Such detailed questions about specific bodily violations are quite uncommon in later interviews.

Table 3.1: Parent and question topics derived from Boder's 16,360 interview questions. Created by Michelle Lee and Todd Presner. Interactive visualizations of Boder's questions can be seen by using the QR code or the Tableau link: hrl.pub/46e8d7.

Parent Topic	Question Topic	Question Count	Percentage of Parent Topic
Body violations, mistreatment	mistreatment, trauma (and reactions to)	166	25.27%
	hygiene, toilet facilities, body violations	156	23.74%
	arrest, beating	113	17.20%
	sickness, disease, illness	111	16.89%
	hospital, doctor	75	11.42%
	tattoos, yellow star	36	5.48%
Concentration and death camps; mass killing, Auschwitz	death, killing, gassing, crematoria	176	33.85%
	killing, shooting, and death	169	32.50%
	Auschwitz	113	21.73%
	prisoners	62	11.92%
Ghettos, transportation, deportation	escaping, leaving, being evacuated, fleeing	278	47.68%
	transportation and deportation	213	36.54%
	ghetto experiences	92	15.78%
German perpetrators/ Nazis	Interactions with SS and SS actions	172	45.50%
	Interactions with and feelings about Germans, Aryan identities	142	37.57%
	encounters with Germans	64	16.93%
War and military	military, soldiers, and construction	123	45.05%
	outbreak of the war, events of war	110	40.29%
	war destruction	40	14.65%
Behavior, decisions, agency	collective actions vs. individual agency	302	42.72%
	actions, choices, and intentions	211	29.84%
	behavior, treatment, and aftermath	194	27.44%

Parent Topic	Question Topic	Question Count	Percentage of Parent Topic
Work	payments and wages	149	35.22%
	professional work and trade	142	33.57%
	factory work, forced labor, business	132	31.21%
Daily life, living conditions	food, eating, hunger	225	21.33%
	clothing and material objects	180	17.06%
	birth, living situation, camp life	165	15.64%
	living quarters (homes, barracks)	162	15.36%
	daily life activities	110	10.43%
	sleeping arrangements	105	9.95%
	music, song	69	6.54%
	smoking, cigarettes, bartering	26	2.46%
	fuel	13	1.23%
Families (men, women, children), relations with other people	women (mother, grandmothers, sisters, aunts, wife, daughters)	232	17.46%
	questions about men	193	14.52%
	men (father, sons, brothers, husband, uncles)	189	14.22%
	family (background, what happened to)	159	11.96%
	references to women	153	11.51%
	children, childhood	146	10.99%
	marriage, marital relations, family	118	8.88%
	men and women	78	5.87%
	how many people in family	61	4.59%
School and religion	Jews and fate of Jewish community	204	27.02%
	Jews and Jewish identity, false papers	158	20.93%
	writing, language, inscriptions	126	16.69%
	studying, learning	94	12.45%
	Christians, church, religion	87	11.52%
	schooling	86	11.39%

(continued)

Table 3.1 (*continued*)

Parent Topic	Question Topic	Question Count	Percentage of Parent Topic
Witnessing; reasons, processes, and skepticism	interviewer trying to understand reasons, skepticism	296	56.06%
	witnessing events	232	43.94%
Postwar, liberation, future	liberation, end of war	221	63.32%
	Palestine, Judaism, kibbutzim	128	36.68%
Ethnic groups, nationalities	Russia, Russians	171	21.14%
	Polish, Poland, Poles	154	19.04%
	Germans, Germany, and German language	149	18.42%
	America, Americans	119	14.71%
	France, French	78	9.64%
	Baltic states and Sweden	76	9.39%
	Italy	31	3.83%
	Switzerland	31	3.83%
Narrative and meaning	questions of meaning	279	36.09%
	tell me/describe . . .	184	23.80%
	introductions, storytelling	162	20.96%
	longer questions about unique Holocaust experiences	148	19.15%
Factual clarifications	clarifications, mostly geographic and people	451	35.32%
	factual clarifications	398	31.17%
	short negation questions (factual)	234	18.32%
	closed-ended, factual questions, mostly yes-no questions	194	15.19%
Time markers and duration	how old (age)	171	29.38%
	time (month, year), when	147	25.26%
	how long (lengths of time)	132	22.68%
	shorter durations of time (hours, days, weeks, months)	104	17.87%
	night	28	4.81%

Parent Topic	Question Topic	Question Count	Percentage of Parent Topic
Quantities (how much, size, numbers)	numerical quantities (mostly people)	127	29.74%
	how many (people)	125	29.27%
	numerical quantities and dates	103	24.12%
	quantities (size, weight, amounts, distance)	72	16.86%
Where; places and geographic locations	where	412	33.17%
	locations and activities in streets, cities	173	13.93%
	Paris, France	150	12.08%
	countryside (forest, fields, and farms)	136	10.95%
	geographic locations, camp names/locations	135	10.87%
	to and from cities and countries	120	9.66%
	Lager (names, conditions, factual details)	116	9.34%
Who, what, why, how	short questions about processes	366	22.75%
	what, how	344	21.38%
	what	241	14.98%
	who	225	13.98%
	what happened (next)	224	13.92%
	why, how	209	12.99%
Nu, yes, ok	nu	606	29.08%
	yes	1478	70.92%

At the same time, certain topics are rarely probed by Boder, such as experiences before the outbreak of the war, childhood, the rise of antisemitism leading to persecution, emotional trauma, and feelings or reflections about the survivor's experiences.[45] Although Boder poses direct questions about antisemitism and pogroms only about a dozen times, he asks a handful of survivors about the antisemitic trope of blood libel, the effect of discriminatory laws (including being forced to wear the yellow star, confiscations of property, aryanization of businesses, and differential schooling), experiences of isolation based on religion, and possibilities for fighting antisemitism. However, he does not ask such questions consistently. One probable reason is that Boder was not interested in broader, explanatory historical narratives; instead, he was focused on the direct effects of catastrophic violence on the witnesses.

The cluster we labeled as "collective actions vs. individual agency" is particularly interesting, since the algorithm returned 302 questions that we thought involved or connoted agency; however, the algorithm cannot distinguish between different types of agency (such as when Boder is asking about actions the Nazis took against the Jews versus instances of Jewish agency, reaction, and resistance). Except for the last one that we manually moved, all of the following questions were algorithmically clustered together: "And how could you jump off?"; "And where did you get the uniforms?"; "And who was the resistance against?"; "How did you get over the wires?"; "Did they search you?"; "How did they choose those people?"; "How did they treat people?"; "Where did they execute them?"; "What was done to the men who blew up the gas chamber?"

While most of the clusters appeared to be thematic topics, the algorithm also determined a number of clusters that seem to be based on *how* Boder asked the question. For example, 234 short negation questions are all grouped together, regardless of topic: "The hair wasn't cut?"; "The Lager was never bombarded?"; "You were not arrested . . ."; "There was no water?"; "And nobody stopped you, nobody?"; "There were no knives or forks?"; "You were not permitted to go to theaters, to movies?" (the last was a question about antisemitic laws). Nearly two hundred questions phrased as imperatives ("tell me/describe" questions) were also clustered together: "Tell me everything"; "I am asking your opinion"; "Describe it in detail"; "Please tell the facts" — although these open-ended questions rarely generated long narrative answers.

Sometimes Boder asked comparatively long questions about the survivor's Holocaust experience, which we labeled generically as "longer questions about unique Holocaust experiences." These were grouped together algorithmically and tended to be quite hard for survivors to answer. For example: "And so tell us please why you were arrested, where you were, of what country you were a citizen, and how you fared personally in Buchenwald"; "So please, tell us some special episodes about life in France or about the resistance and we shall fill the so and so few minutes"; "Well, now I want you to tell me everything that happened to you from the moment when the Nazis had taken Warsaw to the moment when you had been liberated in Paris"; "Now, Mr. Josephy, if someone asked you, or if you would write a book, what would you want to tell us as the main points of your experiences, from 1938 until the liberation?"; and "What do you think shall we tell them [the Americans] about all these displaced people and deportees?" For the last question, survivor Bella Zgnilek answered in English after a notable pause: "Well, I will just send them regards, and I am happy that not everybody of the Jews went through such a hell."

Finally, the algorithm grouped together about three hundred questions that we labeled as "Boder trying to understand reasons, skepticism." These questions tended to have a skeptical or incredulous tone, in which Boder tried to understand something or find out the reasons for something that may have happened contrary to expectation. For example: "And you think that having no relatives in America, it would be possible for you to travel there?"; "How do you explain that the SS men were not killed?"; "But how could an SS man think that anybody would intentionally go to the Ghetto?"; "Did you not try sometimes to hit back?"; "Did they not threaten you?"; "And you didn't know what was going on there?"; "Now, it is true that the Gypsies were not even gas-killed?"; "How can so many people cross the border illegally?"; and "Do you really believe that one can eat ten liters of soup?"[46]

Decades later, some of Boder's interviewees were asked about his tone and interview style. Abraham Kimmelmann, for example, emphasized the importance of trust and the bond with the interviewer, saying that he needed "a confidant . . . someone, who I think, who I feel is worthy, of hearing my story."[47] He felt that Boder "was empathetic" because he "was interested not only in knowing, in learning about, he was interested in feeling the subject . . . that he was passionate about it, that it was a subject he was touched by." At the same time, Kimmelmann also says that he felt Boder was trying to "manipulate" him to take part "in some scientific, technological test, on the device." He also alludes to Boder's skepticism—for example over hunger and how much starving people could eat ("Do you really believe that one can eat ten liters of soup?" was a question Boder posed to Kimmelmann). Kimmelmann says that he told Boder, "You should believe it, when people tell you factual things, it was all real."[48]

Janine Oberrotman (at the time, Janine Binder) says that she was very "vulnerable" during her interview with Boder and felt that Boder spoke in a "condescending way" like "a German professor or a Russian professor before the war."[49] At the same time, she expressed "great admiration" for him because he was among the very first people who wanted to hear her story and had the "determination, the stamina, and interest" to listen to it. However, she was less positive in her assessment of Boder's interview style in her 2016 Dimensions in Testimony interview, saying "he would turn back and he would make comments about me and my responses, and some of the comments were negative. So that made me, put me into a position of . . . what should I say? Adversarial position, that would be a good word. At the end, I finally became indifferent and I answered him in such a way as to please him. And I hope I did."[50]

Finally, Jack Bass (at the time, Jürgen Bassfreund) said that Boder was like "a general talking to a sergeant" and recalled the experience as "more like an interrogation than an interview."[51] Shaking his head, he says Boder was primarily interested in posing factual questions, firing off questions such as "where were you born, how long did you live there, what came next, what did you do there, what did you do?" Joan Ringelheim, the interviewer from the USHMM, played part of the original interview and pointed out to Bass that Boder also tried to give him advice about emigrating to the United States as well as information about American schools and professional training programs. Boder even encouraged him to get in touch when he arrived. Bass agreed with Ringelheim's suggestion of Boder's expression of "caring" and that he was "being more human . . . a little warmer," despite not recalling this part of the original interview.

Between Collection Building and
Humanistic Computational Analysis

Almost as soon as Boder returned to the States, he began the work of translating, transcribing, marking up, disseminating, and analyzing the interviews—work that would occupy him for the rest of his life. As he undertook the arduous task of relistening to the testimonies in order to translate, transcribe, and annotate them, it soon became clear that he had a novel, big-data challenge on his hands: namely, to develop the protocols for curating, publishing, and analyzing the first collection of audio-recorded Holocaust survivor testimonies. While he did not articulate the challenge in quite those words, he did argue that it was "no exaggeration to state that never before have verbatim recorded narratives been presented as a form of literature" and that to do so required the development of new techniques for both translation and analysis.[52] This involved using two Peirce wire recorders in tandem such that the first machine allowed the translator to listen to the original testimony, while the second machine would be used to record the translation in real time, sentence by sentence. As he explained in *I Did Not Interview the Dead*, the translator was "constantly aware of the moods and emotions of the narrator," which Boder recorded and annotated in his markup of the typed transcriptions.[53] The need for new techniques of analysis arose, he suggests, from the fact that "the language habits [of the interviewees] show evidence of trauma" and that "the recollection of episodes of unparalleled stress definitely [contributed] to the peculiar verbal structure and the discrepancies in time and place found on occasion in the narratives."[54] He concludes his book's introduction by providing a preliminary outline of his "trauma index," according to which he intended to assess each narrative "as to the category and number of experiences bound to have a traumatizing effect upon the victim."[55] As we will see, one of his eventual goals (which was partly realized) was to "evaluate each of [the] traumas and to weigh their impact on the personality" using methods of "the professional social scientist."[56]

But before indexing and assessing the traumas conveyed in each of the narratives, he hoped that his translations would help "develop an art of listening to authentic recordings, and find new methods of appreciation of verbally reproduced narratives."[57] To facilitate the "art of listening" through the translations, Boder developed an extensive mark-up language to annotate the narratives in terms of the emotional state of the interviewee, changes in their verbal delivery of the narrative, and various technical issues that interfered with or found their way onto the wire recording (such as planes flying overhead, people interrupting the interviews, dogs barking, problems with the microphone, or difficulties with the wire spools). Lack of clarity—bracketed in the transcripts as "inaudible," "unclear," "unintelligible," or variations of lack of "understanding"—is the annotation used most frequently by Boder in marking up the recordings (over 2,500 times). It is second only to "technical" issues and observations related to the recordings, including Boder's framing comments for each interview. Beyond that, he drew attention to variations of the voice and emotional state of the interviewees (and sometimes his own) through a wide range of annotations, including: laughter, chuckling, crying, stammering, coughing, whispering, mumbling, sighing, sobbing, screaming, and singing, in addition to annotations about pauses, breaks, and faster or slower speech.[58]

As he created the translated and transcribed corpus of survivor narratives in the early 1950s, Boder decided to adopt the overarching term "topical autobiographies" to refer to the interviews as a whole. The term "topical autobiographies" was coined by Gordon Allport in 1942 and refers to the first-person, narrative description of a single, pivotal event or topic in a person's life, rather than a chronological overview of an entire life story.[59] According to Allport, topical documents represent "an excision from the life" and tend to "[focus] on the effects of one social event." Such documents "[invite] comparison, abstraction, and generalization" and "generally exist in *collections* gathered with a view to comparative study and inductive use."[60] Indeed, Boder's individual interviews gave rise to a collection of eyewitness reports that not only provided detailed historical insights into the Holocaust as an event, but also prompted a comparative framework for the analysis of trauma through the development of a traumatological lexicon and a general model for studying hedonic experiences.

Allport argues that the "questionnaire-guide" is "virtually indispensable for topical autobiographies" because it allows the interviewer "to define the scope of his inquiry for the subject," focusing on what should be included and excluded using *Leitfragen*, or guiding questions. He anticipates that verbatim "sound recordings" will become more and more widely used due to their fidelity, permanence, and ability to produce an objective record; however, he notes, as Boder later realized, their "dimensions are staggering" if the recordings remain unedited, since "the reader [or listener] is confronted with all the patient's wanderings, false starts, repetitions, lacerations of syntax and grammar."[61] Far from being a problem to be overcome or somehow fixed through editing, the traumatized language of the survivor narratives was precisely what interested Boder from the perspectives of psychology and linguistics.[62] Indeed, the "staggering" scale and complexity of the corpus of narratives was one of the key reasons he began to develop computational methods for analyzing Holocaust testimonies.

While Boder endeavored earnestly to construct a historical understanding of the range of experiences reported by the survivors and to bring this knowledge to a wider lay public, his disciplinary training in psychology brought another set of interpretive methods to the interviews. He was not only interested in "what happened," but also "how" the interviewees put their experiences into language: How could these narratives reveal insights about the kinds of traumas suffered? Could these narratives point to more general theories of trauma, language, and personality? How could quantitative methods from the psychological sciences and linguistics be used to analyze the narratives and even "compute" trauma?

Boder was probably the first to ask these questions of Holocaust testimonies, but he was not the first to ask such questions within the field of psychology. In fact, since the early twentieth century, a tension over methodology was a through line in the field: On the one hand, Freudian psychoanalysis tended to prioritize hermeneutical models in which the interior life of the individual could be probed through narrative; scientific psychology, on the other hand, tended to prioritize an informatics approach in which individual cases could be compared and generalized to develop broader, statistical laws.[63] The latter might be based, for example, on "frequency of word usage, syntactic patterns, and semantic profiles vis-à-vis other documents in the collection."[64] Because he wanted to find out how personal, autobiographical, and subjective documents could be used to advance the study of trauma, Boder pursued both methods.

In the 1940s and 50s, Boder was not alone in creating a corpus of personal documents and developing a set of tools for analyzing those documents in the context of the psychological sciences and psychotherapy. He wanted to measure the frequency and severity of the traumas reported by survivors (a data-driven, statistical effort), but he also wanted to understand how trauma was narrated in terms of linguistic choices and specific modes of expressivity. Because of his interest in the linguistic analyses of the interviews, Boder pursued a set of methods for identifying and measuring distress and relief within the narratives, focusing on both the content and the frequency of certain kinds of words and semantic features of the narratives. Building on the work of psychologists John Dollard and O. Hobart Mowrer who developed statistical methods for scoring and measuring tension, discomfort, and relief within personal documents, Boder and his graduate students applied these methods to the interviews in order to diagram and interpret fluctuations in the expressive language used by the interviewees.[65] Discussed in more detail below, the "Discomfort-Relief Quotient" (DRQ) was a quantitative method for computing and visualizing "fluctuations of emotional impact within the interview."[66]

In the 1957 addenda to *Topical Autobiographies*, Boder offered a summary statement of the corpus-building and analytical work completed to date. Although he indicates that he focused "predominantly . . . on the task of setting as many interviews as possible on paper," he also reports the following methodological approaches and analytical results: first, the development of the concept of "deculturation";[67] second, the construction of a traumatic inventory; third, the creation of an evaluative traumatic index for the appraisal of the amount and degree of traumatic content; fourth, the design of a general traumatological lexicon; and fifth, a partial linguistic analysis of the interviews.[68] With the exception of the publication of a single essay in 1954 called "The Impact of Catastrophe," this work is only documented in unpublished papers, presentations, graduate student theses, and about a dozen grant applications and reports made during the 1950s. Boder supervised three master's students—Polly Hammond, Alice Brown, and Audrey Uher[69]—who completed their degrees at IIT in psychology using a selection of the translated interviews. All three applied the quantitative analytical methods developed in conjunction with Mowrer, Dollard, Allport, and others in the burgeoning field of scientific psychology.

Part of what Boder realized very early on was the importance of a multidisciplinary approach to studying the Holocaust using interpretative methods from both the social sciences and the humanities—in his case, psychology, linguistics, and literary studies. His analyses are informed by the hybrid methodological approach advocated by Allport, in which statistical features of the interviews were coupled with interpretations attuned to historicity and literary language. He also realized that he had a challenge of scale: the number of testimonies, the hours of auditory material, and the hundreds of thousands of words in nine languages. In an unpublished manuscript interpreting the testimony of one particular interviewee named Anna Kovitzka, Boder writes: "[T]he point by point analysis of these unique documents is a task of the future. It shall require the efforts of more than one investigator and the collaboration of experts of most divergent scientific fields."[70] The evaluation of the events and their emotional impact, the indexing of the different experiences, the cataloging of the psychological and cultural factors, and the articulation of the forces behind certain behaviors and attitudes gave rise to "a scientific and literary adventure—a form of *experimental* comprehension." It required both systematic analysis from the social sciences and literary analysis attuned to "the verbalization of caleidoscopic [*sic*] events." Like the complexity of the events themselves, he argues that the formal structure of his interpretative essay will reflect "a combination of styles akin to the newspaper column, radio script, motion picture scenario, and newsreel soundtrack."[71] In many ways, Boder is suggesting that the scale, scope, and complexity of the modernist event, as Hayden White later called it, required modernist modes of historical emplotment to represent and make sense of it.[72]

Kovitzka, a thirty-four-year-old Polish Jew from a relatively affluent family, survived Auschwitz but lost most of her family during the Holocaust, including her young baby. Before her deportation to Auschwitz, Kovitzka escaped the Grodno ghetto with her husband and attempted to find a way to save their newborn. She gave the baby to a Christian Polish woman who was later denounced by a neighbor before the baby was killed. Conducted in Germany on September 26, 1946, the hour-long interview, spoken with urgency in a highly traumatized Yiddish, covers about eight years and jumps between her hometown of Kielce, hiding and passing along the Polish-Soviet borders, escaping the Grodno ghetto, being sent to Auschwitz, and, finally, at the end of the war, being driven back into Germany on a death march, and ending up after the war in Wiesbaden, where she is interviewed.

In his analysis of her interview, Boder provides an overview of what he understands of the Holocaust and tries to embed her individual story in a much broader, Pan-European context. He takes quotations from Kovitzka's narrative and interprets them both "closely" and at a "distance": for instance, with reference to Freud, he focuses on the absence of the word "mother" from her narrative as potentially indicative of the "repression" or "blocking" of memories that are "superpainful"[73] before talking more generally about the process of "deculturation," the breakdown of familial and social units, the multitude of horrors unleashed by the Nazi regime, and the near-total destruction of the Jewish communities of

Europe. Boder seems to toggle the view, so to speak, from the individual case to the general experience writ large in order to develop a language for characterizing both the specific violence experienced by Kovitzka and the magnitude of the Holocaust as a historical event whose contours, lessons, and legacies are yet to be comprehended.

In addition to trying to extrapolate many of the events of the Holocaust from her individual testimony, Boder pays attention to the testimony's linguistic and literary dimensions, specifically to what is omitted from the narrative and her "inability to find the proper words for the adequate description of nonconventional grotesque events."[74] The absences, narrative jumps, and structural discontinuities—with regard to chronology and place—are especially significant for him. While he admits that some of this could be due to "the interruption of the interviewer," he proposes an explanation rooted in the "psycho-physiological properties of the human organism," which tends to follow reports of climatic violence with relative emotional relief.[75] Here, Boder introduces a statistical methodology to quantify the "rhythmic altering of Discomfort-Relief elements" in the course of Kovitzka's narrative. Derived from the work of Dollard and Mowrer, measuring the "Distress-Relief Quotient" (DRQ) will occupy an important place in Boder's analytical work and that of his students because they saw it as a way of explicating the interrelationship between memory, emotion, and the narrative language of trauma.[76]

And, as if to concretely demonstrate his cross-disciplinary approach, he then cites a portion of Samuel Coleridge's poem "The Rhyme of the Ancient Mariner" to help illuminate Kovitzka's guilt and conditions of survival.[77] He tries to understand the "incoherent" nature of parts of her narrative and how "memories of the actual grievous events . . . are intertwined with turbulent feelings of guilt" that stemmed from her decision to give up her child, before suggesting that "the [German's] satanic logic" might have compelled some parents to save themselves over their children.[78] Although Boder acknowledges that not every action can be fully explained or understood, he reintroduces his "traumatic index" as a set of identifiable traumas suffered by survivors. He turns back to Kovitzka's language and emotional expressivity, which alternates, on the one hand, between being "definite, matter-of-fact, and technical" and "[weeping] convulsively" and "[sobbing] violently" on the other.[79] While he does not delve further into these variations of her language, he concludes the essay by speculating about the ethical stakes of publishing the survivor narratives: "[T]he reading and painstaking analysis of the verbatim recorded and verbatim translated reports" may give lay people "the opportunity for self-projection into the events of history." The interviews could help others develop empathy with those who suffered as well as a sense of aware-ness that may help recognize "the seeds of social ills" before they culminate, once again, in catastrophe.[80]

Quantifying Trauma

Shortly after he started the transcription and translation work, Boder began to develop a unique index for classifying different types of trauma and a process for encoding the narratives by traumatic experiences. The early versions of the trauma index broke down "the personal sufferings of those who survived into about 40 psychological and social categories each of which represents a specific injurious experience."[81] In the only research article that he published on this work, "The Impact of Catastrophe: Assessment and Evaluation," which appeared in *The Journal of Psychology* in 1954, Boder articulates his broader analytic goals: first, to undertake a content analysis attuned to trauma; second, to analyze the linguistic aspects of the narratives; third, to develop a generalizable methodology to quantify trauma; and fourth, to undertake a comparative narrative analysis of wire-recorded interviews with sufferers of the 1951 Kansas City Flood, a natural disaster that displaced more than half a million people and destroyed tens of thousands of homes.[82] Far from leveling differences, Boder emphasized the need to understand the specificity of "man-made disasters" that are "*historically unpre-cedented* and *unique in occurrence*" versus "nature-made disasters within a friendly and intact environment."[83]

In the early 1950s, he worked with a team of student researchers at IIT and later at UCLA to develop a system to rate each trauma by severity and then to encode each narrative based on the frequency of traumatic experiences men-tioned. Boder sought to "derive the method of analysis from the historically and culturally almost unprecedented contents of the interviews themselves."[84] Alto-gether, they identified forty-six traumas grouped into eight categories focused on socioeconomic and geographic traumas, cultural and affective traumas, medical-related violence, labor-related traumas, direct bodily violence, violence related to movement and transportation, and finally deprivations related to food, clothing, and cleanliness.[85] In a preliminary computation of the traumas identified in Jürgen Bassfreund's testimony, for instance, we can see how the method was initially de-veloped (Figure 3.7). The unit of analysis (shown in the left-hand column) is the typewritten page, each numbered one through forty-five. In the next column he lists the number of unique traumas per page, which happen to sum up to forty-five. Each trauma T corresponds to a preassigned value V, which is determined by the

Bassfreund   Milieu

PP	T	V		Trauma list #		
1	=	=		1	‖‖‖‖///	8
2				2		
3	1	3		3		
4				4	‖	2
5				5		
6				6	/	1
7	2	2		7		
8	2	3		8	‖‖‖/‖	7
9	3	35		9	‖	2
10				10		
11				11	/	1
12	2	10		12		
13	1	2		13	‖	2
14	1	32		14		
15	1	3 2		15		
16	2	2		16	‖‖	3
17	3	6		17		
18	2	10		18	‖‖‖	4
19	2	3 4		19		
20	1	2		20	/	1
21	1	32		21		
22	1	8		22	/	1
23	2	3 4		23		
24				24		
25				25		
26	1	4		26		
27	1	3		27		
28	1	4		28	/	1
29	2	3		29		
30				30		
31				31	/	1
32	1	2		32		
33	2	80		33	‖‖‖///	8
34	3	28		34		
35	2	2		35		
36				36		
37	3	35		37	‖	2
38				38		
39				39		
40	1	3		40	/	1
41				41		
42	1	1		42		
43				43		
44				44		
45				45		
46	45	362		46		
47						
48						

FIGURE 3.7: Preliminary accounting of trauma in Jürgen Bassfreund's interview (c. 1952). Courtesy of the Drs. Nicholas and Dorothy Cummings Center for the History of Psychology, University of Akron (Box 1, M11).

severity of the trauma. Each of the forty-six traumas has a preassigned severity rating—ranging from one to thirty-two in geometric sequence—based on a shared "empathy" methodology. These are listed out by "trauma codes" in the far-right columns, and the corresponding numbers indicate how many times a given trauma occurs in the interview. Using an approach called the "Q-technique" for correlating the subjective opinions of different persons, Boder assigned each trauma a value based on how his "judges" (members of his research team and students he employed) rated the trauma's severity.[86] In other words, the severity ratings were assigned after reaching consensus about which traumas the judges believed would affect them the most and the least. Based on the valuations of the different traumas, the sum of their severity comes to 362 in this preliminary analysis of Bassfreund's interview.

As the process was further refined, Boder and his students marked up the narratives by identifying and coding the different traumas, line by line and page by page, based on the experiences narrated by the survivor and whether the traumas were personally suffered (P) or part of the general milieu (M) (Figure 3.8). He points out that the "traumatic frequency" is not a linguistic record of fluctuations in narrative expressivity (as measured, for instance, by the DRQ) but rather an index of the individual, reported occurrences of each trauma. At the same time, he recognized some of the challenges faced in encoding the trauma categories, not least of all the fact that the narratives are "laden with affectivity, disruptions of chronological continuity by flashbacks, and often [cover] within an hour or two of reporting five years or more."[87] In essence, Boder was trying to develop an integrated methodology that linked quantitative measurements of trauma with qualitative interpretations of narratives inflected by emotion, discontinuity, and the condensation and displacement of violent memories.

In his published article, Boder described the process of encoding and calculating "personal" traumas and "milieu" traumas for the narratives of ten displaced people—five Jewish and five non-Jewish—in accordance with the rating system he developed.[88] The survivors are: Julius Klüver, Dimitri Odinets, Anna Prest, Ioan Kharchenko, Anna Braun, Fania Freilich, Fela Lichtheim (Nichthauser), Anna Kovitzka, Jürgen Bassfreund, and Jack Matzner. According to Boder, the sum of the personal and milieu traumas yielded "the traumatic load," something that he broke down into extensive, spreadsheet-like tables with frequency and value ratings for each survivor (Figures 3.9–3.10). The highest severity rating is thirty-two, which is assigned to "indiscriminate beating/killing," while the lowest severity rating is one, which includes forms of debasement as well as various cultural, social, and hygiene-related deprivations. In the table, "indiscriminate beat-

Socio-economic and geographical

1. Removal/relocation of person from environment (eviction/deportation)
2. No adequate substitutes for removed stimuli
3. New, unpredictable stimuli
4. Break-up of the family group
5. Exclusion from original social group
6. Confiscation of personal property, money

Cultural-affective

7. Death of relatives and unknown fates
8. Blocking or restriction of responses
9. Creation of prolonged states of terror
10. Abolition of traditions of decency and dignity (bodily care)
11. Depersonalization
12. Abolition of religious worship
13. Abolition of funeral rites, dignity of dead
14. Blocking of habits of writing or reading
15. Prohibition of any expression of hope
16. Perfidy and betrayal

Medical

17. Roll calls lasting for hours in elements
18. Absence of sympathy for sick
19. Failure to remove ill from barracks
20. Forcing patients to share beds
21. Making living lie with dead
22. Surgery without anesthetics
23. Unnecessary operations
24. Body cavity examinations in search of jewelry or metal
25. Threats of X-ray examinations
26. Emasculation of men and sterilization of women
27. Absence of dental care

Labor

28. Requiring forced or slave labor
29. Overtaxing physical conditions
30. Forcing prisoners to steal

Direct bodily violence

31. Lack of sleep or rest
32. Corporal punishment/group punishment
33. Indiscriminate beating and killing
34. Forced attendance at floggings/killings
35. Punitive work and punitive sports
36. Constriction of bodily space

Appearance, cleanliness, and dress

37. Insufficient clothing
38. Lack of soap and water
39. Conditions for lice and vermin
40. Brutal shaving and delousing; tattooing

Transportation

41. Long marches and starvation
42. Overcrowded boxcars without facilities
43. No toilet facilities
44. Impossibility of removing the dead

Food

45. Compulsory changes in nutrition, extreme reduction of food/water
46. Failure to provide facilities for eating

In January, 1945, the lager was abandoned. We were *transported* to *Shimberg*. These were all small villages, stations, that received us, until we came to the lager *Bergen-Belsen*. En route we had not dozens, but *hundreds of deaths*. People who *were old and sick and weak, and unable to stand the march, would fall on the road. So we marched on and on . . . and then one night we arrived in Bergen-Belsen* (Boder 8, p. 214).

Coding: (1) "We were transported. . . ." Imposed removal from one place to another, covered by trauma No. 1 of the TI. *We*—a personal trauma. Therefore, the coding symbol is 1P. (2) *Shimberg* is an intermediate stop-over (not a camp, not a prison)—not coded. (3) The trip from Shimberg to Belsen is a continuation of "We were transported . . ."—not coded. (4) *Bergen-Belsen* is a concentration camp and the interviewee was part of the *collective target*—coding 8P. (5) "En route . . ." *hundreds of deaths*. This was a prolonged march on foot akin to a death-march. It indicates a *different aspect*, although of the self-same transport, coding 41P. (6) **Deaths of "other people" as a consequence of the march, 32M.** (7) "People who were old and sick . . ." —lack of sympathy for the sick and no hospital provisions, 18M. (8) "So we marched on and on . . ." restatement of a self-same fact previously coded—no coding. (9) "And we arrived in Bergen-Belsen"—reference to self-same fact previously coded—no coding.

FIGURE 3.8: Boder's encoding of Jack Matzner's testimony by forty-six trauma categories. Annotated by Todd Presner. Quote from David P. Boder, "The Impact of Catastrophe: I. Assessment and Evaluation," *The Journal of Psychology* 38 (1954): 10–11.

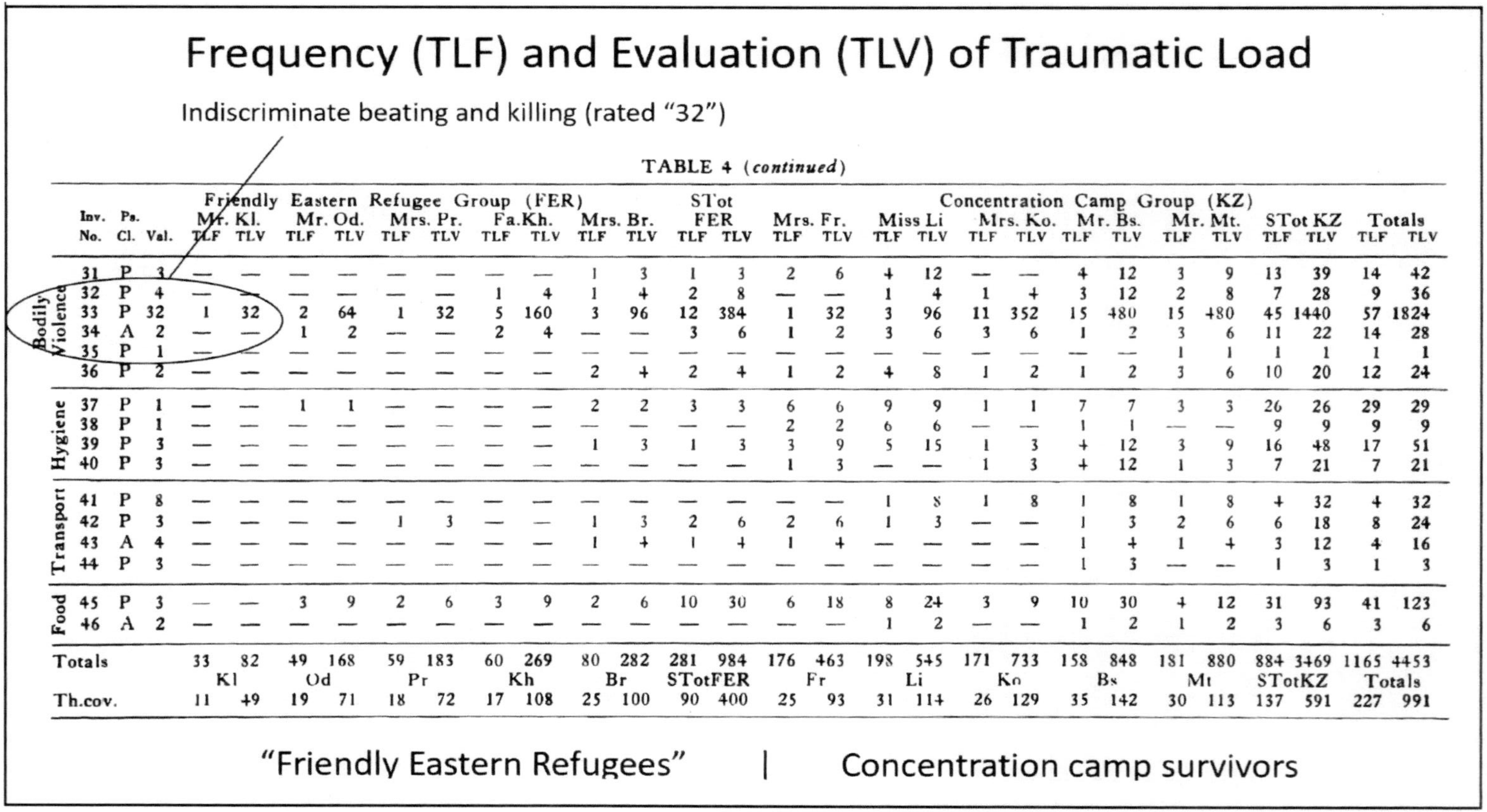

Frequency (TLF) and Evaluation (TLV) of Traumatic Load

Indiscriminate beating and killing (rated "32")

TABLE 4 (*continued*)

Inr. No.	Pa. Cl.	Val.	Friendly Eastern Refugee Group (FER)												Concentration Camp Group (KZ)												Totals	
			Mr. Kl TLF	TLV	Mr. Od TLF	TLV	Mrs. Pr TLF	TLV	Fa.Kh TLF	TLV	Mrs. Br TLF	TLV	STot FER TLF	TLV	Mrs. Fr TLF	TLV	Miss Li TLF	TLV	Mrs. Ko TLF	TLV	Mr. Bs TLF	TLV	Mr. Mt TLF	TLV	STot KZ TLF	TLV	TLF	TLV
31 P	3		—	—	—	—	—	—	—	—	1	3	1	3	2	6	4	12	—	—	4	12	3	9	13	39	14	42
32 P	4		—	—	—	—	—	—	1	4	1	4	2	8	—	—	1	4	1	4	3	12	2	8	7	28	9	36
33 P	32		1	32	2	64	1	32	5	160	3	96	12	384	1	32	3	96	11	352	15	480	15	480	45	1440	57	1824
34 A	2		—	—	1	2	—	—	2	4	—	—	3	6	1	2	3	6	3	6	1	2	3	6	11	22	14	28
35 P	1		—	—	—	—	—	—	—	—	—	—	—	—	—	—	—	—	—	—	—	—	1	1	1	1	1	1
36 P	2		—	—	—	—	—	—	—	—	2	4	2	4	1	2	4	8	1	2	1	2	3	6	10	20	12	24
37 P	1		—	—	1	1	—	—	—	—	2	2	3	3	6	6	9	9	1	1	7	7	3	3	26	26	29	29
38 P	1		—	—	—	—	—	—	—	—	—	—	—	—	2	2	6	6	—	—	1	1	—	—	9	9	9	9
39 P	3		—	—	—	—	—	—	—	—	1	3	1	3	3	9	5	15	1	3	4	12	3	9	16	48	17	51
40 P	3		—	—	—	—	—	—	—	—	—	—	—	—	1	3	—	—	1	3	4	12	1	3	7	21	7	21
41 P	8		—	—	—	—	—	—	—	—	—	—	—	—	—	—	1	8	1	8	1	8	1	8	4	32	4	32
42 P	3		—	—	—	—	1	3	—	—	1	3	2	6	2	6	—	—	—	—	2	6	2	6	6	18	8	24
43 A	4		—	—	—	—	—	—	—	—	1	4	1	4	1	4	—	—	—	—	1	4	1	4	3	12	4	16
44 P	3		—	—	—	—	—	—	—	—	—	—	—	—	—	—	—	—	—	—	1	3	—	—	1	3	1	3
45 P	3		—	—	3	9	2	6	3	9	2	6	10	30	6	18	8	24	3	9	10	30	4	12	31	93	41	123
46 A	2		—	—	—	—	—	—	—	—	—	—	—	—	1	2	1	2	—	—	—	—	1	2	3	6	3	6
Totals			33	82	49	168	59	183	60	269	80	282	281	984	176	463	198	545	171	733	158	848	181	880	884	3469	1165	4453
Th.cov.			Kl 11	49	Od 19	71	Pr 18	72	Kh 17	108	Br 25	100	STotFER 90	400	Fr 25	93	Li 31	114	Ko 26	129	Bs 35	142	Mt 30	113	STotKZ 137	591	Totals 227	991

Row group labels (left margin): Bodily Violence · Hygiene · Transport · Food

Annotations: "Friendly Eastern Refugees" | "Concentration camp survivors"

FIGURE 3.9: Table 4 from David P. Boder, "The Impact of Catastrophe: I. Assessment and Evaluation," *The Journal of Psychology* 38 (1954). Annotated by Todd Presner. Reprinted with permission from Taylor & Francis Ltd.

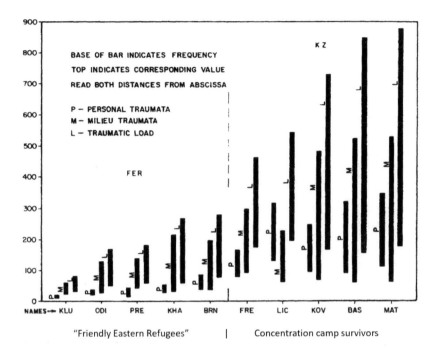

FIGURE 3.10: Figure 3 from David P. Boder, "The Impact of Catastrophe: I. Assessment and Evaluation," *The Journal of Psychology* 38 (1954). Reprinted with permission from Taylor & Francis Ltd.

ing/killing" is a trauma that occurs once in Kluver's narrative, whereas it occurs eleven times in Kovitzka's narrative, and fifteen times in both Bassfreund and Matzner's narratives. The numbers across give the distinct occurrences of trauma with their corresponding severity by survivor as well as provide the total traumatic load values for each of the two groups. Not surprisingly, the total traumatic load suffered by the concentration camp survivors is more than four times that of the "Friendly Eastern Refugees" (FER) group, and in specific categories such as "bodily violence," the concentration camp survivors reported this trauma twenty-six times more than the FER group.

While Boder concludes his article with the hope that his methodology for measuring the impact of catastrophe might be applied more generally to analyzing the psychological toll of any disaster, he still considers the project as an "exploratory," "experimental reading" and expects to supplement it further with content-based, linguistic analyses and more comparative work.[89] He points out that quantitative, statistical data can occlude certain things and argues for the need to go back to the interviews to understand the specificity of the traumas and try to explain them in the context of the survivors' personal experiences. As Boder writes, referencing Allport's blended methodology: "[A]lthough pooling of data may give a useful set of insights, such pooling is bound to obliterate greatly the [idiographic] characteristics of the individual components."[90] Hermeneutical interpretations, attuned to the survivor's language, expressivity, and experiences, are also needed. He further underscores this point when he concludes: "Useful as these [statistical] indices may appear for the short-cut appraisal of catastrophic situations they are by far insufficient for the assessment of individual interviews and the discovery of valid content differences between them."[91]

Although Boder indicates that a second article on "the linguistics of catastrophe" is forthcoming, this article was never published. However, components of such an approach can be found in some of the documents in the archives (including preliminary notes, grant applications, and grant reports that he wrote in the 1950s) as well as the master's theses of his graduate students, Hammond, Brown, and Uher. In fact, the graduate students performed the preliminary analysis of all of the interviews that were used in Boder's "Impact of Catastrophe" article.[92] They did so by applying the "Distress-Relief Quotient," the "Density of the Distress Relief Quotient," the "Adjective-Verb Quotient," and the traumatic severity ratings to visualize and interpret the language of the narratives.[93] According to Boder, the purpose of the "Distress-Relief Quotient" (DRQ) is to measure the "rhythm" of a narrative according to "emotional fluctuations" that can be identified by language usage.[94] Guided by human reading and judgment, the idea of assigning numerical valuations to words that connote "distress" and "relief" has certain similarities with dictionary-based approaches to "sentiment analysis," a field of natural language processing that tries to characterize emotions, opinions, evaluations, or sentiments within a text.[95] The difference, however, is that the distress and relief terms were derived directly from the survivor narratives, not decontextualized and assigned a timeless value.

In addition, his wife, Dora Boder, began to manually "compute" certain testimonies, attuned to word counts in questions and answers, the number of definite and indefinite articles, and the use of first-person, second-person, and third-person pronouns (Figure 3.11). Based on grant reports that Boder submitted in the early 1950s, it seems he was interested in exploring how "various type-token analyses" could be used to characterize trauma and analyze "the language of catastrophe."[96] Frank J. Smith, a graduate student working with Boder (but who did not write a thesis with him), helped collate and process much of the data related to the calculation of trauma in the individual narratives as well

Memorandum on Pronoun Count of the Abe Kimmelman Story*

Summary of Number of Words in the Entire Story

Total number of pages	126
Lines per page	25
Av. number of words per line	12
Av. words per page	275
Approx. word total	34,650
Approx. number of "question" lines	409
Approx. total number of words used in questions	4,908
Approx. number of words used by Abe	29,742
Total number of definite articles	1,694
Total number of indefinite articles	901
Total number of articles	2,595
Total number of words (not including articles)	27,147

Percentage of the Various Pronouns of Total Number of Words used by Abe and of Total Number of Words not Including Articles.

Pronoun	n	% of Total (rounded)	Sub-total	% of Total not Incl. Art.	Sub-Total
I	719	2.41		2.65	
Me	99	.33		.36	
Mine; my(self)	168	.56		.62	
Total 1st. person (sing.)	986		3.30		3.63
We	489	1.64		1.80	
Us, our(s), our(selves)	176	.59		.65	
Total 1st. person (pl.)	665		2.23		2.45
Total 1st. person (sing. and pl.)	1,651		5.53		6.08
You, your(s), yourself(ves)	202	.68		.74	
Total 2nd. person (sing. and pl.)	202		.68		.74
He, his, him(self)	618	2.08		2.28	
She, her(s), her(self)	178	.60		.66	
It (referring to animals)	1	.003		.003	
It (referring to inanimate objects)	1	.003		.003	
Total 3rd. person (sing.)	796		2.69		2.95
They, theirs, them(selves)	805	2.71		2.97	
Total 3rd. person (sing. and pl.)	1,601		5.40		5.92
Total of all pronouns	3,456	11.61	11.61	12.74	12.74

* Actual word count taken by Mrs. Boder.

FIGURE 3.11: Word and pronoun counts in Abraham Kimmelmann's interview by Dora Boder, memorandum by Frank J. Smith, n.d. (c. early 1950s). Box 26, David Boder Papers, Special Collections, Charles E. Young Research Library, UCLA.

as the severity evaluations using the Q-technique.[97] Finally, three graduate students in psychology submitted master's theses under Boder's guidance between 1951 and 1952.

Hammond's thesis, "The Psychological Impact of Unprecedented Social Catastrophes: An Analysis of Three Topical Autobiographies of Young Displaced Persons," examined the narratives of Jürgen Bassfreund, Fela Nichthauser, and Abraham Kimmelmann using a combination of "qualitative and quantitative systems of analysis."[98] She draws on Dollard's "criteria for life history"; Dollard and Mowrer's "Discomfort-Relief Quotient" (DRQ); the "Discomfort-Relief Density Quotient" (DRDQ) developed by herself, Boder, and Uher; the Adjective-Verb Quotient (AVQ) developed by Boder; and, finally, the traumatic index developed by Boder. Uher's thesis, "The Psychological Impact of Unprecedented Social Catastrophe: An Analysis of Four Topical Autobiographies of Mature Displaced Persons," focused on the narratives of Kovitzka, Freilich, Matzner, and Kluver—each of whom was in their thirties or forties at the time their stories were recorded in 1946.[99] In addition to using Dollard's criteria for life histories, the DRQ, the DRDQ, the AVQ, and the trauma index as methods of analysis, she also investigated the usage of personal pronouns (first-person singular and plural, second-person singular and plural, and third-person singular and plural), and what she calls "allness" terms, which referred to all-encompassing words such as "everyone," "nobody," "every," "never," and "absolutely" in the course of the narratives.

In Uher's page-by-page analysis of Kovitzka's narrative (Figure 3.12), she counts ninety-two mentions of trauma, which she links to twenty-three different categories in Boder's traumatic index.[100] These traumas include the breakup of the family unit and Kovitzka's separation from her parents, the death of relatives, the evacuation of the ghetto and massacre of the Jews (represented as peaks in the DRQ on pages 7–8), her attempts to save her newborn baby, her deportation to Auschwitz and experiences of protracted states of terror, including her self-identification as a "Musselman" who lost all will to live (represented as peaks in the DRQ on pages 16–17), and, finally, her reflections of loss and loneliness after liberation (represented as peaks in the DRQ on pages 28–30).[101] Based on a set of calculations attuned to word scores and frequency, this graphical representation of Kovitzka's narrative was intended to visualize the rhythmic fluctuations between distress and relief elements characteristic of the language of trauma.

And lastly, Brown's thesis, "Analysis of Five Topical Autobiographies of Christian Faith," used the narratives of Braun, Prest, Kharchenko, Odinets, and Kluver, the same "Friendly Eastern Refugees" that Boder would later use in his 1954 "Impact of Catastrophe" article.[102] Building on an experimental methodology

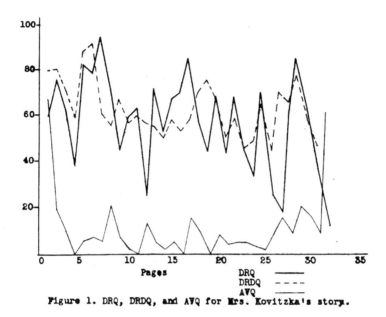

Figure 1. DRQ, DRDQ, and AVQ for Mrs. Kovitzka's story.

FIGURE 3.12: Anna Kovitzka's interview analyzed by page for DRQ, DRDQ, and AVQ. Audrey Uher, "The Psychological Impact of Unprecedented Social Catastrophe: An Analysis of Four Topical Autobiographies of Mature Displaced Persons" (January 1952), 9 (converted for legibility).

suggested by Dollard and Mowrer in which they propose shuffling the pages of the narrative to assign the DRQ to each page,[103] Brown arranged the manuscript pages of each interview in a random, disconnected order (as smaller textual units) and then asked the judges to rate the trauma on each individual page.[104] The purpose was to evaluate the agreement (or lack thereof) of the different trauma ratings assigned by the judges.[105] Brown also computed the DRDQ, DRQ, and AVQ for the five narratives page by page and visualized them through a series of graphs to show changes over narrative time.

While their findings may ultimately be limited, I want to underscore the significance of the team's exploratory methods to measure linguistic features, patterns, relationships, and structures within the corpus of interviews. As a group, they pioneered the use of computational methodologies to interpret testimonial narratives, including what we now call "close" and "distant" reading, statistical feature analysis, and data visualization. Far from antithetical to psychoanalysis, hermeneutics, or philosophy, Boder's team sought to measure the linguistic elements of narratives in order to develop interpretations that could be applied more generally to the entire corpus of interviews, or, for that matter, to any corpus of testimonies. In creating and curating a transmedia archive, marking up the interviews, and computing a wide range of elements in the interviews specific to language, affect, and trauma, Boder and his team were doing what we would now call "digital humanities"—but without the physical, computational, or disciplinary infrastructure to support it.

Although Boder planned to write a follow-up essay called the "Language of Catastrophe," none of this research was ever completed and nothing was ever published of it, possibly because of the challenging computational work involved in creating the data (counting by hand), limited funding, and, eventually, his declining health. In his final years, he focused his attention on developing a "Traumatological Lexicon," a roster of different traumas that could be studied across disciplines and potentially across cultures.[106] While the initial idea was introduced in the late 1940s and derived from the "traumatic inventory" created to encode the interviews, his ambitions for the "traumatological lexicon" were more universalizing, as he now sought to document and understand experiences of suffering that transcended time, place, and cultural and social context.

In this regard, the traumatological lexicon was to cover the widest range of human experiences, including war; man-made and natural catastrophes; family life; industrial, economic, and political aspects of life; physical handicaps; delinquency; problems specific to age groups; and race. Boder outlined three steps in its creation: first, the identification of traumatic experiences from a wide range of publications (such as *The American Soldier*, a major, multivolume study that pioneered methods of social psychology), interviews with displaced people and disaster survivors, psychotherapeutic materials, interviews with war prisoners, case histories (particularly of people who faced challenges due to physical disability, economic situation, or "racial status" in society), court materials, and adjustment studies (industrial, domestic, and intergroup studies). Next came the evaluation of the traumatic experiences using "a bio-mathematical treatment" that aimed to classify the traumas by severity using a geometric scale.[107] Based on a theory of what he called "half bells" (a statistical distribution model), the traumatological lexicon could help characterize the type of trauma and be used to measure its impact attuned to frequency, severity, proximity, physical impact, and emotional toll. And, finally, the trauma ratings had to reflect their context or "traumatic proneness," specifically what he called the "intrafield" and "interfield" evaluation for each event.[108]

The "Evaluative Traumatological Lexicon," as he called it in a 1956 grant application, aimed to produce "rosters of sufferings or deprivations . . . which designate experiences capable of frustrating, impairing, or disrupting to various extents and degrees the adjustment of a person to the processes of biophysical or social life within the framework of physical endurance, subjective attitudes, and culturally determined standards of dignity."[109] In other words, Boder was interested in creating an inventory of traumas that were disruptive to the body, imperiled social life, and impugned the value and dignity of human life. His proposed material for the "traumatological content analysis" not only included interviews, autobiographical reports, recorded narratives, and questionnaires developed by relief organizations, but also works of American literature by the likes of Tennessee Williams, William Faulkner, Ernest Hemingway, and others.[110] Literary content in the form of narratives that reflected the complexity of human experiences and emotions would potentially yield thousands of themes from which his team would produce classifications amenable to quantitative analysis.

In the late 1940s, Boder began his analysis of the DP interviews with close readings and singular voices (exemplified, for example, in his interpretation of Kovitzka's "tale"); however, his final years were spent doing whole corpus analysis aimed at understanding larger structures and shared experiences. This kind of inductive reasoning, made possible by certain quantitative methodologies, turned out to be at odds with how Holocaust testimonies were subsequently interpreted in fields such as history, literary studies, philosophy, media studies, and cultural studies. Computational, statistical, and social science approaches (even when integrated with humanistic, historical, and literary analyses) were not, until quite recently, considered methods of "experimental comprehension." At the same time, Boder was a comparatist who sought to place Holocaust testimonies in conversation with testimonies that bore witness to other human sufferings and histories of trauma.[111] In so doing, he needed to shift the scale and perspective from the analysis of individual interviews to the creation of a comparative, traumatological lexicon that could, potentially, be applied to the human species. He even imagined the creation of "a Team or Council" to promote the creation of traumatological inventories in various countries and that they "would shoulder the responsibility for [the] integration of the material as a whole" as well as keep it "revised and extended." This could lead "in the course of time [to] a sufficient body of scientifically assembled material for the scientific elaboration of a *Cultural History of Values*."[112]

When Boder brought qualitative and quantitative methods together to study narrative and trauma, he laid the foundation for what we call the "ethics of the algorithm." Fully aware of the dangers of a purely quantitative or scientific-statistical approach, Boder and his students sought to develop computational methods to analyze Holocaust testimonies within a capacious, multidisciplinary, humanistic framework. It was to be a "scientific and literary adventure," a speculative, experimental form of analysis and judgment that would be realized more fully in the future. For Boder, these testimonies—both the individual interviews and the analysis of the whole corpus—held forth the hope of contributing to the understanding of something broader about the human experience. Made possible by humanistic methods of computation, Boder's fully zoomed-out view sees new things and aims to generate practical knowledge derived from the manifold violations of human dignity. Ultimately, at this nexus of practical knowledge and propositional methods are ways of developing a cultural history of values to answer ethical questions.

Two Methods of Counter-indexing the "Gray Zone"

N-Grams and Semantic Triplets

With Anna Bonazzi and Lizhou Fan

On August 27, 1946, Boder conducted a four-and-a-half-hour interview with an eighteen-year-old Jewish survivor by the name of Abraham Kimmelmann. It would be the longest and most detailed of his interviews. Kimmelmann relays how he endured forced labor and concentration camps for over four years before being liberated in April of 1945 from Buchenwald. Raised in a Hasidic family in the small Polish town of Dąbrowa Górnicza in Upper Silesia (just forty kilometers north of Auschwitz), Kimmelmann spent most of the war in satellite labor camps affiliated with the concentration camp of Gross-Rosen. Characterized by Boder as one of the "Buchenwald Children" (due to his arrival—on a death march—in Buchenwald at the end of the war), Kimmelmann met Boder in Geneva, Switzerland, at a training school aimed at helping young DPs develop professional skills. Conducted over three recording sessions, the interview was not only Boder's longest and most detailed, but it would become one of his most significant for exploring the nature of testimony, witnessing, and historical truth.

Speaking in German, Kimmelmann began the interview by trying to disabuse Boder of the belief that the experiences of the camps can be definitively, thoroughly, and unequivocally told. Any truth, he says, will always be partial, and there are many, incommensurate truths that exist simultaneously. Before Boder even begins asking questions, Kimmelmann reframes the interview by articulating his understanding of the nature of testimonial truth and the impossibility of recounting things "how they really were":

> You told us before when we were eating what some boys from the Lager [camp] have told you so far. And that they told it to you in different ways, that one said that it was relatively good and that the other reported that he

was very badly off; and in spite of that both have told you the truth. Now you have to make it clear to yourself, that they have not only told you the truth but that they are not able to relate everything the way it really was. Because if you look back to history, or if one writes a book about something, so it is usually said that one writes always more than is true. But in this case it is entirely in the reverse. One can never tell enough and present the things how they really were [*wie es in Wirklichkeit war*].[1]

Boder responds by saying that this is why he is talking to "many" people, "so from the little that I get from everyone, the mosaic, a total picture can be assembled" (*von jedem ein bisserl, das ganze Bild, das Mosaik, das ganze Bild zusammenstellen*).[2] While Kimmelmann obliges to answer Boder's questions, his responses, as we will see, are at variance with Boder's desire to get the "total picture" because Kimmelmann refuses to resolve the contradictions at the heart of many of the experiences he will narrate with intense self-reflexivity. As the interview proceeds, Kimmelmann will continue to raise doubts about the possibility of truly conveying what he and others went through, reinforcing the dubiousness of any attempt to equate testimonial narratives, memories, and historical events.

And yet, for all their importance in Kimmelmann's testimony, these doubts, ambiguities, uncertainties, and narrative fragments are almost entirely absent in Boder's index of Kimmelmann's interview. In fact, when we scrutinize the 209 indexing terms keyed to the 128 typewritten pages, what we see is an extensive, noun-based ontology enumerating Kimmelmann's account of "what happened": geographic locations, people, objects, activities, and events related to the Holocaust. To be sure, these indexing terms—"confiscations," "food," "starvation," "ghetto," "work," "physical mistreatment," "raids," "police," "Gestapo," "deportations," "Appells," "bathing," "hair cutting and shaving," "punishment," "killings," and "crematories"—represent the main subjects of his interview and, altogether, help the reader to form a coherent picture of brutal mistreatment and suffering. But among Boder's enumeration of topics, Kimmelmann's reflections on the uncertainty of testimonial narratives, the complexity of human behavior, and the moral ambiguities of survival are hardly to be found.

For all its usefulness as a finding aid, Boder's index obscures what Primo Levi will later call "the gray zone"—those spaces of complexity and ambiguity that blur sharp distinctions between victims and perpetrators, foil historical lucidity, and undermine moral clarity.[3] Perhaps this is most evidenced by the fact that Boder found nothing to index on page two of Kimmelmann's testimony where he questioned the very premise of testimonial truth and the ability to narrate things as they really were. Instead, Boder commences his index with the facts at hand: the two locations (Geneva and Dąbrowa Górnicza) and an organization (ORT) referenced on page one and the first discussions about "children," "curfews," and "passports" on page three. We might ask: why should this matter? The answer, in short, is that indexing systems—both human- and machine-created—tell us what is worth hearing. They form the basis of any "search" within an archive and thus determine what can be readily found and known.

In what follows, we will first discuss Boder's approach to topical indexing and situate its achievements as well as its shortcomings in the context of his broader work of early Holocaust testimony collection. After that, we will explore two different approaches to counter-indexing that are text immanent—that is, they are derived directly from sets of words in the transcripts rather than from a secondary scaffolding meant to summarize experiences or find discrete mentions of keywords. The first approach uses N-grams to identify the frequency of recurring semantic phrases in the narrative; the second approach uses semantic triplets to index and visualize expressions of agency (reports of who did what to whom). In both cases, we sought to explore computational approaches to indexing that were derived directly from narrative features of the text. As we show below, the results draw attention to the prevalence of the "gray zone" by focusing attention on elements of the narrative that are marked by ambiguity, uncertainty, and self-reflexivity.

On Indexing Systems

Because of the sheer size and complexity of oral history collections, indexing systems are critically important for accessing content and running search queries. Transcribed pages or temporal segments of an oral history can be effectively tagged with names, dates, events, places, organizations, and various topical headings. These noun-based ontologies form the taxonomic structure of most indexing systems and finding aids. Attuned to the objective realm of what was said, they help make the general content of an oral history discoverable and accessible to listeners. Today, when users enter keywords into an empty textbox, search and retrieval works because the content is described by a standardized controlled vocabulary. However, far from objective, indexing systems are propositional, contingent, and sometimes political, highlighting certain themes and epistemic decisions while obscuring others.[4]

Not surprisingly, in the realm of text mining, most entity-recognition software packages, such as OpenNLP (Apache Software Foundation 2017) and spaCy (Explosion AI 2020), privilege noun-based ontologies. They identify proper names, organizations, geographic locations, historical events, dates, units of time, quantities, and other numerical units, such as percentages and times of day. But one of their fundamental limits is the focus on extracting isolated elements (primarily nouns) rather than larger semantic units that describe what people did, what was done to them, and how they put those descriptions into narrative sequences.[5] As such, we want to ask: In what ways can oral histories be mined computationally to index how survivors narrate behaviors and actions? And what might these approaches to indexing uncover or highlight that conventional approaches to indexing have variously forgotten or obscured?

When Boder published his book *I Did Not Interview the Dead* in 1949 (a compendium of eight interviews), he had already developed a preliminary index of traumatic experiences and a set of trauma categories, which he intended to evaluate for their impact on the speakers' personalities. This index would grow dramatically in the years to come and become part of a series of indexes that he would develop for identifying a range of topics in the testimonies: a "subjects and situations" index with more than three hundred entries; a "geographic and ethnic" index with over four hundred entries; a "persons and organizations" index with close to three hundred entries; and a "trauma inventory" of forty-six types of trauma and violence experienced by survivors, supplemented by 116 "interpretative expansions" describing the traumas and an "alphabetic roster" of 377 items for indexing the traumatic content of the interviews. For the first three, the entries were keyed to the typewritten and translated interviews in *Topical Autobiographies*, his 3,194-page anthology of seventy interviews that he translated, typed, and self-published.[6] Although never completed, Boder also planned a "psychological and anthropological index" in which he would "attempt to code the factual experiences and attitudes of the narrators and the reported behavior of their fellow men (prisoners, guards, local authorities, personnel of liberating armies, etc.)," thus placing the experiences of the survivors in a network of behaviors and actions.[7]

The intellectual achievement of these topical indexes is significant, since they were the first ones to make sense of the narrative content of Holocaust testimonies at this scale. In the 1950s, professional Holocaust history was still in its infancy and the collection of primary source materials, while started in earnest immediately after the war,[8] was still in the very early stages of processing and organization. Together with collaborators Dr. Dora Neveloff Boder, Sandy Schuckett, Donald M. Procter, and Bernard Wolf, Boder created an intellectual scaffolding to characterize the content of more than three thousand transcribed and translated pages of testimonies keyed to identifying events, places, people, objects, and trauma. The entries included variations, usages, subcategories, and intertextual references, which, altogether, formed a kind of information system for making sense of the unprecedented narrative content of the interviews (Figure 3.13).

Index - Part I
Subjects and Situations - Second Typing

- 4 - (3108)

Children, (continued), 287, 323, 332, 348, 358, 367, 440, 450, 499, 510, 536, 605, 621, 706, 718, 836, 849, 965, 1112, 1131, 1211, 1220, 1242, 1287, 1305, 1327, 1372, 1423, 1507, 1513, 1575, 1585, 1636, 1659, 1711, 1787, 1807, 1905, 1927, 2000, 2022, 2070, 2194, 2234, 2263, 2332, 2353, 2418, 2540, 2595, 2619, 2636, 2664, 2650, 2676, 2685, 2697, 2723, 2746, 2765, 2786, 2792, 2797, 2810, 2816, 2832, 2856, 2866, 2929, 2985, 3009, 3025, 3056, 3065

Churches, 133, 221, 248, 258, 317, 484, 653, 1548, 2621, 2677, 2693

Clergy,
Catholic, 1086, 3042, 3067,
Greek Orthodox, 433, 668
Jewish, 488, 2538, 2698
Protestant, 1550

Clothing, 82, 100, 152, 164, 189, 252, 263, 271, 291, 304, 317, 324, 348, 357, 366, 381, 397, 450, 468, 611, 793, 826, 841, 856, 873, 1180, 1222, 1320, 1427, 1528, 1593, 1652, 1661, 1724, 2053, 2062, 2273, 2310, 2346, 2555, 2582, 2614, 2635, 2654, 2676, 2742, 2803, 2907,

Collaborationism, (see also turn-coats), 487, 593, 655, 674, 772, 837, 1083, 1683, 1727, 1749, 1857, 1909, 2264

"Combat", (French newspaper), 771

Communication, restrictions of, verbal, written, 103, 139, 347, 402, 430, 607, 650, 764, 944, 1516, 1626, 1756, 1886, 1959, 2356, 2381, 2510, 2583, 2658, 2703, 2953, 2991, 3045, 3058, 3094

Communists, (see also Bolsheviks), 426, 493, 553, 589, 635, 651, 969, 1837, 1911, 2913, 3081

Community councils, Jewish, 16, 49, 135, 176, 253, 285, 310, 962, 1089, 1147, 1290, 1790, 1906, 1955, 1989, 2190, 2296, 2438, 2539, 2615, 2709, 2751, 2887, 3004

Compelled wanton mistreatment of fellow prisoners, (physical and otherwise) 55, 101, 518, 546, 2540

Concealment of objects, 534, 2701

Concentration camps, list of, (for references, see separate entries in Part II of INDEX)
Allerich (?)
Altengrube
Ampfing (?)
Aschaffenburg
Aschersleben
Aussig
Auschwitz
Barta
Barth
Belzec
Bergen Belsen
Biata (?)
Bicki (?)
Birkenau
Birkenheim
Blechhammer
Bomer
Breslau
Buchenwald
Buna
Burgau
Czestochowa
Dachau
Danzig
Dora
Drancy
Freising
Flossenburg
Funf Teichen
Furstengrube
Gabesdorf

Figure 3.13: Sample page of Boder's "Subjects and Situations" index. David Boder, *Topical Autobiographies of Displaced People* (1957), David Boder Papers, Library Special Collections, Charles E. Young Research Library, UCLA, 3108.

In the prefatory materials for the index, Boder provides a few caveats about its use and scope: first, the indexes make no claim of "complete coverage" and, instead, represent an "extensive sampling" prepared with the other four project collaborators, which may account for certain inconsistencies; secondly, the first occurrence of a given term or concept is indexed, but the team did not repeatedly index a term on subsequent pages unless it reoccurred more than nine pages later; third, the index sometimes introduces terms (such as "perfidy") to "conceptualize a given situation," even though the exact word is not used by the interviewee; and, finally, "items repeated with extraordinary frequency" (such as "Jews," "Germans," or "war") are not indexed.[9]

The "subjects and situations" index contained more than three hundred entries and represented the first controlled vocabulary for indexing everything from shared experiences like deportations, selections, and killings to deeply subjective and personal experiences such as screaming and wailing. Of the seventy testimonies comprising *Topical Autobiographies*, the most frequent subjects and situations indexed are shown in Figure 3.14.[10] The left side of the graph shows the distinct number of testimonies in which the term is indexed, and the right side shows the total number of pages in which that term is used (for instance, "food" is indexed in fifty-three distinct testimonies, and there are 113 total instances of indexing across the corpus).[11] Among the most frequently discussed and indexed topics are: food, travel, work, children, liberation, deportations, evacuations, selections, killings, and physical mistreatment. These kinds of indexing counts help us appreciate the range of topics covered in Boder's corpus of testimonies, correlate mentions of different topics across individual testimonies, and, finally, compare topics across testimonial archives, as we will see in chapter 4.

We also sought to know how thoroughly the interviews were indexed by calculating the number of indexing keywords used per thousand words of narrative. In the next visualization (Figure 3.15), we can see the absolute counts of indexing keywords as well as the ratio of keywords to words of spoken narrative. Of the seventy interviews in *Topical Autobiographies* (the only ones Boder indexed), we see a range of eleven indexing keywords per interview at the low end and 209 indexing keywords at the upper end, the latter representing Kimmelmann's testimony. Even though it is the longest, Kimmelmann's interview only contains 5.97 indexing terms per thousand words, making it, as it turns out, one of the least indexed interviews. Among the highest (at 23.39 indexing terms per thousand words) is Boder's interview with Bella Zgnilek, a twenty-two-year-old Polish Jew. While this particular interview is indexed quite thoroughly, it is, in fact, a fairly anomalous interview because Boder actually spoke more than Zgnilek, who spoke 1,582 words versus his 1,667 words. In the span of just over twenty-three

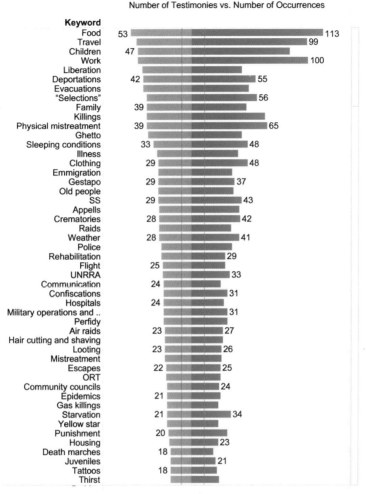

Number of Testimonies vs. Number of Occurrences

FIGURE 3.14: Frequency of Boder's indexing keywords by number of testimonies and occurrences. Created by Lizhou Fan. Interactive visualization on Tableau: hrl.pub/8a0386.

minutes (making it one of the shortest interviews he conducted), Boder asked her 150 questions, ranging from questions about her family and their fate, her deportation to Auschwitz, and her camp experiences to postwar work, reflections, and intentions. In general, the vast majority of ratios are between five and fifteen indexing keywords per thousand words of interviewee narrative.

In addition to these general topics, the index also contains references to a number of subjects that later testimonies may have considered taboo, including discussions

FIGURE 3.15: Indexing ratios for seventy interviews in *Topical Autobiographies*. Count is the number of indexing keywords. The ratio is count divided by total words in the testimony. Created by Lizhou Fan and Anna Bonazzi. Interactive visualization on Tableau: hrl.pub/48b111.

Highlighted tooltip:

Name: Abraham Kimmelmann
ID: 56
Keywords: 209
Words: 35,024
Keywords to words ratio: 0.00597

Treemap cells:

- Hildegarde Franz — Keywords: 57 — Ratio: 0.02437
- Anna Braun — Keywords: 63 — Ratio: 0.01156
- Roma Tcharnabroda — Keywords: 104 — Ratio: 0.01817
- Nechama Epstein-Kozlowski — Keywords: 192 — Ratio: 0.01416
- Charlotte Schultze — Keywords: 31 — Ratio: 0.01287
- Raisel Meltzak — Keywords: 25 — Ratio: 0.01268
- Adam Krakowski — Keywords: 36 — Ratio: 0.01263
- Udel Stopnitsky — Keywords: 161 — Ratio: 0.01201
- Ludwig Hamburger — Keywords: 71 — Ratio: 0.01200
- Jacob
- Bella Zgniek — Keywords: 37 — Ratio: 0.02339
- Bertha Goldwasser — Keywords: 66 — Ratio: 0.01795
- Victor Ferdinansk — Keywords: 25 — Ratio: 0.01410
- Raisel Roset — Keywords: 18 — Ratio: 0.01155
- Adolph Heisler — Keywords: 51 — Ratio: 0.00966
- Bernard Warsager — Keywords: 88 — Ratio: 0.00947
- Fania Freilich — Keywords: 93 — Ratio: 0.00904
- Ephraim Gutman — Keywords: 81 — Ratio: 0.00896
- Anna Paul — Keywords: 44 — Ratio: 0.00885
- Fela
- Samuel Isakovitch — Keywords: 63 — Ratio: 0.01587
- Edith Zierer — Keywords: 31 — Ratio: 0.01408
- Jaques Matzner — Keywords: 180 — Ratio: 0.02194
- Irena Rosenwasser — Keywords: 94 — Ratio: 0.01112
- Esther Krueger — Keywords: 39 — Ratio: 0.00855
- Mendel
- George Kaldore — Keywords: 93 — Ratio: 0.00739
- Pinkhus
- Dimitri Odinets — Keywords: 31 — Ratio: 0.00724
- Friedrich
- Marko Moskovitz — Keywords: 32 — Ratio: 0.01558
- Ernesto Moeller-Arnold — Keywords: 42 — Ratio: 0.01370
- Janis B. — Keywords: 18 — Ratio: 0.01105
- Max Sprecher — Keywords: 71 — Ratio: 0.00849
- Julius Kluver — Keywords: 49 — Ratio: 0.02075
- Anna Kaletska — Keywords: 109 — Ratio: 0.01344
- Jola Gross — Keywords: 31 — Ratio: 0.01096
- Valerius Michelson — Keywords: 46 — Ratio: 0.00820
- Leon Shachnovski — Keywords: 11 — Ratio: 0.00685
- Otto Feu... — Keyw... 55 — Ratio 0.006
- Joseph Ferber — Keywords: 25 — Ratio: 0.00665
- Polia Bisenhaus — Keywords: 37 — Ratio: 0.01505
- Israel Unikowski — Keywords: 93 — Ratio: 0.01027
- Sigmund Reich — Keywords: 36 — Ratio: 0.00799
- Edith Serras — Keywords: 68 — Ratio: 0.00659
- Alexander Gertner — Keywords: 115
- Solomon Horowitz — Keywords: 44 — Ratio:
- Abram Perl — Keywords: 28 — Ratio:
- Isaac Ostland — Keywords: 104 — Ratio: 0.02015
- Hadassah Marcus — Keywords: 98
- Nathan Schacht — Keywords: 19 — Ratio: 0.01317
- Kalman Eisenberg — Keywords: 84 — Ratio: 0.00985
- Jurek Kestenberg — Keywords: 74 — Ratio: 0.00795
- Henja Frydman — Keywords: 75 — Ratio: 0.00552
- Helen Tichauer — Keywords: 76 — Ratio: 0.00541
- Isaac Wolf — Keywords: 52 — Ratio:
- Jacob Wilf
- Clara Neiman — Keywords: 49 — Ratio: 0.01840
- Helena Neufeld — Keywords: 41 — Ratio: 0.01456
- Jurgen Bassfreund — Keywords: 113 — Ratio: 0.01301
- Julian Weinberg — Keywords: 83 — Ratio: 0.00971
- Nelly Bondy — Keywords: 67 — Ratio: 0.00772
- Jacob Minski — Keywords: 67 — Ratio: 0.00642
- Ioan Kharchenko — Keywords: 22
- Benjamin Piskorz
- Rachel
- Jacob Oleiski

of "compelled wanton mistreatment of fellow prisoners (physical and otherwise),"
"perfidy," "cannibalism," "dead-handlers" ("Toten-commando," now known as the
Sonderkommando), references to "urine, alleged drinking of," and nearly two dozen
references to "screaming, collective, including wailing" (3,105–20).[12] The index
also gives two dozen references to "Community Councils, Jewish" (across the seventy interviews) but does not provide any insights about their actions or decisions,
or what particular people did. At the same time, the keyword "police" includes
"compelled mistreatment of fellow prisoners" but does not allow a reader to understand who was involved in such actions, how they happened, and why. This
undifferentiated category "police" obscures both the differences and relationship
between the German police and the Jewish police, the latter of which was sometimes forced to cooperate, through the Jewish Community Councils, with the
German police and the Gestapo in rounding up Jews. The nature of this collaboration, what it means to act in a state of violent coercion, how to talk about it, and
whether to pass judgment on such actions turns out to be a central part of Kimmelmann's testimony.

Although some of these taboo topics are, in fact, referenced in Boder's index of
Kimmelmann's testimony (including "perfidy" indexed once, "Community Councils, Jewish" indexed twice, "compelled wanton mistreatment" indexed twice, and
"police" indexed four times), the indexing terms themselves tend to downplay,
rather than foreground, the complexities of such behaviors, not to mention Kimmelmann's own struggle to describe and judge these organizations, their leaders,
and the actions they undertook. Later articulated by Levi as the "gray zone," these
actions blurred the strict boundaries between victims and perpetrators in a world
corrupted by Nazi terror and "moral collapse."[13] Kimmelmann's testimony, we
argue, refuses to "reduce the knowable to a schema" or "simplify history" into clear
binaries;[14] instead, he describes a world of indecipherability in a narrative form
that is also suffused by these very uncertainties.[15] In what follows, we describe two
algorithmic methods of indexing aimed at surfacing these ambiguities and complexities that remain hidden when we rely only on the manually curated keywords
as finding aids. The first approach focuses on N-grams (word sequences within the
narrative) and the second approach focuses on semantic triplets.

Indexing with N-Grams

N-grams are short segments of *n* words or characters in a text. For example, a
sentence like "the Jewish Council got a call from the police"[16] can be split into
bi-grams like "the Jewish" or "Jewish Council," tri-grams like "the Jewish Council"

or "Jewish Council got," quad-grams like "the Jewish Council got" or "Council got a call," and so on. These snippets, when sorted by frequency and grouped according to certain criteria, are useful in identifying frequent expressions, sentence structures, and similar content patterns within a text. N-grams are a classic tool of computational linguistics and have long been used for text analysis and content mining in large data collections.[17] Working with these units, longer than individual words but shorter than sentences, paragraphs, or pages, we can identify patterns of expression and specific phrases that rotate not only around nouns, but also around verbs, adjectives, and adverbs (which tend not to get annotated as their own categories as much as nouns). Most importantly, looking at N-grams can help us identify content categories we may not have been looking for at the outset, either because they have to do with narrative structure more than with keywords, or because the content to which they point may be unexpected.

As a semiautomated method, N-gram-based indexing presents the strengths and weaknesses of both automated categorization and manual analysis: while the identification of significant categories follows more traceable and objective criteria than a manual approach, the selection and naming of those categories still require human judgment. Moreover, this method relies heavily on frequency, which can sometimes be misleading: a significant expression is not necessarily frequent in a text, and a frequent one may not necessarily be significant. Boder, for example, made the explicit choice not to index words like "Germans" or "Jews," as explained above, precisely because he judged them to be too frequent. Still, our analysis suggests that sometimes elements of a testimony that are both frequent and significant emerge through an N-gram-based approach while they do not easily stand out in a manual or keyword-based analysis. This is partially so because we may not interpret frequent expressions the same way if we analyze a text manually versus computationally: during a close reading of a text, we might notice frequent words like "Germans" or other clusters of similar thematic expressions, while we might fail to notice frequent expressions that look like a linguistic accident more than a specific "topic." For example, this is the case with common expressions like "I don't know" or "I don't remember," as we will see below. We might even tune them out during close reading, or we might not immediately see why they are relevant; however, when a frequency-based index shows us the relative weight of this category of expressions, we might look at them differently and focus more closely on the survivor's expressive choices.

The frequency-based approach, despite its limits, helps us question assumptions about what constitutes the "content" of a testimony. While keyword-based indexing focuses on what survivors *say*, mostly in terms of nouns and events, it does not look at *how* they say a certain thing, or what they choose *not to say*. By using alternative indexing methods, we may want to look at interviews not only as repositories of historical evidence, but also as personal stories that center the survivor's state of mind and help us understand how testimonial narratives developed and what we might be overlooking. Pacing, language choices, narrative structures, insistence, uncertainty, and silence all play a role in the expression of a unique and historically situated memory. What would a content index look like if it was built with frequency-based terms? To be sure, N-gram-indexing (like all frequency-based methods) really shows its potential in the analysis of text corpora or collections that are too large to be analyzed by hand: in those cases, frequency numbers are higher, making them more expressive, as frequency differences vary by orders of magnitude, and the overall distribution of word counts tends to be closer to the ideal limit of natural language. Moreover, the size of the corpus helps similarities and content patterns emerge in numerous disconnected texts. At the same time, using frequency to index the content of a single text has advantages, too: it can be a step to take before (or even instead of) close reading, as it helps us readjust our expectations of what the interview will be about, and it can also be used to double-check or better interpret N-gram results from a larger sample.

Before looking at an alternative analysis of Kimmelmann's interview, let us focus on the way N-grams are computed, cleaned up, and grouped together to build an indexing system. Kimmelmann's interview, like the other interviews from the Boder corpus, is available online as a recording with an XML-encoded German-language transcript and an English translation.[18] Each interview transcript was transposed to XML format and annotated with Boder's original information about the interview's date, location, and languages, as well as the survivor's name, age, and religion. We further annotated the interviews line by line, adding automatically derived data about the speaker, language, and speed of the dialogue in each line.[19] The text was annotated with Treetagger, a Part-Of-Speech (POS) tagging tool that identifies grammatical parts of speech such as nouns, verbs, adverbs, adjectives, and so forth.[20] In order to reduce the noise among N-grams, semantically weak expressions that did not contain at least a non-auxiliary verb, a noun, or an adjective (like the phrase "*and then they*") were excluded from further analysis.

POS annotation relies on context and frequency of a word within a text, so it works better on longer texts and does not yield sensible results if applied to short text snippets like an N-gram. For this reason, the text was first annotated as a whole and then segmented into N-grams, with each word carrying its POS tag (e.g., "*meine*-adjective, *Mutter*-noun"). The text was segmented into N-grams of two to six words:[21] for example, the sample sentence mentioned above, "the Jewish Council got a call from the police," was split into units as short as "Council got" and as long as "got a call from the police." Each segment was marked by line to enable us to trace it back to its original text.

These segments were then counted and sorted by frequency to identify the most common ones. While a segment like "call from the" may appear once or twice in the whole text and not carry any particular meaning, more frequent N-grams like "the Jewish Council" or "from the police" may tell us more about the interviewee's story. However, two drawbacks of raw N-grams need to be addressed to get a reasonably accurate and usable frequency count: frequency underestimation in some cases and overestimation in others. On the one hand, the presence of slightly different versions of the same expression (like "*ein jüdischer Miliz*" vs. "*die jüdische Miliz*") leads to the risk that a frequent phrase might get lost among many variants and appear less frequent than it really is. On the other hand, the overlap of N-grams of different sizes derived from the same sentence makes rare expressions appear more frequent than they really are. For example, we might be led to believe that the town of Bensburg is incredibly important in Kimmelmann's testimony because there are 212 N-grams that contain that word, but in reality, he only mentions the town twenty-five times. Most N-gram instances of this word are snippets of the same sentence: for instance, from the sentence "*Essen war billiger als in Bensburg*" ("food was cheaper than in Bensburg"),[22] we may obtain N-grams like "*war billiger als in Bensburg*," "*billiger als in Bensburg*," "*als in Bensburg und*," and so on.

To improve the reliability of the frequency count, similar N-grams (like "*jüdische Gemeinde*" and "*bei der jüdischen Kultusgemeinde*," both designating the Jewish community council) were identified and grouped together using a similarity algorithm.[23] Any two N-grams were considered to be passably similar if they fulfilled these conditions: their similarity score was greater than or equal to 0.75;[24] they came from different lines of the interview, or if they came from the same line, they were not subsets of each other (such as "*und meine Mutter*" compared to "*ich und meine Mutter*"). The remaining N-grams were then manually analyzed to identify frequent units that potentially indicate the main themes or expressions of the interview, as well as units that may match the similarity criteria on a formal level but without carrying a comparable meaning.

A comparison between Boder's own annotations of Kimmelmann's interview and the N-gram-based results clearly shows the benefits of an alternative content indexing system (Figures 3.16 and 3.17). Boder indexed the interview by page,

Keywords
1 ___ 8

FIGURE 3.16: Boder's indexing of Kimmelmann's interview. Created by Anna Bonazzi. Interactive visualization on Tableau: hrl.pub/ee406b.

Keywords
18 ████████████ 166

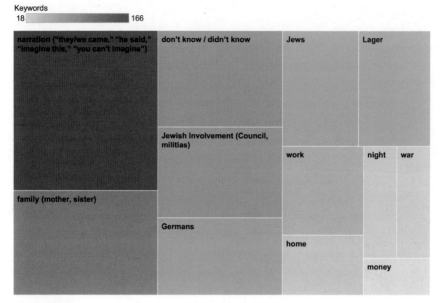

FIGURE 3.17: N-gram-based indexing of Boder's interview with Kimmelmann (1946), in *Topical Autobiographies*. Created by Anna Bonazzi. Interactive visualization on Tableau: hrl.pub/21edc8.

primarily focusing on nouns that he found particularly significant (personal names, geographic locations, objects, and events). The eight most frequently indexed terms in Kimmelmann's testimony are: "Auschwitz," "work," "food," "punishment," "travel," "weather," "Bensburg," and "killings." While these terms give us a broad perspective on the themes of the interview as well as specific references to data and traumatic events, they do not really capture what Kimmelmann is talking about or how he expresses himself. A look at the results of N-gram-based indexing done on the same interview (Figure 3.17) shows that several significant aspects of the interview escape a predetermined keyword-based approach.

N-gram-based categories return a very different image of what this interview is about. First of all, we see an emphasis on the expressive choices Kimmelmann made to narrate his testimony.[25] He is not just answering Boder's questions, but building a narrative that draws the listener into his experience and introduces a wide network of characters (as we can easily confirm with a close reading of the interview). Many of his expressions show that his testimony sets the stage for dialogue and attempts to bring in other people's speech ("he said," "they said," "he thought," "they didn't say"), relay sequences of events and movement ("went in," "came in," "took us"), or show glimpses of time passing and key moments ("the time had come," "the hour had come," "the day had come"). Kimmelmann not only relates what happened, but he often invites Boder to see things from his perspective, repeating expressions such as "imagine this," "picture this," and "you can't imagine." Kimmelmann's testimony is a story populated by many characters, and two of the most common ways of introducing them are what we labeled "talking" N-grams and "movement" N-grams. Movement is a peculiar category in this narration, in that it represents both a topic and a structural feature of the interview. As an indexing category, it helps the reader glimpse an important topic of Kimmelmann's testimony, which is rich in episodes describing travel, hiding, escaping, and particularly the uncertainty of unfinished travel plans just before capture. At the same time, this movement category overlaps with the more structural narrative categories of the index, and signals the presence of a rich network of characters in addition to Kimmelmann and his immediate family. Together with expressions of talking ("he told me," "they were saying"), movement expressions serve as "enter character" tags, thanks to their repetitive nature, making the index a source of both direct and indirect information for the reader.

While a more detailed analysis of each N-gram occurrence might help sort these movement expressions into separate categories of more metaphorical versus more concrete movement (like "it came to a point" vs. "they came in"), that would also defeat the purpose of using the index to show the presence of fuzzy but undeniable groups of related expressions. The decision to group these expressions together and interpret them as a "narration" or "narration and travel" category necessarily relies on subjective judgment, but N-grams help maintain a degree of distance and objectivity by allowing us to see these phrases as a cohesive and highly frequent category. Far from being just a cosmetic trait of Kimmelmann's speech around "real" topics, these expressions *are* a topic: they set the stage and contextualize Kimmelmann's responses; they call for empathy and involvement; they reference other people's speech; and they express uncertainty about the listener's ability to really understand. These narrative expressions are a central feature of Kimmelmann's act of testimony and serve to underscore his doubts about the entire interview process.

Another key category that emerges from this visualization is Kimmelmann's interest in the agency and moral involvement of other Jews in the events he experienced. The blurring of the strict boundary between victims and perpetrators under Nazi occupation is a question of great concern for him. For example, he often talks about the actions of "Jewish militias" and the ambiguous roles of the "Jewish Council," which acted as intermediaries between the Nazi authorities and the Jewish community. The latter term refers to the forced governance and administrative councils (commonly called the *Judenräte*) responsible for overseeing the ghettos, implementing Nazi policies and orders, and providing basic services for the Jewish communities. More broadly, Kimmelmann is concerned with the morally gray area that individual Jewish leaders found themselves in when they had to decide what they were willing to do to protect themselves and their families, as well as what they did for their community under excruciating circumstances in attempting to save lives through compliance with orders. In this case, N-grams offer an indirect way to capture this theme in Kimmelmann's narrative.[26] N-grams, of course, cannot capture Kimmelmann's specific opinions on or observations about these organizations, which are quite nuanced and vary throughout the interview, but what N-grams do achieve is a spotlight effect: They are a simple and powerful way to show the prevalence of this theme in his testimony and thereby open up spaces for further investigations.

Labeling Kimmelmann's concern over Jewish involvement as an indexing item is far from obvious, especially because Boder hardly draws attention to this category. He does index a few mentions of the Jewish Council, perfidy, and authorities like soldiers and police, but his indexing system does not offer a way to grasp Kimmelmann's focus on the moral questions of collaboration under coercion or people's potential for violence and exploitation given certain conditions. At the time of Boder's interview project, establishing facts and grasping the enormity of these events took priority over examining the reactions of people caught between moral choices. Today, depending on the personal, social, and political context of our acts of listening, we may be hesitant to acknowledge (or unable to hear) a topic like this, so it might still go unremarked during manual indexing. The frequency-based approach, on the other hand, allows this topic to emerge on its own, because it identifies the topic as a cohesive category of related expressions whose frequency is too high to be ignored. N-grams make it easier to see, name, and index this topic, leaving it up to the listener to decide how to explore or interpret it.

A third category that stands out in Kimmelmann's interview is the "I don't know/I didn't know" cluster, also observed in a separate analysis of Boder's corpus as a whole.[27] The strong presence of this category, even in an interview that is mostly self-regulated and contains comparatively few direct questions, highlights the narrative role of uncertainty and reticence in early Holocaust testimonies like this one. These are not cases in which Kimmelmann simply does not know the answer to a specific question. Kimmelmann shows reticence or gaps in his present understanding of the situation with expressions like "I don't know," "still today I don't know," or "I don't want to [tell/say] more." Often, he directly evokes the impressions he had at a certain point of the story, using phrases like "didn't know," "knew nothing," "without knowing," and "knew nothing anymore."[28] In this case, using N-grams allows us to identify a category of silent or missing content that can shed light on the way survivors formulate their experiences into language. Once we know that silence, reticence, and uncertainty are a widespread category in early interviews like Boder's, we may want to track this mode of expression in testimonies from later times and different locations in order to understand how a survivor's own narrative evolves in response to what they learn and elaborate over time. We may also want to go back to the text and examine the points where these uncertainties emerge, to try to understand how and where witnesses show their gaps of knowledge as well as the way they frame their own story within a broader historical context.[29]

As these three examples show, N-gram-based indexing helps us center the survivors' words and expressivity and expand indexing to include structural, seemingly inconsequential aspects of testimony. N-grams are only one of the possible tools we may use to enrich traditional ontology-based indexing. While N-grams look at text in terms of sequential expressions, we can also look at a text in terms of its expressions of agency (who did what to whom). In this case, rather than indexing sentence snippets, we index structures abstracted from a sentence, or "semantic triplets," to show the way witnesses represent actors and agency in their stories.

Indexing Agency through Triplets

This approach to indexing focuses on networks of agency—namely, reports of what people (or groups) did and what was done to them. As described in detail in chapter 6, we use natural language processing (NLP) to extract "semantic triplets" from the testimonial narratives by identifying grammatical units consisting of a subject, verb relations (like active, passive, or active but coerced actions), and one or more objects or object phrases. For example, "They [the Gestapo] posted announcements on all of the streets" is a triplet expressing the active agency of the Gestapo, while "we had to stand all night" is an expression of a coerced action. Using our own algorithm built from spaCy's natural language processing methodology, we extracted more than 2,000 triplets from Kimmelmann's 128-page testimony and characterized them according to the type of speech employed: active speech, passive speech, speech about coerced actions, speculative speech, evaluations (or opinions), and orientation (or context). When possible, we further characterized the objects by lemma (the principal root of a word) and manually disambiguated pronouns in order to link related agents together in a network diagram. For the purposes of this experiment, we used Boder's English translation for generating the triplets, but consulted the German original for each triplet used in the analysis below to be sure that the semantic meaning was properly captured, that the translations of subjects and objects were consistent, that pronouns were (to the extent possible) properly disambiguated, and that the related triplets were clustered together.[30]

We can examine triplets in a specific segment of Kimmelmann's testimony (such as a single indexed page) or across the entire testimony. Starting with the former, we see that Boder uses the indexing term "screaming" on page 99 of the testimony. From that term alone, it is hard to know exactly what is going on. Triplets help us to distill the specific forms of agency expressed in this section of narrative. Here, Kimmelmann is talking about forced laborers, including himself, being beaten in the camp. The screaming echoes nightly throughout the barracks of the camp as prisoner functionaries (the *Lagerältester* and their *Helfer*, or auxiliaries), some of whom were also Jewish, beat their fellow prisoners under the watch of the German camp commandant (*der Wachhabende, der Deutsche*).[31] At this time, Kimmelmann was a forced laborer in Markstadt, one of a hundred subcamps outside of Gross-Rosen, building roads and laying railway tracks. He and twenty-five other prisoners slept in a barrack that they were required to clean nightly or risk being beaten. In his translation, Boder groups the prisoner functionaries together using the term "Lager trusties," possibly because Kimmelmann uses the terms *Lagerältester* and *Helfer* somewhat interchangeably to refer to prisoners who were delegated—by the German camp commandant and SS—to carry out violence against their fellow prisoners. The screaming referred not only to the indiscriminate beating meted out nightly on the bodies of the victims, but it also signaled the creation of a broader system of terror in which certain other prisoners were degraded into complicity with Nazi violence. In short, this is a description of what Levi would later call the "gray zone."

In Figure 3.18, we see the seventeen triplets (without correcting for syntax) that were extracted computationally from page 99 of Kimmelmann's testimony. In this synchronic visualization, the indexing term "screaming" is now deeply contextualized in the gray zone of the narrative. The Lager trusties beat the prisoners nightly, and Kimmelmann recounts hearing the screams: "The Lager trusties were beating in another barracks the outcries the screams would be heard"; "I would never fall asleep without hearing uh-uh"; "one would hear the outcries, the screams"; "I cannot describe it." While "screams" are directly mentioned twice

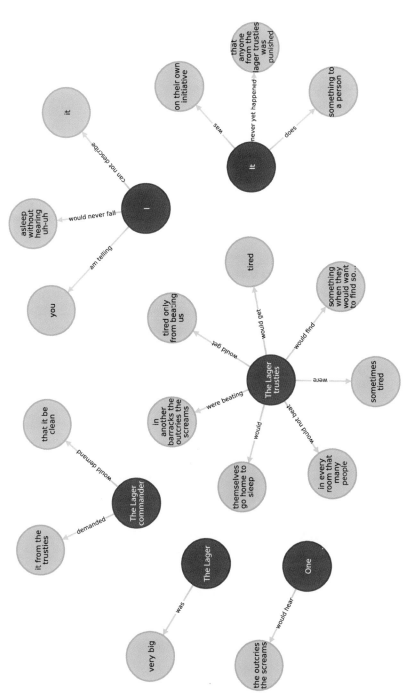

FIGURE 3.18: Triplets from one page of Boder's interview with Kimmelmann (1946), in *Topical Autobiographies*. Created by Lizhou Fan and Todd Presner.

and referenced a third time by the sound "uh-uh," these triplets draw attention to the subjects doing the action (the Lager commander and the Lager trusties), the actions themselves (demanding, beating, becoming tired), and the objects of those actions. And just as importantly, Kimmelmann is part of the story, both in terms of his perception of the events themselves and his attempt to describe them in narrative form to Boder (even as he says, "I cannot describe it").

Beyond just a single page, describing and confronting the "gray zone" runs throughout much of Kimmelmann's testimony. Here, we can use triplets to link together diachronic elements of the narrative. References to *"die jüdische Kultusgemeinde"*—variously translated by Boder as "Jewish community council," "Jewish council," "central council," and "Jewish Cultural Commonwealth," and indexed twice by Boder as "Community Councils, Jewish"—occur thirty times in Kimmelmann's testimony (including the shortened variations of *"Zentrale"* and *"Zentralgemeinde"*). Kimmelmann also speaks, in this context, of the roles played by the Jewish militia (*die jüdische Miliz*), a particular (although unnamed) Jewish militiaman, and the Jewish police (*die jüdische Polizei*) in carrying out such orders. The cooperation of the Jewish councils, the Jewish police, and the Jewish militia—all coerced administrative formations—continues to be controversial and debated since some have argued, like Hannah Arendt, that the complicity of Jewish leaders with the Nazis sealed the fates of countless Jews.[32] As others have pointed out, these decisions of compliance were made by individuals in situations of extreme coercion and precarity who tried to protect the Jewish communities by cooperating with Nazi orders.[33] For example, the leader of the Jewish council of Sosnowiec and regional administrator of dozens of local Jewish councils, Moshe Merin (referred to as "Moniek Merin" by Kimmelmann), cooperated in numerous roundups and selections, believing that forced labor would save a larger portion of Polish Jewry. At the same time, he employed the Jewish police to undermine Jewish resistance, even turning over leaders of the Jewish Underground to the Gestapo.[34] He was sent to Auschwitz-Birkenau in one of the last transports from Sosnowiec in July of 1943, where he was killed.

Boder indexes "Community Councils," "perfidy," and "police" on several pages of Kimmelmann's testimony, as well as "Moniek Merin" in the people index. Beyond these factual mentions, we learn nothing else from the index about "the incredibly complicated internal structure" of the gray zone.[35] In the following figures, we attempt to diagram, distill, and interpret some of that complicated internal structure (Figures 3.19–3.20). These network visualizations depict forty-four interrelated triplets across Kimmelmann's testimony related to the Community Councils, the German and the Jewish police, the Jewish militia, a

FIGURE 3.19: Triplets from Boder's interview with Kimmelmann (1946) related to "Jewish militia," "Jewish police," and "Jewish Community Council." Created by Lizhou Fan and Todd Presner.

Jewish militiaman, and Moniek Merin.[36] All the words—reproduced in the form of semantic triplets—were said by Kimmelmann and surface an extraordinarily complex set of relations. The dark nodes are subjects, while the light nodes are objects; arrows indicate the direction of the vectors of action. We manually clustered related subjects and objects together.

At the center are triplets said by Kimmelmann about the Gestapo, the Germans, and the German police. The German police created a Jewish militia, created a Jewish police, and simply notified the Jewish Community Council about actions. Moving outward we see clusters of actions, reported by Kimmelmann,

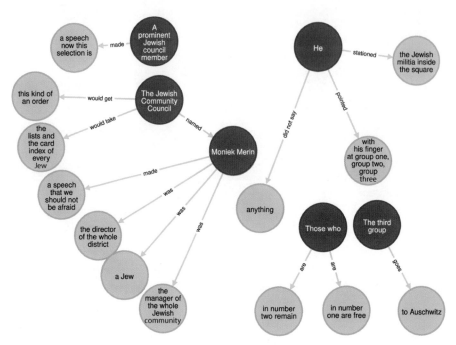

FIGURE 3.20: Additional triplets from Boder's interview with Kimmelmann (1946) related to "Jewish Community Council," including Moniek Merin and a second prominent Jewish council member. Created by Lizhou Fan and Todd Presner.

about the Jewish militia and a particular Jewish militiaman. Kimmelmann explains what the organization did (kept order in the streets, carried out orders, helped round up Jews, participated in raids) and what one specific Jewish militiaman did. He is clear that the Jewish militia and Jewish police were forced organizations created by the Germans. The triplets relating to the Jewish militiaman in the upper right belong to an experience witnessed by Kimmelmann in which this militiaman mistreated a fellow Jew for not making sufficient room for him to board a tramcar. He relates this behavior more generally to the function of the Jewish militia who, unlike the German occupiers, had intimate knowledge of the local Jewish community, which is why the Germans relied on the Jewish militia and Jewish police to locate Jews who may have been hiding in the city.

In the second visualization (separated for the sake of legibility), we see triplets related to the Jewish Community Council, a prominent member of the council, and Moniek Merin. The Jewish Community Council received the lists and card indexes of the Jewish inhabitants from the Nazis. When roundups took place,

Kimmelmann indicates that the leaders of the Jewish Community Council participated along with the Jewish militia. Although continuous with Kimmelmann's descriptions of Merin's actions and a speech made by another prominent council member designating the selection of the three groups, the pronoun "he" is not entirely clear in this section of Kimmelmann's narrative, as there is a break in the wire recording.[37] We leave this pronoun as such to respect the uncertainty that Boder described in his annotation of the translation.

These visualizations of triplets open up interpretive pathways that allow one to trace the interconnections between actions by reading the edges and nodes: For instance, starting with the German police at the center, we might move upward to the creation of the Jewish militia and from there to how they served the Jewish Community Council, and then to the latter's role in receiving orders and taking the lists and card index of every Jew for identification. Rather than a one-to-one reflection of Kimmelmann's narrative sequence, the network diagrams give rise to a multiplicity of readings and relationships that, together, form an impression of the "gray zone."

To reflect on the ethical questions in creating these visualizations, we need to take a step back and enumerate the decisions at every level, from the creation of the testimony to the algorithmic processing of the text. These start with the questions Boder asked to Kimmelmann and the answers Kimmelmann felt comfortable giving. The subsequent decisions include what Boder "heard" when he translated and indexed the interview and, today, what we are attuned to when we read the transcript or listen to the testimony. Similarly, our algorithmic approach extracts triplets and N-grams by attending to particular semantic units, which in turn have been corrected for completion and accuracy by us with reference to the original German recording. We then decided how to label the clusters, group the triplets, and present contextual associations. The ethical principles on which all these decisions rest are grounded in honesty and accuracy, to the best of our knowledge, but they are ultimately all choices. For this reason, the gray zone is also a concept that might apply to the contingency and partiality of any interpretative process.

Far from evidencing sharp distinctions and moral clarity, the visualizations bear witness to a corrupted world tinged by various degrees of complicity, collaboration, and ambiguity. Kimmelmann provides insight into the ways in which human character was degraded when the Jewish Councils, the Jewish militia, and the Jewish police, with their vastly minor power, participated with the Nazis in carrying out raids, selections, and deportation orders. Visualizing the triplets within a network of actions shows that the Lager, like the ghetto, had "innumerable frontiers" that were, ultimately, "indecipherable."[38] As Levi writes with respect to the leader of the Lodz Jewish council, which could easily apply in the case of Merin and this network diagram: "A story like this is not self-contained. It is pregnant, full of significance, asks more questions than it answers, sums up in itself the entire theme of the gray zone and leaves one dangling. It shouts and clamors to be understood, because in it one perceives a symbol, as in dreams and the signs of heaven."[39] Seeing Kimmelmann's narrative descriptions rendered as networks of actions and agencies is disconcerting precisely because it raises more questions than it ultimately can answer. It unsettles historical simplicity, refuses epistemological clarity, and "[confuses] the need to judge."[40]

Rather than passing judgment or trying to render it clear and understood, Kimmelmann opted, like Levi, to reflect on the moral ambiguity of the Jewish Community Council leaders and his own fallibility. He recognized the impossible situation they were in under Nazi terror and the fatal compromises of cooperation made in the hopes of saving lives. He reflected on the nature of human beings in extreme situations and said the following:

> One could see people, intelligent people, educated people, learned people, of whom one could never think that they are capable of certain things, or of such things. Nevertheless, the conditions of the Nazi terror have led them to a complete change. . . . And if I want to judge such a person, I put myself into his situation. I imagine what would I have done if I would have been in his place? . . . But one can never be sure that if it would come to it, that one would simply have replied, "I don't want to do it." Because a human being is only a human being. If one stands over him with a gun and he is being threatened—if you don't do that you shall lose your life—one cannot be responsible for the deeds that one may perpetrate. And in such light one also has to see the Jewish militia.[41]

Kimmelmann reflected on his own fallibility, without passing moral judgment, as much as he was pained by the circumstances and actions he described.[42] In the final analysis, the gray zone is never fully understood, but it is all-too-easily obscured, left unindexed, and forgotten. As we tried to demonstrate in this project, N-grams and semantic triplets are two computational text analysis methods that can help us render such aspects of the narrative visible—and are, themselves, informed by a whole host of decisions that might be said to characterize the computational "gray zone" as well. In both cases, far from offering up definitive clarity, we are left to confront and think through the polyvalent meanings of the gray zone.

4

Through the Lens of Big Data

A MACROANALYSIS OF THE USC SHOAH
FOUNDATION'S VISUAL HISTORY ARCHIVE

Containing more than fifty-five thousand individual testimonies and over seven million tables of metadata, the USC Shoah Foundation's Visual History Archive (VHA) is the largest digital archive of Holocaust and genocide testimonies in the world. As of this writing, the VHA contains interviews with more than fifty-two thousand Jewish survivors of the Holocaust, as well as several hundred survivors of the Armenian genocide, 102 survivors of the Nanjing Massacre, and 123 Tutsi survivors of the Rwandan genocide. It also contains a range of additional perspectives on the Holocaust and genocide, including hundreds of interviews with other victims of the Holocaust (Sinti and Roma survivors, eugenics survivors, Jehovah's Witness survivors, and homosexual survivors) as well as interviews with over a thousand rescuers and aid providers, over two hundred political prisoners, and hundreds of liberators.[1] The videos range in length from several minutes to more than ten hours, although most are between one and three hours in duration. Altogether, they amount to over 120,000 hours of testimony. It would take a viewer about thirty years to watch every testimony, assuming one watched for twelve hours a day, 365 days of the year (and could understand more than forty different languages). The totality of the digital archive—that is, its sheer scale when measured in terms of hours of recorded testimony—is simply not comprehensible to the faculties of human listening. Thus, the database exists to organize, categorize, and search the content of the testimonies. As a highly structured information system, the archive's database includes a robust set of indexing and search terms that link keywords, derived from a thesaurus of more than sixty thousand words, to one-minute segments of video, as well as biographical information about each interviewee, maps of places mentioned, additional documentation (such as photographs), and, in some cases, full transcripts of the testimonial narratives.

Focusing on the USC Shoah Foundation's Visual History Archive, this chapter employs various methods of "macroanalysis" to examine the interrelationships between narrative, data, and information architecture. The central questions concern the creation and structure of digital archives. What is at stake—ethically and epistemologically—when survivor narratives are transformed into data? How might computational methodologies for analyzing big data shed light on the underlying structures of the digital archive and give rise to new, interpretative narratives? What can we learn about the genre of Holocaust and genocide testimony—in terms of both structure and content—when the narratives are visualized from the standpoint of their data? And what can we learn about the development of the digital archive from the standpoint of its indexing systems and data structures? Finally, how can such systems and structures be used (and variously reimagined) to search within the digital archive to yield new insights and analyses? In answering these questions, we indicate how all the choices embedded in the creation of narrative, data, data structures, indexing systems, and information architectures have ethical and epistemological consequence.[2]

Initial Views of the Corpus as a Whole

To characterize the overarching narrative structure of the testimonies in the USC Shoah Foundation's Visual History Archive, one of the first things we decided to do was to visualize the corpus of Jewish Holocaust survivor interviews from the standpoint of its metadata. Using the indexing terms attached to each testimony, we visualized when, in a given testimonial narrative, particular indexing terms were used to describe the content. These preliminary views could give us insights into the indexing system as well as the relationship between the testimonies' narrative structure and content. At the highest organizational level, the indexing terms fall into about twenty "parent" categories such as daily life, health, discrimination, movement, captivity, feelings and thoughts, and still and moving images. Under all of these broad categories are more granular terms known as "children." Captivity, for example, includes camp experiences, which, in hierarchical fashion, includes further terms such as camp abortions, camp adaptation methods, camp brutal treatment, camp clothing, camp medical experiments, camp resistance, and dozens of other terms.[3] As part of the interface, the indexing system is particularly important since any "subject search" of the content in the archive is based on querying and filtering terms derived from the index (Figure 4.1). The interface facilitates the discovery and navigation of content as well as enables multifaceted searching and sorting of the results.

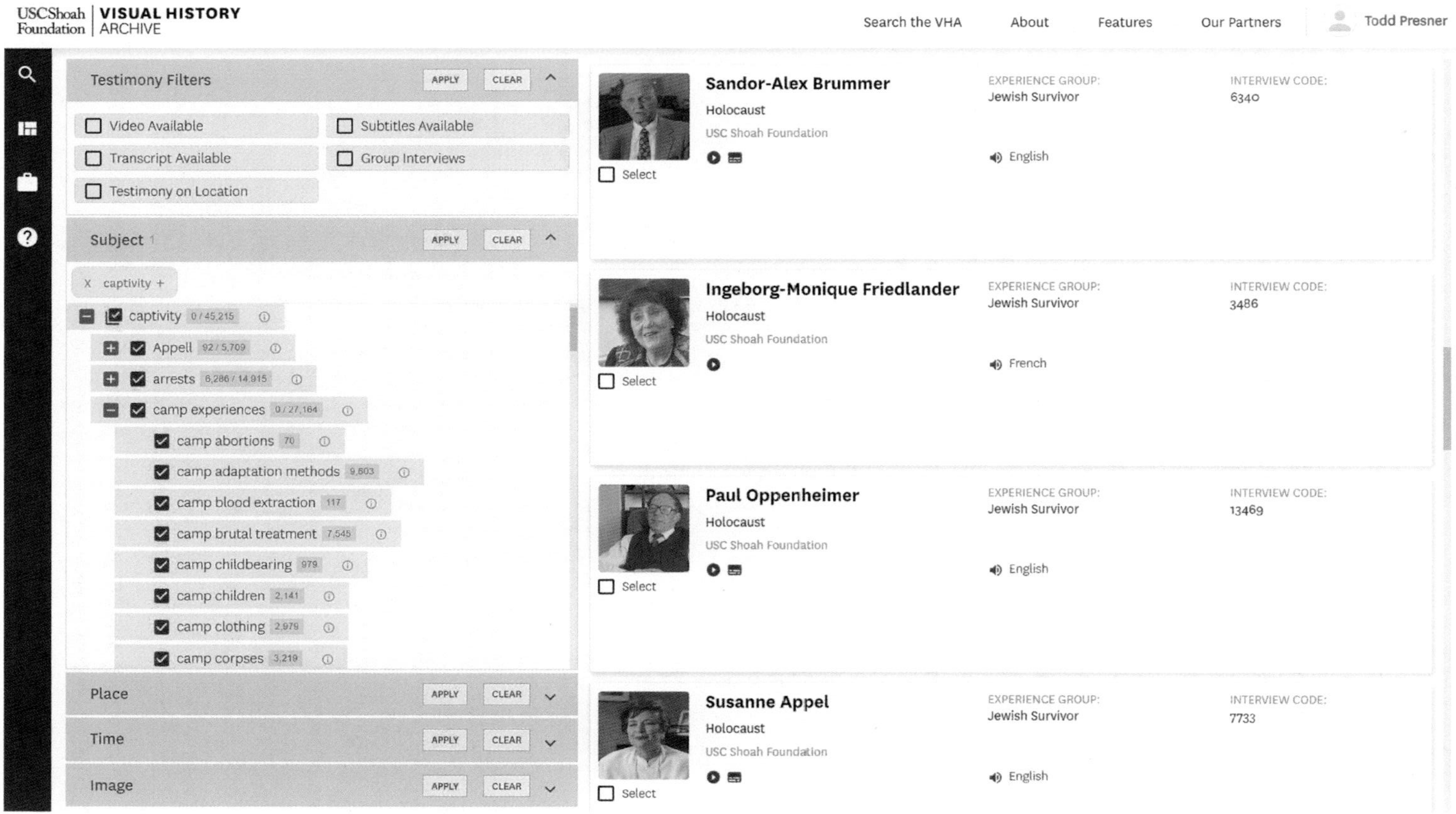

FIGURE 4.1: Screenshot of the USC Shoah Foundation Visual History Archive interface with indexing terms related to "captivity," April 2023. Visual History Archive, USC Shoah Foundation, https://vha.usc.edu.

The following visualizations are based on the general indexing categories developed by the USC Shoah Foundation to organize the more than sixty thousand genocide-related concepts and experiences described in 44,429 Jewish survivor testimonies in the Visual History Archive (Figures 4.2–4.6).[4] Each visualization shows two hundred different testimonies along the y-axis; time is shown along the x-axis, divided into one-minute segments (as per the indexing guidelines of the foundation). A red box means "yes" (that a given parent category was mentioned at that moment in the testimony) and a white box means "no" (that it was not). Any given segment can contain multiple indexing terms, and thus a red box may appear at the same time marker to indicate more than one category.

A few things become apparent from these visualizations. Certain general categories (and, hence, their specific topics) crop up significantly more frequently in the course of the testimonies. Places, for instance, are marked-up significantly

FIGURES 4.2, 4.3, 4.4. 4.5, AND 4.6: Frequency of parent indexing categories over narrative time in two hundred VHA testimonies. Derived from data provided by the USC Shoah Foundation Visual History Archive. Visualizations created by David Shepard, Yoh Kawano, and Todd Presner.

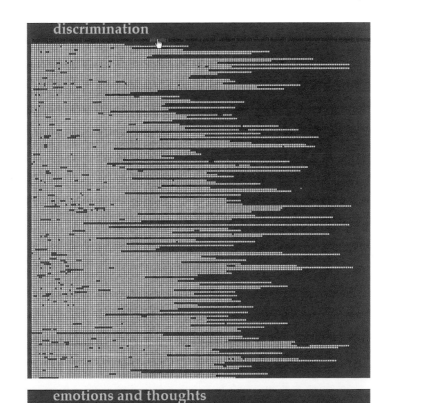

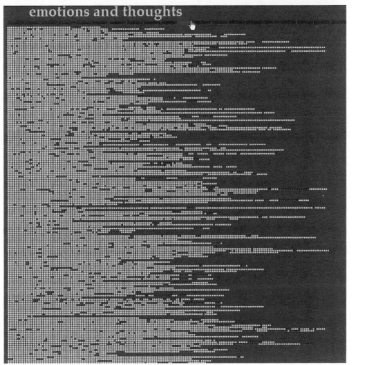

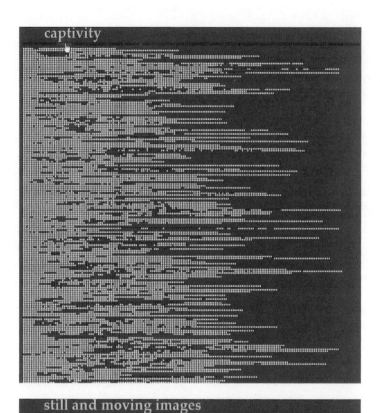

captivity

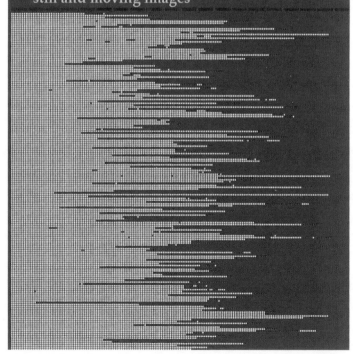

still and moving images

more often than discrimination or emotions and thoughts, likely indicating that places are both mentioned more frequently and indexed more frequently than other categories. Almost all testimonies begin with mentions of time and place, which makes sense as a starting point for a survivor's life story. We can also track some general structural trends in the narrative arc of the testimonies: discrimination tends to cluster in the first third of the testimonies, often keyed to experiences of antisemitism before the outbreak of the war; captivity tends to cluster in the middle; and still and moving images tend to cluster in the final segments, often connected to discussions of present-day life and the survivor showing pictures of family. Part of the reason for this is that the goal of the interview was to produce a story-like narrative that followed the chronology of the survivor's life, beginning with experiences in the prewar period before moving to the war and the Holocaust, and, lastly, the postwar period, which concludes with a segment with family members and a future message.

Far from providing definitive answers about narrative structure and content, visualizations like these—based on a simple binary of "yes" or "no" for a given category—can be used to explore the corpus and detect patterns that would not be visible when viewing the testimonies individually.[5] We can also ask questions that prompt us to move from a "zoomed out" perspective to an individual survivor's narrative account. For instance, why are "still and moving images" shown in the middle of a few of the testimonies and what do they depict? Which survivors narrate their story by starting immediately with experiences of captivity (rather than anything else, such as their experiences of childhood or life before the war)? Which survivors discuss captivity the most and the least? Which testimonies are indexed most and least with "emotions and thoughts" and does this correspond to differences in how a survivor narrates his or her story? How are the discussions of discrimination different when that indexing tag comes up toward the beginning of a testimony versus at the end? To answer these kinds of comparative questions, we need views onto the data in the archive as a whole.

Called "distant reading" by Franco Moretti or "macroanalysis" by Matthew L. Jockers, this kind of large-scale, structural analysis is often contrasted with close, hermeneutical readings of texts because it uses algorithmic calculations to illuminate overarching patterns within a corpus.[6] For Moretti, distance is "a condition of knowledge" because it allows a scholar to "focus on units that are much smaller or much larger than the text: devices, themes, tropes—or genres and systems."[7] In other words, the perspective of distance allows us to see different things than the perspective of closeness, which is characterized by attentive, detailed reading. By confronting scale, "distant reading" reveals structures, patterns, and trends that are not discernable when the focus remains on just a handful of close readings of individual testimonies. Jockers analogizes this to microeconomics and macroeconomics, where the latter "is about the study of the entire economy" as opposed to "the economic behavior of individual consumers and individual businesses."[8] Macroanalysis uses quantification to study "trends and patterns . . . aggregated over an entire corpus" and thus "places the emphasis on the systematic examination of data, on the quantifiable methodology."[9]

As we suggest below, the stakes extend far beyond revealing structures, patterns, and trends: Because macroanalysis is derived from whole-corpus analysis, it can potentially facilitate a certain democratization of witnessing. Instead of limiting ourselves to a very small and highly defined canon of works (probably less than a couple hundred), macroanalysis is performed by a computer and can easily bring together thousands of works, if not far more.[10] Of course, we have to ask what, precisely, is read, understood, and heard by a computer, and how do we interpret such processes? Indeed, this is a question that we confront throughout this book. As we argue here, "close" and "distant," micro and macro need not be pitted against one another; instead, zooming in and zooming out can be complementary, recursive approaches that enable new knowledge.

Moving from two hundred testimonies to 44,529 testimonies, the next visualization is based on the metadata associated with all the Jewish Holocaust survivor testimonies in the VHA, which were equally divided into one-minute segments when the USC Shoah Foundation performed the indexing. Called a "time stream" by us, the visualization shows the relative weights of each of the twenty-three top-level indexing terms as a percentage of narrative time in the testimonies. It is based on a series of calculations of the relative probability that a given topic was spoken about at a particular percentage point in the testimony. To compute these probabilities, we first divided up all the testimonies into one hundred segments (as percentages) and then traveled up the thesaurus hierarchy to determine all the parent indexing terms that corresponded to each of the one-minute segments contained within a given percentile. From there, we calculated the probability that a given parent term would occur at a particular percentage of the testimony and assigned relative weights for each of the top-level terms. The twenty-three top-level indexing categories are shown as percentages that have been normalized relative to one another and thus depict the frequency with which they are indexed across the testimonial narratives in the entire corpus. The results are shown in Figure 4.7.[11]

This visualization indicates that about 70 percent of these 44,429 testimonies start by talking about "time and place" in the first few minutes (or at least the first few percentage points of narrative time). Roughly the same number will end with

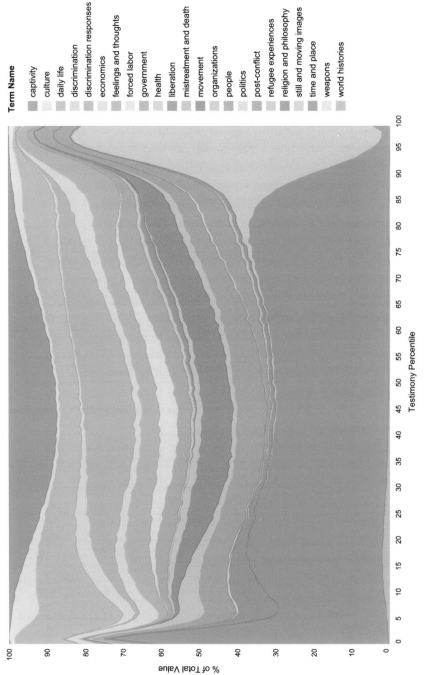

FIGURE 4.7: Time stream of parent topics in 44,429 Jewish Holocaust survivor testimonies. Derived from data provided by the USC Shoah Foundation Visual History Archive. Created by Lizhou Fan, David Shepard, and Todd Presner. Interactive visualization on Tableau: hrl.pub/fd8aed.

Term Name

captivity
culture
daily life
discrimination
discrimination responses
economics
feelings and thoughts
forced labor
government
health
liberation
mistreatment and death
movement
organizations
people
politics
post-conflict
refugee experiences
religion and philosophy
still and moving images
time and place
weapons
world histories

"still and moving images" (generally survivors showing pictures of their family), although we cannot say whether these are the same testimonies. In-between, experiential categories like daily life, movement, captivity, forced labor, discrimination responses, and mistreatment and death are spoken about—and may co-occur at the same percentage point in a given testimony and across the corpus of testimonies. The visualization gives relative weights to both how often and when a top-level indexing category occurs. For instance, daily life, religion and philosophy, and culture all co-occur more frequently in the first 20 percent of the testimony, around the time when discrimination and discrimination responses begin to become significant. Categories such as captivity (including prison, ghetto, and camp experiences), mistreatment and death (including executions and killings, corpses, and brutal treatment), movement (including transfers, deportation, forced marches, and flight), and discrimination responses (including camp adaption methods, hiding, escape, and suicide) roughly correspond to the middle third of the testimonies. Captivity, discrimination responses, and movement follow quite similar curves, indicating that the chances that they are spoken about and co-occur are greater in the middle portions of the testimonies. Liberation is spoken about comparatively less and almost always in the second half of the testimony. Categories such as post-liberation, feelings and thoughts, and, most of all, still and moving images occur most frequently in the final 20 percent of testimonies.

In broad brushstrokes, these results suggest the extent to which the USC Shoah Foundation succeeded in creating testimonies that followed a chronological, story-like structure.[12] This effort of narrativization began with what is called a "Pre-Interview Questionnaire" that aimed to help the interviewers to elicit a chronological "road map" of the survivor's "life story."[13] The Pre-Interview Questionnaire, generally filled out with the interviewer about a week before the interview took place, is an extensive biographical overview of the survivor's family background as well as facts related to the survivor's prewar, wartime, and postwar life.[14] In addition to family history, it includes information about locations lived, languages spoken, educational level, occupational history, military service, political and religious identity, and organizational history. It also includes the specific wartime experiences of the survivor including ghettos, camps, hiding, resistance, refugees, and death marches, which (as relevant) will be part of the interview. In general, the interviews were to be divided into questions that focused 20 percent on life before the war, 60 percent on life during the war, and 20 percent on life after the war, which is where family pictures (still and moving images) were shown.

These kinds of visualizations can guide our exploration of the structure of testimonies and help us to ask interpretative questions about the archive itself:

At what point in the course of a testimony do certain experiences tend to wax and wane (for instance, when do discussions of daily life and culture become surpassed by captivity and discrimination responses)? And, alternating between a distant and close reading, we might ask: Which testimonies adhere to this general narrative pattern and which ones deviate from it (and where)?[15] Which indexing terms occur most (or least) frequently in which testimonies, and what is the relationship between those subjects and the narrative structure?[16] And taking a step back, we might wonder why these topical indexing categories (as opposed to ones focused on agency, sound, or performance, for instance) are privileged? Such questions can also help us appreciate the heterogeneity and variation of testimonial narratives within a given corpus, not to mention allow us to compare across corpora and archives. As such, we might ask: do other testimonial corpora in the VHA, such as those from the Rwandan genocide, the Nanjing Massacre, or the Armenian genocide, follow similar distribution patterns of topics and, if not, how might we account for the differences? Finally, what does it mean that certain narrative paradigms and indexing protocols developed for the Holocaust are now applied to other testimonial corpora?

Before delving into these questions, we first need to better understand the overall information architecture, the structure of the database, and the descriptive metadata, since the visualizations are only as good as the data used to generate them. While all of these indexing terms were derived from a thesaurus that took decades to develop, it is important to remember that the indexing itself was fundamentally an interpretative process completed by human listeners trained to do indexing.[17] That process was intended to be replicable across the entire corpus of Holocaust and genocide testimonies because the thesaurus, indexing system, database structure, and interview and recording conventions were designed to be modular in the sense that they can be applied to testimonies about other genocides. Since the possibilities and limits of the data correlate directly to the possibilities and limits of the visualizations, we need to better understand the human decision-making process at each stage of the creation of the digital archive as an information system. It is here that we now turn.

Indexing and Database

While the media-specificity of Holocaust testimony has been well researched—ranging from Boder's wire recordings to the use of film, cassette tape, and various modes of audiovisual documentation[18]—there is comparatively little literature on the digitization of the Holocaust archive and the accompanying transformation

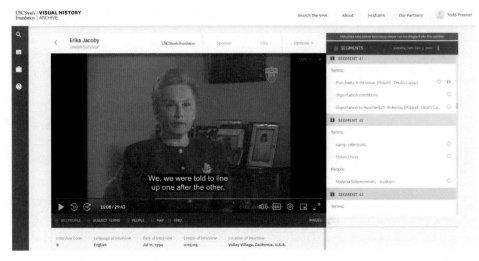

FIGURE 4.8: Visual History Archive interview interface. Erika Jacoby (July 11, 1994), interview 8. USC Shoah Foundation, https://vha.usc.edu/testimony/8.

of testimonial narratives into structured data. With regard to the USC Shoah Foundation's VHA, this is particularly noteworthy because the very condition of possibility for watching any testimony is the information architecture standing behind the testimonies themselves. This information architecture consists of several components: first, there is the interface itself, which runs in a web-browser, allowing a user to type in names or select experiences, filter the content of the testimonies, and listen to segments of video testimony (Figure 4.8); behind that, is a relational and structured query language database (SQL database, for short) in which content is organized into tables, records, and fields (Figure 4.9); all of these tables of data were inputted after the videos were indexed with keywords and other associated information was manually entered (such as the information on the questionnaires that each survivor had to fill out before the interview took place). But before this indexing could happen, standards and protocols, derived from the National Information Standards Organization's Z39.19 standard for the construction, format, and management of monolingual controlled vocabularies, provided the guidelines for how to index the content of the videos and what to index.[19] This standard governed the creation of a unique thesaurus to consistently describe the content through a controlled vocabulary and thereby facilitate its search and retrieval. A special piece of software called a "video indexing application" or a "cataloguing facility" was developed to do this.[20] Beyond that, we have the hardware, such as the archive servers and storage servers, where the videos are stored in digital formats for streaming in a video player.

SegmentID	KeywordID	TestimonyID	IntCode	TapeLabel	Label	TypeID	TypeLabel	InTimeCode	OutTimeCode	InTapenumber	OutTapenumber	ShortFormID	PiqPersonID
513665	16328	299	8	Erika Jacoby	deportation to Auschwitz II-Birkenau (Poland : Dea...	5673	deportation to concentration camps	00:10:00:00	00:11:00:00	2	2	2	354695
513672	12044	299	8	Erika Jacoby	camp selections	877	selections	00:11:00:00	00:12:00:00	2	2	2	354695
513672	14233	299	8	Erika Jacoby	Poland 1944	5677	countries by time period	00:11:00:00	00:12:00:00	2	2	2	354695
513681	14280	299	8	Erika Jacoby	loved ones' separations	5324	personal life activities	00:12:00:00	00:13:00:00	2	2	2	354695
513681	15144	299	8	Erika Jacoby	grandparents	4847	family members	00:12:00:00	00:13:00:00	2	2	2	354695
513688	10853	299	8	Erika Jacoby	camp intake procedures	4194	camp procedures	00:13:00:00	00:14:00:00	2	2	2	354695
513703	15088	299	8	Erika Jacoby	camp living conditions	3931	living conditions	00:15:00:00	00:16:00:00	2	2	2	354695
513720	7562	299	8	Erika Jacoby	Krakau-Plaszow (Poland : Concentration Camp)	5811	German concentration camps in Poland: verified	00:17:00:00	00:18:00:00	2	2	2	354695
513720	16159	299	8	Erika Jacoby	transfer to Krakau-Plaszow (Poland : Concentration...	5674	transfer to concentration camps	00:17:00:00	00:18:00:00	2	2	2	354695
513720	16297	299	8	Erika Jacoby	transfer from Auschwitz II-Birkenau (Poland : Deat...	5675	transfer from concentration camps	00:17:00:00	00:18:00:00	2	2	2	354695
513735	10926	299	8	Erika Jacoby	camp forced labor	5751	forced labor	00:18:00:00	00:19:00:00	2	2	2	354695
513735	15169	299	8	Erika Jacoby	construction forced labor	5751	forced labor	00:18:00:00	00:19:00:00	2	2	2	354695
513735	19597	299	8	Erika Jacoby	camp prisoner physical conditions	5404	general health conditions	00:18:00:00	00:19:00:00	2	2	2	354695

Figure 4.9: Indexing metadata related to Erika Jacoby's testimony (SQL tables). Visual History Archive, USC Shoah Foundation, https://vha.usc.edu/testimony/8.

For every survivor, we essentially have three texts: first, the video testimony itself, consisting of a spoken narrative and video recording; second, when available, the written transcript made from the spoken testimony; and, third, the rows of metadata about the testimony in the database. In the coming chapters, we will analyze the first two texts in detail. For this chapter, our text will be the third, namely, the structure and content of the records in the database. As shown in the screenshot of the organization of the database (Figure 4.9), every survivor is assigned a TestimonyID and an Interview Code (IntCode). The testimony is broken into segments, which are generally one-minute in length and given a unique SegmentID. Each SegmentID is correlated with at least one KeywordID, which, in turn, corresponds further to what is called a TypeLabel in the index hierarchy. For example, Segment 513735, which plays over minute 18:00–19:00 of Tape 2, has three KeywordIDs, which correspond to three indexing labels: camp forced labor, construction forced labor, and camp prisoner physical conditions. These labels (called "children") fall under TypeLabels (called "parents"), in this case "forced labor" and "general health conditions." Some minutes of testimony (such as minutes 14:00 and 16:00) have no SegmentIDs and thus no indexing labels.

In essence, the database structures, organizes, and standardizes the metadata for computational processing. In the words of Johanna Drucker on the significance of such metadata structures: "Arguably, few other textual forms will have greater impact on the way we read, receive, search, access, use, and engage with the primary materials of humanities studies than the metadata structures that organize and present that knowledge in digital form."[21] This is certainly true of the VHA, whose knowledge model is fundamentally aimed at the transformation and disambiguation of narrative into descriptive data amenable to computational processing. While this transformation is ostensibly the opposite of what historians usually do (namely, create narratives from data by emplotting source material, evidence, and established facts into a narrative), we will argue that the ethics of the database is a function of the degree to which it enables new narratives and interpretations. Not unlike Arendt's concept of natality, the ability to give rise to new narratives opens possibilities for promoting action, new beginnings, and human plurality.[22]

We will start with the global architecture of the USC Shoah Foundation's Digital Library System, which was originally developed by Samuel Gustman, the chief technology officer. It consists of the following elements: data capture (starting with the transfer of the video tape to digital formats and cataloguing); the storage of data (both the videos themselves and the indexing server that knows where all the catalogue metadata is); and finally, the interface to play, search for, and distribute data and its related content. In what follows, I will be focusing on that realm of information architecture between the user interface and the server storage—in other words, the metadata, the data structures, and the database, which condition any search within the archive. It is precisely here that we see a fundamental dissociation of the presentation of the content (that is, the testimonies and the interface to watch them) from the information architecture, database, and metadata scaffolding that lies behind the content. Such a dissociation is not unique to the VHA but bespeaks a common practice in digital archives and online library systems more generally, perhaps stretching back to Claude Shannon's theory of information as content neutral.[23] In the words of digital humanities scholar Alan Liu applying the media concepts of Friedrich Kittler, "the discourse network 2000"[24] organizes information by the "separation of content from material instantiation" such that "the content management at the source and consumption management at the terminus [are] double-blind to each other."[25] To put it differently, the content of the testimonies knows nothing of the information architecture because the database is supposed to function as a seemingly neutral container to put content in and organize it for efficient search and retrieval. The goal of this information system is to transmit content as noiselessly and objectively as possible to a receiver or listener.

Between 1996 and 2002, ten separate patents were filed by inventor Samuel Gustman and the Survivors of the Shoah Visual History Foundation, the assignee, for the VHA information architecture. The inventions include the following: a "Method and Apparatus for Cataloguing Multimedia Data," several patents for a "Method and Apparatus for Management of Multimedia Assets," a "Digital Library System," and finally, a "Method and Apparatus for Cataloguing Multimedia Data." Some of the patents—such as the "Digital Library System" and "Method and Apparatus for Management of Multimedia Assets"—have been referenced by more than seventy other patents from companies such as Xerox (for developing a browser-based image storage and processing system) and Microsoft (for semiautomatic annotation of multimedia objects). In 2011, the USC Shoah Foundation granted an exclusive right to all ten of its patents to Preservation Technologies, a company with a specialty in audiovisual preservation, media transfer, digital archiving, and media streaming.

The first patent, "Method and Apparatus for Cataloguing Multimedia Data," was filed in 1996 and established the method for indexing the testimonies and creating a search and retrieval system for their playback. To understand its intended modularity and generalizability, I quote the summary of the invention: "The invention catalogues data such as multimedia data. A catalogue is a collection of one or more catalogue elements. An index is used to access a catalogue. An element of a catalogue has one or more attributes. An attribute provides information that can be used to search for, answer questions about, and navigate through a catalogue. . . . Attribute elements and attributes are used to build an index that can be used to facilitate catalogue access."[26] This summary can be elucidated using a diagram from the patent itself (Figure 4.10). At the top are video segments, generally chunked into one-minute units; they contain narrative elements (sentences and phases) said by the interviewee. These phrases have a number of different attributes: they mention particular people (and the particular information about the person is stored in the database); they contain particular keywords (which may already exist in the thesaurus, or may need to be added, hence, "proposed keywords"); and, most importantly, the keywords have a certain hierarchy that can be contained in more general "types." Altogether, the keywords and types form a catalogue consisting of an index of attributes connected to phrases uttered during segments of video. This is the metadata scaffolding or "metatext" that resides behind the videos themselves.

Within the index, there are three different kinds of relationships that can exist between any two (or more) indexing elements, and these relationships form the "pillar" of the index, according to Gustman: inheritance, whole/part, and associative relationships.[27] Inheritance relationships are characterized by "is . . . a" (for example, in the patent, he cites a "Ford Bronco" that is a "car," where the specific keyword is "Ford Bronco" and the type is a "car").[28] The second relationship is whole/part (for example, cars and tires); and the third relationship is associative (such as "car" and "driver"—where neither "is" the other, and they are not in a whole/part relationship). Applying this logic to the USC Shoah Foundation's thesaurus under the top-level indexing term "captivity": "camp barter" is one of several "camp adaptation methods"; "camp shoes" are a part of "camp clothing"; and "camp corpse disposal" is associated with "camp corpses." These structuring principles derive from the application of a specific standard (Z39.19) to consistently and unambiguously describe "content objects" (the survivor testimonies) in order to produce a monolingual controlled vocabulary (the thesaurus) to facilitate their search and retrieval.[29]

The goal of the standard, as explained in its documentation, is to provide "guidelines for the selection, formulation, organization, and display of terms that together make up a controlled vocabulary" for the purposes of "knowledge management" and "knowledge organization."[30] As in most vocabularies of this kind, nouns—people, places, things, and events—are privileged, rather than adjectives, verbs, or adverbs. One problem, as we will see, is that many things get left out or

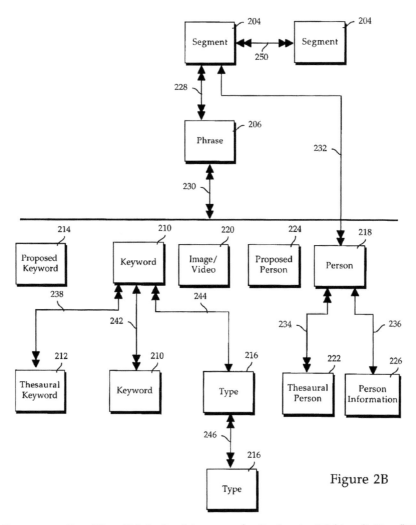

Figure 2B

FIGURE 4.10: Detail from "Method and Apparatus for Cataloguing Multimedia Data," US Patent 5,832,495, November 3, 1998.

cannot be adequately captured by the thesaurus's nested hierarchy. Perhaps a more vexing problem is that the thesaurus introduces a structuring epistemology that may be at loggerheads with the performative dimensions (such as voice and gesture) that are also part of the testimonial narrative. Moreover, expressions of agency are not determinative factors for index categorization, and therefore "camp medical experiments" and "camp resistance" both fall under the parent term "captivity," even though the former describes actions of the perpetrators and the latter describes actions of the victims. Although such distinctions certainly will become clear through advanced searching and listening, our team developed a new approach to identifying, indexing, and visualizing expressions of agency (see chapter 6).

It is important to underscore that none of the testimonies in the USC Shoah Foundation's VHA was automatically tagged with keywords; instead, every component of the cataloguing system—from the development of the indexing terms and the thesaurus to the database itself—was created by the staff working at the foundation who listened to all the testimonies and indexed them according to the guidelines developed by the foundation. This is because the index was derived from the videos, not from transcripts, and thus it is a time-based markup system in which the unit of markup is the "one-minute segment." In fact, the keyword indexing system—which consists of a thesaurus term (or terms) linked to a particular segment of video—is, to date, the *primary* way to search the content of the testimonies (as the vast majority of videos do not yet have transcripts). On average, testimonies have about 120 indexed terms associated with one-minute segments (although many have more and many have less), yielding millions of tables of data.

To develop the descriptive metadata, the USC Shoah Foundation employed about fifty indexers who worked for several years watching each and every video using a specially developed application (also patented) that allowed the human indexer to assign a keyword to a video segment. Keywords were assigned to the narrative content of the video from the thesaurus and, at the same time, new keywords could be proposed to describe experiences not already in the thesaurus.[31] For the first five thousand testimonies, the segments were variable in length and could be determined by the indexer; however, this was quickly replaced by another system (used for the remaining forty-six thousand testimonies), in which the Video Indexing Application would automatically "chunk up" the testimony into discrete one-minute segments and prompt the indexer to assign a keyword. The segmentation of the video was automated and standardized, but the assignment of the keyword was determined by a human listener.

Not every minute-long segment, however, has a keyword, something that often indicates the continuation of the previous keyword but may also signal, according to the USC Shoah Foundation staff, "the lack of indexable content."[32] Lack of indexable content can mean many things, such as conversational or colloquial speech without historical or factual content, the interviewer asking a question that needs clarification, a survivor repeating himself or herself, a pause in the conversation to reflect or search for the right words, an emotional moment, noise, silence, or even content that the indexer may not want to bring to the foreground (such as racist or sexist sentiments). In other words, indexable content is manifest content, in a declarative or imperative mode—in general, what is literally said. The richer and more complete the indexing metadata is, the more it can be used to add to and supplement our analysis of the testimonies, pointing us not only to the uniqueness of certain stories or experiences, but also providing a chance to comparatively analyze the meta-structures of the testimonial archive as a whole.

While its aim is objectivity and neutrality, it is important to underscore that a human listener decided what to index and what not to index; a human listener decided what thesaurus term to use and what thesaurus term not to use; and a human listener decided if a given narrative segment should be described by a keyword or not. This is fundamentally an interpretative process with epistemological and ethical consequence. With the application of the data ontology, the narrative is turned into structured data for computational processing in order to facilitate search and discovery. In this regard, it is exactly the opposite of the problem that Berel Lang bemoaned about the use of figurative language and aestheticization "adding to" the factual reality of the events;[33] here, we are speaking about subtracting from or abstracting of the narrative told by the survivors. In other words, the "neutral language"[34] of the thesaurus's controlled vocabulary removes narrativity: from the dialogical emplotment of the experiences in sentences, phrases, and words in response to the interviewer's questions, to the tone, rhythm, and cadence of speaking, to the physical gestures, emotive qualities, and expressiveness of the voice and face (see chapter 5).

"Indeterminate data," such as "non-indexable content," must be given either a null value or not represented at all. How, for example, does an indexing term such as "miscellaneous footage" reveal the inability to assign meaning within a database structure?[35] Or, how might emotion be represented to allow database queries? While certain feelings, such as helplessness, fear, abandonment, and attitudes, are tagged in the database, marking up emotion and parsing it according to inheritance, associative, and whole/part relationships seems ill-advised at best.[36] Databases can only accommodate unambiguous enumeration, clear attributes, and definitive data values; everything else is not—and perhaps should not be—in the database. The point here is not to build a bigger, more totalizing database but that the database—as a framework for organizing knowledge and meaning—reaches its limits precisely at the limits of the transformation of human experiences into computationally tractable data.

So that leaves us with a critical question: what do we need databases for? With regard to the USC Shoah Foundation's VHA, the database exists to provide meaningful access to the testimonies at a scale that is both tailored and comprehensible to a human viewer whose faculties of attention and knowledge (most likely) preclude decades of viewing and listening. A relational database, by definition, functions by virtue of the relations or cross-connections between the data in the database. As such, the database can give rise to infinitely many search queries and thereby allow innumerable combinations that identify larger thematic issues, reveal patterns and structures, and create new associations between experiences that may not otherwise be considered together. And, finally, computational analysis can provide insights and perspectives that human listening cannot, precisely by the way in which the former allows a kind of "distant listening" based on the whole of the archive rather than a selection of representative or canonical testimonies. It is potentially more democratizing since the stories and data of many more (or even all) survivors in the VHA can be harnessed at once for analysis.

The following two visualizations (Figures 4.11–4.12) are examples of network relations based on just one hundred testimonies, in which names are connected to the keywords indexed in the testimonies. The large circles (nodes) are the names of survivors, which vary in size based on how many indexing terms are associated with the testimony. Smaller circles (also nodes) represent indexing keywords, and they vary in size based on their frequency. All the lines (edges) connect keywords either directly to a survivor or to an intermediate node, which then connects to all the survivors where that keyword was used as an indexing term. The thicker the line, the higher the frequency of use; the larger the circle, the more keywords are associated with the person. Keywords at the center are more common (and this also moves the person to the center); keywords describing less common experiences are pushed toward the periphery. In this particular example, two survivors, Armando Moreno and Arie Leopold Haas, appear on the periphery with comparatively fewer lines connecting the keywords in their testimony to those of other survivors. Among this group of one hundred survivors, they are connected to each other via multiple (but infrequently used) keywords: various mentions of Italy between 1940 and 1943, Italian police and security forces, and hospitals (a keyword also shared with four other testimonies). The fact that the line for "Italian police and security forces" is twice as thick to Haas as it is to Moreno indicates that Haas's testimony has twice as many mentions of this keyword as Moreno's testimony. In the visualization, Haas has the most individual keywords that are unique to him, including terms such as: enforced residence, Christian religious observations, church attendance, and Castelmassa (a municipality in Northern Italy). This is because the experiences he describes in his testimony—being an Italian

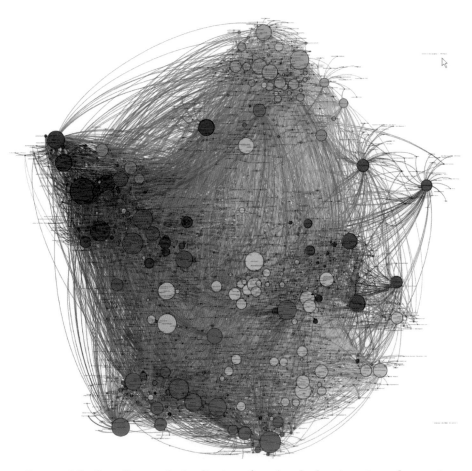

FIGURE 4.11: Overall network visualization of one hundred testimonies and approximately ten thousand indexing keywords. Created by Todd Presner and Zoe Borovsky.

Jew who was hidden, who converted to Christianity, who attended church—are ones that are less typical, at least when compared to the experiences of others in the archive. In fact, when querying the full VHA database, we find that only 746 testimonies of Jewish survivors (out of more than fifty-four thousand) are tagged with the keyword "church attendance."

The graphic was generated by a data visualization program called Gephi, which used a force-driven clustering algorithm to determine "communities" based on topics mentioned. From the one hundred testimonies, it detected sixteen different communities based on shared keywords such as nationality, places mentioned, or shared experiences. While the communities are not named, the clusters

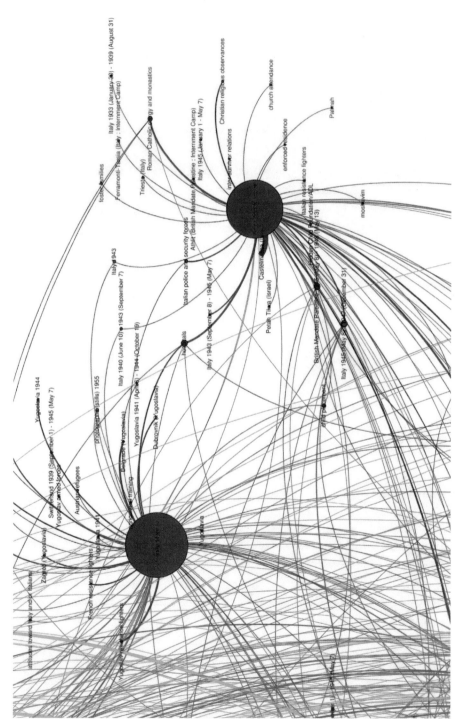

FIGURE 4.12: Detail of network visualization. Created by Todd Presner and Zoe Borovsky.

help us to appreciate the frequency (and infrequency) of certain keywords. Algorithmically generated data visualizations like these might provide new starting points for delving into the millions of records in the database and seeing connections that a human eye or ear could not possibly detect or track. In this particular case, we can identify "outlier" experiences or noncanonical stories that help us reassess certain assumptions or provide a more differentiated set of perspectives on the archive.

Of course, this kind of computational analysis is only as good (or as bad) as the data themselves. The fact remains that the VHA testimonies are not equally well indexed; the metadata differ (sometimes quite significantly) from testimony to testimony; and the testimonies themselves vary tremendously in length, structure, and content. Moreover, the indexing categories can sometimes occlude the specificity of certain experiences, such as different forms of agency and action, not to mention more subjective forms of self-expression such as figural language, voice, intonation, and performativity. We need to bear this in mind by recognizing that the visualizations enable us to explore questions rather than elucidate determinative truths. And even if these metadata were computationally generated in ways that were attuned to these aspects of the testimonies, this would not radically alter the cautionary note being sounded here: at some level, we are always talking about human-created artifacts—whether the metadata and indexing categories, the thesaurus, the testimonies, the search algorithms, or the system architecture of the digital archive itself. They all need to be interpreted in order to understand the structuring epistemologies, decisions, values, and views encoded at every level into the testimonies and the larger infrastructure of the digital archive.

While acknowledging these limitations and caveats, the querying of the database through faceted searching (something that allows a user to apply multiple filters) can reveal sites of overlap and linkages between experiences, thereby prompting new research questions and explorations. Because the VHA's interface facilitates such faceted search and discovery, an infinite number of navigational pathways can be taken. I would contend that the possibility of infinite "queryability" of the relations in a database is, in fact, a critical part of its ethical dimension because it gives rise to new narratives, interconnections, and interpretations. Consider, for a moment, the alternative: more than fifty-five thousand atomized testimonies searchable by unique identifiers such as name or record ID but without the ability to traverse orthogonally through the tables, indexing keywords, and testimonial narratives. The "thicker" the relations and intersections are between tables, the more possibilities there are for interconnection, extensibility, discovery, and interpretation. The potential to facilitate an ever-deeper relationality among the data in a database is one of the conditions of possibility for an ethics of the algorithm precisely because those relationships pluralize the archive and humanize the data through new modes of listening, reading, composing, and interpreting the testimonies.

As Lev Manovich asked in *The Language of New Media*: "How can our new abilities to store vast amounts of data, to automatically classify, index, link, search, and instantly retrieve it, lead to new kinds of narratives?"[37] As an explicit uptake of Manovich's question of how classification, indexing, search, interlinking, and retrieval can lead to new narratives, the USC Shoah Foundation's VHA allows users to create their own project narratives from the search results, essentially, building remixed and hybridized narratives from any number of constitutive narrative segments. In this regard, we see a symbiosis between narrative and database, such that the paradigmatic structure of the database contributes to the syntagmatic possibilities of combination at the heart of narrative.[38] And I would point out that this is not fundamentally different from what historians already do: make selections from the trove of archival sources in order to combine elements together to form a narrative. With every query, the database performs a selection that enables a combinatory process and, hence, literalizes an instance of historical emplotment. The metadata database of the USC Shoah Foundation's VHA thus represents a kind of "paratext" to the testimonial text insofar as it can be reordered, disassembled, and reassembled according to the constraints and possibilities of computational logic.[39]

In addition to this logic of query-ability and reordering, computational modes of representation allow us to "toggle" between the singular and the global, the individual experiences of particular eyewitnesses and all the experiences as recounted by the survivors, which in this case is the summation of all the data in the VHA. The latter does not represent the reality of "the Holocaust" (as a complete or total event) but rather the totality of what is in the archive, and therefore, can only present structures, patterns, and globally oriented visualizations of data. But, again, this is not very different from what historians do, insofar as they emplot events at various levels of "zoom" in order to convey different kinds of meaning. In other words, we "toggle" back and forth between macro-level accounts of the totality of the archive (zoomed out) and micro-level accounts of individual experiences (zoomed in), which are, by their very nature, defined by specific experiences, perspectives, forms of spectatorship, language, and so forth. Saul Friedländer's "globally oriented inquiry" into the history of the Holocaust not only examines the encompassing "ideological-cultural factors" and mythologies of the Nazi regime while recounting the scope of the destruction in terms of events, actions, and numbers (such as geographic scale and communities of people), but he also calls upon the individual voices and personal chronicles of diary and letter writers. The aim of this toggling is "to illuminate parts of the landscape . . . like lightning flashes," and thereby "pierce the (mostly involuntary) smugness of scholarly detachment and 'objectivity.'"[40] This kind of scaling suggests certain parallels between the compositional practices of historians and those enabled by computation.

So, what might macroanalysis mean for the USC Shoah Foundation's VHA? For one thing, it shifts the focus away from the tiny fraction of memoirs and testimonies of survivors that are generally read, listened to, and taught. We tend to privilege a very small canon of witnesses, whose stories stand in—rightfully or not—for the stories of almost everyone else. We know Elie Wiesel, Anne Frank, and Primo Levi, but what about Erika Jacoby, Arie Leopold Haas, Armando Moreno, and the tens of thousands of other testimonies in the archive? In this regard, extrapolating structures, trends, patterns, frequencies, and correlations from the entire database produces epistemological claims that are grounded in the experiences of exponentially more people. At the same time, macroanalysis has ethical consequences since it can facilitate a certain democratization of witnessing in which all testimonies are granted equal importance and weight. Enabled by ever-thicker data relations, faceted browsing and searching allow us to discover interrelations, develop new practices of listening, and chart new pathways through the testimonial archive.

Macroanalysis across Corpora

While whole corpus analysis has the potential to facilitate a democratization of witnessing, macroanalysis can also be applied across testimonial corpora to ask comparative questions about the changing constitution of testimony and the meta-structures of the archive. We might ask ourselves: What is the significance of a generalizable, digital framework for producing, marking up, and archiving genocide testimonies? What does it mean when the methods of the USC Shoah Foundation become a kind of a paradigm for producing, marking up, and archiving testimony? What ethical issues are raised, for example, when the Holocaust becomes the paradigmatic genocide for creating a digital infrastructure and other genocides are situated within that infrastructure? On the other hand, we might ask: in what ways can that digital infrastructure grow and change to reflect the specificity of experiences and narratives from other genocides, including ones that may depart significantly from assumptions about public testimony, memory, and storytelling that are central to how the genre of Holocaust testimony has evolved?

As a comparative heuristic, we can examine the frequencies of the top-level categories for the testimonial narrative arcs of sixty-seven Tutsi survivors of the Rwandan genocide and 246 survivors of the Armenian genocide (Figures 4.13–4.14). Both of the "time streams" were created using the 2019 data provided by the USC Shoah Foundation's VHA. As with the Jewish survivor experience group (see Figure 4.7), we divided the testimonies into one hundred segments (based on percentage) and identified all the keywords in a given percentage by traveling up the hierarchy to the parent-level indexing term. We then calculated the overall probability, by victim group, that a given term would be used at a particular percentage point in the testimony. The time streams visualize the twenty-three indexing terms, weighted with respect to one another at each percentage point of narrative time. The lack of "smoothness" among the Rwandan and Armenian genocide visualizations is the result of a significantly smaller sample size for each victim group.

The Rwandan testimonies were recorded using the conventions established by the USC Shoah Foundation and subsequently marked up in accordance with its indexing guidelines. At the level of the metadata, the general narrative structure of the Rwandan genocide testimonies appears to be similar to that of the Jewish survivors of the Holocaust. After "time and place," the category of "daily life" makes up the largest set of indexing terms for the first 20 percent of the testimonies. At around this time, "discrimination" begins, and "discrimination responses" figure prominently throughout the remainder of the testimonial narratives, as they do with Holocaust survivors. For historical reasons reflecting the rapidity of the brutality and the perpetration of violence, the category of "mistreatment and death" takes precedence over "captivity." The largest indexing categories in the last 20 percent of the narratives are "post-conflict" and "feelings and thoughts." But unlike the Holocaust testimonies, "still and moving images" are indexed in just the final segments and, even then, they remain a comparably insignificant category. This category represents a convention introduced to allow survivors to show pictures of their loved ones.

Rather than detecting underlying "truths," computational methods can help us develop preliminary interpretations by shifting the scale of analysis. There are many factors—including linguistically and culturally specific factors—that we would need to examine, such as: when and where the testimonies were recorded in relation to the events themselves, the questions asked by the interviewers, the

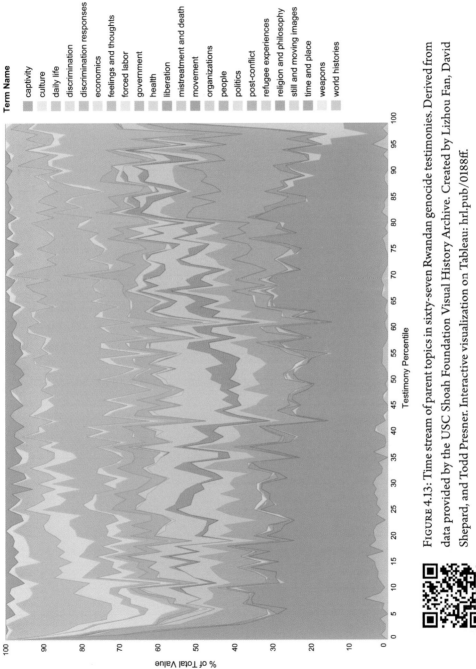

Term Name

- captivity
- culture
- daily life
- discrimination
- discrimination responses
- economics
- feelings and thoughts
- forced labor
- government
- health
- liberation
- mistreatment and death
- movement
- organizations
- people
- politics
- post-conflict
- refugee experiences
- religion and philosophy
- still and moving images
- time and place
- weapons
- world histories

FIGURE 4.13: Time stream of parent topics in sixty-seven Rwandan genocide testimonies. Derived from data provided by the USC Shoah Foundation Visual History Archive. Created by Lizhou Fan, David Shepard, and Todd Presner. Interactive visualization on Tableau: hrl.pub/0188ff.

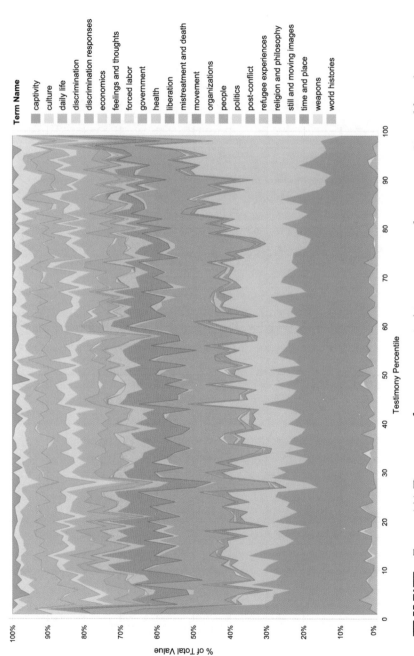

FIGURE 4.14: Time stream of parent topics in 246 Armenian genocide testimonies. Derived from data provided by the USC Shoah Foundation Visual History Archive. Created by Lizhou Fan, David Shepard, and Todd Presner. Interactive visualization on Tableau: hrl.pub/cfea69.

sociocultural situations that inform the genre of testimony for survivors in non-Western contexts (including its recording conventions and publicness), and the critical issue of bearing witness to gender and sexual violence. This is particularly significant in the Rwandan, Armenian, and Nanjing survivor testimonies where sexual violence is a prevalent part of what the survivors experienced or witnessed firsthand. With attention to frames such as these, we might examine differences in "feelings and thoughts"—for example, in testimonial narratives across gender and genocides—perhaps sparking questions about what can and cannot be expressed publicly about violence in particular cultural contexts as well as whether, when, and how such expressions are spoken.

At the same time, we might also pose questions about the globally convergent or divergent development of the genre of testimony, the indexing systems, and the digital databases themselves. To put it more sharply: What does it mean when the interviewing and recording techniques, the indexing methodologies and categories, and the information infrastructures are built on a platform that has been "generalized," so to speak, for all survivor testimonies?[41] How can the heterogeneity and differences—historical, cultural, linguistic, social, and more—be preserved in a system that appears to offer a singular model for producing and preserving testimony? How might other forms of public testimony—such as those developed in the Gacaca courts of Rwanda or the site-specific memorial halls in Nanjing where survivor testimonies are displayed in proximity to victims' bones—present alternative narrative forms and frameworks for bearing witness that engage survivors (and, potentially, perpetrators) in ways that differ from one-on-one interviews? At the same time, to return to the testimonies of David Boder, we might also ask how the genre of Holocaust testimony has changed over time in terms of the recording and interview protocols, the range of questions asked, the answers given by survivors, and the narrative strategies employed to bear witness. In other words, how can aggregate forms of macroanalysis help us recognize testimonies that "look" and "sound" different from those recorded by the USC Shoah Foundation?

To address these questions, we return to the visualization of the top-level indexing categories used by the USC Shoah Foundation to mark up the Armenian genocide testimonies that were created by the Armenian Film Foundation (Figure 4.14). These testimonies were mostly filmed in the 1970s, 80s, and early 90s, before the USC Shoah Foundation existed. Under the leadership of the Armenian Film Foundation's founder, Dr. Michael Hagopian, nearly four hundred survivor and eyewitness accounts of the Armenian genocide were recorded on 16mm tape.[42] The Armenian Film Foundation entered an agreement with the USC

FIGURE 4.15: Stills from Armenian genocide testimonies. Hrahad Harout and Shooshanig Shahinian (February 11, 1984), interview 53525, minute 4:51, https://vha.usc.edu/testimony/53525; Dr. Vahe Churukian, Vahan Churukian, Efronia Attikian, Dr. Giragos Churukian and Arpiar Missakian (September 16, 1984), interview 55399, minute 2:17, https://vha.usc.edu/testimony/55399; Avedis Khantzian (July 17, 1985), interview 53230, minute 1:30, https://vha.usc.edu/testimony/53230; Rose Apelian (May 6, 1992), interview 53182, minute 31:42, https://vha.usc.edu/testimony/53182. Armenian Film Foundation and Visual History Archive, USC Shoah Foundation.

Shoah Foundation in 2010 to digitize the tapes and make them available as part of the Visual History Archive. As part of this effort, the USC Shoah Foundation indexed them according to its guidelines. The testimonies are generally much shorter (most are under one hour and some are just a few minutes in length), and almost none are chronological life stories. As a genre, they are much more experimental and use multiple camera angles, multiple locations, diverse narrative formats, and a wide range of experiences—from survivors filmed among artwork in a home studio to family dinners, literary readings, outdoor walks, performance pieces, and more conventional testimonial interviews (Figure 4.15).

As an indexing category, "still and moving images" is especially prevalent throughout these testimonies because the USC Shoah Foundation marked up the creative effect of the camera and the editing process (zooming, panning, lighting, dissolving, and cutting). This markup is actually a recognition by the Foundation that the camera is doing important interpretive work and is not merely a neutral, technological means by which the testimony was captured. By contrast, in the testimonies filmed by the USC Shoah Foundation, the camera, sound, and lighting were supposed to "achieve a consistent look to all the interviews" by capturing the survivor in "a very soft 3/4 key look."[43] Almost all the USC Shoah Foundation interviewees are filmed in their homes, sitting comfortably on a couch or a chair in their living room, speaking with an interviewer who remains off-camera. Except at the end, the camera almost always remains focused on the interviewee's face and torso. In fact, any movements of the camera were strictly forbidden because the foundation believed "such camera moves would add editorial content to the testimony, thereby compromising its historical validity."[44] Such markup for the Armenian genocide testimonies highlights the standardization—and perhaps normalization—of the recording and interview techniques later developed by the USC Shoah Foundation.[45]

This standardization of the testimonial genre is not only evident in the recording protocols (ranging from camera guidelines to interview questions and narrative structure) but also in the thesaurus and descriptive metadata that form the indexing system. That indexing system, as suggested earlier, is guided by a realist, historical epistemology derived from a factual framework of things said by the interviewee about the experiences of genocide. This means that named entities such as people, geographic locations, organizations, governmental and military bodies, time periods, and events take precedence over marking up and indexing the range of expressive forms, narrative approaches, and representational strategies used by survivors. Disregarding vernacular speech, figurative language, voice, affect, false starts, repetitions, silence, and various unwanted or misunderstood elements, the indexing system elevates manifest content above all else. And while such content is certainly important to provide a framework for understanding the genocidal event, the indexing system cannot account for latent content—the figural, the subjunctive, the tone of questioning and doubt, the grain of the traumatized voice, the expressiveness of the body, and the very acts of telling (and failing to tell)—that marks the contingency of testimonial speech acts. This is something that we can see quite clearly when we toggle between distant and close analysis of the Armenian genocide testimonies.

Let's start zoomed all the way out. Although the whole corpus visualization of the Armenian genocide testimonies (Figure 4.14) shares a number of structural commonalities with those of the other corpora, we also see a number of unique aspects: Certain indexing terms, such as "still and moving images," run across the entire length of the narrative (to describe the videography and the actions of the camera), while other indexing terms, such as "liberation" and "post-conflict," are almost entirely absent. This may indicate the struggle of recognition of the Armenian Genocide more broadly, not to mention the fact that survivors were not "liberated" formally from captivity or oppression when the killing stopped; it may also indicate that they were simply not asked about such experiences. Rather than ebbing and flowing as a function of narrative time, many of the major categories (excluding "time and place," which becomes smaller, and "still and moving image," which becomes bigger) persist across the testimonies in roughly similar ratios. These include "daily life," "discrimination responses," "feelings and thoughts," "government," "mistreatment and death," "movement," and "people." This may be due to the fact that the testimonies do not follow a common narrative arc and, instead, vary tremendously in terms of length, structure, and narrativity.

We now turn to four Armenian genocide testimonies that were originally recorded by the Armenian Film Foundation and have since been archived, indexed, and made accessible within the USC Shoah Foundation's information architecture: those of Khoren Davidson, Zabel (Rose) Apelian, and Hrahad Harout and Shooshanig Shahinian (who were interviewed together), and Avedis Khantzian.[46] With regard to interview strategy, all four interviews start somewhat abruptly with the interviewer asking the survivors to revisit the core of the genocidal experience. Once the clapperboard signals the start of the recording, the first question asked of Davidson is: "What did you see?" Apelian is told: "Ok, start telling your story." After about two minutes of family banter, laughing, and dishes clanging, the interviewer says to Harout and Shahinian, "everyone go ahead" and someone else adds "okay you can start." Similarly, once the recording begins, Khantzian is told: "Okay, you can start." The responses by the survivors vary, and each one begins telling his or her story in ways that are deepened and reworked in subsequent takes. The recording process, which documents everything from the interview protocols to lighting, scene setting, and directions between the film crew and interviewer, is never hidden from view or edited out. While new details and narrative strategies are added in each take, there is also a certain amount of repetition as each interview proceeds. Sometimes the interviewer (or a family member) intervenes in the survivor's narrative, interrupting and asking for clarification, or asking the survivor to retell a particularly traumatic event or prompt a particular story. And unlike the interviews conducted by the USC Shoah Foundation that strive to explicitly encompass the interviewee's "entire life history, usually recounted in chronological order,"[47] the Armenian Film Foundation's testimonies are closer to Boder's "topical autobiographies," focusing primarily on the specific events of the genocide in a wide variety of narrative and filmic forms.

The testimony of Khoren Davidson (born in 1896) runs a little over one hour and was recorded in August of 1977 and February of 1986. Like other testimonies in the Armenian Film Foundation collection, some of the video is missing and parts consist only of the audio track. Interviewed by Hagopian, Davidson speaks in English, Armenian, and Turkish. Far from a life narrative or chronology, the testimony is a montage of memorial vignettes. These include his description of taking pictures to document atrocities committed by Turkish soldiers including sexual assaults and mass killings, changing his name to Turkish and converting to Islam, surviving the end of the war as a practicing city physician, and later freeing hundreds of young women from harems. At one point on the audio track, he breaks down describing the sight of thousands of corpses floating down the river. Since the video appears not to have been captured correctly, the interviewer asks him "to say it again," which he does, performing, perhaps unintentionally, the trauma of repetition at the heart of testimony (minutes 17–20). He later recounts the memory in Armenian, recalling, with his eyes closed, the image of corpses flowing down a waterfall on the Euphrates River (minute 58). Part of the testimony also includes a brief history of the Armenian people from Zeytun, which is included in the middle of his personal narrative. Closing his eyes, the testimony ends with him singing songs in Turkish that recount the sadness of family separations.

Zabel (Rose) Apelian was born in 1907 in the United States to an Armenian family who went back to Turkey around 1914. She tells the interviewer about the harrowing experiences of her family moving their belongings out of the city on wagons that were plundered by Turkish soldiers who arrested, tortured, and killed her parents. She is separated from her younger sister and eventually ends up in an orphanage after being refused aid by various Christian Armenian individuals and organizations who might have helped her. While repeating parts of her testimony multiple times for the different takes, her story progresses in a kind of cyclical fashion until the camera zooms in on her tattoos in the final two minutes of her testimony. On her arm are tattoos of a cross and image of Jesus, which mark her as a Christian Armenian.[48] At this point, Apelian does not say anything; instead, the camera pans and zooms around her body as she holds her tattooed arms above her head, as if to display the stigmata and suffering of Christ. These segments of her testimony are indexed as "miscellaneous footage," a category that obscures the emotional weight of these silent, performative parts of her testimony. Her testimony concludes with the camera moving over a sequence of historical photographs and parts of her birth certificate, also indexed as "miscellaneous footage."

The testimony of Hrahad Harout and Shooshanig Shahinian is thiry-seven minutes in length and filmed at a dinner table with five other family members. The interviewer and camera are mostly situated in the adjacent room, although sometimes the camera enters the room and films close-ups of Harout, Shahinian, or other people asking questions. The testimony primarily focuses on the roles of Harout and Shahinian as members of the Armenian resistance involved in the Defense of Van in 1915, an organized resistance against the Ottoman Empire's attempts to massacre and starve the Armenian population of the Van Vilayet. Harout speaks about the political movement of Armenian liberation and his personal involvement in the armed resistance, while Shahinian mentions how she helped the fighters by providing medicine, carrying messages, and playing Armenian revolutionary songs and music. The interviewer and family members frequently intervene to ask questions, interrupt the stories, and sometimes even encourage the survivors to "get to the point, get to the point" (minute 22). The conversation concludes with a discussion of the death of a betrayer of the Armenian resistance and the feelings of Harout and Shahinian about their memories of hope that motivated the resistance.

At only eight minutes in length, Avedis Khantzian's testimony is among the shortest in the entire VHA collection, but it is also one of the most powerful and haunting. Situated in his art studio, he gives the same testimony twice, in two subsequent takes: He describes the various jobs of townspeople, the experience of seeing people rounded up, and how he was saved by his aunt who was a shoemaker. He uses the term "Holocaust" twice to describe what happened to the Armenians and the fact that he was saved from death by his aunt.[49] Around minute six of his testimony, he begins to talk about being marched out of town, witnessing groups of people forcibly separated, and seeing unburied corpses. Visibly shaking on camera, he breaks down in tears and says: "One night we heard . . . I can't go on . . . I'm sorry I can't go on" (minute 6). Almost two minutes of silence follows, with the camera only showing his art, particularly a painting of a woman holding a child with a family and a skull on the ground. The testimony ends with a close-up on someone's hands, presumably Khantzian's, thumbing through a Bible. The ending sequences of his testimony have been given the following indexing terms: "Armenian genocide testimony sharing reluctance," "sadness," the various movements of the camera ("tilt," "reverse zoom," and "zoom"), and "miscellaneous footage."

Khantzian does not—and perhaps cannot—offer a narrative testimony of what he saw and experienced. His trembling voice and silence testify to finding no words or narrative language to answer the interviewer's questions and describe his experiences. To apply Armenian Studies scholar Marc Nichanian's words, this is a testimony that refuses "to make the event manifest in the orb of the civilized world."[50] How, then, do we open up spaces for listening to what is anything but "miscellaneous footage"? What methods allow us to find it, hear it, and appreciate it? How might we mark up silence without filling it in, so to speak, with determinative meanings and, at the same time, not reduce or dismiss it as "non-tractable data" that does not compute?[51] As we will see in the next chapter, computational listening can help us find variations in voice, including moments of silence, that may help us become closer listeners and thereby prompt us to develop new ways of indexing and searching within testimonies.

Although macroanalysis does not help us interpret Khantzian's testimony, it can show us the extent to which his testimony differs from the narrative patterns derived from the other 245 testimonies, even if the indexed segments do not move beyond the manifest content of the testimony. Khantzian's testimony exposes not only the limits of testimony as a narrative form to represent the factuality of the past but also the structuring epistemologies embedded in the digital archive, the database, and the information architecture. Nichanian is particularly attuned to the burden placed on the survivor to try to fashion—in words and images—the truth of what happened, to offer "proof" to those who were not there, or more problematically, to those who actively deny that genocide even happened. He explains that "the genocidal will wants to destroy the fact, the factuality of the fact" because it is an event "that negates and denies its own factuality" by making it (almost) impossible to bear witness.[52]

Testifying to genocide by making "the event manifest in the orb of the civilized world" thus represents an impossible demand on survivors to testify to negation.[53] For this reason, Nichanian does not evaluate testimony for its capacity to offer proof, substantiate facts, or present the past as it really was, as might be demanded by historians or institutional archiving projects. Instead, he seeks to overcome this realist injunction in favor of testimony as art and literature,[54] freeing survivors from the burden—and shame—of having to offer "proof" for the sake of the archive: "Shame, in sum, is to make testimony play the role of the archive for proof or for memory. Shame is transforming testimony into archive."[55] Asking Khantzian to give "proof" and participate in recounting a realist narrative ("how it really was") only gives rise to trauma, silence, and shame. In Nichanian's words: "It is shame that survives. It is shame that testifies."[56] The testimonial genre all too often prioritizes "what happened," and the indexing system of the digital archive follows suit by marking up factuality, sometimes at the expense of all else.

As a group, the four testimonies differ substantially from one another in terms of length, narrative content, structure, voice, performance, and the content of experiences represented. As evidenced in their experimental approach to narrative strategy, interview process, and visual documentation, the interview and videography methodologies of the Armenian Film Foundation demonstrate a much wider range of possibilities for the testimonial genre. By toggling between distant and close views, we can bring into relief the fundamental decisions that have now become second nature in the recording of witness testimony (interview questions, narrative structure, and filming strategies) as well as underscore how the decisions about the descriptive metadata and the database structure result in a certain "normalization" of witness testimony as a genre. Macroanalysis exposes and perhaps helps us to break this normative frame.

To further characterize how the testimonial genre has changed over time, we will bring back the testimonies recorded by David Boder and the indexing systems he developed during the late 1940s and early 50s. When Boder indexed his interviews, he did not have access to a standardized, hierarchical vocabulary for describing the experiences narrated by Holocaust survivors. At the same time, the genre of "Holocaust testimony" did not exist in the way we understand this term today. To highlight some of these differences, we might devise a "time stream" of the seventy interviews Boder indexed as part of *Topical Autobiographies* derived from the data ontology of the USC Shoah Foundation's thesaurus.[57]

To do so, I first assigned one of the twenty-three "parent terms" from the USC Shoah Foundation's thesaurus to each of the 960 indexing terms that Boder used in his manuscript.[58] This was a manual process by which I took all of Boder's indexing terms and gave them a top-level "parent term." While some of Boder's indexing terms fit neatly into the USC Shoah Foundation's rubric, others did not or required more investigation to figure out what Boder had in mind when he used a certain term. For example, I assigned the parent term "captivity" to his indexing term "weather" after realizing that the latter term referred to weather-related conditions in concentration camps (such as during Appells or forced labor) or during death marches. Similarly, "books" was assigned to the parent term "discrimination," since Boder used this term to index "the use and forbiddance" of books. Other terms, such as "dead handlers" and "dungeons" certainly fit within the parent term "mistreatment and death," but they also bear witness to

Boder's attempt to create neologisms to describe the horrors of the camps. Today, the former term is known as the "Sonderkommando" (Jewish prisoners forced to remove and burn bodies from the gas chambers). The term "dungeon"—as used by Boder interviewee Jaques (Jack) Matzner—seems appropriate to describe his experiences imprisoned in an underground cellar filled with water. Finally, some terms such as "insanity," "screaming," "out-group status," and "TAT test" are unique to Boder's index, and they could only be approximated by the Shoah indexing terms. "Insanity," "out-group status," and "TAT test" (a psychology test that Boder administered to an early group of interviewees) are all terms meant to describe or elicit "feeling and thoughts" among the survivors, so that parent term was chosen; "screaming" was indexed using "mistreatment and death," referencing the context in which the term appeared.

In the following visualization (Figure 4.16), we can see the distribution of the top-level indexing categories over the more than three thousand pages comprising Boder's seventy testimonies in *Topical Autobiographies*. The visualization provides a sense of the topics that were spoken about and indexed the most and the least. Looking horizontally, we can see that the most frequently indexed categories are: "time and place," "people," "mistreatment and death," "daily life," and "captivity." Looking vertically by color, we can see which categories co-occur within a given testimony. Two of the top-level USC Shoah Foundation categories—"refugee experiences" and "still and moving images"—are not used at all simply because the testimonies were taken in 1946 and were not filmed. The experience of displacement and the sheer fact of being in a DP camp were taken as given by Boder and not indexed as such, although many of the survivors talk about their intention to immigrate to the United States or Palestine. True to Boder's intention to gather "topical autobiographies," it is striking how few broad, contextual indexing terms are used: culture, economics, politics, religion and philosophy, and world histories hardly come up in the assignment of indexing categories.[59]

Using the USC Shoah Foundation's indexing terms, our team then computed the probabilities that a given parent term would occur at a particular percentage point in the testimonies. The result is shown in Figure 4.17. While this "time stream" visualization has certain similarities to the others (such as the importance of "time and place" in the first part of the testimonies), there are a number of salient differences. First, categories of violence such as "captivity," "mistreatment and death" and "movement" occur far more frequently, and they persist across the entire narrative. "People," "organizations," and "health" are marked up more often (the last being marked up more frequently in Boder's interviews than in any of the other corpora), while categories attesting to broad

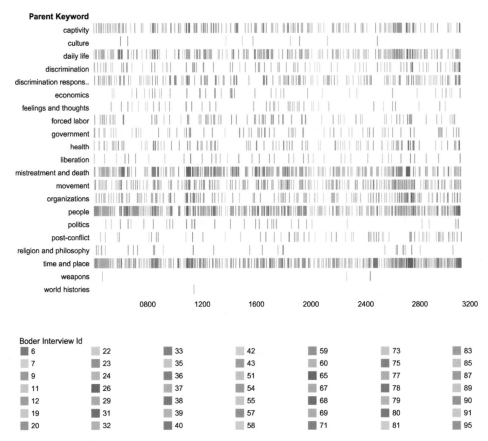

Parent Keyword

FIGURE 4.16: Distribution of top-level indexing terms across Boder's *Topical Autobiographies.* Created by Lizhou Fan and Todd Presner. Interactive visualization on Tableau: hrl.pub/c7d4c2.

historical awareness such as "world histories" are completely absent. Perhaps more significant is the general lack of narrative coherence indicated by the variance of categories that co-occur throughout the testimonies and especially in the final 20 percent of the testimonies. Unlike the Jewish Holocaust testimonies created by the USC Shoah Foundation—which often start with categories such as "daily life" and "religion and philosophy," followed by discrimination, discrimination responses, movement, and captivity, and then tend to conclude in the final 20 percent by discussing life after liberation, feelings and thoughts, and, most of all, showing still and moving images—Boder's testimonies are fragmented into many possible categories, in many ways closer to the Armenian

David Boder's *Topical Autobiographies* (70 testimonies)

Term Name
- captivity
- culture
- daily life
- discrimination
- discrimination responses
- economics
- feelings and thoughts
- forced labor
- government
- health
- liberation
- mistreatment and death
- movement
- organizations
- people
- politics
- post-conflict
- religion and philosophy
- time and place
- weapons
- world histories

% of Total Value

Testimony Percentile

FIGURE 4.17: Time stream visualization derived from Boder's *Topical Autobiographies*. Created by Lizhou Fan and Todd Presner. Interactive visualization on Tableau: hrl.pub/1a9205.

genocide testimonies. For both, it is difficult to discern a generalizable, story-like narrative arc. Even at the end of Boder's testimonies, far from reaching a common closure, categories such as "daily life," "people," "mistreatment and death," "time and place," and "organizations" are all likely to appear.[60] While this fragmentation can be attributed to many factors, including the comparatively small sample size, Boder's changing approach to interviewing survivors, and perhaps even to the incompleteness of his indexing system, it is also probable that he and his interviewees are struggling to develop a narrative form to create meaning within the uncertainty of the immediate postwar period. The genre of spoken Holocaust testimony did not yet exist in the way it does now because paradigms for interviewing, narrating, recording, and indexing testimony were just beginning to be established through experimentation.

Another way to examine the differences is to focus on just a few parent terms across several corpora, rather than looking at all twenty-three parent terms at once. Using Tableau, we can extract and compare whichever indexing categories we want and thus track their relative weights with respect to one another across the corpora. In the following example (Figure 4.18), we focus on just five indexing categories relative to their frequency with respect to one another: "captivity," "culture," "forced labor," "mistreatment and death," and "post-conflict." For the USC Shoah Foundation's Holocaust testimonies, a clear narrative arc emerges: the first 20 percent focuses primarily on "culture" while the last 20 percent focuses primarily on "post-conflict." In between, experiences of captivity make up the overwhelming majority of what survivors are likely to talk about, with experiences of forced labor and mistreatment and death occurring in the middle third of the narrative. Interestingly, the category of "mistreatment and death" is the smallest relative to the other four categories as well as relative to its weighted occurrence in each of the other corpora.[61] While Boder's testimonies seem to be somewhat bookended by discussions of "post-conflict" (he will often start and finish in the 1946 moment), "mistreatment and death" as a category relative to the other four is markedly dominant, while "culture" is almost completely absent. In both the Nanjing and Rwandan testimonies, "mistreatment and death" also dominates right from the outset, with captivity occurring significantly less (and forced labor being largely absent due to the historical specificity of the events themselves). They both end in the post-conflict moment in the last fourth of the testimonial narrative. This last category—"post-conflict"—is almost entirely absent from the Armenian testimonies, perhaps owing to the lack of acknowledgment and closure that persisted up until the time the testimonies were recorded. At the same time, the category of "culture" increases across the narrative

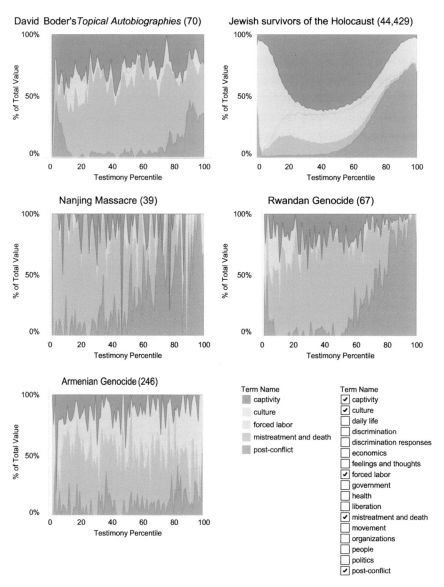

David Boder's *Topical Autobiographies* (70)

Jewish survivors of the Holocaust (44,429)

Nanjing Massacre (39)

Rwandan Genocide (67)

Armenian Genocide (246)

Term Name
- captivity
- culture
- forced labor
- mistreatment and death
- post-conflict

Term Name
- ☑ captivity
- ☑ culture
- ☐ daily life
- ☐ discrimination
- ☐ discrimination responses
- ☐ economics
- ☐ feelings and thoughts
- ☑ forced labor
- ☐ government
- ☐ health
- ☐ liberation
- ☑ mistreatment and death
- ☐ movement
- ☐ organizations
- ☐ people
- ☐ politics
- ☑ post-conflict

FIGURE 4.18: Comparison of relative frequencies of five indexing categories across five testimonial corpora. Derived from data provided by the USC Shoah Foundation Visual History Archive. Created by Lizhou Fan and Todd Presner. Interactive visualization on Tableau: hrl.pub/76300a.

arc of the testimony corpus, perhaps owing to the ways the testimonies were filmed to document aspects of Armenian culture and history.

Although there are significant differences in the size of the five corpora, some of the broad contours of the experiences indexed in the survivor testimonies can nevertheless be detected in these visualizations. They help us to begin to see generally and, therefore, demand that we not only "zoom in" to comprehend the specificity of testimonial narratives but that we also ask critical questions about how the data and narratives were created and structured. The visualizations may also prompt new research questions about the genre of testimony, the interviewing priorities and protocols, and the processes of indexing. In the final analysis, we must historicize and probe the interviewing, recording, archiving, and indexing methodologies as well as interrogate how testimony is rendered into computationally actionable data in the first place. As I have endeavored to show here, all of these decisions have epistemological and ethical consequences.

We will conclude by entertaining a series of speculative questions that aim to reimagine the representational structures of the database vis-à-vis the specific experiences of bearing witness, testifying, surviving, and narrating. Is it possible for a database to embody the fragility of life as reflected in the uncertainty, ambiguity, and figurative qualities of narrative? How might the database preserve (rather than undo) the hauntedness that informs so much of testimony? In other words, how might a database be open to the haunt of the past, the trace of the unknown, the spectral quality of the indeterminate, and, simultaneously, be oriented to the uncertainty of the future, or what Jacques Derrida calls "the spectral messianicity" at the heart of the archive?[62] This means the database, like the entire information architecture, is not a neutral container to store or put content into, and the goal of the information system is not simply to noiselessly and seamlessly transmit factual content to receivers. Instead, the database must be conceived through the same ethical optic as engaging with the testimonies and, therefore, fundamentally connect the intentional acts of bearing witness to the information architecture, the data ontologies, the data structures, the indexing systems, and the distant witnesses who are engaged in a participatory mode of listening. Such a notion of the archive specifically disavows the finality of interpretation, preserves ambiguity, and constantly situates and resituates knowledge through varying perspectives, indeterminacies, and differential ontologies.

Building on the innovation already in place for faceted searching within the VHA, we might, for example, imagine how fluid data ontologies might work, allowing multiple thesauruses that recognize a range of knowledge, standards, and listening practices. These may be community-based descriptions that function to multiply descriptive metadata and foster practices of redescription.[63] Similarly, what if verbs that connected action and agent, experience and context were given more weight than hierarchies of nouns primarily in associative relationships? What if a more participatory architecture allowed for other listeners to create tags that could unsay the said, or at least supplement the indexing categories and keywords associated with the segmented testimonies? Or, more radically, what if the user interface was generated by network graphs or visualizations, such that listeners did not just type words into an empty search box or select indexing terms from the list hierarchy but rather could browse the entirety of the archive in a dynamic way based on communities of experience, narrative structure, or even silences, gaps, and so-called non-indexical content?[64]

Such structures of saying and unsaying the database would constantly reinterpret and reinscribe the survivors' stories in ways that not only place the listener into an active relationship of responsibility to testimony but unleash a potentiality of meaning in every act of "saying" and "browsing." Narratives would be heard in their polyphony, with some listeners hearing some things and others hearing quite different things. Through these acts of saying and unsaying, which are, according to Emmanuel Levinas, marked by an "allegiance" and "exposedness" to the other, the responsibility to the other might become part of the ethics of the information architecture itself. We might call it: "Otherwise than the Database, or Beyond Essence" because it moves beyond an accounting of the manifest, factual content of the testimony.[65] Rather than considering the information architecture, data structures, and databases to be content agnostic, how might they be deeply tied to ethics and the contingent meaning-making and interpretative practices at the heart of the humanities?

The challenge resides in imagining a kind of computational architecture that not only deconstructs any assumptions of mathesis operating behind the digital archive and imposed on top of the cultural record but also propels an approach to information, the database, and the archive that preserves the ambiguous, the unfinished, the differential, the multiple, and the spectral. Such a database functions less as an objectivist container and more like a contingent refuge that is always open and growing, such that the infinite diversity of individual experiences will give rise to new data, new analyses, new perspectives, and new narratives. We have the opportunity to build and explore digital archives at a scale that constantly reinterprets and reinscribes the survivors' stories. Indeed, we will never be done listening, watching, and analyzing the testimonies because there is always more—a surplus of meaning—that is never finally captured, tagged, and marked up. And this is what an ethics of the algorithm would foster: a perpetual process of writing and rewriting, interpreting and reinterpreting, listening and relistening.[66] Through ever-thicker relationships between data and narrative, saying and unsaying, indexing and visualizing, it is possible for computation to facilitate a new ethics of listening. One way to do this is by moving between the whole of the database and the individual testimonies, transforming both in a never-ending, dynamic process that gives rise to new narratives and new data. In this sense, the ethics of the algorithm might begin with both close and distant analysis: that is, by listening to the individual testimonies one by one *and* by developing ways to comprehend them in aggregate—all the way up to more than fifty-five thousand at once.

5

The Haunted Voice

ON THE ETHICS OF CLOSE AND DISTANT LISTENING

Reconsidering the Testimonial Voice of Abraham Bomba

Because of his central role in Claude Lanzmann's film *Shoah* (1985), Abraham Bomba is widely known as the Jewish barber who was forced to work in Treblinka cutting women's hair shortly before the women were gassed. In the film, Lanzmann famously stages Bomba's testimony in a Tel Aviv barbershop in 1979 in order to evoke memories from late 1942 and early 1943, when Bomba was imprisoned in Treblinka. With various patrons in the scene, Bomba cuts the hair of a man (a friend of his from Częstochowa) while discussing how he was chosen to work in Treblinka and his feelings about cutting the hair of victims. Lanzmann asks Bomba to imitate the motions, which he does by demonstrating the movements of his hands and the scissors. As Bomba starts to break down under the stress and emotional toll of the interview, he tells Lanzmann that he cannot continue. After about a minute of silence, Lanzmann says to him: "Go on, Abe, you must go on. You have to. Please. We have to do it. You know it." Lanzmann continues to film Bomba as he wipes sweat from his brow and protests that he cannot go on. Lanzmann prods him again: "You have to do it. I know, it's very hard. I know, and I apologize. Please, let's go."[1] After nearly two minutes of silence (interrupted by Bomba's protestations and frustrated asides in Yiddish to his friend whose hair he is cutting), we become voyeuristically sutured to his testimony of trauma.[2] Bomba finally speaks. He tells Lanzmann that he and the other barbers would try to spend a few extra seconds with family and friends before they were gassed.

This scene has been discussed extensively in the voluminous critical literature on *Shoah* for the way Lanzmann seems to capture the "kernel of trauma," to use Michael Renov's words. The cutting of hair enacts "the repetition of the gesture" and unleashes Bomba's buried memories, while the camera functions as "an incitant to confession."[3] Dominick LaCapra points out that Lanzmann's interviewing strategy is to bring the survivor back "to the scene of victimization and traumatization," but he notes that this is sometimes achieved through "intrusive questioning."[4] Other commentators, such as Shoshana Felman, see Lanzmann as challenging, transgressing, and breaking "the silence of the witness's death" for the sake of truthfulness and history. She argues that Lanzmann, as an interviewer and inquirer, assumes the role of "a transgressor, and a breaker, of the silence" to ensure that the story is liberated, recounted, and historicized.[5]

But as Brad Prager has cogently argued, Lanzmann's interview with Bomba was highly controlled and shaped in order to construct Bomba as "truth incarnate," even if that meant creating one specific, highly staged scene from a panorama of possible memories and experiences.[6] In fact, Bomba relayed hours and hours of testimony to Lanzmann during their conversations in New York and Tel Aviv prior to the filming of this scene. Their conversations in Tel Aviv—which ranged widely from the first deportations from the Częstochowa ghetto, his arrival in Treblinka, his escape from the death camp, and his return to Częstochowa to tell others what was happening and help organize the ghetto uprising, to his reflections on Zionism, Jewish resistance, and religious Jews—are preserved in the three and a half hours of outtakes not included in the film.[7] The Lanzmann scene of Bomba cutting hair while recounting his experiences in Treblinka essentializes one particular part of Bomba's personal story of survival above all else—and to the exclusion of all else.[8] It not only represented what Lanzmann chose for Bomba to perform in front of the camera, but it also encapsulated the director's intention to film the breaking of the silence that he had also constructed. So, we might ask ourselves the following: If we listened differently to Bomba's spoken testimonies, what might be heard beyond this scene of silence and confession? Might we recenter the singularity of Bomba's voice?

In 1996, at the age of eighty-three, Bomba sat for a three-and-a-half-hour interview with Louise Bobrow, a volunteer for what would later become the USC Shoah Foundation's Visual History Archive. Filmed in his home in Monticello, New York, the testimony follows the chronological structure of the life interview established by the foundation as a paradigm for recording survivor testimony. As one of the earlier testimonies filmed by the Shoah Foundation, it is indexed by theme, rather than by one-minute segments. Over the course of seven tapes, Bomba is asked nearly five hundred questions and gives relatively short answers.[9] In the third tape, Bomba mentions how he was one of five people selected by the Nazis to work in Treblinka from transports that consisted of eighteen thousand people. Over the next hour, he speaks extensively about the command structure and functioning of the camp, including specific camp personnel, the brutality and living conditions in the camp, and the development of plans among some of the prisoners to escape. At the beginning of the fourth tape, the interviewer says to Bomba: "You mentioned you were also assigned to cutting the women's hair . . . How did that work?" Bomba explains, somewhat matter-of-factly: "They assigned us to cut off the hair of the women before they were gassed. . . . We have benches. The women were all naked. They were sitting on the benches. And we had to do our job. They shouldn't be suspicious that they're going to be killed."[10] The interviewer follows up with several other questions, including whether they were supplied with cutting instruments, where they stood in relation to the gas chambers, and if he ever spoke to any of the victims before they were gassed.

Despite the extreme horrors that Bomba describes and the wide range of questions the interviewer asks him over the course of the interview, there is—perhaps surprisingly—only a small amount of variation in his speaking voice. He speaks slowly, consistently, and deliberately, often struggling with and sometimes correcting his English grammar, as if translating experiences from another language. If we examine the audio recording of their conversation, we can look at the overall variations in vocal intensity by plotting the average audio output in terms of relative decibels over time (top of Figure 5.1). We see that the vocal intensity of the entire recording fluctuates by approximately ten decibels over the duration of the testimony (a relatively minor amount considering the length of the conversation, the topics, and the two speakers). For this visualization, the MP3 files were sampled for decibel level every 250 milliseconds and then plotted as averages at fifteen-second intervals. The obvious low points that occur approximately every thirty minutes represent the pauses for six tape changes, as these recordings were done on thirty-minute betacam tapes. The associated spectrogram (bottom of Figure 5.1) shows decibel by color and the full frequency range of the audio over time (represented as minutes along the x-axis).[11]

These visualizations provide a distant, zoomed-out representation of the testimony's sonic record and point to one significant variation: The auditory highpoints of Bomba's testimony come in the seventh tape, near the beginning of the third hour of his testimony, where we see two fairly prominent peaks. It is here that Bomba recites two Yiddish poems. His voice is clearly raised and the phonological specificity of the Yiddish language can be heard in his distinct articulation. This is where Bomba's voice is truly his own—unmediated by Lanzmann, Bobrow, the conventions of film and oral histories, or the English language. This sonic variation

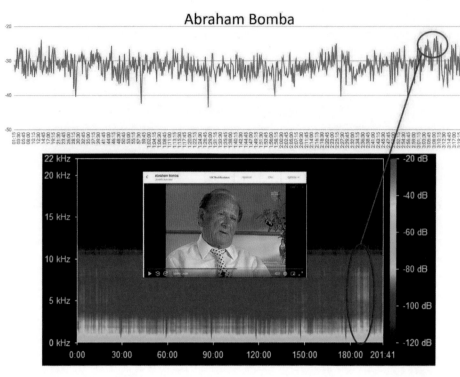

FIGURE 5.1: Voice intensity plot (decibel levels over time) and spectrogram of Abraham Bomba's VHA testimony. Created by Campbell Yamane and Todd Presner. Abraham Bomba (Aug 14, 1996), interview 18061, Visual History Archive, USC Shoah Foundation, https://vha.usc.edu/testimony/18061.

demands that we shift from distant listening to close listening in order to interpret this code-switch. When he completes his reading of the second poem, his voice drops dramatically, as he quietly reflects—in English—on the events described and tries to provide a summary to the interviewer.

Near the start of the third hour of his Shoah Foundation interview, Bomba reaches for several sheets of paper and prepares to read the two Yiddish poems that he wrote in the Częstochowa ghetto (see the appendix to this chapter for transcriptions and translations of both poems).[12] But before he begins, he is interrupted several times by Bobrow who wants assurances that he wrote the poems himself, while in the ghetto, and that he will read them in Yiddish, a language, we find out, she does not understand. She asks Bomba if he is going to read them in Yiddish, and he responds: "In Yiddish. That's all in Yiddish. In, in English I don't write. In anything else I didn't write, only those two."[13] Bomba tries to translate the title of the first poem, "Nekome" (revenge), but cannot come up with the English equivalent.[14] He says: "I would say, take advantage of the, of the thing what you went through, where you were sent. And there will come, there will come a time when you take not exactly advantage. But you will fight against them. You will hate them. And you will live the time when you will be liberated. It's a very, I would say it is very nice. I got two of them."[15] Within the context of his narrative testimony, the poems appear as an acoustic figura, allowing us to hear the anticipation of a future that has now been fulfilled, as Bomba has lived and speaks of the time of liberation—and perhaps revenge—imagined in his poems.[16]

He proceeds to read "Nekome," placing the emphasis on the call, repeated three times in the poem, to remember to take revenge. After finishing the first stanza, he stops himself and quickly confirms with Bobrow, "You don't understand nothing from it," to which she asks, "Is that what you translated before, what you said before is that what that meant?" He responds, "Yeah." The exchange takes place over less than six seconds. The sounds, of course, register but the meaning does not. He continues to read the poem for the camera, perhaps knowing that the testimonial storage system will capture it for future listeners. After offering a brief summary in English, he reads the second poem, which, he says, comes from a different time and recounts the day of the Nazi "action" that began the liquidation of the Częstochowa ghetto.[17] Both poems are left out of the transcript prepared by ProQuest.

In another figural interpretation, the phrase "You don't understand nothing from it" is not just directed at Bobrow, but also, it turns out, at the future transcribers, indexing systems, and descriptive metadata—all of which exclude the Yiddish words spoken by Bomba. Although segment forty is tagged with the indexing terms "Creative works, interviewee original works, and literary recitals," the poems are marginalized within the testimonial record: their content remains uninscribed, untranslated, unnamed, and unfindable through any semantic search. To be sure, the audio sampling algorithms do not "understand nothing from it" either, as they have no way to judge meaning, evaluate significance, or decide about value; however, they do reveal sonic differences. They indicate to us that there is, in fact, something to understand here; we are obligated, as it were, to listen and try to figure it out. In short, computational tools and algorithmic analyses do not provide us with answers or meanings, but they can identify differences, prompting us to listen to what has been excluded or relegated to the margins.

Using a software package called Praat, we created a series of spectrograms (Figure 5.2) of Bomba's Yiddish voice.[18] Praat is a speech analysis software package

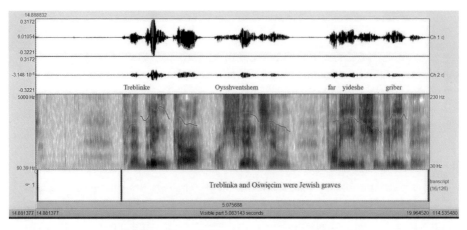

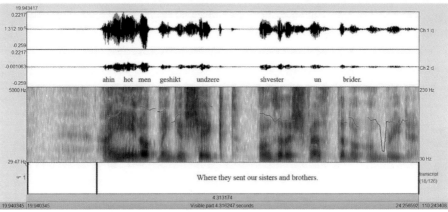

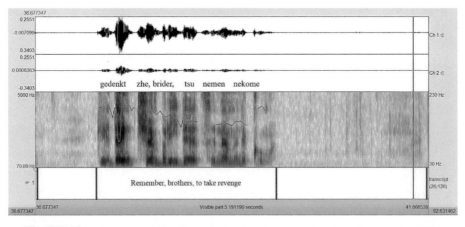

FIGURE 5.2: Spectrogram made using Praat from Bomba's reading of his poem "Nekome." Channel one is Bomba (first mic), and his voice comes through channel two, the mic on Bobrow, as well. Created by Richard Wang and Todd Presner. Both of Bomba's poems can be heard on our project website (https://holocaustresearchlab.com/book/chapter-5) or by using the QR code.

used widely in linguistics. When a sound file is imported into the program, its phonetic features can be analyzed as a waveform (a visual representation of intensity or loudness) and a spectrogram (the frequency of how a sound signal varies over time as well as its energy). Voice qualities, such as glottal activity, are also evident in the spectrograms. The poem "Revenge" is structured in three stanzas with rhyming couplets, culminating at the end of each stanza with a plea for Bomba's Jewish brethren to remember the value of revenge and to take revenge after the war. The poem begins with an "I" recounting the Nazi actions that sent millions of "our sisters and brothers" to their death in Treblinka and Auschwitz. Bomba's voice is at its softest at this point, and we notice a marked drop in pitch and slight dilation of time as he speaks this line. The poem, then, engages a "you": "If you want to know what happened there, then ask those who escaped." Those who escaped and survived the war will not only bear witness through testimony and poetry, as Bomba does, but they must also remember to take revenge: "*Gedenkt zhe, brider, tsu nemen nekome.*" Separated by distinct pauses while breathing, these words—condensed into a single phonetic unit—are uttered like a mantra with rhythmic variations at the end of each stanza. The space between exhalation and inhalation represents a kind of "breath-unit" that is visualized as a moment in time by the spectrogram.[19]

Bomba's second poem is untitled and reads as a testimonial elegy for the Częstochowa ghetto and the thousands of Jews deported to Treblinka during the first waves of the liquidation. The first deportations from Częstochowa took place beginning on September 22, 1942, the day after Yom Kippur. Bomba describes the terror and uncertainty of the roundups and reflects on what was still the unknown future: "We didn't know this yet / But from us Jews, only a bit of trash [*a bisl mist*] would be left." He recounts how the gendarmes and Jewish police chased people through the streets, separating families, forcing them into cattle cars, and beating them. Bomba's immediate family was spared from the first deportation and sent home, where they are overcome by contradictory emotions of "joy and sorrow." But shortly before Sukkot, the second wave of deportations took place, when he and his family were rounded up and thrown onto trains. The poem's accusatory tone establishes networks of complicity between the German Nazis, the collaborating Ukrainian guards, the Christian Poles, and the Jewish ghetto police. His poem bears witness to a multitude of atrocities suffered in the most dehumanizing way on the day of the action: being laughed at, being shoved into trains as human trash, and finally being spit on through the little window of the cattle car.[20] The poem ends with the humiliation and uncertainty of being loaded into a cattle car bound for Treblinka. It bears witness from a subject position within the deportation train.

Decades after composing the poems, Bomba described his arrival in Treblinka in the institutional testimonies he gave to the United States Holocaust Memorial Museum and the USC Shoah Foundation as well as in the outtakes filmed by Lanzmann for *Shoah*.[21] He tells how the men and women were separated on the ramp in Treblinka, which was the last time he saw his mother, wife, and child. In the outtakes, he indicates that these memories are "very painful," and that having to "go through it again" is difficult but that he is doing so for the sake of "history." In the outtake, Lanzmann interrupts him and says: "You have to, you have no choice."[22] Bomba proceeds to describe the family separations and the fate of the people from the transport. While he later speaks to Lanzmann about his experience working as a barber in Treblinka, the poems do not express this experience at all. Instead, the poems focus on documenting the liquidation of the Częstochowa ghetto, the family separations, the feelings of humiliation and terror, his eventual escape, surviving the war, and his intention to take revenge.[23] Lanzmann's Bomba, on the other hand, represents the essentialization of a single experience presented as the traumatic opening of a wound for the world to see.

But Bomba also bears witness in another voice, one that Lanzmann seems to have never heard. Not only are the two poems the auditory highpoint of his entire three-and-a-half-hour USC Shoah Foundation testimony, but they are the only time Bomba speaks in his own voice, unprompted by the questions asked by an interviewer. He speaks with determination to bear witness in the Yiddish language, with words he composed from within the event and delivered orally decades later. It is *not* his silence—so famously recorded, canonized, and broken by Lanzmann—but his own voice calling forth to be heard, in words from a language almost extinguished, once again, from the record. And even before we interpret the semantic meanings of the poems, the sounds of his voice and the phonological uniqueness of the Yiddish language resonate in our ears and on the spectrogram. The voice calls forth in its difference from all that came before. If there is a "truth incarnate" of Bomba's testimony, it is not the theatrical staging of his silence, but rather his voice articulating the sounds of resistance in Yiddish.

Between Phonetic and Semantic

We began this chapter with a reappraisal of Lanzmann's representation of Bomba to explore a process of listening to variations in both the semantic and phonetic records of spoken testimonies. It is a process informed by—but not reducible to—computation, measurement, and quantification. In what follows, we argue that computational tools can facilitate an ethics of distant witnessing by drawing our attention to the radical particularity of the sonic record. This approach is exactly the opposite of trying to generalize, extrapolate, or predict something from a corpus of voices. Instead, we are interested in using technology *to pause the flow of speech* and model a form of listening to the smallest, most fine-grained moments of vocal expressivity in a testimony: the pitch of a single word, the air exhaled in a sigh, the silent gaps between speech, the percussive interruptions of code-switching, or the altered cadence of the voice.[24] These moments allow us to attend to and listen to more than one voice. This happens through a relational reciprocity between voice and ear that is mediated by digital interfaces, computational analyses, and data visualizations. As Adriana Cavarero argues, voice—as a cry, call, or invocation to the other—"is always *for* the ear, it is always relational."[25] The question is what this means when the voice comes to us via a digital interface and when we use a software program to identify, visualize, and listen to these fine-grained, radically particular elements of the human voice.[26]

To be sure, algorithms and computational calculations can reduce the expressive potential of phonation to mere measurements that, in turn, could be transformed into bare data used to track, predict, or police. Always cognizant of the risks of this dialectical potentiality, we seek to model an approach to computation that, instead, redirects attention and attunes our listening to the individual, micro-expressivities of the voice.[27] An ethics of the algorithm necessitates that our attunement to difference results in modalities of listening that humanize the other and preserve the singularity of the human voice *in the data*. Rather than devising algorithmic methods that rest upon extrapolating and generalizing from data outputs, we proceed by listening to some of the many voices from the vast corpus of testimonies. In this sense, we take inspiration from Louise Amoore who argues with regard to algorithms: "I cannot know the essence of the other as a cluster of attributes, and when the algorithm presents me with the likelihood of their attribution, I must begin again from their singularity."[28] When we do so, we use computational tools and algorithmic methods to listen differently because we place ourselves into relationship with the infinite singularity of the other and the infinite multiplicity of the testimonial voice.[29]

Let's start by addressing the question of why we would want to use any form of computation to facilitate close and distant listening. As we saw in the last chapter, the extant protocols for searching within recorded testimonies are almost exclusively drawn from semantic content: historical facts, named entities (places, people, organizations), and various subject terms used to describe narrative content. These structure and guide our listening. One of the fundamental limits of such thing-based ontologies is the focus on the literalism of "the said," to refer back to Emmanuel Levinas's formulation, rather than the process of "saying." In the realm of "the said," semantic meanings are privileged, and they must be fixed for the sake of facilitating accurate search and retrieval. This process prioritizes variations of "being" (what "is" or "was") and tends toward objective, manifest content, factuality, and various degrees of closure. These things are fairly easy to compute and conform to a model of computation grounded in generating knowledge, facts, and answers. The process of "saying," however, is always more complicated, more vexing, and harder to parse, since it focuses our attention on interpreting the uncertainty of language, the expressive variations in the human voice, the fragility of the reluctant witness, the processes of articulating haunting or traumatic memories, and the vulnerable trust between the interviewee and the interviewer. How might deeper links be forged—computationally and humanistically—between ontologies of "the said" and processes of "saying," between semantic content and phonetic meaning, between manifest expressions and latent content, between the literalism of ontology and the phonetic figuralism of "hauntology"?[30]

In her reflection on the erasure of voice in the history of Western philosophy, Cavarero argues that "the devocalization of logos" goes hand-in-hand with the privileging of mind over body, the semantic over the phonetic, and the universal over the particular.[31] Citing Levinas's distinction between "the said" and "the saying," Cavarero argues that "philosophy has always focused on the Said" and "never asks after *who* is Saying."[32] In so doing, it privileges linguistic systems and ontologies grounded in factual content ("the what"). As she argues further: "The more speech loses its phonic component and consists in a pure chain of signifieds, the closer it gets to the realm of truth."[33] Not unlike the conventional functioning of databases and algorithms, speech devoid of the particularity of *phone* presumes (quite falsely) to be the universal, the objective, the neutral, the scientific, the factual, and the manifest.

The phonetic, however, is a chance to undo such rationally organized structures. Through both the face and the voice ("the how"), the processes of saying are contingent and relational ("why" and "for whom"), demanding forms of close listening and interpretation. The phonetic also exposes us to the other, as one might approach a neighbor or even "[inhale] the air that the other exhales." Acts of breathing—like acts of saying and listening—rest upon the proximity of one human being to another, thereby giving rise to an "ethic of the for-the-other."[34] It is sound and breath that precedes the meaning of narrative, for it is sound that first reaches out to us. As the German Jewish poet Paul Celan once said with regard to poetry (and the poetic voice more generally): poems are cast out into the world and make their way toward someone "standing open," ready to listen, and addressable.[35] Relational ethics begins with both the face and voice of the other. And in the case of digitized testimonial archives, the face and voice come to us via a web interface.

As we saw earlier, the USC Shoah Foundation's thesaurus for indexing testimonies is mostly composed of named entities in the semantic realm of the said (not unlike many such archives). However, the thesaurus also includes a number of terms for indexing "feelings and thoughts," as well as other subjective, psychological reactions such as "testimony sharing reluctance." More recently, the transcripts prepared by ProQuest mark-up silences and pauses in the testimonies as well as emotional expressions (such as crying) and performative acts, including singing and literary recitals, all of which would not be found in a transcript that focused exclusively on what was literally said.[36] The creators of the transcript have also added commas, ellipses, dashes, quotation marks, question marks, exclamation marks, and periods, and occasionally removed stuttering or misspoken phrases. Non-English words tend to be omitted entirely (at least for now). In transcribing the voice, the flow of spoken words, often uttered in long, run-on, or grammatically broken sentences, has, to a certain extent, become regularized into discrete, semantic units. This also can make the testimonies more structured and computationally tractable.

Attention to voice, affect, and performativity in Holocaust testimonies is not new and can be found in early radio broadcasts and in the interviews recorded by David Boder.[37] In the transcripts comprising *Topical Autobiographies*, Boder marked up many aspects of the voice and the performative aspect of his interviewees, including the survivors' emotional state and emotional expressiveness, the qualities of the voice, silences and gaps, levels of articulation, and the speed at which the interviewee spoke. While not consistent, his annotations kept track of a number of vocal and emotive expressions, which we grouped under the following categories: low voice/high voice, low pitch/high pitch, trembling voice, stammering or mumbling voice, whispering, laughter/irony, irritable, screaming/upset, crying, and pause/silence.[38] In his studies of trauma, Boder was already trying to parse the expressive, sonorous qualities of the human voice side-by-side with the semantic content of the narratives.

Within the field of Holocaust studies more broadly, attention has been given to various aspects of voice and aurality in survivor testimonies, especially song, poetry, and the prevalence of multilingual expressivity and code-switching.[39] In reflecting on the Yale Testimony Project (later renamed the Fortunoff Archive for Holocaust Testimonies), Geoffrey Hartman characterized testimonies as "oral memoirs" and described the guiding principles as "giving survivors their voice . . . and giving a face to that voice."[40] He added that the "'embodiment' of the survivors, their gestures and bearing, is part of the testimony" and this "expressive dimension" is captured through audiovisual recording technologies.[41] However, beyond underscoring the importance of capturing vocal and gestural expressivity, Hartman never developed methods for analyzing this expressivity. While his approach sought to center the eyewitness accounts of Holocaust survivors, it tended to conflate the sonorous dimensions of the voice (*phone*) and metaphorical approaches to voice: giving voice to stories, voices standing in for those extinguished, and the obligation to listen to different voices.

Other scholars have emphasized modalities of code-switching in testimonies to underscore the importance of changes in narrativity. In her analysis of song in Holocaust testimonies, Leah Wolfson, for example, argues that the encounter between "speech and song—or, between language and lyric—creates a new space for a new kind of testimony to emerge."[42] More recently, in her analysis of intertextuality and code-switching in testimonies, Hannah Pollin-Galay has argued that "Holocaust testimony collections are not only archives of story, but of sound."[43] The Yiddish language, as a "narrative theme and shadowy specter," bears witness to displacement, trauma, and transnational memory, which she traces through attentiveness to aurality, accent, and semantic interpenetration between languages.[44] Oftentimes, as Pollin-Gallay points out, Yiddish is relegated to the margins of testimony (and the past more generally) because it is considered a vernacular idiom that is a vestige of the "old world," disassociated with political life, and gendered in ways that fix it as subservient to national languages like English or Hebrew. As we saw with Bomba, Yiddish functions as a distinct register "to give the Jewish past a specific character, a name, a face, and a sound"[45] because it bears witness to a lost cultural and linguistic texture, in which precarious, traumatic, and uncertain bridges can still be built between the prewar identities of survivors and listeners today.[46]

We are thus interested in investigating the performative dimensions of testimony that are not usually described by the keyword data in the index and, similarly, are not readily findable when reading a standard transcript.[47] But what is at stake in using computational methods to help us interpret the performative aspects of a testimony such as the "grain" of the voice (the bodily aspects of speaking that result in changes in loudness, pitch, cadence, and timbre), interruptions (the pauses, sighing, and stammering of the interviewee, as well as those interjections or interruptions of the interviewer), breath and articulation, the rhythm of speech patterns, the code-switching between languages, and the silences and gaps?[48] The motivation should not be driven by a call to standardize vocal analysis or subject the voice to a controlled vocabulary in an attempt to track or measure its norms and deviations. Nor should it result in quantifying features of voice and performance to define correlations (such as a certain pitch equates with a certain emotion, or a particular gesture indicates a certain meaning, or that breathy striations on a spectrogram adduce particular kinds of trauma). Instead of creating generalized and de-individuated extrapolations from algorithmic outputs, an ethics of the algorithm necessitates that we use the outputs to attune ourselves—as distant witnesses—to the singularity of the voice in order to create opportunities for ongoing relationality, listening, and interpretation. In other words, we must ask: can there be computationally guided forms of empathetic listening that avoid reductive datafication and empiricist extrapolation?

From Distant to Close Listening

Distant listening is a mode of interpretation in which we, as tertiary witnesses, use a range of computational tools and algorithmic methods to identify patterns and differences in the sonic record.[49] Examining certain contours of the voice (such as loudness, pitch, and moments of silence), the algorithm exports a spreadsheet of measurements and values that can be plotted in the form of a graph, waveform, or spectrogram.[50] We began by visualizing changes in vocal intensity and pitch in a group of testimonies using an open source acoustic spectrogram analyzer called Spek. The example below comes from Erika Jacoby's testimony (Figure 5.3). The height of the bars corresponds to pitch (y-axis) and

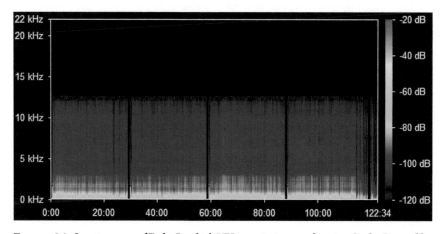

FIGURE 5.3: Spectrogram of Erika Jacoby's VHA testimony made using Spek. Created by Campbell Yamane and Todd Presner. Erika Jacoby (July 11, 1994), interview 8, Visual History Archive, USC Shoah Foundation, https://vha.usc.edu/testimony/8.

FIGURE 5.4: Screenshots from Renee Firestone's VHA Testimony (1994/1995). Renee Firestone (October 11, 1994, and January 26, 1995), interview 151, Visual History Archive, USC Shoah Foundation, https://vha.usc.edu/testimony/151.

is measured as the average frequency of the whole audio track per minute of testimony (x-axis). The color variations correspond to changes in decibel level, with areas of green indicating a louder output. Tape breaks can be seen quite clearly every thirty minutes. The spectrogram of Jacoby's testimony evidences little variance, except in the last minutes when she shows family photographs. After she introduces each picture, the videographer films for several seconds in silence, which accounts for the drop in decibel level and pitch in these moments.

Another way to perform distant listening is essentially the inverse of visualizing the voice—namely, to identify silence in the vocal record.[51] The testimony of Renee Firestone, recorded in Los Angeles on October 11, 1994, was one in which we listened for silence (Figures 5.4–5.6).[52] Firestone, a Czechoslovakian Jew deported in 1944, was a survivor of Auschwitz-Birkenau and experienced the loss of her family during the Holocaust. Her testimony is among a small number in the corpus that includes a second interview filmed on location: the last forty-three minutes were filmed in Auschwitz-Birkenau, without an interviewer, on January 26, 1995, the day before the fiftieth anniversary of the liberation of the camp.[53] The testimony thus consists of two parts: her life story, told in her home in a dialogical fashion to the interviewer, Simon Frumkin, and a set of personal monologues in Auschwitz-Birkenau, in which she discusses the specific places of the camp where she was imprisoned and reflects on the significance of Holocaust testimony today.

Looking at a visualization of silences in the audio track of her testimony shows a couple of things (Figure 5.5). First, the testimony, like other testimo-

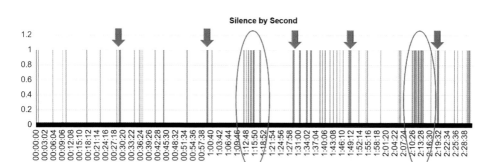

FIGURE 5.5: Moments of silence in Renee Firestone's VHA testimony (1994/1995). The arrows show where tape breaks occurred. Created by Campbell Yamane and Todd Presner.

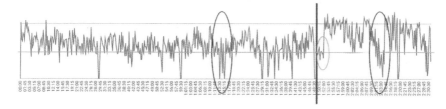

FIGURE 5.6: Voice intensity plot of Renee Firestone's VHA testimony (1994/1995). Created by Campbell Yamane and Todd Presner.

nies filmed by the Shoah Foundation, is divided into thirty-minute segments, which reflect the length of the tapes used for recording. Second, the silences in the audio track are indicated by bands, with the thinnest lines representing three seconds of silence and the thicker lines representing incrementally longer periods of silence. Her October 1994 testimony ends after one hour and forty-nine minutes. The eleven lines in tape four mostly occur during the time she reflects on her "future message" and shows pictures of herself and her family. The testimony filmed on location in Auschwitz-Birkenau begins after that and is organized as a series of reflections filmed in different parts of the camp, beginning with a description of her family's arrival on a cattle car and their separation during the selection process. The second visualization (Figure 5.6) shows the variation in voice intensity across both parts of her testimony. The average decibel level of the testimony filmed on location is higher given the strong wind blowing during most of her testimony and the need to speak louder while outside.

Within the audio of the testimony are two particularly significant areas of silence: the first (encircled) occurs around one hour and thirteen minutes, when she describes the death of her father shortly after the end of the war in a hospital in Terezin. The second moment of prolonged silence (also encircled) occurs over a period of three minutes (starting at two hours and ten minutes) when she walks around the remains of Crematorium V in Birkenau. These plots cannot, of course, tell us anything about the content, meaning, or significance of these two moments of silence, as they merely show us a distinct drop in decibel level. The patterns and differences in the vocal intensity plot call for a hermeneutic of close listening and attunement.

Firestone's testimony on location in Auschwitz is remarkable for many reasons, not least of all for the profound shifts in the nature of the testimonial narrative and the fraught auditory expressions of disbelief and silence. At around one hour and fifty minutes, the first part of her testimony on location begins with an extreme wide shot of the entrance to Auschwitz-Birkenau, looking out from the railway tracks to the camp entrance, before zooming in on Firestone walking alone along the ramp. It is winter, and the wind is blowing hard into the microphone, muffling her voice as she attests:

> My name is Renee Firestone. When I was brought here fifty years ago, my name was Renee Weinfeld. I was brought on these tracks, on a train full of cattle cars with my parents and with my fourteen-year-old sister. I—I am listening to the wind and hear the wind blowing here, and the quiet terrain. I can still hear the sounds of the masses of people that were pouring out of the cattle cars. I can still hear the cries of children looking for their parents and for—for parents looking for their children. It is still in my ears. I hear—I hear this mother yelling: "Hanela, Hanela, where are you?" And then I turned back to the cattle car and I called for my little sister. And I took her off the cattle car and in seconds I moved around and my parents were gone. And then we were the two of us, separated, outward, collapsed. Our life has changed forever.[54]

This scene lasts a little more than three minutes, and is clearly indicated as a relative low point on the voice intensity plot but without silence. The audio contains a mix of diegetic, ambient sounds (the howling wind muffling Firestone's voice) and Firestone's auditory ekphrasis in which she describes the range of sounds lodged in her memory: the sounds of the masses of people, the cries of the children, the yell of parents looking for children, and her own calls to her little sister.

After three minutes, the scene cuts and the audio changes. While the wind persists, her voice is much louder and clearer, as she prepares to take us into the camp itself, along the formerly electrified wires, and toward the delousing "sauna." She describes the delousing process, how her hair was shaven, the electrified wires, and eventually her separation from her sister. The auditory low points of her testimony occur several minutes later as she walks around the remains of Crematorium V. Trying to make sense of the ruins of mangled metal and brick, Firestone says that her mother and little sister were probably killed here. She wonders where the gas chamber was and notices parts of the "elevator" that brought bodies up to be burned in the ovens. The camera pulls out and shows a stand of birch trees in the background, and we hear the distinct sounds of birds chirping off-screen. Words now fade, and she sighs, as her voice cracks: "I don't know what I can say about it . . . I, I don't know how I can speak about it." She asks us to imagine if the ruins of the crematorium "could speak, if they could tell the stories, if the souls could speak here." She then sighs, saying: "I can't speak, I can't describe it," before pausing and saying that "here I can only pray for my mother's soul, for my sister's soul, and that they are resting in peace, because I am not." She stands still and weeps silently, looking down at the ground, and for several seconds that follow, we hear only her gentle breathing and the birds chirping somewhere in the birch trees. The scene ends with her inviting the listener to follow her to "the pits [to see] something else you will not believe."[55]

To be sure, these silences could be heard by simply listening to the testimony, and thus the question of why we need computation needs to be raised, especially because such methods of distant listening (spectrograms, vocal intensity plots, graphs of silence) could easily reduce the voice to mere measurements and even bare data. Distant listening achieved by an algorithm, which, by definition, knows nothing of the content, runs the risk of exteriorizing data about the voice and potentially turning the survivor into a kind of "vocal specimen," if it is not accompanied by empathetic, close listening. And yet, without some form of distant listening, moments of silence, changes in voice, nonverbal language, or paralinguistic cues all go missing when we are guided solely by semantic content (topics, themes, events, people). One possible idea would be to include annotations that mark up silence, voice, emotional expressivity, and perhaps even "the wind" and "the birds."[56] But these indexing terms also run the risk of presenting themselves as exteriorized, devoiced data. As it stands, the segment of Firestone's testimony in which she walks among the remains of Crematorium V is indexed by the USC Shoah Foundation with terms that document the objective and factual content ("the said") but do not capture any of the acts of her "saying": "Auschwitz II-Birkenau (Poland: Death Camp), camp crematoria, location video footage, loved ones' fates, Panstwowe Muzeum Auschwitz-Birkenau, Poland 1989

(June 5)–2015 (August 5), post-conflict persecution site visits, Julia Weinfeld—mothers, Klara Weinfeld—sisters."[57] The factuality of objective semantic information (rendered as search terms) flattens and even suppresses the emotional expressivity of Firestone's testimonial voice and the traumatic memories she records for posterity.

At the same time, we need to be mindful of any presumption of having finally decoded and "dispelled . . . the opaqueness of 'deep memory,'"[58] as if computational tools can reveal a definitive, underlying truth. The way forward is not merely to build a bigger, ever-more-comprehensive index or to measure more and more attributes of the human voice; instead, we want to facilitate a multiplicity of modalities for *differential listening*. In other words, instead of having just one entry point into a testimony based on indexing terms and "subject" keywords, we are suggesting that we use computational methods to continuously "turn over" testimonies and digital archives, thereby creating new pathways to search, discover, listen, and engage with testimonies. The analysis that follows is just one example of how we might do this. We leverage algorithmic methods to make particular vocal moments visible and searchable, while attuning our listening to their uniqueness and singularity. We describe several ways we can move from distant to close listening by hearing more than one voice—something, we argue, that is possible when we use computation to pause the flow of speech and focus on the multiplicity of voices embodied in singular utterances. The ethics of being a distant witness, then, is not about collecting more and more data to produce a definitive explication but about a transformation in the way we listen, opening up the possibility of connecting "what is said" to "how it is spoken" and thus placing ourselves, at least momentarily, within a technologically mediated, middle space of articulation with the person testifying.

Below is a visual representation of Erika Jacoby's vocal intensity over the five tapes comprising her testimony (Figure 5.7). Running just over two hours in length, the extreme low and high points, which occur approximately every thirty minutes, signal tape changes and the calibration of the color and audio levels at the start of each recording (usually with a multi-second beep). The final minutes represent the parts of her testimony in which she shows photographs of her family and briefly identifies who is in them. Looking at the overall audio contour, we were drawn to the part of her testimony around minutes 41–43, where the decibel levels are at their lowest points in the entire spoken testimony. The keywords in the database tell us objectively "what" is being described: her family was deported in a freight train, and they arrived on the ramp in Auschwitz-Birkenau

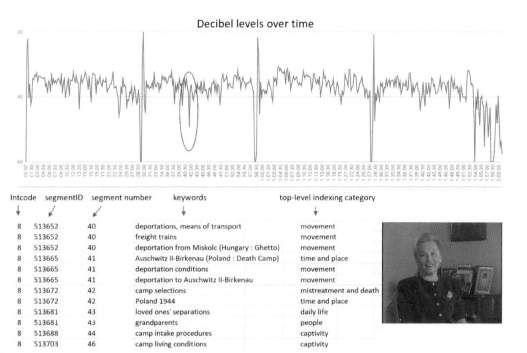

FIGURE 5.7: Voice intensity plot of Erika Jacoby's VHA testimony, with indexing terms for segments 40–46. Created by Campbell Yamane and Todd Presner. Erika Jacoby (July 11, 1994), interview 8, Visual History Archive, USC Shoah Foundation, https://vha.usc.edu/testimony/8.

in 1944 where they were selected and separated. But these keywords indicate nothing about her emotion, her delivery, her voice, or the fact that a critical decision she describes at this moment (for her mother not to hold another woman's baby) saved her mother's life. The keywords tend to guide our listening, and as finding aids, they help us to locate some of the manifest content of what is said in the testimonies.

To be sure, camp selections, loved ones' separations, and camp intake procedures are discussed at this moment in Jacoby's narrative. Her grandparents are sent in one direction, and she is sent in another. During the course of the selection, she is briefly separated from her mother, but they are both chosen for work by Josef Mengele. In addition to the semantic content of the narrative in which she describes "what happened" to the interviewer, something else happens in her telling of this traumatic scene on the ramp: Her voice cracks and briefly trembles; she looks up and, then, appears to look past the interviewer while raising her right hand as if to say goodbye to her grandparents again. She then says— fifty years later, in English—what she said in Hungarian to her grandparents on the selection ramp: "I see you tonight." Those four words embody a translated and transformed memory, articulated this time in slightly broken English, and followed by about eight seconds of silence. She takes a deep breath, closes her eyes, exhales, leans forward, and adjusts herself in the chair, as if to muster the courage and disposition to continue her testimony.

The transcript used for the video annotation reads: "And I waved to them. And I said, I'll see you tonight. [PAUSES FOR 8 SECONDS]."[59] Here, her speech has been corrected; proper punctuation and capitalization have been added; and the traces of her breathing have been removed. While the pause is quantified in duration, it is not understood as a breath unit. In fact, this standardization and regularization of her voice renders it remarkably flat. For this reason, we need to develop ways to listen to both the voice and the breath. This entire part of her testimony is spoken in a tone of questioning, in which the emotional pull of reimagining and narrating the trauma of family separation can be heard in the creakiness of her voice. The marked striations on the spectrogram (Figure 5.8) are evidence of glottal activity (low airflow through a constricted glottis) resulting in a creaky voice.[60]

Represented by these two spectrograms, these thirteen seconds of testimony are fraught with meaning and phonetic significance. First, there is the diminuendo of the three "I"s, which steadily decrease in size and intensity: from "I waved to them," to "I said," to the quietest, least intense articulation of the "I" in the phrase "I see you tonight." On the spectrogram, we can see a marked decrease in the intensity and amplitude of each instance in which Jacoby says "I." Second, the spectrogram shows the hesitant pauses, the white spaces, and the breath between the words, which is longest before she says, "I see you tonight." Thirdly, the entire spectrogram is full of vertical striations, indicating how Jacoby's voice has become choked up by the passage of air through her vocal folds. Lastly, and perhaps most profoundly, is the significant pitch change on the word "tonight," turning it into a question ("will I see you tonight?") not just of the past but also of the present.

Those four words are said simultaneously in more than one voice: the memory of her fifteen-year-old self, speaking to her grandparents in Hungarian on the ramp at Auschwitz in 1944, not knowing these would be the last words she would ever speak to them; the voice of a traumatic and translated repetition—articulated in English, fifty years later—of those same words, said in her home to the interviewer, in which both speaker and listener know the fate of her grandparents; and finally, a reflective, uncertain, and perhaps even exterior voice in which Jacoby is

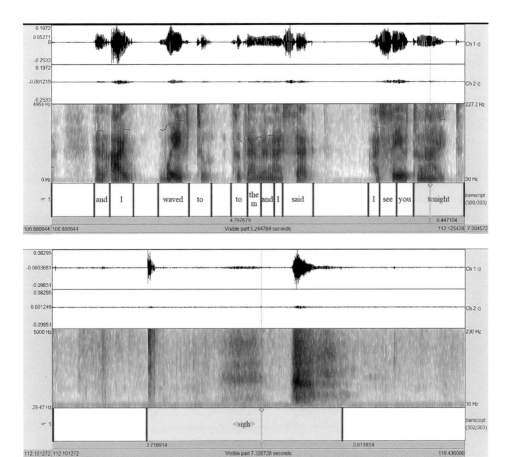

FIGURE 5.8: Spectrograms of Erika Jacoby's VHA testimony (1994, tape 2, minute 12:00), visualized using Praat. Created by Richard Wang and Todd Presner. The recording keyed to the spectrogram can be played on our website (https://holocaustresearchlab.com/book/chapter-5) or by using the QR code.

both testifying and questioning *how* to testify. When she says, "I see you tonight," it does not sound like a declarative statement of intent but rather like a trembling question. The pitch of her voice attains its peak at the word "tonight," perhaps to wonder how, in 1994, she can say and make sense of those traumatic words for the sake of bearing witness in the present. Not unlike Lawrence Langer's analysis of the survivor's "divided self" that "speaks from *in medias res*" and in another voice "detached from past and present," there is more than one voice in Jacoby's seemingly singular vocal expression.[61] In the sonic record, we hear Jacoby's voice simultaneously speaking from within, outside, and beyond the action described.

The second spectrogram is both a "pause" and a visualization of Jacoby's breath: her inhalation and exhalation. It shows a unit of breath in which she inhales deeply, a slight pause as she holds her breath, and then an exhalation of breath that diminishes in intensity over the next three seconds. The breath represents the transition between her narrative of family separation and the remainder of her story of survival in Auschwitz with her mother. The spectrogram captures this moment of respiratory release, as the black striations fade into gray and white over these brief moments of time. Perhaps, paradoxically, computational speech analysis might bring us back to the body, to reembody the voice and breath of testimony, as it were, by signaling the mortality of the human body and visualizing the ephemerality of vocal expressivity.

Ethics at the Limits of Algorithmically Generated Data

Far from offering definitive explanations, dispelling uncertainties, or arriving at truth through the factuality of measurements, these methods are intended to open up spaces of interpretation and differential approaches to listening. But as we calculate sonic variance in a whole testimony or across a corpus of testimonies, we need to ask: how do we avoid the risk of the other becoming merely "an 'example' of some set of finite qualities derived from the gradients of norm and anomaly of others?"[62] Data gradients, we argue, are not inherently unethical (and may, indeed, help us appreciate heterogeneity and variance), but they can become so when a definitive meaning and action is attributed to a particular output, or when the infinite multiplicity of the other is reduced to a finite set of measurements. The danger comes when an algorithm identifies outliers for action by isolating a series of attributes and passing a judgment about the meaning of those attributes. In what follows, we will explore how an ethics of the algorithm demands something else—namely, human judgment to scrutinize the processes and outputs of the algorithm in order to interpret what is recognized and open up new possibilities to guide our acts of close listening.

Starting again with the perspective of distance, our team investigated the relationship between changes in volume (decibel level) and changes in rhythm or speaking cadence (as measured by word count per minute). In one testimony, Moshe Taube describes his family and childhood in Poland. He mentions that he came from a family very fond of music, ranging from opera and classical music to Jewish folk songs. Suddenly, he laughs and smacks himself

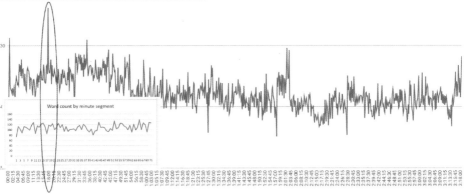

Decibel Levels over Time

Word count by minute segment

FIGURE 5.9: Voice intensity plot and word count per minute of Moshe Taube's VHA testimony. Created by Campbell Yamane and Todd Presner. Moshe Taube (March 7, 1996), interview 13063, Visual History Archive, USC Shoah Foundation, https://vha.usc.edu/testimony/13063.

on the forehead as if a deep memory had just come back to him at that moment: the Jewish folk song "Im ein ani li mi li" (If I am not for myself) comes to his mind, and he proceeds to sing the song and explain its significance in the Pirkei Avot.[63] The marked decibel high point during his singing follows a relative low point in the word count per minute, which corresponds to the rousing of his memory (Figure 5.9).[64] His rendition of the song is a remarkably uplifting, even buoyant moment, which functions as an auditory flashback that he performs in the testimony.[65] As Leah Wolfson astutely argues with regard to song in Holocaust testimony: "The performance of the song blends both past and present in a single moment. The songs unite seemingly opposing concepts: death and survival, narrative and interruption, and the chronology of history with personal memory."[66] In this sense, they "sound" differently from the rest of the testimony and represent a moment in which the survivor "retreats back into memory."[67]

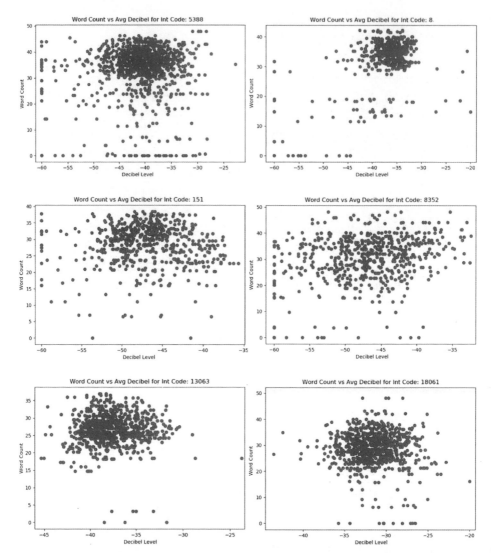

FIGURE 5.10: "Sonic consistency" visualizations for testimonies of Robert Ness, Erika Jacoby, Renee Firestone, Efraim Hoffman, Moshe Taube, and Abraham Bomba. The scales for word count and decibel level are relative to each testimony. Created by Campbell Yamane and Todd Presner.

This mode of detecting variation attuned to word count, decibel level, and pitch can also be used to examine the overall sonic consistency or variation of a testimony. To explore this idea, we devised an algorithm to measure volume and speaking cadence every fifteen seconds and to output the results as scatterplots. We plotted decibel level against words per minute for a small group of English-language interviews (Figure 5.10). Four dots were drawn for each minute of testimony, corresponding to the sampling frequency for volume (averaged every fifteen seconds) linked to word count (measured by minute and divided by four).[68] The visualizations depict the overall sonic consistency or inconsistency of a testimony, potentially prompting questions about variations in sound, including voice, delivery, and expressiveness. The single dots that are far outliers in each testimony are moments that generally correspond to tape changes or the end of a testimony when the survivor is showing photographs. The algorithm cannot, of course, tell us what the changes mean, only that there are variations. There are many reasons for changes in decibel and word counts, such as a testimony filmed in different locations, the emotive or expressive qualities of the voice, the tempo of recounting a particular story, code-switching or multilingualism, the nature of the questions being asked and answered, the interviewer's questions and interventions, or sometimes simply issues with the technical equipment.

In these visualizations, the more highly concentrated the dots are in one particular region, the more consistent the delivery of the testimony. The more dots are spread out horizontally, the more the testimony adduces variation in loudness; the more the dots are spread out vertically, the more the testimony adduces variation in speech tempo (words per minute). And finally, the more the dots are spread out in both directions, the more the testimony delivery varies widely by both of these metrics. Fewer dots indicate a shorter testimony and more dots indicate longer testimonies. They provide an overview of the sonic consistency (or inconsistency) of a given testimony and, through comparison, allow us to identify differences. It is at this point that the algorithm stops because its calculations have reached completion. The outputs might be grouped according to degrees of consistency or inconsistency, perhaps to create a larger data profile and draw attention to the outliers. But the data are not the end, and we do not learn more about the testimonies until we choose to delve into the micro-expressivities of the voice that gave rise to the outputs. In other words, if we are interested in enlarging our listening, we cannot stop at the calculation of a set of attributes; we must, instead, attune ourselves to the other's particularity by examining *what lies behind the dots.*

Robert Ness, a Polish-Jewish survivor of several forced labor and concentration camps in Estonia (interview code 5388, in the upper left of Figure 5.10), gives one of the longer testimonies in the corpus at four and a half hours in duration. Based on these two indicators, his delivery evidences significant variance. Listening to his testimony reveals that it is acoustically remarkable because he is an exceptionally animated storyteller. As he engages with the interviewer and responds to questions, he often ventriloquizes key moments in his story, raising and lowering his voice, leaning forward and backward, furrowing his brow, and sometimes moving his head and hands in and out of the frame as he gesticulates. His testimony is replete with multilingual references and quoted dialogue in Polish, Russian, German, and Yiddish. And finally, the last two tapes of his testimony are a "supplemental interview" consisting of discussions and performances of a series of songs that he sings in Russian, Polish, and Yiddish.

At one point in his testimony, Ness theatrically imitates the shouts of a Nazi officer as he describes how he survived in the Lagedi forced labor camp in Estonia. The Nazi officer had, ostensibly up until then, protected Ness because he spoke German and served as a runner in the camp. During an anti-Jewish roundup, Ness thought the officer was now targeting him, but the officer actually helped save his life.[69] Ness recalls that he went into a line of prisoners who he thought were going to be transferred from the camp, but the officer shouted at him: "*Raus!*" [get out!]. Ness disobeyed and got back in the line. The officer shouted at him again: "*Raus!*" And then, a third time: "*Raus!*" (Figure 5.11). In his testimony, Ness laughs about the three instances of "*Raus!*" and adds that the word was uttered as the most "Nazi Deutsch *Raus*" possible.

The spectrograms show the expulsion of Ness's breath each time he says "*Raus!*": a percussive burst of intensity coming from deep within his throat to form a rolled "r" (a voiced uvular fricative) and ending in a stream of breath as he finishes the "s." As Ness imitates the Nazi officer yelling at him, this multilingual insertion shifts us back to the scene of the camp in a surprising way: the order to "get out!" saved Ness's life, while the sounds of the order are uttered with a derisive humor that suggests Ness's own distance from the events. Indeed, these are not the sounds of *his* words, but in performing them, he has in certain ways made them his own.

Another time, toward the end of his testimony, as he is reflecting on his own survival and the price he paid, Ness cites the principle that there is no statute of limitations in Germany for prosecuting Nazi criminals and, then, passionately declares: "We will get you [Nazis] down until you die and starve and then maybe burn you on top of it, so be sure that you don't get up from your grave."[70] Speaking about two and a half times as fast as before, his cadence is thirty words in 8.75 seconds. Expressed in a tone of great passion, the words "down," "die," "starve," and "burn" are articulated with rhythmic intensity, as shown by the decibel levels, pitch changes, and the alternating, dark striations on the spectrogram. The emphasis on "burn" (a word articulated with the loudest intensity and highest pitch) signals his desire for vengeance on any Nazis caught. Ness's final phrase, "so be sure that you don't get up from your grave" functions as an afterthought, said in a significantly quieter and lower pitched voice, although at a faster cadence than the previous part of his statement (Figure 5.12).

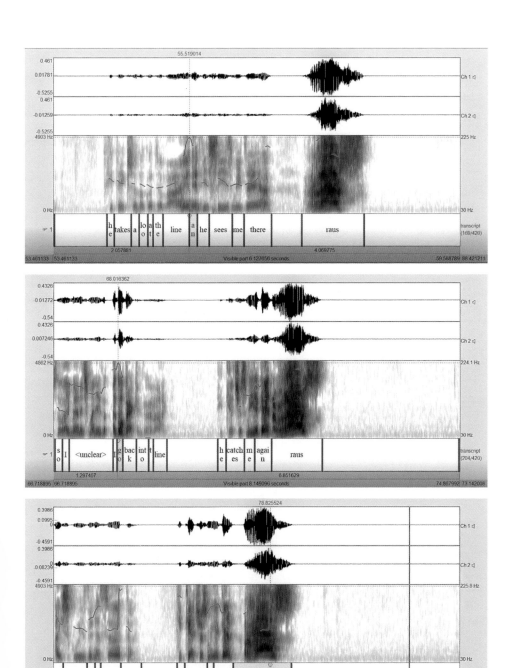

 FIGURE 5.11: Robert Ness's VHA testimony (October 31, 1995), tape 5, minute 20:00, visualized using Praat. The highlighted words are pitch highpoints in these sections. Created by Richard Wang and Todd Presner. Visual History Archive, USC Shoah Foundation, https://vha.usc.edu /testimony/5388. The recording keyed to the spectrogram can be played on our website (https://holocaustresearchlab.com/book/chapter-5) or by using the QR code.

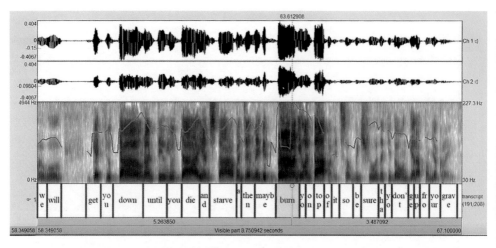

FIGURE 5.12: Robert Ness's VHA testimony (1995, tape 6, minute 17:00), visualized using Praat. Created by Richard Wang and Todd Presner. Visual History Archive, USC Shoah Foundation, https://vha.usc.edu/testimony/5388.

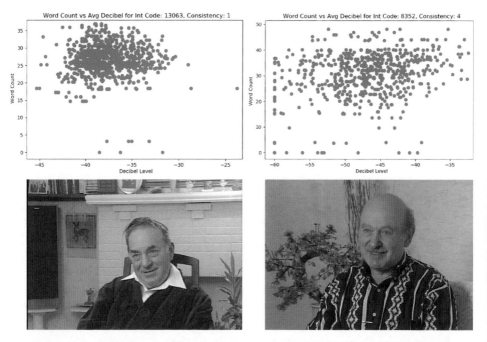

FIGURE 5.13: Comparisons of the sonic consistency visualizations for Moshe Taube and Efraim Hoffman. Created by Campbell Yamane and Todd Presner. Moshe Taube (March 7, 1996), interview 13063, https://vha.usc.edu/testimony/13063; Efraim Hoffman (November 5, 1995), interview 8352, https://vha.usc.edu/testimony/8352. Visual History Archive, USC Shoah Foundation.

Moving again from the data outputs to the particularity of the voice, we can compare Taube's testimony to that of Efraim (Fred) Hoffman, one of the more variant testimonies that we analyzed, as measured by the changes in volume and speaking tempo (Figure 5.13). At the end of the first hour and throughout much of the second hour of his testimony, the variance of Hoffman's cadence vacillates significantly, sometimes by more than one hundred words per minute over just a few minutes of narrative time (Figure 5.14). These changes in tempo are also accompanied by changes in loudness and numerous pauses in narration. However, when relying on the indexing terms in the database (such as the factuality of "camp intake procedures," "camp hunger," "camp diseases," "camp family interactions," "camp prisoner physical conditions," and "camp hospitals"), we have little indication of the emotional intensity of Hoffman's struggle to tell about his arrival in Auschwitz[71] and the deterioration of his father's health.[72] The memories of violence and loss saturate the narrative delivery and are signaled by the pauses, silences, breath turns, and stammering of his voice. The variance of these acts of

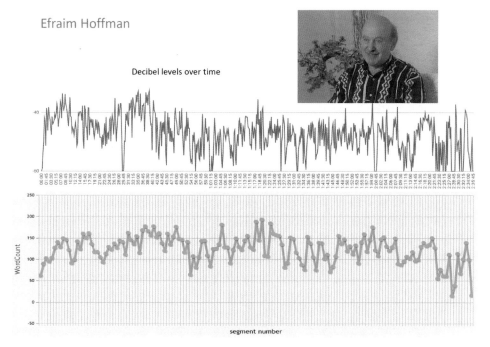

FIGURE 5.14: Efraim Hoffman's vocal intensity plot and word count per minute of testimony. Visualizations created by Campbell Yamane and Todd Presner. Efraim Hoffman (November 5, 1995), interview 8352, Visual History Archive, USC Shoah Foundation, https://vha.usc.edu/testimony/8352.

"saying" is almost entirely muted by standardized keywords or in a narrative transcript accounting for what was said.

Over the course of the third tape, Hoffman recounts being transferred with his father from Auschwitz to Buchenwald and then to a subcamp called Rehmsdorf, where they both worked as forced laborers. He details grueling work digging ditches, laying cable, standing for hours during roll calls, and being tortured and punished. He describes how his father became weaker and weaker, his face and legs becoming so swollen that he could not walk anymore. He says that he told his father to go to the camp hospital in the hopes that he will recover. The transcript is as follows: "My father started getting weaker and weaker. [CRYING] I could see he wasn't going to make it. [CRYING] So I told him to go up to that hospital. Maybe he will be there a couple days, he will feel better, he will come out."[73] In the spectrograms of this part of his testimony (Figure 5.15), we see the condensation and compression of Hoffman's words—the account of his father's deteriorating health shortly before he is murdered—separated by much longer pauses of crying, in which he is choked back with emotion, grief, and silence. He concludes the account of his father's death by telling the interviewer that, one day, all the sick people were simply taken away and gassed (Figure 5.16). He says in a very faint voice: "They killed them out." He, then, takes a breath and switches to a much more pronounced, reflective voice that emphasizes that he is now entirely by himself: "So here I was left all alone, a soul with these strange people in a strange world."[74] The marked striations on the spectrogram indicate the difficulty of putting this memory of radical isolation into words. Unlike a transcript, the visual structure of a spectrogram keys our attention to the gaps in the spoken voice, allowing us to perceive the ephemeral traces of the breath, the tempo of speech, and the changing qualities of the traumatized voice.

By attuning our listening to the micro-dimensions of spoken testimony, we retrieve voices and forms of expressivity that may have otherwise been consigned to oblivion. To do so, we must listen for more than one voice. Hoffman is telling the story of the death of his father and its effect on him as a boy, while reflecting upon and being affected by the telling of the story. When we listen to the radical particularity of the sonic record, we hear how testimony is delivered in more than one voice because the subject is—at once—within, outside of, and affected by the act of testifying. We might say, then, that these are the vocal signs of what Roland Barthes and Hayden White have called "middle-voicedness," that is, a grammatical category of speaking (or writing) in which the subject is interior to and affected by the actions related.[75] Although Barthes and White refer to the middle voice in writing, there seems to be a "middle-voicedness" in spoken

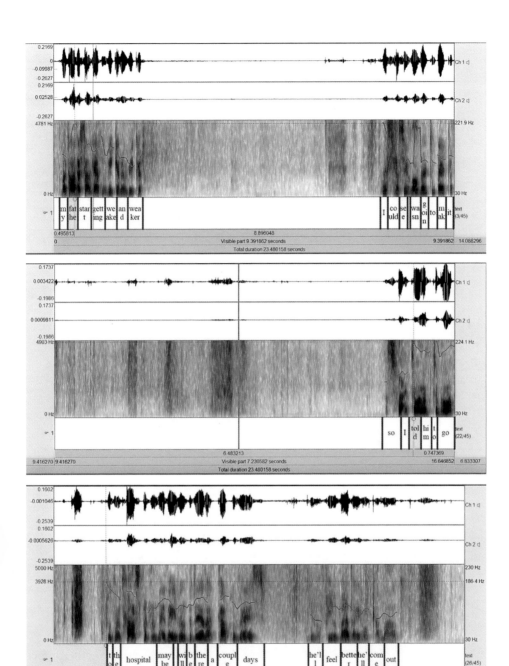

Waveform/spectrogram annotation labels:

Panel 1:
m y | fat he | star t | gett ing | we ake | an d | wea ker ... I | co uld e | se sn | wa oi n | g oi to | m ak | it text (3/45)

0.495813 | 8.896048 | 9.391862 | 14.088296
0 | Visible part 9.391862 seconds | Total duration 23.480158 seconds

Panel 2:
so | I | tol d | hi m o | t | go text (22/45)

9.416270 | 6.483213 | 0.747369 | 16.646852 | 6.833307
Visible part 7.230582 seconds | Total duration 23.480158 seconds

Panel 3:
t ol e th | hospital | may be | wi ll | b e | the re | a | coupl e | days ... he'l l | feel | bette r | he' ll | com e | out text (26/45)

0.871943 | 5.966008 | 23.480158
16.642207 | Visible part 6.837951 seconds | Total duration 23.480158 seconds

Figure 5.15: Efraim Hoffman's VHA testimony (1995, tape 3, minutes 27:00–28:00), spectrograms made using Praat. Created by Richard Wang and Todd Presner. Visual History Archive, USC Shoah Foundation, https://vha.usc.edu/testimony/8352. The recording keyed to the spectrogram can be played on our website (https://holocaustresearchlab .com/book/chapter-5) or by using the QR code.

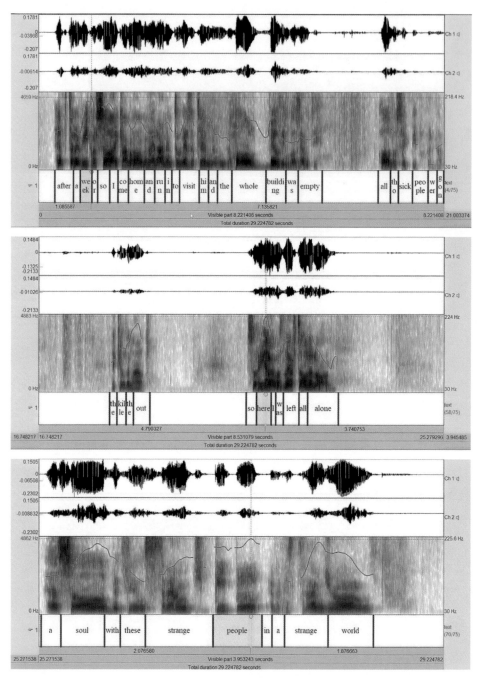

FIGURE 5.16: Efraim Hoffman's VHA testimony (1995, tape 3, minute 29:00), spectrograms made using Praat. Created by Richard Wang and Todd Presner. Visual History Archive, USC Shoah Foundation, https://vha.usc.edu/testimony/8352.

testimony. It is characterized by a particular use of language in which the survivor—through testifying—becomes a subject who not only remains within the action (even as certain parts of the testimony are conveyed through distance and reflection) but is simultaneously affected by and (re)constituted through the very acts of testifying. Perhaps, then, because of its quantitative precision, computational analysis can help us attend to middle-voicedness by attuning our listening to the multiplicity of the testimonial voice.

Coda: The Dialectic of Datafication

While language may reach certain limits in trying to ascribe adjectives to the voice or index sound, computation can quantify a multitude of dimensions of the voice, for better and for worse. From almost the moment that voices could be recorded on storage and playback devices, attempts have been made to quantify, measure, and visualize the voice. In the second half of the nineteenth century, machines such as the phonautograph, modeled on the middle ear, were used to inscribe sound waves and allow scientists to study sound vibrations.[76] By the start of the twentieth century, collections of "vocal fingerprints"—derived from "the rhythm of the voice"—were being created and used by criminologists, anthropologists, and linguists.[77] Not unlike the ways that photography was used to support phrenology and eugenics by aiding the quantification of facial features to create typologies, voice recordings were used to correlate criminality and pathology with ethnicity and physiology.[78] As Xiaochang Li and Mara Mills have argued: "By the early twentieth century, 'vocal portraits' were indeed added to archives of criminal records in police departments across Europe and the United States. Captured voices served a number of forensic purposes, from identification to physiognomy."[79]

By the 1940s, sound spectrograms were deployed in forensics and helped accelerate the development of "voiceprinting" technologies aimed at transforming speech into data. Physiological aspects of the voice could be quantified into tables enumerating a wide variety of vocal characteristics such as phonation and articulation in order to build databases for speaker identification and, eventually, "large-scale statistical data collection."[80] While the efficacy and accuracy of speaker identification have been contested (not least of all because the voice changes over time), law enforcement and defense companies today tout "voice forensic systems" that use massive voice databases and AI to identify speakers and analyze speech by parameters such as gender, age, language, region, ethnicity, and emotion.[81] Such systems have no intention of relating to the unique particularity of the other; they only require measurements as a means to some other end.

This ambition of measuring and quantifying the voice for recognition, character, and identification has been around for nearly a century. According to Li and Mills, the early twentieth-century "sound archive" gave way to the "acoustic database," in which speech and voice were absorbed into "the domain of computational pattern recognition" based on statistical indexing, rather than linguistic and semantic analysis.[82] These data-driven systems incorporated a wide range of approaches drawn from signal processing, information theory, and probabilistic statistics to quantify vocal variance for purposes of surveillance, security, and behavioral monitoring. This, then, is the dialectical underbelly of the algorithm: a computational approach to quantifying the infinite variability of the voice into "machine-trackable patterns" based on decomposing and recombining "spectrographic readings . . . to facilitate automatic indexing, searching, sorting, and retrieval."[83] In divorcing the voice from both the body and narrativity, the voice was transformed into bare data to be placed within machine-readable databases. The singularity of the individual and the particularity of the micro-level vocal utterance became absorbed into macro-level statistical systems.

In effect, voice-printing "exteriorizes" the voice (and human expressivity more generally) as something that can be measured, quantified, stored, and compared in order to do other things with it: deduce characteristics and behaviors, derive cultural patterns or traits, identify criminality or deviance, or track and surveil people. In creating massive voice files, the attributes of the particular are aggregated and analyzed to form generalized patterns that can then be used to measure deviations. In trying to derive general laws or typologies from contingent traces, individuals go missing, potentially reducing people to bare data. For this reason, this is precisely antithetical to the approach we took here. In fact, what the results of our voice analysis indicate is that we cannot correlate, predict, or extrapolate from singular vocal records without doing violence to the individual.

In 1955, around the same time Boder was completing much of the analytical work of his interviews, a team of researchers at the Center for Advanced Study in the Behavioral Sciences began a project called "The Natural History of an Interview."[84] Eventually bringing together dozens of researchers in fields that included psychiatry, linguistics, anthropology, communications, information studies, cybernetics, and media studies, the purpose of the project was to develop scientific tools for analyzing face-to-face communication, particularly the voice and nonverbal movements of the body, what anthropologist Ray Birdwhistell called "kinesics." The central way they did this was through the microanalysis of filmed interviews focused on transcribing, annotating, and analyzing every behavior, movement, interaction, and speech act. Although not, strictly speaking, computational, the researchers used technology (primarily film) to analyze human expressivity in ways that tended to treat people as specimens, not unlike the large-scale data-collection efforts behind voice-printing and statistical vocal portraits. By fastidiously documenting and characterizing every micro-level expression of an interaction (the articulation of each word, the specificity of a gesture or movement), they sought to use micro-analysis to extrapolate macro-level behaviors, characters, and traits. The researchers believed that the cataloging of all human movements and vocal expressions was foundational for a science of behavior that could abstract truths. In fact, Gregory Bateson, one of the founders of the field of cybernetics, situated this research within a group of convergent information studies fields emerging after World War II that aimed to study the science of behavior and human interactions. Bateson argued that the "major justification" of the group's procedures was the "assumption that the microscopic will reflect the macroscopic."[85] As such, the ultimate (and unrealized) goal, as articulated by Norman McQuown in the foreword to *The Natural History of the Interview*, was nothing short of establishing "the foundations of a general theory of the structure of human communicative behavior."[86]

Informed by an ethics of relationality and particularity, our approach to computational voice analysis is situated against these grand ambitions. But we enumerate the risks here in order to acknowledge that any kind of datafication of human attributes, especially the uniqueness of voice, has a dialectical underbelly. In our analysis of the voice in Holocaust testimonies, we drew a limit at extrapolating or generalizing anything from the individual vocal recordings of Holocaust survivors. When we undertake "distant listening"—through vocal intensity plots, acoustic spectrograms, the identification of silence, or visualizations of voice variability—it is to attune our listening to *who* is speaking, to identify differences in *how* speakers articulate their story, and to position us as distant witnesses attending to the particularities of vocal expression. By listening to what has been said through the multitude of acts of saying, our analyses aim to proliferate meanings and interpretations.

But all measurements of voice or human expressivity run the risk of reduction and datafication, including the ones in this chapter. The process we followed was to move from distant to close listening and to avoid extrapolating something macroscopic from micro-level expressions. We used computational speech analysis tools and algorithmic methods to pause the flow of speech and find differences that open up spaces for listening, commentary, and interpretation.[87] An ethical measurement or quantification of voice must not turn survivors into data specimens to be used for some other end, cut off from the ear that apprehends those voices, sounds, and measurements. Since survivors bear witness in both narrative language and forms of paralanguage (vocal inflections, voice qualities, paralinguistic cues, silences, changes in timbre and articulation, and a wide range of expressive sounds and gestures produced by the body), we sought to attune our listening to a combination of phonetic and semantic meanings.

By themselves, algorithms and computational methods cannot "listen"—in the sense of empathetic understanding, involvement, and obligation—because they have no relationality to who or what is being heard. And just as importantly, they are not affected in the process of listening. But algorithms and computational methods can open up spaces for interpretation and meaning-making because of the ways they identify, quantify, and track variations. These tools do not merely have to be "a processing of information . . . reduced to formulas and rules of method" but can be part of an approach to distant listening that results in what LaCapra calls "empathetic unsettlement."[88] Resisting closure and definitive understandings, we use technology to listen for the radically particular and attune ourselves to the differential voices of the survivor. There are many ways to do this, and the propositional methods examined in this chapter are examples of digital humanities approaches. When we bring together the semantic and the phonetic, we aim to foreground the uniqueness of the body: the traumatized body, the body in pain, the body that speaks, the body that sighs, the body that goes silent, the body that breathes, the body that cries, the body that stammers, the body that shouts, but also *our* body—the body that listens. All of these sounds are captured by and encountered through forms of technology for us to attune our listening.

Perhaps every testimony has more than one voice, apprehensible through phonation as a kind of middle-voicedness in which the subject is both inside the action and changed through the acts of testifying. The subject of testimony is in the scene, reflecting on the scene, and bearing witness for secondary and tertiary witnesses, while being affected in the very process of testifying. This is not something that can be accounted for in indexing systems focused on the factuality of "the said" or the semantic content of the narrative. Because the subject of testimony speaks in more than one voice, the testimony ought to be heard through more than one modality of listening. These other voices are specifically recognizable in phonation rather than in semantics, and they evidence, to apply Langer's conceptualization, "a split voice," "another voice," and "a divided self."[89]

Much like the ethical stance that Saul Friedländer creates for his historical narrative (to let in the voices of victims, as jolts and particular perspectives, bearing witness in their own words), our listening needs to let in the sounds of the voice and tarry with the sonic dimensions of the testimony.[90] Rejecting omniscient narration and formalized objectivity, White characterizes this as Friedländer's "middle-voicedness."[91] Distant listening by algorithm and computation may also have a middle-voicedness when the tertiary (or distant) witness is involved in—and also affected by—acts of listening. There is no "neutral" (devocalized) voice to tell the story, and there is no "neutral" (deauralized) ear to hear the story. As such, we need to move beyond "neutral" data to represent expression and listening. Mediated by technologies of storage and analysis, voice and ear remain inside the telling and the listening. Both are affected relationally and give rise to new spaces of encounter. This mediation—between voice and ear, between distant and close, between phonetic and semantic, between data and narrative, between algorithmic and humanistic—can form a foundation for an ethics of distant witnessing.

נקמה	REVENGE
Abraham Bomba	**Abraham Bomba**
Transcribed by Miriam Koral	*Translated by Todd Presner*

איך וועל אייך די געשיכטע דערצײַלען כּסדר	I will tell you the story again and again
כאָטש וואָס דאָס איז "אַקציע" ווייסט דאָך איעדער.	Though everyone knows what an "action" is.
טרעבלינקע, אוישוועענטשעם פֿאַר ייִדישע גריבער	Treblinka and Oświęcim were Jewish graves
אַהין האָט מען געשיקט אונדזערע שוועסטער און ברידער.	Where they sent our sisters and brothers.
און אויב ווילט איר וויסן וואָס דאָרט איז פֿאָרלאָפֿן	And if you want to know what happened there
דערפֿרעגט שוין די מענטשן וואָס זענען אַנטלאָפֿן	Then ask those who escaped.
עס מוז דאָך ווער בלײַבן אויף נאָך דער מלחמה	Someone must remain when the war is over
געדענקט זשע, ברידער, צו נעמען נקמה.	Remember, brothers, to take revenge
זע, עס טרעפֿט שוין איינער—ער פּרובירט צו אַנטלויפֿן.	See, someone is coming—he tries to escape.

ער גייט צו די דראָטן און וויל אים
איבערקויפֿן.

He goes to the wires to bribe one of them.

געלט שפּילט קיין ראָלע, ער האָט עס גענוג,

Money plays no role, he has enough,

ער גייט צו די דראָטן מיט לאַנגזאַמע טריט.

He goes to the wires with slow steps.

נאָר פּלוצלינג אַ שאָס, עס ווערט אים פֿינצטער פֿאַר די אויגן

But suddenly a shot, he becomes faint—

ער ליגט שוין פֿון שמערצן צוזאַמענגעטרויטן

He falls down, curled up in pain.

דאָס אומשולדיקע בלוט שרײַט און עס רופֿט:

Innocent blood cries out and calls:

"נקמה, נקמה, געדענקט אָן דעם גוט."

"Revenge, revenge, remember its worth."

איצט וווינען מיר אין ה'ס'ג, אין האָלצענע הײַזער—

Now we live at HASAG, in wooden houses.—*

זיי זענען אונדזערע באַקליידער און אונדזערע באַשפּײַזער.

They give us clothes and sustenance.

אַמעריקע אײַלט זיך נישט, ענגלאַנד האָט צײַט,

America is in no hurry, England takes its time,

די רוסן זיי גייען, אָבער זיי זענען נאָך ווײַט.

The Russians are coming but they are still far away.

און ווידער אַן אַקציע אין מיטן דער נאַכט,

And another action in the middle of the night,

500 קרבנות אויפֿן בית־עולם געבראַכט.

Five Hundred Jewish victims were killed.

פֿאַר דער וועלט זאָגן זיי זיי פֿירן מלחמה

To the world they say they are waging war,

אָבער קומען וועט דער צײַט פֿון נעמען נקמה.

But the time will come to take revenge.

---

* After escaping from Treblinka and returning to Częstochowa in the summer of 1943, Bomba was deported to the Hugo Schneider Aktiengesellschaft (HASAG), a forced labor camp at a German ammunition factory, where he survived until the end of the war.

UNTITLED SECOND POEM
Abraham Bomba
Transcribed by Miriam Koral

UNTITLED SECOND POEM
Abraham Bomba
Translated by Todd Presner

געשען איז דאָס אַ טאָג נאָך יום כיפּור—	It happened a day after Yom Kippur—
אַ געשריי, אַ גוואַלד, עס איז נעבעך ביטער.	A scream, a cry, the situation is dreadful.
אַן אַקציע האָט זיך בײַ אונדז אָנגעהויבן,	An action had begun where we were,
מיר שטייען אַלע און גלאָצן מיט די אויגן.	We all stand there, our eyes wide open.
מיר האָבן נאָך דאָס נישט געוווּסט	We didn't know this yet
אַז פֿון אונדז ייִדן וועט זײַן אַ ביסל מיסט.	But from us Jews, only a bit of trash would be left.
מיר הייבן אָן לויפֿן איבער די גאַסן,	We start running through the streets,
אין אַלע עקן שטאָט שטייט אויסגעשטעלט וואַכן.	And on every corner of the city guards are watching.
צו דער אַרבעט פֿון דער געטאָ לאָזט מען נישט מער,	Going to work from the ghetto is no longer allowed,
די זשאַנדאַרמען האַלטן גרייט דאָס געווער.	The gendarmes have their weapons ready.
אין די גאַסן לויפֿן ייִדישע פּאָליציי,	And the Jewish police run through the streets,
טרײַבן אַרײַן אין הויז מיט אַ געשריי.	They barge into homes shouting:
"פֿלוצלינג, די און די גאַסן זאָלן ייִדן אַרויסגיין	"All Jews get out immediately on this and that street.
און וואָס דאָרט וועט זײַן וועט איר באַלד זען."	And you will soon find out what happens next."
מענער רעכטס און פֿרויען לינקס, טוט מען יאָגן,	Men are chased to the right and women to the left,
אָדער אונדז פֿירט מען שוין דערשאָסענע אויף אַ וואַגן.	Or we will be shot and forced into a cattle car.
די ביסט שוין בײַ די בעטאַלאָריע אויך,	You too are already at the designated spot.

דעם אויף רעכטס, אַ פּאַטש, יענעם אויף
לינקס, אַ קאָפּיע אין בויך.

This one on the right, a slap, that one on the left, a kick to the belly.

די אויסגעוויילטע זענען אין דער פֿאַבריק
אַרײַן,

The selected ones go to the factory,

און אונדז יאָגט מען צו דער באַן.

And they chase us to the train.

מען צײלט אונדז איינס, צוויי, דרײַ, פֿיר
פֿינעף,

They count us, one, two, three, four, five,

נאָר שנעלער מיט דעם ייִדישן טינעף.

Move faster, you Jewish filth.

אַזוי זענען מיר צו דער ראַמפּ
אָנגעקומען,

This is how we arrived on the ramp,

אָבער די וואַגאָנען זענען שוין געוועזן
מיט אַנדערע קרבנות פֿאַרנומען.

But the cattle cars were already full with other victims.

מע באַפֿעלט אונדז צוריק אַהיימגייין—

They command us to go back home—

אין די גאַסן, אַ פֿרייד מיט אַ געוויין.

In the streets, both joy and sorrow.

דער האָט זײַן משפּחה; יענעם, נישט
באַשערט.

This one has his family; that one wasn't so lucky.

מע זאָגט אַז די אַקציע האָט
אויפֿגעהערט.

It's said that the action has stopped.

די שוואַרצע שטייען ווייטער אויף די
גאַסן

The Nazis are in the streets again.

זיי הערן נישט אויף צו שיסן, דערבײַ
טוען זיי לאַכן.

They keep on shooting, laughing all the while.

אַזוי איז אַדורך דרײַ טאָג, און הער בײַ
זיך ס׳איז געווער

And three days went by like this, with sounds of weapons

און עס איז אַ פֿרישער קלאָג.

And it is a new misfortune.

אַחוץ דעם ערשטן וואָס מ׳האָט געשיקט
טראַנספּאָרט,

Besides those sent in the first transport,

האָט מען צוויי טויזנט דערשאָסן אויפֿן
אָרט.

They shot two thousand on the spot.

איצט האָט מען אונדז ווידער געפֿירט צו
דער באַן,

Now they brought us back to the train,

און ווי אַ באַלעם האָט מען אונדז
געוואָרפֿן אַרײַן.

And like rubber balls, they threw us in.

און אַז מיר זענען שוין אין וואָגן אַריבנגעקומען	And as we were shoved into the cattle car
האָט מען אַ סך ייִדישע לעבנס צוגענומען.	Many Jewish lives were lost.
אין וואָגן זענען מיר צו הונדערט מאַן,	We are in a cattle car with a hundred people,
און נישט יעדער וויסט וואָס פֿון אונדז וועט זײַן.	And no one knows what will become of us.
איינער זאָגט צו דער אַרבעט, דער צווייטער, אין פֿײַער,	One person says we are going to work, another says into the fire,
און דערווײַל האָט יעדער בײַ זיך וואָס עס איז אים טײַער.	And meanwhile, everyone holds tight what is dear to them.
פֿון דער ראַמפּע פֿאָרן מיר צו דער שטאָט	From the ramp we travel to the city
דאָ ווערט מען געוואויער אונדזער קלאָג.	Here we learn of our misfortune.
איין קריסט שפּײַט צו אונדז דורכן פֿענצטערל אַרײַן,	And through the little window, a Christian spits on us,
נאָך טרעבלינקע, בראַכט אויס אַ צווייטער אין געוויין.	"To Treblinka," another bursts out with a cry.

Source: Abraham Bomba (Aug 14, 1996), interview 18061, Visual History Archive, USC Shoah Foundation, tape 7 (http://vha.usc.edu/testimony/18061).

What Were Survivors Asked?

Using Machine Learning to Constellate 89,759 Interviewer Questions

With Michelle Lee

Since the end of the war, Holocaust survivors have been asked thousands upon thousands of interview questions.[1] Among other things, those questions aimed to document the truth of what survivors experienced, how they perceived and learned about various events, how they and others reacted and behaved, how they dealt with trauma, and what meaning they hope will come from their experiences. The purpose of this digital project is to propose a machine-learning methodology to examine nearly ninety thousand questions asked during the foundational years of four archives: 16,360 questions asked by David Boder in 1946 to 111 survivors; 16,396 questions asked to the first 192 interviewees of what would later become the Yale Fortunoff Archive (1979–1983); 16,426 questions asked to 146 interviewees by the Survivors of the Shoah Visual History Foundation between 1994 and 1996; and, finally, 40,577 questions asked by people using the Dimensions in Testimony (DiT) platform (August 2018 through April 2021) to interact with three Holocaust survivors.

For the first three archives, we sought to keep the total number of questions about the same for the sake of comparison. DiT, on the other hand, is an open-ended platform in which new questions are constantly being asked by users. For all four, we decided to focus on a set of interviews that were done in the early years of each archive or project. Although interview methodologies evolved and became more standardized over time, these early interviews provide important insights into the formation of the future archival collections.[2] Moving from a single interviewer to a handful of interviewers to hundreds and soon thousands, and now potentially tens of thousands of interviewers or more, we can trace a remarkable set of continuities—and a remarkable set of critical shifts—in the priorities, topics, and interests of interviewers. While some of these shifts can be attributed to generational changes and expertise, the topics also show the prevalence and recession of certain themes and narrative strategies over time.

What can we learn by comparing questions asked by interviewers over more than seven decades? What topics were addressed most and least frequently, when, by whom, and to whom? What questions (and how many) were asked about specific experiences, such as deportation, mistreatment, or liberation? What questions were specific to a particular moment, and what new topics and interests have emerged over time? Which interviewees were asked the least and greatest number of questions, and which ones were asked about the least and greatest number of different topics? In a given corpus, are there any salient differences in terms of questions posed to men versus women?

Our analysis is guided by a digital humanities methodology developed for parsing, clustering, and classifying semantic meaning in big data. In our case, we are working with a dataset consisting of 89,759 questions (totaling 616,185 words) and 89,654 answers (totaling 7,339,138 words).[3] The questions come from a total of 452 testimonies. To begin to investigate and pose answers to the questions above, we needed a method to cluster together similar questions to compare topics and narrative strategies over time. The machine-learning methodology described below provides an algorithmic model to generate what we call "subjunctive metadata"—that is, possible and plausible outputs for large-scale, comparative analysis. Those outputs rest upon various layers of training and interpretation, including decisions about clustering, labeling, and visualization. We consider this to be distinct from "factual metadata," in which an algorithm makes determinations through counting or template matching of digitized documents.[4]

As we explain, our results could have been somewhat different depending on the parameters and specifications used. It is important to underscore that we are *thinking with algorithms*, not setting them free on a dataset and hoping they will return automatically with "factual" or "correct" results. Classification—whether by human, machine, or both—rests on a series of decisions that give rise to certain ways of knowing and structuring knowledge.[5] We document and discuss those decisions below. Rather than considering our results as definitive and final, we see them as algorithmically guided, propositional constellations. They allow us to ask and, with certain caveats, pose answers to research questions at scale as well as interrogate the use of a machine-learning methodology for analyzing humanistic big data.

Question Extraction and Interview Methodologies
from the Four Corpora

To extract the interview questions, we started with testimony transcripts from the four different archives and filtered the data to lines spoken only by the interviewers. We excluded lines said by the camera crew, annotations or commentary added to the transcripts, or any bracketed comments meant to provide clarification for readers or listeners. The interviewer lines included both interrogative sentences and imperative sentences ("tell me about" or "please describe") prompting the interviewee to speak. Then, we used a sentence tokenizer to separate sentences in each line and save them in a Python list.

For the Boder corpus, we extracted the questions he asked to 111 interviewees, namely Jewish survivors of concentration camps and non-Jewish war refugees.[6] Many of Boder's questions seemed to be directed at fact-finding, as he sought to understand reasons for what happened, how the survivors reacted, and what was done to them. Some questions were open-ended and elicited long narrative responses, while others were simple yes/no questions. Still others expressed degrees of skepticism or disbelief. Some topics were particularly important for Boder, while other topics were scarcely addressed, partly owing to the framing of his conversations as "topical autobiographies," as opposed to "life interviews" (see chapter 3).

The vast majority of the early interviews completed for the Holocaust Survivors Film Project and the Video Archive for Holocaust Testimonies at Yale (later integrated into the Yale Fortunoff Archive) were conducted by Laurel Vlock and Dori Laub, either alone or together. The remainder were conducted by about two dozen additional interviewers, some of whom collaborated directly with Vlock and/or Laub in the interview process. These early interviews were done in English between 1979 and 1983 with survivors living in the United States. Noah Shenker points out that although the archive's interview protocols were not formalized until 1984, "there are nonetheless some fundamental consistencies among the interviews recorded at Yale and its affiliate projects since the establishment of the archive in the 1970s."[7] Both the videographic and interview protocols were meant to "emphasize the primacy of the witness" and develop modes of "active listening" to open up pathways for the survivor to articulate traumatic memories.[8] This is further underscored by Joanne Rudof, who began working with the testimonial archives in 1984. She described the interview training to be "based on Laub's methodology of empathic and knowledgeable listeners following the lead of the survivors rather than using questionnaires or journalistic techniques in which the 'interviewer' controls the narrative."[9] While certain topics (such as prewar and postwar life) were not covered as extensively in these early interviews as in later ones, Rudof argues that "these early recordings are of inestimable value since they often represent the first time survivors and witnesses had spoken at length of their experiences to anyone other than fellow survivors."[10]

As the Fortunoff Archive's interviewing approach developed over time, the importance of "giving survivors their voice," to use Geoffrey Hartman's words, would become paramount.[11] According to the website of the Fortunoff Archive, its interviewing methodology "stresses the leadership role of the witness in structuring and telling his or her own story."[12] Emphasizing the sanctity of the bond between the listener and the survivor, Hartman writes that the interviews are "intended to 'open the book' of the survivor's mind ... [by] recording the psychological and emotional milieu of the struggle for survival, not only then but also now."[13] As such, questions are meant to allow the voice of the survivor to come through, while opening up spaces of encounter in the present with the deep and traumatic memories of the past.[14]

For the Shoah Foundation interviews, we chose 146 English-language interviews amounting to 16,426 questions, all of which were recorded in the United States between 1994 and 1996.[15] While these interviews are just a tiny fraction of the fifty-two thousand interviews conducted by the foundation worldwide in the 1990s and early 2000s, they represent some of the very first interviews that the foundation recorded in the United States, and they played an important role in developing its interview methodology.[16] That methodology was developed "in consultation with Holocaust historians, psychologists, and experts in the field of oral history" and sought to create a coherent narrative that covered life before the war, life during the war and the Holocaust, and life after the war.[17] Interviews tended to conclude with the survivor showing photographs (and naming who is in them), answering reflective questions, and offering a future message.

Following a general chronology, the interviewer prepared "topical questions" that corresponded to the specific experiences of the survivors in the three life moments. For instance, prewar questions might include education, schooling, family life, religion, and early experiences with antisemitism; life during the war varied according to the survivors' specific experiences, but generally included life under German occupation and, as applicable, experiences such as ghettos, deportation, concentration camps, family separations, forced labor, and hiding; life after the war included topics such as displaced persons camps, emigration, professional work, and family; and, finally, reflective topics addressed larger questions about meaning, legacy, and messages to future generations.[18]

Initiated by the USC Shoah Foundation in 2014, Dimensions in Testimony (DiT) is a digital platform in which users can ask questions to survivors through an interactive form of volumetrically captured testimony. All of the answers were recorded during a carefully scripted, multi-day interview. However, users of the DiT platform—either in a formal museum setting or online through the "IWitness" portal—do not have access to any of the interview questions used during the recording. Instead, the platform is trained to match questions asked by users to the most appropriate, prerecorded answer (see chapter 7). Our team was provided with the original interview questions used in the recording, the answers given by the interviewee, and all the questions (called "utterances") asked by users who have interacted with three survivors on the DiT platform: Renee Firestone, Janine Oberrotman, and Anita Lasker-Wallfisch (2018–2021). Our analysis below focuses only on the user-generated questions asked to these three survivors: 40,577 questions. There is no identifying information associated with the users who posed the questions.

Since these user questions were transcribed by an automatic speech recognition (ASR) algorithm, there were errors and misspellings in some of them. We performed an iterative process to remove user utterances that were unintelligible or not questions by applying general rules such as removing phrases with less than two words, removing nonsensical phrases, and keeping questions or interrogative statements based on frequent keywords we found in the corpus. When the semantic meaning was clear and an answer was played, we corrected obvious spelling errors in the ASR. Since we wanted to focus on the use of the platform for generating and posing new questions, we made the decision not to include the questions asked by the interviewers during the original recording process.

Methodology: SBERT Sentence Embeddings and K-Means Clustering

To identify the topics covered in the extracted questions, we used a neural network algorithm developed by Google called Bidirectional Encoder Representations from Transformers (BERT).[19] BERT is a contextual language model trained on English-language Wikipedia and BookCorpus novels. It was developed for understanding search queries in natural language expressions. In 2020, BERT powered nearly every English-language Google search and was also developed for dozens of languages across the world. Since BERT's language model has been touted for its ability to learn words in context and parse the intent behind queries, we thought it could be used to help cluster together similar questions.

To test this out, we employed the following process: We first uploaded the CSV file of each corpus's interview questions into a Google Collaboratory notebook to apply the Sentence-BERT (SBERT) Python framework, which is based on the original BERT algorithm.[20] The idea behind utilizing SBERT was to take advantage of its computational efficiencies alongside BERT's bidirectional nature, which allows the embeddings to be contextually informed by the words and phrasing of each question or sentence. We took the column of questions from the CSV and saved it into a list, which was the desired input format for the algorithm. Then, we computed sentence-level embeddings on the list of questions with the pretrained model "bert-base-nli-mean-tokens." This pretrained BERT model was applied to produce embeddings for each question in our dataset. The output was a fixed size, 768-length embedding vector for each of the 89,759 questions.[21]

After the embeddings were produced, we performed K-Means clustering to group similar questions together. We chose the K-Means clustering algorithm because it is a relatively simple method that scales well to larger datasets. It is also an unsupervised machine-learning model, which would allow us to investigate how questions were grouped together without manually labeling the data beforehand (something that is needed for supervised approaches).[22] After some experimentation, we settled on a hundred clusters ($k = 100$) for each corpus, which we believed would capture and cluster most of the topics among the questions in each dataset.[23] Every question was assigned to only one cluster.

Similar to topic modeling, the algorithm does not name the topics or assign any kind of semantic meaning; it simply tells us that it has determined that certain questions can be gathered together in a cluster. It is up to us to figure out if we agree and to assign labels. We defined "a cluster" as a grouping of questions determined computationally by SBERT and K-Means clustering. After confirming similarities among questions within a given cluster, we assigned a label, which we called a "question topic."[24] Proceeding corpus by corpus, we created a total of 310 question topics for the 89,759 questions. We also created twenty-five "parent topics" to group the topics together.

It is important to note that the embeddings generated by SBERT (the vectors) are the same each time, but the clusters are not.[25] With K-Means from the scikit-learn Python library, similar questions were grouped together using a recursive process based on the Euclidean distance similarity measure between embedded data points. Most clusters appeared to be coherent with this process. However, as we describe below, there were some problematic results, and a few clusters did not make much sense within the context of experiences of the Holocaust. We suspect this may be because the initial SBERT embeddings were produced from a general, pretrained model (Wikipedia and BookCorpus), as opposed to a Holocaust-specific corpus.

After the clustering algorithm grouped the questions based on the individual SBERT embeddings for each of the four corpora, we manually reviewed the clusters. We exported the results into a spreadsheet to assign topic labels to the clusters, combine or split apart certain clusters, and, to the extent possible, correct obvious errors and problematic groupings. The last step involved reading and reassigning what we considered to be incorrectly clustered questions. At the same time, because not every question fit comfortably into a topic, we sometimes used broad descriptions to refer to heterogenous groupings of questions. While the overall process could potentially be used to produce training data for a future Holocaust and genocide-specific machine-learning model, we also found certain limitations and problems that need to be addressed (and are discussed below).

Comparisons across Four Corpora

To explore changes in interview methodologies, questions, and topics over time, we developed a series of interactive visualizations in Tableau (Figure 5.17). The visualizations function as generative abstractions through which we can observe similarities, scrutinize groupings, and query arrangements. Far from depicting a definitive truth or factual certainty, the visualizations function as constellations or lenses for relational thinking because they allow us to see, query, and compare results at a scale that would not be possible otherwise. We offer a multiplicity of visualizations through which readers can explore the 89,759 interview questions in various contexts: by comparing the questions in a given corpus, by comparing the questions across corpora, by exploring the questions and answers in sequence within a testimony, and by exploring testimonies by question topics.

The first visualization depicts four bubble charts organized according to the twenty-five "parent topics," which contain 310 distinct question topics, for all 89,759 interview questions. Larger bubbles indicate questions that are asked more frequently (using exactly the same phrasing), while smaller bubbles indicate uniquely worded questions. For instance, prompting questions (such as "Yes?," "Well?," and "Nu?"), as well as "What?" and "Why?" are the basic questions that Boder asks the most often. For the Fortunoff Archive, the most frequent questions include "What did you see?," "Why?," "How?," and variations of "What did you think?" For the USC Shoah Foundation, the most frequent questions are about names ("What was her name?" and "What was his name?") and narrative sequence ("What happened?" and "Then what happened?"). For the Dimensions in Testimony corpus, the most frequent questions are pleasantries

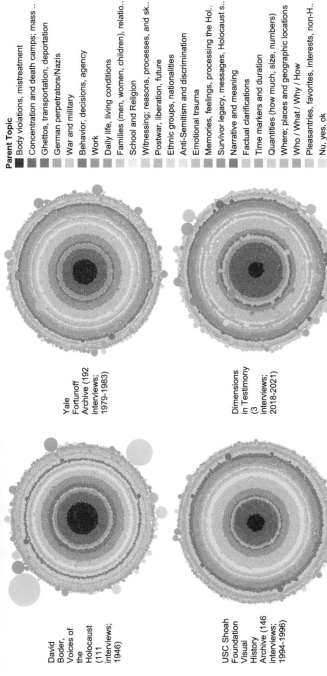

Parent Topic
- Body violations, mistreatment
- Concentration and death camps; mass ..
- Ghettos, transportation, deportation
- German perpetrators/Nazis
- War and military
- Behavior, decisions, agency
- Work
- Daily life, living conditions
- Families (men, women, children), relatio..
- School and Religion
- Witnessing; reasons, processes, and sk..
- Postwar, liberation, future
- Ethnic groups, nationalities
- Anti-Semitism and discrimination
- Emotional trauma
- Memories, feelings, processing the Hol..
- Survivor legacy, messages, Holocaust s..
- Narrative and meaning
- Factual clarifications
- Time markers and duration
- Quantities (how much, size, numbers)
- Where; places and geographic locations
- Who / What / Why / How
- Pleasantries, favorites, interests, non-H..
- Nu, yes, ok

David Boder, Voices of the Holocaust (111 interviews; 1946)

Yale Fortunoff Archive (192 interviews; 1979-1983)

USC Shoah Foundation Visual History Archive (146 interviews; 1994-1996)

Dimensions in Testimony (3 interviews; 2018-2021)

Corpus	Parent Topic (Distinct Count)	Question Topic (Distinct Count)	Interviewee (Distinct Count)	Count of Question	Distinct count of Question
David Boder, Voices of the Holocaust (111 interviews; 1946)	20	93	111	16,360	12,621
Yale Fortunoff Archive (192 interviews; 1979-1983)	24	92	192	16,396	13,969
USC Shoah Foundation Visual History Archive (146 interviews; 1994-1996)	24	85	146	16,426	14,782
Dimensions in Testimony (3 interviews; 2018-2021)	24	114	3	40,577	24,898
Grand Total	25	310	452	89,759	64,578

FIGURE 5.17: 89,759 interview questions by corpus, visualized as twenty-five parent topics. Created by Michelle Lee and Todd Presner. Interactive visualization on Tableau: hrl.pub/c826db.

(such as "How are you?," "What's your favorite color?," "What's your favorite food?") followed by questions about age (variations of "How old are you?"), "Where are you from?," "How did you survive?," and "Do you hate the Germans?".[26] A little more than half the questions in Dimensions in Testimony (24,898 of 40,577) are unique questions, and still many of those are grammatical variations of one another. This stands in contrast to the institutional archives where the vast majority of interview questions are uniquely phrased.[27]

Besides depicting every question by parent topics, the visualizations also show the proportional relationships between parent topics. Who, what, where, when, why, and how questions (including quantities, time markers, and geographic clarifications) form the outer ring of each of the corpora: 24 percent of Boder's total questions fall into these clusters; 21 percent of the Fortunoff questions are in these clusters; 19 percent of the USC Shoah Foundation questions are in these clusters; but they represent less than 10 percent of the questions asked in Dimensions in Testimony. This could be explained by its users being less familiar with (or perhaps less interested in) the conventional biographical dimensions of the testimonies, such as the temporal and geographic contours of the survivor's life story in relationship to the Holocaust. Instead, we see an interest in "pleasantries," a topic that includes introductions ("how are you today?"), goodbyes ("thank you so much for sharing your story"), "favorites," and "interests" (movie, song, color, food, book, joke, hobby, holiday, and so forth). This parent topic (pleasantries, favorites, interests, and non-Holocaust questions) is unique to the Dimensions in Testimony project and bespeaks the contemporary engagement of students and the general public with the platform.

Prompting questions ("Yes?", "Okay?", "Nu?") are common in Boder's corpus (about 13 percent of the total questions), while pleasantries are common in—and unique to—the Dimension in Testimony corpus (almost 10 percent of all questions). Certain parent topics such as emotional trauma, antisemitism and discrimination, memories and feelings, and survivor legacy are completely absent in Boder's corpus, but comprise 20 percent of the questions in the Fortunoff Archive testimonies, 18 percent of the questions in the USC Shoah Foundation, and 17 percent of the questions asked by users of Dimensions in Testimony. Although Boder sought to quantify and analyze trauma within his corpus of interviews, he rarely asked direct questions about the emotional impact of trauma, feelings, memories, or reflections. By contrast, questions that open up an empathetic space to discuss trauma and probe deep memories were critical to the ways the founders of the Fortunoff Archive articulated their interview goals. The vast majority of Fortunoff interviews include questions that we labeled as "interviewer trying to understand reasons, actions, and events; disbelief," "feelings and thoughts," "recalling memories, dreams, incidents, people," "isolation, loss, nega-tion questions," "learning from the past; reflecting on the Holocaust, feeling and meaning," and "emotional trauma, fear, anxiety, fright."

Questions about family, school, religion, work, behavior, and daily life are found in proportions that are roughly equivalent across the four corpora (26 percent of Boder's questions, 26 percent of Fortunoff questions, 27 percent of USC Shoah Foundation question, and 31 percent of questions asked in Dimen-sions in Testimony). Finally, questions about concentration and death camps, body violations, ghettos, deportations, and German perpetrators/Nazis comprise 13 percent of Boder's corpus of questions, 12 percent of the Fortunoff Archive, 9 percent of the USC Shoah Foundation, and 14 percent of the Dimensions in Testimony questions. The variation might be explained by the specific experi-ences of the survivors interviewed, as well as the decisions by the interviewer (including present day curiosity) to hone in on and ask such questions.[28]

We can also trace—at least in broad brushstrokes—trends in the distribution of parent topics across the four corpora (Figure 5.18). In this visualization, we see that questions about family not only comprise the largest overall parent topic (with 11,669 total questions), but the percentage of questions about family has steadily increased over time: from 8.12 percent of questions in Boder's corpus, to 12.02 percent of the Fortunoff Archive questions, to 13.30 percent of the USC Shoah Foundation questions, to 15.24 percent of the questions users asked in Dimension in Testimony. The pie charts on the left are color-coded by corpus according to the absolute number of questions in each of the clusters (pie slices) comprising the par-ent topic. While Boder did not ask questions in the parent topic that we called "memories, feelings, and processing the Holocaust," we see a decline in the frequency of asking such questions, from 11.85 percent of questions asked by interviewers from the Fortunoff Archive to 10.81 percent of questions asked by the USC Shoah Foun-dation to 4.85 percent of questions asked by users of Dimension in Testimony. By contrast, we see a significant increase in the frequency of asking questions about concentration and death camps, Auschwitz, and mass death (9.10 percent of all ques-tions asked in Dimensions in Testimony). Using the Tableau visualization, we also observe an increase in interest in questions related to antisemitism and discrimina-tion; survivor legacy, messages, and Holocaust significance; and postwar, liberation, and future, perhaps indicating a growing interest to relate the Holocaust to con-temporary social issues and future educational possibilities.

These trends need to be taken with a grain of salt since they are contingent upon a number of things: first, they are a function of the data that we used, which is confined (except in the case of Boder) to the foundational years of each archive and to a group of 452 Holocaust survivors; second, as we discuss in more detail

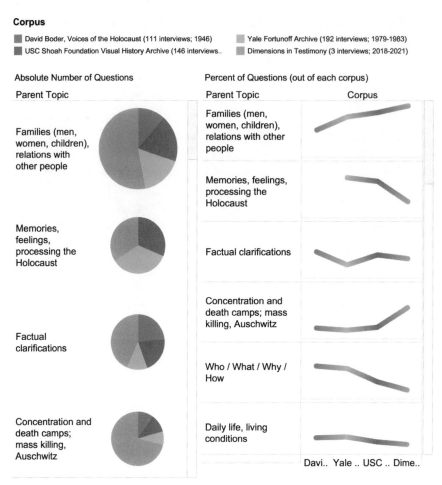

Corpus

- David Boder, Voices of the Holocaust (111 interviews; 1946)
- USC Shoah Foundation Visual History Archive (146 interviews..
- Yale Fortunoff Archive (192 interviews; 1979-1983)
- Dimensions in Testimony (3 interviews; 2018-2021)

Absolute Number of Questions — Parent Topic

Percent of Questions (out of each corpus) — Parent Topic / Corpus

Families (men, women, children), relations with other people

Memories, feelings, processing the Holocaust

Factual clarifications

Concentration and death camps; mass killing, Auschwitz

Who / What / Why / How

Daily life, living conditions

Davi.. Yale .. USC .. Dime..

FIGURE 5.18: Parent topics distribution and trends. Created by Michelle Lee and Todd Presner. Interactive visualization on Tableau: hrl.pub/1fce56.

below, the machine-learning methodology for calculating the embeddings has certain shortcomings, and the precise composition of the clusters changes with each iteration of the clustering algorithm; and thirdly, the named parent topics group together many related, but ultimately still distinct, questions. Far from revealing deep truths, these visualizations function as generalized lenses to constellate and interpret big data. They are heuristics for thinking and for asking comparative, contextual questions at scale.

Filterable by corpus, the next interactive visualization (Figure 5.19) shows all 310 distinct question topics for the 89,759 questions (rather than just the 25 parent

Question Topic	
significance of survival, reasons; lat..	1,102
learning from history; legacy and m..	1,070
food, eating, hunger	943
liberation	908
where	860
clarifications, mostly geographic an..	850
hiding, escaping, falsifying identity	819
message for the future, learning fro..	810
how (processes, events), who was i..	683
where are you from/born	672
ghetto experiences	664
death and killing	645
short follow-up questions/clarificatio..	626
nu	606
worst memory, painful experiences ..	599
tell your story, lessons to learn from..	591
names and language	545
what year, time of year	495
coping with loss; feelings of guilt, for..	494
what happened (next)	490
Jewish identity, Judaism, Israel, Zio..	484
interactions with and perceptions of ..	474
miscellaneous questions	467
anti-Semitism, hatred, and persecuti..	465

FIGURE 5.19: Exploration of 310 question topics. Created by Michelle Lee and Todd Presner. Interactive visualization on Tableau: hrl.pub/20b47b.

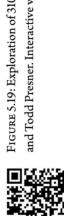

topics). The question topics are grouped by parent topics (indicated by color) and nested by size from the upper left to the bottom right. When a given question topic occurs across more than one corpus—for instance, the 943 questions about "food, eating, hunger"—the questions can be compared across each corpus in which that topic occurs (Figure 5.20). To be sure, the questions are not exactly the same. In this example, the Boder and DiT questions are factual queries (what did you eat in the camps), while the Fortunoff question is about how the hunger felt, and the Shoah Foundation question concerns how food was acquired.

For the Fortunoff Archive, questions about memories, feelings and thoughts, remembrances, reflections, and emotional trauma take precedence—in terms of question frequency—over specific questions about concentration camps, mistreatment, death, and killing. Three of the six most frequent question topics concern what we called the "interviewer trying to understand reasons, actions, and events; disbelief," "feelings and thoughts (then and now)," and "learning from the past; reflecting on the Holocaust, feelings and meaning." These question topics seem to accord with the goals of the archive to foreground the voices and experiences of the survivors by "opening the book" of the survivor's mind to delve into the psychological and emotional milieu of their struggle for survival, to reference Hartman again. Among the questions in these topics are: "What did you feel?," "When did you start feeling you could talk about it?," "What do you feel now about—about the memories that—that you live with?," "Do you believe that people can learn from history?," "What do you think about now when you think of having come through this experience?," and "Of the 230 people that came to your bar mitzvah, no one is alive?" (to which the survivor answers with a flat-out "no").[29]

Different from thematic topics (such as family, food, or mistreatment), the algorithm identified a cluster of questions in both the Boder and Fortunoff Archives that seemed to reflect *how* the questions were being asked, specifically a tone of disbelief or incredulity in which the interviewer sought to elicit rational explanations for actions—or nonactions—in the face of extreme violence.[30] For example, the following questions were asked in the early Fortunoff Archive interviews (and were very unlikely to be asked later on): "Why didn't you leave?," "You didn't think about sneaking out from the wall?," "Why didn't you escape?," "Why didn't the Jews leave with Czechs?," "Why do you think peop—gangs of Jewish children didn't—didn't organize and fight these gangs of—of Brownshirts since they were children and you were children and they weren't armed?," "Do you think that the population really could not have known anything about what was going on inside—on inside there?," "Did you ever try to talk to any of the guards or any of the people that were in charge?," "You couldn't see what was happening?,"

Exploration of Question Topics

Corpus
(All)

Highlight ...   Highlight Question Topic

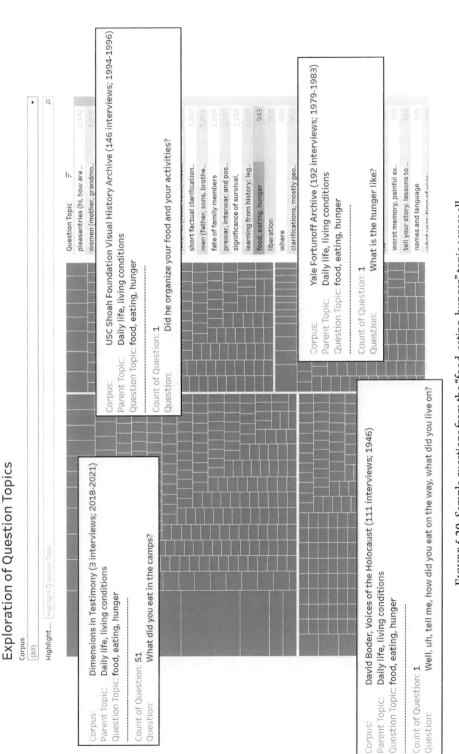

Corpus: Dimensions in Testimony (3 interviews; 2018-2021)
Parent Topic: Daily life, living conditions
Question Topic: food, eating, hunger
_____
Count of Question: 51
Question: What did you eat in the camps?

Corpus: USC Shoah Foundation Visual History Archive (146 interviews; 1994-1996)
Parent Topic: Daily life, living conditions
Question Topic: food, eating, hunger
_____
Count of Question: 1
Question: Did he organize your food and your activities?

Corpus: Yale Fortunoff Archive (192 interviews; 1979-1983)
Parent Topic: Daily life, living conditions
Question Topic: food, eating, hunger
_____
Count of Question: 1
Question: What is the hunger like?

Corpus: David Boder, Voices of the Holocaust (111 interviews; 1946)
Parent Topic: Daily life, living conditions
Question Topic: food, eating, hunger
_____
Count of Question: 1
Question: Well, uh, tell me, how did you eat on the way, what did you live on?

Question Topic   ⌄
pleasantries (hi, how are ...   2,140
women (mother, grandmo..   1,900
                                      1,267
short factual clarification...   1,251
men (father, sons, brothe..   1,234
fate of family members   1,195
prewar, interwar, and pos..   1,102
significance of survival,   1,070
learning from history; leg..
food, eating, hunger   943
liberation   908
where   860
clarifications, mostly geo..   815

worst memory, painful ex..   599
tell your story, lessons to ...   591
names and language   545
what was time of war   496

FIGURE 5.20: Sample questions from the "food, eating, hunger" topic across all
four corpora. Created by Michelle Lee and Todd Presner.

"They couldn't run away?," "Why didn't you want to run away so they didn't take you at that point?," "Instead of getting on the wagon and going to the ghetto, why didn't you run into another town or the woods?," and "How is it that no one seems to remember what Dr. Mengele looked like?" Presumably because of the expression of disbelief in the interviewer's question, the survivor replies to the last question as follows: "Because everybody—can you picture yourself coming in from a halfway normal life, coming into a madhouse? Coming into something like this? Can you picture yourself being lucid? It's impossible. You were fuzzy. You couldn't believe it. That's not happening. That's unreal. I'm dreaming. That's the feeling everybody must have had. That's why we don't remember so clearly the face. Because it's just unreal. It couldn't be. In this day and age? The cultured people—the German people doing this to other people? You couldn't conceive it. Your brain didn't take it in. That's all—just didn't take it in."[31]

Individual Corpus Dashboards in Tableau

For each corpus, we created a series of dashboards that allow researchers to drill down further into the data: first, all the questions organized by parent topic as a filterable bubble diagram; second, a heat map of all question topics asked to each interviewee; third, a "time stream" of questions asked to each interviewee according to the narrative time of the interview, along with their answers; and fourth, a gender breakdown of question topics and answer lengths.[32] Below, we use the early Fortunoff testimonies to introduce the first three dashboards and the Boder corpus to introduce the fourth; however, space will not suffice to discuss all fifteen visualizations. Instead, the reader is encouraged to interact with each of the live visualizations on our project website (http://holocaustresearchlab.com) under "Digital Project 2."

The first dashboard is a constellation of 16,396 questions asked to the first 192 survivors interviewed for the Fortunoff Archive (Figure 5.21). Each "bubble" represents a uniquely worded question, and the size of a bubble represents how many times the question came up. The bubbles are organized in a ring-like formation by the color corresponding to twenty-four parent topics, which contain each of the ninety-two individual question topics. From the center, reds and oranges are questions related to mistreatment and killing, prisoner experiences, German perpetrators, war experiences, bodily violations, arrest, deportation, and ghetto experiences; blues represent questions about behavior, work, religion, school, and family; greens represent questions about ethnic groups, nationalities, and liberation; yellows and browns represent clusters of questions related to anti-semitism, emotional trauma, memories, and survivor legacies; grays and beige

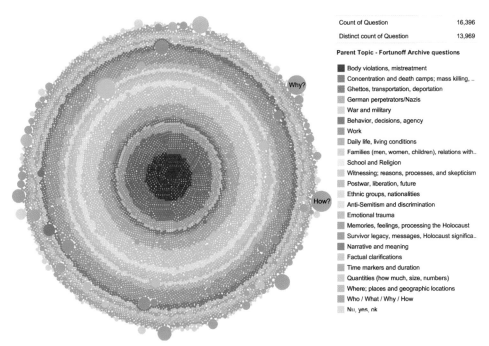

Count of Question | 16,396
Distinct count of Question | 13,969

Parent Topic - Fortunoff Archive questions

- Body violations, mistreatment
- Concentration and death camps; mass killing, ..
- Ghettos, transportation, deportation
- German perpetrators/Nazis
- War and military
- Behavior, decisions, agency
- Work
- Daily life, living conditions
- Families (men, women, children), relations with..
- School and Religion
- Witnessing; reasons, processes, and skepticism
- Postwar, liberation, future
- Ethnic groups, nationalities
- Anti-Semitism and discrimination
- Emotional trauma
- Memories, feelings, processing the Holocaust
- Survivor legacy, messages, Holocaust significa..
- Narrative and meaning
- Factual clarifications
- Time markers and duration
- Quantities (how much, size, numbers)
- Where; places and geographic locations
- Who / What / Why / How
- No, yes, ok

FIGURE 5.21: 16,396 Interview questions from the Yale Fortunoff Archive. Created by Michelle Lee and Todd Presner. Interactive visualization on Tableau: hrl.pub/27bd8e.

colors in the outer ring represent factual information (time, quantities, locations). Mousing over a bubble brings up the text of the question, the cluster to which it was assigned, and the number of times the question was asked.

The next visualization, the topic heat map, illustrates the number of question topics and the frequency in which a given topic occurs within an interview (Figure 5.22). Both the topic (on the x-axis) and interviewee (on the y-axis) are organized in descending order: The topics asked about most frequently are on the left, while the topics asked about least frequently are on the right; similarly, interviewees asked the highest number of questions are at the top, and interviewees asked the fewest number of questions are at the bottom. The darker the squares, the more questions an interviewee was asked about a particular topic. For example, Donia W. was asked 240 questions in seventy out of ninety-two topics, with the most questions (nineteen) asked in the topic "interviewer trying to understand reasons, actions, and events; disbelief."[33] Using the time stream visualization (Figure 5.23), we can read the questions and answers in narrative sequence as well as sort them by question topics. One such question in this topic

X-axis represents "Question Topic" and is ordered by the topic with the most number of questions to the least.
Y-axis represents "Interviewee" and is ordered by the testimony with the most number of questions to the least.

Number of questions

1 ▮▮▮▮▮ 22

Question Topic

Interviewee

Interviewee	Topics tot.	Questions tot.
Hela S.	83	286
Hilde C.	80	301
Pincus and Syl..	77	285
Michael R.	77	250
Leo G.	77	271
Walter K.	73	212
Elizabeth F.	72	173
Marta R.	71	200
Libby and Sidn..	70	198
Harry M.	70	201
Donia W.	70	240
Suzanne R.	69	172
Gina E.	69	240
Murray C.	68	150
Harry T.	68	153
Rosalie W. and..	67	195
Lepa M.	66	174
Irene S.	66	149
Esther R.	66	169
David and Soni..	66	143
Abraham B.	64	146
Millie W.	63	153
Lois and Abrah..	63	139
Eva B.	63	173
Ernestine T.	63	153
Edith H.	62	160
Pauline M.	61	134
Lotte S.	61	128
Gustav R.	61	162

FIGURE 5.22: Question topic heat map for 192 Fortunoff Archive interviews. Created by Michelle Lee and Todd Presner. Interactive visualization on Tableau: hrl.pub/5268f.

Parent question topics in narrative order and sorted by date of interview

Interviewee

April
- Bronia K.
- Erich K.
- Varda H.

May
- Celina S.
- Eva B.
- Leon W.
- Otto K.
- Renee H.
- Sally H.

July
- Abe and David F.
- Abraham P. and Morris P.
- David and Rosa G.
- Emina N. and Miriam W.
- Jack P.
- Leon and Molly N.
- Leon G.
- Menachem S.
- Mendel S.
- Walter S.

Start Date of Interview 1979

August
- Abe and Sari B.
- Alex F.
- Betty C.
- Elizabeth F.
- Eva K.
- Frania R.
- Joseph L.
- Michael R.
- Rosalie W. and Jolly Z.
- Rudy F.
- Schifre Z.
- Stanley S.
- William R.
- Zoltan G.

S..
- Ludwig F.

November
- Bronia and Nathan L.
- Donia W.
- Kochevit P.
- Lotte S.
- Marta R.
- Niusia A.
- Olga S.

December
- Dori K.
- Helen K.
- Isaac A.
- Joseph K.
- Kurt I.
- Rose and Aaron M.

200   400   600

Line Number

Body violations, mistreatment

Concentration and death camps; mass killing, Auschwitz

German perpetrators/Nazis

Ghettos, transportation, deportation

War and military

Behavior, decisions, agency

Work

Daily life, living conditions

Families (men, women, children), relations with other p..

School and Religion

Witnessing; reasons, processes, and skepticism

Postwar, liberation, future

Ethnic groups, nationalities

Narrative and meaning

Factual clarifications

Time markers and duration

Quantities (how much, size, numbers)

Where; places and geographic locations

Who / What / Why / How

Nu, yes, ok

Anti-Semitism and discrimination

Emotional trauma

Memories, feelings, processing the Holocaust

Survivor legacy, messages, Holocaust significance

FIGURE 5.23: Visualization of all questions by topic for 192 Fortunoff Archive interviews. Created by Michelle Lee and Todd Presner. Interactive visualization on Tableau: hrl.pub/64fc86.

was asked by Vlock: "But why didn't they give you work that needed to be done? Why give you work that didn't need to be done?" Donia W. answers: "Aye, look, your question is like, you never was in Auschwitz. Yeah, I understand, yes. But uh, SS, I repeat you. [unintelligible] And power, you know what this is, power? When you have power, in men or, or human, you know what it is?"[34]

Arrayed against the potential of digital fragmentation, the "time stream" visualization (Figure 5.23) not only depicts all the questions and answers in narrative sequence, but also color codes the questions by topics, thereby allowing a user to search all the interviews by question topic. Searches can be initiated on any one of the ninety-two question topics using the "highlight question topic" feature. The longer the time stream, the more questions the interviewee was asked, but the number of questions does not necessarily correspond to longer narrative answers. Each time stream can be fully resolved and examined on its own by clicking directly on it. The interviews are organized chronologically by the date they were conducted (on the y-axis), and each colored sliver represents a question asked during the interview (on the x-axis), colored by parent topic. The denser the colors are, the more questions asked; the less dense (the more white spaces), the more the survivor is speaking. This visualization functions as a kind of remediation of the archive, since it allows readers to gain a synoptic view of the early Fortunoff interviews and also hone in on individual questions and answers by topic within the course of each interviewee's narrative.

For the last dashboard, we return to David Boder's corpus so that we can examine differences in how a single interviewer posed questions to men and women (Figure 5.24). In terms of the overall breakdown, the number of questions Boder asked to men and women were directly proportional to how many men and women he interviewed: 10,122 total questions asked to seventy male survivors, and 6,238 total questions asked to forty-one female survivors. The tree map visualization represents all ninety-three topics arranged according to the absolute number of questions in each topic. The larger rectangles represent individual topics, split into two sub-rectangles by gender. Topics are shown in descending order of the number of questions from top left to bottom right. The sizes of the sub-rectangles represent the gender distribution of questions for a topic. At the same time, color density represents the median answer length by gender within the topic. The darker the color, the longer the answers. The visualization allows us to see if men or women were asked more (or less) questions about certain topics and if men or women gave longer (or shorter) answers.

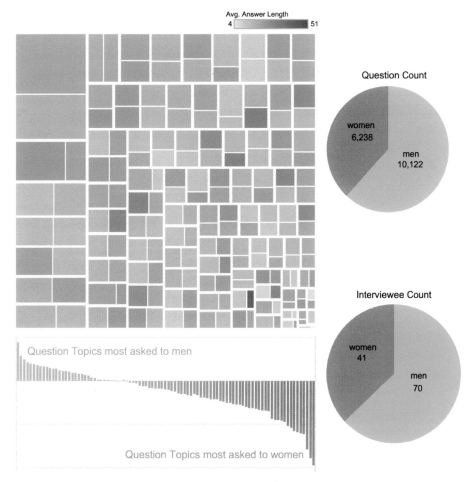

Avg. Answer Length
4 ☐ 51

Question Count

women
6,238

men
10,122

Interviewee Count

women
41

men
70

Question Topics most asked to men

Question Topics most asked to women

FIGURE 5.24: Gender dashboard of 111 interviews conducted by David Boder (1946). Created by Michelle Lee and Todd Presner. Interactive visualization on Tableau: hrl.pub/f05047.

Hovering over each rectangle in the tree map, the pop-up box reveals the percentage of men and women, respectively, who were asked questions about a given topic. For example, 76 percent of women (thirty-one out of forty-one) were asked about "children," whereas 40 percent of men (twenty-eight out of seventy) were asked about the same topic. In fact, female survivors were asked about "men (father, sons, brothers, husband, uncles)," "children, childhood," and "women (mother, grandmothers, sisters, aunts, wife, daughters)" at rates that were, respectively,

39 percent, 36 percent, and 31.5 percent higher than male survivors. Men, on the other hand, were much more likely to be asked about factual information related to specific events during the Holocaust, such as the topics "to and from cities and countries," "longer questions about unique Holocaust experiences," and "closed-ended, factual questions, mostly yes-no questions" at rates that were, respectively, 18 percent, 12 percent, and 10 percent higher.

Manually Reassigned Topics and Errors in the SBERT Clustering Process

Manually reviewing the clustering results for nearly ninety thousand questions was a formidable but necessary task to help us document the usefulness of the algorithm. Since we are *thinking with* algorithms rather than setting them free on testimonial narratives, we needed to scrutinize, correct, and, as far as possible, understand the results we were getting. The manual data review process took at least a hundred hours and involved not only naming (and renaming) question topics and clusters but also experimenting with changing the algorithm's parameters and determining if cluster assignments "cohered" around a topic and why. The manual review and cleaning process involved human labor and the application of domain-specific knowledge by Presner and Lee. We attuned our review to factual errors (such as misrecognized names or geographic locations), erroneous associations (when the algorithm brought two unrelated topics together), and redundancies (clusters that could be combined rather than separated).[35]

For our manual reassignments, the correction rate was 6.49 percent (or 1,061 questions) in Boder's corpus, 4.75 percent (or 780 questions) in the Fortunoff corpus, 3.64 percent (or 597 questions) in the USC Shoah Foundation corpus, and 1.61 percent (or 652 questions) in the Dimensions in Testimony corpus. More reassignments certainly could have been made. The most coherent parent topics—that is, ones that had the lowest percentage of being incorrectly assigned by SBERT and regrouped—were about "quantities (how much, size, numbers)," "who/what/why/how," and "ethnic groups, nationalities." We found two primary problems with using SBERT, both of which may derive from the fact that the algorithm is not trained on a Holocaust-specific corpus. The first problem concerns specific types of questions being miscategorized in topics; the second problem, which is more difficult to resolve, concerns how the algorithm created overly general clusters in certain instances and overly specific clusters in other situations.

The first issue we encountered was that certain types of questions were consistently being miscategorized because SBERT was trained on a monolingual corpus and does not recognize certain words, proper names, or historically specific terms.[36] Unknown words are sometimes separated into subwords and certain compound terms are not considered together. For example, Bedzin is a town in Poland (and not part of the topic "sleeping arrangements"); "nun" is a German adverb (and does not belong in a topic about women); "the Joint" is shorthand for the Joint Distribution Committee (and does not belong in a topic about crematoria or fire); "Hamburger" and "Gross" are proper names of people interviewed; the "Canada squad" and "Canada detail" refer to prisoners sorting Jewish belongings in Auschwitz (not the country); and "cattle cars" have nothing to do with farms or animals. For the last, interviewers used many different words to refer to the deportation vehicles, including "railways," "railway cars," "RR cars," "trains," "cattle cars," "freight trains," and "trucks." Not all of these terms were clustered together algorithmically as forms of transportation for deportation.

The second, more problematic issue was a handful of clusters that aggregated distinct experiences in ways that obscured what the interviewer intended by the question. Initially, the algorithm grouped anything to do with writing and inscriptions together in a single category. This included written documents, books, reading, and language, as well as tattoos and forced markings on victims' bodies. We manually split this cluster apart to isolate questions about mistreatment (tattoos and forced markings). Another initial cluster that combined too many experiences focused on destruction, bombing, and annihilation. We separated out war destruction from the destruction of people and the annihilation of the Jews, attuned, to the extent possible, to the intentions of the interviewer. The same problem was identified in differentiating between professional work (either before or after the Holocaust) and forced labor during the Holocaust. Under the parent topic of "work," we separated the question topics into "professional work and trade," "forced labor, factory work," and "payments and wages" (a category of questions asked uniquely by Boder).

In the Boder corpus, the SBERT embeddings could not reliably distinguish between "ovens" used to burn people, "stoves" used for cooking, "gas" used for transportation versus annihilation, and a "pot" placed in a deportation train for collecting human waste.[37] At the same time, it is worth underscoring that Boder, too, was struggling to understand what the survivors were telling him, as these experiences were still being documented in 1946, and a definitive conceptual and historical vocabulary—in any language, let alone in English—did not yet exist. His questions are sometimes awkward (including debatable translations) and probe details in ways that were unlikely to be asked later ("What did they look like burning?," "What do you mean by 'went through the chimney'?," "Did the chimneys smoke?," "And what fires were outside the crematories?," "Could the crematory be seen burning?," "Were they also sent through the gas chambers?"). The original embeddings and all of our reassignments are documented on our project website.

Reflections on Shortcomings and a Problem of Racial Bias

One shortcoming with this analytical model is the fact that each question was only assigned to one cluster, even though some questions could belong to several categories or none at all.[38] For instance, Boder's question "Were many SS arrested when the Americans came?" could, potentially, be clustered under "arrest" (although we considered that cluster for victims being arrested), "Americans" (although that cluster mostly asked about survivors' intentions of going to America), "interactions with the SS and SS actions," or "Germany, Germans." Knowing the context for this question, we manually moved it under "liberation, end of war," while the algorithm had previously grouped it with questions related to "killing, shooting, mistreatment and death." The algorithm does not have any historical context for rendering its decisions—in this case, American soldiers trying to track down and arrest Nazis at the end of the war for their crimes. Or to take another example from Boder: "Tell me, how were the Jews gathered together, how were they transported, what did your family do, and what happened to your family?" The algorithm put this question in the cluster that we named "Jews and fate of Jewish community, Jewish culture," which is appropriate, but it could also be "transportation and deportation" and "family (background, what happened to)." For future iterations of this clustering algorithm, some questions could be assigned to multiple categories, perhaps by using a weighted scoring mechanism for multiple clusters.

A related shortcoming is that the algorithm treats each question as a discrete "document" rather than part of a broader context or dialogue that unfolds sequentially. While an interviewer may sometimes jump from topic to topic or from question to question, in many instances, the questions follow the structure of a narrative or chronological sequence. As such, follow-up questions tend to be part of a series of questions on the same topic. The algorithm is not programmed to consider this potentiality, and generic questions (such as "Yes?," "When was that?," "And then what happened?," or "Who was there with you?") will not be connected to the specificity of a prior or subsequent topic, such as "escaping" or "hiding"). At the same time, some questions are completely unassignable without context. To address this, it would make sense to explore the possibility of using transcript segments to assign generic questions to specific clusters or to concatenate certain questions together as a topic.

While we cannot (yet) say whether a Holocaust-specific training model for SBERT would result in better results and more precise clustering, we did detect a troubling racial bias in one of the clusters returned by the algorithm. Since BERT was originally trained on BookCorpus novels and English-language Wikipedia, the training data for the model also include racist expressions, sexist stereotypes, and derogatory associations that can get replicated downstream in the clustering assignments.[39] This has been documented quite extensively in the critical literature on BERT.[40] Although we cannot determine precisely why or how the algorithm made the following decisions, we were struck by the danger of an "algorithm of oppression," to apply Safiya Noble's apt phrase, replicating a racial bias through problematic semantic associations.[41]

In our data, we found the algorithm to have inherited and replicated a racial bias in the analysis of two separate corpora. In both the Fortunoff Archive question analysis and the USC Shoah Foundation question analysis, the algorithm identified a cluster of questions which we named "ghetto experiences." For the former, the two hundred questions all mention the word "ghetto" in reference to the experience of Jews sent to and in ghettos ("And you had to move to the ghetto?," "Were there children in the ghetto?," "What did you take with you into the ghetto?," "Was the ghetto surrounded by walls, by fences?," and "What was life in the ghetto like, as time went on?"), but the algorithm also clustered seven additional questions that had nothing to do with the Jewish ghetto experience: "What happened to the black kid?," "How did Black Monday start?," "What did you think about the black American who—," "You mean black people?," "What did you think when you realized this person had black skin?," "And how many wore black neckties?," and "How many wore the black neckties?" In parsing the USC Shoah Foundation data, a similar result appeared: in addition to the 213 questions that explicitly mention "ghetto," the algorithm also included the following questions in the results cluster: "How many black students were there in your class?," "Was there a black market?," "Did he wear a black coat?," and "A black frock coat?"

While we cannot know for certain how the algorithm determined the similarity of the embedding scores in these cases, the underlying problem appears to be a racial bias within the training data that is being passed downstream. First, the algorithm determined that "ghetto" was associated with the racial category of "black" (Black kid, Black American, black skin, Black students).[42] There is no justification for this association. And second, the algorithm determined that all mentions of black, regardless of meaning or context, should be associated together, as if they were all "black" (black market, black neckties, black coat). While we manually moved these questions into other clusters, it does not solve the problem of bias in the training data and those biases being replicated in the embedding calculations that are ultimately inscrutable for users of BERT.

To be sure, these racial biases can be corrected and the algorithm can be adjusted not to replicate those specific results.[43] But the more vexing question remains: How many unremarked and undetected biases—be they over race, gender, sexual orientation, ability, religion, ethnicity, age, nationality—make their way into models based on BERT or other large language models? And what happens when those models—informed by and built upon compromised data—are deployed in other settings to make decisions, pass judgments, enforce rules, and, ultimately, structure the social world in ways that are discriminatory?[44] Here, we might follow Hoyt Long, who writes, citing Timnit Gebru and others, "Race in the machine . . . is always going to be a function of what we feed it."[45] After all, the algorithm "learned" its racial bias from the racial biases already codified in the cultural records and language of humankind (books and Wikipedia). It was trained on and by us. For this reason, the algorithm may also function as a broken mirror held up to our own cultural and social history.

Concluding Thoughts

The methods of analysis in this chapter present a combination of possibilities and perils for using machine-learning algorithms in the humanities. Even though BERT is touted as a generalizable model for natural language processing (and seems to be successful, by our estimation, in parsing meaning and intention in the vast majority of our data), we certainly should not accept the results on blind faith. Like the human beings who created the algorithm and data upon which it was trained, BERT also contains biases and worldviews that are embedded into the system in ways that may ultimately defy human scrutiny. At every stage, there is a series of human and computer decisions, from the training of the language models and the embedding calculations to the computation of the clusters, the human labeling, and the structuring of the data visualizations. As Louise Amoore writes: "Though the mathematical propositions of algorithms cannot be made fully legible, or rendered accountable, they can be called to give accounts of the conditions of their emergence."[46] Indeed, we have endeavored to give such accounts, as best we can, of the conditions of the algorithm's emergence, our own epistemic decisions, and the ethical questions that arise at the nexus of human and algorithm.

For this reason, the resulting constellations are best described as *subjunctive metadata*—namely, possible and plausible outcomes given the constraints of the model, the iterative nature of the clustering algorithm, and our own efforts of human curation and interpretation. The results are mostly replicable, although the outputs are not exactly the same in each iteration of the algorithm. Differences are a function of the specifications for calculating the vector embeddings, the determination of the parameters for the clustering algorithm (such as the number of clusters), the manual assignment of topic labels and naming conventions, the manual correction and curation of some of the results, and the arrangement of the results into interactive visualizations. We have not overcome or eradicated the "errancy" of the algorithm; instead, we keep track and document it. We make it visible, and we discuss it—in order to "[attend] to how these moments give accounts of algorithmic reason."[47] But rather than seeing this as a deficiency, we consider the contingency of the outputs to be a critical part of humanistic data analysis and digital humanities as a field.

At the same time, as our analysis and visualizations show, the results offer a number of possibilities for exploring concrete questions around Holocaust memory and history, especially vis-à-vis the changing nature of testimonial narratives, interviewing protocols, and institutional archiving projects. Patterns and trends can be discerned at various scales and, simultaneously, we can zoom into the questions asked in individual interviews with new insights about topics covered, question frequencies, narrative structures, and gender differences. The flexibility of the Tableau dashboards allows users to explore, filter, and constellate the interview questions in a format that would be nearly impossible otherwise. Our data visualizations are thus heuristics for thinking because they open up ways of distilling, perceiving, and attending to differences and similarities through processes of human judgment linked to forms of algorithmic decision-making.

6

Algorithmic Close Reading

ANALYZING VECTORS OF AGENCY IN HOLOCAUST TESTIMONIES

With Lizhou Fan

Introduction

Accounts of survival given by Holocaust victims are replete with wide-ranging descriptions of agency. While these descriptions often reflect being the object of the decisions, actions, and will of the Nazi perpetrators, they also reflect various degrees of self-determination in the face of brutality. As one listens to or reads testimonial accounts, one cannot help but be struck by the range of everyday actions described by survivors as they remember the past and decide how to embed their experiences into a narrative form. While general subject headings such as discrimination experiences, deportation, mistreatment, and liberation are useful for orienting listeners within the contours of a testimony, we usually cannot know what survivors say they did—and what they say was done to them—without listening to or reading the testimonies individually. Until we delve into the testimonies themselves, we cannot understand how specific actions fit within a broader network of reactions, behaviors, and evaluations expressed by the survivor, including varied and sometimes countervailing vectors of action.

While we will not frame our analysis, strictly speaking, in terms of actor-network-theory, we are interested in documenting clusters of agents and actions by attending to semiotic relationships and expressions of agency in survivor testimonies. In this sense, considering actors within networks of associations and relationships overlaps with parts of Bruno Latour's approach.[1] As Latour writes with regard to some of the key questions in actor-network-theory: "Which agencies are invoked? Which figurations are they endowed with? Through which mode of action are they engaged? Are we talking about causes and their intermediaries or about a concatenation of mediators?"[2] To answer such questions and locate "agencies" within Holocaust testimonies, we need an approach that differs significantly from conventional subject indexing since such terms rarely indicate how people report they behaved, what they and others did, whom their actions affected, how they say they reacted, and what options for action they considered open and possible. At the same time, seemingly simple and straightforward reports of agency are far more contingent, uncertain, embedded, and fallible than may first appear. Indeed, these reports may reveal surprising networks of actions and reactions that compel us to rethink and reinterpret the range of possible forms of agency.

Derived from the Latin verb *agere*—meaning to set into motion, drive forward, or to lead—agency is a term that is usually connected with freedom of action. In fact, Hannah Arendt will explicitly connect "action" with "the principle of freedom" in *The Human Condition* because she considers action to be a kind of deliberate "insertion" of ourselves into the world in order to drive a change or make a difference.[3] As she further explains, action and storytelling are fundamentally interlinked because the record of actions forms history, "the storybook of mankind [*sic*]."[4] Insofar as actions can be told as stories, "the web of acts and words" gives rise to networks and relationships of possibility, records that bear witness to human existence, plurality, and natality (the capacity of human beings to begin something new or unprecedented).[5] Giving testimony embodies this sense of agency because it is an act of freedom predicated on the hope that the story will be received and memorialized as part of the record of human acts and deeds. The telling of the story allows human actors to "reveal actively their unique personal identities and thus make their appearance in the human world," something that corresponds to human "distinctiveness" while actualizing the "human condition of plurality."[6] From our perspective as distant witnesses engaged with apprehending these webs of acts and words, what methods might we use to document, listen to, and understand such expressions of agency?

As we prepare to focus on descriptions of agency within survivor testimony, we may wonder: What did the capacity to act mean in the context of Nazi despotism or within a concentration camp, where individual action, spontaneity, and freedom were systematically eradicated? While survivor testimonies certainly bear witness to the human capacity to obliterate the spontaneity, actions, and lives of others through the perversion of the principle of freedom, testimonies also bear witness to much more than domination and submission. We also find myriad concrete accounts of action and reaction that document possibilities for agency, even in the most extreme circumstances. Through a reflexive language of meaning-making, survivors translate memories of action into expressive forms of narrative, in which complex networks of action and possibility begin to emerge.

The purpose of this chapter is thus to listen to and investigate representations of agency in Holocaust testimonies. To do so, we undertake what we call "algorithmic close reading" in order to ask: How can information extraction algorithms help us find, index, and analyze expressions of agency in Holocaust testimonies? What can text mining and network visualization add to our understanding of the range of agencies expressed by survivors of the Holocaust? What can be learned from the identification and indexing of microhistorical accounts of agency?[7] To answer these questions, we will use methods of natural language processing and network analysis to visually interpret expressions and patterns of agency.[8]

Being able to do so has significant consequences and many applications in understanding the content of a testimonial narrative or oral history in which speakers describe what they did and what others did to them. While individual testimonies can, of course, be parsed manually for expressions of agency, computational approaches allow us to search, query, and correlate disparate narrative elements in ways that use complex networks and visualizations to analyze such expressions. And if we are to scale up to dozens, hundreds, or potentially even thousands of testimonial narratives that describe events and the various agents involved, computational tools are imperative for organizing the multitude of agents, vectors of action, relations, and objects. As legal scholar Renana Keydar has argued, mass atrocity requires "mass testimony," but courts have yet to figure out how to truly integrate quantity and a "plurality of voices" in the legal process.[9] Developing models both to "read" the testimonies individually and to ethically assemble shared experiences—what we will call "testimonial ensembles"—not only has possible legal consequence (such as the creation of computationally enabled forms of mass witnessing of mass atrocity) but also fosters new historical questions attuned to variations in scale and scope.[10]

In the pages that follow, we employ a method for extracting and classifying what we call "semantic triplets" or expressions of agency in Holocaust testimony transcripts.[11] By an expression of agency, we mean the specific description of an action that is "doing something" and "making some difference to a state of affairs."[12] The algorithmic process of identifying and classifying these expressions of agency results in the creation of a new paratext that supplements the way we read and search the transcript. To demonstrate our prototype, we focus on four salient testimonies given by Auschwitz survivors at different points in time and show how the analysis of expressions of agency, particularly everyday acts of resistance and defiance, can contribute to the writing of "microhistories" of the Holocaust. Building on methods of natural language processing and a combination of rule-based and machine-learning algorithms, we show how semantic network analysis can be used to analyze agency and thereby provide insights about what people report they did and what was done to them.

After discussing a series of interpretive networks to visualize expressions of agency, we turn to the construction of "macrohistorical" accounts of agency. Using filterable spreadsheets to query tens of thousands of semantic triplets as well as experimental interfaces to visualize relations among groupings of semantic triplets, we focus on how hundreds of Jewish survivors remember experiencing antisemitic discrimination in the years leading up to the Holocaust. The result is what we call a "testimonial ensemble," a multivoiced testimony created from the words of individual witnesses.[13] In the project discussion following this chapter, we turn to the ethics of creating a "testimonial ensemble" using multiple survivor accounts of a singular experience: specifically, the ways in which twenty-eight Auschwitz survivors remember and narrate the actions of a Belgian-Jewish victim named Mala Zimetbaum. While the story of Mala Zimetbaum's escape from Auschwitz, her subsequent capture, and public execution are fairly well-known and documented in Holocaust historiography, we present a reconfigurable testimonial ensemble as a possible model for how algorithmic forms of critical fabulation can help us create new narratives for mass witnessing and memorialization.

Algorithmic Reading: Between Distant and Close

Stephen Ramsay defines "algorithmic criticism" as a kind of "criticism derived from the algorithmic manipulation of texts." It uses computational tools and algorithmic calculations "to assist the critic in the unfolding of interpretive possibilities."[14] Far more than just instructions for processing inputs and creating outputs, algorithmic criticism is generative because it uses the "forces of constraint" built into computation—logic- and rule-based calculations, enumeration, classification—to open up new avenues of interpretation. For Ramsay, building on the insights of Jerome McGann, this might take the form of textual "deformance," which reorders, restructures, paraphrases, classifies, enumerates, translates, or extracts textual elements to create new paratexts.[15] As Ramsay elegantly sums up the attitude of the "algorithmic critic": they are "unperturbed" by the fear that "criticism is being naively mechanized, [or] that algorithms are being pressed beyond their inability" because they open up new interpretative possibilities for textual scholarship.[16]

Our algorithmic work functions similarly: we take a text created through human and/or machine listening ("the transcript"), and using rule-based methods, we create a new paratext consisting of what we call semantic triplets.[17] Semantic triplets are a text-immanent way to computationally identify and index descriptions of agency within oral histories. A semantic triplet is a grammatical unit consisting of *subjects*, *relations*, and *objects*. *Subjects* are units consisting of nouns, primarily people (but sometimes non-human agents), pronouns, and proper names, as well as the direct modifiers of the subject. *Relations* are verb units including one or more verbs, related prepositions, and modifiers like adverbs. *Objects*, both direct and indirect, and object clauses include a broader range of parts of speech, from regular nouns to adjectives, adverbs, and more. For example, experiences of discrimination may be expressed as coerced actions in the form of triplets: "We had to wear the yellow star," "They told us to give away all the furs and jewelry," or "They closed our business." Experiences of deportation may be expressed through passive constructions: "We were loaded onto trains" or "I was shipped to Auschwitz." And experiences of liberation may be expressed through forms of active agency: "We went back to our town," "I broke into a house," or "We were looking for our family." Of course, each of these experiences can be expressed through a wide range of actions and forms of speech.

To analyze the grammatical structure of each sentence in a transcript, we relied on the dependency parsing tools of spaCy, an open source Python library for natural language processing, to give each word a part-of-speech tag and arrows to show the dependency parsing.[18] Using spaCy in tandem with our own rule-based algorithms, we created parsing trees and categorizations for each semantic triplet, as shown in the two examples (Figures 6.1 and 6.2). For instance, "My father had to leave his home"[19] is a semantic triplet that indicates a coerced action: he was forced out of his home by agents (the Nazis) who are not named in this grammatical construction. Active constructions, on the other hand, can present a trajectory of action in which the subject is the agent: for example, "I removed the yellow patch," "I went across to the Russian side," or "I must save my child." In each of these triplets, the subject is the agent who did something: She took off the "yellow patch" (the Star of David that marked her as Jewish); she went across to the Russian side (escaping the ghetto); and she expressed the intention to save her child. These actions are clear examples of individual agency that intended to make a difference in a state of affairs marked by a litany of violence and coercion. The semantic triplets not only indicate what kind of action the subject pursued, but

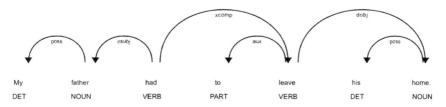

FIGURE 6.1: Example of a parsing tree of a coerced action in Anna Kovitzka's testimony. Created by Lizhou Fan.

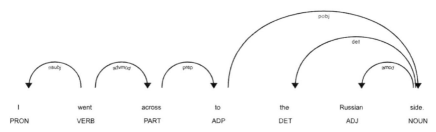

FIGURE 6.2: Example of a parsing tree of an expression of active speech in Anna Kovitzka's testimony. Created by Lizhou Fan.

also, within the context of the narrative, give us information about "where" in the interview and narrative sequence such vectors of action were described by the survivors as possible.

For the triplets output, we divided descriptions of agency into four subcategories: active speech, passive speech, coercion/necessity, and speculative/modal speech. Active and passive speech are, respectively, actions reported by the subject and actions done by others to the subject; coercive speech may have an active structure but a passive meaning since it represents something the subject was either forced to do or had to do (out of necessity); and, lastly, speculative speech, often expressed through modal verbs, represents an uncertain or imaginary action, or a statement of possibility, desire, ability, or futurity. We added two more categories that are not expressions of agency but expressions of evaluation and orientation that use the syntactic structure of a triplet. Evaluation triplets are expressions of judgment (of oneself, another person, or a situation) by the speaker, while orientation triplets provide contextual information generally employed to orient the interviewer or listener in the events of the story. Although these six categories are not perfect or definitive, they help to characterize the general kinds of speech expressed by semantic triplets. We summarize and provide examples of triplet characterization in Table 6.1.[20]

Table 6.1: Six categories of triplet characterization with examples. Created by Lizhou Fan and Todd Presner.

Categories		Examples
Agency	Active	I removed the yellow patch.
	Passive	I was shipped to Auschwitz.
	Coercion/necessity	My father had to leave his home.
	Speculative/modal	They could consummate the terrible deed.
Evaluation		I am not ashamed.
Orientation		I remembered a Christian woman.

Methodology Close-Up

The overall process for extracting semantic triplets can be summarized as follows: using the text processing pipeline provided by the spaCy API, the sentences in the testimony transcripts are first tokenized into words and punctuation marks.[21] Next, we used the pretrained models in spaCy to obtain linguistic metadata that are tagged for parts of speech and parsed into syntactic dependencies. We further used Named Entity Recognition (NER) to determine the categories of nouns (for instance, people, organizations, geopolitical entities, dates, and so forth). As a whole, this Natural Language Processing (NLP) pipeline serves as the foundation for the extraction of semantic triplets. Using the NLP Pipeline in spaCy, we created our triplet extraction system by using a combination of chunk parsing, also known as partial parsing, and a set of customized rules using the built-in noun chunk function and a customized matcher of verb chunks. Our extension includes more parts of speech as the possible components around core nouns, verbs, and adjectives, and we link the chunks together to check if a sentence was fully processed.[22]

With this method, we can extract hundreds (and sometimes thousands) of semantic triplets from each testimony. Some sentences may contain multiple triplets, such as this sentence: "I went with her down to the door, and there I stood across the street, hidden in the gate, and I saw how my child was lying on the snow." In this example, four triplets were extracted: "I went with her," "I stood across the street," "I hidden [sic] in the gate," and "my child was lying on the snow." When extracted, not every triplet is grammatically correct, and some will necessitate manual corrections. It is also important to remember that the testimonies were spoken narratives, which were transcribed (and sometimes translated) by human editors who added punctuation as well as capitalization. Regularized punctuation and segmentation (or lack thereof) affect the outcome significantly.

Not unlike the back-and-forth waves of the "rule-based" and "neural-based" methods in artificial intelligence, we went through a zigzag process in experimenting with which information extraction methods work best for our research process. In our initial attempts, we used the OpenIE extractor API, but it gave too many choices with lower accuracy than we wanted.[23] After much experimentation, we switched to a rule-based system, which is what we used to present the examples that follow. We used two approaches for objects: the first was to prioritize the direct object and include "context terms" that are syntactically related; the second was to extract fuller "object phrases," which we call "meticulous chunk parsing." In order to reduce information loss when parsing longer sentences, we need to include, in a separate column for each triplet, what we call "context terms." We defined the context terms as all the related lexical chunks other than those included in the extracted triplet. In the first triplet above ("I went with her"), the contextual chunks are the following words: the door, the street, the gate, my child, the snow. The context is especially important when we want to understand an action embedded in a complex sentence and create network diagrams from the triplets.

While the contextual terms will capture indirect objects and multiple direct objects, as well as help make sense of reversed order expressions, the "meticulous" chunk-parsing method allowed us to improve the accuracy of triplet extraction in many long or complicated sentences, including ones that are not grammatically correct or complete. Here, we used a set of finer-defined rules to extract noun and verb chunks, which added a layer called the "segment level" for chunk-boundary decision-making. By using this method and the functionalities in the Python package Textacy,[24] we were able to improve the accuracy of subject, verb, and object identification. For example, in this sentence spoken by Jack Bass (Bassfreund), "And then they did some—used some kind of delousing agent, they poured all over us," our initial process found no triplets because the sentence is spoken with breaks that make it difficult to connect the subject ("they") to the verbs and objects.[25] Our "meticulous" extraction method was able to find the triplets in this sentence based on its algorithmically annotated segments. The full sentence is first segmented into two parts, based on punctuation, and inside of each segment, a complete triplet is extracted, as shown in Figure 6.3. This sometimes makes the object chunk of the triplet slightly longer, but it allows for greater rates of success.

Once extracted, the triplets are characterized according to six categories: active speech, passive speech, coercive speech/necessity, speculative/modal speech, evaluation, and orientation. This characterization is derived partially from William

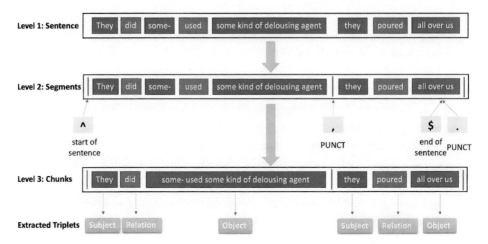

FIGURE 6.3: Example sentence with grammatical incompleteness.
Created by Lizhou Fan.

Labov and Joshua Waletzky's sociolinguistic model of narratives, where clauses are characterized by temporal organization (the order in which the subject narrates events and actions in the story), evaluative description (personal assessments by the narrator), and contextual orientation (information provided by the narrator that helps orient the listener).[26] The basic characterization system happens in spaCy, whereby the algorithm takes tokens consisting of the Relation Verb Chunks (R) and Object Noun Chunks (O). For each token in both R and O, there is retrievable syntactic information including (but not limited to) a part of speech (POS) tag, a dependency tag, and the lemma form of the word. We then use a straightforward lexicon- and rule-based mechanism to assign verb characterizations, as shown in the triplets AEO algorithm below (Figure 6.4).

Finally, disambiguating pronouns presents a major challenge in creating network visualizations of expressions of agency. We experimented with using NeuralCoref, a Python package that annotates and resolves coreference clusters using a neural network.[27] However, this pretrained language model is based on out-of-domain text data and is only effective about half the time. We decided, instead, to create our own machine-learning model of coreferencing by fully annotating seven testimonies using BRAT, a web-based annotation tool that allows customized labels for entities and coreferences.[28] Inspired by the annotation process of entities and coreferences in an English literature dataset, we used a customized set of entity types, including named people, groups, communities, geographic locations, organizations, and political entities.[29]

Algorithm 1 Triplets AEO Algorithm

Input: Spacy Tokens for a Relation R and Spacy Tokens for an Object O, Evaluation
Verbs $list_{evaluation}$, Orientation Verbs $list_{orientation}$, Speculative Action Verbs $list_{posact}$
Output: Triplets AEO Category C_{AEO};

1: # Step 1: Initialization
2: Initialize 0 Integers as Status Identifiers, including $r_{has\_evaluation}$, $r_{has\_orientation}$,
r_{has_posact}, r_{has_be}, r_{has_have}, r_{has_to}, r_{has_neg}, r_{has_VBG}, r_{num_verb}, o_{is_adj}, and o_{has_no}
3: # Step 2: Value Assignments for R
4: **for** $r \in R$ **do**
5:     **if** lemma of $r \in list_{evaluation}$ **then** Assign 1 to $r_{has\_evaluation}$
6:     **else if** lemma of $r \in list_{orientation}$ **then** Assign 1 to $r_{has\_orientation}$
7:     **else if** lemma of $r \in list_{posact}$ **then** Assign 1 to r_{has_posact}
8:     **else if** lemma of r *is word be* **then** Assign 1 to r_{has_be}
9:     **else if** lemma of r *is word have* **then** Assign 1 to r_{has_have}
10:     **else if** lemma of r *is word to* **then** Assign 1 to r_{has_to}
11:     **else if** semantic dependency tree tagger of r *is label neg* **then** Assign 1 to r_{has_neg}
12:     **end if**
13: **end for**
14: # Step 3: Value Assignments for O
15: **for** $o \in O$ **do**
16:     **if** lemma of o *is word no* **then** Assign 1 to o_{has_no}
17:     **end if**
18: **end for**
19: **for** $o \in O$ **do**
20:     **if** part of speech tagger of o *is label ADJ* **then** Assign 1 to o_{is_adj}
21:     **end if**
22:     **if** part of speech tagger of $o \in$ *labels NOUN, PROPN, PRON* **then** Assign 0 to
o_{is_adj} and end For loop
23:     **end if**
24: **end for**
25: # Step 4: AEO Category Decision
26: **if** $r_{has\_evaluation}$ and o_{is_adj} **then** $C_{AEO} =$ Evaluation
27: **else if** r_{has_posact} **then** $C_{AEO} =$ Agency_Possible
28: **else if** $r_{has\_orientation}$ **then** $C_{AEO} =$ Orientation
29: **else if** r_{has_neg} or o_{has_no} **then** $C_{AEO} =$ Orientation
30: **else if** r_{has_have} **then**
31:     **if** r_{has_to} **then** $C_{AEO} =$ Agency_Coercive
32:     **else** $C_{AEO} =$ Orientation
33:     **end if**
34: **else if** r_{has_be} **then**
35:     **if** o_{is_adj} **then** $C_{AEO} =$ Evaluation
36:     **else if** r_{has_VBG} **then** $C_{AEO} =$ Agency_Active
37:     **else if** $r_{num\_verb} > 1$ **then** $C_{AEO} =$ Agency_Passive
38:     **else if** $r_{num\_verb} = 1$ **then** $C_{AEO} =$ Orientation
39:     **end if**
40: **else** $C_{AEO} =$ Agency_Active
41: **end if**

FIGURE 6.4: Basic verb characterization algorithm. Created by Lizhou Fan.

Once the annotation was complete, we employed David Bamman's coreference
BERT model for training.[30] The trained model was then used to disambiguate pronouns, focusing especially on references to family members, perpetrators, and
groups. While not perfect, we found that our model identifies about five times as many
pronouns from the testimonies as NeuralCoref, and, of these, it correctly predicts
more than twice as many. The model works well for the pronouns "he" and "she,"

while "they" and "them" are often hard to disambiguate. As documented in our GitHub repository, creating lists of entity types and their associated pronouns ahead of time improves the accuracy (for instance, Mengele = "he" and "him," or grandparents = "they" and "them"), but the process still requires extensive human checking and was not accurate enough to deploy generally.

In the examples discussed in this chapter, we start with our "context-based" approach to triplets extraction for individual testimonies before employing the "meticulous chunk method" for large-scale extraction of triplets across the testimonies. The latter method, with longer object chunks, is also used for the creation of "testimonial ensembles" in the last part of this chapter and the subsequent project description. Here, we also use the coreferencing model and quantify its success rate.

Indexing Agency Using Semantic Triplets

We might begin by asking: why semantic triplets? The answer, in short, is that they represent the fundamental grammatical units for expressions of agency. While conventional indexing is important for finding overarching themes and topics, it relies on the creation of a secondary scaffolding for searching within the testimonies, almost always focused on named entities (mostly nouns). By indexing semantic triplets, we can link and analyze multiple vectors of action. This attunes our reading (and listening) to complex networks of agents, relations, objects, and contexts. As a prototype, we apply this method to four testimonies to show how indexing semantic triplets opens up new interpretations built on the analysis of networks of agency. In the first part of the discussion, we primarily use the "context-based" extraction method for its comparatively simpler identification of objects and clustering. In the second part of our discussion, we turn to testimonial ensembles and use the "meticulous" extraction process to retrieve longer and more complete object phrases.

To give an overview of the results and show how we can work with semantic triplets using network diagrams, we begin with a testimony by Jürgen Bassfreund, a German Jewish survivor first interviewed by David Boder.[31] Conducted in Munich in 1946, Bassfreund's interview describes the rise of Hitler in Germany, the deportation and death of his mother, and the horrific conditions he endured while being transferred between multiple concentration camps, including Auschwitz. We chose this particular interview because Bassfreund—who later changed his name to Jack Bass—was reinterviewed by the USC Shoah Foundation in 1997, in his home in Alabama. The first interview was conducted in

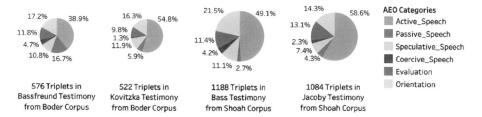

FIGURE 6.5: Distribution of triplet speech categories in four testimonies. Created by Lizhou Fan.

German, and the second was in English.[32] Our next example comes from the interview Boder conducted with Anna Kovitzka in 1946.[33] The fourth interview is with Erika Jacoby, a Hungarian Jew who was deported to Auschwitz with her family in the summer of 1944.[34]

In Figure 6.5, we show statistical summaries of the triplets in each of the testimonies. The triplets were algorithmically extracted from the transcripts, assigned categories by speech type, and manually checked by us for accuracy. The size of each pie chart is scaled to the number of triplets in each transcript. Boder's interviews are shorter than the Shoah Foundation interviews (and, of course, end in 1946, rather than the 1990s). Due to the large number of triplets, we needed to develop ways to categorize and cluster the results. This entailed categorizing the triplets into six types of speech, assigning victim or perpetrator identities (when unequivocal) to subjects and objects, and experimenting with using a Wordnet-based characterization of the objects to cluster them by lemmas. For the "context-based" method of triplet extraction, 7 percent of the triplets were manually corrected. Corrections were made when the extracted subjects, verb relations, or objects were wrong or incomplete. In addition, about 15 percent were manually deleted from the original output because the triplet did not make grammatical sense.[35] To better analyze the triplets and their characterization, we created an interactive triplets dashboard in Tableau (Figure 6.6), which brings together the triplets spreadsheet, an object lemmas bubble plot, and many other filters. Users can also compare the "context-based" (original) extraction process with the "meticulous" extraction process, which has more results and better overall performance (approximately 8 percent of the triplets were corrected and about 7 percent were omitted because they were ungrammatical).[36]

As a finding aid, dashboards such as this one help us query and sort the triplets by interview, subject, object, speech type, and more. In the dashboard, we see

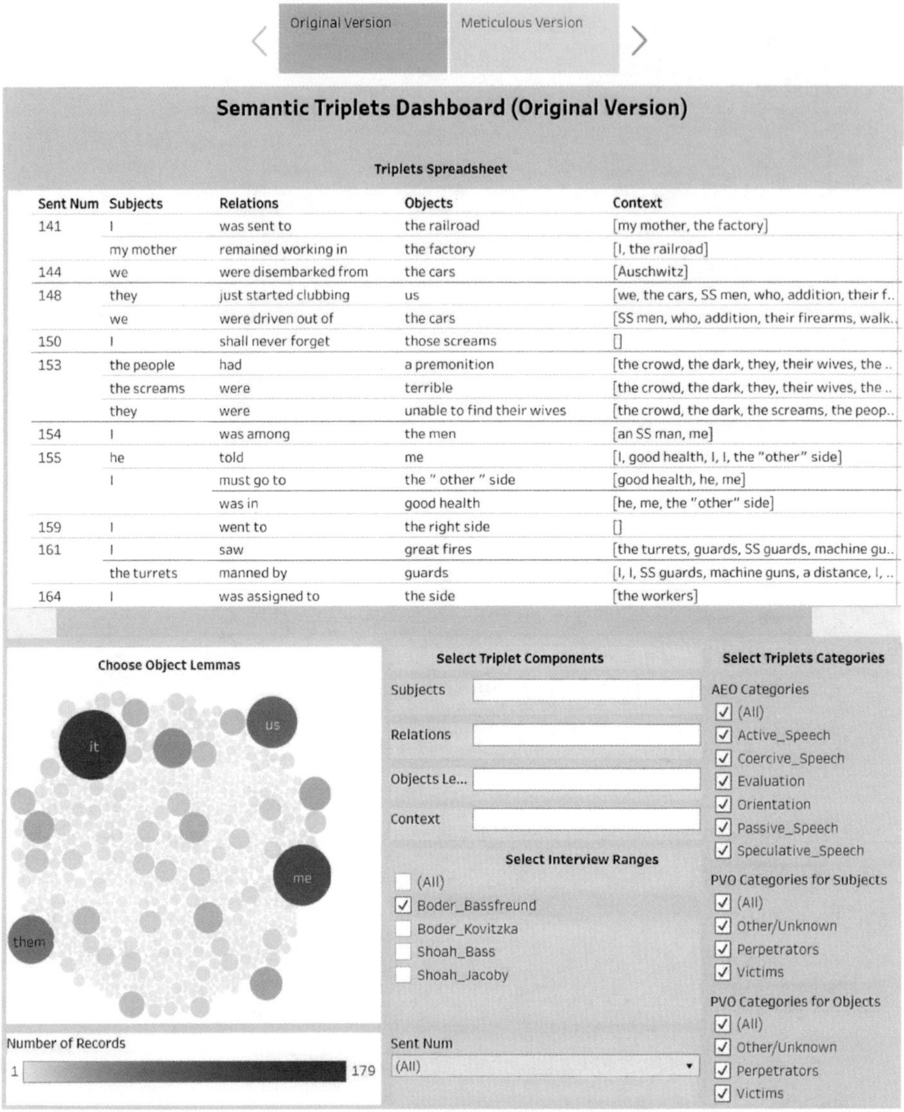

< Original Version   Meticulous Version   >

Semantic Triplets Dashboard (Original Version)

Triplets Spreadsheet

Sent Num	Subjects	Relations	Objects	Context
141	I	was sent to	the railroad	[my mother, the factory]
	my mother	remained working in	the factory	[I, the railroad]
144	we	were disembarked from	the cars	[Auschwitz]
148	they	just started clubbing	us	[we, the cars, SS men, who, addition, their f..
	we	were driven out of	the cars	[SS men, who, addition, their firearms, walk..
150	I	shall never forget	those screams	[]
153	the people	had	a premonition	[the crowd, the dark, they, their wives, the ..
	the screams	were	terrible	[the crowd, the dark, they, their wives, the ..
	they	were	unable to find their wives	[the crowd, the dark, the screams, the peop..
154	I	was among	the men	[an SS man, me]
155	he	told	me	[I, good health, I, I, the "other" side]
	I	must go to	the " other " side	[good health, he, me]
		was in	good health	[he, me, the "other" side]
159	I	went to	the right side	[]
161	I	saw	great fires	[the turrets, guards, SS guards, machine gu..
	the turrets	manned by	guards	[I, I, SS guards, machine guns, a distance, I, ..
164	I	was assigned to	the side	[the workers]

Choose Object Lemmas

(bubble chart with labels: us, it, me, them)

Number of Records

1 ▬▬▬▬▬▬▬▬▬ 179

Select Triplet Components

Subjects   [ ]

Relations   [ ]

Objects Le...   [ ]

Context   [ ]

Select Interview Ranges

- ☐ (All)
- ☑ Boder_Bassfreund
- ☐ Boder_Kovitzka
- ☐ Shoah_Bass
- ☐ Shoah_Jacoby

Sent Num

(All) ▾

Select Triplets Categories

AEO Categories
- ☑ (All)
- ☑ Active_Speech
- ☑ Coercive_Speech
- ☑ Evaluation
- ☑ Orientation
- ☑ Passive_Speech
- ☑ Speculative_Speech

PVO Categories for Subjects
- ☑ (All)
- ☑ Other/Unknown
- ☑ Perpetrators
- ☑ Victims

PVO Categories for Objects
- ☑ (All)
- ☑ Other/Unknown
- ☑ Perpetrators
- ☑ Victims

FIGURE 6.6: Interactive dashboard showing a selection of semantic triplets from Boder's interview with Jürgen Bassfreund (1946). Created by Lizhou Fan and Todd Presner. The dashboard, with over three thousand triplets extracted from four testimonies alongside the original sentences, can be seen on Tableau: hrl.pub/8a1e46.

triplets related to Bassfreund's description of his arrival in Auschwitz, the selection process, and the violence of family separations. They evidence a wide range of speech acts, including active speech about other people's actions ("they just started clubbing us"), passive speech ("we were driven out of the cars" and "I was assigned to the side"), coercive speech ("I had to go to the right side"), speculative speech ("I shall never forget those screams"), evaluation ("the screams were terrible"), and orientation ("the people had a premonition"). The last two also include the contextual terms "the crowd," "the dark," and "their wives," which are part of the sentence from which these triplets are drawn. A search for semantic triplets can be initiated on any term, category, or type of speech within a given testimony or across a group of testimonies. The dashboard represents a powerful way to examine the semantic specificity of the accounts of agency across the testimonies.

Another way triplets can be used is to identify instances of different types of speech. For example, leading up to and following his deportation to Auschwitz, we can visualize all the passive and coercive statements made by Bassfreund in which "we" is the subject (Figure 6.7). There are over thirty such instances of passive and coercive speech in this section of his interview (about ten typewritten pages). Bassfreund emphasizes, with precise language, what was done to him and the Jewish community by the Nazis, including: "We were surrounded by the Elite Guard," "we were moved into railroad cars," "we were loaded into wagons," "we were driven out of the cars," "we were loaded on big trucks," "we were rubbed with kerosene," "we were marked with the triangle," "we were shoved into barracks," and "we had to stand for days."[37]

We can now show how our approach to semantic triplets extends and deepens topical indexing by pairing the triplets with the human-created indexing terms. As developed by both Boder and the Shoah Foundation, we see a significant continuity in terms of topics and themes (places, time periods, people, conditions, and events) used to index the testimonies. For instance, on pages 292–93 of Bassfreund's testimony in *Topical Autobiographies*, Boder indexed the testimony with the following terms: "bathing," "clothing," "hair cutting and shaving," "professional criminals," "confiscations," "punishments," and "tattoos." Similarly, in segment 25 of Bass's testimony, we see the following indexing terms from the Shoah Foundation: "Auschwitz I (Poland: Concentration Camp)," "camp forced labor," "camp latrines," "camp living conditions," "camp selections," "Poland 1941 (June 21)–1945 (May 7)," "prisoner hair cutting forced labor," "transfer from Auschwitz III-Monowitz (Poland: Concentration Camp)," and "transfer to Auschwitz I (Poland: Concentration Camp)." While these topics certainly give us

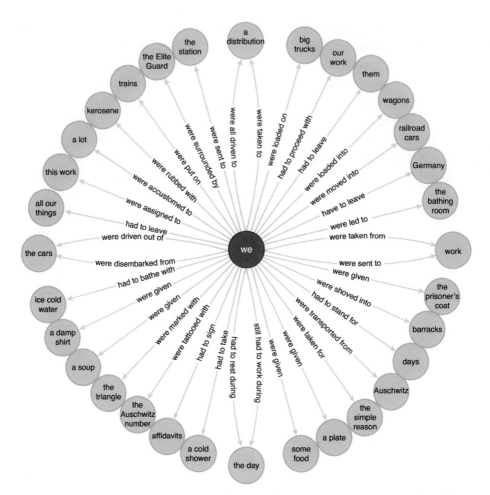

FIGURE 6.7: Passive and coercive triplets from Bassfreund's interview with Boder (1946), with "we" as subject. Created by Lizhou Fan and Todd Presner.

guidance for finding the overarching places, dates, conditions in captivity, movement, and forced labor, the indexing is not at the level of sentences or clauses and, therefore, we do not really know what Bassfreund/Bass did or what was done to him. In Figure 6.8, we produced a corresponding list of just a few of the triplets derived from these specific parts of his testimonies. The interrelated set of triplets provides information about unindexed subjects and agents (both victims and perpetrators), unindexed actions ("written on," "picked up by," "worked in," "filled," "sent"), and unindexed objects ("the formation," "their stomach," "a truck," "the crematories," "human hair," "mattresses," "packages," and "a mountain").

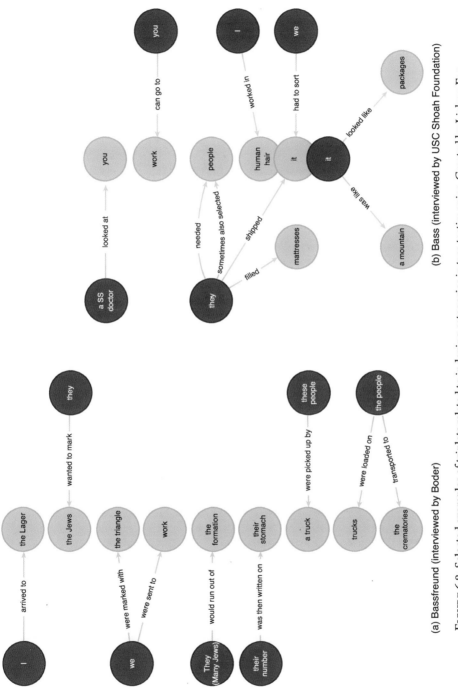

(a) Bassfreund (interviewed by Boder)

(b) Bass (interviewed by USC Shoah Foundation)

FIGURE 6.8: Selected examples of triplets related to indexing categories in two testimonies. Created by Lizhou Fan.

Altogether, they point us to ways of using the extracted semantic triplets to read, mark up, and index testimonies by integrating microhistorical accounts of actions taken by both victims and perpetrators.

Semantic Triplets as Microhistories: Acts of Jewish Resistance

In the foundational historiography of the Holocaust, Jewish victimhood was all too often equated with Jewish passivity. This view found its way into many of the earliest and well-known accounts of the Holocaust, such as those by Raul Hilberg and Bruno Bettelheim, who claimed that Jews put up little to no resistance against the Nazis.[38] And when resistance was spoken about, such as in Hilberg's later writings, it was typically limited to well-known instances of armed resistance to Nazi violence, such as that of the partisans in the East, the uprisings in Treblinka and Sobibor, the Warsaw or Vilna ghetto uprisings, or the Sonderkommando rebellion in Auschwitz. In the years since, the claim of Jewish passivity has been subjected to significant scrutiny and largely debunked.[39] We know that resistance took many forms and occurred in every conceivable context, from local protests and formal civil petitions during the early Nazi years to battles in forests and ghettos, weapons smuggling and rebellions in camps, and wide-ranging acts of intellectual and spiritual resistance during every phase of the Nazi extermination effort. The latter included documentary and archive building projects, such as Emanuel Ringelblum's Oyneg Shabes Archive in the Warsaw Ghetto, as well as diary, memoir, and letter writing, such as the testimonial accounts buried by members of the Sonderkommando in bottles at Auschwitz.[40]

Recent scholarship has turned attention to documenting the range of everyday, seemingly ordinary acts of resistance by individuals. One historian at the vanguard of this reappraisal of Jewish agency is Wolf Gruner, who has delved into numerous police and municipal archives in Germany to uncover the wide range of acts of defiance, opposition, and protest by Jews living in Nazi Germany.[41] In his studies of "microhistories," he has unearthed thousands of examples of Jews mounting both formal and informal protest, ranging from the filing of petitions and government complaints to outright acts of defiance, such as sitting on benches marked "Aryan only" or refusing to use the forced middle name of "Israel" or "Sara," to physical and armed resistance against Nazi officials.[42] For our purposes here, we are interested in using our computational method to identify networks of semantic triplets that bear witness to underappreciated or largely unknown acts of everyday resistance within Holocaust testimonial narratives. Our argument is that triplets point to a wide range of small-scale actions that would otherwise go unremarked, since they do not, generally speaking, rise to the level of what might be indexed as "acts of resistance." Oftentimes, these actions are not even considered to be "indexable content," and thus they are extremely difficult to locate without computational means.

Example 1: Erika Jacoby

After being deported to Auschwitz and separated from her grandparents on the arrival ramp, Jacoby and her mother are selected for the slave labor camp. Their heads are shaven; they are deloused; and they are given meager clothes. Most of Jacoby's testimony, then, focuses on everyday life in Auschwitz, including forced labor, sleeping conditions, food rations, violence, and abuse. While the associated triplets bear witness to her struggle for survival, our index of expressions of agency in Jacoby's testimony also extracted a unique group of triplets. As shown in Table 6.2, after one passive construction, we see five successive, active constructions and one triplet characterized as "orientation" (a computationally assigned category in which the speaker offers explanatory information about something that happened). This strange and astonishing action is not marked up or identified in any way through conventional topic indexing. Jacoby relays the story in just a dozen sentences, comprising about thirty seconds of her two-hour testimony. And yet it is a stunning act of defiance, risk, and agency.

Table 6.2: Triplets from Erika Jacoby's testimony. Created by Lizhou Fan and Todd Presner. Erika Jacoby (July 11, 1994), interview 8, Visual History Archive, USC Shoah Foundation, https://vha.usc.edu/testimony/8. (segments 52–53)

Subjects	Relations	Objects	Category
We	were	taken to a bath	Passive speech
we	were going by	a German officer's area	Active speech
I	saw	a swimming pool	Active speech
I	jumped out of	the line	Active speech
I	dove into	the swimming pool	Active speech
I	swam across	the pool	Active speech
They	didn't shoot	me	Orientation

Here is the portion of the testimony with a little bit of context to set up the scene and reflect on its meaning:

> We stayed six weeks in Auschwitz. We had many, many interesting events that happened to us in Auschwitz. I just want to tell you one that was very important. And I don't think I have time to describe Auschwitz. And I'm sure that it's well known. But we were—one, one day, we were taken to a bath. We were taken to a bath about once a week or once every other week. And as we were marching, we were go—we were going by a German offi-cer's area. And I saw a swimming pool. And I jumped out of the line, and I dove into the swimming pool. And I swam across the pool, and I got back. And they didn't shoot me, and I survived. But of course, my mother almost died. I mean, it was such an irr—irresponsible act from my part. But I was young, and I, I needed to be alive. And I did that.[43]

Indeed, there were at least two "pools" on the grounds of Auschwitz I and II constructed out of cement. They were built as reservoirs to store water and fight fires rather than be used for swimming. When Jacoby arrived in Auschwitz in the summer of 1944, these reservoirs would have been complete. The Shoah Founda-tion tagged these segments of Jacoby's testimony with the following keywords: "camp intake procedures," "camp prisoner marking," "camp family interactions," "loved ones' contacts," "prisoner external contact," and a single person tag, her mother, Malvina Salamonovits. Judging by these tags, one might expect her dis-cussion to focus on procedural elements of the camp, perhaps coupled with how she and her mother survived together. There is nothing in the indexing that would indicate jumping out of line, diving into the pool, and swimming across it. While we can certainly read or hear Jacoby talking about this experience if we happened to land on this part of her testimony, it remains *an unindexed action*, which other-wise submerges a significant act of resistance and memory of agency. Through computational extraction of triplets, we can index, hone in on, and appreciate this defiant act of self-determination.

After Auschwitz is liberated by the Soviet army, Jacoby relays that she and her mother left the camp in search of food and safety from sexual assaults by Russian soldiers. Over the next three and a half minutes (1:18–1:21, segments 78–81), she describes a set of actions that helped her and her mother survive. She also tells of acts of revenge and anger committed by her sixteen-year-old self. Two of the three segments are tagged by the Shoah Foundation as "food acquisition" and "looting" (the third is not tagged at all). These topical terms convey little about the agency involved and the kinds of actions that a listener may want to search and find in her testimony. In Table 6.3, we reproduce the full set of thirty-six semantic triplets that our methodology identified over these three minutes. All forms of agency are included as well as all subjects and objects.

The "we" subject refers to Erika and her mother, and through pronoun disambiguation, we also see that "she" refers to her mother. While "food acquisition" and "looting" are indexing terms that refer to the overall set of content, they tell us nothing specific about what Erika and her mother did in the days after liberation; they tell us nothing about the vectors of agency and reasons for their actions; and they tell us none of the details of the actions conveyed in her testimony. And perhaps more pointedly, the indexing terms tend to obscure more than they reveal: far from abstract topics, "food acquisition" involved the specific act of stealing and eating a pig (a non-kosher act of desperation for survival), while "looting" was connected to Jacoby's immediate postwar actions, which reflected personal anger, acts of revenge, and the longing for a "normal life." The objects she takes from a home are symbols of family life, domesticity, and normalcy: a white tablecloth, an apron, and a little silver cup. Her act of "looting" is to take these everyday, material objects from somebody's home, the first possessions that she acquires after liberation from Auschwitz.

Example 2: Anna Kovitzka

For our second example, we return to Kovitzka's story and begin where she describes her efforts to save her baby girl who was born in the Grodno ghetto. With her husband, she managed to escape the ghetto in the hopes of finding someone to care for her child. Shortly after giving up the child to a Christian woman who promised to protect her, Kovitzka was deported to Auschwitz. Examining the indexing terms used by Boder to mark up her testimony, we see a wide range of themes and topics, including: geographic locations (Wiesbaden, Kielce, Grodno, Slonim, Lvov, and Auschwitz), living conditions and objects (epidemics, starvation, thirst, illness, sleeping accommodations, and clothing), people (children, Gestapo, prisoners of war, family, and "Gypsies"), and events (looting, childbirth, burials, flight, killings, escapes, work, bathing, rebellion, and Appells, or roll calls in camps). The last group of events certainly raises questions about actions, but without further analysis, we cannot know who was looting, escaping, working, rebelling, or even giving birth to a child. Moreover, without delving into the testimony, we cannot uncover specific vectors of agency (such as reports of who did what, how, and to whom).

Table 6.3: Erika Jacoby triplets. Created by Lizhou Fan and Todd Presner. Erika Jacoby (July 11, 1994), interview 8, Visual History Archive, USC Shoah Foundation, https://vha.usc.edu/testimony/8. (segments 78–81)

Subjects	Relations	Objects	Time
we	got out of	the camp	1:18
we	went into	town	1:18
we	looked for	a house	1:18
we	found	a very beautiful home	1:18
we	occupied	it	1:18
we	couldn't lock	the door	1:19
we	barricade	it	1:19
they	broke into	the stores	1:19
I	shoved	a lot	1:19
we	had	a canvas bag	1:19
we	passed by	a butcher store	1:19
I	took off	half a pig	1:19
I	carried	it	1:19
my mother	saw	it	1:19
she	cooked	the pig	1:19
we	ate	it	1:20
we	got	sick	1:20
I	was trying to find	a way	1:20
We	stayed in	this town	1:20
I	want to mention to	you	1:20
I	didn't bring	it	1:20
I	have	a memento	1:20
I	broke into	a house	1:20
I	had	so much anger	1:20
I	expressed	that anger	1:20
I	went into	that house	1:20
I	broke	the piano	1:20
many people	went into	homes	1:21
I	did not want	anything	1:21
I	took from	the house	1:21
I	took	a white tablecloth	1:21
I	took	an apron	1:21
I	took	a little silver cup	1:21
it	had	the initials	1:21
I	kept	it	1:21
I	longed to establish	a normal life	1:21

Table 6.4: Anna Kovitzka triplets around "escapes" using "context-based" chunk method. Created by Lizhou Fan.

Subjects	Relations	Objects	Context terms and coreferences
I	went over	the wires	second attempt, my man, me, the child, her
my man	handed	the child	I, the wires, the second attempt, me, I, her
My man	set up	a chair	me
He	raised	one wire	manual coreference: he = my man
He	handed	the child	me; manual coreference: he = my man
I	went out in	the street	
I	removed	the yellow patch	

By examining the semantic triplets around the topical indexing term "escapes," we can illuminate the specific agency described by Kovitzka in this part of her testimony. The triplets indicate the actions taken by Kovitzka and her husband to escape the ghetto to save their child: they "went over" the wires, "set up" a chair, "raised" one wire, "went out" in the street, and "removed" the yellow patch. In each case, we see active speech describing a set of actions that occurred in the context of escaping the ghetto, even after she had earlier reported that sixteen Jews were killed at the gate in a first attempt to escape. While this section of the text is indexed by Boder as "escapes," "curfew," "fences," and "yellow star," the acts of escaping the ghetto through the wires, removing the yellow Star of David, and going out on the street represent expressions of everyday resistance that can be specified through computational text analysis attuned to semantic triplets. Table 6.4 shows the results from our original extraction process, including the "context terms" that occur alongside the direct object and manually defined coreferences for pronouns. Table 6.5 shows the "meticulous chunk method," in which fuller object phrases were extracted, with coreferences algorithmically assigned using the experimental machine-learning process described in the methodology.

Triplets in Semantic Networks

Moving beyond sequential outputs in tables, we will now demonstrate how networks of semantic triplets can be used to interpret patterns of agency and relationships throughout a testimonial narrative. Of the 522 triplets identified

Table 6.5: Anna Kovitzka triplets around "escapes" using "meticulous" chunk method and algorithmic coreferencing of pronouns. Created by Lizhou Fan.

Subjects	Relations	Objects
I	went	over the wires in the second attempt
my man	handed	me the child
I	carried	the child
My man	set up	a chair for me
My man	raised	one wire I crawled
They	had	no electric wires
My man	handed	me the child
I	went	out in the street
I	removed	the yellow patch

in Kovitzka's testimony, the term "child" is among the most frequent terms to occur throughout the triplets as both subject and object as well as part of the "contextual information" retrieved by the algorithm. The latter set of triplets does not contain the word "child," but because that term is part of the whole sentence, it functions as a lexical association and points us to additional, related triplets. Following the logic of a graph database, we can create and examine the network relations between the triplets and their sentence-level contexts. To show how this might work, we used Neo4j (a network visualization tool) to create a network graph of the triplets in the testimony associated with the term "child" (Figure 6.9).[44] Rather than simply searching for discrete mentions of thematic or topical terms, we are able to render visible the complex set of network associations between a single key relation: "I" and "child." But more than just linked terms, the triplets allow us to see the multiple interrelations between agents and objects involved in the actions of trying to save her child.

Far from being a definitive representation, the network visualization is an interpretive model that helps us consider the relationships of action that made a difference and brought about distinct events. We made the decision to place the speaker, Anna Kovitzka ("I"), at the center of the network as the primary actant who relays that she did certain things and provided reasons for her intentional acts. Her child and her decisions to try to save her child are the object of most of her thoughts and actions, but many other subjects, relations, and objects are linked to the child, opening up a complex social network of contin-

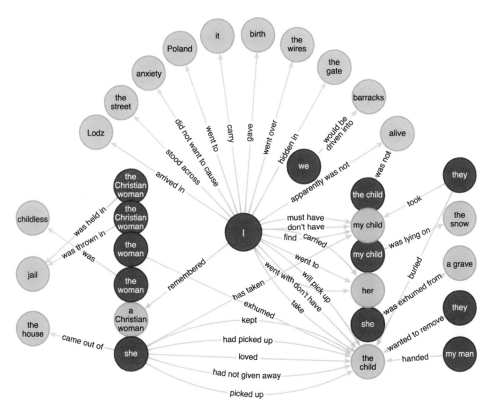

FIGURE 6.9: Network of triplets containing "child" in Kovitzka's testimony. Created by Lizhou Fan and Todd Presner.

gent relations. Kovitzka's single mention of remembering "a Christian woman" opens up a space of possibility. In addition to human actants and objects, there are also non-human objects, places, and assessments (jail, childless, house, gate, wires, street, snow, grave) that form the periphery of the network and establish its material, social dimension.

In all, this network diagram shows thirty-eight triplets related to the term "child." "The child," "my child," or "her" is most frequently an object (light colored nodes), and only three times is "the child," "my child," or "she" a subject (dark colored nodes). Disturbingly, as a subject, the child is lying in the snow, not alive, and was exhumed. But as an object, the child is kept, loved, picked up, taken, handed, held, and saved by various people. And perhaps more revealing are the triplets that do not include the key term "child" but are either directly linked to the subjects and objects at the center of the network or indirectly linked to other objects and relations (and, in one case, floating freely as a contextual element). Starting with the linked triplets, we find a number that describe Kovitzka's escape from the ghetto and her decision to give the child to a Christian woman: "I went over the wires," "I remembered a Christian woman," "I stood across the street," and "I hidden in the gate." In addition, we see a number of triplets around the node "she" (which refers to the Christian woman),[45] evidencing actions Kovitzka directly observed as well as found out after the war: "She came out of the house," "she has taken my child," "she picked up the child," "she had not given away the child," "she loved the child," and "she kept the child."

If we look at the indirectly connected triplets derived from the adjacent contextual terms, we see a number of reported actions that Kovitzka discovered after the war, when she went back to Poland to look for her child: "The Christian woman was thrown in jail," "that Christian woman was held in jail," and "the woman was childless." These indirect triplets help to clarify some of the other triplets, including, "They took my child," "They buried the child," and "the woman exhumed the child." After the Christian woman who promised to protect her child was denounced, the child was killed by the Nazis and apparently buried in a Christian cemetery. Kovitzka found out from a friend of the Christian woman that the child was exhumed after the war and moved to a desecrated Jewish cemetery.

Our interpretive model takes Kovitzka's expressions of agency as "traces of a network . . . that renders the movement of the social visible to the reader," to use Latour's articulation. For him, "a network is a tool to help describe something," not a thing that exists out there in the world.[46] In practice, this means identifying and assembling expressions of agency that show mediation, association, action, transference, and relationality. Derived directly from the spoken language of the survivor, the resulting network is both a process and product of interpretation. The network is an interpretive act made possible by a combination of algorithmic methods of information extraction and humanities visualization. Not unlike Andrew Piper's method of diagrammatic reading of literary texts, the network—as a visual diagram—functions as "a drawing that connects two different sign systems . . . a paratextual form that draws together disparate things to understand them in a conditional way." In our case, the network diagram "draws together" semantic triplets into a kind of contingent, "perspectival totality."[47]

Attuned to her descriptions of the actions she and others took to save her child, the network diagram is thus a summary of the traumatic loss at the core of Kovitzka's testimony.[48] Visualizing the semantic triplets in the form of a network diagram allows us to identify, index, and interpret these critically important and tragic actions at the center of her narrative. While the visualization provides a modicum of synoptic clarity, we want to underscore that these actions conveyed by Kovitzka emerge throughout the entire testimony and are spoken in a language permeated by raw emotions. Although the intentions of the actions taken by her and others do not change, the emotional valences of the words are only hinted at in this diagram. Indeed, they may help sharpen our listening and reading by linking together unaccounted and unindexed actions and, ultimately, point us back to the richness and tragedy of her spoken testimony.

Toggling between Microhistories and Macrohistories of Antisemitism

In the last sections of this chapter, we will explore a method for using semantic triplets to compose and visualize "testimonial ensembles" that bear witness—through many voices—to macrohistorical dynamics. How might we use the semantic triplets from individual testimonies to give voice to shared experiences across hundreds or even thousands of testimonies?[49] The ability to toggle or shift the scale has significant implications for how we think about, study, and analyze historical events, especially events of mass atrocity, which are, by definition, experienced by large numbers of people, potentially creating a framework for a "mass testimony."[50] The ability to toggle the view from an individual witness's account to aggregate perspectives on events and then back again to individual accounts preserves the integrity of the singular witness testimony while opening up new possibilities for comparison and collective analysis.

Below, we focus on one macrohistory from the survivor testimonies: How do approximately one thousand Holocaust survivors from across Europe remember having experienced antisemitism in the late 1930s and early 1940s? What knowledge can be gained and what principles should be followed in bringing together these accounts? How can spreadsheets and visualizations of semantic triplets help us responsibly create a "testimonial ensemble" that bears witness to the Pan-European experiences of antisemitism and, at the same time, preserve the individual voices? Finally, what unique reactions to antisemitism—especially small-scale or microhistorical acts of resistance—can we find among the many witness accounts?

For our demonstration here, all the testimonies that we used were recorded in English by the USC Shoah Foundation in the late 1990s and early 2000s and include survivors from Germany, Poland, Czechoslovakia, Hungary, France,

Belgium, and other countries. We honed in on the segments of the testimonies that were manually tagged by the Shoah Foundation with keywords related to the broad categories of "discrimination" and "personal prejudice" as well as the segments immediately before and after these tags. In terms of narrative sequence, the vast majority of these tags occur in the first quarter of the testimony, which, following the intention of the Shoah Foundation to create a chronological life narrative, generally connote the period before the start of World War II or before the ghettoization and deportation of Jews began in a given country.[51] Under these tags are keywords that reference various experiences of antisemitism, such as anti-Jewish measures, anti-Jewish laws, school antisemitism, and religious antisemitism. They do not, however, tell us about the specific experiences of antisemitism or reveal the range of actions that constituted the broader cultural and social milieu. The contribution of our computational methodology is to bring into the foreground the specific actions of and reactions to antisemitism.

We used the tags for guidance to identify the relevant segments in 1,053 English language transcripts. Our algorithm extracted 61,450 semantic triplets from these segments of the survivor testimonies.[52] Of these, nearly half (28,713) were classified as "active" speech expressions; 20,468 were classified as "orientation" (generally information, knowledge, explanations, and observations by the witness rather than direct experiences); 1,542 were characterized as expressions of "coercion/necessity," which include things the speaker was forced to do or had to do;[53] 2,248 were classified as "passive" expressions, mostly actions that happened to the speaker or targeted members of the Jewish community; 4,567 were speculative/modal expressions, generally expressions of potentiality, desire, or possibility; and finally, 3,912 were classified as "evaluation" (expressions of how the witness felt or assessed a situation). These categories are not absolute, fixed, or always correct, as they were algorithmically assigned with the aim of helping human readers navigate scale and aid interpretation. Moreover, most of the individual triplets are not reports of specific antisemitic actions (or reactions to them) but rather narrative elements of a broader historical description.

Given the large number of results, we filtered them by combining subject and speech categories, as described previously. For example, querying only the triplets with "we" as the subject in the coercive and passive speech categories, we retrieve eight hundred triplets, such as the following: "We were thrown out of public schools," "we had to close the gates because this was the start of a pogrom," "we had to wear a yellow star," "we had to hand in this crystal radio," "we had to give up all our pets," "we had to observe the curfew," "we had to sit on separate benches," "we had to jump off the sidewalk," "we were attacked by 10, 15 of the Hitler Youth," "we were spat at on the street," "we were degraded to the status of the dogs," "we were usually assaulted with stones," "we were thrown out of our home," "we had to hand in all the bank accounts, all the jewelry," "we had to leave our apartment," "we have to pay because we killed their god," and "we were barred from certain sections of the city." Taking just one of these experiences ("we had to wear a yellow star"), we can also filter by object ("star") to see how hundreds of witnesses describe being forced to wear the star or identify their businesses by a Jewish star. Among the many responses are people who also describe "hiding," "covering," "not wearing," or having "removed" the star. We start to gain a broader, collective, and differentiated perspective that would not be possible without many accounts and many voices being brought together. And although these specific triplets are pulled out of the context of the individual testimonies, each triplet is always linked back in the spreadsheet to the specific narrative segment and sentence said by an individual. This trackback is a way of preserving the coherence of the testimony in the face of what could become a form of narrative fragmentation.[54]

From the 61,450 semantic triplets, we used the passive and coercive triplets as "pointers" to first identify and highlight specific antisemitic actions. We then moved syntagmatically through the spreadsheet to understand more of the context for each passive and coercive action reported. The results bear witness to experiences of isolation, deprivation, humiliation, fear, blame, and violence. Altogether, they help us perceive a wide range of actions and reactions under the general subject headings of "discrimination" and "personal prejudice." As an ensemble, the triplets paint a picture of a Pan-European social and political field as it starts to radically and violently contract.[55]

To facilitate viewing the results and show how individual witness accounts can be used to construct a collectively shared experience, we created a smaller, curated spreadsheet used for the visualizations discussed below (Table 6.6). Bringing together a multitude of fragments of memory from the life stories of many different individuals, a multivoiced testimony functions as an ensemble. Unlike the singularity of an individual testimony that unfolds linearly and covers a life story through an interview, a testimonial ensemble is a union of many different voices brought together to bear witness, in this case, to a Pan-European experience. In other words, it represents the assembly of a collective voice, which algorithmic processes coupled with human curation can help to compose. In our sample interfaces, the witnesses come from all over Europe, and they attest to the multitude of antisemitic laws and practices that radically isolated the Jews across

Table 6.6: Sample results from a filtered spreadsheet used for network visualizations: 268 witnesses and 607 semantic triplets. Created by Todd Presner. The full spreadsheet can be found on our project website.

Speaker	Subject	Relation	Object
Frances Gelbart	we	could not walk	on the streets
Frances Gelbart	We	had to walk	on the streets near the gutters
Rose Schindler	they	put	a curfew
Rose Schindler	we	had	a lot of restrictions
Rose Schindler	we	had to wear	the Jewish star on our arms
Rose Schindler	if somebody	did have	a radio they would have to hide it in the basement
Arthur Stern	the Jews	have to sit	in the last row unless they want to be beaten
Alex Stern	we	were really isolated	from the Christian community
Bronislaw Zajbert	somebody	could tell	it was a German we would have to step off the sidewalk and bow
Bronislaw Zajbert	we	had to wear	the Star of David yellow the front the back of our dress clothes the outside our garments
Liz Manning	they	made	them clean the streets with toothbrushes
Renata Adler	They	had	signs dogs bicycles Jews not allowed
Frederick Baar	Everybody	had to wear	an armband
Frederick Baar	Then you	have to turn	in all the silver gold jewelry
Frederick Baar	Then you	have to turn	in furs cameras then radios
Moshe Taube	I	had to put	on a band with a Magen David Star of David
Moshe Taube	I	could not ride	in any trolley
Moshe Taube	I	could not take	any buses
Richard Pick	they	were singing	songs against the Jews
Paul Goldstein	all Jewish enterprises	had to have	a sign
Paul Goldstein	we	were taught	the Christian prayers the Hail Mary the other prayers
Gerda Frieberg	they	sweep	the streets the sidewalks
Gerda Frieberg	we	had to wear	the Star of David
Gerda Frieberg	you	could not leave	your home without it
Gerda Frieberg	any silver	had to be delivered	to the police

Speaker	Subject	Relation	Object
Gerda Frieberg	They	meticulously made	a list of what you gave them
Judith Adler	you	have to put	on a yellow star
Judith Adler	we	had to wear	a yellow star
Eli Stern	we	had to wear	yellow arm bands we would made
Fred Roer	the Jews	have to walk	in the street
Fred Roer	You	had	curfews
Fred Roer	You	had to have	special ID cards
Fred Roer	You	had to wear	your star
Joseph Gringlas	We	could not swim	with the Gentiles in same river

Europe throughout the 1930s and early 40s. We then turn to documenting microhistorical accounts of reaction and resistance across the testimonies.

In this screenshot of a network visualization (Figure 6.10), we see a zoomed-out view of all 607 semantic triplets expressed by 268 survivors. Nodes are subjects and objects, and edges (linkages) are verb relations. Clusters of nodes indicate shared subjects or objects (such as "we," "they," "to the movies," or "on the sidewalk"). The single nodes along the periphery are unique and do not share nodes or edges with any other triplet in this set. Zooming in allows us to delve into individual clusters, such as "we" and "they," the two main clusters in the spreadsheet (Figures 6.11–6.12). For each triplet, we show the entire sentence in which that triplet is contained, the name of the speaker, and a link back to the testimony from which the triplet was extracted. The verb relations (edges) connecting two nodes are shown when a user hovers over or clicks on a given triplet.

The second experimental visualization (Figures 6.13–6.14) brings together the voices of survivors narrating specific memories of antisemitic discrimination under Nazi occupation. We used the same spreadsheet of 607 discrimination triplets to go back to the specific segments in each testimony's transcript where a discriminatory experience was described though a coercive or passive semantic triplet. We then extracted those segments—both words and voices—and used them to create an experimental interface for reading and hearing the accounts. Inspired by the National AIDS Memorial online and the Dutch Jewish Monument, we sought to develop a prototype for an open-ended, nonlinear "generous interface" that allows users to begin to experience the scale of the events being described[56]—in this case, the pervasiveness of antisemitic violence preceding the

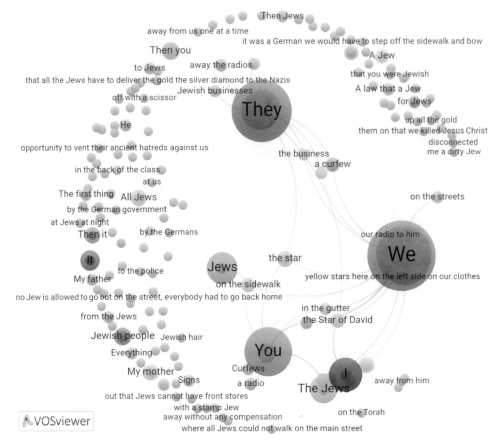

FIGURE 6.10: Network visualization of 607 semantic triplets derived from the Visual History Archive, USC Shoah Foundation, built using VOSviewer (https://app.vosviewer.com/). Created by Jack Schaefer and Todd Presner. Full documentation, including how to recreate the visualization, is available on our project website (https://holocaustresearchlab.com/book/chapter-6/). An interactive prototype can be viewed on the website or by using the QR code.

Holocaust. Users can scroll through the faces in any order, clicking on a survivor to bring up a specific quotation from the testimony, which can be read as well as heard in the survivor's own voice. Links can be followed to take users to the full testimony in the USC Visual History Archive, or users can click through the faces to create a testimonial ensemble.[57] While only an excerpt of the 1,053 testimonies and the thousands of semantic triplets that document antisemitic actions and

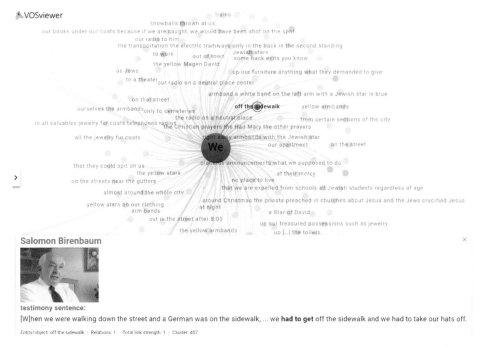

FIGURE 6.11: Zoomed-in network cluster around "we" node. Created by Jack Schaefer and Todd Presner. Salomon Birenbaum (Mar 13, 1998), interview 39917, Visual History Archive, USC Shoah Foundation, https://vha.usc.edu/testimony/39917.

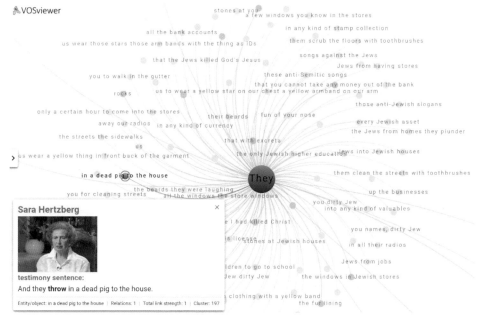

FIGURE 6.12: Zoomed-in network cluster around "they" node. Created by Jack Schaefer and Todd Presner. Sara Hertzberg (Mar 15, 1995), interview 1511, Visual History Archive, USC Shoah Foundation, https://vha.usc.edu/testimony/1511.

FIGURE 6.13: Experimental interface derived from testimonies in the Visual History Archive, USC Shoah Foundation. Created by Chereen Tam. An interactive prototype can be viewed on our project website (https://holocaustresearchlab.com/book/chapter-6/) or by using the QR code.

reactions, the experimental interface creates a visual form to experience a multi-voiced testimony that bears witness to a Pan-European, political and social field of discriminatory violence.

Microhistorical Acts of Defiance

Even as the field of possibilities constantly mutated and contracted with ever newer forms of disenfranchisement and antisemitic discrimination, many survivors also recount microhistorical actions of resistance and personal responses to antisemitic violence. We can also use the full spreadsheet of semantic triplets to locate examples of these individual reactions and small-scale acts of defiance. As we saw earlier, these actions—often expressed in just a sentence or two—are unindexed as specific actions, even if the segment is tagged with a general topic heading such as "anti-Jewish measures" or "school antisemitism." Without delving into the narratives, we cannot know "who did what and to whom" since no keyword search will retrieve these actions. Our semantic triplets algorithm extracts and helps characterize such expressions of agency.

To find such microhistorical acts of defiance, we began by filtering the spreadsheet of 61,450 semantic triplets from the 1,053 survivor testimonies by ones with "I" or "we" as subject and active forms of agency (excluding the most fre-

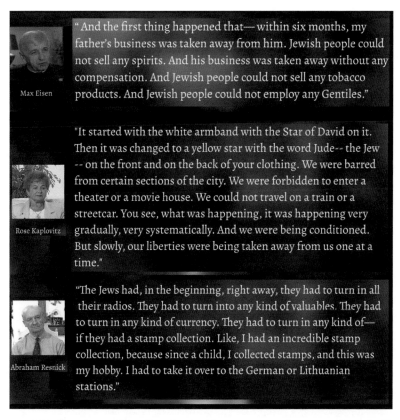

Max Eisen

" And the first thing happened that— within six months, my father's business was taken away from him. Jewish people could not sell any spirits. And his business was taken away without any compensation. And Jewish people could not sell any tobacco products. And Jewish people could not employ any Gentiles."

Rose Kaplovitz

"It started with the white armband with the Star of David on it. Then it was changed to a yellow star with the word Jude-- the Jew -- on the front and on the back of your clothing. We were barred from certain sections of the city. We were forbidden to enter a theater or a movie house. We could not travel on a train or a streetcar. You see, what was happening, it was happening very gradually, very systematically. And we were being conditioned. But slowly, our liberties were being taken away from us one at a time."

Abraham Resnick

"The Jews had, in the beginning, right away, they had to turn in all their radios. They had to turn into any kind of valuables. They had to turn in any kind of currency. They had to turn in any kind of— if they had a stamp collection. Like, I had an incredible stamp collection, because since a child, I collected stamps, and this was my hobby. I had to take it over to the German or Lithuanian stations."

FIGURE 6.14: Experimental interface showing three testimonial segments from the Visual History Archive, USC Shoah Foundation: Max Eisen (February 15, 1995), interview 942, tape 1, minute 21:31–21:41, https://vha.usc.edu/testimony/942; Rose Kaplovitz (April 3, 1995), interview 1858, tape 1, minutes 22:39–23:19, https://vha.usc.edu/testimony/1858; Abraham Resnick (March 31, 1995), interview 1975, tape 1, minute 26:19–26:45, https://vha.usc.edu/testimony/1975.

quent verbs of "was," "were," "had," "have," and "went"). This left a filtered spreadsheet of about eleven thousand semantic triplets, which were read manually—focusing on verbs—to locate unique actions of resistance and defiance.[58] The active triplets could, then, be used to point us back to the fuller text in the testimonial narrative. For example, Stanley Krakowski, a Polish Jew, says: "I destroyed the radio" and "I broke it in the courtyard." He then recounts obtaining the keys to someone else's apartment and surreptitiously listening to their radio. ("I used to listen to stations from other countries"). The active verbs ("broke," "destroyed," and "used to listen to") with "I" as subject all occur in the context of a coerced action: "All the Jewish people have to give the radios."[59] Krakowski is, in fact, not the only survivor who recounts breaking the radio rather than turning it in to the Nazis. Below, we enumerate a series of other instances of unindexed acts of resistance to antisemitic violence.

Many survivors convey experiences of getting into fights while in school and various acts of fighting back. Roman Ziegler, for example, talks about getting into fights with Polish Christian kids: "I gave somebody bloody noses," he says. Rose Minsky, a Polish Jew, remembers boys throwing stones at her. She says that she "threw one stone" back at a boy from the "Gentile section" of Warsaw, but when the stone hit him in the head and caused him to bleed, she recalls running home and being scared that he would come after her. A Polish Jew named Halina Strnad, in recalling childhood antisemitism, says in passing: "I climbed chestnut trees," "I collected a lot of chestnuts," and "I fought with them," referencing throwing chestnuts at antisemitic boys from the town's German school. Bernard Zelinger, a Polish Jew, remembers fights between Jewish kids and Christian kids in school. Although small and short, he says he was "very, very strong physically" and that he still has "scars here from hitting somebody and breaking a tooth." Stephen Howard, a Polish Jew, remembers getting into "fisticuffs with kids in school." Alex Gross, a Czech Jew, remembers being attacked, along with his brother, by a group of Hitler Youth. He says that they "managed to get some stones and somehow crawled under the mud and started bashing their heads in." He adds, "We left all of them bleeding."[60]

Resistance within school took many forms, not just fighting back physically: Ruth Rack, a German Jew, recalls assemblies in which her teachers made the students stand on a platform and say "heil Hitler." She says: "I used to say it 'dreil litler,'" which was intentionally "gibberish" and that she used to "say it very softly, because I didn't want to say heil Hitler." Henrietta Diament, a Polish Jew, recalls an incident in school in which she was called a "dirty Jew" by a Polish girl in her class. She responded by saying, "You are dirty," and goes on to explain, "I took two inkwells," and "I spread [the ink] on her head." Other survivors remember acts of speaking out publicly in school, such as Magda Marx, a Hungarian Jew, who recounts how she stepped "up to the platform where the teacher should be" and told a group of Christian students who had just made antisemitic comments: "Shame on you what you said." Emphasizing her pride in being Jewish, she tells her fellow students: "I will be a princess. Because I have proof that I am a descendant of King David." Helmut Gruenewald, a German Jew, remembers his teacher saying "it was the fault of the Jews" that Germany lost World War I. He stood up in class and said: "I believe you are not right. My father was fighting on behalf of Germany. Two of my uncles lost their lives." He was then beaten for his insubordination. Morris Beschloss, a German Jew, remembers being kicked out of school after Kristallnacht—but before leaving, he got up in front of the class to make a speech condemning the Nazis: "I made a violent speech hoping that the filthy French would come in there and kill them and that the Russian Cossacks would come with their curved swords." The teacher dragged him out of class, telling his classmates that he was "crazy" in the hopes that they would not report him.[61]

Erika Jacoby articulates resistance in terms of personal betterment: after she was kicked out of school, she says that she "decided to study languages," teaching herself German, Hebrew, and English. Ruth Oppenheimer, a German Jew, said that after Jews were barred from attending concerts and going to movies, she was "starved for music," so she "sometimes snuck into a church to hear music." Paul Goldstein, a Belgian Jew, yoked physical survival and resistance together. After his parents helped him and his brother change their names and go into hiding with a Gentile family, he recalls going to church and behaving as good Christians. In addition to a series of triplets that recall being taught Christian prayers and saying the Hail Mary, he recalls a fountain in the church from which the Jewish children, deprived of food and water, used to drink: "As a matter of fact, I didn't mind going to that church because that church had some kind of a—of a grotto, a little altar to some miraculous—miracle-performing saint, and there was a little fountain there with—with—with water, and since we were really deprived of food and drink, it was an opportunity to quench our thirst, so that was a good side of going to church." Despite the pauses and stuttering in the sentence, our process extracted six triplets from this sentence, including "I didn't mind going to that church," "we were really deprived of food and drink," "it was an opportunity to quench our thirst," and "that was a good side of going to Church."[62]

Finally, numerous survivors remember taking off the yellow star or the armband that they were forced to wear in public after 1941 to identify themselves as Jewish. Roman Ziegler says, in the context of going out to get some potatoes and fearing being denounced: "I removed my armband"; Eugene Feld says: "I did not wear it," "I refused to wear it," and "I traveled without knowing I am a Jew." Henri Wittelsohn says: "I wore the star, but I hid the star as much as I could hide the star." Another survivor, Anita Karl, remembers her father telling her mother after they were forced to wear the star in the ghetto: "You are not sewing that in shame"—instead, "you are sewing that with pride." Henry Oertelt, a German Jew who grew up in Berlin, recalls how "a loose corner of this dumb star could cost you your life." He describes engineering a star shape out of a tin can to which he attached a cloth Star of David with a clasping pin: "I took one [of] those stars" and "I glued it onto that metal piece." He did this, he says, so that he could attach and remove it from his clothes at will, thereby allowing him to attend concerts and soccer games.[63]

All told, these small-scale acts of resistance—initially extracted and characterized algorithmically in the form of semantic triplets—help us appreciate the range and diversity of individual acts of resistance, which may otherwise have gone unnoticed. The process, however, is not automatic, and we cannot simply set the algorithm free and expect it to tell us what is interesting, important, or worth knowing about. In concert with human judgment and interpretation, the algorithm functions as a heuristic, a tool for text analysis and decision-making, with both epistemological and ethical consequences at each stage of extraction, visualization, and interpretation.

Because we used the USC Shoah Foundation's metadata tags related to discrimination and anti-Jewish measures to identify the parts of the testimonies that describe antisemitic actions and reactions, our process still relies on human indexing to first identify the relevant segments related to antisemitism. Going forward, another approach would be to supplement human indexing with machine indexing to include actions that come from any part of a testimony, especially those parts that have not been indexed or tagged with keywords. This process may also enhance human indexing, allowing us to find actions that human listeners may have overlooked, ignored, or simply not registered. But the challenge of doing so is somewhat analogous to finding needles in a haystack since we need even more robust ways to filter and classify the massive number of triplets, which sometimes exceed several thousand per testimony.

Before concluding, we will examine one more example of an extraordinary act of resistance that demonstrates this challenge. Near the beginning of their conversation, the interviewer asks Rose Minsky: "Did your family attend any of the cultural activities, the theater or shows?" She speaks briefly about how much her father loved the Jewish theater before she recalls how much he also loved listening to music on the radio. This reminds her of the expensive radio their family had bought on installments, which was kept in a big cabinet. She then says that the family had to give up everything—furs, jewelry, money, the radio—to the Nazis in 1939. But rather than give up their radio, the family decided to take it down to the basement, chop it up into pieces, and put it down the sewage drain as an act of defiance. In the testimony, Minsky makes a chopping gesture with her arms (Figure 6.15). She ends with a reflection: "So my father said, don't worry, children.

FIGURE 6.15: Screenshot of Rose Minsky (December 7, 1994), interview 422, Visual History Archive, USC Shoah Foundation, https://vha.usc.edu/testimony/422.

Don't cry. If we're going to survive, if we're going to live, there will be another radio. That was his last—his words."[64] Tagged only with the name of her father, Simcha Rotkelichen, the actions described in this three-minute segment (taking the radio down to the basement, chopping it up with an ax, and putting it down the drain) are not findable through any standard keyword search process. Like Jacoby's spontaneous act of jumping into the pool at Auschwitz, it remains an unindexed act of defiance.

Even though most of the triplets were correctly extracted from this segment of the transcript, these microhistorical acts of individual resistance still remain hidden in a spreadsheet of thousands of other triplets (Figure 6.16). How can we surface such fascinating and defiant microhistorical actions? One way that we have already explored is to consider certain triplets as "pointers" to larger groups of unindexed actions and reactions. For instance, filtering Minsky's testimony by "agency coercion/necessity" results in fifty total triplets, of which two ("we had to give up everything to the Germans" and "we had to pay one more installment") point syntagmatically to a sequence of connected actions related to what the family did with its radio. Other modes of filtering—such as by subjects, speech categories, object lemmas, and wordnet synsets—can facilitate further search and discovery. The identification of these fugitive acts (such as chopping the radio and putting it down the drain) falls to human readers to filter, read, and judge in ways that can help bring these microhistorical actions to the foreground. In the final analysis, the algorithm cannot tell us what is important and worth knowing about, but it can help facilitate a process of search, discovery, and characterization.

	subjects_coref	relations	objects	texts	speaker	AEO_cat
376				But then Hitler came out in -- came in in September,1939.	RM	
377	We	had to give	up everything to the Germans	We had to give up everything to the Germans.	RM	Agency_Coercion/Necessity
378				Fur coats, radios, jewelry, money.	RM	
379	all of a sudden	became	their property	Everything all of a sudden became their property.	RM	Agency_Active
380	we	paid	already the radio	So my father -- we had to pay -- we paid up already the radio.	RM	Agency_Active
381	We	had to pay	one more installment	We had to pay one more installment.	RM	Agency_Coercion/Necessity
382	I	won't give	them this radio	And my father said, I won't give them this radio.	RM	Orientation
383	my father	could not hide	it	But he couldn't hide it either.	RM	Agency_Speculative/Modal
384	It	was	a big cabinet	It was a big cabinet.	RM	Orientation
385	So my mother	came	up with an idea to take the radio down to the basement	So my mother came up with an idea to take the radio down to the basement	RM	Agency_Active
386	So my mother	to chop	it up in small pieces	So my mother came up with an idea to take the radio down to the basement	RM	Agency_Active
387	it	go	down in the drain	So my mother came up with an idea to take the radio down to the basement	RM	Agency_Active
388				That's what we did.	RM	
389				And we all started crying.	RM	
390	We	loved	that radio	We loved that radio so much.	RM	Agency_Active
391	We	had	so much enjoyment	We had so much enjoyment.	RM	Orientation
392	my father	stays	with an ax	And all of a sudden, my father stays with an ax.	RM	Agency_Active
393	I	still can see	it	I still can see it, the way he chops the radio.	RM	Agency_Speculative/Modal
394	my father	chops	the radio	I still can see it, the way he chops the radio.	RM	Agency_Active

FIGURE 6.16: List of sequential triplets from Rose Minsky's testimony describing the chopping of the radio, with subject coreferences (tape 2, minutes 16:37–17:43).

An ethics of the algorithm does not outsource human judgment to an algorithm; instead, it uses algorithms as analytical tools for exploration, attunement, and interpretative co-creation.

Limitations and Further Steps

While our process of extracting and characterizing triplets creates new paratexts that enable us to index and visualize testimonies by descriptions of agency, there are a number of limitations and shortcomings. The major issue is that semantic triplets can sometimes truncate narrative expressivity and nuance due to their grammatical simplicity. Below, we will identify and discuss a number of limitations as well as indicate some possible next steps.

One challenge concerns certain sentences with dependent, relative, or conditional clauses, which are not always captured completely or may be broken apart in the course of the triplet extraction method. This problem can be seen in conditional statements or ones that begin with a form of negation. For example, this sentence spoken by Bassfreund is turned into three triplets: "And it was already night and the SS opened the doors and said if we throw out the dead bodies we shall get some food." Getting food from the SS is dependent upon the victims being forced to throw out dead bodies from the train. Although the triplets are captured individually, maintaining the specific contingency of the actions and understanding the reasons for them requires that they are read together as larger, sequential units. One way to address this problem is to keep triplets within larger narrative segments once they are extracted.

Although network analysis produces new narrative orderings that allow us to apprehend and understand relationships across a testimony or corpus, taking a triplet out of context can render it meaningless or dramatically change the meaning. To address this problem, we preserve the narrative sequence of the triplets in our extraction process since the context for a triplet matters both within an individual sentence and between sentences. For instance, Bass says: "Well, you could tell. These guys were very rough and very bad. They used to beat you up, and scream, and holler, and push you. And hit you with a—a rubber—piece of rubber there. It looked like a rubber hose." By itself, a triplet derived from the last sentence would make no sense. Our triplet extraction method maintains the contiguity between the description of the men (former criminals who the Nazis put in place as supervisors in camps) so that the last triplet ("it looked like a rubber hose") continues to make sense within the context of this description of brutality. When we examine triplets within network diagrams, these sequential groupings and narrative trackbacks are ways to maintain narrative continuity and meaning.

Another basic challenge that we face is extracting triplets from fragmented, vernacular speech, which the process sometimes has trouble parsing. Survivors may switch from first-person narration to second or third-person narration; sometimes the sentences contain incomplete thoughts, repetitions, or stutters (often represented through variations of punctuation such as dashes, ellipses, and parentheses); and sometimes survivors quote the speech of others directly or indirectly. The triplet extraction process has no way of telling if a triplet refers to the quoted or attributed speech of someone else. For example, Anna Kovitzka says: "Once my man said: 'I can't make peace with them. Our child must be saved even if we two shall die.'" While two triplets are extracted ("I can't make peace with them" and "our child must be saved"), the triplets are not attributed to her husband because the phrase "once my man said" is not part of either triplet, although it is something said by Kovitzka while quoting her husband.

Going forward, we hope to create a better finding aid and visualization tool, perhaps through an indexing dashboard supported by a triplets database and connected to existing topical metadata. Researchers could then query and visualize through the same interface to find expressions of agency and generate associated networks. Such an interactive dashboard would combine the flexibility of curation in a Tableau dashboard with a Neo4j network visualization. At the same time, we are continuing to explore how searching for "agency" within a narrative can complement standard thematic and topical searches through network clustering and categorization of triplets.

The process of extracting, characterizing, and visualizing semantic triplets thus represents a kind of algorithmic "close reading" that creates a searchable paratext derived from the original transcript. That paratext is an index of the expressions of agency in a given testimony. Although "distant reading" remains a powerful approach for statistically summarizing the content of a corpus, digital humanities scholars have amply warned against the seduction of "delegating observation" and "delegating interpretation" to machines.[65] This is why we argue that human judgment and human interpretation go hand-in-hand with algorithmic processes. The algorithm does not provide answers, meaning, or judgments of value and importance. We use some of the algorithmic tools of distant reading (large-scale text analysis attuned to patterns, classifications, and clusters) to enable us to undertake close readings and perform interpretative queries at scale. It is up to us to figure out the meaning or significance of any description of agency in the context of an oral history, a network, or a corpus.

Computational methods and algorithmic analyses of big data do not get us closer to an underlying truth but rather offer new interpretative frameworks and heuristics for thinking. To apply the succinctly elegant words of Andrew Piper who says that "number is a lens,"[66] we might say: "Algorithm is a lens." In much the same way that quantitative analysis is a hermeneutic (among other hermeneutics), algorithmic text transformations allow us to ask certain kinds of questions and get certain kinds of answers. Far from excavating deep truths or fostering definitive facts, they function as lenses for thinking, exploring, analyzing, and interpreting. Computational indexing of agency shifts the scale of analysis to individual mentions of agency and networks of actions, helping us read and listen to testimonies in ways that deepen our understanding of what people report they did and what was done to them. In the final analysis, the ethics of the algorithm can be evaluated by the degree to which these algorithmic processes and outputs humanize the survivors, add new layers of meaning and knowledge to the cultural record, and foster relational modes of listening that help redress historical injustices.

Mala Zimetbaum and the Creation of a Testimonial Ensemble

Accounts of the Jewish heroine Mala Zimetbaum are legion. The story of her efforts to help female prisoners in Auschwitz, her daring escape, her capture, and, finally, her public torture and execution are mentioned in scores of accounts given by survivors who knew Mala, interacted with her at the camp, or witnessed her final moments.[1] She is even depicted as the martyred heroine in the first, full-length Holocaust film, *Ostatni etap* (*The Last Stage*), directed by Auschwitz survivor Wanda Jakubowska.[2] While the general contours of her biography and fate are known, the specific details of her actions survive (when they do so at all) in the heterogeneous accounts given by individual survivors in their personal testimonies.[3]

Because the Nazis repudiated Mala's actions and extinguished her voice in an attempt to erase her existence, we might ask: How can we develop a listening practice that would allow us to hear—from the diversity of survivor voices—who she was, what she did, and what was done to her? What might it mean to assemble those accounts algorithmically in ways that are morally responsive to the historical records? Far from adding up to a coherent whole, the many, polyphonic voices point to the possibility of constructing a "testimony ensemble" of someone whose life is known only through the testimony of others. While the testimonial ensemble remains far from complete (as still more accounts could be included), the point of this project is to show how the methodologies of computational text analysis and interactive visualizations can give rise to a generative form of collective witnessing and fabulation.[4]

Mala was a Polish-born Jew who grew up in Antwerp, Belgium. In September of 1942, at the age of twenty-two, she was arrested and sent to the transit camp of Malines. Shortly thereafter, she was deported to Auschwitz. Because she was fluent in multiple languages, she was chosen by the SS as a translator and "runner" to coordinate information and send messages across the massively sprawling Auschwitz camp system. She received the tattoo number of 19880 and was stationed in the women's camp in Birkenau. Mala used her relative privilege to help women in the camp get clothing, food, and better work duties. According to many testimonial accounts, she erased numbers from selection lists and provided the women with clothing, extra food, and information. Her subterfuge helped save many lives.

Together with a Polish prisoner named Edek Galinski, she planned an escape from the camp in the summer of 1944.[5] After stealing clearance certificates and donning SS uniforms, Mala and Edek managed to escape but were soon caught and returned to the camp. They were kept in punishment bunkers for weeks before both were scheduled to be executed on the same day in the men's and women's camps, respectively. The camp prisoners were called out to watch the executions and speeches were given by the SS officers berating the prisoners about the consequences of escape. Before Mala could be killed by the SS officers, she took a razor blade and slit her wrists in an attempt to commit suicide. One of the guards tried to stop her, and she famously slapped his face while shouting that their time of reckoning was near.[6] She was carted around the camp for the prisoners to see before she was either shot or burned alive in the crematoria.[7] Edek was hanged in the men's camp and also tried to take his own life before he was killed by the SS officers.

As far as we know, there are no extant, first-person testimonies given by Mala Zimetbaum herself.[8] The story of her life, her actions, and her tragic demise are to be found only in the accounts given by various survivors of Auschwitz-Birkenau. The earliest audio-recorded accounts were given in 1946 by two women interviewed by David Boder: Henja Frydman and Edith Serras. While much in these two accounts lines up, there is also a degree of divergence that raises interesting questions about what happened to Mala. Both women agree that Mala was a "messenger" who had privileges in the camp and that she used those privileges to help other prisoners. Frydman says that "Mala saved me from the gas" because Mala excluded her from a list of condemned prisoners; Serras says that Mala "organized soup" for the women and "used to erase their numbers" from selection lists. Frydman reports that when Mala was returned to the camp after her escape, she was placed in a bunker for six weeks where she was repeatedly interrogated. After that, Mala was brought to an assembly before the whole camp that was orchestrated by the *Lagerführerin* (SS officer Maria Mandel), the work service leaders, and various German SS officers. There, Mala was to be hanged, according to Frydman. But before she could be, she cut her arteries with a razor blade in an attempt to take her own life and then slapped the face of the unnamed work service leader. Mala was thrown in a cart, taken to the crematoria, and "shot by the chief of the crematoria [Otto] Moll."[9]

While the account given by Serras corroborates the integrity of Mala, Serras focuses more on the escape itself ("she donned the clothes of an SS woman") and what she considered to be its historical significance: namely, the fact that Mala would tell the world about "how the gassing proceeds" at Auschwitz. According to Serras, Mala planned to "transmit letters" and "propaganda" by dint of her "political connections," so that the prisoners would no longer be "cut off from the world." These hopes were dashed upon Mala's capture, and Serras provides an account of her final moments: a speech given by Mandel admonishing escape, Mala cutting her arteries with a razor blade, the attempt by the work service leaders to stanch the blood flow, and, finally, Mala being removed in a cart destined for the crematorium. But in contrast to Frydman, Serras says that Mala was shot "by one of our own," another prisoner, rather than being "burned alive" and "conscious of her death," as Mandel had wanted. Serras says she and the other female prisoners were "happy" to learn of the fellow prisoner's "compassion" because they did not want Mala to endure more "sufferings."

From just these two accounts—recorded on the same day, August 7, 1946, but apparently not in the presence of one another—we gain valuable knowledge about who Mala was, what she did, the significance of her actions, what happened to her, and who was involved in carrying out her public execution. The two testimonies are largely complementary, although they do not cover exactly the same terrain, and there is a striking disagreement about how she died: either she was killed by the chief of the crematoria, Otto Moll, or shot out of compassion by another prisoner, ostensibly a member of the Sonderkommando stationed at the crematoria.[10] Her compassion for fellow prisoners and her defiance of the Nazis are not, however, in question, although Serras, unlike Frydman, describes her reasons for escape within a broader, world-historical narrative of consciousness-raising about the atrocities taking place in Auschwitz.

While it would be useful—certainly in a legal context—to be able to compare and potentially adjudicate many different witness accounts as part of an evidentiary or fact-finding process, I am interested here in modeling how an algorithmically created testimonial ensemble can augment the scale of witnessing and underscore the multiperspectival, polyphonic possibilities of testimonial narratives. In what follows, I will describe a computational methodology of narrative creation and analysis that brings together a multiplicity of voices and perspectives to create new possibilities for attending to testimonies. Unlike an individual testimony where the autonomy of the singular account is preserved through a fixed and linear narrative structure (often with a single point-of-access, with a clear beginning, middle, and end), a testimonial ensemble extracts pieces of many different testimonies and brings them together in an interactive, reconfigurable, montage format. Because a testimonial ensemble is composed of many different accounts, it is, by definition, polyphonic and even cacophonic, as the different accounts may not fully align with one another. They may even be contradictory to one another. We start with a close analysis of a single testimony to explain the process by which "semantic triplets" (clause-level expressions of agency) are algorithmically extracted from testimonial narratives.[11] After that, we discuss the affordances of scale and "algorithmic fabulation," attuned to filtering and narrative recomposition, to show how many different, possible testimonial ensembles can be created.[12]

Our testimonial ensemble consists of portions of twenty-eight individual witness testimonies in six languages: Yiddish, German, Hebrew, French, English, and Ladino. Of these, twenty-five are recorded interviews; one is a trial transcript; and two are written testimonial accounts (Wieslaw Kielar and Giza Weisblum). Twenty-five were given by women, and three were given by men. The earliest recorded interviews were conducted by David Boder on August 7, 1946, with Edith Serras and Henja Frydman. Both of these interviews were conducted in Yiddish and German at the Jewish Committee home for adult Jewish refugees in Paris, France. The next account was given by Raya Kagan in 1961 during her witness testimony at the Eichmann trial. Weisblum's testimony was published in 1967 as part of an anthology edited by Yuri Suhl.[13] Kielar's testimony was first published in Polish in 1972 and translated into German and English shortly thereafter.[14] Four testimonies come from the US Holocaust Memorial Museum (three in English, one in Hebrew). Nineteen testimonies come from the Yale Fortunoff Archive (eight in French, five in Hebrew, five in English, and one in Ladino). Except for one from 1984, the USHMM and Fortunoff testimonies were done in the 1990s and early 2000s. The French, Hebrew, and Ladino testimonies were translated into English, and when English-language testimonies or translations (from German and Yiddish) already existed, they were checked against the original recordings.[15] A full accounting of the testimonies can be found at the end of this chapter and on our project website.

To date, there is no federated search across corpora that could have brought together these diverse accounts of Mala Zimetbaum; however, they are fairly easy to identify individually since institutional archives (Voices of the Holocaust at IIT, USHMM, Fortunoff, and the USC Shoah Foundation) have tagged names of people mentioned in testimonies, and proper names can be easily found through named-entity recognition. While we used simple searching to find the relevant segments, in the future, the development of federated search protocols, built on linked open data, should allow researchers to query across many different archives simultaneously. This could potentially work even for testimonies that are not formally tagged with metadata, provided the transcripts (or perhaps the semantic triplets) allow users to search by strings of words, intersecting networks, or shared experiences.[16]

After translating the interviews that were not already in English, we created transcripts of just the segments in which Mala was expressly discussed. These segments were not necessarily contiguous and sometimes involved the aggregation of multiple testimonial segments (and the removal of segments about other topics). These transcripts were structured to follow uniform rules: punctuation marks were added (commas, periods, apostrophes, quotation marks, and ellipses); spellings were rendered consistent and, in a few cases, corrected;[17] specific German terms were left untranslated (such as *Lagerführerin*); interviewer questions were not included, although in a few cases where the interviewee's answer would not be comprehensible otherwise, a reference from the interviewer's question was included in the answer to obviate non-referential sentence fragments; and, finally, pronouns were left un-disambiguated, since this process would be performed by our machine-learning process (and be manually verified afterward).

Before we delve into the results, we might wonder: What questions prompt the interviewees to talk about Mala in the first place? Survivors sometimes talk about Mala because of a question asked by the interviewer, while other times, interviewees remember the actions of Mala in the context of their own survival. With regard to the former, the interviewer asks Chaja G. the following question: "The names of the people, in your collective, would you share them with me?" After she mentions Mala, the interviewer follows up with additional questions about her: "Regarding Mala, could you go back to that and your first contact with Mala? That was your first contact with her, correct?" and "What did you all think about Mala's authority or power, rather, to help you, to save you?" The interviewer asks Itta W. a question about public executions that prompts her to talk about Mala: "We heard some stories regarding public executions in the camps and that an Orchestra would play. We know that sometimes at public executions the orchestra had to play?" Other survivors are asked about resistance, such as Mania W., who is asked by the interviewer: "Were you aware of any group in the camp that tried to band together and rebel in any way?" And similarly, Rivka K. talks about Mala after the interviewer asks: "Did you have plans to escape?" On the other hand, Hella Rosenbaum talks about Mala after the interviewer asks her: "Were there instances of women in crisis? Feeling depressed?"

Other survivors recall Mala in the context of narrating memories from Auschwitz, such as Benita H. who says to the interviewer, "I don't know if you have heard of Mala Zimetbaum." Frieda K. says, "Maybe you've heard of Mala, this Belgian woman who, who, who tried to run away?" as she discusses work in the Canada Block and her luck surviving in the camp. Edith Serras and Henja Frydman both discuss Mala in the context of their own survival in the camp, the latter of whom attributes her survival following a three-month stay in the camp hospital to Mala, who erased her name from a list of women condemned to the gas chamber. Finally, Yaakov F. replies with the story of Mala following a question from the interviewer asking if "there were some things you'd wanted [to still say] . . ." He says: "Yes, there are some things that I wanted to say, a memory that has remained of the heroine Mala from Belgium."

All told, we began by creating an aggregate narrative consisting of nearly three thousand sentences (totaling about twenty-eight thousand words) from twenty-eight different testimonial accounts. But this aggregate narrative is *not* a "testimonial ensemble" for our purposes here, since the former only involves the initial assembly of a narrative and would not be much different from "cutting and pasting." To make a testimonial ensemble, we computationally transformed the text of this aggregate narrative into a paratextual set of testimonial fragments called "semantic triplets." The semantic triplet represents the unit of data from which we build new narratives. From the individual sentences, 2,450 triplets were extracted and put into a spreadsheet organized by a set of searchable and reconfigurable data relations. Besides disambiguating pronouns and standardizing the spelling of names, no new words were added to the triplets; however, the triplets were extracted, tagged, grouped, and reordered in new ways. As we will see below, this is because a testimonial ensemble can be infinitely queried and recombined to focus on certain events, subjects, relationships, types and parts of speech, interviewees, and various other parameters. It is generative insofar as it gives rise to new narrative possibilities, networks, associations, and relationships, which allow us to read in ways that would be improbable, or even impossible, if we simply read an aggregate narrative from start to finish. While the testimonial ensemble fits within the interpretative landscape of a "remix," the individual semantic units—in the precise words of the interviewee—are always held together and remain attributable. This faithfulness to the testimonial utterance remains throughout the transformational process. What is new is the way that they can be searched, reordered, recombined, and grouped. In this regard, the rich traditions of cinematic montage and modernist literature are more properly the inspirations for a testimonial ensemble.[18]

From a Single Testimony to a Testimonial Ensemble

To demonstrate the process concretely, let's begin by looking closely at a single excerpt from Edith Serras's testimony on Mala Zimetbaum. Having removed Boder's questions and interjections, we can examine how the following excerpt was transformed from a narrative transcript into a spreadsheet of relations organized as semantic triplets. Serras says about Mala:

> She should tell how she managed to escape, with whom she had political connections on the outside. But she told them nothing. One day, we all returned in the evening from work. We were lined up in the Lager, and in the middle of the Lager, they erected a gallows, to hang. And Mandel, the SS woman who mistreated the whole Lager, and she was a very mean woman. But Mandel liked Mala very much. So she said, "This Jewish Mala, in whom we had such great confidence, has escaped. So there has come an order from German, from Berlin, that a Jewish woman who dares to escape from our Lager must be hanged." In that moment Mala had a razor blade in her hand. And she cut several of her arteries. The work service leader saw that she was cutting up her arteries because she did not want to go to her death by their hands. She wanted to die of her own death. So the work service leader ran over to her, and he grabbed her by both hands. He twisted her hands so that the blood should not run out. So she stood up and slapped him twice. And she said, "I take on you the last vengeance for my sisters and brothers and children." And we heard it, and we saw it. The work service leader gave an order. She was bleeding. She was dying. She should be killed alive, that is, she should be burned alive. She should be conscious of her death. So she was taken in a little cart. Her body was taken to the crematorium. But in the crematorium, she was shot to death by a prisoner who worked in the crematorium. Because he said, "Mala does not deserve to be burned alive." She was the greatest Jewish heroine, who had done so much good.[19]

The spreadsheet in Figure 6.17 shows the results of the algorithmic textual transformation of this narrative excerpt into a set of triplets (row numbers 1284–1309) characterized by type of speech. Each semantic triplet consists of subjects (column D), relations (column F), and objects (column G). The machine-learning coreferencing process disambiguates pronouns in the subject and object columns

ntNt	speakers	subjects	subjects_coref	relations	objects	objects_coref	texts	AEO_cat	t_c	t_cu	f_c	f_cu
1284	Edith Serras	she	Mala	had	political connectio	political connections on the outside	She should tell how	Orientation	0	0	0	0
1285	Edith Serras	she	Mala	told	them nothing	them nothing	But she told them n	Agency_Active	0	0	0	0
1286	Edith Serras	we	we	all returned	in the evening fror	in the evening from work	One day, we all retu	Agency_Active	0	0	0	0
1287	Edith Serras	We	We	were lined	up in the Lager in t	up in the Lager in the middle of the Lager	We were lined up in	Agency_Passive	0	0	0	0
1288	Edith Serras	they	they	erected	a gallows	a gallows	We were lined up in	Agency_Active	0	0	0	0
1289	Edith Serras	she	Mandel	was	a very mean woma	a very mean woman	And Mandel, the SS	Evaluation	1	1	1	1
1290	Edith Serras	Mandel	Mandel	liked	Mala	Mala	But Mandel liked M	Agency_Active	0	0	0	0
1291	Edith Serras	we	we	had	such great confide	such great confidence	So she said,' This Jev	Orientation	0	0	0	0
1292	Edith Serras	that moment Mala	Mala	had	a razor blade in hea	a razor blade in her hand	So there has come a	Orientation	1	0	1	0
1293	Edith Serras	she	Mala	cut	several of her arte	several of her arteries	And she cut several	Agency_Active	0	0	0	0
1294	Edith Serras	The work service leader	The work service leader	saw	that she was cuttir	that she was cutting up her arteries	The work service lei	Agency_Active	0	0	0	0
1295	Edith Serras	She	Mala	wanted to die	of her own death	of her own death	She wanted to die o	Agency_Speculative/Modal	0	0	0	0
1296	Edith Serras	So the work service leader	So the work service leader	ran	over to her	over to Mala	So the work service	Agency_Active	0	0	0	0
1297	Edith Serras	he	the work service leader	grabbed	her by both hands	Mala by both hands	So the work service	Agency_Active	0	0	0	0
1298	Edith Serras	He	the work service leader	twisted	her hands so that t	her hands so that the blood should not run	He twisted her hanc	Agency_Active	0	0	0	0
1299	Edith Serras	I	I	take	on you the last ver	on you the last vengeance brothers children	And she said,' I take	Agency_Active	0	0	0	0
1300	Edith Serras	we	we	heard	it	it	And she said,' I take	Agency_Active	0	0	0	0
1301	Edith Serras	we	we	saw	it	it	And she said,' I take	Agency_Active	0	0	0	0
1302	Edith Serras	The work service leader	The work service leader	gave	an order	an order	The work service lei	Agency_Active	0	0	0	0
1303	Edith Serras	She	Mala	should be killed	alive	alive	She should be killed	Agency_Speculative/Modal	0	1	0	1
1304	Edith Serras	she	Mala	should be burned	alive	alive	She should be killed	Agency_Speculative/Modal	0	1	0	1
1305	Edith Serras	She	Mala	should be	conscious of her d	conscious of her death	She should be consc	Agency_Speculative/Modal	0	1	0	1
1306	Edith Serras	she	Mala	was taken	in a little cart	in a little cart	So she was taken in	Agency_Passive	0	1	0	1
1307	Edith Serras	Her body	Her body	was taken	to the crematoriur	to the crematorium	Her body was taken	Agency_Passive	0	0	0	0
1308	Edith Serras	she	Mala	was shot	to death	to death	But in the crematori	Agency_Passive	0	1	0	1
1309	Edith Serras	She	Mala	was	the greatest Jewisł	the greatest Jewish heroine	Because he said,' M.	Evaluation	1	0	1	0

FIGURE 6.17: Triplets related to Mala Zimetbaum from an excerpt of Edith Serras's interview with David Boder (1946).

(columns E and H, respectively). Not every coreference is assignable or certain (and sometimes they are incorrectly assigned). As such, certain rows are flagged for manual curation. This happens when a coreference is uncertain (most often a question of who "they" refers to) or when a triplet is uncertain, often due to the nature of vernacular speech or the speaker quoting the speech of someone else. Columns AO and AP show when a manual change was made (0 = no change; 1 = change) to the triplet extraction and pronoun disambiguation, respectively.[20] Column I gives the original text before the triplet extraction. Column K refers to the verb categories for the relations in column F (orientation, agency_active, agency_passive, agency_speculative/modal, agency_coercion/necessity, and evaluation). All of the columns can be filtered, allowing for granular searches across the testimonial corpus.

Unlike listening to a spoken narrative or reading a transcript, the spreadsheet of semantic triplets facilitates a different kind of reading experience. While we may still read linearly and sequentially, we do not have to proceed this way since the columns can be read in any spatial order (for instance, we might read the verb relations in column F vertically). And more than that, we can filter by any attribute in a column. We might, for example, filter the subjects_coref column by perpetrators (Mandel, the work service leader, the SS men) to focus on what Serras said the Nazis did to Mala, although this will be partially incomplete since Serras conveys the orders from Mandel without referencing her direct speech: "She should be killed alive," "she should be burned alive," and "she should be conscious of her death." As such, we want to clearly flag a risk of this approach: namely, the fact that individual semantic triplets can become decontextualized when they are read out of order and may not make sense without adjacent triplets.

Employing the search-and-filter features of the entire spreadsheet, we can export a set of triplets according to various parameters. The network diagram in Figure 6.18 shows Mala as the subject and includes only the triplets labeled as "orientation" and "evaluation"—that is, triplets that provide contextual or background information and triplets that express the interviewee's judgment about someone or something. In terms of the latter, Serras considered Mala to be smart, beautiful, logical, and nice, and she characterizes her as "the greatest Jewish heroine." She was "a girl," in her twenties, who had political connections to the outside world, and was of great political value, presumably not only to the resistance movement, but also to the Nazis because she knew so much about the inner workings of the camp. At the same time, Serras says that Mala was "devoted to" and "preoccupied with us," indicating the depth of her relationship with other Jewish prisoners who she had also helped.

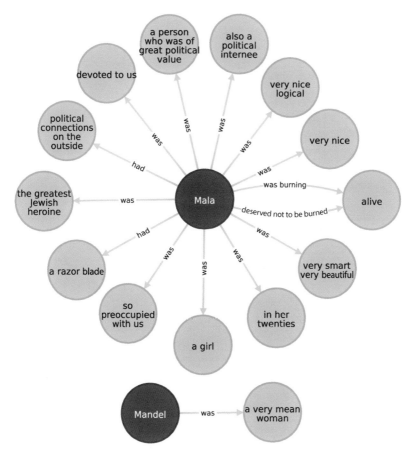

FIGURE 6.18: Network diagram of "evaluation" and "orientation" triplets with "Mala" as subject (Edith Serras's testimony). Created by Lizhou Fan and Todd Presner.

The second network diagram shows what Mala did and what was done to her, according to just the testimony of Serras (Figure 6.19). All the triplets take Mala as the subject and indicate a wide variety of objects using active speech, passive speech, expressions of coercion or necessity, and speculative or modal verbs. As such, this diagram is a synoptic visualization of the different actions, desires, and intentions in which Mala is the subject of Serras's testimony. It is the totality of Serras's spoken expressions about what happened to Mala, what was done to Mala, what the Nazis intended to do to Mala, and what Mala wanted according to a single witness: Edith Serras.

In this visualization, we see the following. First, there are triplets describing her situation in Auschwitz and attributing active agency to Mala: Mala worked

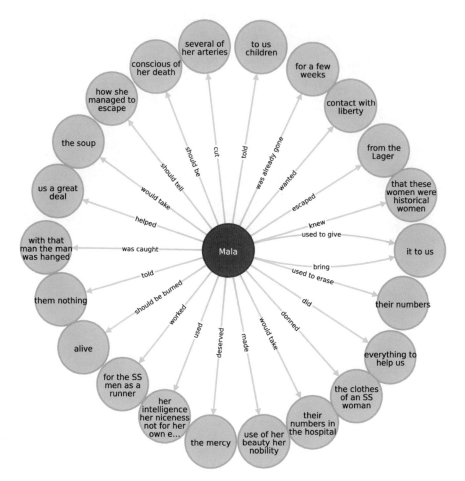

FIGURE 6.19: Triplets with "Mala" as subject from Edith Serras's testimony. Created by Lizhou Fan and Todd Presner.

for the SS men as a runner; Mala used to erase the numbers of fellow prisoners; Mala donned the clothes of an SS woman; Mala escaped from the Lager; Mala cut several of her arteries. Second, there are triplets in which Serras describes Mala's knowledge and represents her intentions: Mala knew that these "historical" women were condemned to death; Mala wanted contact with liberty; Mala wanted to die her own death. Third, there are Serras's descriptions of the intentions of the SS to punish Mala: Mala should be burned alive; Mala should be conscious of her death. Fourth, there are Serras's assessments of what should or ought to have happened to Mala: Mala should tell how she managed to escape; Mala deserved mercy. The network diagram synthesizes what Serras remembers of Mala's agency, what Serras thinks Mala knew and wanted, what Serras thinks the SS officers who punished Mala intended, and what Serras thinks should have happened to Mala.

This is the algorithmic logic by which we transformed the twenty-eight testimonial segments about Mala into a paratextual spreadsheet of 2,450 semantic triplets.[21] If we focus just on Serras's account of Mala as subject, we see about three dozen semantic triplets. But when we expand to twenty-eight testimonies, we have 351 semantic triplets with Mala as subject (and dozens more if we include "she," "the girl," "the runner," and other terms that reference her subjectivity). This output is not easily rendered into a static visualization, and thus we employed the affordances of an interactive dashboard in Tableau to allow readers to search and filter the triplets in many different ways: by interviewee, by subject, by verb, by verb categories (speech type), by objects, and by three preconfigured categories that can be filtered as subjects or objects: perpetrators, Mala, and Mala and Edek. As a reconfigurable and extensible approach to algorithmic fabulation, the testimonial ensemble has the visual form of an amoeba-like aggregation of variously sized and colored nodes (Figure 6.20).

Among the questions we might ask are: What did the witnesses say about who Mala was? What did they say Mala did or desired to do? What did they say happened to Mala? What did others do to Mala and which people are named as agents? What did the witnesses say should have happened to Mala? While many of the answers are corroborative of one another, there are a few that add unique information not mentioned in any other testimony as well as some that are contradictory. Far from being something to overcome, these (minor) contradictions demonstrate the contingency of the witnesses' perspectives, the subjectivity of memory, and the inability for us to finally adjudicate the truth of Mala's life story. For instance, Benita H. says that Mala knew Yiddish but "did not know German" and that she did "not know how to work the machines." Most other witnesses say that she was fluent in German, along with several other languages, and her multilingualism is precisely what helped her survive. While others do not speak about her ability to work machines, it is certain that she helped the women acquire positions in the Canada Commando where they worked, largely indoors, sorting the goods taken from Jews condemned to the gas chambers. Another witness, Alice Jakubovic, says that Mala was a "leader type" but "not smart" because she "went over the limit," a point of view not represented by most of the other women, who recall only her intelligence, bravery, empathy, and heroism. Finally, no one seems to know how she ultimately died: Did she succeed in taking her own life? Was she shot by a member of the SS? Was she hanged? Was she killed by a member of the

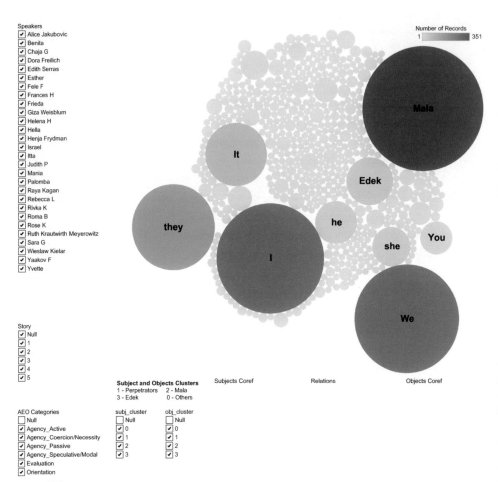

Speakers
- ☑ Alice Jakubovic
- ☑ Benita
- ☑ Chaja G
- ☑ Dora Freilich
- ☑ Edith Serras
- ☑ Esther
- ☑ Fele F
- ☑ Frances H
- ☑ Frieda
- ☑ Giza Weisblum
- ☑ Helena H
- ☑ Hella
- ☑ Henja Frydman
- ☑ Israel
- ☑ Itta
- ☑ Judith P
- ☑ Mania
- ☑ Palomba
- ☑ Raya Kagan
- ☑ Rebecca L
- ☑ Rivka K
- ☑ Roma B
- ☑ Rose K
- ☑ Ruth Krautwirth Meyerowitz
- ☑ Sara G
- ☑ Wieslaw Kielar
- ☑ Yaakov F
- ☑ Yvette

Story
- ☑ Null
- ☑ 1
- ☑ 2
- ☑ 3
- ☑ 4
- ☑ 5

AEO Categories
- ☐ Null
- ☑ Agency_Active
- ☑ Agency_Coercion/Necessity
- ☑ Agency_Passive
- ☑ Agency_Speculative/Modal
- ☑ Evaluation
- ☑ Orientation

Subject and Objects Clusters
1 - Perpetrators   2 - Mala
3 - Edek   0 - Others

subj_cluster
- ☐ Null
- ☑ 0
- ☑ 1
- ☑ 2
- ☑ 3

obj_cluster
- ☐ Null
- ☑ 0
- ☑ 1
- ☑ 2
- ☑ 3

Number of Records
1   351

FIGURE 6.20: Interactive visualization of testimonial ensemble of Mala Zimetbaum with sample triplets that include "Mala" as subject. Created by Lizhou Fan and Todd Presner. On Tableau: hrl.pub/bc2fa6.

Sonderkommando, in an act of mercy? Was she burned alive in the crematorium? Was she trampled to death by the SS? These are some of the possibilities recalled by the different witnesses.

In addition to Mala as subject, the other major subject nodes in the 2,450 triplets are "I," "we," and "they." The 273 "I" statements establish the perspectives of the witnesses and include background, personal experiences, feelings, memories, and knowledge. The 265 "we" statements bear witness to shared experiences and collective actions, including acts of solidarity among the prisoners (singing, helping one another, sharing food, planning, and resisting), collective witnessing

Int ..	Sent..	Speakers	Subjects Coref	Relations	Objects Coref
2	322	Frieda	Mala's job	was to take	girls from the hospital to bring girls
	323	Frieda	Mala's job	to distribute	girls to the right places
	324	Frieda	Mala	would escort	the officers in the morning every block after the roll call
	327	Frieda	Mala	helped	me
	330	Frieda	Mala	helped	me bathe
	331	Frieda	Mala	brought	me to the block
	334	Frieda	Mala	was doing	her job
	336	Frieda	Mala	did	it as her duty her job
	337	Frieda	Mala	came to take	me
	339	Frieda	Mala	told	her to look for me
5	606	Israel	Mala	went	back for her mother
	637	Israel	Mala	was burnt	alive
6	648	Palomba	Mala	was	a very accomplished woman
	649	Palomba	Mala	had caught	the attention of the Germans
	650	Palomba	Mala	performed	kataskopeia espionage
	654	Palomba	Mala	plotted	with those who arrived on the trains
	657	Palomba	Mala	would report	on what was happening in the Lager
	661	Palomba	Mala	remained sitting	in there for several days
	663	Palomba	Mala	had spent	a month in the bunker
	669	Palomba	Mala	suddenly produced	a knife
	670	Palomba	Mala	cut	her veins
	672	Palomba	Mala	spat	on the German
	676	Palomba	Mala	was	Belgian
	678	Palomba	Mala	simply reported	on what was going on inside the camps
	681	Palomba	Mala	was	the Belgian
	684	Palomba	Mala	was	very courageous
7	692	Helena H	Mala	was	already in Krakow
	693	Helena H	Mala	had dyed	her hair
	694	Helena H	Mala	was	Kramer 's translator
	699	Helena H	Mala	dyed	her hair
	701	Helena H	Mala	also had	a nose job in spite of everything
	708	Helena H	Mala	cut	her veins
8	743	Roma B	Mala	was	a marvelous person
	745	Roma B	Mala	was	well educated very intelligent
	746	Roma B	Mala	worked	in the office
	747	Roma B	Mala	was	very active
	750	Roma B	Mala	had	a Polish boyfriend
	755	Roma B	Mala and Edek	were caught	in Katowice
	765	Roma B	next to Mala	were standing	two German soldiers
	777	Roma B	Mala	got	a razor
	778	Roma B	Mala	cut	her wrists with a razor
	781	Roma B	Mala	cut	her wrists
9	798	Itta	Mala	cut	her wrists
	800	Itta	Mala	killed	herself
	801	Itta	Mala	was	someone that everyone knew in the camp the first Laeuferin
	808	Itta	Mala	saw	my feet Mala said we are going to give you some shoes
	810	Itta	Mala	did	something for me

("we saw a Jewish prisoner raise a hand against a German"), and collective suffering.[22] The subject "they" mostly refers to unnamed Nazi perpetrators and includes statements such as "they called the entire women's camp to assemble,"

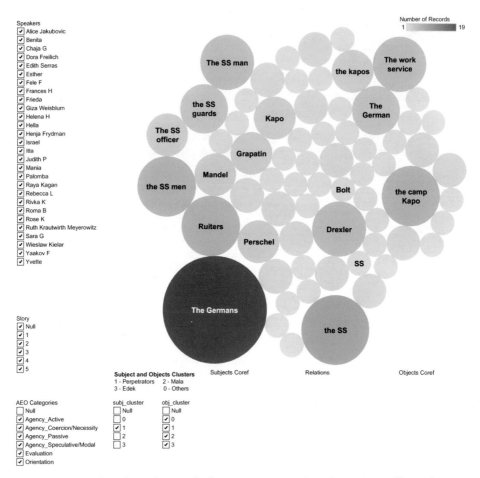

FIGURE 6.21: Sample triplets in which perpetrators are the subject. Created by Lizhou Fan and Todd Presner.

"they put Mala into a cart," "they broke her arm," "they grabbed her by the head," "they put her up on the scaffold," and "they burned her."

While the algorithm could not usually disambiguate the pronoun references in these "they" statements, we did curate a category of subjects and objects called "perpetrators," which includes every named Nazi perpetrator in the triplets as well as categories of agents involved in carrying out the atrocities in Auschwitz (the SS men, the SS guards, the Germans, the SS, the Kapos, the work service leader, the dogs, and so forth). It can be visualized by toggling the relevant filter in the interactive Tableau visualization (Figure 6.21). Among the named perpetrators mentioned are SS officer Maria Mandel (the *Lagerführerin* of the women's

Int ..	Sent..	Speakers	Subjects Coref	Relations	Objects Coref	
1	53	Chaja G	the SS	thought	that you were already someone	▪
	73	Chaja G	Drexler	went	on like Mala was a part of everyday life	▪
	76	Chaja G	So Drexler	did not understand	how Mala could do that	▪
	175	Chaja G	the kapos	would laugh	so hard that they then said	▪
	176	Chaja G	the kapos	give	some water to the little Belgian girl	▪
	194	Chaja G	three SS officers	looking	over us	▪
	196	Chaja G	two or three SS officers	were	not tender to begin	▪
	197	Chaja G	two or three SS officers	were	drunk we would hide to avoid getting hit	▪
	231	Chaja G	the Germans	moved	us	▪
	282	Chaja G	the Germans	calmed	down for a while	▪
	300	Chaja G	the Germans	were	not as hard on us	▪
	301	Chaja G	the Germans	got	scared since we were able to bomb a building	▪
	302	Chaja G	the Germans	still came	to get us to work and carry rocks	▪
2	316	Frieda	the supervisor of the Canada Bl..	sent	someone to me to see if I was alive	▪
3	383	Rebecca L	The Germans	brought	them back to the camp him to the men 's camp Mala to our camp	▪
	385	Rebecca L	the Germans	tortured	Mala	▪
	386	Rebecca L	the Germans	hit	Mala	▪
	387	Rebecca L	the Germans	really tortured	Mala to make Mala talk	▪
	395	Rebecca L	An SS guard	spoke	to everyone present	▪
4	442	Sara G	The three kapos	were	german commanders who treated us rather well	▪
	444	Sara G	The female kapo	was	a german prostitute who was very proud	▪
	486	Sara G	the SS	took	their gun	▪
	487	Sara G	the SS	shot	this nice Polish girl	▪
	491	Sara G	The SS guards	trusted	Mala	▪
	492	Sara G	Drexler	trusted	her the head of the female SS	▪
	520	Sara G	the SS guards	were looking	for them	▪
	522	Sara G	the SS guards	were looking	in the office in the toilets	▪
	524	Sara G	the SS guards	noticed	that Mala wasn't here	▪
	525	Sara G	Drexler	was	so furious	▪
	547	Sara G	The SS officer	wanted to make	a speech saying that if we dared to escape	▪
	550	Sara G	The SS officer	realized	what was happening	▪
	551	Sara G	The SS officer	twisted	her wrist	▪
	575	Sara G	Drexler	was	the head of the German surveillance	▪
	576	Sara G	Drexler	had said	that they were going to burn her alive	▪
5	628	Israel	the Germans	were looking	for secretaries for the SS	▪
6	658	Palomba	The Germans	eventually found	out what she was doing	▪
	659	Palomba	The Germans	put	her in the bunker	▪
	664	Palomba	The Germans	sentenced	her to death	▪
	668	Palomba	The Germans	told	Mala to come and greet death	▪
7	697	Helena H	Kramer	also wanted	her to be pretty	▪
8	744	Roma B	even the Germans	had	a lot of appreciation for her	▪
	753	Roma B	The men	kept	us for hours they counted you stand they counted	▪
	782	Roma B	One of the Germans	realized	what was happening	▪
10	854	Frances H	Kapo	is	a Latin word for head	▪
	856	Frances H	the kapos	liked	Mala	▪
	859	Frances H	The German kapos	had	the power	▪
	863	Frances H	a German soldier or kapo	fell	in love with Mala	▪
14	960	Judith P	the German SS women	liked	Mala	▪
	961	Judith P	the German SS women	took	Mala into the office to work	▪
16	1017	Rose K	The Germans	burned	her body in the crematorium	▪
18	1073	Esther	The SS	were	in admiration of Mala	▪

camp), SS officer Margot Drexler (women's camp administration), SS-*Unterscharführer* Johann Ruiters (work service leader in the women's camp), SS-*Oberscharführer* Wilhelm Boger (escape department of the Gestapo), SS doctor Johann Kramer, and SS-*Unterscharführer* Richard Perschel (women's labor camp director).

For instance, some witnesses describe Mala's various roles as a translator and intermediary in relation to the SS: "Mala would escort the SS officers in the

Mala Zimetbaum: Between Kinship and Death

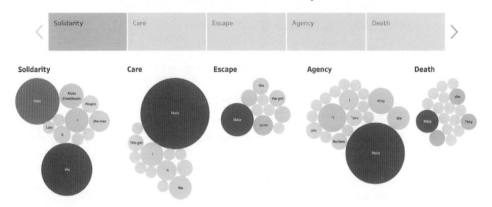

FIGURE 6.22: A critical-algorithmic testimonial ensemble in five parts. Created by Todd Presner and Lizhou Fan. Interactive visualization on Tableau: hrl.pub/b43054.

morning [in] every block after roll call," "Mala would carry messages from one SS to another," "Mala was a page like an errand runner between the Germans," "Mala succeeded in making everyone like her, even the SS." Others testify to acts of violence: "Ruiters took her hand," "Ruiters struck Mala on the head with his revolver," "Ruiters beat her on her back she could not speak," "Boger would extract all the information [Boger] wanted from his victims," "They held a major roll-call Maria Mandel the *Schutzlagerfuehrerin* made a speech," "Frau Mandel ordered that a handcart be brought," "Mandel beat Mala with a gun," "Drexler had said they were going to burn her alive." Drawn from the accounts of multiple witnesses, these narrative fragments—in the form of computationally extracted, tagged, and filtered semantic triplets—testify to the specific actions of the perpetrators. Collectively, they illustrate the potential of a testimonial ensemble to proliferate witness perspectives and give rise to new, scalable possibilities for generating a "mass testimony" about events of mass atrocity.[23]

Inspired by Judith Butler's interpretation of *Antigone*, I decided to curate a five-part story that takes some of the triplets from the twenty-eight witness accounts to emplot a testimonial ensemble in the form of a collective narrative (Figure 6.22).[24] It is a work of critical-algorithmic fabulation.[25] Not unlike Antigone—a figure of defiance and feminist agency who, ultimately, made the decision to take her own life rather than die at the hands of political power—Mala's defiance of Nazi authoritarianism takes the form of a wide variety of political and linguistic acts. These acts of defiance culminate in her decision to slit her wrists with a razor blade and slap the face of SS officer Ruiters. Several witnesses also recount words she spoke: "I shall die as a heroine," "you will die as a dog," "I have told people on the outside," and "the day of reckoning is near." At the same time, the testimonial ensemble of the twenty-eight survivors also bears witness to the multiple ways that Mala—not unlike Antigone—represents and creates forms of kinship that transgress traditional familial and social norms. These forms of kinship are primarily grounded in an ethic of care. Mala's voluntary—and risky— acts of care saved the lives of numerous prisoners, while she acted strategically within a precarious network of relations across the women's and men's camps. These ultimately led to her escape with Polish prisoner Edek Galinski, and, after her arrest and return to Auschwitz, to her final decision to take her own life rather than be publicly executed by the Nazis. Mala's actions—as reported by the twenty-eight witnesses—not only expose what Butler calls "the socially contingent character of kinship"[26] but also, through voluntary bonds of caring and solidarity with other prisoners, gave rise to new possibilities for kinship in one of the most precarious and heinous places on earth: Auschwitz-Birkenau in 1943–1944.

The size of the singular "Mala" node is telling in this story, as it grows and shrinks to reflect the changing relationship between Mala and other subjects in each of the five chapters. In the "solidarity" chapter, "Mala" is roughly equivalent to the "we" subject, while in the chapter on "care" Mala is nine times larger than the other nodes, and in the chapter on "agency" Mala is more than four times the size of the rest of the subject nodes. This size difference correlates with witness fragments that attest to the centrality of Mala's decisions and actions in that part of the chapter. While the number of triplets is quite small in both the "escape" and "death" chapters, Mala is also diminished as subject, as both events are singular actions, not sustained expressions of agency and care that the witnesses attributed to her character.

Starting with the first chapter, the story describes forms of solidarity between women in the so-called "shoe commando" (part of the Canada Block responsible for sorting seized goods). Chaja G. says that the women "shared everything with each other," including the "one toothbrush" that they had for their collective. She even says the women sung anti-fascist songs in order to entice the Nazis to shoot them, rather than be sent to the gas chambers. Sarah G. says that Mala helped hide women and materials—including dynamite—smuggled into the camp. Itta W. speaks of Mala providing her with shoes for her swollen feet. Rebecca L. says that although she had "nothing in common" with Mala owing to their age difference, Mala nonetheless put her in a "good barrack." When Chaja G. says that "we were Mala's children" [*nous étions les enfants de Mala*], she is not only expressing gratitude for Mala's care and protection, but also pointing to a form of kinship that was not based on blood or familial relations. Instead, Mala's kinship was the product of a shared fate between women and men, Jewish and non-Jewish prisoners; it consisted of practices and relations to nurture life.

The second chapter of the story focuses on Mala's ethic of care. Chaja G. says that Mala "made arrangements" for a group of women to go to the Canada Commando, thereby helping "to save [them]." Frieda K. says Mala helped her "bathe," and she worked to "distribute girls to the right places," especially when they were in the camp hospital. Palomba F. says that Mala "plotted with those who arrived on trains" to get women to safety, and Sarah G. says, "Mala helped Polish girls, Russian girls, Jewish girls, wherever these girls came." Esther S. says, "I do not know how many people Mala saved." As a messenger, translator, and runner, Mala created formal and informal networks throughout the camp that not only enabled active forms of resistance but also created bonds of community and caring that were life-giving. According to Rivka K., Mala "helped save girls" and often "thwarted the Germans." As Edith Serras recalls, this manifested itself concretely in Mala's decision to bring extra soup to prisoners and to record—and later erase from selection lists—the "numbers" of girls who were sick in the hospital and would otherwise be condemned to the gas chamber.

The middle chapter on "escape" provides a composite of perspectives on how she escaped, many of which build on Mala's relative privilege and the trust that she established with the SS over time. According to Rebecca L., Mala had certain "resources" to acquire "valuable things" in the camp and that, as Sarah G. and Judith P. recall, the SS guards "trusted" and "liked" Mala. While the female witnesses knew that Mala ran away with a non-Jewish Polish political prisoner, only Wieslaw Kielar, another Polish political prisoner, was fully aware of the plan that was hashed out with his compatriot Edek. Kielar observed part of the escape, which was coordinated with another prisoner named Jurek. According to him, Mala was "helpless, pale with fear and completely confused," and needed to be "propelled . . . in the direction of a potato bunker" near the guardhouse where they successfully exited the camp in disguise. His assessment of her state of mind, conveyed to him after the fact by Jurek, bespeaks the daring and danger of their escape.

After she and Edek were captured and returned to Auschwitz, the chapters on agency and death focus on Mala's final acts of defiance under extreme duress. Supplied with a razor blade by the collective (according to Sarah G.), Mala attempts to take her own life, rather than be executed at the hand of the Nazis. The razor blade that she used to slit her wrists was, according to Alice Jakubovic, given to her "by Sally . . . in case [Mala had] to cut her veins." While the majority of witnesses say otherwise, Itta W. claims that she succeeded: "Mala killed herself," a testament to her final act of self-determination. Many of the witnesses recall Mala slapping the face of SS officer Ruiters (Palomba F. adds that she "spat on the German," too), as he tried to grab her arms and stop the blood flow. Fele F. says she "cursed them in good German," while other witnesses say that she spoke directly to them. Dora Freilich, recalling Mala's words, says that she declared to the women assembled for her execution: "I have told people on the outside." Edith Serras remembers Mala saying: "Children, I was here in the Lager to help you." According to Yaakov F., who would not have been present, she said: "I saw the end of them." While none of these linguistic acts will ever be verified, they each bear witness to the meaning attributed to Mala's acts of defiance. Before she died, Giza Weisblum says that the "SS taped her mouth with adhesive" in a final attempt to silence her voice.

Roma B. underscores the uncertainty of how she died: "Some say they burned her" while "some say she was gassed like the others." Regardless of how she ultimately died, "Mala would not give them the satisfaction of hanging her," according to Frances H. However, Ruth Krautwirth Meyerowitz remembers it differently and says that "they hanged this poor woman," while Fele F. says that "she went to the gas." Israel M. says, "Mala was burnt alive." Although Mala was killed, her deeds remain in language and memory because her words and actions gave rise to new social arrangements, new political possibilities, and new forms of kinship in the face of extreme violence. Denied her humanity and freedom, she speaks to and against power through acts of care and solidarity. If Mala, like Antigone, is "the occasion for a new field of the human, achieved through political catachresis, the one that happens when the less than human speaks as human," she speaks and acts through radically precarious forms of kinship that open up an "unprecedented future."[27] Even as it remains partial and unfulfilled, this future is embodied in—and accessible through—the dozens of witness testimonies.

While we can certainly read or listen to these testimonies one by one, an algorithmically created, testimonial ensemble connects, configures, and amplifies the contingency of survivor voices and memories in ways that allow us to tell poetic stories of the past. By transforming and proliferating individual testimonies into reconfigurable spreadsheets of semantic triplets and then, from there, into testimonial ensembles, a collective form of witnessing begins to emerge: "Mass testimony."[28] As a plurality of voices, testimonial ensembles are modernist forms of representation that arise from the impossibility of telling "any single authoritative story about what really happened."[29] The curated story, "Mala Zimetbaum: Between Kinship and Death," is a recombinant, paratactical form of collective memory and algorithmic fabulation. It makes no claims to be the definitive account, and it certainly provides no closure. There is no omniscient narrator or outside perspective to be found that would allow us to definitively adjudicate the many, different (sometimes competing and contradictory) narrative fragments. Indeed, many other stories could have been told using the generative possibilities of the platform or by including additional testimonial accounts.

It is precisely this proliferation of possibilities that constitutes the ethics of a testimonial ensemble. Not only can we ask questions about "what is remembered" (who Mala was, what happened to her, what others did to her), but we can also create a speculative narrative form that allows us to ask new questions about "what could have, should have, ought to have, or might have been."[30] Far from flattening differences or attempting to capture the past "as it really was," the algorithmic generation of a testimonial ensemble facilitates the multiplication of stories by deepening knowledge and bringing more voices and perspectives to bear on the historical record. At the same time, it allows us to ask new questions about the knowledge we already have and the ways we conventionally think about individual testimonies. Perhaps the testimonial ensemble of Mala Zimetbaum points to the (future) development of a memorial praxis for creating multiscalar, mass testimonies that document, analyze, and narrativize the erasures and silences of mass atrocities.

Credits:

Testimony segments in English from the Yale University Fortunoff Video Archive for Holocaust Testimonies: Roma B. (April 8, 1999; hvt-3863), tape 2, minutes 25:42–29:32 (https://fortunoff.aviaryplatform.com/collections/5/collection _resources/3910); Frances H. (December 13, 1992; hvt-2525), tape 1, minutes 45:08–47:56 (https://fortunoff.aviaryplatform.com/collections/5/collection _resources/2582); Judith P. (March 8, 1993; hvt-2548), tape 2, minutes 29:42– 35:30 (https://fortunoff.aviaryplatform.com/collections/5/collection_resources /2605); Rose K. (February 12, 1987; hvt-0841), tape 1, minutes 39:00–43:00 (https://fortunoff.aviaryplatform.com/collections/5/collection_resources

/907); Mania W. (August 18, 1994; hvt-2623), tape 1, minutes 40:06–43:10 (https://fortunoff.aviaryplatform.com/collections/5/collection_resources /2680).

Testimony segments in French from the Yale University Fortunoff Video Archive for Holocaust Testimonies, translated by Kendell Clarke: Chaja G. (May 8, 1995; hvt-4022), tape 1, minutes 1:17:18–1:33:36; tape 2, 4:32–9:40, 50:42–1:01:00 (https://fortunoff.aviaryplatform.com/collections/5/collection_resources /4067); Rebecca L. (June 24, 1992; hvt-1976), tape 3, minutes 00:29–8:36 (https://fortunoff.aviaryplatform.com/collections/5/collection_resources /2040); Sarah G. (May 20, 1992; hvt-1980), tape 3, minutes 11:27–15:09, 17:50– 22:30, 27:00–38:02 (https://fortunoff.aviaryplatform.com/collections/5 /collection_resources/2044); Israel M. (December 2, 1992; hvt-2981), tape 1, minutes 38:16–40:40; tape 3, 47:30–50:05 (https://fortunoff.aviaryplatform .com/collections/5/collection_resources/3035); Itta W. (March 10, 1997; hvt- 4083), tape 2, minute 49:49–53:00; tape 3, 39:10–42:00 (https://fortunoff .aviaryplatform.com/collections/5/collection_resources/4127); Yvette B. (March 3, 1993; hvt-2672), tape 3, minutes 16:30–20:20 (https://fortunoff .aviaryplatform.com/collections/5/collection_resources/2729); Benita H. (March 16, 1999, hvt-4192), tape 8, minutes 11:50–16:00 (https://fortunoff .aviaryplatform.com/collections/5/collection_resources/4235); Esther S. (No- vember 24, 1993; hvt-2827), tape 1, minutes 30:30–33:05 (https://fortunoff .aviaryplatform.com/collections/5/collection_resources/2881).

Testimony segments in Hebrew from the Yale University Fortunoff Video Ar- chive for Holocaust Testimonies, translated by Rachel Smith: Frieda K. (April 29, 1993; hvt-3539), tape 4, minutes 26:04–28:02 and 42:54–44:47 (https:// fortunoff.aviaryplatform.com/collections/5/collection_resources/3587); Helena H. (Jan 8, 1991–July 13, 1991; hvt-3248), tape 10, minutes 15:00–17:20 and 25:42–27:40 (https://fortunoff.aviaryplatform.com/collections/5/collection _resources/3297); Rivka K. (May 21, 1992; hvt-3342), tape 5, minutes 37:25– 40:25 (https://fortunoff.aviaryplatform.com/collections/5/collection _resources/3391); Fele F. (May 1, 1992; hvt-3341), tape 4, minutes 35:37–38:44 (https://fortunoff.aviaryplatform.com/collections/5/collection_resources /3390); Yaakov F. (March 9, 1989–May 7, 1991; hvt-1841), tape 16, minutes 1:00–12:45 and 19:03–20:20 (https://fortunoff.aviaryplatform.com/collections /5/collection_resources/1907). Testimony segments in Ladino from the Yale University Fortunoff Video Archive for Holocaust Testimonies, translated by Kyle Rosen: Palomba F. (June 4, 1993; hvt-2779), tape 1, minutes 44:10–48:40

(https://fortunoff.aviaryplatform.com/collections/5/collection_resources/2833).

Testimony segments from the US Holocaust Memorial Museum: Dora Freilich (October 24, 1984; RG-50.462.0007), tape 3, minutes 23:55–30:50 (https://collections.ushmm.org/search/catalog/irn508628); Ruth Krautwirth Meyerowitz (February 20, 1990; RG-50.030.0161), tape 2, minutes 9:48–12:50 (https://collections.ushmm.org/search/catalog/irn504659); Alice Jakubovic (August 27, 2002; RG-50.030.0469), tape 6, 16:04–19:12, 20:46–23:10; tape 8, 24:13–30:08; tape 9, 00:45–3:18 (https://collections.ushmm.org/search/catalog/irn511521); Hella Rosenbaum (October 26, 2000; RG-50.120.0380), tape 6, minutes 16:54–18:05 (https://collections.ushmm.org/search/catalog/irn509363), translated from Hebrew by Rachel Smith.

Raya Kagan testimony at the Adolf Eichmann trial (June 8, 1961; session 70), available online: https://www.youtube.com/watch?v=TtXJNcwT1cE (37:00–44:00); German trial transcript (session 70): Adolf Eichmann Trial Collection, Leo Baeck Institute Archives and Center for Jewish History (Box 1, Folder 13, page 148), available online: https://archives.cjh.org/repositories/5/archival_objects/491667.

Henja Frydman and Edith Serras interviews: David Boder, *Topical Autobiographies of Displaced People* (1957), box 12, David Boder Papers, Library Special Collections, Charles E. Young Research Library, UCLA, 575–639 and 1302–66. Quoted segments come from pages 625–28 and 1356–65. The recordings are from: "Voices of the Holocaust," Illinois Institute of Technology, Paul V. Galvin Library: https://voices.library.iit.edu/interview/frydmanH and https://voices.library.iit.edu/interview/serrasE.

Text Sources: Giza Weisblum, "The Escape and Death of the 'Runner' Mala Zimetbaum," in *They Fought Back: The Story of Jewish Resistance in Nazi Europe*, ed. and trans. Yuri Suhl (New York: Schocken Books, 1967), quotations come from pages 182–88; Wieslaw Kielar, *Anus Mundi: 1,500 Days in Auschwitz*, trans. Susanne Flatauer (New York: Times Books, 1980), quotations come from pages 224–55.

7

Cultural Memory Machines and the Futures of Testimony

With Rachel Deblinger

We begin the final chapter by returning to where this book started—namely, with another set of conversations with Holocaust survivor Fritzie Fritzshall. We do so in order to situate the Dimensions in Testimony project within a broader field of technologies that have transformed how testimony is created, stewarded, and accessed. At the same time, we reconsider the cultural and technological conditions of possibility that grounded her hope that she would still be able to answer questions three hundred years from now. To be sure, we cannot possibly imagine how many migrations, upgrades, and transformations the platforms and data would have to undergo to make such an experience possible, nor can we possibly predict what users will know or want to ask of Holocaust survivors in hundreds of years. In what follows, we foreground the technologies of the digital archive in order to think through the significance and implications of the massive innovations that are not only informing how and what we know about the past but also how we relate to the dead.

To do so, this chapter explores a range of media practices and computational technologies that enable us to interact with Holocaust testimonies in profoundly different ways than any of the prior technologies we examined. We start by analyzing data from tens of thousands of interactions with Dimensions in Testimony while situating the platform within the contemporary context of cultural memory machines and human-computer interactions.[1] Far from being simple, straightforward, or neutral, algorithmic culture machines are, as Ed Finn has argued, "sprawling assemblages involving many forms of human labor, material resources, and ideological choices."[2] We need to understand how these cultural memory machines work, what decisions went into building them, and what futures they unfold for relating to the dead. After analyzing the Dimensions in Testimony (DiT) project, we turn to Holocaust testimonies created by machines and people other than survivors. Here, we focus on two social media projects—@ eva.stories on Instagram and the St. Louis Manifest project on Twitter—before discussing the use of generative AI in creating personal archives, structuring access to the past, and finally creating testimonial-like narratives using the unfathomable affordances of large language models. We conclude by underscoring the importance of digital provenance and refocusing attention on the question of ethics at the intersection of human and machine.

Gaps in the Archive

Like Todd, I—Rachel Deblinger—also "talked" with Fritzie Fritzshall after her death. But unlike Todd, I had also interviewed her before. In 2008, I interviewed Fritzie in a small room in the storefront space of the Holocaust Memorial Foundation of Illinois, the precursor to the current Illinois Holocaust Museum and Education Center (IHMEC), as part of an assignment for an oral history course in graduate school. Just a year before, I had worked with Fritzie at the IHMEC as a development assistant. Fritzie was not yet the board president, but she was an active member of the board, and she and I had grown close over the years. When I asked Fritzie why she was sitting for the interview, she responded very quickly: "I agreed to be interviewed today because I love you."[3]

At the time, I understood that asking her to sit for the interview meant reawakening her nightmares. She had always been honest about this, even over the many years when she spoke to museum visitors and school children. Just as she "told" Todd: each time she speaks, "it opens a wound." Like many of our students, I also found that it was emotionally easier to ask questions to Fritzie through the computer interface, without opening up those nightmares for her. This is no small barrier. My notes from the interview in 2008 detail a moment when Fritzie started to cry remembering her mother and her brothers who she never saw after Auschwitz. At the time, she apologized; then I apologized. There was a long break, and Fritzie said, "You know it's funny, it's this many years later and you say I can stand up and talk about this, it's okay. It's not okay." And then I promised: "Okay, we won't go back there again."[4] I pulled back, not as an interviewer, but as a friend that did not want to be the cause of pain to someone I loved.

On the one hand, this suggests that my "interview" with the algorithmically accessible Fritzie can be more open. I ask her about her relationship with her father after the war and about the fate of her mother. I hear stories I had not heard before about her aunt Bella who helped protect her in Auschwitz and about her husband, who had been a POW during World War II. But, on the other hand, the love we had for each other, the familiarity we shared, opened up other stories— ones I tried to find but failed to hear through DiT. In fact, even in 2008, I had tried and failed to get Fritzie to tell me a story on tape that she had told me once over dinner. Here is that story, as I remember it: Upon returning to her home-town of Klyucharki, Czechoslovakia (now Kliucharky, Ukraine), after liberation, she moved into her grandmother's house with a number of other young survivors as they tried to find family members and stay alive. She told me that at one point, while they were all in this house, she stumbled upon a bra in an old wardrobe, attempted to try it on, and ended up tying it twice around her chest. It was the first bra she had ever worn, and she didn't know it was too big, or how a proper bra should have fit.

This story has stuck with me over the years. More than the moments of trans-port or the selections, this memory exposed for me the loss of her mother, her childhood, and her pivotal teenage years. This story filtered all of these losses down into a sweet and comic moment—of Fritzie remembering herself trying to rebuild her life. And when I interviewed her in a vaguely formal way in that small room in Skokie, I tried to steer the conversation toward this story. But when I asked Fritzie about her hometown, about coming home after the war, instead of telling me about that cabinet and the bra, she spoke angrily of the neighbors in their small town. Her anger was evident in her language, in her choppy sentence structure, and in the way she broke her narrative flow to reflect: "This—this—to this day what I don't understand. We came back as young people. We came back with nothing. Our things were taken away from us. I recognized my aunt's clothes that the neighbors were wearing. They saw us on the street, nobody came to say hello. Nobody said, 'Are you hungry?' Nobody said, 'Are you cold?' Nobody."[5]

Neither version of this postwar reflection—not the lighthearted memory of finding a bra in an old cabinet or the anger of remembering that other clothes (perhaps from that same cabinet) had been stolen by neighbors—is captured in her DiT interview. At least I could not find a way to hear those stories. When I "interviewed" Fritzie on February 21, 2022, almost fourteen years later, I asked about her hometown and the algorithm returned this answer: "I was discrimi-nated against. Our neighbors ignored me. They didn't want to know that I came back." It summed up the story she told in 2008, but without the anger, without the disbelief, and without the reflectiveness. None of the questions I asked— about liberation, about her hometown of Klyucharki, about connecting with her dad after the war—resulted in an answer with any detail about the period of time between liberation and her journey to Chicago.

It is possible that in the archive of Fritzie's multiday DiT interview, there is an answer as detailed and as passionate as the one she gave me in 2008. It is possible that there is even an answer where she opens the wardrobe in her grandmother's house and tries to figure out how a bra works. But I could not find those stories. It is an important reminder that the archive is a privileged site of selected and curated stories, and that although the technology will allow users to interact with some version of the survivors' stories and memories—perhaps long into the future—we will not be able to hear the stories that were never recorded. As Fritzie told me in 2008: "There are certain things survivors will speak about and certain things they will not. When survivors get together and do talk amongst themselves and talk about the camps or whatever, they speak in a different language, they speak about things that will never come out in an interview. It's just a totally different world. I just don't know how to explain it."[6] When I asked if those stories should be recorded for historical purposes, she responded: "Sometimes there are personal things, and, women especially . . ." She left that sentence unfinished.

Indeed, some stories will be heard over and over again, and others will never be heard. To be sure, as Fritzie suggested, these presences and absences are an essential part of both testimony and the archive—and a prerequisite for understanding any engagement with them. But the archive is also a technology, or more precisely, is composed and recomposed through a multiplicity of technologies that do not merely provide access but structure what is known and even what can be known. As we have seen, a central part of *Ethics of the Algorithm* is motivated by the desire to interrogate the structures of the digital archive and surface unheard, underappreciated, or unknown elements of the testimonial record. At the same time, no amount of computation will fill in absences or restore silenced voices. As we look to the futures of testimony, we ought to consider which stories have been preserved, which ones have disappeared, which ones were never recorded, and whether there are ones that might still be known or imagined. As distant witnesses, what are we inheriting, producing, interpreting, or being asked to uphold? Who (or what) should do so and how? And what ethical principles ought to guide those decisions?

Learning from Virtual Survivors?

A few years ago, when Dimensions in Testimony was released through the IWitness web platform, I—Todd Presner—began bringing virtual survivors into the classroom. When living Holocaust survivors could no longer come to visit classes, students had the chance, instead, to interact with Fritzie Fritzshall, Pinchas Gutter, Renee Firestone, Anita Lasker-Wallfisch, and Janine Oberrotman through DiT. Supplementing film, we know that digital archives and interactive platforms such as DiT will soon become the primary access points to spoken survivor testimony. Like a traditionally recorded survivor interview in which the interviewer poses a question and the interviewee gives an answer, the original DiT recordings are linear and have a one-to-one correspondence between question and answer. The difference, however, is that they cannot be accessed that way. In the DiT platform, what is heard is contingent upon the questions asked, and there are sometimes multiple answers to the same or similar questions, some of which may be phrased by the survivor with more (or less) concision or affect. And rather than filmed with a single, static camera in the survivor's home, the initial DiT interviews took place over five days in a studio with over one hundred cameras filming the survivor from many different angles.[7] Since the survivors were captured simultaneously from all sides, their image could be turned into an interactive, three-dimensional, volumetric projection.

Part of the appeal of the DiT platform, students have said, is the autonomy and privacy of the experience—namely, the ability to ask questions on their laptop from their home. They can steer the interaction for as long as they wish and, perhaps, ask a wider range of questions because they feel that they will not be judged or make the survivor uncomfortable. Questions about revenge, hatred toward Germans, and forgiveness tend to be at the forefront of their minds. They also turn to survivors for wisdom and guidance, seeking knowledge they can apply in their own lives, learning about the survivors' hopes for the future, and imagining ways that their generation can combat racism and antisemitism in the world today.

While enthusiastic "interviewers," some users—including many students— also characterized the experience with DiT as "spooky," as if they were talking to a ghost or an AI. Before the interaction starts, survivors in DiT nod their heads, blink their eyes, shift in their seats, and almost seem to wait for a question to be posed. And while the IWitness platform is currently a two-dimensional interaction on the screen, survivors can also be projected—in museums and other exhibition spaces—in three-dimensional form. Not surprisingly, DiT survivors are sometimes asked "who" or "what" they are in this technologically mediated form. Such questions include: "What's it like being an AI?," "Did you die?," "Are you dead?," "Are you still alive?," "Are you alive right now?," "Do you know Dracula?," "Can you tell my computer?," "How do you feel about being preserved like this forever?," "Are you an AI?," and "Do you believe in ghosts?"[8]

Pinchas Gutter has a clear answer to the question of whether he is an AI (he replies: "I'm a real person"), but when I ask more pointedly, "What does it feel

like to be an AI?," his response is that "it feels a little strange when I watch myself
[. . .] but the importance of it as for the future to be able to actually see and hear
and be able to interact with a Holocaust survivor despite the fact that he's just a
hologram is so important because I think it will impact the audience in a much
more forceful way than just watching a film in one- or two-dimensional way."[9] In
fact, during the creation of his DiT interview in 2014, the very first question asked
to him by Stephen Smith, then the executive director of the USC Shoah Foundation, was: "What does it feel like to be the world's first full length hologram?" His
response is that he thinks "it's a privilege . . . and very important for the future,
and I feel very privileged to have been chosen to do that so uh I'm very happy
about it." When later asked in the interview how he would like this "project" or
"exhibit" to be used, Gutter responds that he hopes to see it "distributed in such
a way that it should be available everywhere," particularly when he's "not around
anymore," so that students "have the opportunity of interacting with [him] despite the fact that it's just a hologram."[10]

Even if DiT interviewees are not technically turned into or experienced as
holograms, digital projections evoke a strange and perhaps unsettling familiarity,
precisely because of the pervasiveness of holograms in the broader cultural imaginary. In the popular imagination, holographic technologies tend to conjure up
people coming back to life to deliver messages from beyond the grave (as in *Star
Wars*). Technological dreams of transcending human mortality are tied to re-
demptive narratives of future possibility. Indeed, part of the reason for the spook-
iness is the technology's mimetic effect of life (*bios* and *zoē*) that is simultaneously
death-defying.[11] That is to say, we use our finite human faculties of speech and
cognition to interact with the likeness of a survivor who seems to behave as if
always alive and able to defy the temporal, spatial, and biological facticity of
human mortality. The interactive technologies work in concert with a careful
scripting of responses to produce a reality effect characterized by aesthetic verisimilitude and presence. In the moments of awe and delight when the survivor
answers our question, we are willing, at least for a moment, to suspend judgment
and interact with the platform as if interacting with a living survivor.[12]

To make such an experience as lifelike as possible, the DiT interviewers used
numerous scripting devices. While the Foundation does not create answers, the
survivor is advised to give short answers (less than two minutes), rather than long
narrative responses. Sometimes the same question is asked multiple times to record variations or "script" an answer spoken with more concision, focus, or poise.
For example, toward the end of her DiT interview, Renee Firestone is asked the
following: "Okay. I'm going to ask you to be as brief as you can, but I do know

that this is a long story, so do the best you can . . . Can you tell us how your sister died, when and how you found out? That whole story."[13] She obliges and provides a short, factual answer in seven sentences. That answer is played by the system nearly eight times as frequently as another, much longer and emotionally wrought answer in which she details confronting the doctor who performed medical experiments on her sister in Auschwitz decades after the war.[14]

In addition, many predetermined responses and reactions were also recorded to cast a wide net of possible answers to users' questions. Gutter, for example, is recorded saying "hello," "goodbye," and "thank you" in different languages, including Polish, Hebrew, and Italian; he has multiple answers to the question "What did you have for lunch?"; he recorded dozens of answers to fundamental historical concepts and questions ("What is the Holocaust?," "What is a death camp?," "What is a ghetto?"); and there are numerous prompting questions for users such as "Why didn't you ask me how I survived?" as well as pre-scripted responses meant to keep the interaction focused on the Holocaust ("This is not an appropriate question for me to answer" and "Maybe you can find another topic which I would be prepared to discuss with you"). Other DiT interviewees, such as Firestone, were also instructed to record specific gestural movements that could be used: "Hello, I'm asking you a question. So look over at me. This is for a while and then look back. And then, I'm asking you a question over here. Okay. And you look back. . . . And then, over here. And look back. And here . . . and look back. . . . And a little bit more Simon Says. The first thing is nod yes, a slow nod yes."[15] This scripting and editing is not, of course, unique to DiT (we might recall the staging of testimony throughout Lanzmann's *Shoah*, for instance), but it tends to be forgotten or obscured in the interactive platform, which also aims to create the effect of a seamless verisimilitude to life. Once again, the technological media—like the algorithms and computation more generally—are shaped by human choices and must not be mistaken as somehow objective, value-free, or neutral.

For his DiT interview, Gutter was asked close to two thousand questions (including hundreds of performative prompts), and he provides nearly thirty hours of recorded testimonial answers. In aggregate, this makes his DiT interview among the longest of any recorded Holocaust testimony; however, it is not recorded as—or meant to be encountered as—a chronological life story or singular narrative. Instead, each answer is indexed as a fragment of testimony. Once a given answer is determined to be usable within the system, it is given a clip ID (for instance, "01821_feelings_being_a_hologram.mp4") and becomes part of the database of playable answers. Each time a user interacts with the system, a new version of his testimony emerges as a kind of remix.

Drawing on a database of clips, the system determines which answer to play based on an algorithmic process initiated after the user poses a question. That determination follows a sequence of steps: First, the system uses an automatic speech recognition (ASR) tool to transform the waveforms of a user's voice into transcriptions that are resolved into letters, words, and sentences. Once turned into chunks of text, natural language processing is used to determine the meaning and intention of the question, relying primarily on a pretrained vocabulary of domain-specific terms. The IBM Watson system then decides the best match between the question and a prerecorded answer.[16] After doing so, the system assigns a "confidence score" to that determination. Guided by the confidence scores, human readers check the assignments (either validating or correcting the algorithmic determinations) to better "train" the machine-learning algorithm over time. In the process, variations of similar questions ("What did your father do for work?," "What did your father do for a living?," "What kind of business did your father run?") are clustered together and associated with particular answers, some of which might be weighted more heavily than others. Once the system has assigned answers to about ten thousand questions (all of which are validated or corrected by human reviewers), it is said to be "trained" and will continue to make modest improvements over time.

While users guide the DiT experience by the questions they ask, the system does not create new answers. After the five days of recording with the DiT team, the survivor's answers are fixed. Because the Dimensions in Testimony project decouples questions from answers, testimonial narratives are "remade" and "remixed" each time a user interacts with the system. This results in a new, decidedly modernist testimonial experience characterized by contingency, parataxis, chance, algorithmic determinations, and perhaps "middle-voicedness" (as the user is necessarily part of and likely affected by the interaction). If there is an AI component to DiT, it is the fact that the system becomes better at understanding users' questions and choosing the best—or most probable—answer from a finite database of clips. In other words, the algorithm gets better at accurately modeling the content.

The USC Shoah Foundation provided our team with data related to four DiT interviewees: Pinchas Gutter, Anita Lasker-Wallfisch, Renee Firestone, and Janine Oberrotman. The data consisted of the original transcripts with all the questions asked to the survivor during the recording process, the interviewee's answers, and the clip names; all the user questions asked within the DiT platform ("utterances" or "chatlogs") to Lasker-Wallfisch, Firestone, and Oberrotman between August 2018 and April 2021; and the "confidence scores" of the Watson system in deciding which clip to play for a given question as well as the record of the human review process that determined manually whether the correct clip was played. For the interviewee recording, Gutter gave 1,930 playable answers to 1,419 questions as well as an additional 512 prompts that were instructions to repeat short scripted answers such as "I don't understand what you said," "Could you rephrase that question," "I don't know the answer to that question right now," "This is a topic for another time and place," or "I can tell you a story"; Lasker-Wallfisch recorded 1,856 answers that the Foundation determined to be "playable" from 1,849 questions; Firestone recorded 1,625 answers that the Foundation determined to be "playable" from 1,624 questions; and Oberrotman recorded 518 answers that the Foundation determined to be "playable" from 508 questions. According to the DiT team, interview questions are divided into general questions (which are asked to all Holocaust survivors), focus group questions (aimed at understanding the interests of different cultural groups), education program team questions, the top one hundred questions asked over the life of the DiT system itself, and, finally, interviewee-specific questions (the last of which comprises about 25 percent of the total). For each interviewee, about 20 percent of the total answers were scripted responses for the purpose of directing users within the system.

Our analysis focused on 40,577 user questions for the two-and-a-half-year period in which we have data.[17] It is important to note that no demographic data or identifying information was collected about the users, and there is no way to tell if the same person asked more than one question or heard more than one answer. Beyond the ASR parsing of the user's speech into text, all that is known is the time when the question was logged, the answer played, and, in some cases, the location or modality in which the question was asked (such as at a particular museum or through the IWitness online portal). During this time period, one thousand unique answers were played from Lasker-Wallfisch's DiT interview; 885 unique answers were played from Firestone's DiT interview; and 353 unique answers were played from Oberrotman's DiT interview. These numbers are far less than the questions asked because the same answers tend to be played quite often.

Besides general pleasantries ("hello" or "I am very well, thank you") and variations of "That's a very good question, but I was never asked about it during that project" (played 644 times), Lasker-Wallfisch's most frequently played answers concern her daily routine in Auschwitz (played 538 times), her life and career after the war (played 316 times), the moment of her liberation (played 311 times), the five-minute summary of her story (played 311 times), and her attitudes toward Germany and ordinary Germans (played 299 times). Other answers that were played frequently include responses to how she survived, which concentration camps she was imprisoned in, her family then and today, the fate of her parents, and what she ate in the camps. Notably, nearly five hundred answers have been played only a handful of times (between one and five times).

We might also inquire about what answers—during this period—were never played and, hence, what stories remained unaccessed and unknown. For Lasker-Wallfisch's DiT interview, over eight hundred answers were never played, but about half of these are simply comments, reactions to directions, or scripting devices. The remaining ones, however, are substantive testimonial content and consist of a wide range of fascinating stories that were, during our period of analysis, never heard. Among the many unplayed answers were stories about her sister stealing chocolate in Auschwitz and feeling regret for not sharing it, playing music in front of Josef Mengele, her interactions with Irma Grese at the end of the war, her discovery of letters from her family, her problems with historians, and her reflections on postwar Germany. Of course, these stories may be heard one day should the right question be asked to prompt the system to play the answer. Until then, they will remain hidden in the archive, so to speak, awaiting discovery.

Although the DiT system does not suggest questions or prompt users to ask about certain topics, it would be possible for the platform to indicate how much (or how little) of a testimony has been heard during a given interaction. This might inspire users to prolong their interactions or direct them to clusters of answers that would otherwise go unheard. At this point, however, it is not possible to know how much a given user ultimately heard—or learned—from a DiT interaction since the data is not logged by user but rather by daily interactions. Moreover, the system does not (yet) learn through the course of the interaction.

For the data our team examined, the vast majority of people interacting with survivors through DiT asked questions that were related to the Holocaust or to personalizing their knowledge of the interviewee. For instance, during Holocaust remembrance month in April 2021, Gutter was asked nearly four thousand questions through the IWitness portal and various installations of DiT in museum settings.[18] Probably because of the guided, pedagogical contexts for the interactions, nearly every question was related to his Holocaust experience ("What was life like in the ghetto?," "What is your most painful memory?," "Do you ever have nightmares?," "What happened when you were in hiding?," "How old were you when you were captured?," "What were the death marches like?") or aimed to personalize knowledge of Gutter and his attitudes ("What are some of your hobbies?," "What is your favorite color?," "Do you forgive your captors?," "Do you have any grandkids?," "Now, how do you feel about Israel and the Palestinians?," "Are you a happy person?"). Only a tiny fraction of users abused DiT by asking inappropriate questions (for instance, related to sex) or making overtly anti-semitic comments (for instance, praising Hitler).[19]

With regard to the testimonial answers, it is important to underscore that the DiT system does not "make-up" responses—and, in fact, this is the ethical limit that the Foundation has acknowledged and refused to transgress. The survivors' experience, expressed through their own words and voice, remains central to the testimony's authenticity. According to Smith, the ethics of all USC Shoah Foundation interviews is to be found in the principle of respecting the survivors' testimony: they do not edit the answers; they do not cut the survivors off; and they do not add to their words.[20] Unlike interacting with Amazon's Alexa, Apple's Siri, or ChatGPT, no new answers are ever created to questions, no customizable skills can be taught to change the nature of the interaction, and, at least for now, the system has no "memory" or "futurity" which could be used to guide subsequent interactions. A user cannot resume a prior conversation, and the system does not change the answers played based on a user's past questions or previous interactions. With steady advances in cognitive computing and generative AI, all this is already possible and would mean that the DiT system becomes more like a form of Artificial Intelligence rather than an interactive playback machine for listening to testimony clips. As it currently stands, however, each interaction is a unique experience in which the system uses an algorithmic decision-making process to match a question with an answer.

Perhaps one advantage of this approach is that the continuity (or discontinuity) of questioning falls to the user, who is responsible for guiding the concatenation of the narrative and the testimonial experience. In this sense, the system opens up a space for the distant witness to develop a technologically mediated form of ethical relationality, copresence, and intersubjectivity, not entirely unlike that which guided early interviewers like David Boder, Dori Laub, or Lawrence Langer. Of course, the differences in the technologies underpinning the interaction are massive, and it seems disingenuous (though perhaps reassuring to some) to say that DiT is "just a different form of accessing the same stories."[21] The form of the medium has content—epistemic, ontological, political, aesthetic, and cultural—that fundamentally affects the stories, not least of all because DiT interviews no longer have a predetermined narrative coherence or even a definitive beginning, middle, or end. As we have argued throughout this book, technological platforms such as DiT (and the algorithms, databases, and data that run on them) are never value-free or neutral. Instead, these cultural memory machines function by encoding numerous choices and scripting devices that are themselves grounded in certain epistemologies, values, and worldviews. We can begin to evaluate these technologies when we understand how they work.

The Ghost in the Machine / The Machine in the Ghost

Within the history of AI, Turing's Imitation Test—commonly known as the Turing Test—is often cited as the benchmark for determining the difference between human and machine. If the computer can seemingly "think" and provide answers that make human interrogators believe that they are talking to another human being, the machine is said to be artificially intelligent. But as Simone Natale has argued (in reference to Turing's own writings), the question of AI "is not whether machines are or are not able to think. It is, instead, whether we *believe* that machines are able to think."[22] In other words, the experience with AI is not only "a matter of computer power and programming techniques but also resides—and perhaps especially—in the perceptions and patterns of interaction through which humans engage with computers."[23] In this sense, we might consider DiT within the cultural realm of the Turing Test to the degree that it creates an illusion of copresence, emulates dialogical human interactions, and sometimes elicits empathy and cognitive dissonance from users.[24] Each interaction with a DiT survivor produces a new, personalized narrative about the Holocaust while functioning tacitly as a mini–Turing Test: users tend to suspend disbelief when it succeeds at imitating life and to fault the system when it does not (although we probably ought to judge its success by how much knowledge it imparts and whether it can create a foundation for ethical behaviors).

Running on IBM's Watson supercomputer and using millions of simulated neural networks, the DiT machine matches answers to questions by processing vast amounts of data that have previously been aligned by machine-learning algorithms and human trainers. Because of the scale, complexity, and speed of these processes, they ultimately elude human scrutiny, even as human reviewers train the machine to improve the effectiveness of the speech recognition, language processing, and matching algorithm. As the machine behaves more intelligently over time, the DiT interactions become more "natural," blurring the boundaries between human and machine as well as between past and present. Due to the inscrutability of these machine-learning processes that effectively substitute for the survivor's own decision-making (after all, the survivor is no longer deciding what answer to give or even whether to give an answer), DiT interactions might be said to follow a kind of "ghost in the machine" logic: As front-end users, we cannot get inside the system's black box to know how the answers are being determined algorithmically for specific questions.[25] And to the extent that the interaction is seamless, we may not even suspect the existence of an underlying neural network reanimating mind and body. At the same time, if we focus on the effect of spectrality created by these technologies, DiT functions more like a "machine in the ghost" precisely because of the role of technologies in perpetuating the likeness of human interaction beyond death. The machine (a complex of user interface, a database of video recordings, machine-learning algorithms, data, and servers) animates the survivor, potentially well into the future, by defying human aging, disability, and mortality. In this sense, DiT could be considered part of the posthuman lineage that N. Katherine Hayles critiques as "information [that has] lost its body." Through a technological fantasy of "disembodied immortality," it attempts to overcome "finitude as a condition of human being."[26]

When considered in these dual ways, DiT is part of a larger, contemporary, techno-cultural problematic that uses new technologies to animate ghosts, not only through holographic images (such as rapper Tupac Shakur appearing at Coachella in 2012, sixteen years after his death)[27] or through CGI (such as Carrie Fisher in *Star Wars: The Rise of Skywalker*), but also through the seemingly more accessible technologies of necromancy developed by companies such as Eternime, StoryFile, and Replika to allow us to "talk" to our dead loved ones.[28] Founded in 2014, the tagline of Eternime was: "Who wants to live forever?" The company promised to create "an Artificial Intelligence digital replica of you built from your digital footprint (emails, social media posts, smartphone and wearables data etc.). This digital twin will learn from you, grow with you, help you and, eventually, live on after you die."[29] The co-founder of Eternime, Marius Ursache, expressed its lofty ambitions as follows: "Our end goal is to preserve the thoughts, stories and memories of entire generations and create a library of human memories, one where you could ask people in the past about their individual or collective experiences and thoughts."[30] The Eternime avatar, Ursache touted, would function as a "personal biographer" ingesting everything shared with it in order to produce an AI-powered chatbot after we are dead. Of course, in the commercial sphere, many ethical questions arise over who or what has custody over anyone's "digital remains," to use Tonia Sutherland's formulation, including "questions of race, representation, embodiment, commodification, memorialization, spectacle, and carcerality."[31] As the scandals over Facebook and Cambridge Analytica have made abundantly clear, tech companies hardly have a strong track record of protecting, safeguarding, and overseeing what happens to our personal data at any point in our life or after our death.

In fact, there is much that commercial companies could learn from institutional archiving projects like the USC Shoah Foundation's Visual History Archive and Dimensions in Testimony project, particularly with regard to ethical standards for preserving and disseminating personal stories. As Smith argued, for instance, with regard to the Visual History Archive (and this point would presumably apply to DiT as well), an "ethic of data integrity," which is characterized by "bit-level preservation," is connected with an "ethics of access" and "care behind the metadata."[32] Together, they give rise to a foundation of "*trust* . . . in the *integrity* of the [technological] systems."[33] Smith points out that the expectation of the subjects interviewed for the archive is precisely the preservation of their testimony and its access for purposes of education and research. The testimonies and personal data are never used as a means for someone else's commercial ends because the survivors are not data specimens or data providers. For students and researchers, an ethics of access and data curation are paramount, and this includes teaching students "how to search, retrieve, manage, and use testimony in the context of ethical decision making and online citizenship . . . [such as] ethical editing and video argumentation."[34] Authenticity, truthfulness, and responsible stewardship go hand in hand with preservation and access, especially as synthetic media technologies proliferate.

When DiT interviewees were asked why they participated in the project or how they feel about it, they uniformly expressed the wish to have their stories preserved and available to listeners in the future. Lasker-Wallfisch says that her decision rested on "the technology to actually bring this terrible story [of the Holocaust] into the future."[35] Firestone says, "I think this project is amazing. I don't know how I lucked out to be part of it and I hope that in the future, somebody will see me and remember me."[36] Perhaps Oberrotman put it most enthusiastically, highlighting both the power and promise of such technologies: "I think it's the greatest project under the sun. You are witnesses to history. Without you, there would be . . . who knows, actually? I don't want to speculate. I think you make the people who died live forever. So isn't that power? That's a great power. And we are, I imagine all Holocaust survivors are grateful. I'm especially grateful because I always lamented the absence of knowledge about the Holocaust and now there are books and there, that you are here. So it's amazing, it's a dream of every survivor, I'm sure."[37] Survivors participate in projects like DiT because they want to ensure that their stories will be preserved, transmitted, and remain accessible well into the future. They want to be assured that there will be a "you" encountering their testimony. This is the power and possibility of these cultural memory machines.

Today, a multitude of tech companies have also recognized the great power of trying to engineer ways for people who died to live forever. These include companies focused on ingesting user-created data to generate AI simulations of language, affect, and embodiment, ranging from memory preservation to conversational avatars and digital twins.[38] Since leaving the USC Shoah Foundation in 2022, Smith has served as the executive chairman, CEO, and co-founder of StoryFile, a technology company that produces AI-driven, conversational videos aimed at creating and preserving life stories. According to the value statement on their website: "StoryFile is committed to capturing your life story. We began by preserving important historical testimony—and that includes you, too."[39] In other words, anyone can now create, disseminate, and preserve a testimony in the form of an interactive life story. Through its Conversa platform, video-recorded stories—created by users—are encoded using natural language processing and AI to connect questions to answers. And even as the applications extend far beyond capturing life stories and family legacies (for example, the platform is marketed for sales teams, customer service, employee onboarding, and educational tutorials, among other things), "StoryFile Life" is certainly envisioned as an outgrowth of interactive Holocaust testimonies and is built on many of the same technologies developed for Dimensions in Testimony. According to William Shatner's buoyant promotional message featured on the StoryFile Life website, "everyone has a story to tell" and now those stories can be recorded, accessed, and shared with family and friends who are alive today as well as with people in the future who can ask us questions and hear our answers.[40] The premise is that, one day, we will be "an ancestor" to someone in the future who "hundreds of years from now could reach into the past, to talk with [us], and [we] could talk back." With the StoryFile Life platform, Shatner proclaims, a user can produce an "authentic self for all time" that is transformed through AI into an interactive conversation that transcends time and mortality.

Patented in 2021 as a "Natural Conversation Storytelling System," the invention is a method and apparatus for navigating large multimedia databases using a conversational interface.[41] It uses machine learning and natural language processing to understand contributor responses and facilitate conversations between humans and machines. According to the patent, "With [answer] caching and AI-backed search process, the multi-media interactive story-telling system creates the appearance of a continuous and natural conversation between the inquirer and the contributor who appears digitally in the recording segments. The inquirer can ask questions or input inquiries in a real-time fashion as if it were a live conversation." The interaction is "seamless" and the "conversation maintains visual, semantic and logical continuity throughout the engagement."[42] In other words, the goal of the interactive system is to create the effect of natural conversations, liberated, as it were, from the facticities of human mortality and fallibility.

But the question remains: Can it do so without devolving into a world suffused with disinformation and deepfakes? StoryFile's AI principles are grounded in a "human-centric approach" that aims to "empower people to tell their own stories in their own words."[43] This is an ethical standard that comes directly from the work of the USC Shoah Foundation where the authenticity of the voice and the personal story are paramount. The AI facilitates the interaction by matching questions with answers but it does not create, extrapolate, or invent answers. This stands in contrast to the approach of other companies such as Replika, which uses AI chatbots to learn who we are while ingesting more and more of our data. Replika is marketed, for instance, as an AI replica of ourselves, which is created out of our "thoughts, feelings, beliefs, experiences, memories, dreams." It aims to "become [our] friend" through our data.[44] The more the bot is fed personal data, the more it learns about, talks like, and behaves like us (or, at least, the version of "us" reflected in what we choose to share with it). Ultimately, the "digital avatar" will outlive us, raising the question, once again, of what happens to our digital remains—in this case, when they are algorithmically transformed into AI versions of ourselves. This question has reached a heightened level of urgency given the fact that most of our digital remains (social media posts, emails, photographs, videos, text messages, app usage statistics, location records, wearable data, biometric measurements) are already circulating in the cloud and variously stored on, shared with, or scraped by different corporate platforms.[45]

Even as we grapple with these questions and the ways that AI continues to transgress the ethical boundaries we define, we encounter another ethical demand, namely for these stories to be heard (as opposed to just "preserved," or, worse, "ingested" and "harvested" for some other ends). This demand requires not only the kind of bit-level preservation described by Smith, but also an ethic of access and amplification that allows users to hear and learn from survivor testimonies. And this seems to be one of the most important contributions of interactive platforms such as Dimensions in Testimony. In the next section, we look briefly at two social media projects that create new trajectories for testimony creation and distant witnessing. We reflect on @eva.stories on Instagram and the St. Louis Manifest project on Twitter to discuss how these projects decenter institutional archives and physical sites of memory, opening up testimonial content creation to almost anyone and facilitating access through viewing habits specific to these platforms. Finally, we conclude by confronting some of the epistemological and ethical issues raised at the bleeding edge of generative AI.

Social Media: @eva.stories on Instagram and the St. Louis Manifest Project on Twitter

@eva.stories, a Holocaust memory project built for Instagram, launched in 2019 on Yom HaShoah (Holocaust Memorial Day) by asking: "What if a Girl in the Holocaust had Instagram?"[46] This question was less a counterfactual thought exercise about what might have happened differently had technologies of social media been around in the early 1940s and more an attempt to use Instagram as a platform for (re)telling Holocaust stories.[47] Developed by Israeli businessman Mati Kochavi and his daughter Maya, @eva.stories adapted the diary of Eva Heyman, a thirteen-year-old Hungarian girl killed in Auschwitz in 1944, into a series of short film dramatizations of her life shared as posts on Instagram.[48] The posts take the form of thirty daily "stories," each tagged with a date between February and June of 1944. Composed of still images and period-specific film clips that appear to have been shot with a phone camera, the stories are personalized around events in Eva's life (celebrating her birthday, pursuing a school crush, going out with friends) and her reflections on the broader historical forces enveloping Hungary (Figure 7.1).

Heyman's diary begins on February 13, 1944, and continues through May 30, 1944.[49] Three days after the diary entries end, she was deported to Auschwitz, where she was murdered on October 17, 1944. Her mother, Ágnes Zsolt, survived and, apparently, found the diary in 1945 in Nagyvárad, the town where the family lived. Interestingly, at least one scholar contests the authenticity of the diary, claiming, in fact, that Eva's mother wrote most, if not all, of it shortly after the war, in her daughter's voice, perhaps out of guilt and shame for having survived.[50] Although the diary's voice has been questioned, the truthfulness of its account of historical experiences is not contested. Without resolving the question of authorship, we focus on its remediation.

The diary begins about a month before the Nazi occupation of Hungary and documents the rapid escalation of antisemitic violence—from being forced to wear the yellow star, to being denied entry to the park and forced to give up personal effects, to ghettoization and, finally, deportation. For @eva.stories, the three and a half months chronicled in Heyman's diary were condensed into one day's worth of Instagram posts. The final dramatization ("June") depicts the anguish of Eva and her grandmother in a deportation train, as they struggle to breathe and survive. The film clips imagined in the boxcar eventually fade away as night falls on the train. The screen turns to black, and users are told that when the train reached Auschwitz, Eva had no opportunity to say goodbye to her grandparents. Her hair was shaved off; she was given a number; and when she watched her best friend die, she was utterly alone. On October 17, 1944, Eva was sent to the gas chamber when a guard saw wounds on her feet. The final frame states: "According to testimonies of surviving eyewitnesses, Eva never stopped fighting to stay alive."[51]

When the project was launched, @eva.stories attracted global attention. It had 1.1 million followers as of May 9, 2023, down from 1.4 million followers in

FIGURE 7.1: Screenshots of @eva.stories on Instagram. Mati Kochavi and Maya Kochavi (@eva.stories). Screenshots from Instagram, January 27, 2019, https://www.instagram .com/eva.stories.

May 2020. According to Liat Steir-Livny, it garnered more than three hundred million views globally.[52] The most recurrent critique focused on Instagram as a platform for Holocaust memory: social media was not deemed to be an appropriate place for serious Holocaust commemoration.[53] In response, Kochavi was quoted in several news outlets as saying: "If we want to bring the memory of the Holocaust to the young generation, we have to bring it to where they are. And they're on Instagram."[54] In the years since the initial launch, @eva.stories has also appeared on Snapchat. Through the intentional use of both social media platforms, Kochavi sought to reach audiences who he felt were forgetting or ignoring the Holocaust.

Like DiT and the IWitness educational platform, @eva.stories was created to meet a generation of youth where they are. It uses media forms that are familiar, common, and easily digestible.[55] Survivors interviewed for DiT are told, for example, to respond to interview questions as if they were talking to school-age youth: concise answers and straightforward responses. Students using the IWitness web platform in the classroom learn not only to view but also to create and edit testimonial content.[56] Both projects use technology to respond to the collective anxiety that, as the witness generation passes away, young people do not know enough about the Holocaust and, instead, are becoming further and further estranged from its history.

As a response to this estrangement, it is precisely the use of Instagram that allows Eva's story to feel intimate and personal. The platform narrows the focus of the Holocaust to a single victim and her family. Not unlike other film and theatrical dramatizations (for instance, of the life of Anne Frank), we watch Eva's story unfold—almost to the point of feeling that she overshared, in the way that Instagram accounts often do. It is not just the content of the posts but the fact that the technology intensifies the feeling of closeness because it comes to us on our device and in our personal feed. As viewers, we experience the stories intimately: holding the phone in our hand, with headphones in our ears. We believe we see Eva's eyes in the dark as she cries into the camera; we watch nervously as she stands by the doorframe eavesdropping to learn about her fate. Of course, Eva Heyman left no filmed testimony behind, so we are faced with a number of questions regarding fabulation: Who—or what—can accurately and responsibly make a first-person testimony? Who—or what—should listen to such a testimony, and how? Indeed, we have entered a world in which testimonies can be created using media technologies, decision-making algorithms, and generative forms of art and language that are unmoored from direct experiences—and yet, at the same time, seem to offer us direct access to such experiences. As we have endeavored to show in this book, all choices of emplotment (both human and algorithmic) raise ethical, aesthetic, and epistemological questions that we, as distant witnesses, need to persistently confront.

The conventional ethical claim of video-recorded testimonies, to recall Geoffrey Hartman's argument, was to be found in the creation of a space for intimate, affective, and responsible listening: initially, between the interviewer and the survivor and, subsequently, between communities of listeners who encountered the testimonies. This is also the basis of their authenticity. But one of the challenges is the simple fact that, until quite recently, the vast majority of testimonies were inaccessible without prohibitively expensive library subscriptions (USC Shoah Foundation), special viewing stations, or being on-site (Yale Fortunoff Archive). Archives were wary of putting video-recorded testimonies on publicly accessible platforms such as YouTube out of a fear that this would degrade their seriousness, subjecting them to the ranking systems, comment threads, and popularity contests of the online attention economy, not to mention the fungibility of remix culture.[57] While these concerns are certainly legitimate, the decision to restrict access to thousands upon thousands of hours of video-recorded testimony is also consequential: the more inaccessible the videos, the smaller the community of listeners. This becomes all the more acute when we reckon with the three hundred million views of @eva.stories since its launch in 2019.

If we believe that creating access to the stories of Holocaust survivors is an ethical imperative, we might recognize the success of this project: it made millions of us into confidants, recipients of the story, which became algorithmically stitched into all the other stories on our Instagram feed. As users of social media, those who follow @eva.stories are primed to create and share their own stories as well as observe and interact with other people's lives through their curated images and videos. The platform is built to share images and videos of everyday life with strangers. But with @eva.stories, we follow a Holocaust victim who left behind no video clips of her life and few writings. Until it was imagined, created, and shared, there was no visual archive, only traces that could be assembled through acts of imagination. Distant witnesses not only watch and read but also (re)inscribe, shape, and interpret the stories of the past with the technologies and languages of their present. Today, these technologies are globally networked, multimedia, and algorithmic. And every choice—made by both human and computer—is fraught with ethical questions, aesthetic decisions, and alternative possibilities. We will never know with definitiveness and closure who "Eva" was, what she experienced, what she felt, and what she said to her friends and family; but we can imagine who she might have been, what she might have experienced, and what she might have felt and said—and bring it to others. In other words, imagined in the realm of the subjunctive ("what if . . ."), @eva.stories is another form of critical and algorithmic fabulation created by and for distant witnesses.[58]

We can also see the potential of using social media to create an audience for distant witnessing in the St. Louis Manifest project on Twitter (@Stl_Manifest), an account that memorializes the 1939 voyage of over nine hundred Jewish asylum seekers on the German liner *St. Louis* who were turned away at the US, Canadian, and Cuban borders and sent back to Europe, where 254 of them were

FIGURE 7.2: The St. Louis Manifest project on Twitter. Russel Neiss, St. Louis Manifest (@Stl_Manifest). Screenshots from Twitter, January 27, 2023, https://twitter.com/Stl_Manifest.

killed during the Holocaust.[59] Throughout the twenty-four-hour period of Holocaust Memorial Day and, periodically, when the United States fails to live up to its ideals as a site of refuge, this Twitter feed tweets out the names and fates of individuals who sailed to the United States on the *St. Louis.* The project autotweets, one at a time, the names of those aboard the ship using repeated phrasing to document their fates: "My name is ____. In 1939, I sought asylum at the US border and was turned away. I was murdered in ____." When available, it also includes archival images (Figure 7.2).

The creator, Russel Neiss, wrote the code to scrape the data from the USHMM website and parsed it into a CSV file with the corresponding images, some of which have been added from other archival sources over the years.[60] The bot reads directly from this list. According to Neiss, the bot is set via a cron job (a command-based task manager) to auto-post to Twitter every few minutes once it is activated. Although it could be automated to launch on any day and never be touched again, it is intentionally designed, Neiss says, "to require a person to come in and physically restart it whenever we actually want it to run. This is in part because we modeled it after those Holocaust name reading rituals and believe deeply that remembrance requires action, so we've built that human element into the workflow."[61] The bot always runs on Holocaust Memorial Day, often runs on July 6 (the anniversary of the ship being escorted out of US waters by the Coast Guard), and then at a handful of other times that explicitly respond to contemporary asylum denial and the damage caused by our government's policies on refugees and asylum seekers.[62] Neiss explains, "I think the only 'off' times we have run it were when Biden said he was going to keep Trump level refugee caps in place, when Trump talked about 'sending back' Rep. Omar, and once during the height of the family separation policy during the influx of refugees at the southern border. So it's not about immigration per say, but specifically about refugee policy."

What @eva.stories and @Stl_Manifest have in common is that they center the testimonial creation and reception experiences of distant witnesses to the Holocaust. Social media algorithms create user-centered networks based on predicting what you will want to see and what you will probably like. The algorithms do this by analyzing past behaviors (what you watched, what you clicked on, who you followed, what posts you liked, what you shared) and by extrapolating what would be similar in the future. With regard to @eva.stories or @Stl_Manifest, the degree to which it appears on people's feeds depends on past behavior as calculated by the prediction algorithm—and, in fact, this is precisely why social media can also become an echo chamber, or worse, be weaponized in the service of disinformation campaigns, radicalization, and violence.[63] As we have argued throughout this book, every technology—like every algorithm—is dialectical, with potentialities to both humanize and dehumanize at the same time. We can start to address the ethical and epistemological questions when we attune ourselves to what these human-machine assemblages make possible—what they include and occlude, what they discompose and recompose—and how we attach value to these processes and effects.

Social media operates through the trope of (algorithmic) parataxis: placing content (in this case, about the Holocaust) side by side with all the other content in a user's feed. But one consistent criticism of @eva.stories is that placing the story of a Holocaust victim on social media is inappropriate because it trivializes Holocaust memory.[64] After all, Eva's story may show up next to ads for sunglasses and blouses, photos of your friend's hike, celebrity vacation selfies, and anything else you happen to follow. The same may be said of the St. Louis Manifest project: strange, even jarring, juxtapositions that disrupt mindless scrolling. But perhaps the placement of @eva.stories and @Stl_Manifest between ads and celebrity photos makes the project more impactful precisely because the posts function like digital *Stolpersteine*, causing us to trip over these stories. We are forced—however briefly—to stop and confront a Holocaust victim while going about the everyday business of scrolling through media on Instagram. For a moment, Holocaust memory seems to be radically recontextualized and reinscribed within our everyday visual lives.[65]

In each of the cases discussed here, we are talking about testimonies functioning as cultural memory machines—that is to say, the interviews, film adaptations, archival images, and data are produced, disseminated, and encountered by an assemblage of human choices and algorithmic logics. The machine or an AI did not invent the testimonies, although certain components—particularly, at the nexus of human-machine interaction—are built on AI technologies that change, adapt, learn, and predict over time. Of course, none of us can know how our writings, data, emails, posts, photographs, likenesses, or any other digital (or analog) traces of ourselves will be used in the future—and we have almost no way of controlling those uses. But we can be guided by principles for developing forms of distant witnessing enabled by new technologies. Such principles should bring together an ethics of testimony with an ethics of the algorithm by dignifying the singularity of the individual, amplifying access, preserving authenticity, and creating new possibilities for attentiveness to past injustices.

Concluding Words—On the Edges of New Limits and Possibilities

Ethics of the Algorithm is ultimately a humanistic argument for how computational methods can be used to interpret and perpetuate cultural memory in an age characterized by big data, new technologies, and distant witnessing. All of the methods and practices proposed in this book sought to expand how we—as distant witnesses—apprehend, access, and interpret the memory and history of the Holocaust. Focusing on recorded testimonies, we created new metadata for searching within testimonies; we used statistical visualizations and macroanalysis to characterize and compare corpora; we applied phonetic analysis tools to hone our listening at both micro- and macro-level scales of expressivity; we employed rule-based algorithms and natural language processing to identify expressions of agency and build network graphs; we used semantic triplets and interactive data visualizations to produce testimonial ensembles; we used machine-learning tools and language models to classify tens of thousands of interviewer questions; and we examined how machine-learning algorithms are changing the way we interact with testimonies today.

In so doing, we argued that algorithms and computational methods can help us develop new kinds of attention in which we hear, see, and read differently. *Ethics of the Algorithm* is an argument for thinking with technology in ways that are imaginative, open-ended, pluralizing, and, ultimately, humanizing. At the same time, we argued that humanists need to help guide the development and deployment of algorithmic and computational methods because these methods help us interpret the world, know the past, shape meanings, and make judgments. And while the ethical questions at the heart of this book were applied to and sharpened by the limit case of the Holocaust, they apply more broadly to our digital worlds because they speak to urgent, contemporary issues at the nexus of new technologies, power, and responsibility. In addition to changing how we comport ourselves toward one another, these technologies are also shaping the future of the past, particularly the ways in which we interact with, know, and commemorate the dead.

As I write these words, we stand on the precipice of another watershed moment in the development of algorithms and AI. Generative AI—such as Open-AI's ChatGPT, Bing's AI chatbot, and personal chatbots like Replika—are already primed to ingest all of the data we feed them and produce, among other things, resemblances to human language, echoes of human expressivity, and "replicate" versions of ourselves. AI does so by using complex neural networks to data mine massive troves of human-created information (primarily text and images) in order to compute patterns and render predictions. Some generative AI systems have been trained on massive corpora of images to create works of art or generate images of human faces; still others have been trained to write poetry, compose works of literature, and compete in human-computer debates. In 2022, Amazon announced that Alexa can learn to imitate the voice of anyone, including our dead relatives.[66] Using a machine-learning algorithm called a "generative adversarial network" (GAN), the website This Person Does Not Exist generates photo portraits of people who have never lived.[67] A GAN algorithm pits neural networks against one another using the logic of game theory "to generate high-quality data of significant statistical resemblance to real data."[68] While GANs can be used to create effective training models in fields such as medicine, the algorithm can also be used to produce "deepfakes" of photographs, videos, or texts that may pass as real, making it nearly impossible to evaluate media for their authenticity, accuracy, and truth.

What is at stake when an AI has "learned" to speak as or on behalf of the dead? One app, Hello History AI Chat (released in 2023), purports to do just that: allow users to engage in AI-generated "conversations" with hundreds of historical figures, including Confucius, Leonardo da Vinci, Otto von Bismarck, Paul von Hindenburg, Anne Frank, and Eva Perón.[69] These "life-like conversations with historical figures" raise significant questions about how the perspectives, actions, experiences, words, and ideologies of these figures are represented in the app, which is built on GPT-3 technologies.[70] Beyond general statements about the training data for GPT-3 (books, articles, websites, Wikipedia), there is little documentation about where, specifically, the data is sourced to animate such interactions, let alone the processes of curating the data and structuring the interactions to answer what the algorithm has determined to be "safe" questions.[71] Between the input (a user's question) and the output (the system's generation of a narrative answer), the deeply entangled layers of algorithmic and human decision-making remain hidden from view.

Large language models and the apps built on them, such as Hello History and ChatGPT, produce resemblances to or mimicries of human language by predicting word sequences based on frequency, context, co-occurrence, and semantic similarity from a massive corpus of texts fed into the model.[72] Far from demonstrating an inductive form of reasoning or an experiential form of comprehension, the AI has learned to create language by predicting word combinations. For the AI, these words have no meaning beyond their numerical values used for prediction (but this does not mean that they have no meaning for us). They are "chosen" because the AI's complex parameters have determined that they are likely to be concatenated. There is an ineluctable degree of randomness here, and this also means that a given query will unlikely generate exactly the same output again. We are in the realm of a sophisticated "stochastic parrot," which has learned how to combine probabilistic information.[73] The language model has no intention of communicating experiences to listeners, although we may mistakenly think it does, given the (relative) coherence of the outputs.[74]

At the same time, large language models hide the extraordinary amount of labor, fine-tuning, and decision-making (both human and machine) needed to create the preferred outcomes, all of which are fraught with ethical consequence: scrubbing content, annotating images, labeling results, evaluating text, and ranking outputs (not to mention the training and education of the "labelers").[75] Called "reinforcement learning with human feedback," this process is intended to create ethical guardrails and make the system safe by avoiding what have been determined to be misrepresentations, falsehoods, violent language, biases, or morally dubious information.[76] While this is certainly very important (we might, for example, recall the infamous language of Microsoft's Tay chatbot on Twitter),[77] these are fundamentally ethical and epistemological decisions that underscore the need to scrutinize how social and cultural values are being universally encoded into generative AI. In other words, these judgments and evaluations will become codified and operationalized as the moral code of the algorithm. We should not leave this critical decision-making to corporations and their labor forces since AI is potentially a technology for humankind and, with it, lies the possibility of creating a global public good (after all, it is being trained—for better and for worse—on our collective language, culture, and data).

As I write these concluding words, I want to underscore that generative AI is a massively powerful technology of representation that is still in its infancy. We have no idea where it will lead and what its consequences will be for the future of memory and history. It is possible, for instance, that a defamiliarized form of algorithmically generated fabulation could have the potential to usher in new forms of knowledge through generalization and synthesis, perhaps creating useful representations of historical events and eyewitness accounts that are drawn from previously unrecognized or unknown patterns in massive (and massively different) data sources. It is also possible that what might be called "hermeneutical AI" will truly expand our thinking and interpretative capacities through its attunement to the vast complexity of human cultural records. But right now, we have no reliable way to evaluate the provenance network of the outputs and understand the myriad decisions that have been made along the way. These range from the massive amount of data fed into the AI and the preprocessing of the data to the internal processes of self-supervision that the language transformers have undergone in the training, to the programming of certain ethical guardrails, reinforcements, and preferences that shape the outputs. Every decision raises ethical questions that ought to be documented, thought through, scrutinized, and debated as part of a public sense of judgment and value-making. At stake is nothing short of the common good and our common future.

As we begin to imagine practical—that is, constructive and ethical—futures for AI in the field of Holocaust studies, it seems likely that a large language model could be finetuned, as it were, on a digital archive of sources, which might include testimonies, letters, diaries, historical accounts, and other secondary materials related to the Holocaust. Perhaps digital archives could be "read," "animated," and "interpreted" by AI in ways that generate responses to user queries based on all the textual (and perhaps visual and sonic) sources in that archive? Conventional keyword searching, whether by name, date, topic, or any other indexing term created by human beings, not to mention mark-up and encoding protocols for digital records, may quickly become obsolete, as the AI can (ostensibly) synthesize all the content, generate answers to queries, and help us interpret the massive scale of the human cultural record in libraries and archives. Imagine, for instance, if I could ask any question in the world to an archive of tens of thousands of witness testimonies and get answers that were derived from the narrative structure and content of many, if not all, of those testimonies. This could usher in a compelling form of "mass testimony," in which an AI is able to tap into all the content of an archive and create responses that are increasingly authoritative and accurate.[78] And more than that, what if the AI could tell me precisely which testimonies and archival holdings were consulted in formulating its answer, so that I could listen to the specific individuals and verify the source materials?

Going forward, *digital provenance* will become ever more important in judging the outputs of AI.[79] Provenance refers to the chain of custody, so to speak, and includes the entire documented history of the formation of an object or output that allows us to ascertain its origins and authorship as well as assess its truthfulness. Provenance in the digital world means the documentation of data lineages and data flows, the mapping of algorithmic processes and sequences of operations, the accounting for all the data and guidelines used to train the model, the documentation of the specific parameters and evaluations used to finetune the model, the decisions about the imposition of guardrails and other "reinforcements" for its operation, and the forward and backward reproducibility of the object. This work of "giving an account" (of the algorithm, of the data, of the source material, of the processes, of the training, of the finetuning, of the human labor and decision-making) is inextricable from the responsibility of truth-telling. The processes that led to the AI's output can—and must—be understood and documented, even if that means forensically.

Realized as a partnership between the USC Shoah Foundation and Stanford School of Engineering, the Starling Lab for Data Integrity is a compelling example of how this work of provenance can be implemented in testimony capture, storage, access, and verification.[80] Using encryption technologies, the testimonies (as well as any other media and source materials) can be placed on a blockchain, allowing the images and video to be authenticated and traced back to their original owners and sources. This work of authentication will surely be part of our shared digital futures. Without repudiating AI's transformative potential for content creation and analysis, the danger of AI undermining historical truth and authenticity needs to be opposed, particularly in a field haunted by denial and distortion.

For Holocaust and genocide testimonies, provenance will always end with embodiment. Unlike an algorithmically generated deepfake, at the end of every provenance network of testimony—even as it is remediated, reimagined, and encountered in various digital modalities—is the individual human body that bears witness to trauma and pain. We know that testimonies can be made up and identities invented: think, for instance, of the works of Binjamin Wilkomirski and Misha Defonseca, which intentionally and deceptively mimicked the genre of testimony. But such fictions, made in bad faith, do not negate the authenticity of any other testimony—or of testimony as a genre of attestation. Subjects of testimony make a pledge to tell the truth about what they saw, suffered, and survived. And they do so because they believe that their words, their act of testifying, can have an impact on listeners, on the world today, and on the future. Can there be such a pledge of truthfulness or at least a provenance network for an AI?

As distant witnesses engaging with memory and history in the digital age, we will be guided more and more by digital provenance. How we receive testimony, in what ways it is mediated, whether we understand it, how we access and interpret it, whether we compare it, what tools we use to analyze it, how technologies and people generate and transform it, how we value and attach meaning to it—these are all issues that bring questions of method together with questions of ethics. Trying to answer them opens up a field of possibilities for choices and judgments at the nexus of human and machine. As we constitute and navigate this field of possibilities, we will need to develop, over and over again, an ethics of—*and for*—those sociotechnical assemblages called "algorithms."

NOTES

Preface

1. Anne Burdick, Johanna Drucker, Peter Lunenfeld, Todd Presner, and Jeffrey Schnapp, *Digital_ Humanities* (Cambridge, MA: MIT Press, 2012), 38–39. Since then, the concept of an "ethics of the algorithm" has featured in a number of talks that led to my publication of "'The Ethics of the Algorithm: Close and Distant Listening to the Shoah Foundation Visual History Archive," in *Probing the Ethics of Holocaust Culture*, ed. Claudio Fogu, Wulf Kansteiner, and Todd Presner (Cambridge, MA: Harvard University Press, 2016), 175–202. That essay represents an early version of the fourth chapter in this book.

2. "Bearing Witness" is an annual student program realized in collaboration with Hillel at UCLA, Jewish Family Service of Los Angeles, and the UCLA Alan D. Leve Center for Jewish Studies. Since 2010, I have served as the faculty advisor and taught a course on eyewitness testimony and oral history connected with this program. A documentary film of the survivors who participated in the program was created by Andrew Rosenstein: *Light Out of Darkness* (2018).

3. See the FemTechNet Manifesto (https://femtechnet.org/publications/manifesto/) and the UCLA Million Dollar Hoods Project (https://milliondollarhoods.pre.ss.ucla.edu/). Big Data for Justice is the name of a course I codeveloped at UCLA with the Bunche Center for African American Studies. It empowers students to use computational methods, big data, and data visualizations to investigate, expose, and begin to redress racial inequities in Los Angeles.

4. Here, we take inspiration and guidance from the work of Catherine D'Ignazio and Lauren F. Klein, *Data Feminism* (Cambridge, MA: MIT Press, 2020).

5. This approach to "scaling" is analogous to that pursued by Anne Knowles, Tim Cole, and Paul Jaskot who employ methods of digital mapping and 3D modeling as a way to think systematically without losing the individual. See Anne Knowles, Tim Cole, and Alberto Giordano, ed., *Geographies of the Holocaust* (Bloomington: Indiana University Press, 2014). As Jaskot further argues, digital maps function "morphologically . . . by [giving] form to the relationship of the individual to the systemic." See Paul Jaskot, "The Architecture of the Holocaust: How Art History and Digital Humanities Help Us Analyse Difficult Building Sites," The Frick Collection, October 17, 2017, YouTube video, https://www.youtube.com/watch?v=Nz0HcnsCsg8, minute 10.

6. The exception is Rachel Deblinger's 2008 interview with Fritzie Fritzshall, which preceded the conceptualization of this book and is discussed in the final chapter.

Introduction

1. See Achille Mbembe, *Necropolitics*, trans. Steven Corcoran (Durham: Duke University Press, 2019), 66–92.

2. The use of the term "hologram" has been contested, not least of all by the USC Shoah Foundation itself, which prefers terms such as "volumetrically captured testimony" or "interactive biography." Nevertheless, the recordings in Dimensions in Testimony were conceived originally as "holograms" and continue to be advertised by museums as such. See, for instance, the

promotional video, "What Can a Hologram Tell You about the Holocaust?," Illinois Holocaust Museum and Education Center, April 24, 2018, Vimeo video, https://vimeo.com/266329998.

3. Some of the Dimensions in Testimony interviews can be accessed through the IWitness web portal: https://iwitness.usc.edu/home. Physical installations exist across the world through partner institutions, including the Illinois Holocaust Museum and Education Center, the CANDLES Holocaust Museum and Education Center, the Los Angeles Museum of the Holocaust, and the Nanjing Massacre Museum.

4. The Journey App, an educational resource developed by the National Holocaust Centre and Museum in the UK, allows users to follow in the footsteps of (and make decisions about) a German Jewish boy in Nazi Germany. The Anne Frank House is available as an immersive VR experience, and the memorial museum at Bergen-Belsen has explored the use of augmented reality and geolocation technologies to link historical photographs and documentary evidence to the present-day landscape. The best discussion, to date, of these and other such projects is Matthew Boswell and Antony Rowland, *Virtual Holocaust Memory* (Oxford: Oxford University Press, 2023).

5. See Alexandra Garbarini, *Numbered Days: Diaries and the Holocaust* (New Haven, CT: Yale University Press, 2006); Laura Jockusch, *Collect and Record! Jewish Holocaust Documentation in Early Postwar Europe* (Oxford: Oxford University Press, 2015).

6. See Jockusch, *Collect and Record!*, 33–34.

7. The most comprehensive account of the archive and the work of Ringelblum is Samuel Kassow, *Who Will Write Our History? Emanuel Ringelblum, the Warsaw Ghetto, and the Oyneg Shabes Archive* (Bloomington: Indiana University Press, 2007). Today, the Ringelblum archive is housed at the Jewish Historical Institute in Warsaw. For a broader, transnational history of Jewish archiving practices in the nineteenth and twentieth centuries, see Jason Lustig, *A Time to Gather: Archives and the Control of Jewish Culture* (Oxford: Oxford University Press, 2021).

8. Jockusch, *Collect and Record!*, 9.

9. The first Jewish Historical Commissions began collecting witness testimony in Lublin in 1944. Starting in 1945, the United Nations Relief and Rehabilitation Administration (UNRRA) began working with refugees and displaced persons to assist in repatriation and documentation. From December of 1945 through 1948, the Central Historical Commission in Munich (and its fifty branches throughout the American Zone) collected extensive information and documentation about the fate of German Jewry. For a comprehensive discussion of historical commissions throughout Europe, see Jockusch, *Collect and Record!*

10. As explained in chapter 3, neither Boder nor the survivors he interviewed used the term "Holocaust" (as this term only entered widespread usage in the 1950s).

11. Now fully digitized, the archive is available online at: https://voices.library.iit.edu/david _boder. Boder did not use the term "testimony" but rather called his interviews "verbatim recorded narratives," "reports," "personal histories," and "tales." For more on this, see chapter three of this book and Alan Rosen, *The Wonder of Their Voices: The 1946 Holocaust Interviews of David Boder* (Oxford: Oxford University Press, 2010).

12. Boder completed an unpublished manuscript called *Topical Autobiographies*, which contains English-language transcripts of seventy of his interviews.

13. David Boder, "A Note on Wire Recordings" (1949?), box M11, Drs. Nicholas and Dorothy Cummings Center for the History of Psychology at the University of Akron. Boder expands on these ideas in his book, *I Did Not Interview the Dead* (Urbana: University of Illinois Press, 1949).

14. See Annette Wieviorka, *The Era of the Witness*, trans. Jared Stark (Ithaca, NY: Cornell University Press, 2006); Noah Shenker, *Reframing Holocaust Testimony* (Bloomington: Indiana Uni-

versity Press, 2015); and Jeffrey Shandler, *Holocaust Memory in the Digital Age: Survivors' Stories and New Media Practices* (Stanford, CA: Stanford University Press, 2017).

15. Wieviorka, *The Era of the Witness*, 98–100.

16. For comparative media histories of these testimonial archives, see Amit Pinchevski, *Transmitted Wounds: Media and the Mediation of Trauma* (Oxford: Oxford University Press, 2019); Shenker, *Reframing Holocaust Testimony*, esp. 112–50; and Shandler, *Holocaust Memory in the Digital Age*.

17. A thorough discussion of the media transfer and preservation process can be found under "Project Notes" for Voices of the Holocaust at the Illinois Institute of Technology: https://voices.library.iit.edu/project_notes, accessed November 2021. This summary draws on information from that website.

18. Stephen Smith, "On the Ethics of Testimony and Technology," in *Probing the Ethics of Holocaust Culture*, ed. Claudio Fogu, Wulf Kansteiner, and Todd Presner (Cambridge, MA: Harvard University Press, 2016), 205.

19. For a discussion of the hardware behind the VHA, see Scott Weingart, "Ghosts in the Machine," *Scottbot* (blog), November 1, 2015, http://www.scottbot.net/HIAL/index.html @p=41498.html.

20. Smith, "On the Ethics of Testimony and Technology," 206, 216.

21. See Laub's chapter "Bearing Witness or the Vicissitudes of Listening" in which he famously discusses the case of an Auschwitz survivor remembering "the four chimneys going up in flames" during the 1944 Auschwitz uprising. Laub interprets the woman's story to testify not to "empirical historical facts" (that is, to the fact that only one chimney was actually blown up), but rather to "resistance, to the affirmation of survival, to the breakage of the frame of death." Dori Laub, "Bearing Witness or the Vicissitudes of Listening," in *Testimony: Crises of Witnessing in Literature, Psychoanalysis, and History*, by Shoshana Felman and Dori Laub (New York: Routledge, 1992), 57–74, here 62. However, the accuracy of Laub's own account of this witness's testimony has been subject to intense critique by Thomas Trezise, who argues that Laub not only appears to have created a "composite figure . . . based on the videotaped testimonies of at least three different women," but that he "misquoted and overdramatized" the very parts of the testimony about the Auschwitz uprising in favor of his "own mythmaking." Thomas Trezise, *Witnessing Witnessing: On the Reception of Holocaust Testimony* (New York: Fordham University Press, 2013), 26–27.

22. See Wieviorka, *The Era of the Witness*, 132–33.

23. See, for instance, Christopher Browning, *Remembering Survival: Inside a Nazi Slave-Labor Camp* (New York: W. W. Norton, 2010); Jan T. Gross, *Neighbors: The Destruction of the Jewish Community in Jedwabne, Poland* (New York: Penguin Books, 2002); and Omer Bartov, *Anatomy of a Genocide: The Life and Death of a Town Called Buczacz* (New York: Simon and Schuster, 2019).

24. Browning, *Remembering Survival*, 7, 11.

25. Browning, *Remembering Survival*, 9, 12.

26. Browning's study of the Starachowice slave-labor camps was precipitated by a massive failure of justice in which Walther Becker, the chief of police in the Polish town of Starachowice from 1940 to 1945, responsible for the forced labor camps and the liquidation of the nearby ghetto, was acquitted in 1972 after the judge refused to admit and subsequently discredited all eyewitness testimony due to its supposed unreliability and lack of objectivity. See Browning, *Remembering Survival*, 2.

27. The etymology of "testimony"—and its variations across Latin, German, and Greek—is discussed by Jacques Derrida, "Poetics and Politics of Witnessing," in *Sovereignties in Question:*

The Poetics of Paul Celan, ed. Thomas Dutoit and Outi Pasanen (New York: Fordham University Press, 2005), 65–96, esp. 72–76; see also the discussion in Shoshana Felman, "The Return of the Voice: Claude Lanzmann's *Shoah*," in *Testimony: Crises of Witnessing in Literature, Psychoanalysis, and History*, 204–83. As Giorgio Agamben points out, another word for "witness" is *superstes*, survivor, in the sense of someone who has lived through something and thus can bear witness to it from beginning to end. Giorgio Agamben, *Remnants of Auschwitz: The Witness and the Archive*, trans. Daniel Heller-Roazen (New York: Zone Books, 1999), 17.

28. On similarities and differences, see Carlo Ginzburg, *The Judge and the Historian: Marginal Notes on a Late-Twentieth-Century Miscarriage of Justice*, trans. Antony Shugaar (London: Verso, 1999).

29. Geoffrey Hartman, *The Longest Shadow: In the Aftermath of the Holocaust* (New York: Palgrave, 1996), 133.

30. Geoffrey Hartman, interview by Ian Balfour and Rebecca Comay, "The Ethics of Witness: An Interview with Geoffrey Hartman," in *Lost in the Archives*, ed. Rebecca Comay (Toronto: Alphabet City Media, 2002), 492–509, here 495, 501.

31. Martin Buber, *I and Thou*, trans. Walter Kaufmann (New York: Scribner, 1970).

32. Shoshana Felman and Dori Laub, *Testimony: Crisis in Witnessing in Literature, Psychoanalysis, and History*, 72, 85.

33. Felman and Laub, *Testimony*, 58.

34. Primo Levi, *Survival in Auschwitz*, trans. Stuart Wolf (New York: Collier Books Macmillan, 1993), 60. Laub discusses the importance of "being truly heard and truly listened to" in his discussion of testimony as bearing witness in Felman and Laub, *Testimony*, 67–68.

35. Levinas's seminal works, *Totality and Infinity* and *Otherwise than Being*, posit a philosophy of ethics as a relationship to or care of the other, such that the other is never reduced to the same. He contrasts ethics (a philosophy of relationality) to ontology (a philosophy of being) in order to explicate the violent dimensions of the latter as "a philosophy of power," which subordinates and negates the relationship of the subject to the other. Ethics, on the other hand, is a relationship of trust and vulnerability marked by responsibility to and difference from the other, as characterized, for example, by the fragile relationship between survivor and listener. Emmanuel Levinas, *Totality and Infinity*, trans. Alphonso Lingis (Pittsburgh: Duquesne University Press, 1969), 46.

36. Hartman, "The Ethics of Witness," 492. This ethic of "hearing" also corresponds to the central prayer of Judaism, Shema Yisrael, a call of humble readiness to listen.

37. Dominick LaCapra, *Writing History, Writing Trauma* (Baltimore: Johns Hopkins University Press, 2001), 98.

38. For a thoughtful characterization of "tertiary witnessing" as a possible combination of "spatiotemporal distance and emotional copresence," see Caroline Wake, "Regarding the Recording: The Viewer of Video Testimony, the Complexity of Copresence and the Possibility of Tertiary Witnessing," *History and Memory* 25, no. 1 (Spring/Summer 2013): 111–44.

39. While the capture of Holocaust testimony is largely complete, the documentation work of recording testimony with survivors of other genocides and mass atrocities has accelerated. For example, the global collecting mission of the USC Shoah Foundation includes interviews with Tutsi survivors of the Rwandan genocide, Rohingya Muslim survivors who escaped Myanmar to Bangladeshi refugee camps, and video testimonies of witnesses of the Guatemalan Genocide realized through a partnership with the *Fundación de Antropología Forense de Guatemala*. The work of international organizations such as Yahad-In Unum (http://www.yahadinunum.org/) began by documenting what is now known as "the Holocaust by bullets," the mass execution of more than two million Jews by Nazi *Einsatzgruppen* in the east between

1941 and 1944. Over the past decade, it has broadened to include investigations and documentation related to the disappeared in Guatemala, the Roma genocide in Europe, and the Yazidi genocide in Northern Iraq. The organization has continued to develop and apply its field methodology, which combines forensic evidence with witness and survivor testimonies.

40. For a discussion of the problem of scale, see the section "Macrohistories: Scale and the Digitization of the Holocaust" in Wulf Kansteiner and Todd Presner, "Introduction: The Emergence of Global Holocaust Culture and the Field of Holocaust Studies," in *Probing the Ethics of Holocaust Culture*, ed. Claudio Fogu, Wulf Kansteiner, and Todd Presner, 1–42 (Cambridge, MA: Harvard University Press, 2016).

41. Dan Stone discusses some of the critical challenges and possibilities of the mass digitization of the records in the Arolsen archive, specifically highlighting "the politics of the archive" in terms of naming conventions, searchability, and structuring epistemologies. Dan Stone, "The Memory of the Archive: The International Tracing Service and the Construction of the Past as History," *Dapim: Studies on the Holocaust* 31, no. 2 (2017): 69–88, https://doi.org/10.1080/23256249.2017.1311486.

42. Much of the documentation (such as camp names, dates, locations, inmate and perpetrator information) in the seven volumes comprising the *Encyclopedia of Camps and Ghettos, 1933–1945* is currently being put into structured and searchable databases: https://www.ushmm.org/research/publications/encyclopedia-camps-ghettos.

43. See the documentation projects supported by the Claims Conference, including the Holocaust deportation database, which includes data, historical sources, and testimonies about every transport organized by the Nazi authorities between 1939 and 1945: https://www.claimscon.org/our-work/allocations/red/documentation/.

44. See http://www.yahadinunum.org.

45. See Dori Laub, "An Event without a Witness: Truth, Testimony, and Survival," in *Testimony: Crises of Witnessing in Literature, Psychoanalysis, and History*, 75–93.

46. In the 1990s, the debates over the "limits of representation" focused on the anxiety that poststructuralism might lead to the relativization of the Holocaust and that certain aesthetic forms could potentially undermine or imperil the historical factuality of the past. See the seminal volume: Saul Friedländer, ed., *Probing the Limits of Representation: Nazism and the "Final Solution"* (Cambridge, MA: Harvard University Press, 1992). Today, in addition to debates over the ethics of comparison vis-à-vis postcolonial studies, those debates have shifted to new media forms of representation and computational methods of interpretation. See Fogu, Kansteiner, and Presner, ed., *Probing the Ethics of Holocaust Culture*.

47. LaCapra, *Writing History, Writing Trauma*, 103.

48. LaCapra, *Writing History, Writing Trauma*, 99.

49. See the debates in Friedländer, ed., *Probing the Limits of Representation*.

50. Paul Jaskot, "Hidden Histories: What Digital Technology Reveals about Jews and Germans in Occupied Kraków," Ina Levine Annual Lecture, United States Holocaust Memorial Museum, YouTube video, Jun 23, 2021, https://www.youtube.com/watch?v=igJOnlsvXQc.

51. See Knowles, Cole, and Giordano, ed., *Geographies of the Holocaust*.

52. Connected with the USHMM's *Encyclopedia of Camps and Ghettos*, the "Holocaust Ghettos Project" aims to study ghettoization as an integrated historical and geographical phenomenon. The project brings together an H-GIS comprised of data from more than a thousand camps and ghettos with the linguistic analysis of 1,800 postwar survivor interviews to create a "multilingual gazetteer of ghettos" organized by place names. Cognizant of the epistemological, ontological, and ethical challenges, the project aims to build "data structures designed to hold historically contextualized qualitative and quantitative data." Anne Knowles and Justus

Hillebrand, with Paul Jaskot and Anne Walke, "Integrative, Interdisciplinary Database Design for the Spatial Humanities: The Case of the Holocaust Ghettos Project," *International Journal of Humanities and Arts Computing* 14, nos. 1–2 (2020): 64–80, here 65, 66.

53. For a critical assessment, see Jo Guldi, *The Dangerous Art of Text Mining: A Methodology for Digital History* (Cambridge: Cambridge University Press, 2023).

54. See EHRI (https://www.ehri-project.eu/) and CLARIN (https://www.clarin.eu/). The status of this collaborative work is available on the blog by Martin Wynne, "Using Holocaust Testimonies as Research Data," *CLARIN-UK*, May 30, 2023, https://www.clarin.ac.uk/article/using-holocaust-testimonies-research-data.

55. Gábor Mihály Tóth, *In Search of the Drowned: Testimonies and Testimonial Fragments of the Holocaust* (Yale Fortunoff Archive, 2021), https://lts.fortunoff.library.yale.edu. The quote comes from the essay "Fragments" (https://lts.fortunoff.library.yale.edu/anthology).

56. See, for instance, Jeffrey Kopstein, Jelena Subotić, and Susan Welch, ed., *Politics, Violence, Memory: The New Social Science of the Holocaust* (Ithaca, NY: Cornell University Press, 2023), and Gábor Tóth, Tim Hempel, Krishna Somandepalli, and Shri Narayanan, "Studying Large-Scale Behavioral Differences in Auschwitz-Birkenau with Simulation of Gendered Narratives," *Digital Humanities Quarterly* 16, no. 3 (2022): http://www.digitalhumanities.org/dhq/vol/16/3/000622/000622.html.

57. See Yad Vashem's "Transports to Extinction: Holocaust (Shoah) Deportation Database" (https://deportation.yadvashem.org/index.html).

58. By analyzing data from over one-thousand transports across eight countries, Susan Welch has shown how gender differences inflected survival rates. See Susan Welch, "Using the Yad Vashem Transport Database to Examine Gender and Selection during the Holocaust," in *Politics, Violence, Memory*, chapter 11.

59. Zygmunt Bauman, *Modernity and the Holocaust* (Ithaca: Cornell University Press, 2000).

60. Bauman, *Modernity and the Holocaust*, 100, 102, 103.

61. Bauman, *Modernity and the Holocaust*, 104.

62. Bauman, *Modernity and the Holocaust*, 108, 110.

63. Bauman, *Modernity and the Holocaust*, 220–21. See: Joseph Weizenbaum, *Computer Power and Human Reason: From Judgment to Calculation* (San Francisco: W. H. Freeman, 1976). Weizenbaum criticizes the hegemony of science as the authority of knowledge and urges for "the introduction of ethical thought into science . . . [to] combat the imperialism of instrumental reason" (256). Weizenbaum's critiques are discussed in the next chapter.

1: What Should Algorithms Have to Do with Ethics?

1. This is a core approach of the digital humanities and has been articulated in numerous books including Anne Burdick, Johanna Drucker, Peter Lunenfeld, Todd Presner, and Jeffrey Schnapp, *Digital_Humanities* (Cambridge, MA: MIT Press, 2012); Geoffrey Rockwell and Stefan Sinclair, *Hermeneutica: Computer-Assisted Interpretation in the Humanities* (Cambridge, MA: MIT Press, 2016); Ed Finn, *What Algorithms Want: Imagination in the Age of Computing* (Cambridge, MA: MIT Press, 2017); and N. Katherine Hayles, *Unthought: The Power of the Cognitive Unconscious* (Chicago: University of Chicago, 2017).

2. For an overview of the history of the term "algorithm," from which this summary draws, see the discussion by Taina Bucher, *If . . . Then: Algorithmic Power and Politics* (Oxford: Oxford University Press, 2018), 20–23. A more extensive history is provided by Maarten Bullynck, "Histories of Algorithms: Past, Present and Future," *Historia Mathematica* 43, no. 3 (2015): 332–41, https://halshs.archives-ouvertes.fr/halshs-01215943.

3. Tarleton Gillespie, "Algorithm," in *Digital Keywords: A Vocabulary of Information Society and Culture*, ed. Benjamin Peters (Princeton, NJ: Princeton University Press, 2016), 18–30, here 19.
4. Gillespie, "Algorithm," 22.
5. Gillespie, "Algorithm," 25–26.
6. Robert Kowalski, "Algorithm = Logic + Control," *Communication of the ACM* 22, no. 7 (July 1979): 424–36, here 429. A version of this article is also part of his book *Logic for Problem Solving, Revisited*, ed. Thom Frühwirth (Norderstedt, Germany: Books on Demand, 2014 [1979]), 125–29.
7. Robert Kowalski, "Logic Programming," *Handbook of the History of Logic* 9 (2014): 523–69.
8. Cf. Rob Kitchin, "Thinking Critically about and Researching Algorithms," *Information, Communication, and Society* 20, no. 1 (2017): 14–29, especially 16–17, http://dx.doi.org/10.1080 /1369118X.2016.1154087.
9. Davide Panagia, "On the Possibility of a Political Theory of Algorithms," *Political Theory*, 49, no. 1 (2021): 109–33, here 118.
10. Zachary Horton, *The Cosmic Zoom: Scale, Knowledge, and Mediation* (Chicago: University of Chicago, 2021), 184.
11. Horton, *The Cosmic Zoom*, 184.
12. Bucher, *If . . . Then*, 39. The literature on the nexus of algorithms and social/economic power is enormous. In addition to Bucher, some of the key works include: Shoshana Zuboff, *The Age of Surveillance Capitalism: The Fight for a Human Future at the New Frontier of Power* (New York: PublicAffairs, 2019); Kate Crawford, *Atlas of AI: Power, Politics, and the Planetary Costs of Artificial intelligence* (New Haven, CT: Yale University Press, 2021); David Golumbia, *The Cultural Logic of Computation* (Cambridge, MA: Harvard University Press, 2009); Cathy O'Neil, *Weapons of Math Destruction: How Big Data Increases Inequality and Threatens Democracy* (New York: Broadway Books, 2017); and Virginia Eubanks, *Automating Inequality: How High-Tech Tools Profile, Police, and Punish the Poor* (New York: St. Martin's Press, 2018).
13. Machine-learning algorithms are being deployed to make life-and-death decisions in domains ranging from patient treatment in hospitals and training driverless cars to the conduct of warfare. See Eric Topol, *Deep Medicine: How Artificial Intelligence Can Make Healthcare Human Again* (New York: Basic Books, 2019); Roberto Simanowski, *The Death Algorithm and Other Digital Dilemmas*, trans. Jefferson Chase (Cambridge, MA: MIT Press, 2018); and the report by Human Rights Watch, *Crunch Time on Killer Robots* (Human Rights Watch and IHRC, December 1, 2021), https://www.hrw.org/sites/default/files/media_2021/11/Crunch%20 Time%20on%20Killer%20Robots_final.pdf.
14. The Mozilla Foundation published a report in 2021 exposing how the recommendation algorithms of Facebook and YouTube spread misinformation, amplify hate speech, and radicalize users. Jesse McCrosky and Brandi Geurkink, *YouTube Regrets: A Crowdsourced Investigation into YouTube's Recommendation Algorithm* (Mozilla, June 2021), 5, https://foundation.mozilla .org/en/campaigns/regrets-reporter/findings/.
15. See, for example, Safiya Noble's discussion of the sentencing software used by the company Northpointe in her book, *Algorithms of Oppression: How Search Engines Reinforce Racism* (New York: NYU Press, 2018), 27. Ruha Benjamin discusses the use of the Predpol algorithm by numerous police departments to deploy police in neighborhoods that are disproportionately African American in her book, *Race After Technology: Abolitionist Tools for the New Jim Code* (Cambridge, UK: Polity Press, 2019), esp. 80–84.
16. In a similar vein, as Kate Crawford writes: "To understand how AI is fundamentally political, we need to go beyond neural nets and statistical pattern recognition to instead ask *what* is being optimized, and *for whom*, and *who* gets to decide." Crawford, *Atlas of AI*, 9.

17. Donna Haraway, "Situated Knowledges: The Science Question in Feminism and the Privilege of Partial Perspective," *Feminist Studies* 14, no. 3 (Autumn 1988): 575–99, here 581. Godlike in its totality and infallibility, the view from nowhere obfuscates positionality, situatedness, and the contingency and partiality of knowledge under the guise of rationality and objectivity. On the other hand, "feminist objectivity," writes Haraway "is about limited location and situated knowledge, not about transcendence and splitting of subject and object. It allows us to become answerable for what we learn how to see" (583).

18. Ian Bogust, "The Cathedral of Computation," *The Atlantic*, January 15, 2015, https://www.theatlantic.com/technology/archive/2015/01/the-cathedral-of-computation/384300/.

19. See Frank Pasquale, *The Black Box Society* (Cambridge, MA: Harvard University Press, 2015).

20. Bogust, "The Cathedral of Computation."

21. The literature on the field of critical algorithm studies and AI is enormous. Some of the recent books that have informed my thinking include: Wendy Hui Kyong Chun, *Discriminating Data: Correlation, Neighborhoods, and the New Politics of Recognition* (Cambridge, MA: MIT Press, 2021); Crawford, *Atlas of AI*; Markus D. Dubber, Frank Pasquale, and Sunit Das, ed., *The Oxford Handbook of Ethics of AI* (Oxford: Oxford University Press, 2020); Zuboff, *The Age of Surveillance Capitalism*; Noble, *Algorithms of Oppression*; Benjamin, *Race After Technology*; and Catherine D'Ignazio and Lauren F. Klein, *Data Feminism* (Cambridge, MA: MIT Press, 2020).

22. In *Data Feminism*, D'Ignazio and Klein argue for the need to move from data ethics to data justice precisely because the latter is built on concepts that "challenge power" and "work toward dismantling" power differentials (60). Such movements include the Algorithmic Justice League (https://www.ajl.org/), Data for Black Lives (https://d4bl.org/), the Stop LAPD Spying Coalition (https://stoplapdspying.org/), and organizations like Rappler, led by Maria Ressa. For a discussion of equity and tech innovation beyond Silicon Valley, see Ramesh Srinivasan, *Beyond the Valley: How Innovators around the World are Overcoming Inequality and Creating the Technologies of Tomorrow* (Cambridge, MA: MIT Press, 2019).

23. Louise Amoore, *Cloud Ethics: Algorithms and the Attributes of Ourselves and Others* (Durham, NC: Duke University Press, 2020), 7. See also 5–10.

24. Amoore, *Cloud Ethics*, 5, 7.

25. Amoore, *Cloud Ethics*, 15.

26. Amoore, *Cloud Ethics*, 15.

27. See, for instance, Timnit Gebru, "Hierarchy of Knowledge in Machine Learning & Related Fields and Its Consequences," Spelman College, YouTube video, April 22, 2021, https://www.youtube.com/watch?v=OL3DowBM9uc.

28. See Noble, *Algorithms of Oppression*. These critiques have also been compellingly articulated by Benjamin, Crawford, Eubanks, and Gebru, among others.

29. Michael Kearns and Aaron Roth, *The Ethical Algorithm: The Science of Socially Aware Algorithm Design* (Oxford: Oxford University Press, 2020).

30. Kearns and Roth, *The Ethical Algorithm*, 3–4.

31. The acronym FATE has been adopted by numerous academic and corporate think tanks to address a wide range of ethical issues in AI and machine learning. For a critical assessment of those interventions, see Matthew Le Bui and Safiya Noble, "We're Missing a Moral Framework of Justice in Artificial Intelligence: On the Limits, Failings, and Ethics of Fairness," in *The Oxford Handbook of Ethics of AI*, ed. Markus D. Dubber, Frank Pasquale, and Sunit Das (Oxford: Oxford University Press, 2020), 163–79. In addition, Amoore's notion of cloud ethics "begins with the opacity, partiality, and illegibility of all forms of giving an account,

human and algorithmic" in order to "[envisage] a plurality of venues for ethical responsibility." Amoore, *Cloud Ethics*, 8.

32. Kearns and Roth, *The Ethical Algorithm*, 16–17.

33. Kearns and Roth, *The Ethical Algorithm*, 68, 125.

34. One need only mention the massive disinformation campaigns that utilize the affordances of the platform—including its user networks and recommendation algorithm—to propagate hate speech and falsehoods. Maria Ressa, founder of the online news site Rappler, exposes these practices and defends freedom of the press by using data to fight disinformation campaigns on social media. See Maria Ressa, "Fighting Back with Data," DLD Conference, YouTube video, January 18, 2020, https://www.youtube.com/watch?v=3tt9OvzWvHc.

35. This is certainly the case in fields such as genomics and biology where AI has been deployed to identify variants in the human genome to understand which genes contribute to or cause certain pathologies. In pharmacology, AI is used in drug discovery to screen millions of molecules and predict dosing for experimental drugs. See Topol, *Deep Medicine*, esp. chapter 10. In the domain of law, AI and natural language processing are used to sort through millions of documents during litigation review to identify relevant precedents and cases.

36. Amoore, *Cloud Ethics*, 21.

37. Joseph Weizenbaum, *Computer Power and Human Reason: From Judgment to Calculation* (San Francisco: W. H. Freeman, 1976), 13.

38. Weizenbaum, *Computer Power and Human Reason*, 276.

39. Weizenbaum, *Computer Power and Human Reason*, 256. Weizenbaum goes on to lament that humanity failed to learn from the Holocaust and that the same calculating logic continues to guide mass crimes today: "Humanity briefly shuttered when it could no longer avert its gaze from what had happened, when the photographs taken by the killers themselves began to circulate, and when the pitiful survivors re-emerged into the light. But in the end, it made no difference. The same logic, the same cold and ruthless application of calculating reason, slaughtered at least as many people in the next twenty years as had fallen victim to the technicians of the thousand-year Reich. We have learned nothing. Civilization is as imperiled today as it was then" (256). This paragraph is also quoted by Zygmunt Bauman, *Modernity and the Holocaust* (Ithaca: Cornell University Press, 2000), 115.

40. Weizenbaum, *Computer Power and Human Reason*, 256.

41. Weizenbaum, *Computer Power and Human Reason*, 260.

42. Weizenbaum, *Computer Power and Human Reason*, 236.

43. Weizenbaum, *Computer Power and Human Reason*, 239, 241.

44. They are not, however, unknown or forgotten. See, for instance, Wendy Hui Kyong Chun, *Programmed Visions: Software and Memory* (Cambridge, MA: MIT Press, 2011) who discusses "the power of the computer as metaphor" precisely in the ways that it mixes "rationality with mysticism, knowability with what is unknown" (18); and David Golumbia, *The Cultural Logic of Computation*, who historicizes the belief in (and dissent from) "computationalism," namely "the view that a great deal, perhaps all, of human and social experience can be explained via computational processes" (8). Both cite Weizenbaum's critiques of the seductiveness of computer power. The most significant application of Weizenbaum's critique of instrumental reason in explaining the Holocaust is Zygmunt Bauman, *Modernity and the Holocaust*, esp. chapter 4.

45. Weizenbaum, *Computer Power and Human Reason*, 277.

46. Weizenbaum, *Computer Power and Human Reason*, 280.

47. In the final pages of his book, Weizenbaum quotes a lecture given by C. Oglesby, "A Juanist Way of Knowledge" (1971), in which Oglesby says the humanities "have a greater familiarity

with an ambiguous, intractable, sometimes unreachable [moral] world that won't reduce itself to any correspondence with the symbols by means of which one might try to measure it." Weizenbaum, *Computer Power and Human Reason*, 279 (Weizenbaum's brackets).

48. Human judgment is the topic of Immanuel Kant's second and third critiques: *The Critique of Practical Reason* (ethical judgment grounded in reason) and *The Critique of Judgment* (aesthetic judgment grounded in taste). The faculty of judgment was to be the topic of the third part of Hannah Arendt's *The Life of the Mind*, her last and unfinished manuscript. Her lecture notes on Kant, collected as *Lectures on Kant's Political Philosophy*, include her preliminary reflections. Arendt argues that "one judges always as a member of a community, guided by one's community sense, one's *sensus communis*. But in the last analysis, one is a member of a world community by the sheer fact of being human; this is one's 'cosmopolitan existence.'" Hannah Arendt, *Lectures on Kant's Political Philosophy*, ed. Ronald Beiner (Chicago: University of Chicago Press, 1992), 75.

49. Arendt, *Lectures on Kant's Political Philosophy*, 4.

50. Hannah Arendt, "The Crisis of Culture: Its Social and Political Significance," in *Past and Present: Eight Exercises in Political Thought* (New York: Penguin, 1993), 197–226, here 221.

51. Arendt, "The Crisis of Culture," 220.

52. Arendt, "The Crisis of Culture," 220–21. The German quote is Arendt quoting Kant's *Critique of Judgment*. The translation has been modified from Arendt's translation of "enlarged mentality."

53. In a fascinating article on Arendt and big data, Daniel Brennan suggests that big data "has the potential to be both a tool for thinking and a cover for reason." He points out that thinking—in Arendt's sense—is speculative, open-ended, and imaginative, while science—driven by the quest for knowledge and facts—tends to be about discovering underlying truths. As we are arguing here, algorithms and big data do not have be fixated on knowledge and truth but could be connected with meaning-making, interpretation, and imagining new possibilities. Daniel Brennan, "What Might Hannah Arendt Make of Big Data? On Thinking, Natality, and Narrative with Big Data," in *Who's Watching? Surveillance, Big Data and Applied Ethics in the Digital Age*, ed. Adrian Walsh and Sandy Boucher, Research in Ethical Issues in Organizations 26 (Bingley, UK: Emerald Publishing Limited, 2022), 9–21, here 15, https://doi.org/10.1108/S1529-209620220000026002.

54. Arendt is quoting Kant's *Critique of Judgment* in her *Lectures on Kant's Political Philosophy*, 43.

55. Arendt, "The Crisis of Culture," 223.

56. Hannah Arendt, *The Human Condition* (Chicago: University of Chicago, 1958), 57.

57. Arendt, *The Human Condition*, 57–58.

58. Linda M. G. Zerilli, *A Democratic Theory of Judgment* (Chicago: University of Chicago, 2016), 9.

59. Hannah Arendt, "Thinking and Moral Considerations: A Lecture," *Social Research* 38, no. 3 (Autumn 1971): 417–46, here 446.

60. Arendt, "Thinking and Moral Considerations," 446.

61. Moreover, as Norman Spaulding has argued, algorithms do not have the kind of (human) judgment to resist unjust laws because such judgment is to be found in "the oscillation, in the judge, between necessity and freedom." Human judgments to "obey or resist the law" were, he points out, the basis of every major social movement in the twentieth century, from Gandhi to Martin Luther King Jr. An algorithm, however, does not have the freedom of choice to resist injustice. See Norman Spaulding, "Is Human Judgment Necessary? Artificial Intelligence, Algorithmic Governance, and the Law," in *The Oxford Handbook of Ethics and AI*, 375–402, here 400–401.

62. Hannah Arendt, *Eichmann in Jerusalem: A Report on the Banality of Evil* (New York: Penguin Books, 1977), 287.
63. Arendt, *Eichmann in Jerusalem*, 287, 276.
64. The literal translation is "enemy of humankind." The term originated in maritime law to prosecute pirates and slavers who operated in international waters outside the jurisdiction of nations. Cited by prosecutor Gideon Hausner, the concept was used to justify Israel's capture of Eichmann under universal jurisdiction. When Arendt applied the term to Eichmann, she did so, according to David Luban, to make "a moral and political point, not a jurisdictional one." See David Luban, "The Enemy of all Humanity," *Netherlands Journal of Legal Philosophy* 47, no. 2 (2018): 112–27, here 124.
65. Arendt, *Eichmann in Jerusalem*, 276, 279.
66. Arendt, *Eichmann in Jerusalem*, 293.
67. Arendt, *Eichmann in Jerusalem*, 294.
68. Spaulding, "Is Human Judgment Necessary?," 381.
69. Spaulding, "Is Human Judgment Necessary?," 391.
70. In the words of Ramesh Srinivasan, "Algorithms and platforms 'understand' us through our past behavior, not our future possibilities. Their tools and objectives are computation, permutation, and efficiency rather than creativity, imagination, or soulfulness." Srinivasan, *Beyond the Valley*, 12.
71. O'Neil, *Weapons of Math Destruction*, 204.
72. See, for example, Hayden White's seminal essay, "The Burden of History," in *Tropics of Discourse: Essays in Cultural Criticism* (Baltimore: Johns Hopkins University Press, 1978), 27–50. Whether fair or not, the nineteenth-century philosopher of history, Leopold von Ranke, is often saddled with turning history into a science. To use Ranke's famous words, the historian does "not judge the past" but merely shows "how it really was" (*wie es eigentlich gewesen ist*). Since "the past" was somehow out there, cold facts and scientific objectivity would lead historians to resuscitate the reality of what happened. Ranke proclaimed these words in the preface to his *Histories of the Romantic and Germanic Peoples* (1824). Quoted in Georg G. Iggers, *The German Conception of History: The National Tradition of Historical Thought from Herder to the Present* (Middletown, CT: Wesleyan University Press, 1983), 67.
73. Hayden White, "The Fictions of Factual Representations," in *Tropics of Discourse: Essays in Cultural Criticism* (Baltimore: Johns Hopkins University Press, 1978), 121–34, here 125.
74. White, "The Burden of History," 50.
75. This is the topic of Hayden White's collection of late essays, *The Practical Past* (Evanston, IL: Northwestern University Press, 2014).
76. White, "Burden of History," 41.
77. Hayden White, "The Practical Past," in *The Practical Past* (Evanston, IL: Northwestern University Press, 2014), 10.
78. A "cognitive assemblage" refers to the interconnection between human and technical systems, where "the cognitive decisions of each affect the others." N. Katherine Hayles, "Cognitive Assemblages: Technical Agency and Human Interactions," *Critical Inquiry* 43, no. 1 (Autumn 2016): 32–55, here 33, https://www.journals.uchicago.edu/doi/abs/10.1086/688293.
79. While algorithms can also provide answers to strictly factual questions (for instance, confirming how many times a certain word co-occurs with other words in a text), we are more interested in the exploratory potential of algorithms as tools for thinking in recursive cycles with human interpretation. It is this possibility that N. Katherine Hayles calls "enlarging the mind of the humanities" in *Unthought*, esp. 205–11.

80. Bucher, *If ... Then*, 142.
81. Simone de Beauvoir, *The Ethics of Ambiguity*, trans. Bernard Frechtman (New York: Citadel Press, 1948), 134.
82. The first part of this articulation is derived from Immanuel Kant's famous categorical imperative and has been variously applied by others to underscore the value of human freedom in defining ethical relations and ethical actions. Kant, *Groundwork of the Metaphysics of Morals* [1785], trans. Mary Gregor and Jens Timmermann (Cambridge: Cambridge University Press, 2012). Amoore, for example, argues for a cloud ethics that safeguards each person's "singularity" and "particularity" such that "our encounters with others can never be limited to a finite collection of attributes." Amoore, *Cloud Ethics*, 171–72.
83. De Beauvoir, *The Ethics of Ambiguity*, 44.
84. De Beauvoir, *The Ethics of Ambiguity*, 42–43.
85. De Beauvoir, *The Ethics of Ambiguity*, 156.
86. De Beauvoir, *The Ethics of Ambiguity*, 44, 102.
87. De Beauvoir, *The Ethics of Ambiguity*, 142.

2: Computation That (De)humanizes

1. Arthur Seyss-Inquart, Order No. 6/1941, reproduced in *Die Verfolgung und Ermordung der europäischen Juden durch das nationalsozialistische Deutschland 1933–1945*, vol. 5, *West- und Nordeuropa 1940–Juni 1942*, ed. Katja Happe, Michael Mayer, Maja Peers, with Jean-Marc Dreyfus (Munich: Oldenbourg, 2012), 212–14.
2. While Lentz is not especially well-known in the Nazi bureaucratic machinery, his administrative leadership and writings are discussed by Jacob Presser, *The Destruction of the Dutch Jews*, trans. Arnold Pomerans (New York: E. P. Dutton, 1969), 37–40; Andrew Whitby, *The Sum of the People: How the Census has Shaped Nations from the Ancient World to the Modern Age* (New York: Basic Books, 2020), chapter 4; Rob Bakker, *Boekhouders van de Holocaust: Nederlandse ambtenaren en de collaboratie* (Hilversum, Netherlands: Uitgeverij Verbum, 2020); Edwin Black, *IBM and the Holocaust* (Washington, DC: Dialog Press, 2011), 303–13; and in an online exhibition by the USHMM, "Some Were Neighbors: Collaboration and Complicity in the Holocaust," accessed January 2021, http://somewereneighbors.ushmm.org/#/exhibitions /workers/un2107/description. For an overview of Lentz and the impact of his work, see Bob Moore, "Nazi Masters and Accommodating Dutch Bureaucrats: Working towards the Führer in the Occupied Netherlands, 1940–1945," in *Working towards the Führer: Essays in Honour of Sir Ian Kershaw*, ed. Anthony McElligott and Tim Kirk (Manchester, UK: Manchester University Press, 2003), 186–204. My chapter draws on these sources.
3. See Moore, "Nazi Masters and Accommodating Dutch Bureaucrats," 197; Götz Aly and Karl Heinz Roth, *The Nazi Census: Identification and Control in the Third Reich*, trans. Edwin Black (Philadelphia: Temple University Press, 2004), 65–69; Whitby, *The Sum of the People*, 156–60.
4. J. L. Lentz, *De Bevolkingsboekhouding* (Zwolle, Netherlands: De Erven J. J. Tiji N. V., 1936). For reviews of Lentz's book, see Whitby, *The Sum of the People*.
5. H. W. Methorst, "The New System of Population Accounting in the Netherlands," *Journal of the American Statistical Association* 31, no. 196 (1936): 719–22; H. W. Methorst and J. L. Lentz, "Die Volksregistrierung und das neue in den Niederlanden eingeführte System," *Allgemeines Statistisches Archiv* 26 (1936–1937): 59–84; H. W. Methorst, "The New System of Population Accounting in the Netherlands," *Journal of the American Statistical Association* 33, no. 204 (1938): 713–14.

6. See Methorst, "The New System of Population Accounting in the Netherlands" (1936), 719; and Aly and Roth, *The Nazi Census*, 65.

7. Lentz, *De Bevolkingsboekhouding*, 2.

8. Lentz, *De Bevolkingsboekhouding*, 4.

9. Lentz, *De Bevolkingsboekhouding*, 3.

10. Lentz, *De Bevolkingsboekhouding*, 4.

11. Lentz, *De Bevolkingsboekhouding*, 11.

12. Lentz, *De Bevolkingsboekhouding*, 12. In support of this idea, Methorst argues that personal identity cards will be "supplemented with a number of details noted in the course of life, [which will follow individuals] from the cradle to the grave." These data can include "education received, examinations passed, special talent for art, science, politics, technical science, etc.; physical disabilities, idiocy, lunacy, alcoholic excess, hereditary diseases, feeding during the first year of life, etc." (714). He sees this "system" of data collection to be a boon for "social research" and "science" (714) but never considers how it might be used in the service of the biopolitics of euthanasia and genocide. H. W. Methorst, "The New System of Population Accounting in the Netherlands" (1938). Whitby also cites these passages in *The Sum of the People*, 138–39, 357.

13. While I am not suggesting that bare data are inherent to every census or population registry, the history of national censuses cannot be separated from practices of data collection that measure people by race, fitness, and productivity. As Jacqueline Wernimont has argued, the history of the American census, for example, shows how it "placed citizens within its scope as a measure of state power and placed others [enslaved people and displaced Native Americans] as appendices to the national body, valuable as assets and subject to destruction if so needed" (66). In segmenting the population by race, gender, and ability (such as in the 1850 census, which "[collapsed] physical and mental disability with states of poverty and criminality"), the state could manage everything from citizenship rights to economic productivity (70). Jacqueline Wernimont, *Numbered Lives: Life and Death in Quantum Media* (Cambridge, MA: MIT Press, 2018).

14. Collecting such information about populations was not unique to nineteenth- and twentieth-century Netherlands. As Michel Foucault argued, European governments first became concerned about sex in what he calls the classical age of the seventeenth century in order "to ensure population, to reproduce labor capacity, to perpetuate the form of social relations; in short, to constitute a sexuality that is economically useful and politically conservative" (37). To do so, the state and its various administrative apparatuses developed "a whole web of discourses, special knowledges, analyses, and injunctions," all of which would facilitate economic and political behavior. These later became "anchorage points for the different varieties of racism of the nineteenth and twentieth centuries" (26). See Michel Foucault, *The History of Sexuality*, vol. 1, *An Introduction*, trans. Robert Hurley (New York: Vintage Books, 1990).

15. Foucault, *The History of Sexuality*, 146.

16. Foucault, *The History of Sexuality*, 148.

17. J. L. Lentz, *Persoonsbewijzen: Handleiding voor de uitvoering van het besluit persoonsbewijzen* (Arnhem, Netherlands: Uitg. voor de Vuga door G. W. van der Wiel, 1941), 1.

18. The quote is part of an epigraph that starts his book: "*De verbondenheid van persoon, Persoonsbewijs en persoonskaart waarborgt de administratieve beheersching van het maatschappelijk leven*" ["The interconnection between person, identity certificate, and identity card guarantees the administrative control of social life"]. Lentz, *Persoonsbewijzen*, 1.

19. The most thorough study of the role of civil servants in facilitating the process of registration, isolation, and deportation of the Dutch Jews is Bakker, *Boekhouders van de Holocaust*. Bakker also introduced and edited Lentz's 1944–1945 memoirs: Jacob L. Lentz, *Ambtelijke*

herinneringen, ed. Rob Bakker (Hilversum, Netherlands: Uitgeverij Verbum, 2020). The latter publication, which might be translated as "Official Memories" (in the sense of memories from his service in office), includes Lentz's reflections on the "Registratie van Joden" (Jewish Registry).

20. Jacob L. Lentz, "Registratie van Joden" [c. October 1944], in *Ambtelijke herinneringen,* ed. Rob Bakker, 143–44.

21. As Aly and Roth point out, the Dutch civil servants in the inspectorate's office compared the information in the Jewish registry "with church registers concerning baptisms of Jews and the circumcision lists of the Jewish community" to be sure that no "racial" Jews were left out. Aly and Roth, *The Nazi Census,* 65.

22. According to Moore, Lentz's "cooperation with the Germans was driven not by ideological persuasion or loyalty to those who promoted him, but by a desire for technocratic perfection." Moore, "Nazi Masters and Accommodating Dutch Bureaucrats," 195.

23. Lentz, "Registratie van Joden," 143.

24. Presser describes this process in *The Destruction of the Dutch Jews,* 35–37.

25. May 9, 1940, is the date of Germany's invasion of the Netherlands and, hence, the start of Nazi occupation.

26. As John Guillory writes with regard to the emergence of new genres of writing for the transmission of information in modernity: "The standardized form, for example, discarded the connective tissue of sentences and paragraphs altogether in order to transmit information in a new way: by dividing up the page into fields, by offering boxes to fill or check rather than sentences to write." John Guillory, "The Memo and Modernity," *Critical Inquiry* 31, no. 4 (Autumn 2004): 108–32, here 126. For a broader media and material history of the "document," see Lisa Gitelman, *Paper Knowledge: Toward a Media History of Documents* (Durham, NC: Duke University Press, 2014).

27. Lentz, "Registratie van Joden," 151. Black discusses the charges of sabotage and dereliction of duties in *IBM and the Holocaust,* 307.

28. Lentz, "Registratie van Joden," 152. Black also quotes Lentz on renting a Hollerith installation and gives a detailed account of the interactions Lentz had about the organization of the registry and the use of Hollerith punch cards. Black, *IBM and the Holocaust,* 310–12.

29. Lentz, "Registratie van Joden," 152.

30. Black quotes Hans Calmeyer, Wimmer's expert on Jewish affairs tasked with adjudicating cases of Jewish racial ambiguity, who wrote to Lentz in May of 1941, that "Dr. Wimmer would like to see constructed a register like the Hollerith punch card system," with that ability to sort the Jewish register by age, profession, gender, and race according to degree of blood. He added that the names also had to be organized alphabetically across all municipalities. Quoted in Black, *IBM and the Holocaust,* 308–9.

31. For an international history of the development of the Hollerith punch card system in census tabulation, see Lars Heide, *Punched-Card Systems and the Early Information Explosion, 1880–1945* (Baltimore: Johns Hopkins University Press, 2009); Whitby, *The Sum of the People,* esp. chapter 3. For an overview of how Hollerith punch cards were used in Nazi Germany, see David Martin Luebke and Sybil Milton, "Locating the Victim: An Overview of Census-Taking, Tabulation Technology, and Persecution in Nazi Germany," *IEEE Annals in the History of Computing* 16, no. 3 (1994): 25–39. Aly and Roth discuss how Hollerith punch cards were used in the 1933 and 1939 census in *The Nazi Census.* Finally, for the specific case of Lentz's office using Hollerith punch cards to process the Dutch Jewish registry, see Black, *IBM and the Holocaust,* 308–12.

32. The Hollerith system became International Business Machines (IBM) in 1924. In Germany, the Deutsche Hollerith Maschinen Gesellschaft (Dehomag) was founded in 1911 based on

Hollerith licenses and became a subsidiary of IBM. This history is fully documented by Heide, Whitby, and Black. In Germany, the censuses conducted in 1933 and 1939, the 1938 resident registrations, and the 1939 *Volkskartei* [Registry of People] were processed using Hollerith factories and helped the Nazis identify and locate victims nationally. In addition, numerous governmental and Nazi institutions utilized Hollerith machines for internal, administrative information processing, including the *Reichspost*, the *Reichsbahn*, the Armaments Ministry, the War Ministry, the SS personnel office, and others. See Luebke and Milton, "Locating the Victim," 34–35. Finally, as Black has shown, Hollerith installations were later used to manage and track slave laborers in a number of major concentration camps, including Ravensbrück, Dachau, Buchenwald, and Stutthof. See Black, *IBM and the Holocaust*, 427–39.

33. "Statistische Übersicht" [June 13, 1941], reproduced in Aly and Roth, *The Nazi Census*, 69.

34. Jacob Presser, *Ondergang: De vervolging en verdelging van het Nederlandse jodendom 1940–1945* (The Hague: Staatsuitgeverij, 1965), 64. Oddly, this paragraph is missing from the English translation. Black also quotes from the same report, *IBM and the Holocaust*, 310–11.

35. Presser points out that some people wrote anxious petitions to the *Reichskommissar* in an attempt to evade the fate of being designated as a Jew and reduced to what we are calling "bare data." It is not clear if they were ultimately successful. See Presser, *The Destruction of the Dutch Jews*, 40.

36. Giorgio Agamben, *Homo Sacer: Sovereign Power and Bare Life*, trans. Daniel Heller-Roazan (Stanford, CA: Stanford University Press, 1998), 83.

37. Agamben, *Homo Sacer*, 6, 72, and 114.

38. For an explication of "thick mapping," see Todd Presner, David Shepard, and Yoh Kawano, *HyperCities: Thick Mapping in the Digital Humanities* (Cambridge, MA: Harvard University Press, 2014); and Dana Cuff, Anastasia Loukaitou-Sideris, Todd Presner, Maite Zubiaurre, and Jonathan Crisman, *Urban Humanities: New Practices for Reimagining the City* (Cambridge, MA: MIT Press, 2020), chapter 3.

39. For a breakdown of the roundups in Amsterdam, see Presser, *The Destruction of the Dutch Jews*. The first major roundups of Jews occurred on February 22 and 23, 1941, with several hundred Jews deported to Mauthausen. Subsequent raids took place in June and September of 1941. Regular transports to Auschwitz began in July of 1942 and lasted through the summer of 1944. This data comes from Yad Vashem's "Transports to Extinction: Holocaust (Shoah) Deportation Database" (https://deportation.yadvashem.org/).

40. Friedrich Wimmer, correspondence dated September 5, 1941, reproduced as Document 90, "Die Generalkommissar für Verwaltung und Justiz teilt dem Generalkommissar für Finanz und Wirtschaft am 5. September 1941 das Ergebnis der Registrierung der Juden mit," in *Die Verfolgung und Ermordung der europäischen Juden durch das nationalsozialistische Deutschland 1933–1945*, vol. 5, *West- und Nordeuropa 1940–Juni 1942*, ed. Katja Happe, Michael Mayer, Maja Peers, with Jean-Marc Dreyfus (Munich: Oldenbourg, 2012), 271–72.

41. Wimmer, correspondence dated September 5, 1941, 271, 272.

42. Wimmer, correspondence dated September 5, 1941, 271–72.

43. Following Max Weber's famous articulation of the logic of bureaucracy as objectifying and dehumanizing, Cornelia Vismann argues that "in the domain of instrumental reason, files become the means for the modern, rationalized exercise of legal power" (127). These files "process the separation of the law into authority and administration. They contribute to the formation of the three major entities on which the law is based: truth, state, and subject" (xii). Cornelia Vismann, *Files: Law and Media Technology*, trans. Geoffrey Winthrop-Young (Stanford, CA: Stanford University Press, 2008).

44. See Presser, *The Destruction of the Dutch Jews*, 127–32, 187. Some of the original orders, published as public announcements and placards, can be found in the Bulmash Family Collection

on "The Holocaust in the Netherlands" located at Kenyon College (https://digital.kenyon.edu/bulmash_netherlands/index.2.html).

45. These figures come from Yad Vashem's "Transports to Extinction: Holocaust (Shoah) Deportation Database."

46. Guus Meershoek, "The Amsterdam Police and the Persecution of the Jews," in *The Holocaust and History: The Known, the Unknown, the Disputed, and the Reexamined*, ed. Michael Berenbaum and Abraham J. Peck (Bloomington: Indiana University Press, 1998), 284–300; Pim Griffioen and Ron Zeller, "Comparing the Persecution of the Jews in the Netherlands, France and Belgium, 1940–1945: Similarities, Differences, Causes," in *The Persecution of the Jews in the Netherlands, 1940–1945. New Perspectives*, ed. Peter Romijn (Amsterdam: Amsterdam University Press/Vossiuspers, 2012), 66.

47. Moore, "Nazi Masters and Accommodating Dutch Bureaucrats," 187. In addition to Lentz, Moore describes the actions of Sybren Tulp, the Amsterdam Chief of Police, who personally oversaw the officers who helped locate the Jews, bring them to holding centers, and put them on trains at the Amsterdam Central Station in the late summer of 1942 (193). Moore argues that both men were examples of "deference to authority and unthinking execution of orders" (199).

48. Bakker, "Inleiding: J. L. Lentz, een gezicht van de algehele ambtelijke collaboratie," in *Ambtelijke herinneringen*, 12.

49. Lentz, *Ambtelijke herinneringen*, 65.

50. Lentz, *Ambtelijke herinneringen*, 73–74.

51. Hannah Arendt, *Eichmann in Jerusalem: A Report on the Banality of Evil* (New York: Penguin Books, 1977), 287–88.

52. Bakker, "Inleiding," 12.

53. See Bakker, "Inleiding," 12; Moore, "Nazi Masters and Accomodating Dutch Bureaucrats," 198.

54. Presser, *Ondergang*, vol. 2, 150.

55. The website of the monument is: https://www.joodsmonument.nl/. The original concept for the digital monument was developed by Isaac Lipschits (1930–2008) who sought "to lift victims out of anonymity, by using everything that is known about them to portray them as individuals." The website launched in 2005 and has since become a "living archive" gathering tens of thousands of contributions about the Jewish victims of the Holocaust from the Netherlands. Today, the monument is maintained by the Amsterdam Jewish Cultural Quarter. Quotations come from "This is the Jewish Monument," Joods Monument, July 10, 2017, https://www.joodsmonument.nl/en/page/577141/this-is-the-jewish-monument. For an overview of the history of the monument, see Laurie M. C. Faro, "The Digital Monument to the Jewish Community in the Netherlands: A Meaningful, Ritual Place for Commemoration," *New Review of Hypermedia and Multimedia* (2015): http://dx.doi.org/10.1080/13614568.2014.983556.

56. This decision to organize the victims by last place of residence (as opposed to date of deportation, date of death, or alphabetically by last name, as the Nazi administrators wanted) is telling: first, it binds every victim to the towns and cities in which they lived as Dutch Jews; and second, it rejects an organizational variable used by the Nazis (the alphabetical organization of names by municipality).

57. In addition, a memorial book, *In memoriam* [*L'zecher*] (The Hague: Sdu Uitgeverij Koninginnegracht, 1995), compiled by Hans Joseef ben Michael Bloemendal, provided data. Some of the entries also include death certificates that are specifically correlated with information from the Jewish registry. See https://www.joodsmonument.nl/. For a comprehensive history of the looting of Jewish property and assets in the Netherlands, see Gerard Aalders, *Nazi Looting:*

The Plunder of Dutch Jewry during the Second World War, trans. Arnold Pomerans and Erica Pomerans (Oxford, UK: Berg, 2004).

58. Johanna Drucker, *Graphesis: Visual Forms of Knowledge Production* (Cambridge, MA: Harvard University Press, 2014), 143.

59. For more on the differences between "user" interfaces and "subject" interfaces, see the discussion by Drucker in *Graphesis*, esp. 142–52, here 148. Like the work of new media artists such as Casey Reas and Scott Snibbe that Drucker cites, I consider the interface's "aesthetic dimensions and imaginative vision" to give rise to "a space of being and dwelling" (152).

60. See "News," Stolpersteine, https://www.stolpersteine.eu/en/news/.

61. Each of the bricks can be "adopted" by a sponsor to support the funding of the memorial. See https://www.holocaustnamenmonument.nl/nl/home/.

62. This formulation comes from Paul Dorish, *The Stuff of Bits: An Essay on the Materialities of Information* (Cambridge, MA: MIT Press, 2017).

63. "Live Stream Holocaust Namenmonument Nederland," Holocaust Namenmonument Nederland, YouTube video, September 9, 2021, https://www.youtube.com/watch?v=pdw42t9h5F8.

64. Daniel Libeskind, "Dutch Holocaust Memorial of Names," Studio Libeskind, https://libeskind.com/work/names-monument/.

65. For a comparative, global analysis of the "unmooring" of digital memorials from physical locations, see Eva Monique Zucker and David J. Simon, ed., *Mass Violence and Memory in the Digital Age: Memorialization Unmoored* (Cham, Switzerland: Palgrave Macmillan, 2020).

66. Physical memorials are extensible in certain ways, especially when one considers their ritualistic function in which people leave flowers, photographs, clothing, teddy bears, notes, flags, medals, and much more. The Vietnam Veterans Memorial Collection contains over 400,000 such objects, each carefully cataloged and recorded by the National Park Service (https://www.nps.gov/vive/learn/collections.htm).

67. These numbers come from the 2023 Yad Vashem "Central Database of Shoah Victims' Names" and are somewhat different from the estimates in 1995 (https://yvng.yadvashem.org/). James Young provides a thorough discussion of the history of the memorial competition and the years of controversy that ensued after Helmut Kohl vetoed the first design for being "too big and undignified." See James Young, *At Memory's Edge: After-Images of the Holocaust in Contemporary Art and Architecture* (New Haven, CT: Yale University Press, 2000).

68. Giorgio Agamben, "Die zwei Gedächtnisse," *Die Zeit*, May 4, 2005, 45. Peter Eisenman appears to agree with this assessment in his chapter, "Berlin Memorial Redux," in *Probing the Ethics of Holocaust Culture*, ed. Claudio Fogu, Wulf Kansteiner, and Todd Presner (Cambridge, MA: Harvard University Press, 2016), 304–8.

69. Mark Godfrey, *Abstraction and the Holocaust* (New Haven, CT: Yale University Press, 2007), 244, 246.

70. Godfrey, *Abstraction and the Holocaust*, 249.

71. These and related questions have also been taken up explicitly by historians of slavery and Black Studies scholars who have shown how the arithmetics of the slave trade, racial capital, and demography are informed by dehumanizing "systems of logic" inherent to Western rationalism that extend up to the present-day. See, for instance, Jennifer Morgan, *Reckoning with Slavery: Gender, Kinship, and Capitalism in the Early Black Atlantic* (Durham, NC: Duke University Press, 2021), 42–43; Katherine McKittrick, "Mathematics Black Life," in *The Black Scholar* 44, no. 2 (Summer 2014): 16–28; Jessica Marie Johnson, "Markup Bodies: Black [Life] Studies and Slavery [Death] Studies at the Digital Crossroads," *Social Text* 36, no. 4

(December 2018): 57–79; and Christina Sharpe, *In the Wake: On Blackness and Being* (Durham, NC: Duke University Press, 2016).

72. These terms are drawn from Emmanuel Levinas's eponymous book, *Totality and Infinity: An Essay on Exteriority*, trans. Alphonso Lingis (Pittsburgh: Duquesne University Press, 1969).

73. See National AIDS Memorial (https://www.aidsmemorial.org/interactive-aids-quilt) and SlaveVoyages (https://www.slavevoyages.org/).

74. Mitchell Whitelaw, "Generous Interfaces for Digital Cultural Collections," *DHQ: Digital Humanities Quarterly* 9, no. 1 (2015): paragraph 3, http://www.digitalhumanities.org/dhq/vol/9/1/000205/000205.html. Whitelaw's examples include both experimental interfaces, such as "The Real Face of White Australia" (http://invisibleaustralians.org/faces/), and more conventional interfaces for exploring large collections, such as the National Gallery of Australia's Prints and Printmaking Collection (http://www.printsandprintmaking.gov.au/).

75. Hayden White, "The Modernist Event," in *Figural Realism: Studies in the Mimesis Effect* (Baltimore: Johns Hopkins University Press, 1999), 66–86. He also discusses "modernist events" in Hayden White, "Historical Discourse and Literary Theory," in *The Practical Past* (Evanston, IL: Northwestern University Press, 2014), esp. 80–81.

76. White, "The Modernist Event," 70.

77. White, "Historical Discourse and Literary Theory," 84, 85. Saul Friedländer, *The Years of Extermination: Nazi Germany and the Jews, 1939–1945* (New York: Harper Collins, 2007).

78. Sharpe, *In the Wake*, 69.

79. The animation is also a snapshot in time of ongoing research, which, to date, has located records and details of more than thirty-six thousand slave voyages. See David Eltis, "Methodology," SlaveVoyages, 2018, https://www.slavevoyages.org/voyage/about#methodology/introduction/0/en/.

80. In *Reckoning with Slavery*, Morgan points out that fewer than 10 percent of the slave ship records in the database contain information about sex ratios (31). Since those who created "the ledger and account books . . . [regarded] sex differences among the captives as not worthy of note" (43), researchers are forced to "[extrapolate] from severely incomplete data" (31).

81. Johnson, "Markup Bodies," 64.

82. Eltis, "Methodology."

83. The records are drawn from more than a thousand sources, many of which are held in national archives and libraries, including published and unpublished documentary sources, newspapers, logbooks, and reports. See https://www.slavevoyages.org/voyage/about#sources/3/en/.

84. "About the Enslavers Database," SlaveVoyages, accessed October 2022, https://www.slavevoyages.org/resources/enslavers_about#understanding-database/0/en/.

85. Of the records in the African Origins Database (which are drawn from records between 1819 and 1845), about two-thirds of the captives were male and about one-third were female. Nearly half were under eighteen years old.

86. Johnson, "Markup Bodies," 58, 65. Johnson points out that this methodological work goes back to earlier Black historians, such as W.E.B. Du Bois, who used a mix of quantitative (social science) and qualitative (testimonial) methods (60). Du Bois's data visualizations on "the problem of the color-line," for example, pioneered new methods of social and historical analysis through attention to data design (ranging from maps, histograms, and pie charts to spiral graphs, area charts, and interactive, multimedia plates containing both narrative elements and statistics). See W.E.B. Du Bois, *W.E.B. Du Bois's Data Portraits: Visualizing Black America*, ed. Whitney Battle-Baptiste and Britt Rusert (New York: Princeton Architectural Press, 2018).

87. Johnson, "Markup Bodies," 71.

88. Johnson, "Markup Bodies," 71. Johnson argues for deeper interconnections between Black digital practice, informed by "freedom struggles and radical coalition building," and the digital humanities (58). The projects and labs associated with "LifexCode: Digital Humanities Against Enclosure," which Johnson directs, are compelling examples of this praxis. See https://www.lifexcode.org/.

89. McKittrick, "Mathematics Black Life," 23.

90. Vincent Brown, "Mapping a Slave Revolt: Visualizing Spatial History through the Archives of Slavery," *Social Text* 33, no. 4 (December 2015): 134–41, here 138.

91. Brown, "Mapping a Slave Revolt," 138. Brown expands on this in his discussion of his digital mapping project, "Slave Revolt in Jamaica, 1760–1761: A Cartographic Narrative" (http://revolt.axismaps.com/), and in the article "Narrative Interface for New Media History: Slave Revolt in Jamaica, 1760–1761," *The American Historical Review* 121, no. 1 (2016): 176–86.

92. For example, Morgan discusses the "methodological poetics" of a number of authors such as M. NourbeSe Philip, Robin Coste Lewis, and Douglas Kearney, whose "work provides a road-map both for that which is knowable and that which remains unknown" (193). See Jennifer Morgan, "Accounting for 'The Most Excruciating Torment': Gender, Slavery, and Trans-Atlantic Passages," *History of the Present: A Journal of Critical History* 6, no. 2 (Fall 2016): 184–207.

93. Brown, "Mapping a Slave Revolt," 134.

94. Sharpe, *In the Wake*, 18.

95. Sharpe, *In the Wake*, 14.

96. Sharpe, *In the Wake*, 73.

97. Johnson, "Markup Bodies," 66. She goes on to mention how "black digital practice uses the commodification of blackness during the slave trade as a reference point, building sites, projects, organizations, and tools that resist and counteract slavery's dehumanizing impulses . . . [with the goal of] sustaining black life and shaping black futures" (66). In a similar vein, Ruha Benjamin considers "toolmaking as a practice" for resisting inequities, building solidarity, and imagining more just futures. Ruha Benjamin, *Race After Technology: Abolitionist Tools for the New Jim Code* (Cambridge, UK: Polity Press, 2019), 168.

98. Toni Morrison, "The Site of Memory" [1987], in *The Source of Self-Regard: Selected Essays, Speeches, and Meditations* (New York: Alfred A. Knopf, 2019), 238. With regard to "the unwritten interior life of these people," Morrison likens her work to "a kind of literary archaeology" that relies "on the image—on the remains—in addition to recollection, to yield up a kind of a truth" (238).

99. Morrison, "The Site of Memory," 243.

100. M. NourbeSe Philip, *Zong!* (Middletown, CT: Wesleyan University Press, 2008), 203. *Zong!* is a testament to the 150 Africans killed by the ship's crew, but it is also a testament to the more than 1.4 million captives who were forced onto slave ships but who never disembarked. This number comes from the SlaveVoyages database (https://www.slavevoyages.org/voyage/database#statistics). Sharpe discusses how the dead appear in Philip's book of poems "beyond the logic of the ledger, beyond the mathematics of insurance . . . [by the way she] aspirates those submerged lives and brings them back to the text from which they were ejected." Sharpe, *In the Wake*, 38.

101. Saidiya Hartman, "Venus in Two Acts," *Small Axe* 26 (June 2008): 1–14, here, 11. As she further writes with regard to the empty, one-sidedness of the extant accounts (statistical and financial) of slaves such as Black Venus: "No one remembered her name or recorded the things she said . . . we only know what can be extrapolated from the ledger or borrowed from the world of her captors and masters and applied to her" (2).

102. Hartman, "Venus in Two Acts," 11.
103. Hayden White, "Afterword," in *The Practical Past* (Evanston, IL: Northwestern University Press, 2014), 97. Here, White considers stories in opposition to "algorithms." As we will see in chapter 6 and in the digital project on Mala Zimetbaum, algorithmic forms of fabulation can be used to construct and tell a multitude of new stories with practical—that is, ethical—consequence.

3: David Boder and the Origins of Computational Analysis of Survivor Testimonies

1. The best biography of Boder and the significance of his recordings is Alan Rosen, *The Wonder of their Voices: The 1946 Holocaust Interviews of David Boder* (Oxford: Oxford University Press, 2010).
2. David Boder to Maurice Bisgyer, National Secretary of B'nai B'rith (July 27, 1945), box 1, David Boder Papers, Special Collections, Charles E. Young Research Library, UCLA. Boder wrote this letter as a solicitation for sponsorship of his research trip. The quotes are from pages 2 and 3, respectively.
3. For a history of Holocaust witness testimony, see Annette Wievorka, *The Era of the Witness*, trans. Jared Stark (Ithaca, NY: Cornell University Press, 2006). Rosen discusses the history of the term "testimony" vis-à-vis Boder's audio recordings and argues that Boder's project "compels us to rethink the models of Holocaust testimony and the terms that characterize them." He prefers the term "unbelated testimony" to draw attention to the transitional historical moment in which the interviews were done, something that includes not only the uncertainty of the displaced persons crisis but also the "rawness" of the survivors' memories, the emergence of a new language to characterize the historical events, and the preliminary development of the interview and preservation protocols for testimony collection. See Rosen, *The Wonder of their Voices*, 227–28.
4. Yad Vashem is an exception in this lineage, since it began audio recordings of survivor testimonies in the 1950s and continued that effort until 1989, when it shifted to recording video testimonies. For a comparative overview of the institutional efforts of the Yale Fortunoff Archive, the USHMM, and the USC Shoah Foundation, see Noah Shenker, *Reframing Holocaust Testimony* (Bloomington: Indiana University Press, 2015).
5. See, for instance, his unpublished interpretation of the interview with Anna Kovitzka: "The Tale of Anna Kovitzka: A Logico-Systematic Analysis or An Essay in Experimental Reading" (1949), box 6, David Boder Papers, Special Collections, Charles E. Young Research Library, UCLA. Boder framed the "tale" of Auschwitz survivor Anna Kovitzka in the context of great literary tragedies, including those from Greek and Roman antiquity, as well as Shakespeare, Goethe, and Coleridge.
6. David Boder, "Addenda" to *Topical Autobiographies of Displaced People* (1957), box 12, David Boder Papers, Special Collections, Charles E. Young Research Library, UCLA. In the addenda, Boder quotes himself from April of 1945 (see page 3161).
7. David Boder, "The D.P. Story" (1948), box 3, David Boder Papers, Special Collections, Charles E. Young Research Library, UCLA. He later renamed the book *I Did Not Interview the Dead* (Urbana: University of Illinois Press, 1949), underscoring not only his personal decision to interview displaced persons who survived Nazi atrocities but also the fact that these interviews do not include "the grimmest stories that could be told—[because] I did not interview the dead" (xix).
8. Boder to Maurice Jacobs of The Jewish Publication Society of America (November 16, 1948), box 21, David Boder Papers, Special Collections, Charles E. Young Research Library, UCLA.

9. While not a systematic or centralized effort, audio interviews and oral histories with former slaves were recorded in the 1930s and early 1940s. The Library of Congress documents twenty-three such interviews in their "Voices Remembering Slavery: Freed People Tell Their Stories" (https://www.loc.gov/collections/voices-remembering-slavery/about-this -collection/). The earliest interviews were done between 1932 and 1933 in South Carolina and Georgia; others were recorded in Virginia from 1934 to 1935; three recordings between 1937 and 1940 were part of the Federal Writers' Project of the Works Progress Administration; and about thirteen were done by various fieldworkers in the mid-1930s and early 1940s across Georgia, Florida, and Texas. In addition to these recordings, the Library of Congress collection "Born in Slavery: Slave Narratives from the Federal Writers' Project, 1936 to 1938" contains about 2,300 first-person slave narratives undertaken by interviewers working in seventeen states. In 1927–1928, Zora Neale Hurston undertook and transcribed a unique oral history of Cudjo Lewis, an eighty-six-year-old survivor of the Clotilda, the last slave ship known to have made the transatlantic journey to the United States in 1860, nearly fifty years after slave trade to the United States was outlawed. Although completed in 1931, the interview was rejected by publishers because she refused to standardize Lewis's vernacular diction and dialect. The work was only published in 2018 as: *Barracoon: The Story of the Last "Black Cargo,"* ed. Deborah G. Plant (New York: HarperCollins, 2018).

10. For a comparative media history of Holocaust testimonial archives, including a short discussion of Boder, see Amit Pinchevski, *Transmitted Wounds: Media and the Mediation of Trauma* (Oxford: Oxford University Press, 2019).

11. Boder, *I Did Not Interview the Dead,* xiv.

12. Boder, *I Did Not Interview the Dead,* xviii.

13. Speaking in Yiddish, interviewee Joseph Ferber used the term "Shaarith Hapleta [*sic*]," Hebrew for "surviving remnant," to describe the Jewish survivors as well as the Yiddish term *khurbn,* which is translated in the transcript as "Holocaust" (minute 24). The Yiddish term "grosser khurbn" ("great catastrophe") is also used by interviewee Udel Stopnitsky to describe the evacuation of the Bedzin ghetto on June 22, 1942, and the deportation of the inhabitants to Auschwitz (minute 11). Pinkhus Rosenfeld speaks of a "burned offering" (minute 27), as does interviewee Kalman Eisenberg (minute 23). These interviews are available on the "Voices of the Holocaust" website maintained by the Paul V. Galvin Library, Illinois Institute of Technology: https://voices.library.iit.edu. "Burnt offering" is the literal translation of the term "Holocaust." In his analysis of the interview with Anna Kovitzka, Boder will later adopt the language of "remnant" to refer to the surviving Jewish DPs as "small remnants of an exterminated people." David Boder, "The Tale of Anna Kovitzka," 10.

14. In a report that he wrote to the Illinois Institute for Technology shortly after returning from Europe, he refers to the "verbatim reports of war sufferers in Europe with respect to their personal experiences and outlook for the future." David Boder, "Psychological Survey of the Displaced Persons of Europe" (c. 1947), box 1, David Boder Papers, Special Collections, Charles E. Young Research Library, UCLA.

15. Transcript from radio debate between David Boder and Congressman Ed Gossett: "Should We Close the Gates to Displaced Persons?" (March 30, 1948), box 10, David Boder Papers, Special Collections, Charles E. Young Research Library, UCLA.

16. Quoted in Rosen, *The Wonder of Their Voices,* 150.

17. David Boder, "The Displaced People of Europe: Preliminary Notes on a Psychological and Anthropological Study," *Illinois Tech Engineer,* March 1947, 1.

18. Boder, *I Did Not Interview the Dead,* xii.

19. Digitized audio from unmarked, decaying quarter-inch reel, David Boder Papers, Special Collections, Charles E. Young Research Library, UCLA. The exclamation marks are my own and underscore his emphatic voice.

20. Boder, "Addenda" to *Topical Autobiographies*, 3162.

21. His archives are split between UCLA's Charles E. Young Research Library and the Drs. Nicholas and Dorothy Cummings Center for the History of Psychology at the University of Akron, Ohio.

22. Rosen gives a much more detailed history in *The Wonder of their Voices*, 153–59.

23. Of the twenty-five non-Jewish interviewees, six are not displaced people or survivors: Two are teachers working in the Organization for Rehabilitation and Training (ORT), three were part of the French Resistance, and one is a Spanish refugee taking classes at ORT. Among the Jewish interviewees, one is not a survivor: Judah Golan is a Jewish lawyer and civil servant from Palestine working in the DP camps to help survivors immigrate to Palestine. For the visualizations of the whole Boder corpus, we include these interviews, but we exclude them in any statistical analyses focused on Holocaust testimonies. In the appendix to *The Wonder of their Voices*, Rosen gives a chronology of each person interviewed, including the place and date of the interview and biographical data about the interviewee (age, birthplace, wartime locations, including camps, and interview language) (see 231–40). On our project website (http://holocaustresearchlab.com), our team's metadata spreadsheet can be downloaded and includes most of the above information as well as interview lengths, word counts, number of questions asked, languages spoken as percentage of the interview, aliases, and corresponding pages and indexing terms used by Boder in his manuscript, *Topical Autobiographies*.

24. Copies of the original wire spools were sent to the Library of Congress, which, decades later, procured the technical means to undertake the media transfer of the wire-recorded audio to tape. Later, they were digitized by the Illinois Institute of Technology (IIT) and made available as WAV files through the Aviary platform. The interviews can be accessed on the Voices of the Holocaust website (https://voices.library.iit.edu/). The English translations, annotations, and indexing were done by Boder for the testimonies in his book *Topical Autobiographies* (1950–1957). For more on the transmedia history of the recordings, see Rosen, *The Wonder of their Voices*, 165ff.

25. In his introduction to "The D.P. Story," Boder underscores the "urgency" of the project and points out that he must reckon with "the unavoidable failings of human memory and the fading of emotions due to time" (29). He makes a similar argument in his extended analysis of the interview he undertook with Anna Kovitzka, in which he detected the "unquestionable loss of freshness" and "the dampened emotions" with regard to the scenes of liberation. Boder, "The Tale of Anna Kovitzka," 86.

26. Boder, *I Did Not Interview the Dead*, xii–xiii.

27. All interactive Tableau visualizations in this chapter are available on our project website, http://holocaustresearchlab.com, under chapter 3.

28. For the speaker times and counts, we relied upon the TEI markup created by the Voices of the Holocaust team at the Illinois Institute of Technology. The markup for Boder's testimonies includes the following items: speaker turns, times of speaker turns, languages, geographic entities, camps/ghettos, and glossary terms. We are grateful to Adam Strohm for sharing the XML files with our team.

29. We agree with Johanna Drucker that "data are capta"—that is, data are a function of what was captured and organized using certain measurements and parameters. This does not diminish our belief that the visualizations can give us insights into the qualities of the archive. Johanna Drucker, *Graphesis: Visual Forms of Knowledge Production* (Cambridge, MA: Harvard University Press, 2014), 128.

30. Strangely, Boder says in a self-report for IIT in 1947, "The interviews were uninterrupted, except for rare instances when the story became fantastic enough to promote questioning." Boder, "Psychological Survey of the Displaced Persons of Europe," 2. In fact, from just his own markup of the seventy interviews in *Topical Autobiographies*, which he completed in 1957, he indicates that he interrupted the interviewees over a hundred separate times.

31. The data used for determining this figure can be found on our project website. For consistency of comparison, the word counts are based on the English translations. These include Boder's framing comments, introduction, conclusion, and any commentary made during the interview, but do not include any parts of the interviews marked as "unintelligible." For the first 195 Fortunoff Archive testimonies (from 1979–1983), the interviewees speak 15.3 times as much as their interviewers; for the early Shoah Foundation testimonies (mostly done in the mid-1990s), the interviewees speak 13.3 times as much as their interviewers. Beyond these ratios, we also observe a general trend toward longer interviews, as testimony develops the narrative form of a life story (a point to which we will return in the coming chapters).

32. Toward the end of at least seven other interviews, Boder asks permission to conduct this "experiment" with his interviewees. Unlike a Rorschach test in which subjects are asked to discuss a nonrepresentational inkblot, the TAT images are representational, and the subjects are prompted to provide an interpretation of what is happening in the scene: "What do you see?," "What do these pictures remind you of?," and "What is happening in this picture?" are questions Boder asks. For a discussion of the TAT, see Rosen, *The Wonder of Their Voices*, 185–94.

33. David Boder interview with Polia Bisenhaus (July 29, 1946), Voices of the Holocaust, Illinois Institute of Technology. The original recording can be accessed here: https://iit.aviaryplatform .com/collections/231/collection_resources/17587/.

34. There appears to be gender parity in terms of who is speaking and how much; however, we did find some differences in the topics asked of men versus women. Boder tended to ask women about family (men, women, and children) at a rate much higher than men: for instance, 75 percent of women were asked about children, but only 40 percent of men were. A full gender comparison of the question topics in Boder's interviews can be found on our project website and is further discussed in the Digital Project "What Were Survivors Asked? Using Machine Learning to Constellate 89,759 Interviewer Questions."

35. For the DiT examples, there were 2,113 unique answers played (for three testimonies) but more than forty thousand unique questions asked. For the other corpora, the disparity between the number of questions and the number of answers is explained by the fact that multiple questions are sometimes asked by an interviewer but only a single answer is given (as shown in the Kimmelmann example in Figure 3.4). For this particular visualization, we did not count each question separately but rather as a "unit of speech" (to measure who is speaking).

36. Anna Bonazzi, "Stories of Displacement: Silence and Language in Digital Migrant Interview Archives" (PhD diss., UCLA, 2024).

37. For a list of code-switching instances with time stamps and characterization labels, visit our project website.

38. In *The Wonder of Their Voices*, Rosen analyzes Zgnilek's multilingualism (209–12) and argues that the "choice of language . . . [is] an active shaping force in the content of what is being expressed" (212).

39. The JDC, a US-based Jewish aid organization, had been providing aid to displaced persons and helping resettle Jewish refugees to the United States or Israel.

40. David Boder interview with Otto Feuer (August 22, 1946), Voices of the Holocaust, Illinois Institute of Technology, minutes 19:00–20:00. The original recording can be accessed here: https://voices.library.iit.edu/interview/feuerO.

41. The 111 interviews are all survivors (Jewish and non-Jewish); we did not include the seven non-survivors interviewed by Boder in this analysis. Boder's original recordings, transcriptions, and English translations can be found on the Voices of the Holocaust website: https://voices.library.iit.edu.

42. In addition to Boder's framing comments, we also removed translators' clarifications or observations by Boder not directed to the interviewee. We left the bracketed term "unintelligible," when it appeared, in order to check these questions later for whether there was enough semantic information in them for analysis (in about twenty-five cases, there was not and these were excluded). For the rest (218 questions), we replaced the word "unintelligible" with ellipses and manually reassigned them after the clustering process was completed.

43. When Boder simply repeated single words or phrases spoken by the interviewee, we did not count those as questions. We did, however, extract any line with non-interrogative statements that included the following words or phrases: "tell," "describe," "share," "sing," "message," "photograph," "ask," "did you," and "were you." Sometimes, we found that question marks were not included in the transcripts, and we did not want to overlook these questions.

44. All the data, including the embedding vectors, original clusters, and reassigned questions, can be found on our project website.

45. This can also be explained by Boder's interview framework, which was not intended to record "life histories" but, instead, focus on specific events experienced by the survivors ("topical autobiographies"). As Rachel Deblinger has pointed out, Boder did not need to ask about trauma directly because his interviewees were deeply traumatized. See her chapter "David P. Boder: Holocaust Memory in Displaced Persons Camps," in *After the Holocaust: Challenging the Myth of Silence*, ed. David Cesarani and Eric Sundquist (London: Routledge, 2012), 115–26.

46. Boder manually annotated the English-language transcript to include the words "with laughter" for the last question. Unfortunately, the audio reel for this section is missing. Boder, *Topical Autobiographies*, 85. The question of the fate of "the Gypsies" was posed to Helena Tichauer, who affirmed that they were, in fact, gassed. Boder, *Topical Autobiographies*, 2102. For a discussion of Tichauer's testimony, see Ari Joskowicz, *Rain of Ash: Roma, Jews, and the Holocaust* (Princeton, NJ: Princeton University Press, 2023), 90–91.

47. Oral History Interview with Avraham Kimmelman [Abraham Kimmelmann] (2004–2005), United States Holocaust Memorial Museum, https://collections.ushmm.org/search/catalog/irn518056. Quotations are from the English translation of the Hebrew testimony, 380.

48. Oral History Interview with Avraham Kimmelman, 382.

49. Oral History Interview with Janine Oberrotman (2004), United States Holocaust Memorial Museum, https://collections.ushmm.org/search/catalog/irn514926. Quotations are from tape 10, minutes 22:00–26:00.

50. Janine Oberrotman, Dimensions in Testimony interview (2016), USC Shoah Foundation, https://iwitness.usc.edu/activities/5241.

51. Oral History Interview with Jack Bass (2003), United States Holocaust Memorial Museum, https://collections.ushmm.org/search/catalog/irn514241. Quotations are from tapes 8, minutes 25:00–26:00 and tape 9, minutes 1:00–8:00.

52. David Boder, "A Note on Wire Recordings" (c. 1949), box M11, Drs. Nicholas and Dorothy Cummings Center for the History of Psychology at the University of Akron. Parts of this note are also reproduced in *I Did Not Interview the Dead*. In a grant progress report from 1955, Boder indicates that he was still working on the translations, a task that he says is "much more complex and cumbersome than the one confronting the translators of Dante, Kant, or Kierkegard [sic]" due to the fact that he was translating from auditory material "frequently wrought up by emotions, and narrated in a language traumatized by years of disruption of normal

processes of human communication." David Boder, "Progress Report" on project entitled "Psychological and Anthropological Analysis of Topical Autobiographies of Displaced People Verbatim Recorded in D.P. Camps" (October 28, 1955), box M11, Drs. Nicholas and Dorothy Cummings Center for the History of Psychology at the University of Akron, 4.

53. Boder, *I Did Not Interview the Dead*, xiii.
54. Boder, *I Did Not Interview the Dead*, xiii–xiv.
55. Boder, *I Did Not Interview the Dead*, xviii.
56. Boder, *I Did Not Interview the Dead*, xix.
57. Boder, "A Note on Wire Recording," 1.
58. Boder's annotations have been documented thoroughly by Anna Bonazzi and appear on our project website under chapter 5. Although not always consistent, Boder annotated emotions and voice qualities, and we manually grouped them into the following categories: crying, sigh, pause/silence, whispering, laughter/irony, happy voice, singing/recitation, trembling voice, low voice, voice fading, stammering/mumbling, interruption, hesitation, screaming/upset, loud voice/emphasis, irritable, thinking, slow speech, and high pitch. For more on voice, see chapter 5.
59. Gordon Allport, *The Use of Personal Documents in Psychological History* (New York: Social Sciences Research Council, 1942). Rosen also discusses part of the influence of Allport's work on Boder in *The Wonder of Their Voices*, but does not discuss their convergent methodological and analytical approaches (180–81).
60. Allport, *The Use of Personal Documents*, 81–82.
61. Allport, *The Use of Personal Documents*, 89–90.
62. Rosen, in *The Wonder of Their Voices*, points out that this motivated Boder to publish unedited, verbatim narratives (181). Almost forty years after Boder died, Donald Niewyk published an edited collection of thirty-four of Boder's interviews. Niewyk renders the testimonies more coherent by removing most of Boder's questions, retranslating the interviews into standard English, removing what he considered to be redundant material, and smoothing them out to make them less fragmented and, in some cases, more chronological and thematically coherent. Donald L. Niewyk, ed., *Fresh Wounds: Early Narratives of Holocaust Survival* (Chapel Hill: University of North Carolina Press, 1998), 6.
63. For a thorough history of the development of personality psychology in the early twentieth century, see Colin Koopman's "Algorithmic Personality: The Informatics of Psychological Traits, 1917–1937," in *How We Became our Data: A Genealogy of the Informational Person* (Chicago: University of Chicago, 2019), 66–107.
64. Koopman, "Algorithmic Personality," 104.
65. John Dollard and O. H. Mowrer, "A Method of Measuring Tension in Written Documents," *Journal of Abnormal Social Psychology* 42 (1947): 3–32.
66. Boder, quoted in O. Hobart Mowrer, J. McVicker Hunt, and Leonard S. Kogan, "Further Studies Utilizing the Discomfort-Relief Quotient," in *Psychotherapy: Theory and Research*, by O. Hobart Mowrer (New York: Ronald Press, 1953), 257–95, here 285. Two of Boder's students—Polly Hammond and Audrey Uher—are also cited in the book's bibliography but not in the chapters.
67. "Deculturation" is the antipode to "acculturation," the latter being a term that Boder attributes to the psychologist John Dollard to describe the integration of the human being into groups, social structures, and cultural norms. Deculturation, on the other hand, refers to the "cutting down of a human being to fit into concentration and annihilation camps." Boder, *I Did Not Interview the Dead*, xix.
68. Boder, "Addenda" to *Topical Autobiographies*, 3162.
69. Boder supervised at least three master's students at IIT, each of whom submitted a master's thesis in 1951 or 1952 analyzing a group of his interviews.

70. Kovitzka (given the pseudonym Kaletska by Boder) was interviewed in Germany on September 26, 1946. Boder, "The Tale of Anna Kovitzka," 3.

71. Boder, "The Tale of Anna Kovitzka," 3. Boder's emphasis.

72. Hayden White, "The Modernist Event," in *Figural Realism: Studies in the Mimesis Effect* (Baltimore: Johns Hopkins University Press, 1999), 66–86, here 70.

73. Boder, "The Tale of Anna Kovitzka," 6.

74. Boder, "The Tale of Anna Kovitzka," 7.

75. Boder, "The Tale of Anna Kovitzka," 15–16.

76. Dollard and Mowrer, "A Method of Measuring Tension in Written Documents."

77. Rosen discusses the reference to Coleridge in *The Wonder of Their Voices*, 219–21.

78. Boder, "The Tale of Anna Kovitzka," 52–53.

79. The first quote comes from Boder, "The Tale of Anna Kovitzka," 80. The last two quotes come from Boder's annotation of Kovitzka's translated narrative in *Topical Autobiographies*, 258, 261. These correspond to minutes 26:00 and 32:00 of the audio recording (https://voices .library.iit.edu/interview/kaletskaA).

80. Boder, "The Tale of Anna Kovitzka," 95–96.

81. David Boder, "Psychological and Anthropological Analysis of Topical Autobiographies of Displaced Persons Recorded Verbatim in D.P. Camps" (1951), grant application for Federal Security Agency Public Health Services, box 1, Special Collections, Psychological Museum, University of Akron, 6.

82. David P. Boder, "The Impact of Catastrophe: I. Assessment and Evaluation," *The Journal of Psychology* 38 (1954): 3–50. Boder conducted forty-five interviews with displaced people in the wake of the Kansas City Flood and hoped to use those interviews to further develop the trauma index. He does not equate the experiences and says explicitly that "the flood victims in Kansas are not DPs, neither physically or morally; far from it. They are people who have suffered a stroke of tough luck . . . It is a small island of misfortune within a matrix of two rich cities and a rich and generous country." David Boder, "Memorandum on a Study among Flood Sufferers" (July 25, 1951), box 9, M18, Special Collections, Psychological Museum, University of Akron, 5.

83. David Boder, "Psychological and Anthropological Analysis of Topical Autobiographies of Displaced Persons Recorded Verbatim in D.P. Camps" (1956), box 7, M16, Grant Application to the Department of Health, Education, and Welfare, Special Collections, Psychological Museum, University of Akron, 6. Boder's emphasis.

84. Boder, "The Impact of Catastrophe," 7.

85. In the "Laboratory Manual" for "The Impact of Catastrophe," Boder provides 116 "Interpretative Expansions" for the forty-six traumas and lists 377 "Items in [an] alphabetic roster." The roster, with reference to the interpretations, is intended to be "a tool to assist the trained content analyst in finding the appropriate themes in the inventory" (3152). The Laboratory Manual appears in the addenda to *Topical Autobiographies* as "TRAUMATIC INVENTORY for the Assessment and Evaluation of Interviews with Displaced Persons: A Contribution to the Methodology of Content Analysis and Psycho-Sociological Appraisal of Distress Situations," *Topical Autobiographies of Displaced People* (1957), box 12, David Boder Papers, Special Collections, Charles E. Young Research Library, UCLA, 3141–3159.

86. The Q-technique was developed by the psychologist William Stephenson. O. Hobart Mowrer offers a genealogy and critical history of the applications of the Q-technique in his chapter "Q-Technique: Description, History, and Critique," in *Psychotherapy: Theory and Research* (New York: Ronald Press, 1953), 316–75.

87. Boder, "The Impact of Catastrophe," 9.

88. Boder, "The Impact of Catastrophe," 12.

89. Boder, "The Impact of Catastrophe," 33, 35.
90. Boder, "The Impact of Catastrophe," 32.
91. Boder, "The Impact of Catastrophe," 38.
92. It should be noted that the numbers are not the same, perhaps indicating that the process was further refined over time. Nevertheless, the five Jewish and five non-Jewish interviewees that appear in Boder's article were first analyzed in the student theses (and they are credited in his 1954 article and grant reports). In a grant report that he submitted in 1952, he indicates that, to date, two graduate students have "computed and plotted" the DRQs for eight interviews. Boder, "Progress Report," 3. In a 1954 "Full Statement of Progress," Boder cites all three of the completed master's theses and indicates that some of the students' graphs are reproduced in Mowrer's recent book, *Psychotherapy: Theory and Research*, 2–3. This appears to be true, but they are uncredited in that book (284). Both reports are from box 8, David Boder Papers, Library Special Collections, Charles E. Young Research Library, UCLA.
93. The "Distress-Relief Quotient" is measured by calculating the number of "distress" words on a given page divided by the sum of the distress and relief words on the same page. Dollard and Mowrer explain the method in their article, "A Method of Measuring Tension in Written Documents," 7. Hammond, Brown, and Uher multiplied this number by one hundred. Because a single distress word on a given page (with no relief words) will yield a value of one hundred, the students, with Boder, introduced the "Distress-Relief Density Quotient," which measured the frequency with which distress and relief terms arise as a function of the total words per page. Finally, the "Adjective-Verb Quotient" (AVQ) was based on Boder's master's thesis, "The Adjective-Verb Quotient: A Contribution to the Psychology of Language" (1927/1940), and consists of dividing the number of stand-alone adjectives by action verbs on a given page. This value was also normalized to one hundred.
94. Boder, "Progress Report" (1952), 3.
95. Sentiment analysis packages such as VADER (Valence Aware Dictionary and sEntiment Reasoner) and LIWC (Linguistic Inquiry and Word Count) use predefined lexicons to assign positive, negative, and neutral values to words and produce aggregated sentiment scores for segments of text. The values are fixed and extract the words from their context. These programs identify the words, sum up the valuations, and compute averages for units of text. While such approaches sometimes yielded sensible results in our analysis of Holocaust testimonies, we also found these methods to be quite problematic because words are taken out of context, complex or multiple meanings are not taken into account, and individual words are not sufficient to understand sentiment. These are all things to which Boder's human raters needed to be attuned. More recently, neural networks have been touted for their ability to "decode" complex sentiments using a combination of supervised and unsupervised learning. See Tobias Blanke, Michael Bryant, and Mark Hedges, "Understanding Memories of the Holocaust—A New Approach to Neural Networks in the Digital Humanities," *Digital Scholarship in the Humanities* 35, no. 1 (April 2020): 17–33.
96. Boder, "Full Statement of Progress," 4–5.
97. Smith's name appears on a number of key archival documents including the tabulation of the judges' scoring sheets for assigning severity values to the traumas and the preliminary word counts.
98. Polly Hammond, "The Psychological Impact of Unprecedented Social Catastrophes: An Analysis of Three Topical Autobiographies of Young Displaced Persons" (June 1951), box 30, David Boder Papers, Special Collections, Charles E. Young Research Library, UCLA, 2.
99. Audrey Uher, "The Psychological Impact of Unprecedented Social Catastrophe: An Analysis of Four Topical Autobiographies of Mature Displaced Persons" (January 1952), box 6, M15,

David Boder Papers, Drs. Nicholas and Dorothy Cummings Center for the History of Psychology, University of Akron and the Paul V. Galvin Library, Illinois Institute of Technology.

100. Uher, "The Psychological Impact of Unprecedented Social Catastrophe," 15–16.

101. Unfortunately, we do not have the data used to recreate Uher's calculations of the DRQ, DRDQ, or AVQ.

102. Two are Mennonites (Braun and Kluver) and the other three are Greek Orthodox (Prest, Kharchenko, Odinets). Alice Brown, "Analysis of Five Topical Autobiographies of Christian Faith" (February 1952), box 6, M15, David Boder Papers, Drs. Nicholas and Dorothy Cummings Center for the History of Psychology, University of Akron.

103. Dollard and Mowrer, "A Method of Measuring Tension in Written Documents," 23.

104. Brown, "Analysis of Five Topical Autobiographies of Christian Faith," 12–14, 55.

105. Decades later, the USC Shoah Foundation would use the one-minute segment (rather than the typewritten page) as the unit of analysis for assigning indexing terms to testimonies. However, unlike Brown's approach, this is done in a linear, sequential fashion using a video indexing tool (see chapter 4), which facilitates the continuity of indexing terms over narrative time.

106. David Boder, "The Traumatological Lexicon: A Cross-Disciplinary Project" (April 21, 1955), box 6, M15, David Boder Papers, Drs. Nicholas and Dorothy Cummings Center for the History of Psychology, University of Akron.

107. Boder, "The Traumatological Lexicon," 1.

108. Boder, "The Traumatological Lexicon," 2.

109. David Boder, "Construction (in Part) of a Traumatological Evaluative Lexicon" (August 20, 1956), grant proposal to the Ford Foundation, box 14, David Boder Papers, Special Collections, Charles E. Young Research Library, UCLA, 3.

110. Boder, "Construction (in Part) of a Traumatological Evaluative Lexicon," 7–8. Although derived from the transcultural Holocaust interviews, Boder proposed limiting the "Traumatological Lexicon" to the culture of the United States, and only after the "methods and procedures" were developed for constructing the "evaluative traumatic inventories" could it be expanded to study intercultural differences and similarities (10–11).

111. In certain ways, Boder anticipated some of the comparative methods of (and perhaps controversies over) what is now called multidirectional memory. The seminal articulation of this concept is Michael Rothberg, *Multidirectional Memory: Remembering the Holocaust in the Age of Decolonization* (Stanford, CA: Stanford University Press, 2009).

112. Boder, "Construction (in Part) of a Traumatological Evaluative Lexicon," 16. Boder's emphasis.

Digital Project: Two Methods of Counter-indexing the "Gray Zone"

1. Perhaps without knowing it, Kimmelmann explicitly rejected the historicist dictum made famous by Leopold von Ranke to reconstruct the past as it really was (*"wie es eigentlich gewesen ist"*). David Boder's interview with Abraham Kimmelmann, *Topical Autobiographies of Displaced People* (1957), translated by David Boder, box 12, David Boder Papers, Special Collections, Charles E. Young Research Library, UCLA, 1–128, here 2. The original interview, conducted in German, is available online: https://voices.library.iit.edu/interview/kimmelmannA. Adam Strohm at the Illinois Institute of Technology generously provided our team with an XML mark-up of Kimmelmann's original interview with timestamps.

2. Rosen also discusses Kimmelmann's "reversing" of the terms of the interview in Alan Rosen, *The Wonder of Their Voices: The 1946 Holocaust Interviews of David Boder* (Oxford: Oxford University Press, 2010), 78.

3. Primo Levi, "The Gray Zone," in *The Drowned and the Saved*, trans. Raymond Rosenthal (New York: Vintage Books, 1989), 36–69.

4. See, for example, Urs Stäheli, "Indexing: The Politics of Invisibility," *Environment and Planning D: Society and Space* 34, no. 1 (2016): 14–29; Tonia Sutherland and Alyssa Purcell, "A Weapon and a Tool: Decolonizing Description and Embracing Redescription as Liberatory Archival Praxis," *The International Journal of Information, Diversity, & Inclusion* 5, no. 1 (2021): 60–78.

5. Gábor Mihály Tóth's digital humanities project, "Let Them Speak," represents another example of what we are calling counter-indexing. Using natural language processing and topic modeling, Tóth extracts thousands of testimonial fragments to identify collective experiences such as shame, nakedness, shaking, standing, begging, walking, and many more. These experiences are pervasive across testimonial corpora but are not typically indexed or easily found. See https://lts.fortunoff.library.yale.edu.

6. Boder's full indexes are found at the end of *Topical Autobiographies*, 3105–59.

7. David Boder, "Psychological and Anthropological Analysis of Topical Autobiographies of Displaced Persons Recorded Verbatim in D.P. Camps" (1951), grant application for Federal Security Agency Public Health Services, box 1, M11, Special Collections, Drs. Nicholas and Dorothy Cummings Center for the History of Psychology, University of Akron, 6.

8. See Laura Jockusch, *Collect and Record! Jewish Holocaust Documentation in Early Postwar Europe* (Oxford: Oxford University Press, 2012). Differing from spoken interviews, most of the early, postwar documentation was in the form of written testimonies or questionnaires prepared by historical commissions.

9. Boder, *Topical Autobiographies*, 3105–6.

10. All interactive Tableau visualizations in this chapter are available on our project website, http://holocaustresearchlab.com, under "Digital Project 1."

11. Again, not every page that mentioned "food" would have been indexed if such mentions occurred together over a series of contiguous pages. Based on our analysis of Boder's questions, he asked 159 distinct questions about "food, eating, and drinking" in the seventy interviews in *Topical Autobiographies*.

12. Boder, *Topical Autobiographies*, 3105–20. Rachel Deblinger discusses these and other details of Boder's testimonies, including stories of shame, physical depravity, and violent revenge, that "predate a taboo that might have made testimonies more palatable for large audiences" (122). See her chapter "David P. Boder: Holocaust Memory in Displaced Persons Camps," in *After the Holocaust: Challenging the Myth of Silence*, ed. David Cesarani and Eric J. Sundquist (London: Routledge, 2012), 115–26.

13. Levi, "The Gray Zone," 39.

14. Levi, "The Gray Zone," 36.

15. For an interpretation of Levi, see the discussion by Michael Rothberg, *The Implicated Subject: Beyond Victims and Perpetrators* (Stanford CA: Stanford University Press, 2019), esp. chapter 1.

16. "Nun die jüdische Kultusgemeinde hat bekommen so einen Aufruf von der Polizei." Boder's interview with Kimmelmann, minute 11, line ID 77.

17. See, for example, Christopher D. Manning and Hinrich Schütze, *Foundations of Statistical Natural Language Processing* (Cambridge, MA: MIT Press: 1999); and the discussion of text analysis tools in Susan Schreibman, Ray Siemens, and John Unsworth, *A Companion to Digital Humanities* (Oxford, UK: John Wiley & Sons, 2008).

18. The XML-encoding was done by the Illinois Institute of Technology (IIT), and we added additional mark-up, as described below. The English translation was done by Boder and includes editing by the IIT team.

19. To identify the different languages used across Boder's corpus line by line, two Python packages were used: TextBlob for lines below eleven characters (high accuracy but daily usage limitations) and langdetect for all other lines (high accuracy but only on longer strings; no usage limitations). As Boder's interviews are highly multilingual, it was important to label the languages used in every line. This was also useful to analyze the use of code-switching by survivors.

20. Helmut Schmid, "Probabilistic Part-of-Speech Tagging Using Decision Trees," revised version of a paper presented at the International Conference on New Methods in Language Processing, Manchest, UK, 1994, https://www.cis.uni-muenchen.de/~schmid/tools/TreeTagger/data/tree-tagger1.pdf.

21. We used the "ngrams module" from Python's nltk package, but N-grams can easily be generated in other ways too, such as with the "Phrases" function of the online text analysis platform Voyant Tools (https://voyant-tools.org/).

22. Boder's interview with Kimmelmann, minute 41, line ID 277.

23. SequenceMatcher from Python's difflib, related to the Ratcliff-Obershelp gestalt pattern-matching algorithm.

24. This threshold was set after a few tries and may still be improved.

25. The category of "narration" N-grams includes expressions in three semantic areas: 1) "went/came," 2) "imagine this/you can't imagine this," 3) "he said/she said/one said/they said." A few examples:

1) N-grams following the models *gekommen und* ("came and"), *gegangen und* "went and"), *ist gekommen* ("has come"), and *dazu gekommen* ("it came to that"), including both literal and metaphorical expressions of movement as well as morphologically different but semantically related words like *nehmen* ("take") and *gehen* ("go"): the most frequent instances are *genommen und* (twenty), *gekommen und* (fourteen), *gegangen und* (thirteen), *ist gekommen* (eleven), and dozens of variations like *reingekommen und* (one), *raufgekommen und* (one), *raus gekommen und* (one), plus several expressions of time, like *Zeit gekommen* (one), *Mittagszeit gekommen* (one), *Uhr gekommen* (one), *Minute gekommen* (one).

2) N-grams in the model of *sich vorstellen* ("imagine," "picture for oneself") or its opposite "can't imagine": *sich vorstellen* (ten), *nicht vorstellen* (six), *das vorstellen* (two), *auch nicht vorstellen* (one), *das nicht vorstellen* (one), *mir vorstelle* (one).

3) N-grams in the model of *hat gesagt* ("he/she said"), including related expressions like *hat gedacht* ("he/she thought"): the most frequent include *hat gesagt* (sixteen), *man gesagt* (five), *haben gesagt* (six), *nicht gesagt* (three), *hat man gesagt* (four), *hat er gesagt* (three), *hat mir gesagt* (two), *hat gedacht* (two), *nichts gesagt* (two), *ihm gesagt* (two).

26. The category of "Jewish council" and "Jewish militias" emerges very simply through the frequent repetition of terms related to these two bodies (at least seventy times). In addition to these terms, there are also 151 bi-grams along the model of "* Jews" or "Jewish *" indicating the extent of Kimmelmann's focus on the actions, reactions, and fate of the Jewish community.

1) Militias: there are forty-five mentions of the Jewish militia, the Jewish police, and various Jewish administrators/functionaries, the most frequent being *jüdische Miliz* (fourteen), *die Miliz* (six), *jüdischen Miliz* (four), *jüdischer Miliz* (two), *jüdische Polizei* (three), *der Miliz* (three), *der jüdischen Miliz* (two), *jüdische Ordner* (two), *jüdische Beamten* (two), *jüdischer Miliz Mann* (two).

2) Councils: there are thirty references to the Jewish council, which Kimmelmann mostly calls *jüdische Kultusgemeinde*. Historically, this institution was called the *Judenrat*, but Kimmelmann never uses this word. The context, however, makes it abundantly clear that he is referring to the same institution. Frequent N-grams include *jüdische Kultusgemeinde* (fourteen), *der Kultusgemeinde* (six), *jüdischen Kultusgemeinde* (four), *die Kultusgemeinde* (three), *hat die Kultusgemeinde* (one), *bei der jüdischen Kultusgemeinde* (one), *der Präsident der jüdischen Kultusgemeinde* (one), and other minor variations referring to the Jewish central community (*Gemeinde, Zentrale,* and *Zentralgemeinde*) and its administration.

27. At a previous stage of our research on Boder's corpus, we found that one of the most frequent clusters of expression across the whole collection, regardless of interview, was "I don't know/I don't remember/I don't want to [say/tell]." A visual representation of this category, along with other frequent N-grams, can be found on our project website.

28. The "don't know/didn't know" cluster includes two main categories: past and present (plus related but opposite N-grams like "I did know," "we already knew," etc.).

   1) Past: twenty negative expressions; these include *nicht gewusst* (sixteen), *nicht genau gewusst* (one), *nichts mehr gewusst* (one), *nichts gewusst* (one), *ohne dass ich wusste* (one). Other expressions in the same cluster can be both positive or negative depending on the surrounding context.

   2) Present: twenty-seven negative expressions, *weiß nicht* (nineteen), *will nicht [viel sagen/ mehr erzählen]* (two), *[weiß ich/ich weiß] bis heute nicht* (two), *ich kann [Ihnen] nicht genau sagen* (two), *weiß es nicht* (one), *weiß das nicht* (one).

29. Other examples of the most prominent N-gram-based topics in Kimmelmann's interview are his focus on family, life in the concentration camps, work/money, and night.

   1) Family: 109 bi- and tri-grams primarily about his mother (eighty) and sister (twenty-four), following the model *(*) * Schwester (*)* and *(*) * Mutter (*)* (while he barely mentions his father, who was taken very early on).

   2) Camps: sixty-six bi- and tri-grams following the model *(*) * Lager*, like *das Lager* or *damals im Lager*.

   3) Work/money: seventy-nine bi- and tri-grams following the model *(*) * Arbeit/arbeiten (*)*, like *der Arbeit* (twenty), *zur Arbeit* (seventeen), *schwere Arbeit* (two); plus sixteen bi- and tri-grams on money (*Geld*) or gold (*Gold*).

   4) Night: forty bi- to quad-grams talking about night and nighttime, the most frequent being *in der Nacht* (ten), *der Nacht* (eleven), *erste Nacht* (five), plus expressions like *in einer Nacht* (one), *ich jede Nacht* (one), *während der Nacht* (one) and other variations.

30. An annotated list of the triplets extracted from Kimmelmann's testimony is available on our project website.

31. The German terms come from Kimmelmann's interview with Boder on the Voices of the Holocaust website: https://voices.library.iit.edu/interview/kimmelmannA (minutes 2:37–2:39). In addition, Kimmelmann describes the actions of various Jewish prisoner functionaries on pages 91 and 96–97 of his testimony (corresponding to minutes 2:24 and 2:33–2:34, respectively).

32. Hannah Arendt, *Eichmann in Jerusalem: A Report on the Banality of Evil* (New York: Penguin, 1977), 117ff.

33. Raul Hilberg writes, for example: "German supervisors turned to Jewish councils for information, money, labor, or police, and the councils provided them with these means every day of the week. . . . Members of the Jewish councils were genuine if not always representative Jewish

leaders who strove to protect the Jewish community from the most severe exactions and impositions and who tried to normalize Jewish life under the most adverse conditions." Raul Hilberg, *The Destruction of the European Jews*, 3rd ed. (New Haven, CT: Yale University Press, 2003), 1111–12. The many actions of the Jewish councils across various communities, including their relationship to the Jewish police, are discussed in Michael Robert Marrus, ed., *The Nazi Holocaust: Historical Articles on the Destruction of European Jews*, vol. 6, *The Victims of the Holocaust*, Part 1 (Westport, CT: Meckler, 1989).

34. Leni Yahil, *The Holocaust: The Fate of European Jewry, 1932–1945*, trans. Ina Friedman and Haya Galai (Oxford: Oxford University Press, 1991), 472.

35. Levi, "The Gray Zone," 42.

36. In terms of data-cleaning and curatorial decisions related to the layout of the visualization, we did the following: First, we manually disambiguated subject pronouns ("they" or "he"), when the reference was unequivocal. We left the subject pronoun "he" in one case where it was not entirely clear to whom he referred. Second, we confirmed each English triplet with the German original and translated named organizations consistently; in some cases, minor changes were made to match the original language. Third, we manually juxtaposed triplets that were part of the same narrative theme but did not share a common subject or object. Fourth, we connected triplets together as tangentially touching when they referred to the same subject or object with only a minor grammatical difference. The triplets depicted occur across pages 6, 16–23, and 49–53 of *Topical Autobiographies*, corresponding to minutes 9:30–11:30, 30:00–43:00 and 1:38:00–1:44:00, respectively, of Kimmelmann's recorded testimony.

37. Boder added an annotation to the English translation that referenced the wire break and says that he is not sure to whom "he" refers. Boder indicates that it is "apparently the Gestapo man" who made the selection and placed people into three groups as well as stationed the Jewish militia inside the square. Boder's interview with Kimmelmann, 50. However, there is no mention of a Gestapo man in this segment. From the recording, "he" could refer to Merin: "Also . . . —also um uns etwas zu beruhigen, ist gekommen der Monek [*sic*] Merin, was ich . . . was ich schon vorher von ihm erzählt habe, ich habe erzählt, das war der Hauptleiter der Kultusgemeinde für die ganzen Kreise da. Und er hat eine Rede gehalten, dass wir keine Angst haben sollen, in Wolbronn war das auch so und man hat alle frei gelassen [kein Ton am Tonband—Bruch oder nur übersprungen?] . . . dann mussten wir noch einmal vor der Kommission stehen und die Dritte war nach Auschwitz gegangen. Also der hat nicht gesprochen, der hat nur die Miliz hingestellt—es war im Platz . . . außen war deutsche Polizei, die haben uns bewacht und innen war die jüdische Polizei, die haben alle geordnet, dass es still sein soll. Und der hat mit dem Finger gezeigt—Gruppe eins (1), Gruppe zwei (2) und Gruppe drei (3). Ich will nicht viel sagen, was passiert hat, bis ich an die Reihe gekommen bin" (minute 1:38:00). Several minutes later, Kimmelmann finishes the story and references another Prominent Jewish Council member who declared the selection over and explicitly referenced the same three groups: "Plötzlich steht auf ein Mann, er war Jude, er hat geheißen Smetana, er war auch Einer von den sogenannten Prominenten, in der Sosnowice jüdischen Zentrale. Und er hielt eine Rede und hat gesagt: 'Nun ist die Selektion fertig. Die, die in Gruppe eins sind, die noch frei sind, die gehen noch an einem Tisch durch und die lassen sich den Lichtbildausweis stempeln. Und die Anderen, die in Gruppe zwei, die bleiben noch vorläufig in der Kultusgemeinde in Dabrowa. Die wird man dann noch mal untersuchen. Die dritte Gruppe geht nach Auschwitz'" (minute 1:44:00).

38. Levi, "The Gray Zone," 38.

39. Levi, "The Gray Zone," 66–67.

40. Levi, "The Gray Zone," 42.

41. Boder's interview with Kimmelmann, minutes 24:00–25:00.
42. Rosen also discusses Kimmelmann's reflections and says that his "tempering of judgment against the Jewish police shows a rare moral breadth." He does not, however, analyze the specific statements made by Kimmelmann depicted in the visualization of the gray zone. Rosen, *The Wonder of Their Voices*, 82.

4: Through the Lens of Big Data

1. While the vast majority of the testimonies were recorded by the USC Shoah Foundation in the mid-1990s and early 2000s, the foundation has also partnered with more than a dozen institutions and foundations across the world to preserve and make testimonies accessible (including, for example, collections from Jewish Family and Children's Services Holocaust Center, the Montreal Holocaust Museum, and the Holocaust Museum Houston). Recently, the USC Shoah Foundation has pursued a number of global partnerships to record testimony with survivors of the Guatemalan genocide, survivors of Anti-Rohingya Mass Violence, survivors of the South Sudan Civil War, and survivors of War and Genocide in Bosnia and Herzegovina.
2. The ideas and analyses presented here were performed over nearly a decade, and, hence, they also bear witness to the growth and change of the VHA, including the number of testimonies, the range of experiences, and the metadata related to those testimonies. The earliest analyses were completed in 2012, while the latest analyses were completed in 2022, using a version of the database from May 2019. Because the data provided to us comes from 2019, our analysis uses somewhat fewer testimonies from the experience groups we analyze (Holocaust survivors, Armenian genocide survivors, Rwandan genocide survivors, and Nanjing Massacre survivors).
3. An abridged version of the 2012 USC Shoah Foundation thesaurus (191 pages) can be found here: https://sfi.usc.edu/sites/default/files/docfiles/USC_SF_Thesaurus_101212_0.pdf. Our analysis is based on the 2019 database and thesaurus. The current VHA interface and database have been updated to include the addition and consolidation of a couple of parent categories as well as the separation of search filters for "place," "time," and "image." Any of these fields can also be combined to undertake a multifaceted search.
4. We only used the Jewish survivor testimonies recorded before 2019 by the USC Shoah Foundation (not its partner collections), which were divided equally into one-minute segments for indexing. About five thousand other testimonies were indexed using variable temporal units for segmenting. Those were not included in the analysis below for the sake of keeping the comparisons between testimonies uniform.
5. See the discussion by N. Katherine Hayles on exploratory algorithmic analysis in her book: *Unthought: The Power of the Cognitive Unconscious* (Chicago: University of Chicago, 2017), 208–10. This approach to visualization as a means of doing research through critical inquiry is also central to the work of Richard White and the "Spatial History Project." See https://web.stanford.edu/group/spatialhistory/cgi-bin/site/pub.php?id=29.
6. Franco Moretti first explored this notion of "distant reading" in an article called "Conjectures on World Literature," *New Left Review* (January-February 2000): 54–68. A more thorough and wide-ranging analysis of the practice is found in Franco Moretti, *Distant Reading* (London: Verso, 2013). His collaborator, Matthew L. Jockers, focuses on the possibilities of large-scale literary computing in *Macroanalysis: Digital Methods and Literary History* (Urbana: University of Illinois Press, 2013). More recently, these methodologies have been developed further by Andrew Piper, *Enumerations: Data and Literary Study* (Chicago: University of Chicago, 2018)

and Ted Underwood, *Distant Horizons: Digital Evidence and Literary Change* (Chicago: University of Chicago Press, 2019).

7. Moretti, "Conjectures on World Literature," 57.

8. Jockers, *Macroanalysis*, 24.

9. Jockers, *Macroanalysis*, 24–25.

10. Moretti argues that the vast majority of books are simply never read by human beings, amounting to what he calls the great "slaughterhouse of literature." In his estimation, 99.5 percent of the novels published in nineteenth-century Britain are never read or taught; instead, literary scholars are fixated on a tiny canon of works that are radically unrepresentative of the massive number of books, authors, publishing houses, and markets of that period, and that this fixation on the canon greatly skews our understanding of culture and social history. There is certainly an analogue here with regard to survivor testimonies, as the vast majority is rarely heard by human listeners. Franco Moretti, "The Slaughterhouse of Literature," *Modern Language Quarterly* 61, no. 1 (March 2000): 207–27.

11. All interactive Tableau visualizations in this chapter are available on our project website, http://holocaustresearchlab.com, under chapter 4.

12. For an institutional history of the foundation in relationship to its development of structures and norms for recording Holocaust testimony narratives, see Noah Shenker, *Reframing Holocaust Testimony* (Bloomington: Indiana University Press, 2015) and Jeffrey Shandler, *Holocaust Memory in the Digital Age: Survivors' Stories and New Media Practices* (Stanford, CA: Stanford University Press, 2017).

13. "Interviewer Guidelines," USC Shoah Foundation (2012), accessed July 2021, 4. https://sfi.usc.edu/sites/default/files/docfiles/USCSF_Interviewer_Guidelines_Oct%202012.pdf.

14. See "Survivor Pre-Interview Questionnaire," USC Shoah Foundation (2012), accessed July 2021. https://sfi.usc.edu/sites/default/files/docfiles/USCSF_JSPIQ.ENG_102512_0.pdf.

15. These are questions that Renana Keydar and her team at the Hebrew University's Lab for the Computational Analysis of Holocaust Testimonies have also begun to explore. Rather than using the human-created indexing terms, her team has developed algorithmic methods to segment the testimony transcripts into topics and determine which testimonies adhere to (and deviate from) certain narrative structures. See Eitan Wagner, Renana Keydar, Amit Pinchevski, and Omri Abend, "Topical Segmentation of Spoken Narratives: A Test Case on Holocaust Survivor Testimonies," in *Proceedings of the 2022 Conference on Empirical Methods in Natural Language Processing*, Association for Computational Linguistics, 2022, 6809–21, https://aclanthology.org/2022.emnlp-main.457/.

16. Of the Jewish Holocaust survivors, Dario Gabbai's testimonies (the first recorded in 1996 and the second recorded in 2014) contain the most indexing terms under the parent category "mistreatment and death," owing to the fact that he was a member of the Sonderkommando in Auschwitz. The overall structure of the testimonial narrative still follows a tripartite organization.

17. Part of our team's current research explores how computational approaches to indexing using a combination of non-negative matrix factorization (an unsupervised, "bag-of-words" approach to topic modeling) and BERTopic (a pretrained, transformer model for topic modeling) might provide new possibilities for expanding and regularizing subject indexing. See Keyi Cheng, Stefan Inzer, Adrian Leung, and Xiaoxian Shen, "Multi-Scale Hybridized Topic Modeling: A Pipeline for Analyzing Unstructured Text Datasets via Topic Modeling," *SIAM Undergraduate Research Online* (2022): 25–43, https://doi.org/10.48550/arXiv.2211.13496.

18. In addition to Shenker and Shandler, see Amit Pinchevski, *Transmitted Wounds: Media and the Mediation of Trauma* (Oxford: Oxford University Press, 2019).

19. See *Guidelines for the Construction, Format, and Management of Monolingual Controlled Vocabularies* (ANSI/NISO Z39.19-2005) (Bethesda, MD: National Information Standards Organization, 2005). The metadata—ranging from biographical information about the survivors and the recording of the testimony to the indexing terms—are all in English. The videos, however, are in more than forty languages.

20. See Samuel Gustman and Survivors of the Shoah Visual History Foundation, "Method and Apparatus for Cataloguing Multimedia Data," US Patent 5,832,495, November 3, 1998.

21. Johanna Drucker, *SpecLab* (Chicago: University of Chicago Press, 2010), 9.

22. Hannah Arendt, *The Human Condition* (Chicago: University of Chicago, 1958), 177–78.

23. Claude Shannon's foundational ideas of information theory were articulated in a 1948 article in which the goal of a communication system was to transmit a message over a channel to a receiver with the minimal amount of noise possible. Claude Shannon, "A Mathematical Theory of Communication," *The Bell System Technical Journal* 27 (1948): 379–423, 623–56, https://people.math.harvard.edu/~ctm/home/text/others/shannon/entropy/entropy.pdf.

24. The reference is to Friedrich Kittler, *Discourse Networks 1800/1900*, trans. Michael Metteer, with Chris Cullens (Stanford, CA: Stanford University Press, 1990).

25. Alan Liu, *Local Transcendence: Essays on Postmodern Historicism and the Database* (Chicago: University of Chicago Press, 2008), 216.

26. See the "Summary of Invention," in "Method and Apparatus for Cataloguing Multimedia Data," 3.

27. Conversation with author, February 6, 2012.

28. "Method and Apparatus for Cataloguing Multimedia Data," 10.

29. The thesaurus functions like an "ordered hierarchy of content objects," to use the classic (and not unproblematic) expression introduced by Steven J. DeRose, David G. Durand, Elli Mylonas, and Allen H. Renear to describe the computational transformation of text into ordered and hierarchical structures of information in "What Is Text, Really?," *Journal of Computing in Higher Education* 1 (1990): 3–26, https://doi.org/10.1007/BF02941632.

30. *Guidelines for the Construction, Format, and Management of Monolingual Controlled Vocabularies*, 2.

31. The thesaurus and database structure were designed to be extensible and modular: new terms could be added over time and common terms, concepts, and experiences could be used to index testimonies of other genocides. As the foundation began indexing testimonies from the Armenian genocide, the Nanjing Massacre, the Rwandan genocide, the Cambodian genocide, the Guatemalan genocide, and other contemporaneous atrocities, the thesaurus grew significantly to include relevant place names, cultural references, historical information, ethnic groups, and specific experiences from other genocides. While many indexing terms used to describe the Holocaust are also used to index these testimonies, certain new terms have also been introduced (such as "roadblocks," a key term in the Rwandan genocide testimonies, or "neighbors," a term only introduced, surprisingly, in 2016 and first used to index the Rwandan and Armenian genocides). As the foundation integrates testimonies from other peer organizations (such as San Francisco's Jewish Family and Children's Services), relevant indexing terms from other genocides and experience groups are also being used to tag these newly acquired Holocaust testimonies. In addition to "neighbors," other such terms include "perpetrator remorse" (a term only introduced in 2016) and "reconciliation," which appears in the vast majority of the Rwandan testimonies but is, to date, almost completely absent from the Jewish survivor testimonies recorded by the Shoah Foundation. As such, the experiences of genocide and atrocity in other global contexts might inform what is "seen" and "heard" in Holocaust testimonies. For a thoughtful discussion of some of the challenges involved in

avoiding the "one size fits all" model of producing testimonies of genocide, see Noah Shenker, "Through the Lens of the Holocaust: The Holocaust as a Paradigm for Documenting Genocide Testimonies," *History and Memory* (Spring/Summer 2016): 141–75.

32. Crispin Brooks, conversation with the author, February 6, 2012.

33. Berel Lang, *Act and Idea in the Nazi Genocide* (Ithaca, NY: Cornell University Press, 1992), chapter 6.

34. "Indexing Guidelines," USC Shoah Foundation Visual History Archive (2021), 39. https://sfi.usc.edu/content/indexing-guidelines.

35. As we will see below, the indexing term "miscellaneous footage" (defined as "non-interview footage of various kinds") is used by the Shoah Foundation to mark up about one in five of the Armenian genocide testimonies that were filmed by the Armenian Film Foundation and are now part of the VHA.

36. Many of the terms used to describe emotion were only introduced in 2014 and include: anger, disgust, pride, relief, confidence, fear, happiness, despair, surprise, antipathy, sadness, determination, embarrassment, guilt, jealousy, loneliness, happiness, empathy, and nostalgia. To date, sadness, for example, is only tagged in 187 Holocaust testimonies (out of more than fifty-four thousand) but in more than a third of the Tutsi survivors of the Rwandan Genocide (fifty-four out of 123). The thesaurus and indexing system are works in progress, and the introduction of new terms reflects changes in what is "heard" over time.

37. Lev Manovich, *The Language of New Media* (Cambridge, MA: MIT Press, 2001), 237.

38. Database relationships are foremost paradigmatic or associative relations, to use Ferdinand de Saussure's terms, since they involve rules that govern the selection or substitutability of terms. Syntagmatic relationships are combinatory since they may give rise to narrative. These terms derive from Ferdinand de Saussure, *Course in General Linguistics*, trans. Roy Harris (Chicago: Open Court, 1998). Also, see the discussion by Manovich, *The Language of New Media*, 230–31; and N. Katherine Hayles, "Narrative and Database: Natural Symbionts," *PMLA* 122, no. 5 (October 2007): 1603–8, here 1606.

39. See the discussion by Stephen Ramsay, *Reading Machines: Toward an Algorithmic Criticism* (Urbana: University of Illinois Press, 2011), 85.

40. Saul Friedländer, *The Years of Extermination: Nazi Germany and the Jews, 1939–1945* (New York: HarperCollins, 2007), xvi, xxv–xxvi.

41. Examining the collaboration between the USC Shoah Foundation and the Documentation Center of Cambodia, Noah Shenker has raised some of these critical questions. He is particularly attuned to the use of the "Pre-interview Questionnaire," shared narrative templates, and common indexing strategies, the last of which, as I have also suggested, tend to privilege "the transcribable content of interviews rather than their relationship with the gestural, aural and corporeal resonances that cannot always be reduced to the typed page as 'objective' content." See Noah Shenker, "Through the Lens of the Shoah: The Holocaust as a Paradigm for Documenting Genocide Testimonies," *History & Memory* 28, no. 1 (Spring/Summer 2016): 141–75, here 165–66. On the other hand, Michelle Caswell has argued that comparisons with the Holocaust and the use of convergent archiving approaches for documenting genocide can help "legitimize" a genocide in the eyes of the global community. See her discussion of the Cambodian genocide archives: Michelle Caswell, *Archiving the Unspeakable: Silence, Memory, and the Photographic Record in Cambodia* (Madison: University of Wisconsin Press, 2014). In addition, Rebecca Jinks has examined the overlaps between representations of the Holocaust and other genocides in her book *Representing Genocide: Holocaust as Paradigm* (London: Bloomsbury, 2016). Mostly focused on film, literature, photography, and forms of public memorialization, Jinks examines how representational strategies and tropes from the Holo-

caust have been deployed to represent other genocides. These questions of comparison—and their generative possibilities—are central to Michael Rothberg, *Multidirectional Memory: Remembering the Holocaust in the Age of Decolonization* (Stanford, CA: Stanford University Press, 2009).

42. Our analysis focuses on Armenian genocide survivors recorded by the Armenian Film Foundation, rather than all the interviews (which include descendants, foreign witnesses, and scholars).

43. "Videographer Guidelines," USC Shoah Foundation, 2012, 4. https://sfi.usc.edu/sites/default/files/docfiles/USCSF_Videographer_%20Guidelines_Oct2012.pdf.

44. "Videographer Guidelines" 7. These requirements were not followed absolutely every time, and there are a number of examples of VHA testimonies where the camera zooms into the subject's face, pans to other material (such as a work of art or piece of writing), and occasionally does some interpretive work to set up a scene visually.

45. Shenker discusses the Foundation's videographer guidelines in "Through the Lens of the Shoah," 154–55, as does Shandler, *Holocaust Memory in the Digital Age*, 127–29.

46. Khoren Davidson (Aug 13, 1977), interview 53322, Visual History Archive, USC Shoah Foundation: https://vha.usc.edu/testimony/53322; Zabel (Rose) Apelian (May 6, 1992), Visual History Archive, USC Shoah Foundation: https://vha.usc.edu/testimony/53182; Hrahad Harout and Shooshanig Shahinian (February 11, 1984), interview 53525, Visual History Archive, USC Shoah Foundation: https://vha.usc.edu/testimony/53525; and Avedis Khantzian (July 17, 1985), Visual History Archive, USC Shoah Foundation: https://vha.usc.edu/testimony/53230.

47. "Interviewer Guidelines," USC Shoah Foundation, 15.

48. Armenian women were often tattooed with Christian symbols against their will, so that they could be identified as "other" over the course of the genocidal campaign and targeted for sexual violence. According to her testimony, Apelian's tattoos were done when she was three years old.

49. As Ronald Grigor Suny notes, "Holocaust" was used as early as the 1890s by the *New York Times* to refer to the Hamidian massacres of Armenians and, later, the Adana massacres of 1910. See Ronald Grigor Suny, "Writing Genocide: The Fate of the Ottoman Armenians," in *A Question of Genocide: Armenians and Turks at the End of the Ottoman Empire*, ed. Richard Grigor Suny, Fatma Müge Göçek, and Norman M. Naimark (Oxford: Oxford University Press, 2011), 320 note 47. According to Jon Petrie, the term "Holocaust" was also used in 1913 to refer to the murder of thirty thousand Armenians in 1909. See Jon Petrie, "The Secular Word Holocaust: Scholarly Myths, History, and 20th Century Meanings," *Journal of Genocide Research* 2, no. 1 (2000): 31–63.

50. Marc Nichanian, *The Historiographic Perversion*, trans. Gil Anidjar (New York: Columbia University Press, 2009), 95.

51. In their chapter "What Gets Counted Counts," Catherine D'Ignazio and Lauren F. Klein point out that classification systems—whether computational, conceptual, or physical—always need to be interrogated for the assumptions and beliefs that render data into forms (such as numbers and labels) that make them processable by computers. See Catherine D'Ignazio and Lauren F. Klein, "What Gets Counted Counts," in *Data Feminism* (Cambridge, MA: MIT Press, 2020), esp. 103–4.

52. Nichanian, *The Historiographic Perversion*, 70, 73.

53. Nichanian, *The Historiographic Perversion*, 95.

54. Nichanian, *The Historiographic Perversion*, 94, 114.

55. Nichanian, *The Historiographic Perversion*, 122.

56. Nichanian, *The Historiographic Perversion*, 199.
57. An analogy for this process can be found in digital mapping, where one "map" (or indexing system) is georeferenced to another "map" or indexing system. This process, of course, underscores the power of the basemap's epistemology—that is, the knowledge system of the map (in this case, the Shoah Foundation's VHA) to which everything is georeferenced. But we can also imagine the opposite approach (reverse georeferencing), namely using Boder's indexing terms to index the Shoah Foundation testimonies. Such an approach displaces the normative "basemap," or reference system. For a discussion of this process in digital mapping, see Todd Presner, David Shepard, and Yoh Kawano, *HyperCities: Thick Mapping in the Digital Humanities* (Cambridge, MA: Harvard University Press, 2014), 110ff.
58. There are 318 subject terms, 429 places, and 213 people (excluding the names of the interviewees).
59. "Weapons" is also hardly used, and, in fact, this is a newer parent-level category introduced by the Shoah Foundation in 2019, primarily to account for the role of weapons during genocides. To date, it is very infrequently used by the Shoah Foundation when indexing genocide testimonies.
60. Some of Boder's interviews just end abruptly due to time constraints, technical issues, or interruptions. In the case of Abraham Kimmelmann's incomplete interview, Boder promised to return to Geneva to continue the interview at a later time (but he did not return). After four and a half hours, Kimmelmann is narrating his time in Gross-Rosen in 1945 but is not able to talk about his time in Buchenwald, where he was liberated. In his discussion of the Kimmelmann interview and its publication in an abbreviated format in Boder's book, *I Did Not Interview the Dead*, Rosen remarks about its fragmentary status and pronounced "lack of closure." Alan Rosen, *The Wonder of their Voices: The 1946 Holocaust Interviews of David Boder* (Oxford: Oxford University Press, 2010), 136.
61. This may be explained in a number of ways: First, the 44,429 Jewish survivor testimonies in the Shoah Foundation are life narratives, in which many different topics (from childhood to postwar resettlement) are spoken about. As such, the topic "mistreatment and death" may only be mentioned in a few segments. Second, the corpus represents a very wide range of experiences, and not all survivors recount experiences indexed under "mistreatment and death" (some, for example, fled before their families were deported to camps). And, third, Jewish survivors are about seven times more likely to talk about experiences related to "captivity" than to "mistreatment and death," something that is both a function of their experiences of survival and an artifact of the way the indexing system marks up the content of the testimonies. This stands in contrast to the other corpora where experiences of "mistreatment and death" are spoken about and marked up more frequently relative to the other four categories.
62. Jacques Derrida, *Archive Fever: A Freudian Impression*, trans. Eric Prenowitz (Chicago: University of Chicago Press, 1996), 36.
63. Tonia Sutherland and Alyssa Purcell, for example, have argued for the importance of auditing archival description to undo naming violence and foster community-centered descriptive practices. See Tonia Sutherland and Alyssa Purcell, "A Weapon and a Tool: Decolonizing Description and Embracing Redescription as Liberatory Archival Praxis," *The International Journal of Information, Diversity, & Inclusion* 5, no. 1 (2021): 60–78, https://jps.library.utoronto .ca/index.php/ijidi/article/view/34669/27395.
64. Through processes of "saying" and "unsaying," these questions speak to ways that algorithmic approaches might be able to "pluralize" digital archives. For a broader discussion from the field of critical archival studies, see Frank Upward, Barbara Reed, Gillian Oliver and Joanne Evans, *Recordkeeping Informatics for a Networked Age* (Clayton, Australia: Monash University Publishing, 2018).

65. Emmanuel Levinas, *Otherwise than Being, or Beyond Essence*, trans. Alphonso Lingis (Pittsburgh: Duquesne University Press, 2006).

66. An analogue might be found in Giorgio Agamben's characterization of his book *Remnants of Auschwitz* as "a kind of perpetual commentary on testimony." Agamben, *Remnants of Auschwitz: The Witness and the Archive*, trans. Daniel Heller-Roazen (New York: Zone Books, 1999), 13.

5: The Haunted Voice

1. Claude Lanzmann, *Shoah, Second Era* (New Yorker Films, 1985), minutes 32:00–34:00.

2. Dorota Glowacka argues that the "agonizing silence" is the "culmination of Lanzmann's antimimetic strategy," in which the viewer is "forced to voyeuristically participate" in the breakdown of art and life, in *Disappearing Traces: Holocaust Testimonials, Ethics, and Aesthetics* (Seattle: University of Washington Press, 2012), 118.

3. Michael Renov, *The Subject of Documentary* (Minneapolis: University of Minnesota Press, 2004), 127.

4. Dominick LaCapra, *Writing History, Writing Trauma* (Baltimore: Johns Hopkins University Press, 2001), 98.

5. Shoshana Felman, "The Return of the Voice: Claude Lanzmann's *Shoah*," in *Testimony: Crises of Witnessing in Literature, Psychoanalysis, and Film*, by Shoshana Felman and Dori Laub (New York: Routledge, 1992), 219, 218.

6. Brad Prager, "The Real Abraham Bomba: Through Claude Lanzmann's Looking Glass," in *The Construction of Testimony: Claude Lanzmann's Shoah and its Outtakes*, ed. Erin McGlothlin, Brad Prager, and Markus Zisselsberger (Detroit: Wayne State University Press, 2020), 275–301. As Prager points out, the term, "truth incarnate," comes from Lanzmann's own reflections on Bomba's performance (278).

7. The outtakes are available online through the USHMM: https://collections.ushmm.org/search/catalog/irn1003920. Bomba is noticeably the most emphatic and animated when responding to—and strongly rejecting—Lanzmann's questions about the supposed "blindness" of the Jews to understanding their situation. He condemns the complicity of the Jewish ghetto police, and he repudiates the stereotype that Jews "went like sheep to slaughter." He says that the majority of the Jews were "a good people, honest people, fighting people" (outtake 5, minute 22:00), who survived because they had "a will to live . . . even in suffering" (outtake 5, minutes 12:00–13:00).

8. Alina Bothe, who discusses Bomba's testimony extensively and compares different versions, argues that this is an exceptional and "brutal" scene that contrasts starkly with all of Lanzmann's interviews with Bomba in which Bomba "is composed and maintains narrative sovereignty." Alina Bothe, *Die Geschichte der Shoah im virtuellen Raum: Eine Quellenkritik* (Berlin: De Gruyter Oldenbourg, 2019), 159.

9. In 1990, Bomba gave a three-and-half-hour oral history interview to the US Holocaust Memorial Museum. Conducted by Linda G. Kuzmack, the interview consists of just thirty-seven questions. He gives long, detailed narrative answers to the interviewer's questions, sometimes speaking with barely any pause for ten or fifteen minutes at a time about specific historical events, such as the liquidation of the ghetto, his arrival in Treblinka, or his descriptions of the other men who worked as barbers in the extermination camp (https://collections.ushmm.org/search/catalog/irn504538).

10. Abraham Bomba (Aug 14, 1996), interview 18061, Visual History Archive, USC Shoah Foundation, tape 4, minutes 3:17–4:51: https://vha.usc.edu/testimony/18061.

11. The decibel level plot was created using a custom script written by Campbell Yamane that sampled the audio output of the seven tapes (MP3 files) and averaged the vocal intensity in fifteen-second units. For this testimony, the threshold for silence established at -40 DB (as seen by the tape changes), and all measurements were made with respect to this threshold. The negative values do not signify anything (as this is an arbitrary reference system). The average decibel level was found to be -31.39, and the maximum peaks returned values of -22.82 (at three hours and nine minutes) and -23.47 (at three hours and eight minutes). In fact, six out of seven of the maximum decibel values of the entire testimony occurred in this section of testimony (between three hours and five minutes and three hours and ten minutes, while he is reading his poems). This corresponds to tape 7, minutes 7:20–14:53 (https://vha.usc .edu/testimony/18061). The audio measurements can be found on our project website. The color spectrogram was created using an open-source software called SPEK (http://spek.cc/).

12. Bomba, interview 18061, tape 7, minutes 5:45–15:00.

13. Bomba, interview 18061, tape 7, minute 7:00.

14. Shandler cites Bomba's two poems in his discussion of multilingualism and code-switching in Holocaust testimonies. He argues that "performing [such as poetry, song or music] provides survivors with opportunities to assume control of the interviews with regard to form as well as content," something that applies to sound, voice, and language. Jeffrey Shandler, *Holocaust Memory in the Digital Age: Survivors' Stories and New Media Practices* (Stanford, CA: Stanford University Press, 2017), 114. Bothe also discusses Bomba's inability to come up with an English translation of "Nekome" in *Die Geschichte der Shoah im virtuellen Raum*, citing the contemporary taboo of survivors expressing feelings of revenge (163).

15. Bomba, interview 18061, tape 7, minute 6:00.

16. The notion of "figura" was introduced by Erich Auerbach as a way of describing a historical fulfillment or redemption in which a later historical event fulfills the promise of an earlier one. See Erich Auerbach, "Figura" [1939], in *Scenes from the Drama of European Literature* (Minneapolis: University of Minnesota, 1984), 11–78. Hayden White provides a compelling interpretation of this essay in "Auerbach's Literary History: Figural Causation and Modernist Historicism," in *Figural Realism: Studies in the Mimesis Effect* (Baltimore: Johns Hopkins University Press, 1999), 87–100.

17. Some of the details of the second poem are described earlier in his Shoah Foundation testimony when he recounts the deportation of his family from the Częstochowa ghetto. The interview Bomba gave to the USHMM in 1990 (tape 1, minutes 30:00–39:00) contains many more details and gives the fullest narrative description of the Nazi actions in the Częstochowa ghetto between Yom Kippur and Sukkot in September of 1942 (https://collections.ushmm .org/search/catalog/irn504538).

18. Praat was created and developed by Paul Boersma and David Weenink, "Praat: Doing Phonetics by Computer" [computer program], version 6.2.14, retrieved May 24, 2022, http://www .praat.org/.

19. According to Maya Barzilai, in her analysis of Paul Celan's poetry, "the breath-unit represented for [Celan] not merely the interval at which a line break should appear but also, more broadly, the singularity of the poem as a product of individual breath." Maya Barzilai, "'One Should Finally Learn How to Read This Breath': Paul Celan and the Buber-Rosenzweig Bible," *Comparative Literature* 71, no. 4 (2019): 436–54, here 437. For a discussion of the significance of breath in Celan's poetry and testimonial poetics more comparatively, see Kyle Rosen, "The Speculative Lyric: Poetic Testimonials of Modern Holocausts" (PhD diss., UCLA, 2023).

20. The final lines of the poem are: "And through the little window, a Christian spits on us, / 'To Treblinka,' another bursts out with a cry." This memory of being spit on is also described in

his USHMM testimony: "I was near a little window, where was with wire closed around that people shouldn't be able to escape. I looked through. Most of the people what they did to us, they spit on us" (part 1, minutes 38:00–39:00), https://collections.ushmm.org/search/catalog/irn504538.

21. Claude Lanzmann, *Shoah*, outtake 2, film ID 3198, camera rolls 4–6, https://collections.ushmm.org/search/catalog/irn1003920. These parts were not, however, included in the final film.

22. Lanzmann, *Shoah*, outtake 2, minutes 16:00–18:00. Prager also points out that these locutions uttered by Lanzmann—"You have to, you have no choice"—are essentially reused in his later staging of the barbershop scene in which he films Bomba break down describing the haircutting of condemned women. See Prager, "The Real Abraham Bomba," 287.

23. Hannah Pollin-Galay's forthcoming book, *Khurbn Yiddish: How the Holocaust Changed the Yiddish Language*, analyzes how the trauma of the Holocaust caused a kind of "lingual shock" that resulted in the creation of a new vocabulary to describe its horrors in terms of vulgarities, anger, and poetic truths.

24. For an interdisciplinary discussion of "close listening" to poetry reading and sound performance, see Charles Bernstein, ed., *Close Listening: Poetry and the Performed Word* (Oxford: Oxford University Press, 1998). Bernstein argues that the sounds of a work may be "extralexical but they are not extrasemantic" (5). As such, he not only draws our attention to "the body's rhythms–gasps, stutters, hiccups, burps, coughs, slurs, microrepetitions, oscillations in volume, 'incorrect' pronunciations, and so on," but also to the richness and dynamism of prosody more generally, including distress, rupture, silence, and many other rhythmic forces (14).

25. Adriana Cavarero, *For More than One Voice: Toward a Philosophy of Vocal Expression*, trans. Paul A. Kottman (Stanford, CA: Stanford University Press, 2005), 169.

26. For a useful overview of how "advancements in affective computing, social signal processing, and automatic analysis of non-verbal communication [are] providing us with new tools that can capture the subjective and the emotional content" (6) of oral histories, including a wide range of prosodic features and paralinguistic cues, see Francisca Pessanha and Almila Akdag, "A Computational Look at Oral History Archives," *ACM Journal on Computing and Cultural Heritage*, 15, no. 1 (December 2021), 1–16. https://doi.org/10.1145/3477605.

27. Rather than measuring the voice to "show us something about the universality of vocal functioning" or unlock essential features and signifying patterns, we employ sonic measurements for the ways in which they can help us attend to the particularity of the voice, or what Nina Sun Eidsheim calls the "voice's fine-grained specificity and overall complexity." Nina Sun Eidsheim, *The Race of Sound: Listening, Timbre, and Vocality* (Durham, NC: Duke University Press, 2019), 14, 15.

28. Louise Amoore, *Cloud Ethics: Algorithms and the Attributes of Ourselves and Others* (Durham, NC: Duke University Press, 2020), 171.

29. Within the field of oral history studies, there is a significant literarure on learning to listen differently and apprehend the importance of the unsaid by attending to gaps and silences. We have taken inspiration from much of this history, including the following works: Anna Sheftel and Stacey Zembrzycki, ed., *Oral History Off the Record: Towards an Ethnography of Practice* (London: Palgrave Macmillan, 2013); Sherna Berger Gluck and Daphne Patai, ed., *Women's Words: The Feminist Practice of Oral History* (New York: Routledge, 1991); and Lawrence Langer, *Holocaust Testimonies: The Ruins of Memory* (New Haven, CT: Yale University Press, 1991).

30. The concept of "hauntology" comes from Jacques Derrida, *Specters of Marx: The State of the Debt, the Work of Mourning, and the New International*, trans. Peggy Kamuf (New York: Routledge, 1994).

31. Cavarero, *For More than One Voice*, 33–41.

32. Cavarero, *For More than One Voice*, 28, 29.

33. Cavarero, *For More than One Voice*, 42.

34. Cavarero, *For More than One Voice*, 31.

35. Paul Celan, "Bremer Ansprache," in *Gesammelte Werke*, vol. 3 (Frankfurt am Main: Suhrkamp, 1983), 185–86. The German is "Auf etwas Offenstehendes, Besetzbares, auf ein ansprechbares Du vielleicht" (186). For a timely discussion of Celan's poetic voice, see Kyle Rosen, "The Speculative Lyric."

36. The VHA transcripts are not TEI encoded, and there is no consistent markup of variations in voice or paralinguistic features. Within the digital humanities, Tanya Clement has argued for the need to reevaluate "how we develop metadata frameworks that facilitate access to audio." See Tanya Clement, "Towards a Rationale of Audio-Text," *Digital Humanities Quarterly* 10, no. 3 (2016): paragraph 44, http://www.digitalhumanities.org/dhq/vol/10/3/000254/000254.html. See also the discussion by Pessanha and Salah who present the state of research on computational paralinguistics: Pessanha and Salah, "A Computational Look at Oral History Archives."

37. See chapter 3. As Rachel Deblinger has argued, radio was one of the primary ways that American audiences first encountered Holocaust survivors. In addition to Boder's numerous radio interviews (which often included recorded voices of survivors), Deblinger shows how Jewish organizations such as the United Service for New Americans, the United Jewish Appeal, National Council of Jewish Women, Hadassah, and the Citizen's Committee on Displaced Persons relied on radio to advocate for immigration reform, inspire financial giving, and spread awareness. See Deblinger, *Saving our Survivors: How American Jews Learned about the Holocaust* (Bloomington: Indiana University Press, 2025), chapter 2. In the Israeli context, Amit Pinchevski shows how the live radio broadcast of the Eichmann trial in 1961 was critical in shaping Holocaust memory in Israel. Amit Pinchevski, *Transmitted Wounds: Media and the Mediation of Trauma* (Oxford: Oxford University Press, 2019), chapter 1.

38. Boder's annotations have been documented thoroughly by Anna Bonazzi and appear on our project website under chapter five.

39. The critical literature includes: Leslie Morris, "The Sound of Memory," *The German Quarterly* 74, no. 4 (Autumn 2001): 368–78; Alan Rosen, *Sounds of Defiance: The Holocaust, Multilingualism, and the Problem of English* (Lincoln: University of Nebraska Press, 2005); Noah Shenker, *Reframing Holocaust Testimony* (Bloomington: Indiana University Press, 2015); Jeffrey Shandler, *Holocaust Memory in the Digital Age* (Stanford, CA: Stanford University Press, 2017); Hannah Pollin-Galay, *Ecologies of Witnessing: Language, Place, and Holocaust Testimony* (New Haven, CT: Yale University Press, 2018); and Henry Greenspan, *On Listening to Holocaust Survivors: Recounting and Life History* (Westport, CT: Praeger, 1998).

40. Geoffrey Hartman, *The Longest Shadow: In the Aftermath of the Holocaust* (New York: Palgrave, 1996), 136.

41. Hartman, *The Longest Shadow*, 144.

42. Leah Wolfson, "'Is There Anything You Would Like to Add?': Visual Testimony Encounters the Lyric," *South Atlantic Review* 73, no. 3 (Summer 2008): 86–109, here 86.

43. Hannah Pollin-Galay, "The History of My Voice: Yiddish at the Seams of Holocaust Video Testimony," *Prooftexts* 35, no. 1 (Winter 2015): 58–97, here 59. A fuller treatment is given in her book, *Ecologies of Witnessing*.

44. Pollin-Galay, "The History of My Voice," 60.

45. Pollin-Galay, "The History of My Voice," 73.
46. Shandler also discusses a large number of testimonies from the Shoah Foundation's Visual History Archive where code-switching from one language (often English) into Yiddish occurs. He documents a wide variety of reasons, including the survivors' own relationship to the language and (lost) Jewish culture, as well as performative components in testimonies such as literary recitals, testimonial readings, music, and song. See Shandler, *Holocaust Memory in the Digital Age*, chapter 3.
47. To date, several thousand English-language transcripts have been created from testimonies in the VHA and over one thousand German-language transcripts were created through a partnership with the Freie University in Berlin. Both include XML markup indicating pauses, certain emotional expressions, and other sounds on the audio recording (such as interruptions or background noise).
48. Roland Barthes considers the bodily aspects of the voice to be its "grain." As he explains: "The 'grain' is the body in the voice as it sings, the hand as it writes, the limb as it performs" (188). For the voice, this includes the lungs, the throat, the lips, the tongue, the glottis, the teeth, the mucous membranes, and the nose—and is deeply connected to the act of breathing (183). See Roland Barthes, "The Grain of the Voice," in *Image-Music-Text*, trans. Stephen Heath (New York: Hill and Wang, 1977), 179–89. According to Adriana Cavarero, interpreting Barthes, the voice is "a pivotal joint between body and speech." Cavarero, *For More than One Voice*, 15.
49. Far from static or neutral, technologies that enable distant listening through the visualization of sound patterns need to be, as Tanya Clement has argued, situated within "a hermeneutic framework that allows for different ways of making meaning with sound" in order to "[open] spaces for interpretation." See Tanya Clement, "Distant Listening or Playing Visualizations Pleasantly with the Eyes and the Ears," *Digital Studies / Le Champ Numérique* 3, no. 2 (2013): https://www.digitalstudies.org/article/id/7237/.
50. To be sure, this is hardly new and is intended to set the stage for preliminary analysis. For the long history of visualizing sound as spectrographs and waves, see Jonathan Sterne, *The Audible Past: Cultural Origins of Sound Reproduction* (Durham, NC: Duke University Press, 2003); Joseph Auner, "Weighing, Measuring, Embalming Tonality: How we Became Phonometrographers," in *Tonality 1900–1950: Concept and Practice*, ed. Felix Woerner, Ullrich Scheideler, and Philip Rupprecht (Wiesbaden, Germany: Franz Steiner Verlag, 2012), 25–46.
51. Our process converted the audio signals into a digital output, which was based on a simple "on/off" variable, namely whether there was sound at a given moment or not, in order to identify moments of silence within the course of a testimony. This involved sampling the output every 250 milliseconds to measure decibel level. The results were averaged by second and then a script determined moments in the testimony in which three or more consecutive seconds of silence occurred (a duration that we determined as a baseline for identifying a moment of silence). The results were visualized as simple histograms where the thickness of the line corresponded to the number of seconds of silence at a given timestamp in the testimony. After that, we created basic line graphs ("vocal intensity plots") of the overall variation in decibel level across the testimony.
52. Renee Firestone (October 11, 1994 and January 26, 1995), interview 151, Visual History Archive, USC Shoah Foundation, https://vha.usc.edu/testimony/151.
53. While not typical of VHA testimonies, about 138 Holocaust testimonies include footage taken on location. In addition, several testimonies include a second, later recording, such as the testimony of Dario Gabbai who was reinterviewed by the then director Stephen Smith in 2014.
54. Renee Firestone, interview 151, tape 5, minutes 0:40–2:10.
55. Renee Firestone, interview 151, tape 5, minutes 20:00–25:00.

56. This would be a form of the *phone semantike,* a "signifying voice," to use Cavarero's expression. See Cavarero, *For More than One Voice,* 32. Today, these are questions being confronted in TEI and AudioAnnotate.

57. Renee Firestone, interview 151, indexing terms used for segment 42 (tape 5, minutes 20:00–25:00).

58. Saul Friedländer, "Trauma, Memory, and Transference," in *Holocaust Remembrance: The Shapes of Memory,* ed. Geoffrey H. Hartman (Oxford: Basil Blackwell, 1994), 252–63, here 263. The full quote from Friedländer concerns his view, which I share, that "new forms of historical narrative" or "new modes of representation" in literature and art (and, I would add, new methods of computational analysis) may "probe the past from unexpected vantage points," but they will not "entirely [dispel] ... the opaqueness of 'deep memory'" (263).

59. Erika Jacoby (July 11, 1994), interview 8, Visual History Archive, USC Shoah Foundation, tape 2, 12:04–12:17: https://vha.usc.edu/testimony/8.

60. Although focused on comparing phonation in different languages, Matthew Gordon and Peter Ladefoged discuss the characteristics of the creaky voice in "Phonation Types: A Cross-Linguistic Overview," *Journal of Phonetics* 29, no. 4 (October 2001): 383–406.

61. Langer, *Holocaust Testimonies,* 68.

62. Amoore, *Cloud Ethics,* 171.

63. Moshe Taube (March 7, 1996), interview 13063, Visual History Archive, USC Shoah Foundation, tape 1, minutes 16–18: https://vha.usc.edu/testimony/13063.

64. The word count includes the missing Hebrew words in the transcript created by ProQuest.

65. Taube, who later became a cantor, survived the Holocaust with his father working at a factory affiliated with Oskar Schindler. Both were placed on Schindler's list.

66. Wolfson, "'Is There Anything You Would Like to Add?,'" 86.

67. Wolfson, "'Is There Anything You Would Like to Add?,'" 106.

68. After some experimentation, we decided that averaging out decibel level and word counts in fifteen-second intervals allowed us to visualize variations while minimizing the suppression of either variable. This research was spearheaded by Campbell Yamane and overseen by Presner.

69. Robert Ness, (October 31, 1995), interview 5388, Visual History Archive, USC Shoah Foundation, tape 5, minutes 20:00–21:30: https://vha.usc.edu/testimony/5388.

70. Robert Ness, interview 5388, tape 6, minute 17.

71. Efraim (Fred) Hoffman (November 5, 1995), interview 8352, Visual History Archive, USC Shoah Foundation, tape 2, minutes 24:00–26:00: https://vha.usc.edu/testimony/8352.

72. Hoffman, interview 8352, tape 3, minutes 25:00–31:00.

73. Hoffman, interview 8352, tape 3, minutes 27:00–28:00.

74. Hoffman, interview 8352, tape 3, minute 29:30–30:00.

75. Roland Barthes, "To Write: An Intransitive Verb?," in *The Rustle of Language,* trans. Richard Howard (Berkeley: University of California Press, 1989), 11–21; Hayden White, "Writing in the Middle Voice," in *The Fiction of Narrative: Essays on History, Literature, and Theory 1957–2007,* ed. Robert Doran (Baltimore: Johns Hopkins University Press, 2010), 255–62. As Barthes indicates, "diathesis" refers to how "the subject of a verb is affected by the action." In the middle voice, the subject remains inside the action: "By acting, the subject affects himself, he always remains inside the action, even if that action involves an object" (18).

76. Sterne, *The Audible Past,* chapter 1.

77. Here, I draw on the comprehensive overview of this history from Xiaochang Li and Mara Mills, "Vocal Features: From Voice Identification to Speech Recognition by Machine," supplement, *Technology and Culture* 60, no. 2 (April 2019): 129–60, here 130, https://doi.org/10.1353/tech.2019.0066.

78. For the interconnection between photography, eugenics, and the archive, see Allan Sekula, "The Body and the Archive," *October* 39 (Winter 1986): 3–64.
79. Li and Mills, "Vocal Features," 130.
80. Li and Mills, "Vocal Features," 138.
81. See, for example, Strategic Defense Technology (https://www.stratign.com/). Beyond identification, other AI systems purport to assign values to the voice—such as confidence, honesty, or prevarication—all of which can be used to classify people and develop systems of exclusion.
82. Li and Mills, "Vocal Features," 155.
83. Li and Mills, "Vocal Features," 155.
84. A single book manuscript, *The Natural History of an Interview* (1971), edited by Norman McQuown, is available through the Regenstein Library at the University of Chicago. It includes chapters by McQuown, Henry Brosin, Charles Hockett, Ray Birdwhistell, Gregory Bateson, Henry Smith, and George Trager, which address the hermeneutics of communication, vocal activity, body motion, transcription and annotation, and implications for psychiatry. It appears that they did not work with Boder, but they do cite his article, "The Adjective-Verb Quotient: A Contribution to the Psychology of Language" (1927/1940).
85. Gregory Bateson, "Communication," in *The Natural History of an Interview*, ed. Norman McQuown (Chicago: University of Chicago Library, 1971), 39.
86. Norman McQuown, "Foreword," in *The Natural History of an Interview*, ed. Norman McQuown (Chicago: University of Chicago Library, 1971), 5.
87. In this regard, our approach is also different from recent computational-bioinformatic approaches to studying breath and trauma, such as Salah Almila Akdag, Salah Albert Ali, Kaya Heysem, Doyran Metehan, and Kavcar Evrim, "The Sound of Silence: Breathing Analysis for Finding Traces of Trauma and Depression in Oral History Archives," *Digital Scholarship in the Humanities* 36, issue supplement 2 (October 2021): ii2–ii8, https://doi.org/10.1093/llc/fqaa056.
88. LaCapra, *Writing History, Writing Trauma*, 41.
89. Langer, *Holocaust Testimonies*. These quotes come from the chapter "Anguished Memory," 52, 66, and 74, respectively. Langer does not, of course, use any sort of computational analysis and his focus is not, strictly speaking, on phonation. Through a lens informed by literary theory, he does show, in line with our analysis here, how survivor narratives are composed of more than one voice, often in tension with one another, as they bear witness both within and beyond the events they describe.
90. See the introduction to Saul Friedländer's *The Years of Extermination: Nazi Germany and the Jews, 1939–1945* (New York: HarperCollins, 2007).
91. Hayden White, "Historical Discourse and Literary Theory," in *The Practical Past* (Evanston, IL: Northwestern University Press, 2014), 83. In addition, see Hayden White, "Historical Truth, Estrangement, and Disbelief," in *Probing the Ethics of Holocaust Culture*, ed. Claudio Fogu, Wulf Kansteiner, and Todd Presner (Cambridge, MA: Harvard University Press, 2016), 56.

Digital Project: What Were Survivors Asked?

1. This chapter is based upon research undertaken by Michelle Lee as part of the UCLA Holocaust DH Research Lab under the direction of Todd Presner (2020–2022). The datasets were curated jointly by Todd Presner and Michelle Lee. The Tableau dashboards and methodology were created and designed by Michelle Lee. The chapter analysis was primarily written by Todd Presner through an iterative writing and research process with Michelle Lee.

2. For a thorough institutional history of the Yale Fortunoff and USC Shoah Foundation archives, including the evolution of their respective interview methodologies, see Noah Shenker, *Reframing Holocaust Testimony* (Bloomington: Indiana University Press, 2015), esp. chapters 1 and 3.

3. In 105 instances, no answer was given to a question. In our dataset, there were 64,578 distinct questions and 41,775 distinct answers. The vast majority of "repeated" questions and answers come from the DiT project.

4. For example, Benjamin Charles Lee developed and trained a machine-learning model to classify hundreds of thousands of death certificate reference cards from nearly forty million scanned cards in the Central Name Index (CNI) of the Arolsen ITS archives. As Lee points out, "because card type is an intrinsic property of a CNI card, the classification of CNI cards by type is a task with an *a priori* answer, unlike subjective tasks related to the document's content, such as sentiment analysis or topic modeling." Benjamin Charles Lee, "Machine Learning, Template Matching, and the International Tracing Service Digital Archive: Automating the Retrieval of Death Certificate Reference Cards from 40 Million Document Scans," *Digital Scholarship in the Humanities* 34, no. 3 (2019): 513–35, here 524.

5. Among the vast literature on the epistemic work of classification taxonomies, see Michel Foucault, *The Order of Things: An Archaeology of the Human Sciences*, trans. Alan Sheridan (New York: Vintage, 1994); Geoffrey C. Bowker and Susan Leigh Starr, *Sorting Things Out: Classification and its Consequences* (Cambridge, MA: MIT Press, 2000).

6. The seven interviewees excluded from the analysis here were professionals working with the displaced persons and students completing occupational training side by side with survivors.

7. Shenker, *Reframing Holocaust Testimony*, 28.

8. Shenker, *Reframing Holocaust Testimony*, 28–29.

9. Joanne Wiener Rudof, "Holocaust Testimonies: Problems Analyzed, Promises Fulfilled," *The Journal of Holocaust Research* 34, no. 4 (2020): 288–304, here 294. Organized by Dana Kline, the 1984 "Syllabus for Volunteer Interviewers" included presentations by Vlock and Laub, as well as background readings and historical lectures. It also included a set of "bad" interview questions for discussion, including ones that were deemed to express judgment by the interviewer, offer answers in the question, be "agendized" ("Did your belief in God help you to survive?" or "What do you think of Germans?"), or be inappropriate ("How did you feel?" or "What was the worst thing to happen to you?"). Those questions were, indeed, asked with some frequency in the early interviews analyzed here. The interview training materials are available online: http://fortunoff.library.yale.edu/wp-content/uploads/2018/10/interviewer .training_redacted.pdf (accessed July 2021). Shenker also discusses the archive's training materials and development of its interview methodology, *Reframing the Holocaust*, esp. 32.

10. Rudof, "Holocaust Testimonies," 295.

11. Geoffrey Hartman, "Learning from Survivors: The Yale Testimony Project," in *The Longest Shadow: In the Aftermath of the Holocaust* (New York: Palgrave, 1996), 144. Hartman served as the long-term project director for the archive.

12. See the section on "Interview Methodology" under "Our Story," Fortunoff Video Archive for Holocaust Testimonies, accessed July 2021, https://fortunoff.library.yale.edu/about-us/our -story/.

13. Hartman, "Learning from Survivors," 136, 142.

14. The notion of "deep memory" comes from Lawrence Langer, who served as a long-time interviewer and researcher for the Fortunoff Archive. See Lawrence Langer, *Holocaust Testimonies: The Ruins of Memory* (New Haven, CT: Yale University Press, 1991).

15. In the case of Dario Gabbai, two interviews took place: the first in 1996 with Carol Stulberg and the second in 2014 with Stephen Smith. Since the interviews consist of one file in the Visual History Archive, the questions from both interviews are included in this analysis.

16. The foundation's efforts to interview survivors spanned over twenty countries and involved more than two thousand different interviewers. See "The Interview," USC Shoah Foundation, accessed July 2021, http://sfi.usc.edu/content/interview.

17. As Shenker points out, the "interview protocol mirrors a three-act dramaturgical structure" owing to its cinematic origins. The interview, he argues, aims to create "a form of narrative continuity reminiscent of the traditional Classical Hollywood Cinema paradigm." Shenker, *Reframing Holocaust Testimony*, 119.

18. "Interviewer Guidelines," USC Shoah Foundation (2012), 7–8, accessed July 2021, https://sfi .usc.edu/sites/default/files/docfiles/USCSF_Interviewer_Guidelines_Oct%202012.pdf.

19. See Jacob Devlin, Ming-Wei Chang, Kenton Lee, and Kristina Toutanova, "BERT: Pre-training of Deep Bidirectional Transformers for Language Understanding," *Proceedings of the 2019 Conference of the North American Chapter of the Association for Computational Linguistics: Human Language Technologies, Volume 1* (May 24, 2019), 4171–4186, https://arxiv.org/pdf /1810.04805.pdf. In addition, see Chris McCormick and Nick Ryan, "BERT Word Embeddings Tutorial," *Chris McCormick* (blog), May 14, 2019, https://mccormickml.com/2019/05 /14/BERT-word-embeddings-tutorial/.

20. See Nils Reimers and Iryna Gurevych, "Sentence-BERT: Sentence Embeddings Using Siamese BERT-Networks," November 2019, *Proceedings of the 2019 Conference on Empirical Methods in Natural Language Processing and the 9th International Joint Conference on Natural Language Processing*, Hong Kong, China, 3982–3992, https://arxiv.org/abs/1908.10084.

21. The numerical embeddings can be found on our project website.

22. For a cultural history of the K-means clustering algorithm, see James E. Dobson, *Critical Digital Humanities: The Search for a Methodology* (Urbana: University of Illinois Press, 2019), chapter 4.

23. While we experimented with increasing or decreasing the number of clusters, one hundred gave us results that placed the questions into a manageable number of clusters while still retaining enough specificity. This was largely a trial-and-error process that involved human reading and interpretation of the results. As we describe below, we sometimes combined similar topics during the human review process, and thus the final clusters were as follows: ninety-three for Boder's corpus, ninety-two for the Fortunoff, and eighty-five for the USC Shoah Foundation. Because of the substantially larger number of questions in DiT, we chose 150 clusters for the K-Means Clustering algorithm but reduced it to 114 for the final results after observing significant (and initially surprising) overlap among the clusters. It turned out that the range of question topics was smaller than expected, even though many more questions were asked using DiT. We attribute this to the fact that students and the general public tend to ask a fairly delimited set of general questions to survivors, at least in comparison with experts who are trained on the history of the Holocaust.

24. While not the same, we did refer to the tagging, naming, and indexing conventions used by the various archives as finding aids in developing our topic names.

25. In fact, we reran the K-means clustering more than once for each corpus and noticed minor variations in the outputs. The same mistakes, however, persisted, which we attribute to the calculation of the embeddings.

26. While the last question ("Do you hate the Germans?") was asked 136 times in our dataset, variations of this question (for instance, "Do you hate Germans?," "Do you hate Nazis?," "Do you still hate the Germans?," "Do you hate Hitler?," "Do you hate the German people?," "Do you hate Germans now?") bring the total questions in this cluster to 256. Interestingly, Anita

Lasker-Wallfisch, for example, has two answers to the first question, one of which has been played 127 times and the other of which has been played nine times. She also has different answers to questions about Nazis and Hitler. Presumably, different weights have been assigned to the two answers during the training process.

27. All interactive Tableau visualizations in this chapter are available on our project website, http://holocaustresearchlab.com, under "Digital Project 2."

28. Two of the three Dimensions in Testimony survivors (Firestone and Lasker-Wallfisch) used in this analysis were deported to Auschwitz where they experienced and witnessed extreme mistreatment and violations at the hand of the Nazis; Oberrotman, who lost both of her parents, secured false papers and went into hiding before being sent to Stuttgart as a Polish forced laborer. There are now dozens of Dimensions in Testimony interviewees, representing a wide spectrum of experiences. These include not only Holocaust survivors but also liberators, a survivor of the Nanjing Massacre, and the chief prosecutor at the Einsatzgruppen Trial at Nuremberg. See "The Interviewees," USC Shoah Foundation, accessed September 2021, https://sfi.usc.edu/dit/interviewees.

29. Interview with Kurt I. (December 2, 1979), Yale Fortunoff Video Archive for Holocaust Testimonies (hvt-135), minutes 40:23–40:28, https://fortunoff.aviaryplatform.com/collections /5/collection_resources/208.

30. Critiqued by Primo Levi as "stereotypes" that exposed "the gaps . . . or inability to perceive the experience of others," these and other such questions come from the world of the living and express a tone of inquiry that sought to elicit rational reasons for something done contrary to what the interviewer may have expected, known, or personally experienced. Primo Levi, "Stereotypes," in *The Drowned and the Saved* (New York: Vintage Books, 1989), 157–58.

31. Interview with Bernice S. (May 12, 1982), Yale Fortunoff Video Archive for Holocaust Testimonies (hvt-175), tape 2, minutes 10:54–12:00. https://fortunoff.aviaryplatform.com /collections/5/collection_resources/246.

32. We did not create a gender dashboard for Dimensions in Testimony since the three interviewees analyzed here were all women.

33. In the case of the interview with Donia W., a translator is also part of the conversation with interviewer Laurel Vlock. Non-interrogative statements made by Vlock and the translator to rephrase questions and repeat answers are not part of the question count.

34. Interview with Donia W. (November 4, 1979), Yale Fortunoff Video Archive for Holocaust Testimonies (hvt-74), tape 2, minute 15:23–15:53, https://fortunoff.aviaryplatform.com /collections/5/collection_resources/147.

35. Understanding and critiquing the many roles of human labor in AI has helped construct vitally important labor histories of AI as well as demystify algorithms more generally. As Ian Bogost has argued in his efforts to explicate the workings of algorithms and big data: "Data is created, not simply aggregated, and often by means of laborious, manual processes rather than anonymous vacuum-devices." See Ian Bogost, "The Cathedral of Computation," *The Atlantic*, January 15, 2015, https://www.theatlantic.com/technology/archive/2015/01/the-cathedral-of -computation/384300/. See also Kate Crawford, *Atlas of AI: Power, Politics, and the Planetary Costs of Artificial intelligence* (New Haven, CT: Yale University Press, 2021), chapter 2.

36. The problem of monolingual foundation models has been documented and discussed in the report published by the Center for Research on Foundation Models and the Stanford Institute for Human-Centered Artificial Intelligence, *On the Opportunities and Risks of Foundation Models*, CRFM and HAI, August 2021, esp. 24–27, https://arxiv.org/pdf/2108.07258. While available training data varies by language, Multilingual BERT (mBERT) has been trained and tested on more than one hundred languages using Wikipedia. See the discussion by Nils Reimers and Iryna Gurevych, "Making Monolingual Sentence Embeddings Multilingual

Using Knowledge Distillation," 2020, *Proceedings of the 2020 Conference on Empirical Methods in Natural Language Processing (EMNLP)*, Association for Computational Linguistics, 2020, 4512–4525, https://arxiv.org/abs/2004.09813.

37. We manually separated incorrectly clustered questions, and the adjustments are documented on our project website. It is worth noting that it would also be impossible for a human reader to know what Boder meant by the question "a pot?" without knowing the context of the question and the answer.

38. This observation is analogous to a critique made by James E. Dobson, "Can an Algorithm be Disturbed? Machine Learning, Intrinsic Criticism, and the Digital Humanities," *College Literature: A Journal of Critical Literary Studies* 42, no. 4 (Fall 2015): 543–64. Dobson writes, "The algorithm assumes all data will 'fit,'" and he asks how the algorithm can be deployed against itself to "open holes" for interpretation and sustain ambiguity rather than overcoming it (559–60). See also the discussion of fuzzy, mixed, and multilabel classification in Matthew L. Jockers and Ted Underwood, "Text-Mining the Humanities," in *A New Companion to Digital Humanities*, ed. Susan Schreibman, Ray Siemens, and John Unsworth (Oxford: Wiley Blackwell, 2015), 291–306, here 298, https://doi.org/10.1002/9781118680605.ch20.

39. Emily M. Bender, Timnit Gebru, Angelina McMillan-Major, and Shmargaret Shmitchell argue that the largely inscrutable training data used in deep learning to produce natural language processing models, including BERT, contain innumerable biases and stereotypes that "[result] in models that encode stereotypical and derogatory associations along gender, race, ethnicity, and disability status" (613), in "On the Dangers of Stochastic Parrots: Can Language Models Be Too Big?," *Conference on Fairness, Accountability, and Transparency (FAccT '21), March 3–10, 2021, Virtual Event, Canada*, ACM, New York, NY, 610–623, https://doi.org/10.1145/3442188.3445922.

40. See the Center for Research on Foundation Models and the Stanford Institute for Human-Centered Artificial Intelligence, *On the Opportunities and Risks of Foundation Models*; Bender et al., "On the Dangers of Stochastic Parrots: Can Language Models Be Too Big?"; and Keita Kurita, Nidhi Vyas, Ayush Pareek, Alan W. Black, and Yulia Tsvetkov, "Quantifying Social Biases in Contextual Word Representations," *Proceedings of the 1st Workshop on Gender Bias in Natural Language Processing*, August 2019, 166–72, https://aclanthology.org/W19–3823.pdf.

41. Safiya Noble, *Algorithms of Oppression: How Search Engines Reinforce Racism* (New York: NYU Press, 2018).

42. Noble shows, with regard to Google's auto-suggest results for the phrase "why are black people so," that the word "ghetto" is returned as the ninth most-common association. See her screenshot of January 25, 2013, in *Algorithms of Oppression*, 20. This algorithmic association predates BERT by about five years.

43. Kate Crawford discusses the limits of "debiasing systems" in *Atlas of AI*, 131–33. Safiya Noble has argued that these "glitches" in the system—far from unique or idiosyncratic problems simply to be corrected—are pervasive and even "fundamental to the operating system of the web," in *Algorithms of Oppression*, 10.

44. For a discussion of the implications, see Ruha Benjamin, *Race after Technology: Abolitionist Tools for the New Jim Code* (Cambridge, UK: Polity Press, 2019).

45. Hoyt Long, "Can Algorithmic Bias Teach Us about Race?," *Public Books*, June 28, 2021, https://www.publicbooks.org/can-algorithmic-bias-teach-us-about-race/, as well as his book, *The Values in Numbers: Reading Japanese Literature in a Global Information Age* (New York: Columbia University Press, 2021).

46. Louise Amoore, *Cloud Ethics: Algorithms and the Attributes of Ourselves and Others* (Durham, NC: Duke University Press, 2020), 9.

47. Amoore, *Cloud Ethics*, 167.

6: Algorithmic Close Reading

1. See Bruno Latour, *Reassembling the Social: An Introduction to Actor-Network-Theory* (Oxford: Oxford University Press, 2005).
2. Latour, *Reassembling the Social*, 61.
3. Hannah Arendt, *The Human Condition* (Chicago: University of Chicago, 1958), 176–77.
4. Arendt, *The Human Condition*, 184.
5. Arendt, *The Human Condition*, 188.
6. Arendt, *The Human Condition*, 179, 178.
7. Explored in more detail below, the concept of "microhistories" or small-scale, individual actions comes from Claire Zalc and Tal Bruttmann, ed., *Microhistories of the Holocaust* (New York: Berghahn Books, 2016).
8. For a thoughtful reflection of the possibilities and pitfalls of using natural language processing (and other text analysis tools) in historical research, see Jo Guldi, *The Dangerous Art of Text Mining: A Methodology for Digital History* (Cambridge: Cambridge University Press, 2023). For an argument that brings the humanistic frameworks of narrative theory to natural language processing, see Andrew Piper, Richard Jean So, and David Bamman, "Narrative Theory for Computational Narrative Understanding," *Proceedings of the 2021 Conference on Empirical Methods in Natural Language Processing*, 2021, 298–311, https://doi.org/10.18653/v1/2021 .emnlp-main.26. Using their "minimal definition" of narrativity, our analysis focuses on the elements of narrative in which a survivor describes the agency of someone doing something to someone (300).
9. Renana Keydar, "Mass Atrocity, Mass Testimony, and the Quantitative Turn in International Law," *Law and Society Review* 53, no. 2 (2019): 554–87, here 582.
10. Although his text-mining methodology is quite different (focusing on identifying recurrent expressions and grouping them together using topic modeling), we want to draw attention to Gábor Mihály Tóth's digital project "Let Them Speak," which uses thousands of testimonial fragments to assemble collective experiences: https://lts.fortunoff.library.yale.edu/. In this sense, his project represents a convergent approach to our own. See: Gábor Mihály Tóth, "Recovering and Rendering Silenced Experiences of Genocides: Testimonial Fragments of the Holocaust," *Digital Scholarship in the Humanities* 36, no. 1 (June 2021): 124–36, https:// doi.org/10.1093/llc/fqaa025.
11. In this chapter and in the digital project that follows, the transcripts come from the testimonies recorded by David Boder in 1946, testimonies recorded by the Yale University Fortunoff Archive in the early 1980s, testimonies recorded by the USC Shoah Foundation Visual History Archive in the 1990s and early 2000s, and testimonies recorded by the US Holocaust Memorial Museum (USHMM) in the 1990s and early 2000s.
12. Latour, *Reassembling the Social*, 52.
13. The term "testimonial ensemble" comes from Kyle Rosen, who introduced this term to our lab as a concept for testimonial analysis. The term, discussed later in this chapter, is meant to reference musical ensembles, in which multiple players and voices come together to form a contingent, meaningful whole.
14. Stephen Ramsay, *Reading Machines: Toward an Algorithmic Criticism* (Urbana: University of Illinois Press, 2011), 2, 10.
15. Ramsay, *Reading Machines*, 32–33. Cf. Jerome McGann, *Radiant Textuality* (New York: Palgrave, 2005).
16. Ramsay, *Reading Machines*, 85. Within literary and historical studies, some recent works to explore the possibilities of algorithmic text analysis include: Ted Underwood, *Distant*

Horizons: Digital Evidence and Literary Change (Chicago: University of Chicago, 2019); Andrew Piper, *Enumerations: Data and Literary Study* (Chicago: University of Chicago, 2018); Hoyt Long, *The Values in Numbers: Reading Japanese Literature in a Global Information Age* (New York: Columbia University Press, 2021); and Jo Guldi, *The Dangerous Art of Text Mining*.

17. The idea behind semantic triplets corresponds to the RDF/XML syntax specifications for representing information that takes the form of "triples" (subject-predicate-object expressions). See "RDF/XML Syntax Specification (Revised)," W3C, February 10, 2004, https://www.w3.org/TR/REC-rdf-syntax/; and "RDF 1.1 XML Syntax," W3C, February 25, 2014, https://www.w3.org/TR/rdf-syntax-grammar/#RDF. Triplets are organized by network relations between entities (nodes and directional arrows, or edges). Inspired by the database design of Triplestore and RDF store and their humanistic applications, we have developed our own process of extracting semantic triplets from spoken testimonies and analyzing them in network environments.

18. See dependency parsing: "Linguistic Features," spaCy, https://spacy.io/usage/linguistic-features.

19. This and the following triplet examples are drawn from the testimony of Anna Kovitzka (also known as Anna Kaletzka) in her 1946 interview with David Boder.

20. The examples in the table come from the English translation of the testimony of Anna Kaletzka (Kovitzka) done by David Boder in 1946: *Topical Autobiographies of Displaced People* (1957), box 12, David Boder Papers, Special Collections, Charles E. Young Research Library, UCLA, 244–75. The original recording and transcript can be accessed here: https://voices.library.iit.edu/interview/kaletskaA.

21. In addition to our GitHub repository (https://github.com/lizhouf/semantic_triplets), which provides full documentation and sample data, a more detailed discussion of the semantic-triplets pipeline process can be found in our article: Lizhou Fan and Todd Presner, "Algorithmic Close Reading: Using Semantic Triplets to Index and Analyze Agency in Holocaust Testimonies," *Digital Humanities Quarterly* 16, no. 3 (2022): http://www.digitalhumanities.org/dhq/vol/16/3/000623/000623.html.

22. SpaCy's noun chunk code is found here: https://github.com/explosion/spaCy/blob/master/spacy/lang/en/syntax_iterators.py. This model helps extract base noun phrases from syntactic dependency parsing results. All words with the dependency parsing tags "NOUN," "PROPN," and "PRON" are regarded as the coreference components of a chunk, and all the other related syntactic components are stored alongside the same noun chunk. The "noun_chunks" function serves as a syntax iterator that retrieves all the noun chunks based on the above definition.

23. See "Stanford Open Information Extraction," Stanford Natural Language Processing Group, https://nlp.stanford.edu/software/openie.html.

24. Textacy is a Python package based on spaCy (https://github.com/chartbeat-labs/textacy). We mainly use the "pos_regex_matches" function (now "regex_matches" in the most current version) in its "extract" module, which enables the use of the customized rules when we apply regular expressions for detecting noun chunks and verb chunks.

25. In the earlier interview with David Boder, Bassfreund says, "We were rubbed with kerosene," with respect to the delousing process in Auschwitz. This triplet is easily found; however, in his later interview with the Shoah Foundation, he speaks less clearly about the same process.

26. Cf. William Labov and Joshua Waletzky, "Narrative Analysis: Oral Versions of Personal Experience," *Journal of Narrative & Life History* 7, nos. 1–4 (1997): 3–38.

27. NeuralCoref (https://github.com/huggingface/neuralcoref).

28. Pontus Stenetorp, Sampo Pyysalo, Goran Topić, Tomoko Ohta, Sophia Ananiadou, and Jun'ichi Tsujii, "BRAT: A Web-Based Tool for NLP-Assisted Text Annotation," *Proceedings of the Demonstrations at the 13th Conference of the European Chapter of the Association for Computational Linguistics*, Association for Computational Linguistics, 2012, 102–7.

29. David Bamman, Olivia Lewke, and Anya Mansoor, "An Annotated Dataset of Coreference in English Literature," *Proceedings of the 12th Language Resources and Evaluation Conference*, 2020, 44–54, https://arxiv.org/abs/1912.01140.

30. David Bamman (https://github.com/dbamman/lrec2020-coref).

31. Jürgen Bassfreund, interview with David Boder (September 20, 1946), *Topical Autobiographies of Displaced People*, box 12, David Boder Papers, Special Collections, Charles E. Young Research Library, UCLA, 276–318. Also available through Voices of the Holocaust, Illinois Institute of Technology (https://voices.library.iit.edu/interview/bassfreundJ).

32. German interview: Jürgen Bassfreund (Sept 20, 1946), interview with David Boder, Voices of the Holocaust, Illinois Institute of Technology, https://voices.library.iit.edu/interview/bassfreundJ. English interview: Jack Bass (Jul 9, 1997), interview 30765, Visual History Archive, USC Shoah Foundation, https://vha.usc.edu/testimony/30765.

33. Anna Kovitzka (Kaletska), interview with David Boder (September 26, 1946).

34. Erika Jacoby (July 11, 1994), interview 8, Visual History Archive, USC Shoah Foundation, https://vha.usc.edu/testimony/8.

35. Many triplets evidence the vernacular speech of oral histories, and this sometimes means incomplete thoughts, breaks in sentences, and lack of punctuation. The accuracy of the triplet extraction process often depends on the complexity of the sentence, including whether (and how) the speaker uses relative or subordinate clauses, run-on sentences, reported speech, or indirect speech. Manual review and curation are critical for ensuring accuracy. Recognizing that the process will never be 100 percent complete or correct, we discuss some of the challenges and shortcomings in the last section of this chapter.

36. A spreadsheet of the original sentences, along with the "meticulous triplets" (and record of our corrections), can be found on our project website.

37. Examples in the original German, which all follow the pattern of passive speech in the English translation, include: "Plötzlich waren wir umringt von der Leibstandarte, und wurden dann mit Füßen getreten und in Autos verladen"; "Und dann kamen wieder Autos und wieder wurden wir von der Leibstandarte zu einem ganz entlegenen Bahnhof in Berlin gebracht und wurden dort einwagoniert"; "Wir wurden aus diesen Wagons herausgetrieben"; "Wir wurden mit Petroleum eingerieben."

38. Raul Hilberg, *The Destruction of the European Jews*, 3rd ed. (New Haven, CT: Yale University Press, 2003); Bruno Bettelheim, *The Informed Heart: Autonomy in a Mass Age* (New York: The Free Press, 1960), 263–65.

39. For a comprehensive reassessment, see Michael R. Marrus, "Jewish Resistance to the Holocaust," *Journal of Contemporary History* 30, no. 1 (January 1995): 83–110. In addition, see: Joseph Rudavsky, *To Live With Hope, To Die With Dignity: Spiritual Resistance in the Ghettos and Camps* (Northvale, NJ: Jason Aronson, 1997); Nechama Tec, *Defiance: The Bielski Partisans* (Oxford: Oxford University Press, 1993); Nechama Tec, *Resistance: Jews and Christians who Defied the Nazi Terror* (Oxford: Oxford University Press, 2013); and Rachel Einwohner, *Hope and Honor: Jewish Resistance During the Holocaust* (Oxford: Oxford University Press, 2022).

40. Samuel Kassow, *Who Will Write Our History? Emanuel Ringelblum, the Warsaw Ghetto, and the Oyneg Shabes Archive* (Bloomington: Indiana University Press, 2007); Jadwiga Bezwinska, ed., *Amidst a Nightmare of a Crime: Notes of Prisoners of Sonderkommando Found at Auschwitz*, trans. Krystyna Michalik (Oświęcim, Poland: Publications of State Museum at Oświęcim,

1973). For an analysis of diary writing during the Holocaust, see Alexandra Garbarini, *Numbered Days: Diaries and the Holocaust* (New Haven, CT: Yale University Press, 2006).

41. Wolf Gruner, "'The Germans Should Expel the Foreigner Hitler . . .': Open Protest and Other Forms of Jewish Defiance in Nazi Germany," *Yad Vashem Studies* 39, no. 2 (2011): 13–53; Wolf Gruner, "Defiance and Protest: A Comparative Microhistorical Reevaluation of Individual Jewish Responses to Nazi Persecution," in *Microhistories of the Holocaust*, ed. Claire Zalc and Tal Bruttmann (New York: Berghahn, 2016), 209–26; and Wolf Gruner, "Defiance and Protest: Forgotten Acts of Individual Jewish Resistance," UC San Diego Library, YouTube video, March 19, 2019, https://www.youtube.com/watch?v=bONTGjo7h5w. In this lecture, Gruner draws on survivor testimonies in the USC Shoah Foundation's Visual History Archive, diaries, and letters to paint a more complete picture of Jewish resistance under the Nazis. Wolf Gruner's book, *Resisters: How Ordinary Jews Fought Persecution in Hitler's Germany* (New Haven, CT: Yale University Press, 2023), focuses on the stories of five Jewish people who resisted persecution in Nazi Germany.

42. See Gruner, "Defiance and Protest: A Comparative Microhistorical Reevaluation of Individual Jewish Responses to Nazi Persecution."

43. Erika Jacoby (July 11, 1994), interview 8, USC Shoah Foundation, tape 2, minutes 21:23–22:27. Although unindexed, this action is not unknown. See, for instance, Jon Kean's film, *Swimming in Auschwitz* (2007).

44. While all the edges and nodes were created in Neo4j based on filtering the triplets spreadsheet by mentions of "child," we manually organized the visual layout of the nodes in an effort to demonstrate locally coherent groups of agencies and to enable interpretation. We chose to put triplets in which "I" was the subject at the center, triplets with "child" as a subject or object to the right, and triplets about the Christian woman to the left.

45. Pronouns are not disambiguated in this visualization in order to preserve the specificity of Kovitzka's speech. A simplified model would have aggregated a number of these related nodes.

46. Latour, *Reassembling the Social*, 128, 131.

47. Andrew Piper, *Enumerations*, 21.

48. Rosen also discusses Kovitzka's loss of her of child and situates the story more broadly in the corpus of Boder's interviews for how "loss and death . . . overshadow escape and survival." Alan Rosen, *The Wonder of their Voices: The 1946 Holocaust Interviews of David Boder* (Oxford: Oxford University Press, 2010), 141.

49. Although we follow different approaches, the use of computational methods to characterize shared experiences accords with Tóth's digital humanities project "Let Them Speak." Tóth uses topical modeling and text mining to assemble testimonial fragments that bear witness to collective experiences such as fear, guilt, shame, and numbness as well as recurrent actions such as yelling, beating, standing, and running.

50. See Keydar, "Mass Atrocity, Mass Testimony, and the Quantitative Turn in International Law."

51. When the tag "antisemitism" occurs toward the end of the testimony, it often refers to post-War or even contemporary experiences of antisemitism and discrimination. To maintain the cohesiveness of the historical period leading up to the Holocaust, we did not include those instances in the analysis discussed here. See chapter 4 for more on the narrative structure of the testimonies recorded by the USC Shoah Foundation's Visual History Archive.

52. The full spreadsheet of triplets as well as a curated spreadsheet of 607 triplets related specifically to antisemitic experiences can be downloaded on our project website.

53. "Coercive" expressions can also be expressions of need or necessity, depending on the context. The majority, however, are expressions of being forced to do something against one's will.

54. Tóth does the same for the "Let Them Speak" project, always letting users connect the specific testimonial fragments back to the original testimonies and survivor accounts.
55. The notion of an "ensemble," connoting a multiplicity of voices, is also a way of describing social experiences beyond a single individual. As Étienne Balibar notes in *The Philosophy of Marx*, human beings are not just individuals but can be thought of as ensembles. Quoting Marx's sixth "Thesis on Feuerbach," Balibar introduces the concept of transindividuality to prioritize the social relations in which the human being is embedded: "Human essence is not an abstraction inherent in each single individual. In its reality it is the ensemble of social relations" [*Das menschliche Wesen ist kein dem einzelnen Individuum inwohnendes Abstraktum. In seiner Wirklichkeit ist es das ensemble der gesellschaftlichen Verhältnisse*]. Étienne Balibar, *The Philosophy of Marx*, trans. Chris Turner (London: Verso, 2017). I thank Kyle Rosen for this reference.
56. The idea of a "generous interface" comes from Mitchell Whitelaw, "Generous Interfaces for Digital Cultural Collections," *DHQ: Digital Humanities Quarterly* 9, no. 1 (2015).
57. The outcome of assembling a testimonial ensemble is in certain ways similar to the "project" creation tab in the new USC Shoah Foundation interface. In the latter, users can save segments of testimony (or a testimony in its entirety) as a project for viewing or sharing with others.
58. Although the triplets were extracted and characterized algorithmically, there was no way to "ask" the algorithm to "do" this work for us, as it could not know what constituted a unique expression of an act of resistance. The phrases and verbs used were simply too heterogeneous. This moment represents a critical inflection point for human decision-making.
59. Stanley Krakowski (April 22, 1996), interview 11997, Visual History Archive, USC Shoah Foundation, tape 3, minutes 2:43–3:55: https://vha.usc.edu/testimony/11997.
60. All testimonies come from the Visual History Archive, USC Shoah Foundation, respectively: Roman Ziegler (December 6, 1994), interview 365, tape 1, minute 11:35–11:56: https://vha.usc.edu/testimony/365; Rose Minsky (December 7, 1994), interview 422, tape 2, minute 8:00–8:45: https://vha.usc.edu/testimony/422; Halina Strnad (May 31, 1997), interview 31815, tape 2, minute 6:57–7:03: https://vha.usc.edu/testimony/31815; Bernard Zelinger (June 9, 1995), interview 3097, tape 1, minute 12:30–12:46: https://vha.usc.edu/testimony/3097; Stephen Howard (August 7, 1995), interview 5275, tape 1, minute 7:20–7:34: https://vha.usc.edu/testimony/5275; and Alex Gross (January 24, 1996), interview 11272, tape 1, minute 15:00–16:00.
61. All testimonies come from the Visual History Archive, USC Shoah Foundation, respectively: Ruth Rack (June 9, 1995), interview 3044, tape 1, minutes 9:45–10:16: https://vha.usc.edu/testimony/3044; Henrietta Diament (June 6, 1996), interview 16017, tape 1, minute 16:05–16:24: https://vha.usc.edu/testimony/16017; Magda Marx (July 7, 1995), interview 3757, tape 1, minute 11:30–12:30: https://vha.usc.edu/testimony/3757; Helmut Gruenewald (May 16, 1997), interview 31612, tape 2, minute 17:15–18:07: https://vha.usc.edu/testimony/31612; and Morris Beschloss (April 6, 1996), interview 13860, tape 1, minutes 22:26–23:50: https://vha.usc.edu/testimony/13860.
62. All testimonies come from the Visual History Archive, USC Shoah Foundation, respectively: Erika Jacoby (July 11, 1994), interview 8, tape 1, minute 14:00–14:20: https://vha.usc.edu/testimony/8; Ruth Oppenheimer (November 18, 1995), interview 8962, tape 2, minute 16:40–16:50: https://vha.usc.edu/testimony/8962; and Paul Goldstein (March 15, 1996), interview 13313, tape 2, minutes 20:27–21:33: https://vha.usc.edu/testimony/13313.
63. All testimonies come from the Visual History Archive, USC Shoah Foundation, respectively: Roman Ziegler (December 6, 1994), interview 365, tape 2, minutes 4:30–6:00: https://vha.usc.edu/testimony/365; Eugene Feld (August 19, 1994), interview 68, tape 1, minute 2:53–

3:10: https://vha.usc.edu/testimony/68; Henri Wittelsohn (October 5, 1995), interview 5810, tape 1, minute 11:25–11:32: https://vha.usc.edu/testimony/5810; Anita Karl (December 10, 1995), interview 9899, tape 1, minute 25:15–25:33: https://vha.usc.edu/testimony /9899; and Henry Oertelt (November 21, 1995), interview 7069, tape 2, minutes 21:00– 22:55: https://vha.usc.edu/testimony/7069.

64. Rose Minsky (December 7, 1994), interview 422, Visual History Archive, USC Shoah Foundation, tape 2, minutes 14:57–17:43: https://vha.usc.edu/testimony/422.
65. Underwood, *Distant Horizons*, 157, 158.
66. Piper, *Enumerations*, 39.

Digital Project: Mala Zimetbaum and the Creation of a Testimonial Ensemble

1. The vast majority of survivors who reference Mala Zimetbaum do so by her first name only: Mala. Most did not know her last name or did not remember it correctly. In accordance with these witness accounts, we will refer to her primarily as "Mala."
2. The movie was filmed on location in Auschwitz in the summer of 1947 and first released in 1948. Jakubowska was herself a Polish political prisoner in Auschwitz. In addition to Jakubowska, the screenwriter and numerous members of the cast were female survivors of the camp.
3. The most comprehensive biography is by Lorenz Sichelschmidt, *Mala: Ein Leben und eine Liebe in Auschwitz* (Bremen, Germany: Donat Verlag, 1995), which includes numerous survivor accounts of Mala's life and actions. Ellie Midwood recently wrote a historical novel about Mala Zimetbaum and Polish prisoner Edek Galinski, *The Girl Who Escaped from Auschwitz* (New York: Grand Central Publishing, 2022); Bernard Mark dedicated a chapter to Mala in his book on Sonderkommando writings: *The Scrolls of Auschwitz*, ed. Isaiah Avrech, trans. Sharon Neemani (Tel Aviv: Am 'Oved, 1985). Among the many testimonies, Raya Kagan mentioned the fate of Mala in her testimony at the Eichmann trial in 1961; Mala and Edek's escape is discussed extensively in the autobiography of Wieslaw Kielar, *Anus Mundi: 1,500 Days in Auschwitz*, trans. Susanne Flatauer (New York: Times Books, 1980); and Primo Levi mentions Mala briefly in an essay on "stereotypes" around the possibility of escape and resistance in Auschwitz in *The Drowned and the Saved*, trans. Raymond Rosenthal (New York: Vintage, 1989), 155–56.
4. While our methodologies are different, the idea of using the testimonies of survivors to learn about collective experiences and give voice to "the drowned" overlaps with the intention of Gábor Tóth's digital project "In Search of the Drowned: Testimonies and Testimonial Fragments of the Holocaust," Fortunoff Archive, 2021, https://lts.fortunoff.library.yale.edu /anthology.
5. The most thorough account of the planning of their escape and the escape itself is given by Wieslaw Kielar, a close friend of Edek Galinski who had initially planned to escape the same day. As a non-Jewish, Polish political prisoner, Kielar had certain privileges and mobility in the camp that he used to help facilitate and witness the escape. He also witnessed the public execution of Edek in the men's section of the camp. His account is given in *Anus Mundi*, 224–55.
6. Accounts of what she said vary tremendously and will be discussed in more detail below.
7. Primo Levi says that she slit her wrists with a razor blade and slapped an SS officer, but he says that she was, then, "trampled to death" by the guards and died "on the cart taking her to the crematorium." Levi, *The Drowned and the Saved*, 156.

8. There are postcards and letters that she sent, by coercion, to her family in 1943. In addition, Sichelschmidt reproduces a photograph of graffiti, presumably carved by Mala into the wall of the bunker where she was kept before her execution. See Sichelschmidt, *Mala*, 145.

9. Boder interviewed the women on the same day and makes an annotation about the fact that they both reference a certain "Molly Zinnenbaum" (his transcription and probable translation). Listening to Frydman's testimony, it is quite clear that she says, "Mala Zinnenbaum from Belgium" (minute 2:03:51), but she has the last name wrong. Serras references "Mala from Belgium" but does not know Mala's last name. Boder asks if it is "Zellenbaum" (having just interviewed Frydman), but Serras cannot corroborate. The original wire recordings of both testimonies (in Yiddish and German) are truncated in the middle of their descriptions of Mala. For those parts, we had to rely entirely on Boder's English translations. Henja Frydman and Edith Serras interviews (August 7, 1946): David Boder, *Topical Autobiographies of Displaced People* (1957), box 12, David Boder Papers, Library Special Collections, Charles E. Young Research Library, UCLA, 575–639 and 1302–66, respectively. The quoted parts come from 625–28 and 1356–65. The original (partial) recordings are from: "Voices of the Holocaust," Illinois Institute of Technology, Paul V. Galvin Library: https://voices.library.iit.edu /interview/frydmanH and https://voices.library.iit.edu/interview/serrasE.

10. Starting in 1944, Moll oversaw the crematoria in Auschwitz-Birkenau and was in charge of the Sonderkommando. He was arrested and tried by an American military tribunal shortly after the end of the war. He was found guilty and executed on May 28, 1946, a few months before Frydman and Serras were interviewed by Boder.

11. See chapter 6 for a full discussion of this methodology.

12. While our approach is an algorithmic form of fabulation, the storytelling practices of "critical fabulation" and "recombinant antinarrative" are methodological inspirations for testimonial ensembles. See, respectively, Saidiya Hartman, "Venus in Two Acts," *Small Axe* 26 (June 2008), 12, and M. NourbeSe Philip, *Zong!* (Middleton, CT: Wesleyan University Press, 2008), 204. Both storytelling practices are rooted in the possibilities of subjunctive forms of narration given the absences, fragmentations, and silences of the archive. At the same time, there are important differences to underscore, namely the fact that archives of testimonies from survivors of the transatlantic slave trade do not exist. In addition, Louise Amoore uses the concept of "algorithmic fabulation" to describe the reworking and reimagination of "the arrangements, perceptions, and accounts of the algorithm" for the purposes of "[deepening] the political intensity of what it means to output something into the world." Louise Amoore, *Cloud Ethics: Algorithms and the Attributes of Ourselves and Others* (Durham, NC: Duke University Press, 2020), 158. While we do not rework the arrangements of the algorithm, we do attune its perceptions and rework its outputs.

13. Giza Weisblum, "The Escape and Death of the 'Runner' Mala Zimetbaum," in *They Fought Back: The Story of Jewish Resistance in Nazi Europe*, ed. and trans. Yuri Suhl (New York: Schocken Books), 182–88.

14. Kielar, *Anus Mundi*, selections of chapters 70–77.

15. Boder's English translations of the Edith Serras and Henja Frydman testimonies are part of his manuscript *Topical Autobiographies*, and also available on the Voices of the Holocaust website. While parts of the original sound recordings are available on the website, there are no German/Yiddish transcripts (and thus the missing segments could not be checked). For the rest, the German, Yiddish, and English testimonies were checked by Todd Presner. The relevant parts of the French testimonies were translated by Kendell Clarke; the relevant parts of the Hebrew testimonies were translated by Rachel Smith; and the relevant part of the Ladino testimony was translated by Kyle Rosen.

16. Using transcripts from the Yale Fortunoff Archive, the USC Shoah Foundation, and the USHMM, Tóth's "Let Them Speak" project is already an example of this.

17. In addition to correcting Boder's transcription mistakes, we made the following corrections: Mania W. says Mala's name was "Helen," and we changed it to Mala. Another survivor, Palomba F., seems to call her Bala, and we rendered the name as Mala. Judith P. does not recall Mala's name (she merely references her actions and the French version of Jakubowska's film, *La Dernière Étape*). While we added two references to Mala by name in her transcript, we did not correct any errors in her testimony (for instance, she says "the girl" was Czech). We also added quotation marks for direct speech attributed to other people.

18. Within film studies, there is a long tradition of precisely this kind of analysis and presentation. Parataxis is the governing principle of filmic montage and can be found in some of the foundational films documenting the Holocaust, such as Alain Resnais's *Night and Fog* (1955), Marcel Ophuls's *The Sorrow and the Pity* (1969), and Claude Lanzmann's *Shoah* (1985). In addition, Geoffrey Hartman mentions how the Fortunoff Archive "put together [quotations] in montages of fifteen to fifty minutes" from its collections of witness testimony. See Geoffrey Hartman, "Learning from Survivors: The Yale Testimony Project," in *The Longest Shadow: In the Aftermath of the Holocaust* (New York: Palgrave MacMillan, 1996), 144. More recently, the USC Shoah Foundation's IWitness platform allows students to engage in "ethical editing" of testimonies, a practice that involves splicing together parts of different testimonial videos to tell new stories or create video essays (https://iwitness.usc.edu/sfi/).

19. Edith Serras, interview with David Boder, in *Topical Autobiographies of Displaced People*, box 12, David Boder Papers, Special Collections, Charles E. Young Research Library, UCLA, 1362–1364. Boder's questions were removed.

20. Our algorithm extracted the named entities correctly in Serras's testimony (Mala, Mandel, the work service leader, the SS men) but left pronouns in place when the certainty of replacement was not high enough. Those were manually changed and marked as such. Extracted triplets were corrected twice in this example, once to simplify the subject and once to correct the category of verb (evaluation rather than orientation).

21. The complete spreadsheet can be found on our website, https://holocaustresearchlab.com, under "Digital Project 3." For this project, we determined that 89 percent of the triplets were extracted and characterized correctly, and 91 percent of the coreferences were correct.

22. Leaving out the three male testimonies, the ratio of "I" to "we" statements becomes 173 to 249, showing that "we" statements predominate in the women's accounts. Indeed, only sixteen "we" statements are made by the three men. Although this is only a small sample, the results raise questions about gender differences in speaking about solidarity versus individual actions. This phenomenon has been studied at scale by Gábor Mihály Tóth, Tim Hempel, Krishna Somandepalli, and Shri Narayanan, who argue that "in testimonies of women solidarity and social relations are more probable and more important topics than in testimonies of men" (paragraph 54), in "Studying Large-Scale Behavioral Differences in Auschwitz-Birkenau with Simulation of Gendered Narratives," *Digital Humanities Quarterly* 16, no. 3 (2022): http://www.digitalhumanities.org/dhq/vol/16/3/000622/000622.html.

23. I am not suggesting that algorithmic methods are the sine qua non for a "mass testimony." After all, Christopher Browning read and watched 292 witness testimonies to piece together the history of the Starachowice factory slave-labor camps. Christopher Browning, *Remembering Survival: Inside a Nazi Slave-Labor Camp* (New York: W. W. Norton, 2010). He sought to accumulate "a sufficient critical mass of testimonies that can be tested against one another" (8). Weighing and evaluating the "multiple perspectives," some of which were "conflicting and contradictory" (7), falls to the historian in fashioning a narrative and documenting "a core

memory . . . [that] emerges from a critical mass of testimonies" (9). A "testimonial ensemble"—composed algorithmically of thousands of semantic triplets—functions similarly and allows ongoing filtering, querying, scaling, and reconfiguration.

24. Judith Butler, *Antigone's Claim: Kinship between Life and Death* (New York: Columbia University Press, 2000).

25. The form of the work is inspired by the writings of Hartman, "Venus in Two Acts," and Amoore, *Cloud Ethics*.

26. Butler, *Antigone's Claim*, 6.

27. Butler, *Antigone's Claim*, 82.

28. Cf. Keydar, "Mass Atrocity, Mass Testimony, and the Quantitative Turn in International Law."

29. Hayden White, "The Modernist Event," in *Figural Realism: Studies in the Mimesis Effect* (Baltimore: Johns Hopkins University Press), 66–86, here 73.

30. Not unlike Lisa Lowe's concept of "past conditional temporality" ("what could have been"), which opens up "a space of reckoning" attuned to "intimacies," testimonial ensembles allow us to explore possibilities, uncertainties, and gaps through new forms of narrative and knowledge creation. Lisa Lowe, *The Intimacies of Four Continents* (Durham, NC: Duke University Press, 2015), 175. In an earlier work, I explored possibilities for using the subjunctive form in writing histories of the Holocaust: Todd Presner, "Subjunctive History? The Use of Counterfactuals in the Writing of the Disaster," *Storiografia*, no. 4 (Winter 2000): 23–38.

7: Cultural Memory Machines and the Futures of Testimony

1. The term "cultural memory machines" is inspired by Ed Finn's notion of "culture machines," which he uses to refer to the imbrication of code and culture, algorithms and people, abstractions and materiality, among other things. See Ed Finn, *What Algorithms Want: Imagination in the Age of Computing* (Cambridge, MA: MIT Press, 2017), 47–8.

2. Finn, *What Algorithms Want*, 7.

3. Fritzie Fritzshall interview with Rachel Deblinger, March 17, 2008, recorded in Skokie, Illinois, 01:06.

4. Fritzshall interview with Deblinger, 2008, 40:57–41:40.

5. Fritzshall interview with Deblinger, 2008, 45:12–45:35.

6. Fritzshall interview with Deblinger, 2008, 33:00–34:17.

7. In order to streamline and expedite the filming (particularly on a global scale), most DiT interviews are no longer filmed in such studios, but the lengthy interview process is still quite taxing physically and emotionally. For more on the DiT interviewing process, see Matthew Boswell and Antony Rowland, *Virtual Holocaust Memory* (Oxford: Oxford University Press, 2023), esp. chapter 3.

8. These are examples of questions asked by members of the general public to Renee Firestone, Anita Lasker-Wallfisch, Pinchas Gutter, and Janine Oberrotman between 2018 and 2021. The data were logged by the USC Shoah Foundation and shared with our research team.

9. Pinchas Gutter, Dimensions in Testimony, 2014, USC Shoah Foundation.

10. Pinchas Gutter, External Transcript, 2014, provided by USC Shoah Foundation.

11. Amit Pinchevski, building off roboticist Masahiro Mori's idea of the "uncanny valley," argues that survivor holograms can be located "firmly within the territory of technological humanoids"; however, the more they become humanlike, "any subtle deviation from human likeness provokes eeriness and recoiling" (analogous to the experience of a corpse or a zombie). Amit Pinchevski, *Transmitted Wounds: Media and the Mediation of Trauma* (Oxford: Oxford Uni-

versity Press, 2019), 99–100. In addition, see the detailed discussion of the media history of DiT in: Boswell and Rowland, *Virtual Holocaust Memory*, chapters 1–3.

12. Simone Natale argues that AI technologies function through a form of human-computer interaction that he calls "banal deception," namely mundane and subtle ways that "allow users to embrace deception so that they can better incorporate AI into their everyday lives, making AI more meaningful and useful to them" (7). Among the characteristics of "banal deception," Natale draws attention to the agency of the programmers and developers who create desired effects—in other words, the scripting of interactions (9). See Simone Natale, *Deceitful Media: Artificial Intelligence and Social Life after the Turing Test* (Oxford: Oxford University Press, 2021).

13. Renee Firestone, External Transcript, 2015, provided by USC Shoah Foundation.

14. This number is based on chatlog data from 2018–2021 provided by the USC Shoah Foundation. While slightly different questions may elicit different answers, certain answers can also be weighted more than others during the training process.

15. Renee Firestone, External Transcript, 2015, provided by USC Shoah Foundation.

16. Among prior uses, IBM's Watson system was trained to play *Jeopardy!* using a software called DeepQA developed by IBM Research. Trained on encyclopedia data, Wikipedia, and digitized books, the system's algorithms determine the most likely answer to a factual question. While questions about personal testimony do not, of course, always have single, factual answers, the DiT system makes its determination of what answer to play based on its training and by drawing inferences from the meaning and intention of the questions posed. For more on IBM's Watson, see https://www.ibm.com/ibm/history/ibm100/us/en/icons/watson/.

17. Since this time, the DiT systems have been deployed much more broadly, and thus the data discussed in this chapter are only representative of the period between August 2018 and April 2021. In addition, about six thousand "questions" were excluded from our analysis because they were simply blank or unintelligible, likely due to errors of the ASR. Those questions generally did not elicit content answers but variations of "Can you rephrase that?"

18. Data from "Pinchas Gutter Tagged Utterances," April 2021, provided by the USC Shoah Foundation.

19. Although we might note in passing that people do "test" the platform by asking questions such as "How is COVID-19 for you?" or "What is the square root of 45?"

20. Stephen Smith, interview with Deb Donig for "Memory Drive: The Ethics of Holocaust Memory in the Age of Virtual Reality," October 8, 2021, in *Technically Human*, podcast, https://podtail.com/podcast/the-technically-human-podcast/memory-drive-the-ethics-of-holocaust-memory-in-the/, minute 42.

21. Stephen Smith, interview with Deb Donig for "Memory Drive," minute 54.

22. Natale, *Deceitful Media*, 20.

23. Natale, *Deceitful Media*, 21.

24. For example, as if she could react to discomfort at the moment of their interaction, one user asked Lasker-Wallfisch: "I know this is gonna be a really uncomfortable question, but if you don't mind, I'm really curious about how did you cope with losing family and friends." Data from "Anita Lasker-Wallfisch Tagged Utterances," 2021, provided by USC Shoah Foundation. Noah Shenker and Dan Leopard have also considered the connection between DiT and the Turing Test in their talk, "Beyond the Era of the Witness: The Digital Afterlife of Holocaust Testimony," University of Haifa, 2021. For a broader discussion of the cultural history of the Turing Test, see Natale, *Deceitful Media*, chapter 1.

25. Ed Finn also discusses how machine-learning algorithms have been characterized as "ghosts in the machine" by certain developers in *What Algorithms Want*, 95–96.

26. N. Katherine Hayles, *How We Became Posthuman: Virtual Bodies in Cybernetics, Literature, and Informatics* (Chicago: University of Chicago, 1999), 5.

27. Unlike survivors who consent and opt to be part of DiT, Tupac's death, Tonia Sutherland argues, was "coopted and commercialized" precisely because he "had no agency, no rights, over his digital remains" (438). See Tonia Sutherland, "Remains," in *Uncertain Archives: Critical Keywords for Big Data*, ed. Nanna Bonde Thylstrup, Daniela Agostinho, Annie Ring, Catherine D'Ignazio, and Kristin Veel (Cambridge, MA: MIT Press, 2021), 433–42.

28. The best discussion of the media history of DiT in relationship to the cultural production of holographic images is Boswell and Rowland, *Virtual Holocaust Memory*, esp. 49–56.

29. See "Who Wants to Live Forever?," Eternime, accessed January 2022, https://eternime .breezy.hr/. The company existed from 2014–2018.

30. Marius Ursache, "The Journey to Digital Immortality," *Medium*, October 23, 2015, https:// medium.com/@mariusursache/the-journey-to-digital-immortality-33fcbd79949.

31. Sutherland, "Remains," 438. For an expansion of this argument, see her book: Tonia Sutherland, *Digital Remains: Race and the Digital Afterlife* (Berkeley: University of California Press, 2023).

32. Stephen Smith, "On the Ethics of Technology and Testimony," in *Probing the Ethics of Holocaust Culture*, ed. Claudio Fogu, Wulf Kansteiner, and Todd Presner (Cambridge, MA: Harvard University Press, 2016), 205, 214.

33. Smith, "On the Ethics of Technology and Testimony," 217. Smith's emphasis.

34. Smith, "On the Ethics of Technology and Testimony," 212–13.

35. Anita Lasker-Wallfisch interview (2016), "External Transcript," courtesy of USC Shoah Foundation, Dimensions in Testimony.

36. Renee Firestone interview (2015), "External Transcript," courtesy of USC Shoah Foundation, Dimensions in Testimony.

37. Janine Oberrotman interview (2016), "External Transcript," courtesy of USC Shoah Foundation, Dimensions in Testimony. The ellipses are part of the transcript.

38. See, for example, Deep Brain (https://www.deepbrain.io/), and Forever Identity (https: //foreveridentity.com/articles/).

39. See "Face-to-Face Conversations Across the Boundaries of Time and Place," Storyfile, accessed May 9, 2023, https://life.storyfile.com/storyfile-overview.

40. "William Shatner Introduces StoryFile Life—A New Way to Preserve Family History," StoryFile, YouTube video, October 15, 2021, https://www.youtube.com/watch?v=HVPm GbynBrw. All subsequent quotes are from this video.

41. Samuel Gustman, et al., "Natural Conversation Storytelling System," US Patent 11,107,465 B2, August 31, 2021.

42. Gustman, et al., "Natural Conversation Storytelling System," 13.

43. "StoryFile's AI Principles," accessed January 2024, https://storyfile.com/storyfiles-ai -principles/.

44. "Our Story," Replika, accessed January 2022, https://replika.com/about/story. Not unlike the storyline of the first episode of season two of *Black Mirror*, the background story of Replika, according to the company's founder, Eugenia Kuyda, is the experience of losing her close friend Roman in a car accident. She sought to "reconstruct Roman out of his digital remains" (minute 3:00), and in the process created, what she calls, a Bot that can "listen." According to Phil Libin, "it's the only interaction you can have that isn't judging you" (minute 7:00). As mentioned earlier, this is precisely what students appreciated about DiT.

45. These and related questions are taken up by Sutherland, *Digital Remains*, and Tamara Kneese in *Death Glitch: How Techno-Solutionism Fails Us in This Life and Beyond* (New Haven, CT: Yale University Press, 2023).

46. This section draws on earlier presentations by Rachel Deblinger, including "Remix, Remember, Retweet: Meditations on Holocaust Memory, Social Media, and Antisemitism Online," Misinformation, Media Manipulation, and Antisemitism: Remembrance Symposia at the Columbia University Italian Academy, February 2020, and the Association for Jewish Studies Conference, December 2020. Available online at: https://www.youtube.com/watch?v=ZHo836bfyxI&t=1351s.

47. Of course, if the project is asking us to consider whether having Instagram could have made a difference during the Holocaust, we must contend with what it means to have social media today, including online bullying; the amplification of racist, antisemitic hate speech; and the tracking, profiling, and selling of user data.

48. Mati Kochavi and Maya Kochavi (@eva.stories), Instagram, 2019–present, accessed July 2022, https://www.instagram.com/eva.stories/.

49. Éva Heyman, *The Diary of Éva Heyman*, ed. Ágnes Zsolt, trans. Moshe M. Kohn (New York: Shapolsky Publishers, 1988). Information about the diary can be found on "The Diary of Éva Heyman—Éva Heyman," Yad Vashem, https://www.yadvashem.org/education/educational-materials/books/dear-diary.html.

50. Gergely Kunt, "Ágnes Zsolt's Authorship of her Daughter Éva Heyman's Holocaust Diary," *Hungarian Studies Review* 43, nos. 1–2 (Spring-Fall, 2016): 127–54.

51. Mati Kochavi and Maya Kochavi (@eva.stories), "Eva" story highlight, Instagram, accessed July 2022, https://www.instagram.com/stories/highlights/17877652939352743.

52. Liat Steir-Livny, "eva.stories: Disrespect or a Successful Change in Holocaust Memory?," *Jewish Film & New Media* 8, no. 2 (Fall 2020): 129–52, here 130.

53. Among other coverage, see Natalia Winkelman, "Do Holocaust Stories Belong on Instagram?," *Slate*, May 3, 2019, https://slate.com/culture/2019/05/holocaust-instagram-eva-stories.html; Oliver Holmes, "Instagram Holocaust Diary @eva.stories Sparks Debate in Israel," *The Guardian*, May 8, 2019, https://www.theguardian.com/world/2019/may/08/instagram-holocaust-diary-evastories-sparks-debate-in-israel; Emily Burack, "Can an Instagram Account About the Holocaust Really Impact Teens?," *Alma*, May 2, 2019, https://www.heyalma.com/can-an-instagram-account-about-the-holocaust-really-impact-teens/.

54. Quoted in Oliver Holmes, "Instagram Holocaust Diary @eva.stories Sparks Debate in Israel," *The Guardian*, May 8, 2019.

55. As Steir-Livny points out, @eva.stories is "not the first time the Holocaust has appeared on social media or on Instagram; it is not the first time a Holocaust story has been adapted into a fictitious visual narrative for adolescents." Steir-Livny, "eva.stories: Disrespect or a Successful Change in Holocaust Memory?," 145.

56. See the discussion by Wulf Kansteiner, who considers the ways in which students reframe Holocaust memory in multidirectional ways through ethical editing practices: Wulf Kansteiner, "The Holocaust in the 21st Century: Digital Anxiety, Transnational Cosmopolitanism, and Never Again Genocide without Memory," in *Digital Memory Studies: Media Pasts in Transition*, ed. Andrew Hoskins (London: Routledge, 2018), 110–40, here 120–21.

57. Comments can, of course, be disabled. But rather than just ranking, the recommendation algorithm might usefully predict what testimonies or testimonial segments (such as from the thousands of "hidden" clips within DiT) a user may want to hear based on past behaviors. If you watched this testimony or asked these specific questions, perhaps you would be interested in this testimony or clip, too. This is not fundamentally different from interacting with a human archivist: if you were interested in box two, you might also be interested in box three.

58. While there are differences with Hartman's practice of critical fabulation (most notably, the decision to give voice to Eva's thoughts, feelings, and actions), this speculative form of story-

telling is motivated by absences in the archive and the use of the subjunctive as a grammatical form to imagine who she might have been. See Saidiya Hartman, "Venus in Two Acts," *Small Axe* 26 (June 2008), esp. 11–12.

59. St. Louis Manifest (@Stl_Manifest), Twitter, January 27, 2023, https://twitter.com/Stl_Manifest. The project has about sixty-six thousand followers, many of whom share and retweet the posts.

60. The full passenger list, with the fates of all 937 people, was produced by the USHMM for a 1996 exhibit (https://www.ushmm.org/online/st-louis/).

61. Email from Russel Neiss to Rachel Deblinger, September 17, 2021. Used with permission. The description of the project and subsequent quotes are from this email.

62. The project is intentionally engaged in contemporary political debates over refugees as well as the controversies over Holocaust comparisons. See also Lily Rothman, "The Story Behind a Viral Message About the Holocaust and Refugees," *Time*, January 27, 2017, https://time.com/4651998/stl-manifest-holocaust-remembrance-twitter/?amp=true.

63. See, for example, the critiques of YouTube's recommendation algorithm, which boosts capital by maintaining high levels of user "engagement": Zeynep Tufekci, "YouTube's Recommendation Algorithm Has a Dark Side," *Scientific American*, April 1, 2019, https://www.scientificamerican.com/article/youtubes-recommendation-algorithm-has-a-dark-side/; Lauren Valentino Bryant, "The YouTube Algorithm and the Alt-Right Filter Bubble," *Open Information Science* 4, no. 1 (2020): 85–90, https://doi.org/10.1515/opis-2020-0007.

64. Criticism of @eva.stories quickly reached a fever pitch, and Yad Vashem, the Israeli Holocaust memorial museum and archive, had to address the issue, saying "the use of social media platforms in order to commemorate the Holocaust is both legitimate and effective." Quoted in Isabel Kershner, "A Holocaust Story for the Social Media Generation," *New York Times*, April 30, 2019, https://www.nytimes.com/2019/04/30/world/middleeast/eva-heyman-instagram-holocaust.html.

65. Other commemorative projects function similarly on social media. Featuring photographs and short stories written by family members and friends about people who died of AIDS, the AIDS Memorial project on Instagram (@theaidsmemorial) has over ten-thousand posts with threaded comments, many of which express sympathy, grief, and hope. The posts appear, often unexpectedly, in the context of everything else in one's social media feed.

66. Samantha Murphy Kelly, "Amazon Alexa Will Be Able to Mimic Deceased Loved Ones' Voices | CNN Business," *CNN*, June 23, 2022, https://www.cnn.com/2022/06/23/tech/amazon-alexa-mimic-voice/index.html.

67. "ThisPersonDoesNotExist—Random AI Generated Photos of Fake Persons," This Person Does Not Exist, accessed May 9, 2023, https://this-person-does-not-exist.com/en.

68. Monireh Mohebbi Moghadam, et al., "Game of GANs: Game-Theoretical Models for Generative Adversarial Networks," *Artificial Intelligence Review* 56, no. 9 (September 2023), 9771–9807, https://doi.org/10.1007/s10462-023-10395-6. Davide Panagia discusses GANs vis-à-vis the website This Person Does Not Exist (https://thispersondoesnotexist.com) in "On the Possibility of a Political Theory of Algorithms," *Political Theory* 49, no. 1 (2021): 121–22.

69. "Chat with Anyone from the Past," Hello History, accessed June 2023, https://www.hellohistory.ai/.

70. A generative pretrained transformer (GPT) is a language processing AI model. Developed by OpenAI (https://openai.com/), GPT-3 was trained on forty-five terabytes of plain text, estimated to be trillions of words. Its deep learning neural network contains 175 billion parameters. OpenAI's API allows third-party apps to be developed using its technologies. Built originally on GPT-3, ChatGPT was released to the public in late 2022 by OpenAI. In March

of 2023, it began running on GPT-4, a neural network containing over one trillion parameters. For background about GPT-4, see OpenAI (2023), "GPT-4 Technical Report," March 2023, https://arxiv.org/abs/2303.08774, which includes information about the training, evaluation, and calibration of the model.

71. While the "Hello History" app gives plenty of warnings and occasionally cites sources, it is far from clear where the data come from, how they are vetted, how the tone of the interaction is determined, and what principles inform the AI-generated responses. When I "chatted" with Anne Frank, for example, I was greeted with this message: "Good day to you! I am Anne Frank, a girl who has lived through much hardship and sorrow. When the Nazis came to power in Amsterdam during the Second World War, my family and I were forced into hiding in an attic for two years. Despite the difficult circumstances we faced, I always tried to remain optimistic and find joy in life" (July 11, 2023). The app will only answer what it deems to be "safe questions" about Frank's childhood, family, and time spent hiding.

72. This information is based on the answer given by ChatGPT about how it calculates word probabilities.

73. The seminal discussion of the risks of mistaking the outputs of language models for meaningful text is Emily M. Bender, Timnit Gebru, Angelina McMillan-Major, and Shmargaret Shmitchell, "On the Dangers of Stochastic Parrots: Can Language Models Be Too Big?," *Conference on Fairness, Accountability, and Transparency (FAccT '21), March 3–10, 2021, Virtual Event, Canada*, ACM, New York, 610–623, https://doi.org/10.1145/3442188.3445922.

74. As Bender, Gebru, McMillan-Major and Schmitchell argue: "Text generated by an LM [language model] is not grounded in communicative intent, any model of the world, or any model of the reader's state of mind. It can't have been, because the training data never included sharing thoughts with a listener, nor does the machine have the ability to do that. This can seem counter-intuitive given the increasingly fluent qualities of automatically generated text, but we have to account for the fact that our perception of natural language text, regardless of how it was generated, is mediated by our own linguistic competence and our predisposition to interpret communicative acts as conveying coherent meaning and intent, whether or not they do," in "On the Dangers of Stochastic Parrots," 616.

75. The extensive human labor needed to create the preferred outcomes—defined by OpenAI as helpful, truthful, and harmless—is largely hidden from end users. For a broader discussion of the ways AI is built on outsourced human labor, see the discussion by Kate Crawford, *Atlas of AI: Power, Politics, and the Planetary Costs of Artificial Intelligence* (New Haven, CT: Yale University Press, 2021), chapter 2; and Sarah T. Roberts, *Behind the Screen: Content Moderation in the Shadows of Social Media* (New Haven, CT: Yale University Press, 2019). For a report that includes how ChatGPT outputs are annotated and evaluated, see Josh Dzieza, "AI Is a Lot of Work" *The Verge*, June 20, 2023, https://www.theverge.com/features/23764584/ai-artificial-intelligence-data-notation-labor-scale-surge-remotasks-openai-chatbots.

76. As documented by OpenAI, the language models have been fine-tuned using extensive human instruction to avoid toxic, violent, and untruthful outputs. See "Aligning Language Models to Follow Instructions," OpenAI, accessed June 2023, https://openai.com/blog/instruction-following. For a discussion of the process of aligning language models with human intentions using a model called InstructGPT, see Long Ouyang, et al., "Training Language Models to Follow Instructions with Human Feedback," 36th Conference on Neural Information Processing Systems, March 2022, https://arxiv.org/abs/2203.02155. Many questions still exist about this process since reinforcement learning encodes countless judgments into the AI, which can disproportionately affect certain groups or reinforce the preferences, values, and

knowledge (or lack thereof) of the human labelers and output evaluators. Appendix B of Ouyang's study discusses the selection, backgrounds, and training of the human labelers.

77. Set free on Twitter in 2016, the chatbot learned to spew racist, antisemitic, and misogynistic speech in less than twenty-four hours and had to be shut down by its creators. Matthew Handelman explains that the chatbot essentially learned to algorithmically recombine and redeploy the hate speech fed to it by a coordinated group of attackers (292). As he warns in his compelling critique of algorithmic reason and the story of the chatbot, "One of the first things that an artificial intelligence chatbot can learn on the internet is to deny the Holocaust" (286). Matthew Handelman, "Artificial Antisemitism: Critical Theory in the Age of Datafication," *Critical Inquiry* 48, no. 2 (Winter 2022): 286–312.

78. Although not in the context of generative AI, the idea of "mass testimony" was conceptualized by Renana Keydar, "Mass Atrocity, Mass Testimony, and the Quantitative Turn in International Law," *Law and Society Review* 53, no. 2 (2019): 554–87.

79. I am certainly not alone in calling for digital provenance to assure authenticity. See, for example, "Responsible Practices for Synthetic Media: A Framework for Collective Action" Partnership for AI, February 27, 2023, https://syntheticmedia.partnershiponai.org/. Rather than "unfathomable training data," the authors of "On the Dangers of Stochastic Parrots" explain that such responsibility will have to include intentional acts of curation, documentation, and accountability to reduce real-world harms, biases, and errors. See Bender, Gebru, McMillan-Major, and Shmitchell, "On the Dangers of Stochastic Parrots," 613–15. On documenting datasets, see Emily M. Bender and Batya Friedman, "Data Statements for Natural Language Processing: Toward Mitigating System Bias and Enabling Better Science," *Transactions of the Association for Computational Linguistics* 6 (2018): 587–604, https://aclanthology.org/Q18-1041/.

80. See the Starling Lab for Data Integrity, accessed June 2023, https://www.starlinglab.org/. Stephen Smith discusses the collaboration with the USC Shoah Foundation in "Deepfakes and Holocaust Testimony," USC Shoah Foundation, YouTube video, September 23, 2021, https://www.youtube.com/watch?v=xqUDFAAPjsM.